The Power of Will in International Conflict

The Power of Will in International Conflict

How to Think Critically in Complex Environments

WAYNE MICHAEL HALL

Foreword by Patrick M. Hughes

Praeger Security International

BLOOMSBURY ACADEMIC
NEW YORK • LONDON • OXFORD • NEW DELHI • SYDNEY

BLOOMSBURY ACADEMIC
Bloomsbury Publishing Inc
1385 Broadway, New York, NY 10018, USA
50 Bedford Square, London, WC1B 3DP, UK
29 Earlsfort Terrace, Dublin 2, Ireland

BLOOMSBURY, BLOOMSBURY ACADEMIC and the Diana logo
are trademarks of Bloomsbury Publishing Plc

First published in the United States of America by ABC-CLIO 2018
Paperback edition published by Bloomsbury Academic 2024

Cover photo: Chess Desert Game Over. (Albund/Dreamstime.com)

A catalog record for this book is available from the Library of Congress.

ISBN: HB: 978-1-4408-6612-8
PB: 979-8-7651-2044-6
ePDF: 978-1-4408-6613-5
eBook: 979-8-2161-3111-3

Series: Praeger Security International

To find out more about our authors and books visit www.bloomsbury.com
and sign up for our newsletters.

What barest the exit of that hungry wolf, volition. It can be that man has evolved into asceticism far enough to hold his natural tendencies at bay. It could be that a catalyst has not awakened this day. But know well all ye who dwellith here on this earth, it can be a monster that is held at bay.

—Author Unknown

Contents

Figures and Tables

FIGURES

TABLES

Foreword

"Where there is a will, there is a way."

—Pauline Kael

There are many variations and definitions of the word and the idea it conveys—*will*. Perhaps the best context for this complex and remarkable book is to think of having the resolve and the determination to accomplish a goal or a task. This definition can likely be improved upon and argued over by the reader, but in the context of this instructive examination of one of our most necessary traits by the author, Brigadier General Wayne M. Hall, this is the right way to start.

Will is a continuing element of whatever condition or circumstance to which it is applied. You cannot have success in your endeavors unless you resolve to see them through, no matter what, and you cannot continue to succeed unless you determine to maintain your resolve and to persist in its spirit. It seems to be that simple—and that hard to understand.

One may argue that inflexibility or an inability to recognize changed conditions can be ascribed to excessive *will*, or *will* gone to compulsion or even obsession. That may in some cases be true, but it misses the point. To begin with, *will* is a vital and necessary part of any approach to achievement or accomplishment. No one would think that *will* means an inability (or incapability) to change or to adapt—but they would think that it reflects a strong motivational link to end goals, to end states, and to future possibilities. Most would accept the idea that *will* is a precursor to success.

These ideas seem relatively easy to apply if one is talking about a person. They become more difficult to firmly accept if one is talking about a group, and very complex and challenging indeed if one is talking about the collective *will* of a larger socio-political-military and economic enterprise which could have enough interwoven components of values, beliefs, rules and laws, vital human emotion, and dynamism to send the simple constructs of resolve and determination into a rich stew of conditional and circumstantial vagaries.

One may ask: What is the *will* of our nation in regard to a mortal threat to our sovereign state? It is especially hard to deal with the inherent strength of *will* when its application may involve the likely death or injury of others, or in less dire circumstances, the economic or social failure of another person or a group, as a direct effect of the imposition of *will*. But . . . that is reality. It signals the implication—indeed the absolute fact—that the expression of *will* has consequence. Thus, *will* becomes a powerful force no matter at what level or in which context it is applied.

There are precedents and requirements to the viability of *will*. What one wills must (of necessity) be possible. What one wills must (perforce) be coherent and cognitively acquirable—fitting into the crucible of culture and condition. Without these and other themes of legitimacy, an expression of will may merely be a wisp in the wind of imagination or simply a hope or a wish, without real merit. These formative elements are important specifically because without such supporting structure and substance, *will* may become a malignancy of thought and a forerunner of disaster.

In this beautifully written and very well-researched excursion into the philosophical, and yet the very real, realm of leadership and inspiration, one might find a near-religious experience. One may also tire of the formality of it all and merely come to believe or disbelieve as the ideas and concepts provided herein strike the reader. In the end, it would be hard to deny the capture of the essential logic and the mysterious power of *will* in the evolution of man, in the development of societies, and in the conduct of events—like war and like peace. Once again, "Mike" Hall has taken on an existential topic and has seen into its very soul.

As the reader wends their way through noteworthy historical reference points, brilliant observations by the greatest of minds, and insights so keen as to be definitive, the reader may also discover the inherent truth of this scholarly effort: there is no iron-clad rendition of volition or *will*. We must all come to grips with the sure knowledge that to express *will*, we must assert our belief and describe our intent in clear and uncompromising form. *Will* is perhaps the classic form of decision, and its nature requires that we give it that recognition and that power. This is another gift from Mike Hall.

It is worth noting that *will* has always been an integral feature of humanity, even if the humans at the time didn't fully realize it. Over time, the exercise and expression of *will* have been affected by many changes in context, especially through the modern phenomena of rapidity, remote access, and technical assistance in perception and understanding. As contemporary conditions continue to evolve and as technology continues to change so many elements of our existence, we should expect the commonality of *will* and its practical manifestations—such as decisiveness and adaptability—to change too. *Will* is an enduring quality but also an evolving one.

Part of *will* includes the ethical imperatives upon which any expression of *will* is based. We have long had an issue among humankind regarding circumstantial ethics and the effect of culture and other societal forces which shape the human experience. In this book, the deep and demanding consideration of these issues are fully explored—if not fully reconciled. In some cases, there are no completely right or wrong answers to these challenges.

The Power of Will in International Conflict: How to Think Critically in Complex Environments—If we can somehow comprehend the deeply intuitive, if we can struggle with and come to know the elements of its value, and if we can apply its powers to need—whatever that need may be—then perhaps we can proceed into the future on a firm footing with full confidence in our intent and our perseverance. We may be instantly aware of the application of our *will* toward the juxtaposition of countervailing conditions and views that seek to prevent our *will* from culminating in success. We may also be attuned to the winds of change and the vibrations of life. That, too, is an expression of General Hall's work—he shows us how to be firm in our conviction but how to adapt if such adaptation is required. God knows many of our leaders and many of our fellow citizens—in eventualities large and small—could benefit from this philosophical insight. Unfortunately, few will find the way.

As you read this masterwork of modern meaning and this canon of interior thought, I hope you will appreciate the author's effort as much for the artful spiritual refreshment it may bring as for any elucidation of the theory or science upon which the study of *will* may be based. This book is—and should be—a flowering rendition of thought and belief, idea and feeling, and in the end, instinct and intuition. It is very human and sings to the ages and to the future—with hope.

Patrick M. Hughes
Lieutenant General, U.S. Army (Retired)
Arlington, Virginia
March 15, 2017

Preface

War is thus an act of force to compel our enemy to do our will.[1]

This book involves a long trek out of the dark pit of Plato's Cave.[2] My group is escaping this cave, and while gazing up and away, a light appears even as we struggle up a cluttered trail in a cold, dark, and damp environment. As faint as the light may be, it has the light of knowledge and truth, as it were. My group and I aim to reach the light and bask in its warmth. Our little group pursues fact, reason, truth, and knowledge, but face the climb up a steep and obstacle-strewn path, ever so foreboding, dark, and narrow to reach this light of truth and knowledge. All of us are apprehensive. I lead this journey; I guide two travelers: one is an Über-thinker[3] and one is a

1. Carl von Clausewitz, *On War* (Princeton, NJ: Princeton University Press, 1976), 75.

2. Plato, *Five Great Dialogues*, p. 398. Plato's Cave is an allegory. It comes from the famous Greek thinker, Socrates, and his discourse with his student, Glaucon, in our words, about man, man's propensity to accept data inputs from his senses as true but that he knows to be untrue. He lives in a dark cave where a puppet master shows him false truths through puppet actions displayed as shadows on a wall in the dark cave. Socrates contrasts the corporeal world of everyday living with the intellectual world of thinking and knowledge. The person who does drink in knowledge and truth must go back to the cave and try to help the others think about truth and light. They know that the people who have never left the comfort of the cave and the "truths" therein will renounce his good intentions and attack him for disturbing their equilibrium, their comfortable acceptance of false truths, in the dark gloom of the cave. See Plato, *Republic*, Book VII.

3. *Über-thinker*: Literally, a great or superior thinker. This kind of thinker is trained and educated to triumph in mental combat over any foe, in any domain, at any level of conflict, day or night. This thinker is older and more experienced than a *thought pilgrim*.

thought pilgrim[4] who escaped from their chains in the Cimmerian gloom of Plato's Cave.

Our group starts its climb and struggles up the steep path. Impediments slow us during our advance along the icy pathway through cold winds and brambles clutching at our robes, and oh those wild roses whose sharp thorns tear at our skin. All of us experience mental and emotional ups and downs during the trip—our journey along this narrow and winding path toward the light. The last night as we hid and before our ascent, we decided to learn about the subject of *will* on this journey. All of us can learn, if indeed we muster the humility to exclaim at least to ourselves that our knowledge about this important subject is oh so poor and of low quality. Learning becomes our passion trudging up along the perilous path, and while taking the time to think critically and deeply about this difficult phenomenon of which we know so little, a pledge comes forth in each mind. Learn the intricacies of *will* to be known and recognized as a professional and deep-thinking person. As you shall soon discover, this trip is going to be well worth our mental and physical travail, moving toward the light of pure thought, humping up the ever-so-cold and steep trail toward knowledge.

Off in the distance, perhaps as a gasping knell of an ever-so-faint echo, I hear someone ask, "Why would anybody want to read a book about *will?*" My admittedly simplistic answer to this question is that reading the book provides readers the potential to impose their *will* on other people and to resist a similar action by an adversary. This book helps people learn how to think[5] about *will* and how to bring relating knowledge to life via synthesis and holism.

To help us succeed in our journey, I provide my travelers and my readers with a variety of models. Models help people learn how to think not only about one's use of *will* but also about their adversaries who have their own desire. As one model, I use duality, which comes from Clausewitz's book *On War,* and the metaphor of our advanced thinkers riding the wild pendulum, which metaphorically allows one to swing back and forth—from one arch involving how an adversary reasons, to the other arch involving how a friendly decision maker reasons, and I explain the connectedness between the two. I also deliver the wherewithal to learn how

4. *Thought pilgrim*: A person preparing themselves for "deep thinking" engagements by traveling to their personal "high country," which is conducive to their brand of deep thinking. Younger than the *Über-thinker,* the thought pilgrim is an intellectual apprentice, perhaps a journeyman, but not a master-level thinker.

5. *How to think*: Deep thinking along with intuitive thinking. It means using cognitive elements, theoretical and historical aids, and creativity to perceive, think, plan, and anticipate any adversary in any domain or level of conflict. In an additive way, how to think implies using one's mental prowess to solve complicated problems, resolve issues, assess outcomes of actions, and adapt faster than any adversary.

to think about operational contexts in which conflicts involving bouts of mental combat occur. To focus our attention and energies toward our learning, this preface offers a first glimpse of my 14-element model of *will*. Its design helps one learn how to work with its parts, connections, and intricacies. I also provide you with an 18-consideration model that will serve you well in any type of conflict.

Alas, I make out faint voices sounding from afar, asking, "Why did you write this book?" I answer, "I have been thinking seriously about this topic for the better part of 48 years. It has taken me a long time to reason and then to turn my contemplative outputs into written thoughts that other people can read, understand, and use. So, I can now say without equivocation this book allows, indeed inspires, people to gain perspective about the hungry wolf, volition, and in doing so, to learn about many aspects of strife that reside beneath the undertow of a churning sea that is life and strife."

I must proclaim this book is arduous to say the least. In my defense, the subject is difficult too. People may try to simplify this subject and denigrate its complexity, but if so, they don't speak the truth, and their reticence to embrace the depth and breadth of this great phenomenon perplexes me. Others might claim this subject is too abstract to ever understand. But I have been in the pit of volition and wrestled with the voracious and formidable wolf of volition. Now you know enough about in which direction I will go. Although this book wends a path to make its interwoven complexities understandable and useable, it is not a light beach read. It is metacognition relative to the task at hand one must know and use for reaching and then sustaining high-level thinking via assumptions and subsequent actions and assessments and eventually adaptions sufficient to engage in mental warfare and to win constant battles of wits occurring in all domains and at all levels of conflict—a triumph of our *will*. But at its end, your conclusion will be that the time you spent wrestling with this phenomenon represented in this book has been worthwhile. And, I must add, it has been my honor to write this tome.

With that said, I could be in danger of people avoiding the book because of its provocations, its density of ideas, and its discussions of the complexities of difficult subject matter. But well armed with the power of positive thinking, I have opened the rusty and creaking gate of secrets. My duty now is to guide you on this journey, after which you will never be the same. The industrious and intellectually aggressive reader shall gather this book's insights and ram them into the realm of their experiences and their challenges. With deep thinking, readers can make great intellectual gains. I am confident if you are sufficiently patient to wend your way through the forests of knowledge expressed by my words, thoughts, concepts, and models, in lust for the secrets contained therein, through contemplation and learning you will keep alive the eternal flame of yearning for more knowledge.

Along with my own thinking, I want you to know I liberally borrowed and interpolated thoughts from great thinkers, some alive and many dead, who obviously thought about fragments of my subject. The book though could not have been finished without their help, so I thank my friends from now and so long ago. I worked with 82 books by great captains, theorists, and historians, seeking their thoughts about this phenomenon, and I included references from all. I found what I sought in the actions of some of the great captains in history such as Sun Tzu, Scipio Africanus, Julius Caesar, Napoleon, T. E. Lawrence, Mao Zedong, von Manstein, Giap, etc., though they didn't explicitly capture "how they thought" and "what they thought" about all of the aspects of *will* as they imposed their desires on their adversaries. Caesar's *The Gallic War* helped me move closer to what I sought, but it, too, didn't travel down quite the same road. *On War* provided me with the most assistance.

Some of my thinking is original. I have labored on this book for well over two years. After all, a bell peals in my mind: its message induces inference that it is *will* that mankind has fought about and over from the beginning of time; it continues to dominate conflict today. I forecast it shall dominate future conflict. Even though mankind may try, human beings shall fail to keep the ravenous wolf of volition at bay. Thus, one must learn all there is to learn about volition and use this knowledge as a light to follow while feeling our way into the dark hollow and attempt to learn how to impose our *will* or hold our adversary's impositions at bay.

Our equation is simple—one person wants something another possesses. He exerts his life force and resolve and imposes it through violent action. The recipient of this violence has a choice: either resist or comply. The recipient might wait for his competitor's act of aggressive imposition to justify his own secret desire to kill or take something of value from the aggressor. Thus, a secondary imposition becomes possible, put forth by the recipient of the original aggression. Quite the dance of imposition, counterimposition, and new imposition could happen, often by chance, wouldn't you say?

Now, once again attuned to my context, the cave's breezes bring forth a whisper to my ear: "What is this book *The Power of Will in International Conflict* about?" It is not about willpower, or the will to live, or free will—these topics deserve their own day. Instead, my book involves imposing, gaining, or taking something from a resisting entity or resisting a competitor's efforts to do so. Competition for supremacy or advantage is a recurring phenomenon in human life. People compete for supremacy or advantage over a wide variety of things and situations such as position, presence, action, appearance, dominance, influence, power, wealth, positions, promotions, bonuses, land, resources, and so on.

The subject of this book is a concept, a theory, indeed one of the most important but most neglected theories ever conceived. In my world, *will* is the basis of conflict. One side wins and one side loses, or both sides lose, or both sides declare a draw. But truly, there is no end once the first move is made—even with a "win/win" result, one still finds, in the minds of both parties, the desire to covet what the other owns. With that said, my definition[6] and ensuing discussion of *will* is lengthy but important in our quest to learn its intricacies:

- In the most understandable way I can conceive, it means one person or party imposing their desire, or conceived outcome, on a resisting opponent. This meaning, though, needs more specificity to help us gain more understanding: *The appearance of one's desire, volition, life force—empowered by potency of resolve and willingness to sacrifice, that when yoked with strength of motive and appropriate capabilities, provides action sufficient to accomplish or satisfy an aim, goal, objective, strategy and thereby imposing one's desires over and gaining the acquiescence of a resisting entity or understanding the phenomenon sufficiently to resist such attempts from another human entity.*
- As the most important part of the definition viz., explanatory and working interpretation of this phenomenon, it involves the degree of resolve individuals apply to accomplish an aim, goal, or objective. *Will* appears in one's mind as an oft-powerful, all-permeating presence that clarifies and often releases and empowers one's sublimated desires to either control that which another person possesses or to take what they own, such as wealth, land, power, beliefs, accesses, organization, hilltop, freedom of movement, and so on. This impulse—the desire—once rationalized and articulated, enables its originator to judge the degree of resolve at play relative to the resolve of their adversary, or people whose *will* could be aroused to later involvement.
- If capabilities and strength of motive prove sufficient via assumption, the concerned desire can infect and shape a sequence at the very heart of our topic of discussion—a transformation from passive, chameleon-like, volition to active life force, and a subsequent shift into reality and consciousness via a host of possible impositions of action to satisfy desire. Resolve and sacrifice empower one's rationale and emotions for said appearance to enter the human "keep" where the hungry, potentially powerful wolf of volition strains at its restraints, ripping apart its

6. I could not find a satisfactory definition of *will*. I thus developed my own definition in 2007 and have been improving on it over the intervening years. In fact, the first place I looked for a definition was in the U.S. military's Joint Publication (JP) system and specifically in JP 1-02—DOD Dictionary of Military and Associated Terms. The definition of *will* was not in this compendium of definitions. I also looked for definitions and discussion of *will* in JP 3-0 Joint Operations, JP 5-0 Joint Military Planning, JP 2-0 Joint Intelligence, and JP 2-01.3—Joint Intelligence Preparation of the Operational Environment (JIPOE)—and again did not find *will* either defined or discussed like I discuss in this book.

remaining tatters to cause its release. The appearance of which we speak influences one's deep thinking about strength of motive and capabilities, and in so doing capacitates action sufficient to negate impediments. The infected being applies, by dint of capability and resolve, sufficient pressure and mental acuity in which to accomplish an aim, goal, objective, strategy in a quest for superiority in conflicts certain to occur and in which our thinking moves to triumph. In any action involving conflict, one always finds an apparition-like, restless, "intent," as it were, "acknowledged purpose," necessary to secure a resister's acquiescence to our entreaties.

- *Will* has 14 interconnected, essential elements: 1) life force; 2) purpose; 3) strength of motive; 4) capabilities; 5) determination; 6) perseverance; 7) sacrifice; 8) passion; 9) advantages; 10) disadvantages; 11) imposition; 12) action; 13) assessment; and 14) adaptation. Plan on seeing aspects of this definition and the 14 essential elements model many times throughout the book's pages.

Another whisper in this dreaded cave comes into my mind: "Who should read this book?" My answer: all people who either are now or could be involved in conflict in the future—that is conflict of any type—should not only read, but study, this book. Conflict always involves struggle for dominance. But conflict doesn't have to be one army against another army. It could be friendly conflict, such as a football or basketball game. It could be competing with a friend for a better-paying job. It could be a struggle for ascendancy of power between a husband and wife. Or, of course, such clashes of desires and wants could be hostile, perhaps involving two people or a group of people trying to perform a hostile takeover of a company, or a country trying to abscond with another country's source of wealth, or even a warm-water port. I turned to author and philosopher Ayn Rand, who provides us with a useful idea about our subject:

> It's the spirit you want to loot. I never thought and nobody ever told us how it could be thought of and what it would mean—the unearned in spirit. But that is what you want . . . You want unearned love. You want unearned admiration. You want unearned greatness. . . . Without the necessity of being anything. Without . . . the necessity . . . of being.[7]

Ayn Rand's view of this struggle is raw and ugly, leaving people either emotionally or physically hurt or sometimes even dead. A conflict of colliding interests could play out as two companies battle against one another in a court of law—somebody wins and somebody loses. And, of course, a

7. Ayn Rand, *Atlas Shrugged* (New York: The Penguin Group, 1957), 814.

conflict could be nonviolent steps of compellence[8] in imposing one's goals via inducements, incentives, sanctions, shows of force, or demarches on a resisting entity; for example, trying to force North Korea to be peaceful and to not weaponize their nuclear capability. So a wide range of people in a multitude of jobs and positions in life should read this book—absolutely! It will help them win in contests of all kinds of imposition or counterimposition that surely come their way.

As yet another faint and barely perceptible cry, I hear someone ask, "Why should I care about reading this book?" Is it because there is a kernel of meaning that could grow and become of immense importance? Could it be this subject, regardless of difficulty, is important for any type of security? Can I wrestle the idea to the ground and throttle it long enough to extract its secrets and use them in my life? I say yes! People must be interested in this book and its messages. They had better take care, as each and every day, they stare into the eyes of this hungry and fearful wolf of volition. Forces of aggrandizement, self-interest, hatred, false pride, hubris, greed, retribution, or people forcing their views on other people concerning beliefs in God; or the flow of illegal drugs; or the encroachment of borders; or the hostile takeover of one company by another—all prove themselves at play all of the time and everywhere. So, I ask, "Are you ready to wrestle in these bouts of mental combat under the umbrella of the global war of wits in which we reside?" I ask too, "Are you going to lose because our minds were not prepared for mental combat?" I then throw out a final but ugly question: "Do you believe people to be altruistic in their approaches to life and success?" I say with conviction—no.

I hear a different whisper coming with the dank and fetid air of Plato's Cave, "What are your premises?" Well, here are the six premises I use to frame the substantive thoughts of this book:

1. Practitioners and students of conflict must know *will*'s intricacies and put this knowledge into practice.
2. The importance of *will* is self-evident. It is the central idea of conflict and competition.
3. The subject is difficult to master and put into use; therefore, to succeed, one has to use a method of "how to think" about the subject to comprehend and use its innate powers.
4. To understand and employ this subject I present a thought model. It has 14 essential elements: 1) life force; 2) purpose; 3) strength of motive; 4) capabilities; 5) determination; 6) perseverance; 7) sacrifice; 8) passion;

8. Thomas C. Schelling, *Arms and Influence* (New Haven, CT: Yale University Press, 1966), 79–80. "*Compellence*—is inducing . . . withdrawal, or his [*the adversary's*] acquiescence, or his collaboration by an action that threatens to hurt, often one that could not forcibly accomplish its aim but that, nevertheless, can hurt enough to induce compliance."

9) advantage; 10) disadvantage; 11) imposition; 12) action; 13) assessment; and 14) adaptation.
5. In conflict, the winner always considers their adversary's point of view (this is duality) and the operational context within the clashes occurs.
6. To put forth the highest-quality[9] thinking possible, one must know, understand, and comprehend "connectedness." It requires thinking skills—holism and synthesis.

Cautious and inquisitive people groping about in the dark of Plato's Cave ask me, "What techniques did you use to help learners advance through the heavy brush and numerous obstacles along the trail to the light?" I explain how nine techniques of writing help one move through these clinging vines of stasis in mind and time:

Allegory. An allegory is a story, poem, or picture that can be interpreted to reveal a hidden meaning, typically a moral or political one.[10] In our case I use the allegory of Plato's Cave. I have freed two people from the chains in their cubicles in their bureaucracy of false realities and conventional wisdom running rampant in the dark pits of this cave.

Excursions into my inner sanctum. During breaks while climbing up the trail from the dark pits of Plato's Cave to the sunlight, I take my Überthinker and thought pilgrim and my readers on excursions into my private thinking about a variety of subjects.

High country. I use the high country metaphor as a place where people go to engage in deep thinking (taking the time and expending the mental energy to think about a subject deeply and critically). The idea comes from author and philosopher Robert Pirsig in his book *Zen and the Art of Motorcycle Maintenance*.

Thought models. Throughout the book I provide numerous thought models and explain their elements. For most of these models, I offer graphics to help with understanding and comprehension.

Graphics. I use a variety of graphics throughout the book. There are 23 figures.

Tables. I use seven tables.

9. *Quality*: The degree of excellence in a product, thought, play, book, briefing, solution, and the like. It is judged by identifying a predetermined and defined standard or set of standards derived from the essence of an outcome that acknowledges the purpose of an effort and satisfies the purpose, recognizing the central idea, nub, or core that is the cause of the effect—the output of an endeavor, action, product, a finish place in a track meet, recognizing a good wine, enjoying a good book, or those predetermined criteria with which one judges its degree of goodness.

10. Oxford Dictionaries, Oxford University Press.

Fragments spun into wholes. I often speak about fragments, shards, elements, or parts of wholes. These references and discussions help people learn to think holistically.

Poetry. I use poetry to help explain points, portray situations, or help us think throughout this book.

Quotations. I use the thoughts of many wise people.

Digressions, sidebars, and Chautauquas.[11] I hold discussions with my acolytes, readers, and with even with myself via purposeful digressions, sidebars, and Chautauquas. I use the Chautauqua as Robert Pirsig did in his book *Zen and the Art of Motorcycle Maintenance*, as a vehicle for stopping and mulling over a subject and then discussing what we thought about, or for a private discussion within my mind's inner sanctuary.

A person might ask, "Why do you write about theory and history?" I answer with this thought from a very wise man—physicist John Holland—who says:

> Theory is crucial. Serendipity may occasionally yield insight, but is unlikely to be a frequent visitor. Without theory, we make endless forays into uncharted badlands. With theory, we can separate fundamental characteristics from fascinating idiosyncrasies and incidental features. Theory supplies landmarks and guideposts, and we begin to know what to observe and where to act.[12]

I have found theory to be a useful companion in my intellectual journeys. Along the way I have discovered many a mystery that piqued my interest. When confronted with any mystery, one needs a theory to start solving it, and then one can alter or improve the theory with the knowledge gained from studying the concept. So the term theory means, in my world:

> An abstract or generalizing form of thinking, or the outputs of such thought. The results of theoretical thought present the thinker with a concept or schemata of how something might be, might work, might want to be, might grow into, might come to change, all in the absence or lack of definitive knowledge about the subject in question.

For example, *On War* is a book of theory—the theory of a very complicated and abstract subject, war. The author uses history and his contemplative

---

11. *Chautauqua*: 19th-century annual educational meetings providing lectures, concerts, and dramatic performances during summer months, usually in an outdoor setting (Dictionary.com). Dictionary.com Unabridged. Random House, Inc. http://www.dictionary.com/browse/chautauqua (accessed: October 17, 2017). Robert Pirsig used the term in *Zen and the Art of Motorcycle Maintenance* as a meeting he held with his current and former selves.

12. John Holland, *Hidden Order* (New York: Basic Books, 1995), 5.

excursions as backdrops for his theory. Depending on the context, when you think via theory and history, you might, for example, include generalized explanations of how something works, such as how, when, where, why an adversary may attempt to strike you in the near future. You would need a theory about how you think he might attempt to impose his desires and how he views all 14 elements of our primary model and, of course, his model for his elements of *will*. To note, if you are going to play in this game of mental combat, learn how to deliberate deeply. Deep thinking permeates every nook and cranny of this book to help my acolytes and my readers learn to reason theoretically and practically about a very abstract subject—a heretofore mysterious phenomenon. The prime mover in this learning is thinking. If you don't want to ruminate, you should not be reading this book.

So, I believe we have decided how to proceed. For readers—from all walks of life, military and civilian—who stay the course and proceed on this intellectual journey here are some absolutes—think; learn; question; form mysteries; add ideas to those the author provides; build upon the author's thought models; add to the author's six premises; become thought leaders who help others learn "how to think"; and master *will* to engage successfully in mental combat and win, contributing to winning the overarching war of wits in which America finds itself involved!

Hang on—the journey is going to be wild and tumultuous, but highly stimulating and memorable!

Acknowledgments

First, I thank my very able wife, Sandy Hall, Colonel, U.S. Army, Retired, for her support and ingenious advice in writing this book. She encouraged me to move forward at every twist and turn as we experienced this journey over the past several years. She edited what I wrote many times and always found ways to improve the manuscript. Sandy became so close to what I was thinking that she became adept at offering recommendations for how to interpret my thoughts into sufficient clarity to improve the book. As I wrote the book, it went into a trajectory of thought proving to be new and challenging. With her great intelligence, coupled with her experiences, Sandy understood my thinking, thus joining me on my journey into this Nirvana of thought that is *will*.

Second, I thank my great friend, Paul Tiberi, Colonel, U.S. Army, Retired. He expended a significant amount of time and much thinking as he studied the book's intricacies. Armed with a tremendous understanding of theory, history, and philosophy, Paul provided great insights and ideas that proved most useful; similarly, his insights and suggestions kept me moving to finish this amazingly difficult book. His skillful editing bettered the book and helped the book become more readable. With Paul's fine mind at work and his diligence in thinking about and offering suggestions for improvement, the book ended as I hoped—a useful book of knowledge about *will*.

Third, I thank Dr. Larry Regens, Professor, University of Oklahoma, for his able assistance in writing this book. His thoughts helped to advance the book not only substantively, but also organizationally. In particular, his organizational skills shone brightly, as he advised me on chapter merging and reorganization, all to improve comprehension. Larry read my book three times, and he knows the book's intricacies well. As he travelled so close to the book's core of meaning, he provided numerous useful recommendations from a wide variety of perspectives.

Fourth, I thank Eric Walters, Colonel, U.S. Marine Corps, Retired, for his interest and support in developing this book about *will*. Eric, an avid reader, an eager learner, and blessed with a great mind, read what I wrote as the book developed. Eric always provided remarkable comments about the segments of my book I shared while writing the manuscript. His back and forth with me proved most helpful in attaining the high quality I defined and sought for this book. He imagined how to use the book's ideas in his U.S. Army Command and General Staff College (CGSC) classroom and even in his wargaming efforts.

CHAPTER 1

Introduction

Argument: *In this chapter, I explain the phenomenon of* will. *While age-old, this subject has been ignored and is not defined in U.S. Joint Doctrine. Yet its importance in war and all forms of conflict is undeniable. I prepare the reader to go into depths of meaning about this central idea in all conflict. I prepare readers to think about man's struggles in history and turn what they learn into practice. Anybody who reads this book and practices its admonitions will be armed with a decided edge in future conflicts in any domain, at any level, at any time.*

When one says directly (I'm going to impose my *will* on my opponent) or indirectly (I'm going to slow down and incrementally get what I want over a competitor), what exactly do they mean and against whom? In this work, I present an extraordinary but neglected phenomenon—*will*. Its amazing influence on humankind throughout the ages makes it consequential, mostly because of the misdeeds of its offspring—conflict and war. At a grassroots level, when picking at its nub, one always finds quests for power, hubris, madness, greed, hatred, avarice, retribution, religion, fear, cultural differences, and so on. At a loftier level, consider how the United States tries to impose its national will via instruments of national power. Thus, exerting one's will on a resister takes a variety of influences—diplomatic, economic, military power, scientific know-how, information, culture, industry, technology, academic institutions, geography, and so on. If intelligently used, instruments of power can compel other people, organizations, terrorist groups, dictators, drug gangs, and even nation-states to acquiesce to America's desires. Often, however, America's efforts meet with either formal resistance or resistance via subterfuge and obfuscation. In particular, one can consider North Korea, Iran, Russia, the Taliban, ISIS, and various factions and forces in Syria and immediately understand how difficult it is to impose one's goals when there exist few obvious and effective ways to do so short of direct military force.

As we attempt to impose our way of thinking on other people, should one expect resistance to such an attempted imposition? This question is important. Coercing another human being in charge of a country, company, drug gang, insurgent group, and so forth can be not only difficult when offering incentives and inducements, but also each target can be very different from each other so the inducements and incentives will differ too. First and foremost, know the target. Even if we identify our target to induce, incentivize, or punish, realize this person, or people, or organization will always display many masks of appearance. Peel away the layers of his masks and find the nub of his existence. Explore this nub to find *that which truly matters* that could cause him to acquiesce to our way of thinking.

How do people proceed to know and learn if the pressure point of our attention is an individual, a group (such as in Iran), or a strongman, such as is the case in Russia today? If it is an individual, rarely could he make decisions totally by himself (Hitler, Stalin, and other dictators prove exceptions). Instead, these leaders use trusted advisers to help them think through ramifications, possibilities, dangers, risks, and responses. Interestingly, each side in such a fray can participate in the "game" with resolve to win, as he tries to influence his enemy and their coterie of confidants. An example of what I'm speaking of involves Russia and Ukraine over the past few years. Many forces have been at work and influence a struggle of *wills* in this example—military sensitivities, military necessities, for example, a warm-water naval base housed in the Crimea on the Black Sea, recency of freedom, economic ties, historical views and pressures, richness of the break-away country (Ukraine), security issues, views of the strongman and knowing his actions to bring the Crimea back into Russia.

Another example considering the imposition of *will* involves America's attempts to influence a dictator and his entourage—Kim Jong-un in North Korea. To win, one has to know how their adversary thinks; identify his coterie of advisers and assistants and how they interact; how this coterie thinks (truly thinks); where Kim went to school and what he learned, his family relationships; his pastimes; his aim, goals, objectives, strategies, and tactics; and how he views each of these purveyors of power. In addition, to force Kim to acquiesce to our imposition actions, one must reason about his personality; personal habits; proclivities; trappings of power; "that which truly matters"; his aims, goals, and objectives; and the value he places on their accomplishment. Our Über-thinker and thought pilgrim identify some other aspects of Kim's being so as to have the best probability to cause acquiescence to our supplications. These aspects of our knowledge should, to the best of our know-how and wargaming, consider Kim's values, social mores, worldview, and his and his enemy's military and economic capabilities. One would also have to assess and form conclusions about his life force, self-esteem, confidence, views of technology, mythos—afterlife, legacy, his comprehension of causes and effects, his view of his enemy's motives, his strength of motive, and how he views his opponent's strength of motive. One would have to know Kim's purposes for what he could cause to happen, his view of his own advantages and disadvantages, and his adversary. One has to understand Kim's definition of winning, his determination and perseverance to win, his readiness to sacrifice his people, his passion, and fear of his own removal in a regime change should a full-scale war commence on the Korean peninsula.

I'm sure you can develop more ideas about this kind of thinking involving the targeting of people and their minds to entice or convince them it would be in their best interests to acquiesce to our requests. Remember, I'm speaking of struggles over *will*—one side is trying gain an objective or goal thorough force and another side is resisting or acquiescing. This fight, this conflict, this struggle is the basis for war, security, countering drugs, as all involve this struggle for dominance of one side's desires (thus the freedom to control, reaching a height of power, imprisoning the losers, and so on). We must remember, however, what and how people think is private and thereby difficult to understand. The factors involving this thinking are easy to see and understand but particularly difficult to grapple with in practice. Reasons for such troubles prove easy to understand from a philosophical perspective but more difficult when I speak of pragmatism in actual use.

An example of what one could and should be looking for could be groups or aggregations[1] of varying size. These groups could be financial, religious, organizational, or occupational (media and so forth). My thinking about aggregations comes forth in the following explanation. What I'm talking about involves a sequence that can be either slow or quick. The sequence is additive and goes as follows: In any conflict one finds in the always turbulent operational context, complex adaptive systems (CAS) (dynamic network of many agents, which may represent cells, species, individuals, firms, and nations) acting in parallel, constantly acting and reacting to what the other agents are doing)[2] that are enemies, adversaries, opponents, neutrals, or allies. Thus, one can find one CAS + one CAS = *aggregate*. The merging of two aggregates becomes a *micro-aggregation*. The kludging of two or more micro-aggregations leads to a *macro-aggregation*. Each of these aggregations has some sort of leader, a structure of sorts, a coterie of decision support people, a mass of people, and capabilities that can defend or attack

1. *Aggregation:* The gathering of aggregates into a larger whole. This whole is collective and responsive to accepting more like and disparate elements into its whole. An aggregation enfolds smaller aggregates and unfolds into larger aggregations.

2. The definition, a compendium of thoughts and descriptions, entered my mind when I synthesized the work of John Holland, as cited in M. Mitchell Waldrop, *Complexity* (New York: A Touchstone Book, 1992) 11–12, 176–177, 169, 251–262, and from Holland himself in, John Holland, *Hidden Order* (New York: Basic Books, 1995), 4–12.

in a conflict. As another example, intelligence analysts, subject matter experts (SMEs), and local experts can come together, bond, and form an aggregation of their own to develop sufficient data, information, and knowledge to influence their adversary in ways positive to the imposer. One can also use the combined power of an aggregation to form a supra-virtual intellect, a holistic aggregation involving *a combination of minds, computers, sensors, data, data conduits, knowledge, organizations, and virtual knowledge environments.*

I am sure you surmise that which I describe presents you with a strategy for engaging in any kind of conflict. But people have to understand the purpose of such groupings, as strengths vary according to what one desires to win. These strengths can be created and manipulated via combinations, and even in the coherency of parts in the combinations, and relationships (single or bundles of links) of relative wholes. Thus, one of the most perplexing challenges one finds as they work with considerations of volition involves typologies and their origins. Some questions and answers forming our conceptual framework[3] for this subject help us work our way through this morass. As one question, we could ask ourselves: "Who might serve as our target?" It could be an individual, a group of individuals, a CAS, two CAS, an aggregate, a micro-aggregation, or a macro-aggregation. Interestingly, one's focus for imposing our ideas could be 1) a person; 2) a group of people; 3) an organization; 4) a business; 5) a religious group; 6) a social group; 7) a neighborhood; 8) a sect or tribe; 9) a village; 10) a political group; 11) a military unit; 12) a union; 13) a homeowners association; 14) a decision maker; 15) several decision makers; 16) a judge; 17) a clergy person; 18) a legislative body; 19) a law enforcement organization; and so on. One has to decide with a high degree of specificity who is the target for our imposition actions and calculate the probable reaction. We also forecast an opposing adversary's capabilities to resist and parry our imposition actions. Also, people caught between two fighting forces could decide to take advantage of the melee to impose their desired outcomes, if they have the strength of motive and wherewithal. Any participant in this game always remains wary of the motives of others as the ugly hydra of self-interest always preys upon those conflicting. Once we consider "who" or "what," then detailed planning and timing of imposition actions becomes surprisingly possible.

With an understanding of the primary targets of our *will*, we discern why they are our primary target to first focus incentives and then inducements of sufficient value (from this adversary's perspective) and compellence[4] to

3. *Conceptual framework*: A way of organizing to differentiate concepts, organize ideas, and show/discuss relationships within and with other concepts.

4. Thomas C. Schelling, *Arms and Influence* (New Haven, CT: Yale University Press, 1966), 79–80. "Compellence—is inducing . . . withdrawal, or his [*the adversary's*] acquiescence, or

accept our imposition. In addition, our Über-thinker and thought pilgrim always submerge in deep thinking in their high country of thought to understand their adversary's status via 1) life force; 2) purpose; 3) strength of motive; 4) capabilities; 5) determination; 6) perseverance; 7) sacrifice; 8) passion; 9) advantage; 10) disadvantage; 11) imposition; 12) action; 13) assessment; and 14) adaptation.

It is clear to me that we have not reached the intellectual level I desire. More mental work will appear in my acolytes' minds to provide answers to questions with more specificity. These questions prove critical to success; therefore, it is important for further learning to answer them. Some of these questions involve:

- Do I believe the adversary can resist my efforts to influence? If so, how hard, how long, and with what capabilities?
- How much is my adversary willing to sacrifice and what is his level of passion—important in knowing my enemy in conflict.
- If my adversary chooses to parry my impositions, will he impose his way of thinking on me, as I am embroiled with his parries to stop my original efforts?
- Does my target have its own target in my camp for a specific purpose and intended outcome?
- What is the basis for his possible attempts to impose a desired outcome against me?
- Why should I worry?
- What could go wrong, what could stray awry?
- How might my enemy react or act first in a preemptive mode?
- Could it be that the target of my adversary's intentions might be my condition-setting activities and thus threaten to preempt me with his instruments of power? What can I do to anticipate and forestall his efforts to find my condition setting for my imposition actions and thereby preempt his counters?
- What can I expect the operational context housing the conflict to be like, and who might have the initial advantage?
- Which of the seven domains in which combat/conflicts occur (air, ground, sea, space, cyber, information, and cognition)[5] shall our actions spring forth to enable my desired outcomes to prevail, vibrate, or even aperiodically oscillate?[6]

---

his collaboration by an action that threatens to hurt, often one that could not forcibly accomplish its aim but that, nevertheless, can hurt enough to induce compliance."

5. Note that I added two domains to the five in existence due to their importance in any kind of conflict: information and cognition.

6. *Oscillate*: Appearance of turbulence and change.

- At which of the four levels of conflict—grand strategic (policy), strategic (military), operational, and tactical—do we expect/desire impending battles of imposition and denial efforts to occur?
- How does one synchronize actions across the seven domains and four levels of conflict?
- What characteristics of nonlinearity could prove highly influential to our operational context, in that they could turn our actions and theirs into chaos?
- How can I attain both brief and long-standing advantages over the adversary?
- How can I learn how to think about the thought model of my enemy: against whom do I conflict, what is his strength, why am I attempting to impose my way of thinking on him, and where and when should this effort occur?
- Robustness is an important consideration as I need to determine this following goal—that is to say, if I succeed, do I want my adversary to have the potential to rise from the ashes of his defeat?

How do conflicting organizations figure in this struggle?[7] The answer is, of course, that they play a major role if empowered to focus their energies not only on how and when an adversary could try to resist our imposition, but for the friendly side to "make a deal" or help the adversary retain his honor by not destroying his entire capabilities. The specific capabilities of which I speak involve robustness and resilience. So, I ask my Überthinker and thought pilgrim these five questions: 1) What is the higher order of thinking that comes from our new understanding of the drive of desire, robustness,[8] and resilience?[9] 2) Is resilience an important factor in determining my strength of connectedness and my enemy's? 3) Why would I care about resilience relative to my adversary's and my connectedness one way or the other? 4) Can robustness and resilience succeed without one another? Again, it is good to ask questions, but sometimes either time or knowledge intervenes and precludes good answers to our questions. But

7. Organizations I'm speaking about must be 1) nimble; 2) agile in adjustment; 3) self-organizing even across "turf" boundaries; 4) able to delegate decision making to the lowest levels of their operation; 5) open to innovative and creative ideas (in fact, seek such ideas); 6) aggressive; and 7) able and willing to take risks. In my world, America's hierarchical organizations learn to shift to a "flat, edge-oriented structure with complementary processes" and then are able to switch back to a hierarchical structure and processes when the time is right. I have serious doubts this can happen now, but I am speaking of the ideal, so it goes.

8. *Robust:* Strong and healthy; hardy; vigorous; able to withstand pressure, the winds of change, assaults against one's being.

9. *Resilient:* Returning to the original or roughly similar form or position or capability after being assaulted, attacked, dispersed, bent, compressed, or stretched.

they provide us with "food for thought," as it were, and they provide a powerful motive to learn.

Other questions lurk and cause dissonance in my mind. My mind appeases this intellectual turbulence by asking and answering a simple-looking question but which I find at its core to be profoundly complicated: *What are the most effective and efficient groupings of people in conflicts over will and their organizations, to create the wherewithal to successfully impose my desires on this adversary who resists*? I thus need to examine my basic thinking and theory and turn them into practice by identifying 1) strategic aim; 2) goals; 3) objectives; 4) the right combinations of national and local power and how to employ them to win in engagements, battles, and campaigns; 5) the sources of power with which to plan for and execute sufficient capabilities to succeed; and 6) the range and magnitude of probable enemy/adversarial responses before, during, and after the competition ends.

Still, something remains amiss in our deep thinking and causes me consternation. Could it be a gap or fissure remains in the peaks and valleys of our reasoning? Is imposing our way of thinking different in each individual and grouping? If so, why? Could it be the culture and elements therein? Let us expand our ways to influence individuals and groupings of individuals. In a generic sense, what follows is one of several thought models to use in conflict, regardless of domain, foe, capabilities, cultures, visible and physical implements of strife, and struggles against foes in often diverse operational contexts.

Rational thought helps us design and pick "tools" to succeed through persuasion and sometimes through force (from our adversary's perspectives and thoughts as well as ours).

1. Incentives
2. Inducements
3. Threats via media and revving elements of national power to change the opponent's governing, or better known as the threat of regime change
4. Compellence (coercive diplomacy)
5. Sanctions
6. Shows of force
7. Actual force
8. Waging bouts of mental combat
9. Outthinking adversaries in mental combat, a subset of knowledge war

Wargaming is also important. It is different, though, from the normal course of action wargaming the U.S. military has used for years. This new kind of wargaming—*against the adversary's wargaming*—specifically helps intelligence people, planners, some operations people, and, of course, one or more decision makers. Just a smattering of our considerations includes some very interesting questions: How does the adversary anticipate my attempt to influence? How can we attack 1, 2, or all of the 14 elements of his *will* model? How does the adversary hope to take away pieces of the model? How do our narratives, our proclamations, our calls for unconditional surrender influence this important consideration—fear of alternatives—and what could such fear drive this adversary to do? How does the adversary wargame our wargaming? How does one attack or take away that which truly matters to him (or show the adversary they could lose that which truly matters away from them)? How might the adversary assess and attack what he believes we consider to be that which truly matters to us? How does one proceed to outthink a resisting opponent? Who are the primary actors on all sides? Where and when will the struggle occur?

These struggles undoubtedly come when one can surprise or seize the initiative. Any entity with a bent to win hides the *when, shape, and form* of any particular imposition action. To win, one strives to act first, by preemption, when the recipient of the imposition is discovered performing his well-hidden condition setting for his forthcoming actions. Know why the adversary is imposing actions to fulfill his desires.

This kind of thinking provides our collective intellects and emotions with the impetus to sacrifice, act with passion, persevere, be determined, and know our inner being is connected with purpose and life force of the origins of volition—the birth place of the aggressive actions of which I speak. Our thinking about "how" is, of course, dependent upon our adversary—his persona, aims, goals, objectives, strategies, culture, personality, beliefs, values, view of us, view of technology, *Weltanschauung*,[10] and, of course, how he considers us.

In my experience[11] with conflicts and combat, I often heard people utter pronouncements such as "Our *will* must crush our enemy's; "I must impose my *will* on a particular leader." But these statements cause a diminution of this phenomenon's power due to the ambiguity of the words. I suggest to my acolytes that such people do not know a definition of *will*, much less possess a sufficient understanding of it.

In this chapter, I explained to my readers unless people possess a deep knowledge and comprehension of *will*, they flounder, intellectually and often physically, as they do not know with high exactitude what this powerful word means from their perspective, let alone their antagonist's. Contrarily, I argued, as a combatant, one must know how adversaries think about *will*; they must comprehend this person' understanding of *will*. This

10. *Weltanschauung*: Worldview; holistic conception of the world and universe, human foibles, contexts, and how human beings relate to one's worldview.

11. *Operation Just Cause* December 1989; *Operation Desert Shield/Desert Storm* August 1990–March 1991—Battalion Commander in the 82d Airborne Division for both wars.

understanding helps people assess outcomes of conflicts and the levels of resolve at work. Thus, I discussed and presented a definition and typology for *will*. I introduced sufficient theory for thinking about the enemy/adversary's *will* whom I plan to engage in a contest of *wills*. To win, one must know his enemy, so it goes.

I introduced in this chapter the stalwart columns of strength in my thinking—*wargaming how the adversary is wargaming* to beat us in fights and battles. Warriors know this great phenomenon of *will* and use its intricacies to cause their opponent to yield. I also spoke of knowing how to work with incentives, inducements, and compellence to force an adversary to yield to our desires. To develop and impose our demands and influence our adversary's inferences I expect my readers to identify, study, and understand *will*'s secrets and its essential elements, and then wisely use this knowledge to win. I explained in this chapter, within *will*'s essential elements one discovers how to visualize them in a thought model. Knowing these elements provides our combatants with an inner strength. Thus, people either studying or acting out struggles of *will* must learn these 14 elements, so essential in winning any contest or conflict of arms: life force, purpose, capabilities, strength of motive, perseverance, determination, advantage, disadvantage, passion, sacrifice, imposition, action, assess outcomes, and adapting faster than their competitor. Knowing and exploiting the power inherent to this model shall always enable the knower to possess a massive advantage over any foe.

CHAPTER 2

Theoretical Foundations

Argument: *In this chapter, I define* will *and discuss its importance in conflicts. I explore how it always involves one side seeking to impose their way of thinking on a particular adversary and the another side resisting or acquiescing. I introduce the concept of duality to emphasize thinking about an adversary's views and attempts to leverage intricacies of the phenomenon under our studious examination. I explain how my 14-element model involves collisions in which neither side yields until one or more model elements crumple. I introduce a second model to help you to think about our great phenomenon; it provides 18 considerations to ponder as one plans to fight.*

Why does man seek power? The strong desire to be recognized, to leave something behind, to be remembered burns brightly in all human beings, but more brightly in some people than others. Sometimes it channels into family contrivances, but at other times, particularly with men, life force is more of a physical act or deed. In this, one finds links wending their way through the ages connecting with people who lived in antiquity almost as though there was no passage in time. Entanglement occurs with those coming after us. Man and his life force seek to impose a way of life or thinking on another person, often a resisting person.

Seeking even more depth of thought to help us understand this phenomenon, one can discover a partial answer to this question by bringing to life the thoughts of the German philosopher Friedrich Nietzsche. His interpreter, Frederick Copleston, provides us the following insights from this great mind:

> [C]ategories of reason are also logical fictions and perspectives, not necessary truths, nor a priori forms. . . . For him, even the fundamental principles of logic are simply expressions of the Will to Power, instruments to enable man to dominate the flux of becoming.[1]

---

1. Frederick Copleston, *A History of Philosophy, Volume VII: Fichte to Nietzsche* (New York: Doubleday, 1973), 410.

Will—unpretentious, or is it? My view—it is extraordinarily complicated and difficult to contemplate, let alone to grasp for use in our lives. What happens when humans start to impose their desires on another person or persons? What happens when a friendly decision maker is on the receiving end of an adversary who is attempting to do the same thing? The complexity involved with a fight for dominance of any kind involves a position of superiority over another person or people. Such dominance involves reasons for the mind-boggling and unrelenting aspects of such competition. Struggles over *will* usually involve intangibles such as greed, fear, retribution, desire, lust, religion, narcissism, and even premeditated defenses such as in preemptive strikes. Sadly, human beings have been fighting one another since the first man clubbed another man to take his food and women. Fights always involve *will*; one side commits an aggressive act against another, the other side defends against the imposition or submits. Therefore, allow me to submit my first premise: Practitioners and students of conflict must know the intricacies of *will* and put this knowledge into practice. Nietzsche helps us understand this kind of rationale. As deep thinkers, responsibilities exist and actors prove duty bound to not only grasp this kind of rationale and plan for its implementation in an intellectual sense, but also to place this discovered theme into practice. As one of many distinct cause-and-effect relationships,[2] it helps to know some good reasons as to why people—opponents, enemies, adversaries, business competitors—fight each other:

> Power is enjoyed only as more power. One enjoys not its possession but its increase. . . . Again, they are trying to gain independence through power in a system that encourages dependence and . . . conformity.[3]

Philosopher Arthur Schopenhauer presents a view that buttresses my thoughts on *will*:

> [N]ow if the Will is an endless striving . . . it cannot find satisfaction or reach a state of tranquility. It is always striving and never attaining. . . . Each individual thing . . . strives to assert its own existence at the expense of other things. Hence the world is the field of conflict, a conflict which manifests the nature of the Will as at variance with itself, as a tortured Will.[4]

---

2. Copleston, *A History of Philosophy*, xviii–xix: "The alleged instinct for causality is merely the fear of the unfamiliar and the attempt to discover something familiar in it—a search not for causes, but for the familiar."

3. Walter Kaufmann, *Nietzsche: Philosopher, Psychologist, Antichrist* (Princeton, NJ: Princeton University Press, 1974), 186.

4. Copleston, *A History of Philosophy*, 273–274.

Writer John Steinbeck also lends us some insight into mankind's restlessness even if they have everything—money, youth, looks, smarts—with this short but meaningful thought:

> There's a capacity for appetite . . . that a whole heaven and earth of cake can't satisfy.[5]

If a person chooses to learn only one matter from history, it is this: conflict, cruelty, inhumanity, aggressive behavior, war, suffering, and even death are often the result of man's lust to impose his desires on others—this always has been, and always shall be. Thus, it follows people in the dealings of conflict know a voracious beast is on the loose, and it comes to impose his appetite on you. So beware and heed my admonitions—you need to know *will,* its elements, how they relate, how they float from place to place in my model, the model's inner workings, and how its machinations involve imposing actions (an adversary trying to block or parry the attempted imposition or the recipient of the original blow attempting to impose his *will* in a related, retaliatory action via a new set of actions in the volatility of the nonlinear part of the operational context). In a broad sense, one of the first steps to climb as you start toward the light to understand involves seeing a causal connection between *will* and competition. I now provide you with an excellent thought to disabuse us of the notion that our educated minds and aestheticism will cause other so-enlightened human beings to disavow violence and dissuade people from engaging in overly aggressive competition to impose their way of thinking on you or to gain dominance. It is a dream, and a good one, but naive and impossible to fulfill, as author T. R. Fehrenbach notes:

> Since the dawn of time men have competed with each other—with clubs, crossbows, or cannon, dollars, ballots, and trading stamps. Much of mankind, of course, abhors competition, and these remain the acted upon, not the actors. Anyone who says there will be no competition in the future simply does not understand the nature of man—men must compete.[6]

The first man imposed his *will* with his version of a well-planned action. So, I can safely put forth my second premise: The importance of *will* is self-evident. It is the central idea of conflict and competition. The phenomenon appears as a series of interlocked conceptual rings. This book examines them one by one and eventually conjoins these rings into a whole.

---

5. John Steinbeck, *East of Eden,* audio book, read by Richard Poe (New York: Penguin Classics, June 2003), 157.

6. T. R. Fehrenbach, *This Kind of War* (New York: The Macmillan Company), 659.

Our work here is difficult, but it can help all of us possess and exercise "a way" to either use this marvelous phenomenon or ensure we do not fall victim to this voracious beast, the perpetrator of volition's appetites. Since in a general sense people struggle to think deeply enough in order to comprehend this phenomenon, I address their error of omission with the wise words of French physicist Blaise Pascal:

When we wish to correct with advantage, and to show another that he errs, we must notice from what side he views the matter, for on that side it is usually true, and admit that truth to him, but reveal to him the side on which it is false. He is satisfied with that, for he sees that he was not mistaken, and that he only failed to see all sides. Now, no one is offended at not seeing everything; but one does not like to be mistaken, and that perhaps arises from the fact that man naturally cannot see everything.[7]

The Über-thinker and thought pilgrim had been toiling away under the curse of ignorance in the depths of Plato's Cave until I showed them the light outside of Plato's Cave. But they have to journey up, up, and up to the light of knowledge. I, of course, want to help them learn to cogitate about *will* and many other subjects. So, I converse with them along the way, asking questions and answering their questions using the Socratic method, as one would expect interaction in a lyceum and perhaps even a Chautauqua in America's early days (a mentor interacts with students, asking questions and pressing into one's thinking and causing students to learn to question everything).

As we embark upon this journey, remember, you, the reader, must mentor your bright young stars and explain in a Socratic way each and every day. Even when reaching for our rendition of Pirsig's high ground of thought[8] and use his idea of Chautauqua[9] as a method of conversing within ourselves or among our group, you should feel the weight of moral responsibility to help your wards learn "how to think" as I postulate and propose in this book. Finding one's *high ground* where they can engage in deep thinking is no small matter but essential all the same. Robert Pirsig's *high ground* for ruminating conjoins nicely with another great author's notion, Fyodor Dostoyevsky, who wrote:

It was there that I seemed to hear some mysterious call to go somewhere, and I could not help feeling that if I went straight on and on, and kept going for a long, long time, I should reach the line where sky and earth met and find the key to the

7. Blaise Pascal, *Thoughts*, trans. W. F. Trotter and Charles W. Eliot (Danbury: Grolier Enterprises Corp., 1984), 12.

8. Robert Pirsig, *Zen and the Art of Motorcycle Maintenance* (New York: Bantam Books, 1974), 113.

9. Ibid. p. 247. Pirsig uses Chautauqua practices to converse with his former self.

whole mystery there and at once discover a new life, a life a thousand times more splendid and more tumultuous than ours.[10]

As a Socratic mentor, I do not perform my acolytes' thinking for them. Our relationship, while cordial, is didactic, and thus I am helping them to reason better than they had before. All of us have to crawl and scratch along the difficult precipice out of the pits of Plato's Cave; if one falls over the edge and into the abyss, they promptly return to the cave for more action with the puppet master.[11] Our goal—to reach the light, find truth, and feel the warm sun of enlightenment. Nietzsche's words encourage my thoughts and reinforce my resolve to proceed:

No one can build you the bridge on which you, and only you, must cross the river of life. There may be countless trails and bridges and demigods who would gladly carry you across; but only at the price of pawning and forgoing yourself. There is one path in the world that none can walk but you. Where does it lead? Don't ask, walk![12]

So, I ask in my Chautauqua, why this lack of thinking about the thinking to understand *will*? I do hear some reasons echoing in the vastness of Plato's Cave. Some people, for example, believe it to be too difficult to consider. Some people don't want to expend the energy to reason about a subject this difficult. Others say the subject is culturally dependent, thus mutually unfathomable to the minds of people from different cultures. Others lament the tragedies that have resulted from impositions of volition. I say, how true, but why not develop a way to ponder this important subject to survive the clash of others' efforts to impose their way on you? Why don't we go into depth about *will* in the United States military's command and staff and senior service colleges? Perhaps the secret, the most secret of secret, answers lies in the ancient affliction of mankind, the extremely poisonous and deadly disease of "not invented here."

In my view, this subject has been long overlooked. This is not to say that people don't use the word, and I certainly admit that great leaders do have an innate sense it. But there must be more to it than just an innate sensibility. All of us ordinary people need to take the time and expend the mental effort to think deeply and critically about this marvelous phenomenon. Thus, this is a propitious time to put forth my third premise: *Will* is difficult to master and put into use; therefore, one has to use a method of how to think about the subject to comprehend and use its innate powers. This

10. Fyodor Dostoyevsky, *The Idiot* (Baltimore: Penguin Books, 1955), 85.

11. The puppet master in Plato's Cave shows the shadows dancing in the firelight, which represent the false reality of unenlightened thinking.

12. Friedrich Nietzsche, *Schopenhauer as Educator: Friedrich Nietzsche's Third Untimely Meditation*, trans. Daniel Pellerin (CreateSpace, 2014), 5.

book presents a detailed method for thinking successfully about this topic. With my methodology, one can codify its intellectual and conceptual underpinnings. When one writes the supporting doctrines, organizations, technology, equipment, and experiments, they have a basis for their thinking that lasts beyond a single lifetime.

Alas, I have not found a substantive work that goes into the depth of thinking about this matter—the pool of thought I have dived. Even my hero Clausewitz broke off just a few tantalizing parts and dropped them into places, scattered candies on cookies, in several places in his tome *On War* (e.g., capabilities, strength of motive, value of objective, passion). My mind is helpless with the force of this beck and call—I must write this book about *will*—it is my last effort to help people learn to think about this ravenous, voracious beast.

My admonition and challenge to each of my readers and my two acolytes: Understand and use this knowledge, understanding, and comprehension. Its understanding and your subsequent pondering about and working with its many vicissitudes (changes in context and conditions, which might not be best but appear and influence anyway) provide one or more great advantages for you personally in any conflict. The comprehension of which I speak does not come easily. People must work for it with how-to-think guidelines, as well as how to think deeply[13] and, of course, borrow the ideas of great thinkers who imposed or denied it, wrestling with its sharp claws, though they only spoke or wrote obliquely about this phenomenon—*will*. To help, I provide my fourth premise: To understand and employ this subject to its fullest power requires knowing and using a thought model that has 14 essential elements: 1) life force; 2) purpose; 3) strength of motive; 4) capabilities; 5) determination; 6) perseverance; 7) sacrifice; 8) passion; 9) advantage; 10) disadvantage; 11) imposition; 12) action; 13) assessment; and 14) adaptation. Elements 1 and 2 (life force and purpose) lock into place at the beginning of the model; elements 11 through 14 (impose, act, assess, and adapt) lock into place at the end of the model; the other elements (strength of motive, capabilities, determination, perseverance, sacrifice, passion, advantage, and disadvantage) prove interchangeable.

Alas, my views are so plentiful and heavy in my backpack that I must drop some of them as I trudge up the path toward enlightenment with my wards, the Über-thinker and thought pilgrim. I find myself asking, "Do others think this way? Do others view their thoughts and works as pheromones leading them to backtrack and sweep up the droppings so as to find the core of thought about this subject and many other related subjects of

13. *Deep thinking*: Taking the time and expending the mental energy to think about a subject or problem deeply and critically.

value?" I think so, but let's find out! The author, dramatist, and, I daresay, philosopher Tom Stoppard has this to say about what we drop while moving:

> We shed as we pick up, like travelers who must carry everything in their arms, and what we let fall is be picked up by those behind. The procession is very long and life is very short. We die on the march. But there is nothing outside the march so nothing can be lost to it. The missing plays of Sophocles will turn up piece by piece, or be written again in another language. Ancient cures for diseases will reveal themselves once more. Mathematical discoveries glimpsed and lost to view will have their time again.[14]

During the course of this book I, my alter-ego (when he wants to inject himself), and my two acolytes who escaped from the bottom of Plato's Cave trudge up the path; it is easy to feel and see the cave's insidiousness. People chained in the same position forever, neither looking up nor down, chained in what I can only call an ossuary of the living, a place without intuition, imagination, innovation, and creativity—all the lifeblood of intellectual energy. The prisoners can talk and they can see the puppet master's false truths brought forth by a fire moving as shadows against the wall. It is their only reality. Little do they know of the world outside the cave, but it is there all the same, and it is where they could find truth and enlightenment brought about by the light of knowledge.

Thus, they become conditioned to do things one way, to think one way, to believe truth one way, and to be content with their fates. Learning how to think deeply is difficult by itself, but when I ask you to also learn how to think per se, via synthesis and holism, the task is exponentially larger and more difficult. I talk about deep thinking throughout this book, and I dedicate an entire chapter to how to think about volition's role in conflict. As reasoning people, it is our job, our raison d'être for being in existence, to be moral, be of value, search for truth, be responsible, and shoulder accountability to help future and current leaders learn about the intricacies of this wonderful phenomenon.

An injection of learning to people waging mental combat in a war of wits must occur now. We, as peace-loving people, find ourselves in multiple struggles involving the collisions on a grand scale around the world. It follows that it is imperative to use a rigorous methodology for thinking about this subject. Being careful not to sound shrill, in my view America's best and brightest people must learn about being involved in mental combat in a war of wits to fathom the nature of conflicts in which we find ourselves involved and those in the future. These bouts of mental combat definitely occur in a complicated variety of operational contexts, difficult

14. Tom Stoppard, *Arcadia* (New York: Farber and Farber, Inc., 1993), 42.

because of the tornadic energy emanating from nonlinearity that Clausewitz and Sun Tzu wrote about but did not label as nonlinearity. These confrontations, of course, center on one side imposing their way of life or way of thinking on another resisting side.

Our Über-thinker and thought pilgrim must occasionally "ride the wild pendulum" of duality[15] so they consider the adversary's mind, mental prowess, points of view, empathy, and thoughts about advantages and disadvantages in any contested operational context. This mind realizes that it is only subjectivity one finds no matter what people may say about being objective. When successfully thinking about our topic, one takes into account a macro- or global perspective, as well as a micro-sense such as the conflicts playing out in Afghanistan, Iraq, Israel, Syria, Europe, and the United States' cities. The struggles we see unfolding before our eyes involves adversaries attempting to impose their beliefs on the Western world and parrying of such impositions. Then the original recipient of the first imposition action should block this imposition and invoke their own. This leads to my fifth premise: To win in clashes of *will* the winning participant always considers their adversary's points of view (this is duality) and the operational context within which clashes occur.

But how did mankind take the first step to imposing their desires? What took place to cause the imposer of action to desire something and attempt to take it and thereby accomplish a first condition? The actual first struggle between humans is not unknown, as such clashes have occurred since time immemorial. As such, one looks about for more intellectual verve and depth to the subject and finds a shortage in the supply room; as I mentioned earlier, human beings tend to take intellectual shortcuts and thereby blithely use *will* without understanding what it means, what it could mean, and its implications for human life.

Such struggles often have enormous outcomes for our way of living. It can be a struggle between the darkness and light of human behavior. Shakespeare helps us grapple with our thoughts in this short passage:

> Ah, gracious lord, these days are dangerous:
> Virtue is choked with foul ambition,
> And charity cased hence by rancor's hand;
> Foul subornation is predominant,
> And equity exiled your highness' land.[16]

---

15. *Duality*: The state of being in which one thinks as two connected opposites in motion all the time, and emitting noise and energy as one side interacts with the other. Duality, though difficult to understand and to remember, considers two parts: friendly and adversary (and could increase the numbers in complicated contexts and conditions).

16. Shakespeare, *Henry VI—Part II, The Complete Works of William Shakespeare*, ed. William Aldis Wright (Garden City, NY: Garden City Books, The Cambridge Edition Text, Including the Temple Notes, 1936), 52.

Ah, how true this passage rings even with what today brings. Ambition is on the loose and a force in any human's rationality—sometimes good, sometimes bad. Consider these thoughts:

When cruel life happens, virtue disappears, overcome by foul over-ambition; thanks to life force, purpose, motive quickens their pace, racing forth from the Cyclops' cave, wreaking havoc on the human race. A burden humans bear, allowing the ugly baby into an unforgiving and always critical public's glare, and so human behavior churns on and on, and forevermore; Thus, people pair and prepare for appearances of this beast of despair any time and everywhere.

It is deep thinking that provides our Über-thinker and thought pilgrim insights into human nature and motivation. Our Über-thinker's and thought pilgrim's minds sadly recognize a truism—purely altruistic quests prove rare. Instead they find, at the core of most human actions and impositions of "will," the ugly hydra of self-interest, fully or partially masked, and thereby not always obvious. But in this hydra, there exists a presence, a lingering evil with a voracious appetite to influence outcomes with one sole motivation—self-interest, whether in matters trivial or of life or death. Our rumination always includes self-interest; despite the admonition I hear in my mind to avoid becoming cynical, self-interest is indeed the state of continuity among human kind.

Yet another motivator exists. Though rare, this rationale for seeking to impose their desires on other people or organizations comes to be because the perpetrator likes action—almost a nihilistic rationale in that there is no concrete reason.

In their high country,[17] my Über-thinker and thought pilgrim come to accept a degree of humility because it is a condition conducive to good learning, and with it, they open their minds for reasoning. Humility is, of course, not only relative to Socrates's thoughts but also relative to what the greatest thinker of all time—Goethe—had to say:

There is nothing worth thinking but it has been thought before; we must only try to think them again.[18]

Keeping this truism in mind, in our imaginations during the difficult journey along the narrow and deceit-filled trail from pit to light, I and my brave acolytes visualize and ponder an adversary's true nature and his

---

17. Pirsig, *Zen and the Art of Motorcycle Maintenance,* 112–113.

18. Johann Wolfgang von Goethe, *Maxims and Reflections of Goethe,* Kindle Book, UUID-9ce661f6-11e5-853a=119a1b5d0361, created with Street-Lib Write (http:/write.streetlib.com) by Simplicissimus Book Farm, 27.

sources for his life's energy and creation—thought, rejuvenation, energy, and capabilities. Through the protective shrouds covering the adversary and his thoughts, the enterprising pioneer of deep thinking knows how to ascertain distinctions that set his adversary apart—the adversary's perceptions, thinking, planning, acting, assessing, learning, empathy, and adapting—that is to say, of course, relative to ours. It is at an Über-thinker's and thought pilgrim's high country where a person ruminates about the difficult subject of life force,[19] the principal propellant causing one person to try to impose their way of life upon another.

The high country is where our Über-thinker and thought pilgrim think about the power one finds in one's willingness to sacrifice to accomplish a high-value objective and the strength of motive to endure the necessary suffering to prevail in a struggle—if he believes the effort to win is worth the pain and sacrifice, then passion trumps reason. It is the place where my acolytes can ponder the mystery at hand and discover the purpose of strength of motive one finds within human beings when these acolytes think deeply about all sides and find how the competing sides connect with each other even when trying to destroy one another in a competition or conflict (consider troop-initiated truces such as those between the Union and the Confederacy in the Civil War, and between opposing sides in WWI who declared a temporary stoppage of the insanity of killing one another so as to retrieve the dead and wounded). This brings forth the right time to present my sixth and final premise: To put forth the highest-quality thoughts possible, one must know, understand, and comprehend "connectedness." Connectedness requires the highest condition of holism and synthesis. Connectedness means:

Joined together into a viable and thereby operable whole; linked to one another in a purposeful agreement; parts, pieces, people, organizations, infrastructures linked with one another to build coherence in the parts, pieces, objects, subsystems, micro-aggregations, macro-aggregations comprising a relevant "whole."

My acolytes nod. Regardless, I sense a need for more thinking. So, I explain to them, "In my view we connect to all other human beings. In some ways this connectedness is wonderful, magical, and mesmerizing. In other ways it is deplorable, worthy of weeping, as it dooms humankind not only to share the good but the bad of being oh so human. A deep thinker with knowledge of Donne has certainly read his 'Meditations XVII,' understands and feels the connectedness among us all, and realizes that its positive force allows one to reach the summit of one's

19. *Life force*: Vital force or one's source of energy, strength, with a direct connection *will*—capabilities and strength of motive.

high country and thereby tear away the shackles of intellectual stasis in Plato's Cave."[20]

The long and challenging trek up the trail to enlightenment promises the light of truth and a state of intellectualism sufficient to learn the inner secrets of *will*. But are my acolytes tough and determined enough to endure the climb? With a goodness-oriented attitude, this light will allow them the intellectual basis to ruminate in a pure thinking environment—to work unencumbered by any doctrine of limitation and uncluttered with constraints; lo and behold, they will find the breathtaking vista of holism![21]

I see their tired faces fall as they comprehend the reality of the distance, discomforts, and obstacles along the path they must overcome to ascend from the pits of Plato's Cave to the light of opening far above. But it is here, at one's high country, where one finds freedom of thought—it is where one becomes mentally free in an unfree world. Each person thinking about conflict has a different "high country" where they can enhance their propensity to enter the churning pool I call "deep thinking." It is here that each person can conjure forth one or more adversaries into their consciousness. I hear them saying, "There he is—I see him—he is formidable; he acts and then assesses, then he evaluates, learns, and adapts." So, learn to enter his portal—his mind's eye—and reason as he reasons, see what he sees, taste as he tastes, feel what he feels, touch what he touches, and smell what he smells. Prognostication points out how he might be thinking and planning to protect his soft spots—his pressure points[22]—and how he might view the triumvirate of pressure points, decisive points,[23] and centers of gravity[24] as distinct yet each related.

Figure 2.1 shows a clear multifaceted approach to success—seize the initiative and six other advantages. All conflict occurs in a turbulent—some

20. Plato, *The Republic*, trans. B. Jowett, ed. Louise Ropes Loomis (New York: Walter J. Black, Inc., 1942), 398–428.

21. *Holism*: The theory that the parts of any whole cannot exist and cannot be understood except in their relation to the extant whole or wholes coming into existence via aggregate and aggregation theory. Holistic doctrine maintains that in characteristics of nonlinearity one must consider wholes to be greater than the sum of its parts.

22. *Pressure point*: A sensitive, critical point, weakness, or dispute against which pressure of many persuasions is directed. Actions against pressure points always have a distinct purpose in mind, and the dispenser of said action will certainly have a dedicated effort to see whether the tactics of action against them are working. A pressure point always has a logical connection with the hierarchy of 1) pressure point(s) (important); 2) decisive point(s) (very important); and 3) center(s) of gravity (vital).

23. *Decisive point*: A geographic place, specific key event, critical factor, or function that, when acted upon, allows commanders to gain a marked advantage over an adversary or contribute materially to achieving success (U.S. Joint Publication 3-0).

24. *Center of gravity*: The hub of all power and movement on which everything depends. That is the point that all our energies should be directed against (Clausewitz, *On War*, 595–596).

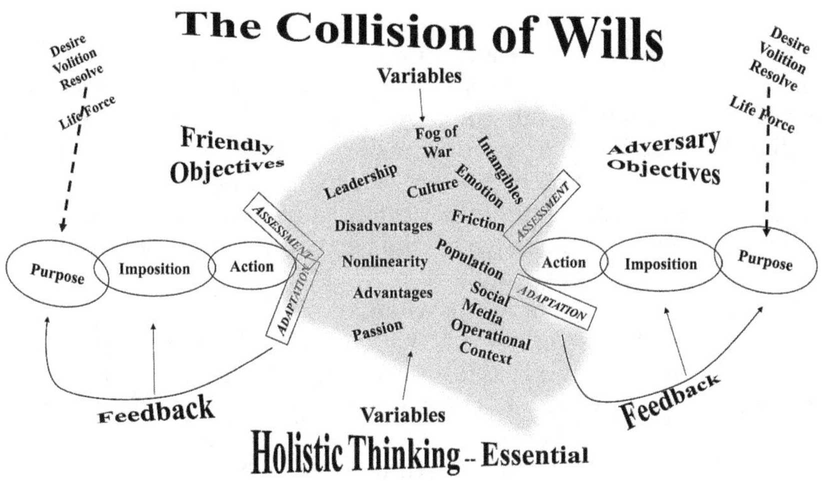

Figure 2.1. Ancient to Present to Future—Collision of *Wills*

would say chaotic—operational context in which one finds the characteristics of nonlinearity at constant play, so use the context for advantage. The clash between decision makers is a top target for one's reasoning. The fight over the dominance of *will* is in the center—as it should be. The graphic thereby depicts areas of thought of high importance that any decision maker must consider and act upon.

Additionally, this graphic shows complexity immediately emerging as foes enter into bouts of mental combat. Each side in such conflict tries to impose their desires on their adversary. But life isn't as easy or simple as conflict experts hope. No, conflicts over imposing and denying always prove far more complicated than one's mind, in its normal pattern of thinking, can conjure; the thinker of which I speak might not recognize traces of its presence or understand the traces if they do pick up on their appearances and meanings. The fight with one another can, and often does, tend to head one's way, in reality as an avalanche demanding instant attendance to the present, forcing the imposed upon to put aside his reasoning about possible causes and effects awaiting him in the future.

While thinking about the last paragraph and its graphic, we search our minds for "ways" to enter the portal, the adversary's mind's eye. Once there, it takes an Über-thinker to do what needs to be done. Learning how to think frees our Über-thinkers to venture deeper and deeper into the musty and dark mines that comprise an adversary's mind, to think like the adversary thinks[25] and employ one's imagination to feel, sense, see, smell, what

25. Wayne Michael Hall, *Think Like the Adversary Thinks*. Unpublished, 2016.

their adversaries feel, sense, see, smell. In this womb protecting and nourishing one live, active, and relative "probability"[26] among many, our Über-thinker's senses lift their intelligence collection receptacles. These receptacles remain on high alert to help the thinker hear, see, sense, feel, taste, and smell even when far removed from the physical location. An Über-thinker also (along with the thought pilgrim) rides a "wild pendulum" swinging like the pendulum of a grandfather clock, at one point reasoning like an adversary (the most difficult part of the pendulum's swing) and swinging back to reason like the friendly side.

It is during this state of mind, when all of one's sensing organs and thought processes rage full of life, that one is suddenly on the prowl for details possibly showing a path to an adversary's 1) pressure points; 2) decisive points; and, hopefully, 3) centers of gravity—the important aspects of his quest to impose his way of thinking or deny the opponent's. They are Janus, looking to the past and to the future to see what they can learn from the past to use again in the future. They arduously strive to see the friendly force through the adversary's eyes. After all, they must surmise that the adversary has put forth serious thought into this endeavor, and he has planned his chosen way to influence them.

Therein lies the rub. If using our advanced thought processes, then we have intelligence collections—human, mechanical, open source, and social media watching for intrusions by the adversary as he tries to size up these three connected aspects of capabilities. If one fails to seek these intrusions early on, it could be too late to deny his strokes and to impose ours. To outthink the adversary, our people anticipate and block or parry the adversary's imposition of his thoughts and dreams. Moreover, friendly decision makers also have the clear task of imposing their way of thinking on their adversary. The adversary surely anticipates the time and direction of such moves and designs thwarting measures. But can he be correct in his designs—hence the need to reason, with errors and misdirection included? Digging a bit further into the increasingly fetid layers of reality and aggressive ambitions, our contemplative person thinks like the adversary thinks. Though admittedly a difficult task, all of us have to learn to reason this way to approach success in such endeavors.

I am introducing the theory of adaptation now, early in the book, because it is of great importance throughout the book and its baseline reasoning. So, adaptation and its relationship with complex adaptive systems (CAS) goes as follows:

- Adaptation. Adjustment and adaptation entwine and prove to be the output or result of a complex adaptive system's co-evolution process.

26. *Probability*: The likelihood something is plausible and doable and also the viability of the possibility of occurrence of an action or event.

Adaptation is a purposeful effort to modify or shape movement, or execute an action due to 1) changes in the operational context and/or to 2) an adversary's reactions and actions as he adjusts to fluctuations in the operational context and/or action of his adversary.

- Adaptation is the final stage or outcome of co-evolution. It comes from learning and evaluating assessment data, information, and knowledge and then doing something one judges to be positive with the knowledge. In this case, the adversary makes a decision about adaptation because of what another agent is doing or has done.
- Adaptation also comes forth from data inputs, sometimes unwanted or unwelcome, from the *operational context*. Weather comes to mind as an example, such as, an unexpected sandstorm during the U.S. invasion of Iraq in the spring of 2003 brought all movement to a halt, when rapidity was the overwhelming tactic and intent of the commander.
- Interestingly, adaptation exudes an aura or glow of positive energy. When people choose to adapt, one has to "see" or "intuit" the implication from adaptation riding the wave of probabilities coming from adaptation forthwith. An action or situation caused adaptation's energy to release and relate to a cause. The action leading to adaptation exerts a positive energy. The energy comes from directed actions with distinct purposes to adapt, which can be positive and active or negative and reactive.

If the CAS receiving data in its assessment process fails to act intelligently on incoming data (from the operational context and/or the adversary's actions or responses), then adaptation turns into a shot in the dark response—the handmaiden of a reactive response to a competitor's acts or non-acts or adaptation. Additionally, when an aggressively thinking decision maker decides and articulates purpose and motive for action, they might seek and grab the "floating" initiative and enable themselves to act first. They also may orchestrate a quest to obtain feedback with which to adapt and thereby open a window of opportunity to achieve the advantages all sides want. With these three elements in place, 1) defining purpose and motive; 2) seeking and grabbing the initiative; and 3) orchestrating an aggressive quest for feedback, then one finds a positive force at work in actions.

It is indeed possible through our minds to venture into a strange, frightening, exciting world—an alternate reality. The presence of this phenomenon preys ever so menacingly on our state of being, but often proves difficult to see and recognize in ours without extensive learning about how to think about the phenomenon. I am asking you to ponder this marvelous phenomenon deeply and carefully, as it is the essence, or better yet, the life-blood of all conflicts and competitions. I'm asking you to learn all you can about this voracious wolf of volition as it is loose having broken free from the leather restraining straps in its keep. It continues to rampage and

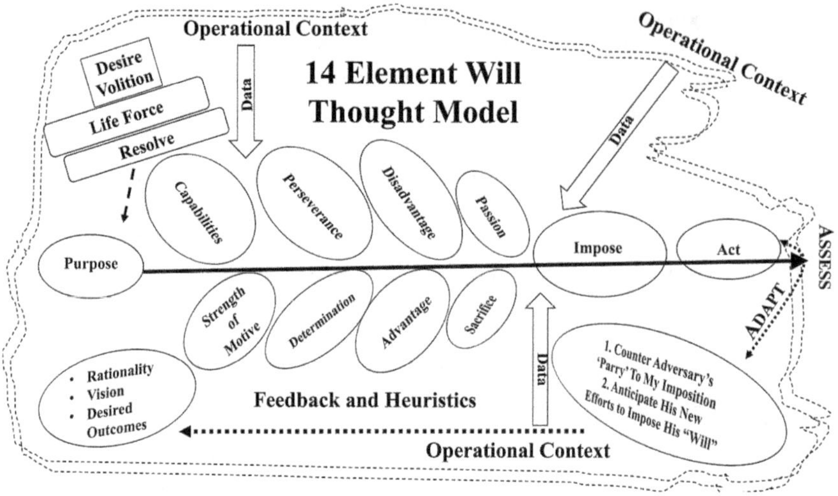

Figure 2.2. Model for Contemplating *Will*

cause death and destruction throughout the world. It is resilient and robust; therefore, it cannot be stomped out as it is, with metaphor aside, the none other than human nature in some people, in some governments, in some religious groups, in some bureaucracies, and so on. To help us think, I developed this simplified model (Figure 2.2).

As we travel through this book, I'll explain the 14 essential elements of this model I developed in all its complicated glory to my readers. Some of these elements prove to be interchangeable in their order but not in meaning. Also, they relate and in fact link to one another. Sometimes not all elements come into play; at other times all elements come into the conflict.

As you can surmise by now, such thinking challenges one's mind. With so many parts and complicated aspects, the task to consider *will* remains daunting. It helps, however, to have this thought model and another to help our thought processes grapple complexity as we move through the book. You might want to copy both this graphic and the one that follows and refer to them while I'm taking you on this journey. This following model puts forth not only another rendition of the 14 essential elements but also introduces the seven advantages I speak of throughout the book. It will help you ponder what to influence to ensure you have the best chance to succeed and the adversary's the best chance to fail thanks to our intrusion into his thought and action cycles.

If people want to stride forth into the cerebral world, intellectual preparation is a must. To understand people and ruminate deeply, using synthesis and holism, along with analysis you must strive to understand the

Table 2.1

18 Considerations of *Will*

Life Force	Passion	Advantage and disadvantage	Value of objectives	Fear of alternatives
Purpose	Pressures	Sacrifice	Constraints	Kinds of *will*
Capabilities	Perseverance	That which truly matters	Pressure points, decisive points, centers of gravity	
Strength of motive	Determination	Affecting CAS adaptation cycles	The marvelous trinity, incentives, inducements	

parts and pieces of this concept, thought, intuition, or characterization. This is deep thinking.[27]

So it behooves you well to know the meadow's green and forested dell—thinking of which I speak remains a complicated spell, but a simple thought it is—this unity of opposites[28] at work before our eyes, a story does it tell.

As another point for your deliberation, I argue: Anybody working with this multifaced phenomenon seriously considers 18 considerations of *will*. One never uses all of them; however, combinations of these considerations coax one's intellect into thinking at a high enough level to start comprehending the subject—you can see these elements in Table 2.1. These considerations are listed in the following table, but realize these considerations constitute the beginning of a thought process to help people learn how to think about this subject. I'm always adding to the list, and I hope you will do the same.

The considerations you see in this graphic stand as vital for one side or the other or both sides in any kind of conflict. Interestingly, the

27. *Deep thinking*: Taking the time and expending the mental effort to think about a subject or problem deeply and critically.

28. *Unity of opposites*: A situation or several situations or conditions in which the appearance, existence, or identity of a commodity, article, belief, understanding, comprehension (or situation) depends on the coexistence of at least two entities or conditions both opposite to and dependent on one another. The ancient Greek philosopher Heraclites first developed this concept ~2,500 years ago.

deep-thinking adversary understands and works a similar approach. On the other hand, as one wargames, they pick considerations most pertinent to the problem. Nothing is ever perfect, so leave some considerations below a hypothetical cutline. Below this line awaits your "risk." You must understand this risk and do what you can to bring its quick demise.

This chapter defined *will* and explained its importance in all conflicts. The book's definition of *will* is *the appearance of one's desire, volition, life force, empowered by potency of resolve and willingness to sacrifice, that when yoked with strength of motive and appropriate capabilities, provides action sufficient to accomplish or satisfy an aim, goal, objective, strategy and thereby imposing one's desires over and gaining the acquiescence of a resisting entity.* Seeking to supplement my thinking and the reader's, I borrowed ideas some of the great thinkers in time: Clausewitz, Nietzsche, Fehrenbach, Pascal, Sun Tzu, Goethe, Pirsig, Schopenhauer, and Shakespeare, among others, to help us understand the nature of the adversary's *will* one grapples with to grasp the magnitude of this concept. In this chapter, I explored *will*'s existence and its commanding presence ever so necessary to fight and win conflicts. Its importance can be found where it lives and resides (life force and resolve). It has been the central idea in war and conflict forever. In this chapter I introduced the concept of duality by explaining how any deep thinker has to ride on a theoretical pendulum, back and forth, from the friendly mind into the adversary's mind, to discern both views of *will* and how one side intends to beat the other in its imposition. I introduced my two acolytes, who join us on the journey from Plato's Cave[29] of darkness to move from distorted reality into the light of truth and knowledge: the Über-thinker and thought pilgrim. In this chapter, I defined a necessary condition of thought for understanding this need to impose their way of thinking and living and grabs for power with what I call deep thinking (taking the time and expending the mental energy to think about a problem deeply and critically). I asked the reader to consider Robert Pirsig's notion of the high country where deep thinkers go to cogitate. The chapter introduced the book's 14 essential element model depicting the essence of our subject. But the key model is when the adversary's and friendly's models collide and neither side yields until one or more of the 14 essential elements withers or dies. In this chapter I stated unequivocally that, in addition to the 14-element model, students of conflicts, warriors, and policy/decision makers who contemplate imposing their desires on a resister must use a model I developed, which includes 18 considerations.

29. I explain the allegory of Plato's Cave in prior footnotes.

CHAPTER 3

Life Force as the Underlying Motivation

Argument: *In this chapter I present the concept of life force. Life force is fundamental to* will; *it is the heart of all conflict, combat, and disputes. It's a wellspring bringing the theory to life and action. I explain how students of war and conflict must study life force to 1) comprehend the phenomenon; 2) affect its inception; 3) stop its momentum; and 4) protect their life force. I provide thinking aids, tables, and models to foster thought. Combatants think about, understand, and experience inception of a coveting desire and its transformation to life force. I provide readers the means to understand* will *in sufficient depth to win.*

Life force is a vital force or impulse of life. It is one's source of vitality, spirit, energy, ambition, and strength. Life force directly links to purpose, capabilities, strength of motive, and imposition of one's desires in a conflict or competition. Life force is one's cradle of energy, strength, motivation, desire, ambition, and even life. Even though we cannot see, feel, hear, smell, or touch life force, it is the starting point and substance for the emergence of *will*. In this regard, life force then becomes the principal propellant causing one person to attempt to impose their way of life or way of thinking upon another person.

At the heart of the hungry wolf of volition, one finds translucent reasoning behind the basic imposition of one's opening gambit—an action-driven view of life force We also find some kind of response—often either a counter to the original imposition or capitulation of some measure. But as deep thinkers, one knows there is far more to *will* than a basic imposition and one or more counters. At the origination of battles over imposing one's desires on a resister and his counter-imposition, our starting point beckons—it calls forth our attention to none other than life force, the dark and murky well of desire from which a person's *will* springs forth, matures, metastasizes, connects, and empowers our 14-element model. All people have life force, as it springs from desire—naturally, it varies in activeness, force, frequency of awakening, and the like. Noted psychiatrist C. G. Jung provides us with this insight from his many years of studying the human mind:

> [W]e seldom find anybody who is not influenced and indeed dominated by desires, habits, impulses, prejudices, resentments, and by every conceivable kind of complex. All these natural facts function exactly like an Olympus full of deities who want to be propitiated, served, feared and worshipped, not only by the individual owner of this assorted pantheon, but by everybody in his vicinity.[1]

Life force knows neither sleep nor quietude. Often, after succeeding in conquering or accomplishing, the instigator grows bored, and then they move on to another target in more situations, with life force showing itself once again. The tether always leads from imposition and action back through the other elements of our model to the essence of the action's origination, the anchor from which the elements connect. It is the nub from which resolve and volition come, and it exclusively belongs to life force. Thus, as a self-evident proposition, I offer this thought—students, planners, thinkers, and decision makers/policy makers must learn to hook to this phenomenon I call life force to ever grasp the *will*'s intricacies. Without it, one only finds parts of the whole.

To learn how to think about life force, the human mind must break free from the oppression of poor thinking always inherent to any rendition of Plato's Cave. The path out is torturous, but our escapees are not Sisyphus.[2] If they reach the sunlight, they experience exposure to enlightenment and truth. They see that their "reality" in the cave was wrong and feel sad knowing they were believers in the wrong truth for years. But in their defense, they had no alternative from which to consider otherwise.

Another angle of thought about life force involves this proposition: life force is the epicenter of the *will* problem. One must understand the sequence of the source of this motion to release its energy via action, which always begins with life force. As Figure 3.1 depicts, our thoughts march from life force through purpose to imposition and action. Later on I'll add more elements to this graphic, but for now, let's keep it simple. Grasping and studying the phenomenon of life force should be an important priority for

---

1. C. G. Jung, "Psychology and Religion: West and East." From *Collected Works of C. G. Jung: A New Anthology of His Writings 1905–1961*, Volume 11, ed. Jolande Jacobi & R.F.C. Hull (Princeton, NJ: Princeton University Press, 1970), 143.

2. *Sisyphus*: A king in ancient Greece who offended Zeus and whose punishment was to roll a huge boulder to the top of a steep hill; each time the boulder neared the top, it rolled back down and Sisyphus was forced to start again.

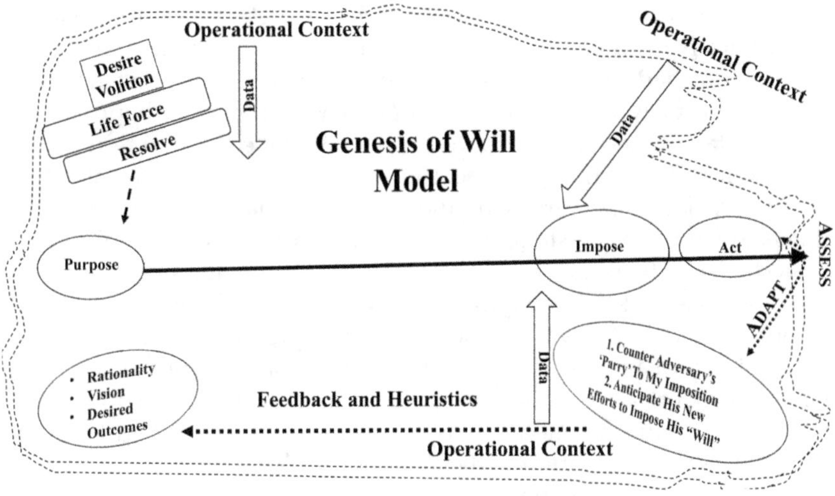

Figure 3.1. Genesis of Imposing *Will* on a Resisting Entity

people who think specifically about enhancing national security and augmenting corporation analytic efforts such as executive security.

Thus, in the following graphic, I provide you with this simple model to elucidate where life force fits relative to 1) purpose, 2) imposition, 3) action, and 4) enforcement to subjugate an adversary or resister to our desires. This model helps us wargame action, reaction, and counteraction cycles of possible behaviors to understand how to win and anticipate how we might beat down this recipient's attempts to deny the imposition in question.

As you can see, the flow of the graphic makes a point in helping us think about the origination of life force. Desire and volition excite life force with resolve, providing strength, which actuates purpose; purpose actuates imposition; and imposition actuates action. If people understand this flow and comprehend its elements and how they fit into the whole, they can realize the presence of a back door, an indirect approach to influence the process. That is to say they can intercede at any point along the path from life force to action. If mental combatants get life force and the flow right, they can look for, find, and stop an adversary's process before it begins. What I'm speaking of is a form of preemption, but the thinking and wargaming load on people who aspire to perform this function in mental combat is significant and intense. Nonetheless it is necessary that people who understand this process model what each waypoint means and implies, and hence have the wherewithal to intercede in the flow of the process. With deep, holistic thinking, one can perform the work and thereby preempt the adversary's life force.

As in all conflict situations, people on each side prefer to ignore unwanted data inputs from their operational context (knowingly, at their peril) because with bad news comes the realization that their planning was wrong. Conversely, contestants in competitive events prove happy to use wanted data inputs from the nonlinear operational context to find advantages. With sufficient thought, operational contexts that seem resolved are always revealed to be turbulent and changing due to the presence and influence of nonlinear systems and the actions coming from complex adaptive systems (CAS) as they co-evolve via assessing and judging the quality of their actions and then adapting their activities, goals, and even organizations. The context always presents wildcards to people carefully planning each step of an endeavor, and they find that sticking with an original plan rarely works.[3] A person seeking to impose their yearning on a resisting force must be intellectually agile due to the changes inherent to co-evolution and adaptation in the operational context.

As a final perspective, because we know that life force exists and we understand its strength and how it "plays" in varying degrees of force, we know that life force can awaken from its indolence, and even while straining at its bonds, can affect purpose, one of the most important elements of our fundamental model. It follows, then, that our people in mental combat must seek an adversary's life force and influence it—optimally before it either partially or fully awakens. If we can influence life force as it transitions from indolence to activity, we can influence the purpose and eventually the adversary's *will* before it becomes a raging, out-of-control monster. My view is this: it is possible to influence our opponent's life force and purpose, thus precluding them from boiling over by keeping them restrained with the chains of diplomacy, economics, pressure from caretakers, inducements, incentives, and military options. Decision makers can preempt, via a scale from small to large, warnings to hurtful punishments, and threatening with increasingly emergent (well disguised at the start and becoming more evident with escalation) and aggressive actions, all tethered to our own menacing, unruly life force that should pose a direct threat to our adversary's.

Before proceeding further, allow me to expand on the earlier operational definition of life force:

[T]he force within an organism responsible for growth, change, and necessary for desirable adaptations. It is a force vital to human growth, improvement, goal accomplishment, and change. It is the energy flowing through human beings, pushing them to achieve, excel, sometimes to merely exist. In some people, this turns into the foundational force that compels them to take what another person possesses but does not want to surrender.

---

3. Helmuth von Moltke, the great German chief of staff, strategist, and warrior, said, "No battle plan survives contact with the enemy."

Life force analysis is essential our intellectual work, as its impact on human beings and to leash or unleash the hungry wolf of volition is beyond important. To understand *will* we must understand our adversary's life force—its origin, its composition, its nature, its aggressiveness, the thin and fragile veneer holding it steady, what restrains it, what unleashes it, the sensitive variables that could cause it to spring forth with enormous energy to covet and take other peoples' property, riches, land, etc. Death is the only obstacle people with an overly strong and flowing life force cannot overcome.

Within life force, one finds the origins of purpose (the reason for existing or acting). In one sense, probably in the sense we can understand best, life force is a beginning to a process with a recursive loop at its finish, meaning the organism learns and its life force can then either adjust or stick with the original life force. In our version of understanding, as I have said several times, life force is the starting point of the effort. For certain, though, to get to the true origin of *will*, one experiences "time travel" to the beginning of the impulse, which could be, of course, how a human baby evolves and weathers gestation in the womb and survives through maturation. In this view, I want you to see the past, present, and future as a whole in which you can move to the past and see what has occurred, move to the future and see what could play out in competitive events, and then drift back to the present and understand how it connects with both past and future. With one eye see the past as it enfolds the present, and with the other eye see how the present unfolds into the future and thereby take action to mitigate obstacles to our process and design obstacles to your adversary's process. In other words, to work with life force, learn to use a dual approach to thinking—time as a progression from life force to purpose to action and then as somewhat of a jumble in which one can bounce back and forth between and among the final to the birth to the middle, but knowing all occur at the same time. Our thoughts take us into life force to understand the presence of an embryo, and it follows that we can possibly affect the action evolving as the desire in life force starts to grow and gain momentum.

This is a discussion of cause-and-effect relationships. Nietzsche admonishes fellow thinkers and readers to understand why outcomes (consequences) of action are important, while also suggesting that we cannot forget the origin of the action (intent) that led to the outcomes. What is the action meant to cause or to do via the cause, link, and effect schema? This is an admonition to pay attention to life force and purpose as the starting points on our journey to understand the impulse to subjugate and aggrandize.

There exists within mankind a force that lives; its energy may be either dim in some people or it may brightly burn in others. The force influences pursuit and satisfaction of one's personal—and collectively, organizational—need to strive, excel, or reach for goals and objectives relative to a strong internal impetus. This impetus involves moving toward self-realization, self-actualization, winning, losing, climbing the organizational ladder, being promoted early, and the like.

The blazingly bright human mind sees this passage and in an instant, hears, at last, the trumpet call heralding knowledge, understanding, and coherence. This sudden, jolting insight thereby allows us to pry open our eyes and minds to that which we seek—that is to say, to roam where life force exists, hides, is contained (in some cases constrained) by layers and wrappings of protection along with multiple masks, such as the innocent, the initiator, the dreamer, the one who desires, the human being conceiving efforts to impose their desires on one or more resisting human beings. We also realize the depth of thinking that it takes to burrow into this conceptual morass and thereby gain insight into the intent of the incipient action or what the action coming into being might be. Once intent comes forth, as a beacon in a turbulent sea, one can attain at least a partial understanding of how to affect the thought appearing as inception and, if extant, how to dam the hole through which the activated and aggressive life force works and pressures this opening to pour eventually into "purpose."

What causes human beings to always want more, to force one's way of thinking on others, to possess a need for power, or to desire more money than any one person could possibly spend? There is more to this than "fate." Why do men, both young and middle-aged, more often seem to be perpetrators of this relentless quest for more? Is it young and middle-aged men who, for the most part, have awakened the scourge of war and conquest to satisfy their desires? Is testosterone the culprit? Do young and middle-aged men impose their urgings from within their being because it is stereotypically expected? Does the need to impose one's desires come with circumstances of the times? Have the young and middle-aged men exerted their efforts to gain power only in times when their country was in dire need of leadership? I don't know the answer to these questions. Regardless, the conundrum remains worthy of consideration. So let us ponder these questions further.

Given that we consider this problem of life force and unpack it just a bit more, some reasons why hyperaggressive people come forth to lead people to enjoin in conflicts involving their need for power or recognition could appear. Would it be nice to possess a list of possible reasons why people leap the boundary between normal ambition and hyperaggression? I think so. Here is a list of such reasons that could very well have implications for you to consider. The goal with this kind of reasoning involves first understanding reason(s) for the awakening or appearance of life force, and second, using the outputs of this mental process to learn about affecting the adversary to force his aberrant life force back into a corral of reasonable human intercourse via inducements, incentives, or other measures. Table 3.1 presents a list showing our minds some possible influencers.

Table 3.1

Possible Influences on One's Life Force

Birth and Context	Courage	Heritage	Legacy	Wealth	Revenge
Parental Sway	Perseverance	Rules	Self-esteem	Notoriety	Jealousy
Communication	Schooling	Expectations	Narcissism	Intolerance	Patriotism
Belief-Destiny	Friendships	Relationships	Psyche	Religion	Pressures
Intellect	Need to Attain	Inheritance	Role of Power	Hatreds	Narrative

I submit to you that one must plumb the depths of good and evil and the wretched conditions afflicting all humans as they live their lives to understand life force. How can we perform the deep thinking necessary to enter into mental combat with an opponent who wants to impose their way of living on America? Are people abdicating the very mental capabilities required to counter such nefarious desires and actions? Have they lost the ability to think because of artificial intelligence, the need to produce products, or bureaucratic tendencies? I cannot in good conscience say that all people are in this condition, but some people become caught in a web of bureaucratic rewards for not creating changes to what is normal and sustainable. Over time, people experience a dissipation of their mental capabilities in this kind of work environment and habitually follow expectations. In huge bureaucratic organizations, the goal is efficiency, not effectiveness. Creative thinking is sometimes frowned upon, as with it comes change, and change proves to be an abomination to a bureaucracy because change is inefficient; costly; and creates the cascading need to change rules, regulations, standing operational procedures, business rules, power positions, and the like. In large bureaucracies, people train on form, processes, protocol, and function but seldom train about how to think or engage in creative thinking, deep thinking, wargaming the adversary's thinking, and the like.

Do we have the intellectual wherewithal and "vitality" to know, understand, and operationalize life force? For the well-intended people in bureaucracies, some become denizens of their environment—they find themselves in a version of Plato's Cave. Day by day, they complain that they don't have time to think. Knowledge workers attend endless meetings and feed the beast with reports, one-page summaries, briefings, processes, forms, routines. They know something is wrong but cannot explain exactly what it is. This feeling, starting out as a minor irritant, becomes a major infection as day by day they feel a loss in their capability to think and learn. This issue compounds with the context always changing and the adversary learning better ways to beat the people and organizations in question.

In my view, the disease is not terminal. People can and should learn how to think, which is a process of education, not training. They need an oasis, their "high country,"[4] a place where they can enter into deep thinking, reflection, critical thinking, and creative thinking about the past, present, future, adversaries, and nonlinear operational system influences on their work and the health of their organizations.

I believe that to understand life force, one has to learn to think deeply. However, as a qualification, I do not advocate a world totally dependent

4. Pirsig, *Zen and the Art of Motorcycle Maintenance*, 112–113.

upon such cogitation. For example, I certainly admit that one finds times where they must believe in their intuition and act or react—this is the focus of two works, both exceptional testimonials to the power of blink think and intuition, *Blink*[5] and *Hare Brain, Tortoise Mind*.[6] No, what I advocate is merging the power of intuition and thought into a "whole," thereby developing individual and organizational approaches to "a way" to actualize the theory of how to think. People in organizations need more than training—they need education to provide them with systems of thought, a philosophy of rumination and learning, the ability to contemplate and feel like other people from other cultures, the ability to create new and better wholes of life. These people must develop sufficient mental prowess to engage in mental combat.

I believe life force to be the principal igniter of countless wars and battles over many millennia. It propels leaders and their followers to act, but always with either implied or explicit reasoning, guided by the hydra[7] of human shortfalls, self-interest, and rationalization. People mask self-interest, but it struggles for dominance and seeps out of its prison within our beings, fingers of hot lava coursing through the arteries and veins of boundless human ambition. When we cut through the words coming from the mouths of these power-driven people who soothe their supporters with a moral sense of right and wrong, it is self-interest that always dominates thinking. At the base of these words—life force—one finds purpose, but not labeled as such. Instead, if thinking deeply and critically, self-interest masquerades as "purpose," and life force acts as a stimulus and catalyst for "purpose" to become strong and demanding on the main actor in our reasoning—*will*. But why have some men been power hungry, with their life force being nothing more than wanting more for the sake of it?

Life force is a source of "being" for all human life. That is to say, as we consider life force, know it to be the basis for movement and change to accomplish goals and objectives. With this thought in mind, one can recognize the presence of three kinds of life force: 1) highly influential and pulsating, 2) normal ambition, and 3) contentment to remain the way they happen to be. Yes, life force exists in all human beings, but in varying degrees of intensity and aggression. For example, very few human beings have the life force of a Scipio Africanus, Hannibal, Caesar, or Napoleon, and thankfully even fewer people have the life force of a Hitler or Stalin.

It follows, with some thought, that a typology emerges for our use. The typology exemplifies people relative to the degree of aggressiveness of life

---

5. Malcolm Gladwell, *Blink* (Boston: Little, Brown and Company, 2005).

6. Guy Claxton, *Hare Brain, Tortoise Mind* (New York: The Ecco Press, 1997).

7. *Hydra*: A monster in Greek mythology that had nine heads. When one head was cut off, two new heads came into being.

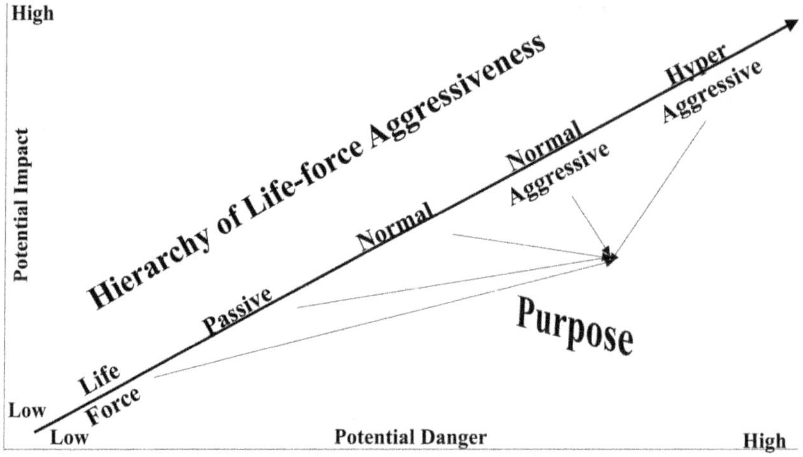

Figure 3.2. Hierarchy of Life Force Aggressiveness

force with, at the extreme right of the continuum, the potential to unleash hyperaggressive people who do anything to impose their wishes upon others. At the other end of our spectrum, passive people live. For the most part, they prove content to live and die as billions of other similar people have done. Next, our thinking takes us to normal people, with normal ambition, with a normal life force causing positive outcomes in everyday living. Next up the spectrum, normal aggressive people appear ever so real and in large numbers. A normal but aggressive life force drives them to achieve, and once they have achieved to achieve again and again, but within societal and cultural constraints. And finally, at the far end of the spectrum, hyperaggressive people appear. They don't number many, but their presence has caused enormous shudders throughout humankind. These people would be like Genghis Khan, Hitler, Stalin, and the Kim family in North Korea. Figure 3.2 shows the progression relative to potential impact along the Y-axis and potential danger along the X-axis.

As such, it is through deep thinking and liberally applying the admonitions in one of my unpublished papers, "Think Like the Adversary Thinks," that we can know and understand the adversary's life force. We can, as contemplative people, dive into the well of knowledge and thought and therein discover the composition of the epicenter of humanness that drives and motivates humans to impose their longings on resisting entities. That epicenter is, once again, life force. Life force is also at play when people find the means to power via making money. I'm certainly not denigrating making money. I'm simply making a point via a hypothetical billionaire's continued need to "play the game" of making more and more money instead of being content, becoming a philanthropist, or just enjoying their billions. If we could peer behind the masks hiding the motivation—indeed, the strength of motivation and the billionaire's capabilities—we would find this person's drive, coupled with life force and "purpose," fueling the engine of avarice always wanting more and more money. At the center of our imaginary billionaire, one finds, of course, that the person likes the trappings money brings (e.g., private jet, multiple homes, limousines, and the like). But digging even deeper, the love of the game of becoming richer every day and love of the process instead of a definitive end-state appear as causes for the effect. Such is the yoke human beings carry around their neck—the cost of being human—but in most cases, people are oblivious to the burden and, sadly, oblivious to life force, purpose, capabilities, strength of motive, and the like in our full-up model depicting *will*'s elements.

As another example, consider the process of gaining and keeping political power by elected officials but who never reach an actual end-state. I have wondered many times why politicians put up with the strain and stress of running for office, being elected, and exercising their political power and facing constant criticisms and then choosing to go through even more election cycles. I found no easy answer to these questions other than a narcissistic self-esteem constantly stroked and buttressed with the ascension to public office. I suspect that the attention politicians receive is intoxicating, as is holding power. In fact, hierarchical bureaucracies encourage the centrifuge of humanness to keep the core of life force active and, when needed, to fuel purpose, capabilities, and strength of motive to impose their longings on their opponent. Once in power, they constantly battle their opponents, real and imaginary, by imposing these longings and anticipating and beating their adversary's counters to the first, second, third, etc., impositions and counters. In their case, it is the political process, along with holding and exercising power as steel is drawn to a magnet, that draws and redraws these people into constant mental combat. Although seemingly invisible and normal to the "players," the perpetual struggle for dominance, power, ways of life, and so forth proves ever so transparent to bystanders in the hinterland. These politicians of whom I speak should read Dostoevsky's *Notes from Underground* and take heed of its sarcasm and truthfulness:

> But man is a frivolous and incongruous creature, and perhaps, like a chess player, loves the process of the game, not the end of it. And who knows (there is no saying with certainty), perhaps the only goal on earth to which mankind is striving lies in this incessant process of attaining.[8]

8. Fyodor Dostoevsky, "Notes from Underground," *Existentialism from Dostoevsky to Sartre*, ed. Walter Kaufmann (New York: New American Library, 1975), 77.

Humans can and should think about, understand, plan, and experience the mental journey from inception of a coveting desire, which is life force, to purpose, to considering capabilities and strength of motive, to connecting all with our newly found understanding and then proceeding to impose one's way of thinking on a resisting person via action. Humans' self-determination and freedom provide the wherewithal to allow their minds to roam and thus to learn in their and others' intellectual contexts. These fortunate people learn about not only the theory, but also the concrete perspectives identified of vitalism. The freedom to roam and create provides people with a two-prong strategy. One prong provides us with a very good way to conceptually think about our subject from our perspective for our purposes. Prong two provides an avenue to attack or manipulate our adversary's thinking and methods for turning thought into action.

When I read the best explanations I could find of life force, I concluded it could be construed as antitechnology. But with more thought, I concluded not so. Instead, we can snatch this definition into our orbit of knowledge and understand that machines, physics, and chemistry cannot do all of a human's mental tasks at this time in history. What machines do well is sort and organize past data and perform repetitious tasks. Machines are even grading school essays now with astounding correlations with human grading. Machines can provide the artificial environments and contexts with which to do what vitalism calls for. In this way, one finds a certain kind of symbiosis between man, machine, and situational context. Machines, however, do not possess life force. Even with this closeness, my conclusions are that machines cannot think about something as abstract as life force. In addition, machines cannot replace the human in solving problems with novelty,[9] anticipating an adversary's actions with high accuracy, detecting and comprehending human nuances and emotions, and most importantly, synthesizing like and disparate thoughts, events, activities, behaviors, accomplishments, and the like into larger and more creative wholes.

But perhaps a somewhat different but related question to our study of life force could be: Can machines learn how to think like humans to consider life force, purpose, imposition, action, and so forth, given advances in technology coming into being? If so, the human being should shape not only the machine's function of thought as it develops, but also the implications and long-term effects on human life as we know it today. Could it be that man has programmed machines to do so much of their thinking and

9. Anthony Goldblum, "The Jobs We'll Lose to Machines—And the Ones We Won't." TED, 2016. Retrieved May 3, 2017, from https://www.ted.com/talks/anthony_goldbloom_the_jobs_we'll_lose_to_machines_and_the_ones_we_won't.

has abdicated responsibility to the machines in hopes the machines design strategies for achieving one's desires? From a practical perspective, such work would take machines of enormous power and the ability to think about not only the mountains of data they sort from the past, but also to work with the mountains of potential data they have to crunch to understand possible future problem sets in a variety of scenarios—and in absence of actual data, to design appropriate strategies for winning conflicts based on hypothetical data as they shift perspective from past to present to the future in some semblance of forward movement. I ask again: Should machines design life force sufficient to drive our comprehension of life force and *will*?

This process happens now. My experience from working with and observing the output of many an intelligence analyst is anecdotal, but it leads me to conclude that society has abandoned critical thinking and critical reading, with each being replaced by the blink think, sound bites, Tweets, Facebook inputs, FaceTime, Instagram, and so on. As a supporting thought, consider author Derek Beres:

> The medium of the Internet, where most people get their information and news on a daily basis, is not designed for nuanced, critical thinking; it incites our brain's reptilian response system: scan it, believe it, rage against it (or proudly repost it without having read the content).[10]

It doesn't take a leap in logic to conclude people do not find serious, deep thinking to be of use any more. Just consider the definition of deep thinking: taking the time and expending the mental effort to think about a subject or problem deeply and critically.[11] The concerted and continuous effort to engage one's mind in this mental process is antithetical to the trend lines flowing in society. Deep think advocates taking the time to reason. Quick think races through intuitive flashes, ideas, data, and even information, but its "employer" does not take the time to reflect and to evaluate, assess, critique, and check data—the propensity is for many a person to accept what they see or hear on the Internet and to see only what they want to see to confirm or deny a hypothesis—an error identified as confirmatory bias.

Do humans have the capacity and the inclination to take the time to think deeply and critically about the wonderful phenomena of life force? What can we do about those fine young minds growing more and more dependent upon computers, the Internet, and the vast sea of continuously

10. Derek Beres, "Can We Think Critically Anymore?" *Big Think*, 2016. Retrieved May 3, 2017, from http://bigthink.com/21st-century-spirituality/can-we-think-critically-anymore.

11. Wayne Michael Hall and Gary Citrenbaum, *Intelligence Analysis: How to Think in Complex Environments* (Santa Monica, CA: Praeger Security International, 2009), 98.

replenishing data? These people are missing the joy of thought and the capability to consider subjects I'm discussing now. In addition, of course, America is missing out on a potential weapon system with which to engage and win in mental combat. We must help our thinkers learn to think about thinking (metacognition) and thereby know how to reason, as it is the other half of the whole that anyone would need to consider very difficult and abstract subjects like "life force" and ultimately the interplay of *will*.

If less and less deep thinking and more and more erring come to bear, they come with the abandonment and atrophy of that which any viable system of security and stability needs now and into the future. That is to say, technical machine progress, though exceptionally great in many functions, can, on the downside, cause erosion of thought, cognition, and reason. Contrarily, America needs to outthink an adversary, any adversary, in any domain or dimension or level, at any time. Its best and brightest should always start their thought processes with their adversary's volition and life force, purpose, etc., as an initial step in any reasoning process. We must possess the mental prowess to outthink the Chinese, Russians, Iranians, North Koreans, terrorists, drug dealers, and others as they come forth, not only with kinetics, but also in mental combat.

It follows then, that the human race must maturely consider the notion of humanism and understand there cannot be an abdication of human primacy in reasoning and synthesizing thinking skills and functions. We cannot wish abstractions and difficult subjects away so machines can perform, with their pizzazz, bells, whistles, and tricks. I'm suggesting this—if we can agree that we must perform thinking sufficient to outperform our adversaries and to do what Sun Tzu proclaims (e.g., attack enemy plans at their inception) and what Clausewitz suggests (a dual force with capabilities and the always human strength of motive at work), it follows that we cannot abdicate our responsibilities for thinking to machines. It is the human mind that is the pinnacle of thought.

It may seem like the adversary uses his machines to impose his desires on us, the friendly force. But at the start of any imposition and in key elements along the line of *will*'s processes, we still find human minds and physical actions at work. The quest to impose one's way of thinking on another resisting entity starts in a human mind; this human's life force provides fuel. This action is resolutely human, and as such, human capabilities must not be allowed to atrophy.

In some cases, the quest to impose one's desire comes forth and acts with an unquenchable thirst for "more." Sometimes death is the only terminal obstacle that people with a hyperaggressive and highly desirous life force cannot overcome. Nonetheless, with sound deep thought, my acolytes can go to the very epicenter of an adversary's life force; consider its purpose, strength, and *raison d'être*, its essential elements via personal history; and then affect it before it "impregnates" the influence of purpose and in turn influence with its long slinking tentacles, the other elements of our 14-element thought model. Details matter when one considers life force. One cannot forget to target it; otherwise, life force wreaks havoc. I'm convinced that mankind remains basically as he was 2,000 years ago with respect to *will*. It can and has become an out-of-control monster, and it is much better to stop the process before it attains mass and finds its velocity and thereby leads to unsatisfactory payment in lives, treasure, and emotional capital.

Now let's bind our loose thought fragments into a whole of meaning as we finish this segment of thought. I have been discussing the concept of life force with you. What can we consider as we craft a summary of this phenomenon?

- First, life force is a phenomenon. It is true and important. It is a wellspring that allows one's volition to come to life. Life force, however, is quite abstract and requires serious mental travail and deep thinking to make sense of what it is, why it is important, and what we can do to either stop or impede its formulation and release or to enhance our own life force and its role in imposing our "will." Nobody can see, hear, smell, or feel life force, yet it is real and highly influential in the amazing progression of a mere idea of coveting what someone else has. Life force can be the basis for a given conflict. When it bursts from its bonds, it allows a dangerous apparition to come into existence. It often involves imposing one's *will* on other parties and using actions that come with capabilities and strength of motive to cause the imposition to succeed and the adversary's efforts to fail, bringing a controversial view of the future into reality, regardless of resistance (invading a country, persecuting a particular minority, forcing our thoughts on a resisting entity).
- Second, our goals in thinking about life force are quite simple: 1) understand the phenomenon; 2) find "a way" via thought to affect life force at its inception; 3) stop its momentum up the chain of process ending with imposing one's needs via action or innuendo; and 4) enhance our own life force and deny the adversary attempts to stall or kill it in its cradle (well of life). The dynamism accompanying some humans or their organizations should cause wariness and worry even when it appears restrained.
- Third, I provided definitions to aid your thinking about this very abstract subject:

  [T]he vital impetus, the creative force within an organism responsible for growth, change, and necessary for desirable adaptations.[12] *It is a force vital to human growth,*

12. Dictionary.com. *Dictionary.com Unabridged*. Retrieved November 6, 2017, from http://www.dictionary.com/browse/elan-vital.

> *improvement, goal accomplishment, and change. It is the energy flowing through human beings, pushing them to achieve, excel, sometimes to merely exist. In some people, this turns into the foundational force that compels them to take what another person possesses but does not want to surrender.*

Thinkers with self-realization and self-actualization—and perhaps even movement beyond self-actualization—find their "high country" where they exhibit the knowledge, understanding, and comprehension necessary to understand how *will* comes into being. The admixture and interplay of these elements, potentialities, and probabilities develop one of many budding means, each of which could influence its maturation.

In this chapter, I discussed the concept of life force. It stands squarely and firmly at the heart of all conflict, combat, and conflicts per se. Life force is a true and important aspect of *will*. It is a wellspring that allows volition to come to life and act (which leads to conflict and colliding forces). Life force is the basis for the start of any conflict, and it lurks in the minds, hearts, and souls of human beings. In pending or actual conflict, life force involves imposing one's way of thinking or living on other parties and using actions that come with capabilities and strength of motive to cause the imposition to succeed and the adversary's efforts to fail (e.g., invading a country, persecuting a particular minority, forcing our thoughts on resisting entity). I explained we must: 1) understand the phenomenon; 2) find "a way" via thought to affect life force at its inception; 3) stop its momentum up the chain of process ending with imposing one's desires via action or innuendo in war or episodes of combat; and 4) enhance our own life force and deny adversary attempts by stalling its growth or killing it in is cradle (well of life). I provided my readers with thinking aids, tables, and models to stimulate thinking. Sadly, I explained, life force strongly burns in some people and compels them to take what another person possesses and ultimately, to enact outright episodes of fighting and struggling with one another—imposer and resister. I explained in the chapter that humans can and should think about, understand, and experience the mental journey from inception of a coveting desire and its degree of resolve, leading to one's life force. The freedom to roam and create provides our thinkers with a two-prong strategy. Prong one helps the reader to understand life force and then how to use it. Prong two provides an avenue upon which to attack or manipulate our enemy's life force and his methods for turning thought into action.

The next part of the book involves the operational context. This topic, although fascinating, is quite different from conventional thinking. Context, in my world, is not the same as environment. I want us to bore into the distinction. Context is what surrounds and influences actions, transactions, interactions—and in our particular study, where the conflict takes place. Operational context is the surrounding "bubble" where conflicts occur; thus, it must be not only known but also combed for any hints of a lurking presence of actual or potential advantage or disadvantage that one side or the other could use to their benefit. In this next chapter, you will learn about two kinds of systems that competitors must cope with: one, which is predictable, is linear, and the other, which is unpredictable, is nonlinear.

CHAPTER 4

Understanding the Operational Context

Argument: *In this chapter I explain my view of operational context; its newness expands current thinking. Context surrounds conflict; it is the surrounding "bubble" in which conflicts occur. I introduce four new kinds of context and a model to aid in using them to understand conflict, fighting, and wars. One system of contexts is unpredictable and largely unfathomable—it is nonlinearity, and it wreaks havoc in all fights. I provide 18 characteristics of nonlinearity one must consider to have success in conflict. I describe how context is a source of valuable data—some desired, some abhorred!*

Operational context has an immense and obvious importance, so the need to attend to our ruminations about this "play land of conflict" almost goes without saying. Operational context houses, enshrouds, and affects everything involved in winning conflicts and competitions. But do people think about context deeply? Not necessarily. A favorite author of mine helps me think about pushing my mind to always discover more—in this case, about the all-important context—

When the mind is satisfied, that is a sign of diminished faculties or weariness. No powerful mind stops within itself: it is always stretching out and exceeding its capacities. It makes sorties which go beyond what it can achieve: it is only half-alive if it is not advancing, pressing forward, getting driven into a corner and coming to blows; its inquiries are shapeless and without limits; its nourishment consists in amazement, the hunt and uncertainty. . . . It is an irregular activity, never-ending and without pattern or target.[1]

---

1. Michel de Montaigne (1533–1592), "On Experience," *The Complete Essays of Montaigne*, unabridged, translator, Donald M. Frame, narrator, Christopher Lane, Audible, Publisher: Brilliance Audio, release date: 09-20-11, https://www.audible.com/pd/Classics/The-Complete

Context has influenced and shaped the outcomes of conflict and competition throughout history. "Does context retain the importance you give it?" my Über-thinker and thought pilgrim ask. My answer: "Yes, and it will be even more important in the future!" Context directly influences people, organizations, conflict, competition, functions, activities, transactions, machines, and so forth. Nothing occurs within a conflict or competition without occurring in a particular operational context's influence—this context sometimes proves beneficial to one side or the other, or beneficial to both sides, and often wrathful to both sides. It is the smart competitor who considers the context to squeeze advantages over an opponent from a sometimes neutral or unfavorable operational context. But, unfortunately, our adversaries do the same. So the winner in the struggle to wrest advantages from the context goes to the side thinking deeply not only from a personal perspective, but also from the perspectives of other actors in this arena of battle.

This consideration involves our intrepid Über-thinker and thought pilgrim accompanying me as eager travelers and learners going through mazes whose solution leads to "a way" for wresting advantages from context while denying an adversary's quest to wrest advantages from this same context. So as we and our adversary compete for the operational context's largess, we sometimes find it obediently giving, sometimes recalcitrant, and indeed sometimes unyielding, unforgiving, even punishing.

Though many people and organizations speak of context and operational environments, approaching comprehension in this topic requires moving into the deep entangling thickets and underbrush of heretofore hidden recesses of the concept of "context" that shall prove difficult to imagine. But we can and should take this journey, as it sets up the rest of our discussion. As such, it picks up on some of the important but dormant aspects of context bypassed in the speed of "doing" rather than "ruminating."

To start, let's ponder some pertinent definitions before we proceed further in our discussion. My definition of context is:

The set (a set is a collection of distinct objects, each considered as an object in its own right but part of a larger whole) of situational influencers that surround, permeate, and influence one's thinking; the thinking of organizations; the activities of a particular event; the arena of action; the place where an operation unfolds; the shape and intensity of any situation; the constrainer of individual actions; or groups of individuals acting.[2]

-Essays-of-Montaigne-Audiobook/B005NC866K?ref=a_a_search_c_lProduct_1_1&pf_rd_p=e81b7c27-6880-467a-b5a7-13cef5d729fe&pf_rd_r=4CCA3YABPV4Z3NTXBDJW&.

2. Please note—this is my definition but I perused many dictionary definitions and synthesized what I read and thought about into this definition.

Consider my view of the word set—an aggregation of objects connecting in a "whole" with one another via links. One finds this "whole" imbued and motivated with purpose via what advanced thinkers describe as "aggregate," "aggregation," and "glue." The glue bonds disparate parts that thereby function as elements of a unified "whole." The glue could be an ideology, a religion, a value, social mores, and so forth. An aggregation is a collection of aggregates. I am merely foreshadowing here and plan to provide you with more thought about and definitions of aggregation theory shortly.

If a person or organization uses the word context, they should understand and use theoretical and historical underpinnings of it. Context describes itself and something bigger and more important than itself, but it is true that a context is a whole but of varying sizes. As you work your way through these thoughts, understand that I designed how to think of methods and approaches to understanding and actually using this idea of operational contexts to focus it and its ideas, concepts, thought models, and intellectual processes to win bouts of mental combat during conflict. Where do these bouts occur? They occur in a highly influential operational context. It follows that we have to understand what operational and context mean. The U.S. military's Joint Chiefs of Staff, in Joint Publication 1-02, uses the term "operational environment" to explain context as "[a] composite of the conditions, circumstances, and influences that affect the employment of capabilities and bear on the decisions of the commander." Joint Publication 2-01, Joint Intelligence Preparation of the Operational Environment (JIPOE), is a well-done document. With that said, it doesn't go into the areas I am introducing in this book; it should include most or all of my chapter on operational context.

The key words include composite, conditions, circumstances, influence, and capabilities. Consider composite as combinations of conditions, circumstances, and influences that blend into a whole that shapes and influences capabilities. This composite involves more than one aspect, object, or thought via action functioning as a whole and via thought as synthesis and holism. Context's influence includes all actors on the stage of conflict under our intense inner eye of consideration. More thought on this subtle but necessary angle of operational context will come later.

Continuing with our discussion, consider the word capabilities:

Potential to perform one or more activities; the means and ability to perform or achieve designed actions through potentialities, demonstrations, scientific experiments and proofs, happenings, individual and organizational acts, group activities, causal outcomes, expenditures of energy, outlays of power, causes to effects to outcomes, disturbing operational and personal contexts, and influences on normal and stable human life.

Of course, context influences capability performance. Consider a "decision maker"—a leader who makes decisions after thinking and planning.

Typically, this person works in a "normal" or "routine" context. Occasionally, though, they have to work in times of high stress. In any kind of situation, a decision maker must pay attention to two things: risk and uncertainty. The object is, of course, to manage risk and reduce uncertainty. Both come into play when one attempts to impose their desire on another resisting party. As you realize by now, many forces and activities/processes interact and produce outcomes in any operational context when conflict occurs. They cause risk to increase and uncertainty to grow for all participants in a conflict.

When we recognize the incredibly important influence of operational context in any activity or conflict, we realize it influences not only capabilities, but also any decision maker's thinking and planning to impose their desires via imposition and action—imposition and resistance always occur in an operational context. So as we push our way through the briar patches in our maze to comprehend 1) relationships among context, competing actors, and turbulent and changing situations and 2) the contextual nature itself to search for value and advantages, one accrues a thorough and deep understanding of operational context. The U.S. military says that understanding the operational environment requires a holistic view, as it encompasses physical areas and factors, as well as the less easily seen information environment. This use of the word "holistic" is apt and right, with one qualification. When people use "holism," they must be cognizant of what it means and implies—this comes by way of deep thinking.

Allow me to explain my admonition: holism is a doctrine in which the whole is greater than the sum of its parts; the parts of any whole cannot exist and cannot be understood except in their relation to the whole. This definition implies the presence of people who ruminate via synthesis[3] and thereby combine seemingly disparate and "at-odds" bits and pieces of data and information and transform those bits and pieces into a new and different whole that I call knowledge. Synthesis and holism prove difficult for some people, so we need to take the advice of a famous thinker whose thought still matters some 450 years later:

> When the mind is satisfied, that is a sign of diminished faculties or weariness. No powerful mind stops within itself: it is always stretching out and exceeding its capacities. It makes sorties which go beyond what it can achieve: it is only half-alive if it is not advancing, pressing forward, getting driven into a corner and coming to blows; its inquiries are shapeless and without limits; its nourishment

3. *Synthesis*: "The cognitive activity that combines elements of contexts, substances, events, electrons, activities, energy, and the like, to create a new, coherent, and better whole." *The American Heritage Dictionary of the English Language*, fourth edition. Retrieved March 3, 2008, from http://dictionary.reference.com/browse/synthesis.

consists in amazement, the hunt and uncertainty. . . . It is an irregular activity, never-ending and without pattern or target.[4]

It is with valuable and current knowledge that decision makers manage risk and lower uncertainty. The synthesis process always encourages a thinker to consider how well combinations affect coherence (how well something works) of the whole itself. In this book, though, knowledge is not the end-all—when we come to knowledge, we come to understanding. When one comprehends, they can find the ever-so-rare wisdom.

To understand and thrive in conflict within operational contexts, you must know quite a lot about synthesis and holism to not only know parts of the context, but also the wholes within it and how they combine with one another to form larger wholes or aggregations. If you study only one part of an operational context, there is no way you can ever understand the holistic nature of the context in which struggles occur. So continuing with this line of thought, it seems to me that we must have people who understand analysis (breaking something apart) and synthesis (putting parts and pieces together into a new whole) operating in the same whole that is our minds. Additionally, people who synthesize naturally and without prompting still need advanced thinking about the operational context, comprehend how they differ from one another, relate to one another, and exist in the same whole. As people use the term holistic, they should understand that in military and many civilian institutions of higher learning, we do not routinely learn how to think about holism and holistic contexts, or even synthesis. In my experience, if any instructor or mentor knows much about metacognition involving synthesis, he or she assumes everybody knows this. This is definitely not the case.

As a related thought, context surrounds and influences all conflict and competitive operations. When humans organize and act to accomplish an outcome, such as using action to impose their desires, they do so in an operation. An operation could be one person (or a cell) who plans to blow himself and a bus to smithereens with a suicide bomb vest. To conduct this action requires planning the bombing, recruiting the conveyer and actor, building the bomb, collecting intelligence, and via command and control, focusing the bomber on their target at the time and place of choosing in the existing operational context. The term operation thus has several meanings. My definition of operation in this book is *an organized and concerted activity involving a number of people, especially members of the military or law enforcement or competing people/organizations.* Operations force us to recognize their importance in successfully implementing our desired choices of acting on another resisting entity. Operations thereby become more and

4. Montaigne, "On Experience," 1958.

more important to us trudging along the path out of Plato's Cave toward knowledge and comprehension.

Before exploring operational context any further, consider its importance. It is obvious that fighting for advantages in the operational context is imperative for success. Overall, it is a place where "disturbing the universe"[5] occurs from minute to minute or day to day, etc., depending on the type of operational context we are discussing. Disturbing the universe is an operational context that occurs via humans: their actions, interactions, transactions, reactions, counteractions. This ripple could come from the environment in the form of environmental interventions (weather, rain, winds, earthquakes). The disturbance could come from nonlinear turbulences. Sometimes disturbing the universe comes from the intercessions and involvements of organizations (e.g., governments, terrorist groups, criminal groups, nongovernmental organizations [NGOs], multinational corporations, etc., in a military conflict). Of course, while plumbing the depths of a sea of what is possible, a discovery enters our minds. That is, disturbances in the universe often come from machines—even an action as tiny as a personal computer passing one datum to a server disturbs a universe (where it originates [action necessary], where it travels, and where it arrives [receptacles grasp the datum and process it], thus requiring an action).

Any actor, whether friendly or adversary, uses an operational context to impose their *will* on a resisting entity, or to resist an adversary's imposition actions. Or they could seek advantages (initiative, tempo, momentum, knowledge, decision, position, and freedom of movement/freedom of maneuver). Any competitor knows they can use context to offset their opponent's strengths and enhance their weaknesses and to blend and secure cover. Adversaries can use the operational context to contain and conceal the always important command and control (C2) and to set conditions for defensive or offensive actions; if on the receiving end, they can use it to deny or parry an adversary's actions. Lastly, one could use the operational context to affect their opponent's decision making.

Context houses, enshrouds, and affects many activities and things that we subsume in our minds and "tune out." An operational context is a "sea of data" where action occurs and conflicts play out. Sadly, no one can gather and understand all data, so our conscious "over-mind" selects what it can work with while our "under-mind"[6] certainly absorbs much more data. It is often in the "cutting room floor" of our minds where true baubles of value exist. It is a place to return to find neglected data to deal with later.

5. T. S. Eliot, "The Love Song of J. Alfred Prufrock," *Poetry: A Magazine of Verse*. Chicago, 1915.

6. Claxton, *Hare Brain, Tortoise Mind*, 116–117.

Or we can force our minds to pay attention to the extant sea of data and actually notice what it is telling us or implying, whether in a large sense or as minutia.

Consider individual contexts and their relationships within any context. I consider individual contexts as membranes (outer "texture" of contexts) that surround and influence organisms within the operational context. To my mind, a person's or organization's complex adaptive system's[7] surrounding membrane is akin to a spherical body. One can peer into and around this membrane, which adapts to its changing contexts and provides data inputs to the CAS within and about its protective shroud. It can and does go into new and larger contexts; it responds to contextual influences there.

Our astute Über-thinker and thought pilgrim know that a larger context always exists around their small bubbles. With the view one gains from a larger context, they can look, sense, see, feel, and imagine ever larger operational contexts vaguely appearing and receding in and out of their sights and consciousness at a distance. They knowingly connect with the micro- and macro-contexts in which they exist and that exist about them. An operational context contains countless striving and counter-striving CASs and CAS-populated organizations. A CAS is a dynamic network of many agents (which may represent cells, species, individuals, firms, or nations) acting in parallel, constantly acting and reacting to what the other agents are doing. The control of a CAS tends to be highly dispersed and decentralized. If there is to be any coherent behavior in the system, it has to arise from competition and cooperation among the agents themselves. The overall behavior of the system is the result of a huge number of decisions made every moment by many individual agents.[8] These CASs

---

7. *Complex adaptive system (CAS)*: A complex, self-similar collection of interacting adaptive agents. The study of CAS focuses on complex, emergent, and macroscopic properties of the system. A CAS is a dynamic network of many agents (which may represent cells, species, individuals, firms, nations) acting in parallel, constantly acting and reacting to what the other agents are doing. This definition is a synthesis of my thoughts and those of John Holland (see M. Mitchell Waldrop, *Complexity* [New York: Touchstone, 1992]; John Holland, *Hidden Order* [New York: Basic Books, 1995]).

8. Holland, *Hidden Order*, 8–42. Please note throughout this chapter that I have been inspired by John Holland's work with CAS. I have applied the core of Holland's thoughts about CAS into my thinking and works. M. Mitchell Waldrop perused Holland's work and discusses CAS in *Complexity: The Emerging Science at the Edge of Order and Chaos*. In this book Waldrop devises a definition of CAS and attributes it to Holland, but I can't help but think he thought about Holland's work on CAS, just as I have done. I, of course, believe I am right in my depiction of nonlinearity, aggregations, CAS, agents, models, sequence of adaptation, and actions being shaped by rules, which drive models of behavior, outcomes, assessment, gathering relevant (to other agents) data, evaluating the data, learning, sharing, and adapting relative to other agents. This is yet but one aspect of my work that is indeed both original and new.

constantly try to impose their desires on one another, with some on the offense and some on the defense. They assess these actions and adapt, all the while watching their competitors and discerning how they responded to action. With some imagination, one recognizes the very nature of CASs and, via the movement of their co-evolution, how they do the following: 1) collide, 2) intersect, 3) careen off one another, and 4) conjoin to form aggregates and aggregations. Thus we can conclude that CAS and co-evolution cause some of the change in the sea of data comprising our micro- and macro-operational contexts. These changes cause normal patterns to break and thus present anomalies to our eyes.

Some of the turbulence and change in an operational context that involves CAS and CAS-populated organizations might be invisible but highly influential. They may be in operational contexts occurring in a domain other than ground, such as air, space, sea, cyberspace, information, and cognition. In these domains, one can most often find multiple related conflicts occurring. But we experience difficulty in discerning all of these comings and goings if our minds only burrow into and notice what our present, personal membrane is involved with. As such, if we dare to peer through the "veil" that apparently clouds our view of larger relationships and combinations of other membranes, one senses and views images coming to our minds—they are contextual spherical bodies. They certainly exist and vary in size, and they surround sentient beings and inanimate objects. They influence combatants pitted against one another in operational contexts in question.

In cities, a relevant operational context contains infrastructure. People need support from the infrastructure in their operational context to live—water, food, shelter, sewage (if available), electricity (if available), public transportation, markets, refuse disposal, businesses, residences, personal transportation, roads, bridges, dams, and so forth. Any infrastructure can be neutral, or it can be a plus or a minus to opposing sides in a conflict or competition. As an admonition, be cognizant of the fickle nature of infrastructure advantage; it can change with the winds of conflict that cause missions and problem sets[9] to appear and change. Change, with its oscillating uncertainty and risk, causes the rise of knowledge gaps, and these gaps trickle down to intelligence analysis and collection operations to cover and certainly affect decision makers with their influence on risk and uncertainty.

Interestingly, activities within a particular operational context can be important as "intangible weapons." Let me explain a little more about this notion. Consider a terrorist who has a presence in a neighborhood that

9. *Problem set*: A challenging problem that either has occurred or will soon occur with numerous sub–problem sets all relating to the macro-problem at hand.

causes angst in the people in their residences, markets, meeting places, and places of worship. But decomposing the situation a bit, we find that the terrorist has a micro-context and a macro-context in which he lives, feels, fears, hates, loves, acts, and so forth. In these views, one finds vulnerabilities worth seeking, finding, and acting on to influence. Our Über-thinker and thought pilgrim must imagine how the terrorist senses, perceives, and ruminates about his personal context and his larger context, how he senses the friendly context, and so on. Or consider a suicide bomber who might detonate a bomb inside a large airport and wreak havoc with a host of cascading, subsequent actions. These actions can become hugely important, sometimes disproportionately important, in that they cause reactive actions due to a rush to judgment, panic, anguish, angst, the fear of economic losses, changes in laws, ascendency of political parties, and so on. This bomber had a personal context. What did they see in their context as they experienced selection, preparation, movement to the target, and as their masters or they detonated the bomb?

Lastly, consider drug operators who might use a city along a border to stage, set conditions, and act (cause and effect) to push drugs into many large cities across this hypothetical border—this context houses their desires to push drugs across the border and receive money, lots of money, within the bounds of high risk and high uncertainty, but huge potential outcomes. Both tangible and intangible effects occur in the country whose people become the targets of the drug operations. There exists in some minds residing in recipients a feeling of hopelessness, resentment, impotence—all contributing to an intangible but real malaise. These outcomes are present in the cause, which establishes sufficient reason[10] for not only the activities involved with condition setting, but also the effect (outcome): successful insertion and distribution of drugs into the target country.

This thought—sufficient reason—is important and it returns to our thinking many times in this book. Therefore, I must provide some explanation for its importance now. I'm providing you with more of Schopenhauer's thoughts on sufficient reason:

> [W]hoever has recognized the law of causation, the aspect of the principle of sufficient reason which appears in what fills these forms (space and time) as objects of perception.[11]

The action and object and the titillation of matter in this case occurs in and influences both micro- and macro-contexts, but these contexts

10. Arthur Schopenhauer, "The World as Will and Idea," *The European Philosophers from Descartes to Nietzsche*, ed. Monroe C. Beardsley (New York: Random House, 1960), 652.

11. Ibid. p. 652.

influence the action, object, and matter. These contexts exist, expand, contract, disappear, and become dormant as their inhabitants move about, act, sleep, and so forth. Our Über-thinker and thought pilgrim must therefore understand these contexts to comprehend the whole of drug operations and how these operations evolve around imposing the operational driven action, which prepares the drugs, moves them across the borders, reaches the streets, and makes contact with the users. To make this happen, drug cartels impose their desires on America and, for the most part, appear to be winning this immense clash of interests. This is a collision of *will*s between the cartels and America's counter-drug and law enforcement contexts—America must win!

OPERATIONAL CONTEXT—PHENOMENOLOGY[12]

The shape, purpose, and activities of context seem self-evident. After all, we live in and respond to influences of one or more contexts every second until death. A variety of contexts provide the playgrounds in which volition comes to life, matures, thrives, withers, and dies—the seasons of life. Nonetheless, let us think a bit more about context. To my way of thinking, any operational context must be considered via sensation, serious cognitive intensity, and imagination. Clearly, when I think of operational context, I view it conceptually and experientially. I do so first to identify and study what makes operational context an interesting phenomenon,[13] and second, to identify and then find the wherewithal to discuss some of the important phenomena at play in any operational context.

While on the trail leading out of Plato's Cave, our belief is, with a high degree of certainty, that the trail leads to knowledge, comprehension, and truth. But I warn my acolytes about the lure and seduction of false knowledge and false truth. Be wary of knowledge, which can be 1) false, 2) deceptive, 3) outdated, or 4) of little or no value. Schopenhauer admonishes us to be skeptics, to be aware of the treachery that often lies at the heart and mind of human beings. Though some people can be pure in motive, most often self-interest turns up to pollute their minds and twist their logic, sometimes convincing them that they are speaking valid knowledge and truth rather than self-promotion and self-deception:

12. Phenomenology, in its simplest explanation, pertains to thinking about experience, or consciousness of an experience, that has affected our minds and feelings. Phenomenology involves thinking about phenomena (things) as they appear in our experience (or through the eyes, minds, and experience of others).

13. *Phenomenon*: An appearance or immediate object (focus) of awareness of action or interaction with other beings—human, organizational, and machine—in experience.

In the idea of perception, illusion may at moments take the place of the real; but in the sphere of abstract thought, error may reign for a thousand years, impose its yoke upon whole nations.[14]

I want you to be skeptics when it comes to placing your trust in subject matter experts (SMEs). Inevitably they have their own self-esteems, agendas, and biases. Though we need "experts," always approach and work with them with your eyes open and your mind questioning and checking, evaluating what they can be instead of what you want them to be.

Context's constant hovering, surrounding presence appears and disappears in our consciousness. When it does strike our fancy with sufficient substance and shape, our over-mind reaches in and snatches it into our conscious mind from its sea of data from within the under-mind.[15] If one's mind is "idle," they would neither see nor sense the invisible context surrounding a person. If, on the other hand, one's mind is active and roaring, fully prepared to race at high speed, one would accordingly adjust their minds to be open, expansive, and alert to nuance. They would therefore open their thinking to synthesis. Human beings need this skill to sense, see, feel, and judge various contexts coming to us, which could be 1) permanent, 2) semi-permanent, 3) partially fluid, 4) fluid, 5) micro-contexts, and 6) macro-contexts as each enfolds and unfolds within our context schema.

All of us live in a personal context. We live, act, transact, interact, travel, and so forth in contexts, some large and complicated, others simple and stable. Because any of several types of context under our consideration prove ubiquitous and "a given," humans or organizations don't take sufficient time to bring surroundings into their consciousness and subsequently fail to think deeply about the meaning of context. All of us need to take the time to ruminate deeply about the influence of context in conflict or competition. Indeed, it is a rare moment when we decipher contexts' elusive meanings and influences from the variety of angles necessary for success. Also, when we unavoidably bring "context" to our consciousness, it is our personal context that comes forth. Thus we need to learn how to think about the way other people think about their personal micro-context and their macro-context. Context surrounds us and influences all we do.

Arguably, everybody at least senses their contextual influences. With only the ever-so-vague condition of "awareness" cloaking that which we deem important yet ignore, context remains vague—a "thing," as "there," but only peripherally or perhaps even as an apparitional presence. Context may be 1) physical or nonphysical, 2) tangible or intangible, 3) visible or invisible, 4) symmetrical or asymmetrical, 5) harmonious or cacophonous,

14. Schopenhauer, "The World as Will and Idea," 659.

15. Claxton, *Hare Brain, Tortoise Mind*, 116–117.

6) odorous or nonodorous, 7) noisy or silent, and so forth. The presence of an operational context sashays about, in various forms, sometimes darting and weaving in and out of our consciousness and at other times remaining to visit.

In any of its forms, when we notice its imperial visage, it is through a rich repertoire of probabilities that helps us realize the striking importance of the phenomenon that is an operational context. With this importance in mind, we can and should learn to influence our operational context in a positive sense and turn it into a negative influence for those who oppose imposition of our aspiration. As students of conflict, advanced-thinking people know and continue to build their knowledge via thought about the variety of operational contexts at play in any particular situation. These contexts move about, in and out of our individual and collective consciousness and subconsciousness—the more sensitive to this movement we become, the more advantages appear where none previously existed.

Even though one may sense the presence of the operational context, it lives, pulses, and influences. Comprehending the wholes that unfold and enfold within its "confines" sometimes proves to be too much to wrap our minds around. Interestingly, any operational context exerts random influences on one's actions and adaptations, moving from positive to negative and back to positive. This kind of quirkiness comes from characteristics of nonlinear systems, which interact with linear systems. All of us always prove susceptible to the influences happening in the context—variables becoming sensitive; co-evolutionary CAS always causing motion, actions, assessments, adaptations, presence and influence of friction, chance, randomness, presence and influence of aggregations; and constant, striving expulsion of energy that the human life force feeds upon. Our view of context could occur in other minds also: in the minds of our adversaries, in the minds of a host nation and populace, and in the minds of businesses and nongovernmental organizations, among others. This means that as we think of the multitude of probabilities flowing along in our river of comprehension and experience, always consider the relativity of operational context to people and organizations, rather than a decidedly simple and reactive friendly-only perspective.

But how to gain this perspective, so alien to our typically shallow mental activities, serves up a mental challenge. So what might be some solutions? One solution is to think deeply and consider how opposing or interloping human beings and organizations 1) perceive, 2) think, 3) plan, 4) decide, 5) act/operate, 6) assess outcomes, 7) evaluate assessment data, 8) learn, and 9) adapt relative to contextual influences. This mental "deep dive" thus becomes a valued approach for understanding operational contexts.

With such thinking, we can start to comprehend the complicated nature of relevant contexts from views of other human beings who find themselves involved in conflict. My reasons for this proposition include the following: 1) these dualistic perspectives, expectations, and interpretations heavily influence operational success; and 2) one's adversary could very well be performing the same kind of thoughts about you and how you consider him relative to advantages and disadvantages of the operational context. This plus and minus focus becomes more intense in our lives when groping for any advantage to overcome a formidable foe and cause their capitulation. We focus on and direct our decisions and subsequent actions on what is important to our decision maker's intent, and in our case, his or her intent lies in either imposing their volition on a resisting entity, or in a reversal of roles: resisting an adversary's imposition actions. Ultimately you and people like you come to believe that mission outcomes depend on deep thinking about the operational context housing the conflict; it is of supreme importance, but only in a complete sense, when we include hard mental work in the adversary's view of their and our operational contexts, as well as our view of the context and how our adversary believes our side thinks about the operational context and their thoughts too—whew, difficult work indeed!

Cultural drivers and shapers always prove important to context. Why? Culture influences co-evolution. I'll cover co-evolution in depth in another chapter in the book, but for now, I provide just a brief paragraph to help us understand aggregates and aggregations relative to operational context. So, here we go. If more than one person (CAS) joins for a mission, say a task or a social outing, the single CAS and its personal context conjoins with other people (CAS) and their personal contexts. They thus form an aggregate (one CAS + one CAS), which is a micro-context. If two or more aggregates conjoin, an aggregation of people (CAS) and their personal contexts are enclosed in a larger operational context (operational because said people have a purpose for congregating and performing some action/activity that requires an operation of some kind). This is a macro-small context. When two macro-small contexts conjoin, one finds a macro-large context.

Thus, one finds a substantial growth to our original reality of context. Instead of one personal context—say a CAS—several increasingly larger and more complicated contexts come together via aggregation's kluging or bonding effects, and we discover a macro-context (origin) that now has a large aggregation as one element of its core. In a simplified explanation, the macro-large context appears in our minds as a large translucent bubble or globule. It is pliable and translucent (if one knows how to truly look, sense, feel, and imagine), and it allows and nurtures smaller and smaller contexts (bubbles or globules) as they kluge in aggregates and aggregations comprising the whole of operational context. The macro-small context holds two or more micro-contexts. The macro-context is our larger immediate context in which our minds choose to operate. Our personal context surrounds us. Each of us has an immediate personal context surrounding us; it moves with us during life.

How one views their contextual bubble and what happens inside it is one of the wonders of being human, given a level of thinking—it is unique to the individual, and this realization should be a part of our daily journey to being aware of consciousness and feeling awe at being intellectually alive. But our work as thinkers involves imagining how our adversary views data interactions, presentations, and happenings occurring in his or her micro-context and how they view and ruminate about the macro-context and its larger macro-context, aggregates and aggregations, and so on. All of this pondering, however, comes through the lens of desire—a desire to dictate outcomes or to resist such a situation.

When people in their contextual "globules" move, their personal context moves with them, and it changes. This personal context exerts influence, in varying degrees of sway and importance, upon the organism itself, second by second, via an invisible mental model residing and working within the consciousness and subconscious of said organism. If one person conjoins with another person, each party maintains their personal context, but the two contexts now relate and induce changes in one another from exchanges of perspectives. Even with this closeness, however, eventually a withdrawal of sorts occurs. In such extrications, each person with their personal context pulls away and reestablishes their singular, contextual whole, awaiting another conjoining or bonding with another person and their personal context. They then perform actions within their own context and, of course, within a larger contextual globule. As a single entity, they are now a CAS underneath a micro-context draped over them. How a person thinks about their personal context; others' personal contexts; and the larger and richer micro-, macro-small, and macro-contexts surrounding this personal context depends on how the person in question perceives, thinks about, and experiences their personal context relative to the existence of increasingly larger contexts. This process ends up being quite subjective, and it is that subjective perspective the hunter uses to pursue their quarry or the quarry uses to anticipate the hunter's actions.

My Über-thinker and thought pilgrim look puzzled and appear concerned. "Listen," I explain, "I understand this thinking is difficult. Regardless, it is important for you to understand and leverage in your upcoming conflicts. We already discussed how a person's context provides data inputs to its person. What I didn't say is that said data inputs cause a person in question to 1) respond, 2) ignore, 3) delay action, 4) seek help, 5) do nothing, 6) twist to advantage, 7) confer with other people, 8) learn more via deep think, 9) adapt, and so on. I hope you surmise that this data, as it streams from personal, micro-large, and macro-large contexts to the organism (CAS), proves to be the point of entrée for data feeds to perception, thinking, planning, decision making, acting, assessing, adapting, etc. These flows from multiple sources of data engage and bring to life the energies one finds in their life force, purpose, capabilities, strength of motive, and so forth in our 14-element thought model. If we reason similarly to our adversary and understand their contextual layers and how they receive and process context-pushed data, we can start to understand how an indirect approach to their mind and actions could be useful. To Sun Tzu's way of thinking, what I'm speaking about constitutes an extraordinary approach into a mental attack rather than a normal approach[16] with the same goal: the adversary's mind.

All of us must remember that an organizational context always surrounds an organization, but its people live and operate in their personal contexts. As such, they bring their personal contexts into and "under" the "bumbershoot" of the organizational context. How long they stay bonded depends on the whole, whose "glue" could be a common purpose—say, going to a movie. Once the movie is over, the small group of people, in a physical sense, breaks apart, and each CAS becomes an individual with their own CAS contexts again. The friends in this example, even though physically separated, remain friends—they remain bonded via feelings, memories, loyalty, emotions, love, admiration, trust, and so on—but although all the threads of this tapestry of entanglement are real, they are invisible.

Consider a nation-state surrounded by regional, national, and global contexts. Global contexts, broad and complicated, generally involve interactions of large linear and nonlinear social, political, economic, technical, informational, ecological, and military systems, to name but a few. To understand and comprehend these ultra-large systems proves difficult. Thus, we must imagine and understand the wholes at work, visualize and perceive them, and know they exist on a much higher level and larger scale than our personal or organizational micro-, macro-small, and macro-large contexts. But one can use the same line of reasoning as they examine global contexts. To understand these large supra-contexts, connect them with the way of visualizing contexts I just covered. Also, link them with a theory of wholes. The smaller wholes (micro-contexts) unfold (spread or unfurl) into a larger whole, while the larger whole enfolds (surrounds or envelops or even swallows) the recently formed smaller wholes. These two entities, now conjoined with wholes within the larger whole, become part of a new, larger whole's bigger, richer, and more powerful whole (macro-context) due to the additive power of synergy and materialization deriving from thinking, deciding, and acting via the doctrine of holism. The largest whole, that of the earth and all its interlaced people, organizations, processes, species, resources, etc., enfolds all and thereby

16. Sun Tzu, *The Art of War*, trans. Samuel Griffith (New York: Oxford University Press, 1963), 91–92.

influences all within its realm. Earth, meanwhile, is a tiny speck that unfolds with other planets and stars and solar systems and galaxies.

It follows that a relevant larger whole within our range of action has a direct influence on smaller CAS, aggregates,[17] and aggregations[18] that constitute the personal, micro-, macro-small, and macro-large contexts. This process I'm describing also influences individuals within their personal contextual membranes as they connect, enfold. and unfold into and out of one another in sometimes asymmetric and asynchronous gyrations, but always with motion and energy, until they exist no more. Even then, certain wholes can live in human minds for millennia. For example, Julius Caesar's The Gallic Wars, and in particular, his description of the battle of Alesia inspire me even today. He died in 44 BCE, so ideas do count, and they live sometimes forever.

The theory of wholes is a powerful and most useful concept to help us understand operational contexts. As we make this assessment, however, and because I assume moral and ethical human beings, always remember

---

17. *Aggregate*: For purposes of this work, an aggregate involves one CAS kluging with at least one other CAS and staying together via glue (which is that which holds both similar and dissimilar aggregates together). When more than one aggregate conjoins with another aggregate, one finds an aggregation. Aggregates and aggregations can subsume and actually assume these features:

- *Velocity*: the time rate of change of position of a body in a specified direction
- *Speed*: rapidity in moving, going, traveling, proceeding, or performing
- *Mass*: aggregate, whole
- *Momentum*: a measure of the motion of a body equal to the product of its mass and velocity

18. *Aggregation*: The gathering of aggregates into a larger whole. This whole is collective and responsive to accepting more like and disparate elements into its whole. An aggregation enfolds smaller aggregates and unfolds into larger aggregations. An aggregation can move and achieve a constantly building velocity. Often the strongest and most impermeable glues holding an aggregation together happen to be emotion, ideology, and religious beliefs.

- AGGREGATION "GLUE": that which holds both similar and dissimilar aggregates together—usually an ideology, emotion, extant condition, religion, belief in racial superiority, and so forth.
- AGGREGATION "PROPELLANT": that which provides velocity and motion to aggregates and aggregations.
- AGGREGATION "IGNITER": that which arouses the passions of sensitive variables or excites. The igniter ignites the propellant.
- SENSITIVE VARIABLE: a variable easily excited and highly influential because of its direct access to the "glue" holding the whole together, such as ideology. It moves at various rates of speed due to its propellant, which is often emotion. Emotions, however, can be the glue of an aggregation as well as the propellant.
- CONTEXT: the set (a set is an assortment of entities, each considered an entity in its own right and as a larger whole) of circumstances, meanings, actions, and potentialities that surround, permeate, and influence people and a particular event, action, operation, situation, action, or aggregation acting in a concerted way to accomplish an aim, goal, objective, strategy, or tactic. The context holds secrets as to why variables become sensitive.

that the system or systems of which I speak are relative to human beings and human endeavors. Otherwise, without humans at work or at play, what do the ideas and concepts and schematics matter? If a tree falls in a forest, does it make a sound?

To understand individual, organizational, and national contexts takes alternative ways of thinking. People have to learn how to think about holism, synthesis, alliances, goals, objectives, resources, constraints, connectedness, entanglements, strategies, and, of course, ways of reasoning tendered by our adversary. We have to know and apply the 14 essential elements of our model. Using how-to-think methods and practices means practitioners of conflict consider, know, and apply the 18 considerations model. In addition, I recognize that examples of constants concerning wholes and contexts wend their way through many countries, organizations, and people. One constant involves money and money-making edifices and the contexts in which they exist and work. Other constants, cultural in nature, seep into and influence all conflict: religion, rule of law and law enforcement, government and politics, stability and security operations, basic subsistence, home life, societal and cultural values, social mores, marriage, views of the world, birth and death, and so on. But never forget—one always, always, always finds none other than self-interest at the center of life. With candid and deep thought, always set your sights on self-interest as the epicenter of being and source of energy for all people, organizations, and ultimately larger systems of organizations, even if some organizations and people purport to be altruistic.

FORCES AT PLAY RELATIVE TO OPERATIONAL CONTEXT

Next, I discuss two important forces at play in any operational context hosting conflict or competition. Let us delve into the first—nonlinearity:

> [T]he study of situations where, in a general sense, cause and effect are not proportional to each other[.][19]

Nonlinear systems possess some oddities that drive the minds of decision makers and their coteries literally wild. Here are a few of these oddities most pertinent to our work: 1) nonadditive; 2) improbability of accurate prediction; 3) small inputs can lead to large outputs; 4) turbulence and change are the norm; 5) causes for effects are difficult to discern; 6) presence and influence of aggregations; 7) presence and influence of sensitive variables; 8) importance of context; 9) presence and influence of complex adaptive

19. *Nonlinear*: https://encyclopedia2.thefreedictionary.com/nonlinear+physics, Retrieved February 23, 2017.

systems; 10) presence and influence of co-evolution; 11) presence and influence of the spooky world of tendency theory; 12) importance of adaptation; 13) sensitive dependence on initial conditions; 14) presence and influence of observed/observer behavior and influence; 15) untidy and changing rules; 16) presence and influence of the edge of chaos;[20] 17) presence and influence of conditions that cause variables to become sensitive and thereby influential; and 18) presence and influence of friction, randomness, and chance.

Of interest to our inquiry, one finds two peculiarly different yet entwined systems in any operational context—one being the disorderly and unpredictable nonlinear system and the other being the orderly and predictable linear system. Each influences competitive action, and each causes one to think differently and thereby use alternative approaches to each of the systems. Maintain a healthy respect and sometimes a trepidation of each, but particularly fear the vagaries one finds with nonlinear systems. It is with nonlinearity where one experiences the whipsaw changes involved with chaos and turbulence and the counterintuitive characteristics. Each characteristic can ruin one's day, so always approach any operational context respectfully and with a propensity to shift focus and actions quickly and with agility as change and truth are certain to plague all entities in their grips.

Another way to help us think about this particular brand of dualism comes from scientist and philosopher Karl Popper. In his view, one can gain an understanding of nature by presenting a concept of clocks and clouds. He states in very succinct language the difference between the two and their need to fold into a whole in this lengthy passage from his lecture "Of Clocks and Clouds":

> My clouds are intended to represent physical systems which, like gases are highly irregular, disorderly, and more or less unpredictable. I shall assume that we have before us a schema or arrangement in which a very disturbed or disorderly cloud is placed on the left. On the other extreme of our arrangement, on its right, we may place a very reliable pendulum clock, a precision clock, intended to represent physical systems which are regular, orderly, and highly predictable in their behavior. According to what I may call the commonsense view of things, some natural phenomena, such as the weather, or the coming and going of clouds are hard to predict: we speak of the "vagaries of the weather." On the other hand,

20. Waldrop, *Complexity*, 12. The edge of chaos is "where components of a system never quite lock into place, and yet never quite dissolve into turbulence, either . . . where life has enough stability to sustain itself and enough creativity to deserve the name of life. The edge of chaos is where new ideas and innovative genotypes are forever nibbling away at the edges of the status quo, and where even the most entrenched old guard will eventually be overthrown."

we speak of "clockwise precision" if we wish to describe a highly regular and predictable phenomenon.[21]

Thus, from Popper's view, clouds and clocks, though different, exist in the same whole. One could go on and postulate that people can be either cloudlike or clocklike, or they could be both clock and cloud. Cloudlike people can be creative, innovative, and not regimented by schedules, precise requirements, and books of guidance like blueprints, maintenance schedules, and the like. Conversely, clocklike people deal with precision. I also interpret these characterizations and apply them to our thoughts about nonlinearity and linearity living and complementing one another, even though different. It is nonlinearity, of course, that proves so indicative of cloudlike people, organizations, and systems, whereas the more predictable and stable linear systems exist and complement nonlinear systems. Robert Pirsig also helps us understand this differentiation between people, organizations, and the like. One set of people he calls classicist and the other romantic. Pirsig is clearly classical, as he enjoys and finds beauty in blueprints and parts manuals as well as maintenance schedules. He would love to work in linear systems. Romantics do not like all the detail. They find things like an entire working motorcycle to be beautiful, but they do not want specific details of how it works. Romantics would love to work with nonlinear systems. Coming to the nub of this comparison and contrast, two opposites working together would be wonderful thing indeed. This following passage helps us understand and gain insight into how two opposites can and should come into one unified whole:

> The world of underlying form is an unusual object of discussion because it is actually a mode of discussion itself. You discuss things in terms of their immediate appearance or you discuss them in terms of their underlying form. . . . A classical understanding sees the world primarily as underlying form itself. A romantic understanding sees it primarily in terms of immediate appearance. . . . Persons tend to think and feel exclusively in one mode or the other and in doing so tend to misunderstand and underestimate what the other mode is all about.[22]

Hmm, I wonder if this passage also provides insight into why people often prefer to design forms before they describe functions and why there is a distinct absence of metacognition so essential for integrating the two. I think so! Pirsig continues on to acknowledge the two and their differences, but in the end argues for them to come together and conjoin into a unified whole where one cannot exist without the other:

---

21. Karl Raymond Popper, *Of Clouds and Clocks: An Approach to the Problem of Rationality and the Freedom of Man*, Retrieved May 2, 2017, from www.the-rathouse.com/2011/Clouds-and-Clocks.html.

22. Pirsig, *Zen and the Art of Motorcycle Maintenance*, 60.

> Classical understanding is concerned with the piles [of sand] and the basis for sorting and interrelating them. Romantic understanding is directed toward the handful of sand before the sorting begins. Both are valid ways of looking at the world although irreconcilable with each other. This is the source of the trouble. **What has become an urgent necessity is a way of looking at the world that does violence to neither of these two kinds of understanding and unites them into one** [emphasis added]. Such an understanding will not reject sand-sorting or contemplation of unsorted sand for its own sake. Such an understanding will instead seek to direct attention to the endless landscape from which the sand is taken.[23]

With nonlinear systems at work, one finds friction, chance, and randomness occurring and exerting influence in any operational context in all domains and dimensions. These three phenomena's existence reaches into the yesteryear of history, to the beginning of time and human conflict; their tentacles stretch and cling to conflict frameworks of even the murkiest of futures and influence activities in any operational context. Let's take a look at some definitions of these phenomena and interpret their theoretical meaning:

- Friction: In my words, unexpected chance events.
- Chance: "The unknown and unpredictable element in happenings that seems to have no assignable cause" [for an effect or outcome].[24]
- Randomness: "Proceeding, made, or occurring without definite aim, reason, or pattern."[25]

These phenomena grow exponentially as conflicts and competition among CAS occur. They "play" and "frolic" in the pastures of nonlinear operational contexts. They live, operate, compete, adapt, and sometimes grow exponentially during their interactions with other CAS; they exist and influence all entities in all operational contexts.

I now want to conclude this section of our journey by providing you with my thoughts regarding a few approaches related to how to think about operational contexts. I want you to realize that one finds many views and characteristics of any operational context. All views are important, but some prove more so than others. It is of no small matter then to reason about the operational context and recognize the most influential characteristics of nonlinearity at play. Contestants determine these levels of importance as friend and adversary struggle to extract advantages from

23. Pirsig, *Zen and the Art of Motorcycle Maintenance*, 70.

24. American Heritage Dictionary. Retrieved May 2, 2017, from www.ahdictionary.com/word/search.html?id=C5243000.

25. Dictionary.com. Retrieved May 2, 2017, from www.dictionary.com/browse/random.

the operational context. But they have to know when said advantage appears.

This acknowledgement occurs with co-evolution—I'll just briefly touch upon this important concept now, foreshadowing its resurfacing in Chapter 13. An adversary could believe his ability to co-evolve might be important to each side as they ponder respective *wills*. The dictionary definition of co-evolution means:

The evolution of complementary adaptations in two or more species of organisms because of a special relationship that exists between them.[26]

Building upon and drawing implications from this dictionary definition, I developed the following working definition of co-evolution:

The evolution of two or more species or organisms (natural or manmade) that interact closely with one another, with each adapting to changes in other(s).

To adapt, the organism needs to assess its actions and behaviors to see what impact they have made on the operational context, competitors, and adversaries. To assess, the organism in question needs to search for and collect relevant data. Once collected, the organism can make sense of, understand, and comprehend data; its derivative *information*; and information's derivative—*knowledge*. Once this synthesis occurs, the organism must evaluate the conclusions turning from intuition into reason/visualization appearing as collusion between experience from one's past and new inputs from gathered assessment data. Then the organism must learn, and it must adapt—all more quickly than its competitors and/or adversaries. It follows that co-evolution is a crucially important aspect of being a complex adaptive system. The implication for our thinking is to teach our minds to think like the adversary is thinking, to interfere with his efforts to search for and find relevant data, to alter data being collected and the conclusions forming in the organism's mind and, of course, to protect against such imposition of desired outcomes by one adversary or the other.

Remember, a resisting side works to block or parry an imposition action and possibly launch a counter-imposition of their desired outcomes at a place and time of least expectation and resistance. Finding the right place and time to strike with the right imposition actions, however, can become obscured by the illusions that cloud our eyes and subsequent thinking. Behind this Veil of Maya[27] one finds reality. Competing knowledge warriors realize they are in conflict for triumph of the *will* but are usually held

26. http://www.dictionary.com/browse/coevolution?s=t.

27. *Veil of Maya*: The delusion of one's understanding of connections and interactions and how an adversary would/could be thinking.

back by their own illusions, which are the result of one's apperception.[28] Again, I borrow from philosopher Arthur Schopenhauer for pushing our thoughts to a higher level:

> It is Maya, the veil of deception, which blinds the eyes of mortals, and makes them behold a world of which they cannot say either that it is or that is not.[29]

Obviously, the veil is complicated. Consider how all humans ingest data from the actions of others, the words of others, the operational contexts abounding in the world. It is one's intellect, with its training and education, apperception (sum total of all of one's experiences), biases, prejudices, worldview, and elements of values and character that comprise our interpretation by ways of a mishmash of data coming to our minds. The trick then occurs as one peers behind the adversary's veil and blocks his attempts to pierce our veil—then and only then can one begin to understand an operational context's characteristics, how it vacuums data, how it transmits data, and how its forces have the potential to make one's days trying.

Our Über-thinker and thought pilgrim want to view behind the curtain so they understand not only the presupposed illusion of operational context, but also its essence (that which is causing the illusion, why it is there, and whether it is a permanent affliction for the purposes of our manipulation of this veil clouding the perceiving aspect of our thought model). They see images of chaos and time and attempt to make sense of it all via rational thought; reflection; sense making; learning the impacts of weather; being cognizant of the presence, influence, and functioning of infrastructure; and seeing an adversary and a populace who purposefully "disturb the universe." Data inputs come to both friendly and adversary receptacles, causing more thoughts, more mysteries, more wonder—to what end, nobody knows, but on and on it goes.

So, if we happen to be the person in the graphic, how can we reason about a very complicated operational context? What can one do to help ourselves think? A few ideas follow:

1. View context as a series of ever-increasing or ever-decreasing sizes (depending upon one's vantage point). The context unfolds into larger bubbles or enfolds smaller bubbles of context, as I introduced earlier.

---

28. *Apperception*: Mental perception, especially the process of understanding something perceived in terms of previous experience. From Webster's Revised Unabridged Dictionary, retrieved June 30, 2008, from http://dictionary.reference.com/browse/apperception. Also, the sum total of a person's experience.

29. Schopenhauer, "The World as Will and Idea," 651.

2. In the field of conflict and competition, a large macro-context houses any conflict, competitive event, and bartering activity.
3. A macro-context can accept smaller mobile contexts that might be passing through, staying, passing over, or becoming stationary instead of being mobile contexts.

If one peers into the depths of a very deep lake containing operational contexts, they find personal, micro- and macro-small, and macro-large contexts. Also coming from these same depths, one discovers variables tending to transform from dormant and docile to raging, flaming, conflagration-sensitive variables. Within such a force, the operational context becomes roiled and violently turbulent, unpredictable, and mysterious. One does know with certainty, however, that one CAS + one CAS = an aggregate; one aggregate + one aggregate = micro-aggregation; one micro-aggregation + one micro-aggregation = a macro-aggregation. In other words, wholes in our operational context can grow, conjoin, and move with astonishing speed. These wholes can continue to grow and even move, sometimes with high velocity and mass that wreaks havoc in the operational context until their power, energy, and velocity diminish, dissipate, and eventually disappear. All of this happens because a seemingly innocuous variable becomes sensitive and starts a chain reaction from sensitive variable, to igniter, to propellant, to aggregation, which binds into a whole via "glue."[30]

In my particular view, any operational context is an arena in which conflict occurs. It is a "bubble" housing struggles between adversarial CAS, each intent on imposing their desire on their adversary CAS. They battle mightily for thought/knowledge advantage and thus decision advantage and perhaps the other five advantages: initiative, tempo, momentum, position, and freedom of movement/maneuver. To understand context as an arena for mental and physical combat, I ask that you remember and account for the different kinds of context you have learned from me: personal, micro-, macro- (small), and macro- (large). Also, contexts may be mobile, stationary, or combinations therein. One mobile context can exist in another, larger mobile context (e.g., a person traveling in an automobile, train car, or airplane). A potentially mobile context can be in stasis or dormancy but still be present within stationary contexts. Macro-contexts can house mobile, mobile + larger mobile, and more permanent structures such as infrastructure. In electronic contexts, one finds small mobile contexts surrounding electrons and packets moving (if propelled) through wires, cables, or via electrons through the air—elements of more

30. Hall and Citrenbaum, *Analysis*, 277–298.

permanent infrastructures that possess both semi-permanent and mobile features. Any thinking person in the field of study or action involving conflict of *wills* always considers nonlinearity. It is a leering specter haunting any operational context; its mere presence sways outcomes of conflicts for superiority.

You must learn to comprehend how adversaries compete with one another, each hoping to win in the battle of supremacy, and each possessing views of advantages and disadvantages lurking in the operational context. So, I ask my indefatigable Über-thinker and thought pilgrim two questions: 1) "What constitutes the main points about operational context you should consider in your decision making?" and 2) "What does your theoretical adversary consider as he mulls over how the friendly decision maker and his knowledge warriors think relative to advantages and disadvantages in the operational context?" My acolytes took some time to think, and they came back to me with the following 15 thoughts, which I judged to be quite good and apropos:

1. Always remember that the forces of nonlinearity are at play in any operational context. Thus one must know, understand, and comprehend nonlinearity at work in the operational context.
2. Always wargame the operational context from different sides to cause it to yield its advantages and disadvantages.
3. Identify how you think about the advantages the operational context presents to your side.
4. Identify how the adversary thinks about the advantages the operational context presents to him.
5. Reconcile the differences between your views and his.
6. Identify how the operational context provides disadvantages to the adversary.
7. Identify how the operational context provides disadvantages to your side.
8. Reconcile the differences between your views and his.
9. Identify how the adversary thinks you think about the advantages and disadvantages the operational context presents to you.
10. Identify how the adversary thinks that you think about what he thinks about the advantages and disadvantages the operational context provides to each side.
11. Identify ways to capitalize on how your adversary thinks about the advantages and disadvantages inherent to the operational context.
12. Identify where and when the adversary could try to use his advantages and exploit your disadvantages that come in the operational context.
13. Decide how to turn your disadvantages from the context into advantages and vigorously turn the adversary's advantages into disadvantages.

14. Remember and account for duality as you consider context and the advantages or disadvantages the operational context presents therein (via each side's interpretation and perspectives).
15. With the phenomenon of duality clinging to and metastasizing in the rapidly expanding recesses of our minds, consider the adversary's mental operations. Keep Sun Tzu's famous dictum in our minds and actions:

> [K]now the enemy, know yourself; your victory will never be endangered. Know the ground, know the weather; your victory will then be total.[31]

I break in to remind them of a few thoughts they need to consider before moving on from our study of the operational context. Battles of perspective violently erupt in operational contexts. These battles involve thinking like the adversary not only about his views of the advantages and disadvantages he gains from operational contexts, but also how you think he thinks about how you think about him. Your thoughts should be akin to this line of thought: First, don't forget how duality/pendulum thinking mitigates those small erosions of perspective coming forth in your logic and bias errors. Second, if you cause your mind to circle back to duality and pendulum thinking, the mere motion of energy through the sea of data in your operational context can keep you thinking about what the adversary thinks relative to their view of operational context. As you perform this mental work, I want you to experience the appearance, sense, taste, and smell superiority and the potential for victory over your adversary when you have created one, or two, or all seven advantages. You won't always possess them, so savor the moment while it lasts. This condition of superiority leads you to satisfy your goals and objectives—winning—but also cautions you to understand, as you gain an advantage or two from the operational context, that you lose an advantage or two. So keep an eye on the whole of your struggle for superiority in the operational context. I'm convinced that finding "a way" to win in this sea of data that is the operational context is offered to people bold enough to perform these recommendations and thereby beat their adversary in mental combat and the overall war of wits.

Context, in my world, is not the same as environment. In this chapter I explained that my view of operational context expands the thinking the U.S. Joint Chiefs of Staff doctrine presents in doctrine as operational environment. I explained that context surrounds conflicts. Operational context is the surrounding "bubble" where conflicts occur; each side combs context for any hints of a lurking presence of actual or potential advantage or

31. Sun Tzu, *The Art of War*, 129.

disadvantage that one side or the other could use to their benefit. As a welcome surprise, I introduced the existence of four new kinds of context and explain how they unfold and enfold into and onto one another. I presented readers with a model to aid their reasoning about these contexts in which one finds varying degrees of conflict, fighting, and even wars: 1) an individual context that surrounds people, 2) a micro-context, 3) a macro-small context, and 4) a macro-large context. In this chapter, I discussed two kinds of systems present in the contexts where competitors grapple in combat with one another—one, predictable and understandable, is linear, and the other, unpredictable and largely unfathomable, is nonlinear. In this chapter, I explained that it is the nonlinear system that wreaks havoc with all efforts to impose one's way of thinking on another side in any kind of fight in any operational context. As such, I provided the reader with 18 characteristics of nonlinearity that always demand attention to be successful in any conflict. Contexts are as opaque bubbles housing fights. A context also proves of foremost importance because of the context's provision of data—some desired, some abhorred! I explain how the great philosopher of war, Sun Tzu, recognized the importance of context as he wisely warns combatants to know the enemy as themselves and to know the terrain and the weather and never know defeat. In the latter portion of the chapter I posed two questions to readers relative to learning how to think about conflict: 1) "What constitutes the main points about operational context housing people in conflicts that you should consider in your decision making?" and 2) "What does an adversary consider as he mulls over how his enemy decision maker thinks relative to finding and exploiting advantages and disadvantages in the operational context?"

CHAPTER 5

Purpose, Capabilities, and Strength of Motive

Argument: *In this chapter, I define purpose. The reader, via thought, learns to enter a hostile mind to identify purpose. I discuss conditions an adversary must set to accomplish his purpose. I discuss the meaning of capability.* "Capabilities" *prove indispensable in winning any fight. But I alert readers' wariness of assumptions about capabilities. One must consider moral and physical domains when pondering capabilities. Strength of motive uses Clausewitzian thinking to explain strength's meaning relative to motive. Strength of motive, always important, rests within hearts and souls of combatants. It cannot be quantified. It remains in a mysterious box—the moral domain of conflict. Both sides in a fight must meld purpose, strength of motive, and capabilities to win conflicts.*

PURPOSE

Coming next, while working our way through the many considerations one must make to think about *will,* we pursue purpose, capabilities, and strength of motive—all of great importance in gaining comprehension of this great phenomenon. As a first step, I explain "purpose." What better way to start than to hear from Clausewitz about the heart of purpose in conflict:

War, therefore, is an act of policy . . . is clear, consequently, that war is not a mere act of policy but a true political instrument, a continuation of political activity by other means. . . . The political object is the goal, war is the means of reaching it, and means can never be considered in isolation from their purpose.[1]

1. Clausewitz, *On War,* 86–87.

Purpose is "the reason, grounds, or cause for which something is done or created or for which something exists." It is a necessary element in the 14 critical elements of *will*. The early part of this chapter helps all of us understand the meaning of this important concept—purpose. Without further ado, let us begin this leg of our journey.

A purpose is the reason why something exists. In our case, I want you to narrow your focus and examine "purpose" in its specific relationships in our learning. Purpose is its impetus and the reason for a person's or organization's or country's imposition of their ways of doing life's functions on a resisting force and countering this adversary's attempts to impose his desires Purpose always deals with two interlocking backdrops: the emotional and the rational. Either attackers or defenders must consider purpose, and both must be countered. Our Über-thinker and thought pilgrim remind me to also consider purpose in light of its power and ability to be a catalyst for volition to turn into *will* and subsequent counters. All of us should study purpose keeping the object of influencing purpose in mind.

As you can see, imposing one's desires is suddenly more than a broad explanation. *Will* has many pieces that contribute to bending an adversary's resistance. Figure 5.1 points out the ominous presence of life force as we discussed in Chapter 3 and rationality—vision—desired outcomes both of which feed into a higher order concept—which is, of course, purpose. There must be a purpose driving the force's action. Desire drives life force, which feeds into purpose and infiltrates the entire model—the rationality, vision,

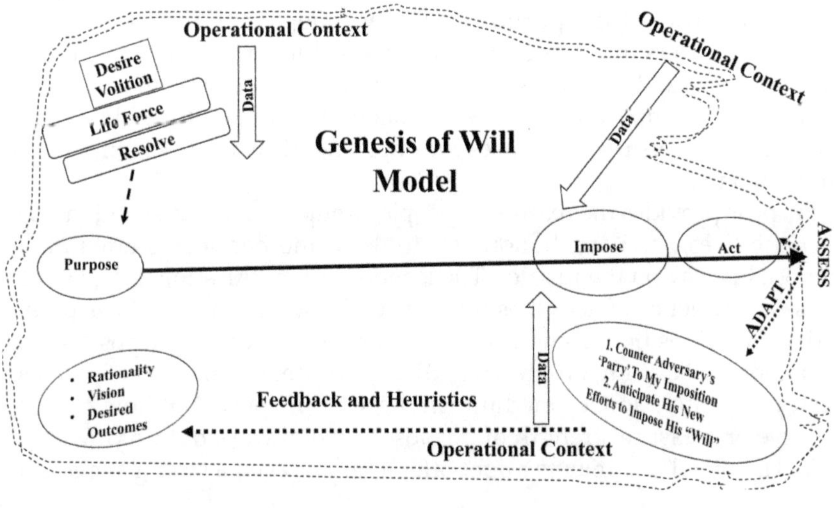

Figure 5.1. Building a Model for Understanding *Will*

and desired outcomes that all come into play. But more elements prove essential—I'll add them to the graphic while moving along in the book.

Purpose has a strength, a capability, and a nub or epicenter in which with rumination our Über-thinker and thought pilgrim can peek into the boiling cauldron of conflict. There they find a recipe for diminishing the potentially enormous power in purpose and thereby diminishing the ardor of strength of motive, and indirectly manipulating capabilities and the abilities. While easing from purpose as an abstraction to purpose as a practical, pragmatic way of reasoning, our focus bores into the basis of purpose relative to strength of motive and capabilities. The basis of purpose has a center of rationality. It is the rationality of the principle of sufficient reason.[2] Basically, it is what one has to attack; it is the center. All of us must realize the importance of anticipating the adversary's desire to attack our purpose. Thus, I hope you realize another important reason for purpose: It directly links with outcome and possible/plausible means one side or the other could employ to reach their desired outcome. This linkage also connects purpose with capabilities. However, while people readily quantify numbers, tons, sorties, weapon systems, and the like, they cannot quantify rationality, values, pride, revenge, ego, hatred, aggrandizement, and so forth.

The purpose or purposes forming the basis or foundation for one's goals involves people, organizations, groups, sects, regions, or nations to support and sacrifice to accomplish a goal or objective. The purpose we consider can be either human or machine. That is, humans think about what they want, what resistance could meet their desires, what they need to do to triumph in obtaining what they want and end up using capabilities emboldened and hardened with strength of motive and why they act in a certain way—their purpose. Thus, as a departure from the past, so far, one considers the start of this logic trail—life force, purpose, strength of motive, capability, imposition, and action (more elements come forth momentarily). Importantly, we remember and therefore think about duality and the adversary's purposes for imposing his way or resisting imposition of ours.

Purpose provides the reason for people, groups, etc., to resist and thereby sacrifice lives, territory, honor, etc., to deny another actor's attempts to impose his way on the resister. The leader's way of thinking, for example, causes a sequence of activities that set conditions and thus allows preparation for imposition of his volition on a resisting foe. A purpose can be strong or weak. With a high strength of purpose, it is more likely to succeed than with a low or medium strength of purpose. But how can one observe or measure strength of purpose? Several ways of thinking could help. Historical documents might offer a hint or even a strong suggestion

2. Schopenhauer, "The World as Will and Idea," 650–651, 656.

of how purpose has influenced decision makers' decisions and how strongly people support their decisions and rationales therein. A review of social media can also help by looking for either direct references or indirect discussions pertaining to purpose.

One has to consider and find the true purpose driving the rationale for imposing one's approaches to life on a resisting party or force. Once our Über-thinker and thought pilgrim discern true purpose, then through thought and action, they can decide the best way to work against the purpose in question and possibly counter. They also know of the presence of the omnipresent unstated purpose—the true driving force behind actions involving setting conditions for or the actual imposition of one's volition on another person or group of people. Quite often, at the heart of the matter of purpose, one finds self-interest. Sometimes, however, people have more than self-interest in mind as they consider purposes. One might find altruism at work too, such as supporting a purpose involving love of one's country, or duty to an ideal, or love of brotherhood. Ernest Hemingway brings this altruism to life in the mind and actions of a fighter in the Spanish Civil War (1936–1939):

> [Y]ou were taking part in a crusade. That was the only word for it although it was a word that had been so worn and abused that it no longer gave its true meaning. You felt, in spite of all bureaucracy and inefficiency and party strife, something that was like the feeling you expected to have and did not have when you made your first communion. It was a feeling of consecration to a duty toward all of the oppressed of the world which would be as difficult and embarrassing to feeling you had when you rear back. . . . It gave you a part in something that you could believe in wholly and completely and in which you felt an absolute brotherhood with the others who were engaged in it. . . . You learned the dry-mouthed fear-purged, purging ecstasy of battle and you fought that summer and that fall for all the poor in the world, against all tyranny for all the things that you believed and for the new world you had been educated into.[3]

Though rare when compared to the usual causes for the often-naked aggrandizement behind actions that impose "*will*," the appearance of altruism does happen. This kind of volition is particularly inspired by religion or duty or nationalism or solidarity with the oppressed, and often involves great personal sacrifice, as when Hemingway's Robert Jordan attempted to destroy the bridge in *For Whom the Bell Tolls* at the cost of his life.

Conversely, for a very good example of how not only seizing power but fighting to keep it can take its toll in one's humanity and humility, see Robert Graves's marvelous explanatory passage about the great Roman emperor Augustus:

---

3. Ernest Hemingway, *For Whom the Bell Tolls* (New York: Scribner, 1940), 235–236.

> The senate were certainly becoming shamefully obsequious in their manners towards him and his family and staff. He disliked the situation . . . and it was true that as long ago as before the defeat and death of Antony he had publically promised to retire when no public enemy remained. . . . But my grandmother [Livia] would never allow him to give up: she would always say that his task was not half accomplished yet, that nothing but civil disorder could be expected if he retired now. . . . And he must not be simple-minded: once out of office and a mere private citizen he was liable to impeachment and banishment, or worse; and what of the secret grudges that the relations of men whom he had killed or dishonoured bore against him? As a private citizen he would have to give up his bodyguard as well as his armies. . . . So he gave in and continued ruling.[4]

What a treasure trove of thoughts for us to digest, while working to understand the bedrock, the deep well of life force and derivative purpose that motivate people to seize and hold power. In this paragraph some appearances strike our thoughts—fear of alternatives, fear of the shame of being thought simple-minded, love of the trappings of power, and a penchant to keep peace in the family and perhaps bend for one's wife's desires, all the while acting strong to his foes and to the Senate.

At other times, one might find people seizing upon purpose to pursue their love of money, but this one generally slips back into self-interest too. Sometimes, however, one finds one or more people or groups committed to a purpose that they surmise would make their god pleased with them. Sometimes purpose comes forth as a villain causing the difference between what people state publicly and how they act. Consider Germany's grand charade with the Sudetenland in 1938. Germany's public statements, propaganda, meetings, and eventually a treaty in October 1938, in which Hitler promised no more land grabs, all masked Hitler's true purpose—to take over all of Czechoslovakia for purposes of exploiting its natural resources, military capabilities, and physical position to flank Poland's southern and eastern borders.

As I age, it becomes all the more difficult to accept explanations of purposes at face value. Most often, ulterior motives prove involved; one just has to scratch beneath the thin veneer of representational humanness to find that which truly matters and therefore the drivers and shapers of behavior and how much one or more people might sacrifice to meet the demands that said purpose suggests. In an individual sense, purpose, with its strengths or weaknesses, influences the winning or losing. Purpose drives a person to succeed in satisfying an aim, goal, or objective. For example, people go to college. The purpose could be multidimensional. One purpose could be to gain knowledge. Another purpose could be to obtain a college degree. Yet another purpose could be to meet people

4. Robert Graves, *I, Claudius* (New York: Vintage International, 1989), 48.

and thus to gain contacts for life after college. If our college student has a strong purpose, then their perseverance to stay the course and graduate in four years is likely. If our college student is a drifter and lacks a strong purpose to either attend or graduate from college, their strength of purpose is undoubtedly weak. Their motivation to graduate is less than the student with a strong purpose and their probability of graduating decreases accordingly.

Let's consider about another example. Consider a dictator. A dictator undoubtedly has multiple purposes behind his actions. For one, this supreme leader wants to rid himself of opponents. To impose his iron rule on his own people, this dictator chooses a purpose of popular adulation. As yet another purpose, the dictator wants to stay in power and to pass it on the power to his progeny. This dictator might also have a purpose of reuniting a divided land—consider the two Koreas today. Or a dictator may have as a strong purpose to retake land historically a part of a particular motherland but lost in treaties. Consider Russia today with their seizure of the Crimea as a good example. It doesn't take a stretch in our individual and collective imaginations to believe that Ukraine could be next on the Russian Bear's list of must-dos.

As we consider purpose, our Über-thinker and thought pilgrim examine some additional approaches to reason about purpose and its relationship to capabilities and strengths of motive. Let's spend a few minutes thinking about these approaches. First, one has to intend to do something to affect an adversary's stated or intended purpose for planning future moves and counters. Second, don't be daunted by how difficult it is to discern true purpose, which can only be found in an opposing leader's heart, mind, and soul, manifested by their behavior. The riddle can only be answered indirectly by surmising individuation of purpose and then aggregating their stated and hidden rationality to discern possible reasons for purpose to come into play in the first place.

To better understand purpose, my counsel to our Über-thinker and thought pilgrim is to ponder the true overarching outcomes in the mind of a hostile entity—military, diplomatic, business, athletic—providing the strength of purpose. As they attempt to think like the adversary thinks, they reason that their adversary would be reasoning about what he should have in place for achieving success and then actually acting or behaving with this overall purpose in mind. To do so, I counsel my Über-thinker and thought pilgrim to consider purposes relative to what follows next—in individuals, in families, in social and religious groups, in business entities (particularly those standing to benefit from tensions or actual enactment of imposition) in neighborhoods, in academia, in multinational corporations, in governmental entities, in the military, in government, in political entities, and, of course, in the mind and hearts of leaders and their ever so elusive intentions.

To understand this logic trail, please recall "duality" and "pendulum" thinking. You must always consider what the adversary is doing to identify purposes and subsequent actions relative to 1) the adversary's view of their own strength of purpose; 2) the adversary's view of their opponent's rationale for and strength of purpose; and 3) how the adversary considers their strength of purpose and their opponent's view of the strength of the adversary's strength of purpose again from the adversary's perspectives. Relativity between the two sides, as I've listed earlier, can allow insights into how one might go about affecting the adversary's strength of purpose, how the adversary anticipates struggles, and how the adversary could counter its enemy's influencing efforts and use them for his advantages. I do think we can begin to measure (crudely) numbers of people buying into the leader's purpose and adopting it as their own. For the most part, though, one has to measure and observe many subtle, nuanced observables whose satisfaction can help us gather enough data so as to turn into information and knowledge, thereby reducing risk and lowering uncertainty. But in the unquantifiable spectrum of competition, nobody can eliminate either risk or uncertainty in anything, let alone something as intangible as human purpose. Next, let us turn our attention to capabilities. Capabilities are, of course, indispensable, as a person may have the volition coming forth in life force and purpose, but without capabilities, life force and purpose remain impotent.

CAPABILITIES

Capabilities enable people to impose their desires on other entities or to resist another person's efforts to dictate their way of living or thinking. Capabilities are often measurable or even quantifiable, but not infinite. Oh, to have endless capabilities, usable in all domains and across all levels of conflict. Such is the ode to God that men sing out as they consider the presence of capabilities in conflict. Somebody needed to explain in the past and still needs to explain to decision makers the omnipresent specter of limitations to any kind of kinetic capability. In addition, we often find the lurking presence and influence of moral constraint against using one's capabilities to the fullest extent possible. The mere notion that one cannot go to the theoretical extreme of a particular capability presents a significant and sobering paradox to all people in conflicts. That is to say one may have capabilities but also lack determination to unleash them on an adversary. Or one may possess adequate determination for winning a conflict but lack the capabilities to do so. Thus, please read my definition of capability:

The means and ability to perform or achieve designed actions or outcomes through a set of observed and measured acts, activities, and influences. It is with application of capabilities and assessment therein in which each side judges how well one side can impose their *will*, with their facilities, performance acumen, quality of faculties, machine performance, human performance, cyber, air, sea, information, cognition, space, and ground power. The same thinking proves true for the defender/recipient of the initial thrust, and absorbing subsequent actions—capabilities, important to any calculus involving probabilities of outcomes in conflicts, influence every decision maker desiring to impose their way on another human, organization, and the like.

People can behave or act or do things with impunity—as long as there is no resistance, limited friction, no inhibitors, or obstacles to such behaviors or actions. If one side, however, anticipates resistance to their actions to impose their volition and their anticipatory work comes true, then resistance occurs. It sometimes results in conflict. Such a fight involves a collision of capabilities. Clausewitz says:

> [M]atch your effort against his power of resistance . . . the total means at his disposal and the strength of his will.[5]

In our time, I believe it's better to think in terms of capabilities here. As an example, consider the Battle of Gettysburg. The North outnumbered the South in troops, cannons, and muskets. They also were more plentifully supplied due to interior lines of communications. The South had the edge in élan and morale as well as low- to high-level leadership, with one exception. That was General Lee's insistence on settling the fight via one last mighty thrust even though he knew the defensive terrain favored the North. During the first two days of the battle, the play of friction and improbabilities contributed to a stalemate. On the crucial second day, when the North's far left flank was out of ammunition, the unexpected happened. Led by Colonel Chamberlain, Union troops from Maine fixed bayonets and repelled the Southern attackers. On the third and last day, Lee thought he could burst through the Union defenses with one final push—so went the infamous Pickett's Charge. The North turned back the tide and annihilated Pickett's division. But the North failed to follow up their victory and did not pursue Lee as he fled south across the Potomac, surviving to fight another day. Thus, when one considers capabilities on the last day, the North's strong defensive positions and numbers of troops trumped the South's edge in élan and overall leadership.

Capabilities today relate to a host of influences other than the physical killing prowess of an army. For certain, one must possess military combat power to "win" in conventional conflicts. But without strength of motive, wars usually don't turn out with advantages in numbers of things only.

---

5. Clausewitz, *On War*, 77.

Consider the immense advantage America had over the Viet Cong and North Vietnam in the Vietnam War. Morale, strength of motive, and determination trumped the physical, quantifiable advantages America held. In a world of hybrid war, multiple missions, complicated problem sets, influence from the media, presence and employment of other elements of power, and other factors comprise one's capabilities. More specifically, I speak of intelligence, morale, training and education, communications, cyber capabilities, logistics, command and control, synthesis of multiple means of national power, social media, cellular and satellite connectedness, decision making, agility, narratives, moral constraints, and speed in acting, adapting, and changing with the vagaries of nonlinear operational contexts, adaptive adversaries, and instant transmission and sharing of data gathered and pushed out by the voracious appetite of the modern media. Capabilities also include intangibles such as morale, leadership, the Clausewitzian "inner mind's eye" of senior decision makers, beliefs, patriotism, and the like. If one side has more of such capabilities than its opponent, then the weaker side has to choose either to resist or to acquiesce to the desires of the stronger side. So capabilities always prove important in designing strategy to act or to resist.

Capabilities, however, prove more interesting than this simple explanation. Capabilities have always been complicated and difficult to understand. For the sake of clarity and argument, let us switch our thoughts from the death and dying of a battlefield to commercial companies. In a commercial situation where one large and rich company wants to merge with a smaller but desirous company, discussions between the two sides occur. If the smaller company resists, it must have the means to withstand the aggressive actions of capabilities belonging to the larger company. Such capabilities could be outthinking the bigger competitor, playing on the arrogance accompanying size and strength (a usual condition, I might add), delay, money, alliances, or even merging with another company and then facing off with the larger company. Each organization should do the following: First, determine their capabilities and power for seizing control of the other company. Second, anticipate what each company could do by way of reaction and what capabilities it has to succeed. Third, if the smaller company resists, parries, or counters the larger company's initial imposition, they must anticipate the first and subsequent parries and do something to bring their capabilities to bear and deny the aggressor's. Fourth, anticipate their competitor's deceptive activities. Fifth, plan or anticipate the smaller company's efforts to entangle—legally, organizationally, monetarily—with the larger company's first effort. The smaller company desires an entanglement to hide their desires and capabilities, all the while preparing to impose their threatening counter on the larger company.

In this effort, the smaller company could very well use what Sun Tzu presents and I call the interaction of opposites—that is to say, the interaction between normal and extraordinary forces entwined and at work emitting energy in the same whole.[6] The smaller company entangles with the larger company's first effort to impose takeover in a hostile takeover by ensnaring their prey with legal, fiscal, and alliance measures and creating multiple pressures on the attacking company's capabilities. At the same time, the smaller company takes the opportunity to attack the larger company and thereby scoop up large amounts of the attacking company's stock, buy their own stock to raise the price of its stock, or purchase a company critical to the operations of the larger company.

What does this mean for each company in our theoretical fracas? First, each company must possess highly trained and educated people who learn to contemplate how their adversary thinks about their opponent's capabilities and each side's view of advantages and disadvantages. Further, each company must possess highly trained and educated people and systems to gather relevant high-quality data, analyze this data, and rapidly turn it into information and knowledge thereby reducing risk and uncertainty.

The company and its intelligence systems also engage in co-evolution.[7] That is to say, let's assume that each conflicting company is a complex adaptive system, or CAS. CAS must endure constant turbulence and change to survive. They beget change via the outputs and use of two kinds of assessments. One involves constantly gathering data the operational context emits and then judging its impacts on 1) themselves (first imposer); 2) their opponent; and 3) their opponent's view of the first imposer. Another involves a constant assessment of their actions as well as those of their competitors' and subsequent assessments. From these assessments, data comes forth. Each company must possess and artfully use the wherewithal to gather assessment data, evaluate said data, turn data into information, and turn information into knowledge, and learn and adapt faster and more effectively than their adversary. Actually, this process is a capability.

Second, leaders and planning people in each company at "war" know how to think about *will* and in particular its two pillars—that is to say each antagonist's capabilities, as well as strength of motive to persevere and triumph in the theoretical conflict from their perspective and the perspective(s) of their opponent.

---

6. Sun Tzu, *The Art of War*, 91–92.

7. *Co-evolution*: Evolution of two or more species or organisms (natural or manmade) that interact closely with one another, with each adapting to changes in the other(s). Note, if one can think about and find how the adversary CAS co-evolves (e.g., assess, collect, evaluate, learn, adapt), it is possible to manipulate the data that the adversary relies upon.

Third, corporate leaders and planning people know and put into operation applicable military theory, as it is all about conflict, and it is conflict in which our two theoretical companies engage. Fourth, each side engages in interactive wargaming so as to ascertain, to the extent possible, their opponent's thinking; planning; actions with their capabilities; and their possible intentions, actions, assessments, and adaptations. They also ponder in their wargaming, of course, a range of possible unexpected consequences coming from the release of the heretofore "bound" energy of all the capabilities I spoke about earlier in a holistic vision and enactment. Our thinkers are mature in their deep-thinking capabilities; therefore, they seek via anticipation possible second- and third-order effects.

Fifth, in any struggle, one can be surprised by black swans (totally unforeseen, huge outcomes),[8] friction (unexpected chance events), randomness, and the sudden appearance and influence of sensitive variables in their actions or activities in the context of their struggle. Friction, randomness, etc., affect how each opponent implements their capabilities in the imposition and counterimposition that represents real competition and conflict. In their thinking, opposing leaders and planners contemplate the axiom "think like the adversary thinks." In no process is this axiom more important than in discerning how an opponent thinks, plans, decides, acts, assesses, develops observables, collects, transforms data into information and then knowledge, evaluates, learns, and adapts. These games represent the tightly bound capabilities and strength of motives of each competitor in a struggle.

Thinkers must be careful when thinking about capabilities. Some capabilities prove quantifiable and affect outcomes in conflict. Others prove quantifiable, but irrelevant. Still other capabilities are not quantifiable—for example, thinking, execution, speed, quality of decisions, thinking like the adversary thinks, influence of culture, and so on—but they certainly affect outcomes. What we notice is there is a moral and physical domain relationship. Be careful. Your opponent must have the strength of motive to use some of his capabilities. There will be limitations on how and what he uses by way of capabilities.

In Vietnam, all quantifiable indicators literally screamed that the Viet Cong and North Vietnamese should have quit and acknowledged that the U.S. imposition of power—troops, tonnage of bombs dropped, artillery shells fired, body counts, logistics—had succeeded. But the North Vietnamese *will* was stronger than that of the United States due to a weak strength of motive in the United States that was directly tied to "purpose." One cannot consider capabilities without including *will*. For certain there

8. Nassim Taleb, *The Black Swan: The Impact of the Highly Improbable* (New York: Random House, 2007), xvii–xxviii.

will be winners and losers in any hostile action in which one side attempts to impose their volition on another side. Capabilities always come into play as we think, wargame, plan, and act. Decision makers choosing whether to use a capability must deal with the entanglement of many 18 considerations that come at us fast and furious throughout the rest of this work.

Now I'll bring in more discussion about strength of motive, which can sometimes overcome a deficiency of capabilities. Though this subject is somewhat abstract—how does one measure morale or even strength of motive?—we can learn how to think about this important subject. As you proceed, consider this question: How does strength of motive relate to capabilities, perseverance, determination, advantage, disadvantage, sacrifice, passion, and so on?

STRENGTH OF MOTIVE

Strength of motive—my, such a tantalizing subject! It is important for our understanding of *will*. Thus, let us take a few minutes to review some definitions. Strength comes to our understanding via four essential explanations or descriptors: 1) a state of being strong; 2) ability to cope with difficult situations; 3) maintenance of an emotional, moral, or intellectual position (stance); and 4) possession of a quality of mind and spirit to persevere against disadvantageous odds or potential cost/loss. Strength provides us with a deeper understanding of the meaning of motive. That is to say, motive by itself means little for the purposes of our discussion without a connection. The connection comes when while examining the term "motive" and discerning questions of importance to our comprehension and use. It is important to discern whether or not one finds a strong or weak motive. Of course, our findings could yield situations where strength of motive is yet a potentiality, but we know the potentiality could become strong and come into being or, with the right anticipatory and preemptive work, could stay stable or weaken. Let us digress for a moment to bring in some thought fragments into our nascent "whole" of comprehension of "strength of motive" with these thoughts, which provide the theoretical framework for the all-important cause, link, and effect relationships that do indeed prove important for our growing comprehension of *will* as its praxis provides the means for precognition, anticipation, and preemption. The theory comes with these few words:

> willing considered as object for the knowing subject . . . the object is the self, as source or subject of volition. And the principle governing our knowledge of the relation between this subject and its volitions or acts of *will* is the principle of the ground (or sufficient reason) of acting. A man acts for motives and the motives for which he acts have their ground or sufficient reason in his character. We

understand the relation between a man's deliberation actions and himself as subject of volition where we see these actions as issuing from the character of the subject.[9]

In this next interesting passage, Schopenhauer takes us on a journey behind the Veil of Maya[10] to seek and find the true core or nub of a particular strength of motive. He is telling us to examine the phenomenal sphere where one finds other spheres of objects (humans) for subjects (other humans). This principle governs relationships between and among phenomena. In review, phenomenon means:

An appearance and subsequent awareness of action or interaction with other entities—human, organizational, and machine—in experience.

Considering the thinking and writing of famous philosopher Immanuel Kant, a phenomenon is a thing as it appears to and is constructed by one's mind, as distinguished from a noumenon, or an a priori thing in itself. It leads us through the labyrinth of our hypothetical adversary's mind and tells us the ground or basis or nub or epicenter of motive lies in man's character (the aggregate of features and traits that form the individual nature of some person or thing; representing a personality type, especially by emphasizing distinctive traits, as language, mannerisms, physical makeup, etc.).[11] It certainly follows that to understand and do something with motive, our Über-thinkers and thought pilgrims must segregate decision makers from their supporting cast of people so as to delve into their characters. Their inner character, hidden by the omnipresent Veil of Maya and the Matryoshka doll,[12] displays multiple masks to hide what goes on in their minds and souls. Thus, our deep-thinking people should know and understand their target character from several different perspectives: their own, their subordinates', their friends', families', acquaintances', lovers', enemies', and so forth.

Now, let us proceed to define motive for the purposes of this devolution into the fundamentals of considering *will:*

That force or energy or other provocative phenomena that causes a people to act in a certain way, do a certain thing, endure deprivations, or operate, or act/behave,

9. Copleston, *A History of Philosophy, Volume VII: Fichte to Nietzsche*, 266.

10. Here is my version of the Veil of Maya. It comes from an amalgamation of thought, my imagination, and mental travail to turn theory into practice (praxis). The Veil of Maya is an illusion of normalcy involving an imaginary veil or mesh distorting their view of reality.

11. Dictionary.com. Retrieved November 30, 2011, from http://dictionary.reference.com/browse/character.

12. A Matryoshka doll is a set of identical wooden dolls of decreasing size placed one inside another.

or perform, usually relative to goal accomplishment, which could be good or evil. [Note—the essence of "motive" involves not only its content or purpose, but also the action and outcomes it causes.]

I dare say "motive" is an important thought in our quest for learning. Motive is sublimated to life force and purpose but infuses the rest of our model with an energy or force tremendously important in waging and winning clashes of interest. This energy or force can only be found in the mind of humans and human-populated organizations. Interestingly, motive is often well hidden behind the masks that an adversary uses to hide his innermost thoughts and feelings. Motive often involves emotional elements and influences—emotion most often defies rational thinking but it influences all the same.

Motive, when combined with strength, provides more specific meaning. We can start to use our reasoning capabilities to empathize, sympathize, and "think like the adversary." That is to say, know what each term means but never look at the two separately. But, I ask myself, am I going into enough depth and borrowing sufficient thought from the masters to conquer this abstract and slippery subject? Rummaging in my mind for a thought to buttress my effort, I found this quote about Schopenhauer's thinking:

> Each individual thing, as an objectification of the one will to live, strives to assert its existence at the expense of other things. Hence, the world is a field of conflict, a conflict which manifests in the nature of the *will* as at variance with itself, as a tortured *will*.[13]

Both words, even when combined, defy quantification, as they are intangible. Nonetheless let us look at Figure 5.2 to see our position in attempting to understand the transformation of desire to reality. From the desire, one has to have a purpose, as previously discussed. But the purpose is not enough—the purpose relates to capabilities and strength of motive. Capabilities and strength of motive, imperative for success, first always relate to one another, and second only come forth with deep thinking about the relationships between our capabilities and strength of motive relative to the adversary's. With this line of thought we are adding capabilities and strength of motive to the equation that leads to the far right—action and assessment of outcomes. This graphic helps us understand what must be done by the convening leader whose vision their subordinates resolve to implement. This imposition does not, of course, happen without the kind of thinking occurring now.

13. Copleston, *A History of Philosophy, Volume VII: Fichte to Nietzsche*, 274.

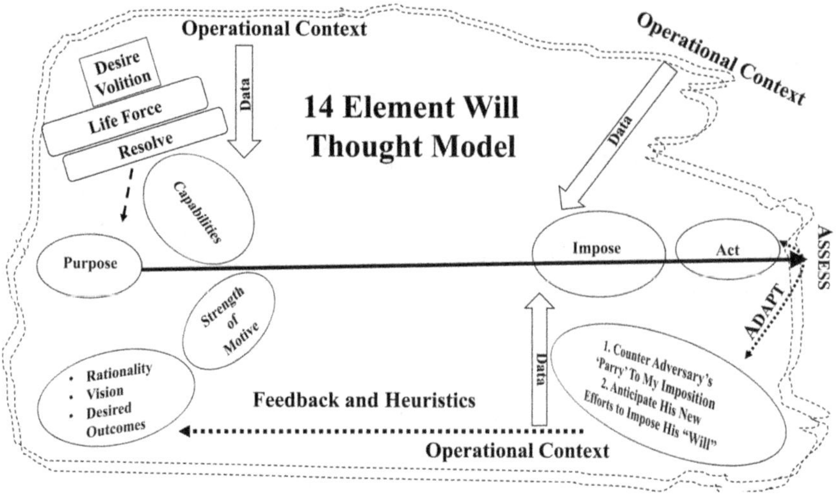

Figure 5.2. Building Out Our Model for *Will*—Motive and Capabilities

Continuing with our inquiry, capabilities and strength of motive exist as concepts to influence and to cause behavior on a sliding scale of intensity and strength. Strength of motive therefore pushes and bullies its way into the realm of the master equation: *will* = capabilities × strength of motive. Strength of motive connects and relates to virtually all of the remainder of our 18 considerations with which planners, operators, and decision makers account for in the mental and physical combat involving successful imposition by one side or and the denial of this behavior by the resisting side. Thus numbers-driven people who want certainty and no risk should not be making decisions—implementing *will* is too risky for them. History is replete with people who didn't know how to think about this matter and, similarly, never learned about the assumptions one has to make to bring it into use. Too many intangibles exist, connect with one another, and influence strength of motive and hence, what one seeks—to influence a resisting party's *will.*

The most difficult part of our mental endeavors involves recognizing the difficulty of trying to observe or measure intangibles such as strength of motive and realizing that there is no easy answer or template for how to proceed to work with and understand these intangibles. Yet we can develop "a way" to ponder the positive side of the challenge—the human mind can indeed perform these mental tasks and win sufficient bouts of mental combat to gain at least a marginal knowledge of capabilities and strength of motive. Further, our acolytes can begin to comprehend how the 14-element model's elements vibrate, leap from one position to another, and move along the model's shaft while denying our adversary the ability to do likewise.

We have previously spoken about assumptions and why using them with capabilities and strength of motive is difficult and risky. All of this is to say, let us proceed, but do so cautiously, with our eyes wide open, and our minds as objective as can be with all our wargaming, Red Teaming, critiques, and sessions with subject matter experts. With that said, our thinking can be wrong and our thoughts about the duality of capability and strength of motive could be at the center of our errors. It follows that our reasoning must be agile, flexible, and astute. Furthermore, one must constantly learn from their mistakes and understand what might have gone wrong if they err and fail. Failure, however, is never an abrupt "end state." Instead, erring is a continuum, and with such a recognition, one must discern how to correct our flawed mental processes.

So we'll move along and use our reasoning powers to learn how to think better about difficult concepts. Thus, let us use Heraclites's unity of opposites and perhaps Sun Tzu's normal and extraordinary forces[14] combinations to gain better comprehension when entangling our capabilities and strength of motive to counter our adversary's efforts. Thus, while working our way through this section, set conditions for connecting our thoughts to the other elements of our thought model. This condition setting sets the stage for us to connect to other parts and pieces of this work on learning and using the 18-consideration model.

I see another word that came from Clausewitz's fertile mind that can contribute to our discussion: *animate,* which, quite simply, means "to bring to life." So how does it relate to strength of motive? Let's first ponder the elements of our definition of motive: force, energy, or other provocative phenomena that cause a people to act in a certain way, do a certain thing, endure deprivations, or operate, or act/behave, or perform, usually relative to goal accomplishment, which could be good or evil. Motive also involves 1) one or more reasons for acting or behaving, especially one [reason] hidden or not obvious; 2) the actual reason [cause] for an outcome [effect]; and 3) the core or nub or pressure point of one or more causes that always link with an effect [outcome].

Strength of motive connotes a distinct need to discern an opponent's keenness to sacrifice to accomplish an aim, goal, objective, or strategy. That is, all of us must gain an understanding of "strength" as it applies to "motive." Though this point is easy to understand in everyday life, it is devilishly difficult to judge and successfully act on in a real-world conflict situation, in a foreign country, in an unfamiliar operational context, and working against a learning, adaptive adversary. Quite simply, strength of motive is subjugated to vagary, as it were, the causal influences that affect and thereby cause a cascading change in the strength of the actual or

14. Sun Tzu, *The Art of War,* 91.

potential motive. The vagary often bursts into bloom from the nurturing influence of culture, from all forms of media, from human beings' beliefs and values, from the silent screaming in one's mind attributable to retribution, from personalities and strength of motive of friendly forces, and from self-assessments involving self-interest.

We can combine these two terms—"strength" and "motive"—and view them in their natural state of being, a composition of one person, several people, families, businesses, religious groups, political groups, action arms such as the military and police, media, or a nation, and so on, that in its combinatorial state constitutes the intrinsic reality. Yes, strength of motive is important. But what is the source of this phenomenon's power? Is there a single source? Is it logical to find and affect this source, whether it is either one or many? In doing so one could break apart or at least cause decay of the various glues bonding the groups, which they could label in ascending order as 1) complex adaptive systems (CAS); 2) aggregates; and 3) microaggregations into 4) macro-aggregations. It is the whole that is most important from a macro-perspective. Second, one can seek to affect one part of the whole, only to find that it is resilient and though diminished for a while, it can reappear stronger than ever. As a quick example, consider the condition of the Taliban in Afghanistan after the initial U.S. attack in 2001—they scattered with many of their leaders and fighters dead. Then, because of the American refocus of priorities heaped on Iraq and neglect of the war in Afghanistan, the Taliban rebuilt and become a stronger force than ever. They had time to learn, co-evolve, and adapt. Let us deliberate this implication. Even when one believes that they have destroyed or neutralized life force, purpose, capabilities, and strength of motive among a group like the Taliban, the other parts of the 14-element model help to bring life back to the elements thought dead but only dormant.

The thought leader working the strength of motive challenge thinks, at a minimum, from three perspectives. The first perspective is micro—it recognizes the importance of individuals' *will* and of motives inherent to human beings and as a centrifugal force: emanating from individual, familial, and social groups. He also considers using a submacro-perspective in which larger and larger groups of people provide the basis for strength of motive and the infectious nature of this phenomenon. Finally, we find our thoughts drifting to a macro-level in which all relevant (to the mission, to an adversary's *will* for the potential to gain or lose strength) large and larger CAS, aggregates, and aggregations form the basis for affecting an adversary's critical elements, whether personal, local, or country combining into larger and larger aggregates, or groups of various sizes and functions. The strength of the various kinds of "glue," such as religious beliefs, values, honor, history, cultural mores and myths, and so on, hold the three elements (perspectives) or concepts together in a macro-sense.

Deep in the gorge of rumination, one understands the difficulties they face and how difficult it is to impose their desire when others resist. One has to think deeply to discern the characters, strengths, and weaknesses of this epicenter of the adversary's *will* from each perspective while keeping in mind that they all belong to the same macro-aggregation (whole). Quite simply, though capabilities can often prove susceptible to quantifiable means of understanding, the other half, the strength of motive, cannot be quantified to the extent necessary to prevail in the extreme. This other half, I posit, is vulnerable to defeat via our mental combat if our people learn to think better than they do today!

Generally speaking, capability and strength of motive gain their strength from entangling with one another. To be certain, one can possess strength of motive but lack capabilities or vice versa, yet only a fool would try to impose strike a stronger entity without a superiority in not only strength of motive but also in capabilities. A high degree of uncertainty roams the operational context, and the tyrant of "risk" looms in storm clouds drifting in and out of the contextual backdrop, but is steadily menacing to the Über-thinker and thought pilgrim's musing all the same. There is a subtle but important consideration entwined with capability and strength of motive. Deep thinking and judgment emerge with primacy from a field of many mental capabilities inherent to human beings one could use for considering strength of motive. "So, what does 'deep thinking' mean, pray tell?" the Über-thinker and thought pilgrim ask. In our world, deep thinking means (I say once again) taking the time and expending the mental energy to think about difficult problems or situations deeply and critically. Judgment means possessing sufficient multidimensional (air, ground, sea, space, cyber, information, and cognitive) acumen to reason and thereby make considered decisions or develop sensible conclusions and recommendations for better decisions than an adversary. It is one's moral obligation to learn to reason and use good judgment to find "a way" to determine an adversary's capability and strength of motive. You must seek, find, and use knowledge not for the simple sake of knowing, but for the sake of achieving advantage to beat an adversary. Or you must possess sufficient knowledge to anticipate your adversary's attempts to impose his volition on you and know how to deny this imposition.

Sometimes one's judgment becomes questionable due to their inability to think deeply, synthetically, creatively, or even via inspired imagination. Also, the presence of errors in judgment and derivative contemplation, planning, execution of action, assessing action, and adapting looms over the context of conflict. Interestingly, this potential for error and mistakes affects all players in a contest or competition. By all players, I mean neutrals, adversaries, and even friendly rivals, such as in other government agencies or commercial corporations. Thus, when I say duality, I am speaking of a wide swath of current or potential competitors, all of which are human and all of which are subject to erring like I list earlier. There are many reasons why this process is fraught with the potential for mental errors, but none are more important than considered judgment. We must always assess the presence of obstacles to our efforts to ruminate and to gain knowledge. Obstacles, natural and manmade, present formidable constraints on the pace of our ascent into enlightenment, truth, and considered judgment.

Of interest to our inquiry, friendly strength of motive is relative to the adversary's strength of motive. You must learn to comprehend how your adversary, the potential resister to your impositions or the originator of their own impositions, views your strength of motive but now out of theory and directly relative to the facing off and assessing from each opponent's view about the other. The imposer strives to discern the adversary's strength of motive, as its truthfulness looms important for any degree of success; they could be attempting to deceive us since they know our side assesses their strength of motive and vice versa. Not only must an imposer have a good estimate of the adversary's capabilities and strength of motive, they must also wargame future states of probabilities of changes in both the adversary's situation and the operational context, as well as his adversary's tactics to keep his strength of motive high, while always causing decay in the adversary's strength of motive. One must also discern the struggles to influence strengths of motive occur by both sides at a frenzied pace, as each recognizes its importance in individual as well as collective collisions and subsequent possible outcomes. Strength of motive is a target and has to be worked against; strength of motive often changes; sometimes one finds the strength of motive analyses have pointed at the wrong elements of the opposition and therefore even the most well-devised and rehearsed preparations and even capabilities stand tall and champ at their bits, these horses of actions. If our Über-thinker and thought pilgrim fail to do their homework and fail to consider strength of motive of the moving pieces constituting the adversary, then they shall undoubtedly err during execution and as they assess the quality of their actions.

I suspect you find what I discuss earlier regarding strength of motive to be straightforward. Nonetheless, people have always made mistakes about strength of motive, and I believe that they always will. Now let us delve for a minute into a very brief discussions of decision makers whose judgment was wrong about strength of motive—if the subject indeed ever entered their minds. We could pick a bevy of culprits with such an examination, but I picked one for our further exploration. Germany's initial invasion of the Soviet Union started on June 22, 1941, and had stalled by December 30, 1941. When Germany invaded, they held significant advantages over the Soviet Union: a seasoned, well-trained, well-led, and victorious army; a superb air force; and excellent leaders. The Soviet Red Army was large but raw and lacking modern weapons. Even more important, the Red Army lacked leaders (many had been purged by Stalin in the 1930s). Although outnumbered by the Soviets, the Germans were better organized and trained. Of interest to our discussion, Germany assessed that the Soviets would quickly fold and the war would be over by Christmas 1941. They based their assessment on assumptions—the swift-moving tanks of the Wehrmacht would overcome the size of Russia; National Socialism was superior to Bolshevik Communism; the invincibility of Hitler; and a lack of *will* in Soviets including inferiority in genetic makeup; inferiority of equipment and organization; and the populations of the Soviets republics' weak strength of motive to sacrifice and resist Hitler's legions. Part of the German assessment came from Soviets' poor showing in the 1939–1940 Winter War in which the minute Finnish army performed incredibly well against a large Soviet invasion until their own heavy casualties, and the mass and weight of the Red Army, overwhelmed them. Also, German planners had known about Stalin's extensive purges of officers whom the Red Army were still struggling to replace. They figured too that many oppressed Soviet civilians would not resist the invasion and even help the invading Germans. And finally, Hitler believed communism to be rotten and doomed to perish.

Well, the Germans had most things wrong. They did not understand the vastness of Russia and the primitive nature of its road networks. Their assumptions, or better said, lack thereof, about Russia's rainy seasons and brutal winters proved devastating. They assumed that the Red Army would quit fighting after incurring large losses—it did not quit fighting. They assumed that Soviet people would come to the German side and help them. Though people in Ukraine initially welcomed the Germans, they soon understood their new role in a greater German world: as slaves. So they resisted and fought and sacrificed well. Most Russians fought for Mother Russia—another element that should have been in German planners' design of assumptions. In addition, German planners assumed that Stalin and his government would either cease to exist or would flee Moscow with the German advance. Although Stalin and his government wavered, they stayed the course and did not abandon Moscow. German planners also assumed that once huge chunks of valuable Soviet farmland, industrial centers, and natural resources came into German hands, this economic loss would cripple the Soviet economy and would push the Soviets toward capitulation. They must have assumed that Soviet losses would subvert the populace's strength of motive. Again, the assumption was wrong. Selecting assumptions relative to strength of motive is difficult because of unknowns about people, their culture, and willingness to sacrifice to win.

Often, people realize that necessary assumptions—how they develop, how they prop up plans and decision making—seem to take on a life of their own and survive and continue to influence far beyond discovery of their speciousness. Poor assumptions can be found at all immense failures of military leaders in past history. Often, human beings cannot seem to understand of the sensitivity of assumptions and their contrivance without keeping being mindful of the duality that Clausewitz spoke of in *On War*:

War, however, is not the action of a living force upon a lifeless mass . . . but always the collision of two living forces.[15]

As I conclude this short discussion of strength of motive, I want to share some further thoughts:

- As one, I want and expect my Über-thinker and thought pilgrim to think deeply and therefore understand the elemental terms in our present discussion: strength and motive.
- As another thought, I put forth the following proposition for your consideration: As our Über-thinker and thought pilgrim ponder strength of motive, they realize that each term—"strength" and "motive"—is weak in its own right, but when one combines the two terms, they become a whole. and the whole is strong and important to any outcome of any conflict. With the insights, find when the words come together as a whole and peek behind the curtain of a complicated play and learn about its innards. Also, silently intrude behind several masks protecting the adversary's secrets of his mind, soul, and heart. See more than one mask, as he often wears them one on top of the other. When quietly peeking behind one of the most protected masks, we discern two interesting insights: 1) what he protects constitutes that which comprises his strength of motive, (from his perspective and what he thinks his adversary's perspective might be); and 2) how he might consider the friendly strength of motive from his view of the friendly perspective (he is seeking to find what we consider to be elements of our strength of motive so as to manipulate them to his advantage).
- As another thought, an interrogative helps explain strength of motive. Is it safe to surmise and so realize via a strong self-induced admonition that we must be cautious about accepting the veracity of mesmerizingly influential assumptions involving the all-important but ever so complicated strength of motive? Could it be that our Über-thinker and thought pilgrim remain in a perpetual state of wariness about how their adversary thinks about his assumptions regarding strength of motive—his and ours? Well, this influential relationship, with culturally imbued parts, entwines and thereby proves difficult for even the best and

15. Clausewitz, *On War*, 77.

brightest people to seek, find, untangle, and understand. This understanding can only come with sustained deep thinking in their version of high country.[16] Once again, though, as our Über-thinker and thought pilgrim ruminate about assumptions involving strength of motive and the possibility they could be wrong, they realize that their adversary makes assumptions too—some valid, others invalid. They realize and set conditions to exploit the adversary's susceptibility to err, as they design and rely upon assumptions regarding strength of motive, both theirs and their adversary's.

- A final thought for you to consider, as you ponder what you learned during this leg of the journey up the slope from the depths of Plato's Cave: The steep slippery slope is littered with damaging arrogance, mental shallowness, disparaging outlooks of stolid reasoning, the disappearance of critical thinking and reading in our general population, specious assumptions, ignoring and even disdaining creativity, and the monotonous beat of the bureaucratic mantra—feed the beast, feed the beast, no time, no time, don't worry about quality, just feed the beast. Continuing with where our journey takes us along this arduous path to the cave's exit and sunlight, once again the flotsam of poor thinking appears—the influence of the basest of biases, the readiness to commit egregious logic errors, and heavy reliance on conventional wisdom[17] that keep the people in their place at the bottom of the dark cave and providing them the puppet master's view of reality. They find the rhythmic beat of the drums of stasis, with its alluring suggestiveness to hold the course steady, "stay in your lane," and push away change.
- A mantra—Out, out, out of this darkness and into the sunlight I seek—becomes my catalyst for working past this variety of obstacles to my progress. Alas, I have only started the journey. I know enough, however, to realize a significant matter of facts. I must add the importance of strength of motive to any effort to understand cause-and-effect relationships, either before they happen or after an effect occurred. If a person knows the motive for an action and how it connects or contributes to imposing one's volition—where it originated, why it originated, who originated it, what the context was during its origination and maturation, and when the motive came forth—then they can possibly understand the adversary's rationale for the effect, but from the perspective of the mind of the originator of the effect. Then our Über-thinker and thought pilgrim can decompose the motive into its constituent elements. Once one has

16. Pirsig, *Zen and the Art of Motorcycle Maintenance,* 112–113.
17. John Kenneth Galbraith, *The Affluent Society* (New York: Houghton Mifflin Company, 1958), 6–17.

> the cause's constituent elements, they can thereby select elements that could contribute to their decision maker's thinking. Their performance always involves first stopping an effect from coming into being—or if the effect has occurred, then using the decomposition of the effect and its elements to anticipate when and where and how a next effect has a high probability of occurring. The protective layering, indeed enshrouding, of this thought is to preempt the action (effect) as it comes into being and to thereby seize the initiative.

Starting with *"purpose"* (of conflict or of attacking and defending), in this chapter, I guided the reader to ponder the true overarching desired assumptions in the mind of a hostile entity that enable his purpose—be it military, diplomatic, business, athletic, and so on. Taken together, they provide strength of purpose. As my readers attempt to think like an adversary thinks, they reason about what he must have in place for achieving success and then actually acting or behaving with this overall purpose in mind. I explained that when one considers the adversary to be doing by way of identifying purposes and subsequent actions therein, one must realize the state of relativity between the two sides; it fluctuates and each opponent's strength of purpose ebbs and flows and must be watched and exploited. In this chapter, I argued that *"capabilities"* prove indispensable in winning any fight. Nonetheless, I warned my readers to be careful how they form assumptions about capabilities, as those assumptions can often be wrong as an adversary could have a distorted view of his capabilities but proceed anyway (e.g., Hitler in WWII). I discuss the meaning of capability and how some capabilities prove quantifiable and others unquantifiable (thinking, morale, quality of decisions). These unquantifiable factors certainly affect outcomes of conflict. So, I, like my hero Clausewitz, exclaimed the absolute need to consider the inextricability and importance in winning of the *moral and physical domain* any time one considers capabilities for volition's sake. I pointed out to my reader both sides in a fight; one must meld purpose, strength of motive, and the determination to use capabilities effectively. I provided historical examples of capabilities sometimes being the wherewithal or nub of origination in the Russo-German war 1941–1945 and the Vietnam War 1954–1975, as intangibles came to play a huge role in both wars. "Strength of motive" is the final discussion point of this chapter. I reminded the readers that it, too, is a key element in the 14-essential element model we discussed in these pages.

In my view, you, my readers, now possess a new and unique discovery thanks to deep thinking in the "high country" of our minds. But we have a long way to travel and many obstacles to navigate in order to reach the end of the path and pass through the exit. With our escape, the notion of bathing in the sunlight of comprehension—reality and the beauty of high-level thinking—bids us forward, and up and up and up . . .

CHAPTER 6

Perseverance and Determination

Argument: *In this chapter, I examine perseverance and determination. Perseverance is* the indomitable continuation, staying power, or resolute completion of a task, deed, or action. *We must study the adversary to discover his level of perseverance in a fight. Determination means* "resolve, resoluteness, firmness of one's fixation on purpose." *Determination, a state of mind, shapes one's physical and mental being; it's "fuel" for perseverance; it's the stimulus one needs to succeed in conflicts.* Appearance[1] *shows determination; it leads to determination's meaning and provides insights into the seriousness of an imposition of* will.

PERSEVERANCE

Perseverance and determination—so important to understand, but so abstract in nature and form. So, let us roll up our sleeves and get to work on improving our understanding of each and why they are related by all the while different. As a first step, I'll work through perseverance. The word sounds simple enough for anybody to understand. After all, we heard the word chanted to us throughout our youth in school, in sports, in learning, and in sticking to a task to completion. All of us reading this work undoubtedly persevered in difficult tasks and bask in an aura of amazing experiences earned while persevering against difficult obstacles and circumstances. As children and adults, one learns the nature of obstacles and recognizes the need to work hard to overcome their often-formidable presence dragging on our morale and our willingness to persevere. Sometimes one perseveres only to find out they took too long and what we sought has long since gone away. Sometimes a single person perseveres in a group.

1. My thoughts about appearance first came forth from Hannah Arendt's *The Life of the Mind*. I have built upon what I learned from her wise mind involving appearance. In truth, I had never thought of appearance as unique images that demand thought until her thinking stimulated my thinking.

All of us have tasted the thrill of victory in perseverance, and all of us, if honest with ourselves, know times of failure in our efforts to persevere. Sometimes, though, stubbornness wins and our perseverance succeeds only to discover a Pyrrhic victory.[2]

One always wants to persevere in accomplishing a goal or objective with high standards—that is to say, with high-quality perseverance of a task or goal or objective. My father used to tell me in so many words—do it right, do it completely with high quality, or don't do it at all. So, as we grapple with the word, one must connect perseverance to quality outcomes. This takes more time, more effort, more desire, and more willingness to persevere but persevere well. We must overcome all self-inflicted human foibles and body-inflicted or friction-inflicted obstacles that must be deposed or scaled. If afraid of something, overcome your fears and persevere.

Perseverance proves essential to all human actions. In the context of conflict in which one side attempts to impose its worldview upon another resisting side, perseverance is ever important—there is perseverance to impose, and there is perseverance to resist. Each side undoubtedly examines perseverance from their point of view and from the view of their adversary. But its appearance is not easy to anticipate, let alone understand. It comes forth hidden by a series of masks, which denies any adversary an easy understanding of its strength or weakness. Yet as we shall see in this chapter perseverance and its appearance always stand as important aspect of winning conflicts.

In history, perseverance has meant pursuing a goal or objective over time—sometimes over may years. The ancient Romans, for example, persevered in their war with Carthage despite enormous casualties and costs in manpower, money, and land. They experienced three Punic Wars with Carthage lasting 118 years, including breaks between war. Rome's hatred toward Carthage had its causal seeds in the first Punic War and the lost souls who fell fighting in the Carthaginian attempts to become the power in the Mediterranean Sea that Rome would eventually become. Hatred, retribution, and lack of mercy all served as one basic purpose—to utterly destroy Carthage, to transcend generations and eventually lead to a strong Rome that persevered over centuries despite the many obstacles and suffering that their people, army, and political beings endured.

What does perseverance mean? My acolytes impishly ask, "Why should we care?" I start my answer with this indomitable quote:

> [T]he need of reason is to give account . . . with greater precision, of whatever there may be or may have occurred. This is prompted not by the thirst for knowledge—the need may arise in connection with well-known and entirely familiar

2. *Pyrrhic victory*: A victory that costs more than it is worth.

phenomena—but by the quest for meaning. The sheer naming of things, the creation of words, is the human way of appropriating and, as it were, disalienating the world into which, after all, each of us is born as a newcomer and a stranger.[3]

It is indomitable continuation, staying power, resolute completion of a task, deed, action, gritty, continued defense against another's intruding volition. You may share some additional thoughts to this list as you ponder perseverance with our Über-thinker and thought pilgrim.

- Perseverance is doing something even if it is difficult.
- Perseverance usually has a time limit after which continuing with a task or action doesn't make sense. But in some cases, the pursuit of a plain and purposeful goal—for example, a goal in which someone seeks to accomplish all their lives in spite of obstacles—perseverance can last a lifetime.
- Perseverance can motivate through thought or via emotion with a resoluteness to complete a task even when faced with severe consequences.

Why does the adversary possess a firmness in staying power? Our Über-thinker and thought pilgrim try to understand the adversary's steadfastness in staying power, which is, of course, yet another aspect of being determined and to what extent. Sometimes, they conclude, the firmness comes with believing in their leadership and following them with resoluteness, regardless of where they might go. Another reason for firmness in staying power could be their resentment against instigators of a foreign or adversarial presence and a perceived smirch against their sense of honor. Or they could believe in their people and not want to let them down.

Our Über-thinker and thought pilgrim have to develop hypotheses and assumptions concerning this firmness and work through the options of what could be instilling the solidifying elements of the firmness in play. Their job, of course, is to determine not only the nature of firmness under examination, but also how to soften or change or influence this firmness. It is via reasoning that our Über-thinker and thought pilgrim become determined and resolute in their own right; they know when they are in mental combat with the adversary. In this combative state of mind, our Über-thinker and thought pilgrim work to understand their adversary's state of mind behind his resoluteness to win or withstand and being unwavering in their support of outcome. Culture, background, education, experience, capabilities, emotional well-being, morale, and the like all count for strands of thought that our Über-thinker and thought pilgrim must weave into a

3. Hannah Arendt, *The Life of the Mind, Volumes 1 & 2* (San Diego: Harcourt, Inc., 1979), e-book, location 1600 of 8237.

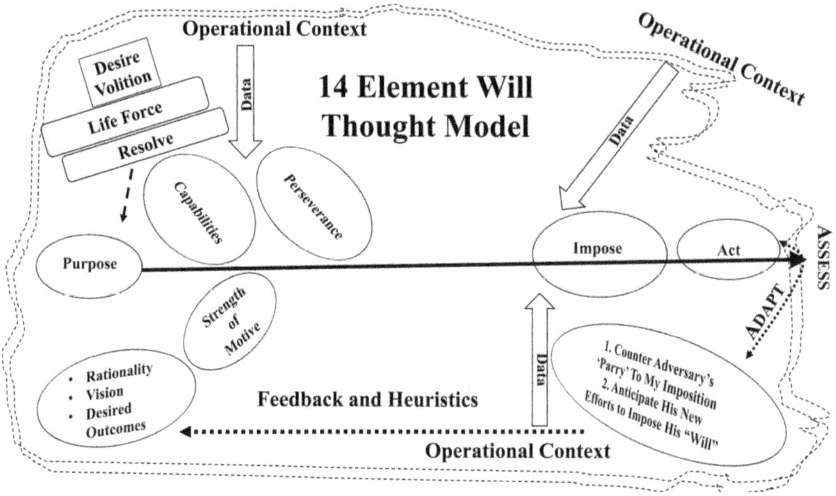

Figure 6.1. Building Out Our Model for *Will*—Perseverance

tapestry of meaning. Again, they consider and answer these questions: Why does this condition exist? How could we assault the firmness and soften its rigidity? What are the strengths and weaknesses of the adversary's actors and their steadfastness in staying power to win? How can one seek, find, approach, and affect each element? How can one consider an adversary's approach to attacking directly or indirectly friendly firmness in staying power?

Relationships involving perseverance. When life force, purpose, capabilities, and strength work with perseverance, they entangle and an amazing energy comes forth. It allows one to prevail against resistance. Perseverance has a distinct and pointed influence on capabilities, strength of motive, and purpose. Figure 6.1 shows parts of our thought model but highlights perseverance.

Our aim is to 1) protect our core of action that holds each of these core elements together as one and thus present an opportunity for gaining much more power due to the phenomena and power of synergy and holism as the elements start working together; and 2) attack our opponent's core of action as he tries to keep his elements (sacrifice, perseverance, passion, and determination, etc.) working as a whole and thereby gain immense power. Such an attack must occur in seven vertical domain silos (in a military sense air, ground, sea, space, cyber, information, and cognition domains) and multiple levels of conflict troughs (strategic [policy], strategic [military], operational, and tactical) with actions synchronized to create the greatest outcomes relative to our subject—*will.*

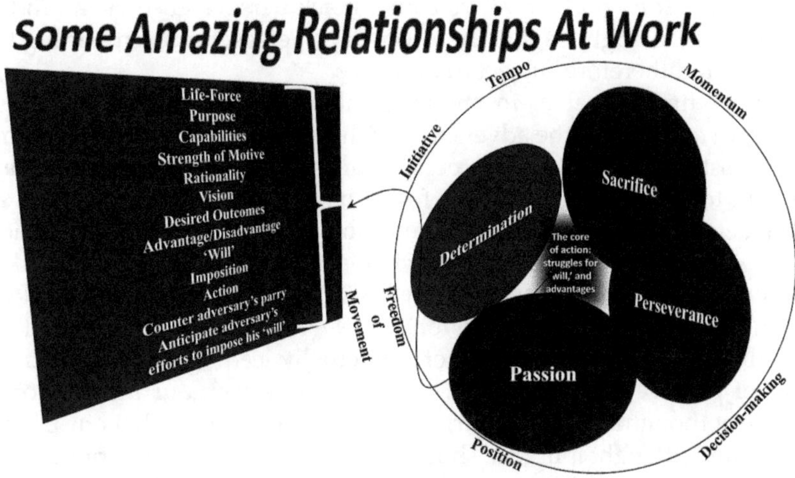

Figure 6.2. Early Important Relationships to Consider

It almost goes without saying that if any side in either a competition or conflict wants to beat their adversary or competitor, they must have a Venn diagram, whose parts connect and work as a whole, as you can see in Figure 6.2.

If one can dominate one or all of the elements comprising the Venn diagram, they often discover a window of opportunity for seizing, retaining, and using seven kinds of advantages: 1) initiative; 2) tempo; 3) momentum; 4) knowledge; 5) decisions; 6) position; and 7) freedom of movement.[4] The struggles for dominance, once again, involve actions/behaviors to affect the adversary in multiple domains and across levels of conflict (tactical, operational, strategic [military], and grand strategic [policy]), all synchronized to create the most significant outcomes possible for influencing how the adversary thinks, his determination, his passion, and willingness to sacrifice.

So we have constant struggles between smart, capable competitors and adversaries not only to consider each of the elements of our Venn diagram, but also to protect theirs and attack to disassemble the whole that is their opponent's efforts in the mental and physical combat associated with imposing one's desires on an adversary while preparing for this adversary to parry this effort and attempt to impose vision on the us, the initiator. But the pathway always leads back to the Venn diagram and also centers

4. Mao Zedong, *On Guerrilla Warfare*, trans. Samuel B. Griffith II (Urbana: University of Illinois Press, 1961), 98.

perseverance. It might be that we could attack perseverance via an indirect approach. It might be that the adversary's perseverance isn't strong to start with and therefore subject to influence.

Since we find ourselves in mental combat—in a war of minds—it is imperative to convince the adversary that his probability of victory is slim and his cost and commitment to perseverance are too high to sustain over time. But to venture forth into the fog of battle requires steady nerves, a vision, determination, and perseverance to win and prove willing to sacrifice to completion. To perform what I am advocating takes thinking like the adversary thinks, knowing his values, understanding his attitudes, and understanding his aim/goals/objectives/strategies sufficiently well to make this subtle entrée into his soft underbelly leading to his pulsating whole of perseverance feasibility. Of course, however, our moves along this line of thought should be surreptitious. It follows then that our Überthinker and thought pilgrim should know this adversary's protective mechanisms (e.g., intelligence analysis and collections) sufficiently well to penetrate his co-evolution and adaptation system without him becoming suspicious. If he does discover our attempts, he could "double" the data outcomes and act out as he reasons you desire, only to be waiting to spring a trap on you via your incursionary methods. The friendly thought warriors thereby emplace believable data from believable sources that represent the adversary's intelligence operations out and about performing what co-evolution demands—a sequence such as act, assess, evaluate, learn, and adapt—and stimulate their "take" with our data in the sea of data extant in the operational context. This insertion requires knowing the adversary's intelligence system well enough to implant the streams and bundles of data packets at the right time. The adversary must seek that which is the "bait" and bite sufficiently hard to be "hooked" into other humans' understanding and measure data with gullibility and credulity that influences his thinking, decisions, and action initiators.

As you see, in mental combat, it is the mind, heart, and soul to manipulate in our time and our domains. One seeks to assault the strength and power of the adversary's 1) purpose; 2) determination; 3) perseverance; 4) willingness to sacrifice; and 5) passion to indirectly assault morale and steadfastness. This shatters such a Venn diagram thought model into glass shards—sharp and dangerous, impossible to put back into a workable "whole" and doomed to remain disconnected for the rest of their time in a particular conflict. Of course, from a duality perspective, the friendly side has to consider their own perseverance and defend it from assaults not unlike Caesar's bloody fight at Alesia in 52 BCE, as he and his men besieged the fortress. In this and other battles, Caesar bravely led fights when his men in combat needed his leadership and example. His perseverance was strong and intoxicated his legions and frightened the trapped soldiers within the fortress. He also had to deal with morality because Vercingetorix (the Gaul adversary leader of the Arverni tribe) eventually pushed women and children into the no-man's land between the fortress walls and the first siege ditch, believing Caesar would have to take them in and thus strain his logistics. Caesar left them in no-man's land ,and eventually Vercingetorix took the women and children back into the fortress. Caesar also had to persevere in the worst of conditions when Vercingetorix called for his external allies to attack the Romans from the rear. Caesar again personally led the fight, and with his cavalry and the killing capability of his legionnaires, he won. He won through discipline, training, superior engineering, his men's belief in Caesar, and his example of leadership, his men knowing the consequences if they failed (death), and, of course, our favorite line of thought, the arrow of 1) life force; 2) purpose; 3) strength of motive; 4) capabilities; 5) determination; 6) perseverance; 7) sacrifice; 8) passion; 9) advantage; 10) disadvantage; 11) imposition; 12) action; 13) assessment; and 14) adaptation.

The implications here should lead you to accepting two kinds of implications at play: 1) distinct and obvious implications; and 2) often invisible but still impregnated with a nascent and subtle implication. That is to say, what one finds is a war of minds in which each mind in the fray tries to outfox their adversary and thereby create advantages in initiative, knowledge, and decision making and possibly the other four advantages (tempo, momentum, position, and freedom of movement). Perseverance is the descriptor, the noun so important for success, and its object adhered to sacrifice, passion, and determination, and resolutely so in the Venn diagram you saw earlier.

Perseverance has variable staying power; its links to purpose, capabilities, and strength of motive always prove essential in winning or losing. A favorite author of mine provides this thought for us to ponder relative to perseverance:

> Permanence, perseverance and persistence in spite of all obstacles, discouragements, and impossibilities: It is this, that in all things distinguishes the strong soul from the weak.
>
> —Thomas Carlyle

The grand question, though, involves the intensity and staying power of perseverance. One must imagine the elements and whole of this question and use experience, reason, trial and error, wargaming, critical and creative thinking, etc., to find what could be key variables forming the basis (the rock bed at the bottom of the still pond, but a pond that experiences aperiodic roiling via influences of nonlinear systems and complex adaptive systems [CAS] co-evolution activities) for considering *will.*

Of course, my Über-thinker and thought pilgrim intensely ruminate to comprehend what an inducement or incentive to influence an adversary's *will* could be. They retreat to the infinite levels of thought, but they remain fully capable of imagining probabilities that are the inducements and incentives at hand floating in, appearing then disappearing, but always presenting possible ways to convince our adversaries to cease their resistance. The floating probabilities involve inducements and incentives that matter to the person upon whom we impose our way of thinking. The techniques a friendly decision maker uses should appear as "a way" for this adversary to gracefully acquiesce to our desire. Lo and behold, pockets of algae appearing passive in our still pond, grow, infiltrate, and cause the formerly stable bed rocks to move. This could influence the intensity and staying power, causing it to waver and decay, thus necessitating other approaches to our objective. What we have at this point is a realistic concern. When one looks deeply into what appears to be the "still pool" of steady and dependable perseverance, they fix upon possible reasons (causes) for variance (effects). Perseverance has as its foundations and sources of energy none other than the slippery slopes of 1) emotion; 2) perception in solidity due to belief in one or more purposes/causes; 3) love of one another; 4) admiration of a leader; 5) ideals about nationalism; and 6) commitment to a religion and its supposed obligations, and so forth. Recognition and adjustment to the truism of power of determination, perseverance, passion, sacrifice, and their definitive linkage to purpose dictates success or failure with respect to concurrence with and acquiescence to a concordant dictating acceptance of our *will* by the adversary and acceptance of the failure—the continuing failure—of his attempts to impose his desires on the friendly side in a future competition.

Thus it follows we can also draw an implication, which should be an inference too: There is no end state. "What, no end state?" the staid and uncreative bureaucratic thinker exclaims. Yes, it is true—with deliberation, we find only states of continuity,[5] in which people, organizations, or countries rebound from defeat and prepare for the next round of encounter. Schopenhauer attests to the validity of this claim with this passage of high-level thinking:

[F]reedom from all aim, from all limits, belongs to the nature of the will, which is an endless striving. . . . Eternal becoming, endless flux, characterizes the revelation of the inner nature of will. Finally, the same thing shows itself in human

5. From an unpublished paper I wrote while attending the National War College from 1991–1992, "Thinking and Planning for the 21st Century." In this paper I discourage the use of "end state" in one's personal and organizational lexicon in favor of the purposefully pointed phrase, "state of continuity," which should cause deep thinking people to realize that we, as human beings, *admit to no end to anything, even with death,* and to break free from the conventional thinking of the prison of the present, and also recognize a next state of being, and the next, and so forth.

endeavors and desires, which always delude us by presenting their satisfaction as the final end of will.[6]

History is replete with such delayed, tired patience in service of revenge, such as in France after their defeat at the hands of Germany in the Franco-Prussian War (1870–1871); in Germany in the interwar years after losing WWI; in a seething Japan with a newly found self-esteem after winning the Russo-Japanese War of 1905 emerging on the world scene with the invasion and occupation of China's industrial area—Manchuria—with the Marco Polo Bridge Incident in 1937, and their subsequent war in China, their attack on Pearl Harbor, and lasting until their ultimate defeat in 1945 with the end of WWII; in the Soviet Union's destruction, theft, rape, and severe governance of their partition of Germany and Berlin in the late days of WWII and during the Cold War—all of these situations serve to help us think about and consider a truism: Perseverance can come, appear, influence, persist, or go into dormancy for its arousal at a later date. When it goes, sometimes it never reappears. In other cases, time can pass with no sign of perseverance only to discover later, sometimes several years later, that perseverance appears to influence and dominate a current conflict from a former fight—interestingly years to centuries ago. During the time of its nonappearance, it could have veered into a "hibernation" or "dormancy" of sorts, awaiting stimuli sufficient to cause an awakening to appear and influence current clashes over the resolve and volition with strands that connect it back into the time and circumstances when first it went into hibernation. The strands of connection stay alive by memories consumed by passion and perhaps even the emotions of anger, hatred, and retribution, such as in the ethnic struggle that occurred in the Bosnian war from 1992–1995 in what used to be Yugoslavia. Here is a short poem by W. H. Auden that in a few lines brings credence to the potential release of the pinned wolf that is volition:

> I and the public know,
> What all school children learn,
> Those to whom evil is done,
> Do evil in return.[7]

Why is perseverance important in our study? Well, conflicts often take time to resolve. Clashes of *will*, therefore, often become contests of perseverance—who can last the longest. An example of this phenomenon is World War I. Long after leaders recognized a stalemate, both sides persisted in staying in the conflict and wearing out the other side so as to cut

---

6. Schopenhauer, "The World as Will and Idea," 681–682.
7. W. H. Auden, "September 1, 1939." From *Another Time* (New York: Random House, 1940).

away at their adversary's perseverance, willingness to sacrifice, passion, and on and on. In the end, Germany's perseverance wore out as well as their capabilities and strength of motive. Thus, they capitulated and retreated to their den to hibernate, as I discussed earlier, until a force of energy awakened and unleashed it with the rise of totalitarianism under the flag of the Nazi movement in Germany.

So what does this mean for our ever-thoughtful Über-thinker and thought pilgrim? Let's unpack this question and see if we can find some important thoughts, thought angles, and thought approaches with which to arm ourselves for future conflicts. As one aspect to be considered, when decision makers experience inception of their vision of a desired outcome, they provide a purpose for the impending attempts to dominate a resisting entity. Along with an effective purpose, they consider subsidiary necessities such as capabilities and strength of motive to bring vision and purpose into being. Inevitably they start thinking with what they desire and how to obtain it even in the case of extreme resistance, which to overcome is antithetical to the beliefs and perhaps existence of the imposer of action. One of these considerations happens to be perseverance. They consider and envision the kind of actions that could occur, and for each they consider perseverance—us and them. Along with designing purpose and recognizing the importance of the life force in its birth and maturation, they consider capabilities and strength of motive. Both of these aspects of our thought model feed into and energize determination and perseverance.

With these two aspects of colliding thoughts and interests our decision maker and his Über-thinker and thought pilgrim recognize, indeed anticipate, pluses and minuses that could accrue to one side or the other. As our decision maker considers actions on a resisting entity, he recognizes the adversary's perspective. He also considers how strong the adversary's strength of motive could be and this side's desire to persevere. With some understanding of the adversary's desire to persevere, our decision maker, Über-thinker, and thought pilgrim reason from the adversary's perspective the strength and steadfastness of his persevering, what persevering would cost him, and what it would look like when done (criteria for success, perhaps). During this contest of strength and perseverance what can our decision maker count on by way of perseverance with his own action people—the people who actually execute the actions on another person who resists? What is their strength and steadfastness to persevere, and what would be the cost to persevere and sacrifice well enough to win?

[An apparition appears and says to its stunned audience] . . . that which you seek hides and sleeps. Awaken and coax this indolent "idea" to stir, come forth; beware of its consequences, as it can cause one to weep.

It is the gaze of perseverance you grasp and view in your mind's eye, allowing a brief peek of outcomes yet to come in conflict's maze.

Address the cost of zeal to persevere and sacrifice while imposing your ever ambitious *will*, ever so real.

Address the link between perseverance and sacrifice on each side, turning violent with the swiftness of an eye's blink. Each side prays to win, but influencing the link allows you to stray from obvious paths, to his soft underbelly, to where his capabilities and perseverance harbor refuge; extinguish your opponent's wrath and cause fear in the people of his capabilities.

Protect yourself from subterfuge, his lies scheming against your desires; use and defend your elements of *will* or die! [The apparition disappears]

Shaken, but quick to regain our composure, we consider what just happened with the apparition. But now, back to the task at hand. Once our decision maker "wrestles this question to the ground" and applies a chokehold on his adversary, he still has to understand the adversary's perseverance from his own view and conclusions of relative strength of motive, and capabilities from the view of each side. That is to say, each side's perspective of relative strength, ability to exert force, and possess sufficient perseverance to win in this bout of colliding ideas. The penchant to err looms large in this battle over perseverance.

Et tu, Brute? Then fall, Caesar![8] So it is with chameleon-like emotion that stands so tall a friend at one moment then, in another, an enemy seeking to charm. Emotion is treacherous. It is fickle—it can appear and affect one side, then the other, then both sides at once. Fickleness and falsehood, nothing new, present in Caesar's time it was, still in ours. It is nearly impossible to understand emotion with reason and logic. Everybody is a slave at some time to their emotions and to those of others. Yet even with our lamentations about its fickleness, density, and opacity, it still lies at the heart of perseverance. One must always engage their best reasoning skills to consider this subject so as to understand its nature and influence.

Continuing on, let us start with learning what emotion means. For the purpose of this work, it's

[a] state of state of being coming from perceiving, sensing, or feeling, but generally not via cognition. Emotion is characterized by intense physical and mental activity, both occurring at the same time, and a high degree of liking or disliking. Emotion can entwine with mood, temperament, personality, disposition, and motivation, and off the cuff action and reaction. Emotion involves sensing and feeling change in one's context and inner drives and feelings, both inured from the

8. Shakespeare, *The Tragedy of Julius Caesar*, 645.

bureaucratic ravages of quantification and inane bureaucratic tendencies and standards of behavior (e.g., do not show emotion or you shall be castigated as weak).

Emotion is the zest and flow of life, of one's energy coming forth usually without thought or via very little thought, but instead bursting from one's inner being—feeling, sensing, experiencing, empathizing, sympathizing—it is the high heartbeat, the cry of anguish, the feeling of surprise, a searing pain of sadness bursting in one's chest; a response that brings into view the happiness actually deriving from one's subconscious and coming into presence and influencing behavior in one's conscious mind; and as a human being (one or more) who experiences and relates (well or badly) to one's circumstances, resultant moods, or relationships with others. Emotion relates to life force, purpose, strength of motive, sacrifice, passion, determination, and perseverance, and closely to *will*.

Emotion always proves vital to conflict, with its many considerations. Yet it is most often ignored by all sides in a fray. Emotion is the answer, meaning, and substance of the fuel and fluid for the moving parts and pieces of our model's essential elements. One finds emotion's "fluid" of life in all these elements. Emotion helps to bond all efforts to impose one's wishes on a resisting entity via a variety of actions. Leaders though keep emotion in check so they can moderate its use in force, power, and energy. They never want emotion to extinguish too early or become out of control, which could allow those who apply force and action to open the door to surprise actions.

The weary travelers on Plato's trail suddenly realize something is missing in their thinking. They start reasoning and surmise if they can attack, manipulate, or dissipate the power of emotion in the adversary and protect the emotion of their friendly people, they might very well have found, through deep thinking, the epicenter of *will*. They deduce that they may have discovered an indirect way—though not the only way—to influence the adversary's *will*, while protecting their own. The Über-thinker and thought pilgrim realize they must traipse off to their high country and deep-think as their minds realize the need to improve with experience and heuristics.[9]

As I mentioned early in this book and want to mention once again, *will* is important because it is why men have been killing each other across many millennia. It involves physical, mental, and emotional struggle. Thus, a significant aspect of this subject must involve emotion. Thus our Über-thinker and thought pilgrim must wrestle it to the ground and work hard to understand its meaning, intricacies, and power to influence, but also

9. *Heuristics*: A person learning on their own recognizance via experience, reflection, reasoning, and applying to their particular situation and context. Heuristics can be short lived, aperiodic, in a pattern, or continuous.

understand what could possibly cause its power to erode. But alas, they find emotion too difficult to imagine, let alone to engage in deep thinking to comprehend its mysterious composition. And too, emotion is a personal thing that has been conditioned and even masked by the person involved via their situation, context, experiences, education, worldview, culture, intellect, and the like.

With these thoughts in mind, our Über-thinker and thought pilgrim focus their study of emotion not only to discern its meaning, but also to understand its capability to vary in its intensity and in its extensive reach into a person's life and well-being, among family, friends, business acquaintances, church friends, and so on. With deep thinking, they discover and thereby focus on a particular kind of emotion, first as individual emotion, then as micro-aggregations of emotion, and then as macro-aggregations, for example, in a movement like the Arab Spring (2010); a large riot like in Ferguson, Missouri (2016); a protest like the Women's March in (2017); large groups of people in an organized democratic political movement (like the Trump win in 2016); a series of political protests such as the anti–Vietnam War protests in 1968; and so forth. All of these events involved conflicts of varying kinds and emotions.

They also find their thinking drawn to one or more particular decision makers and their view of and response to "emotion," how this adversary views his adversary's emotions, extant vulnerability to one's emotions undergoing the ravages of overt and covert manipulation, and how this adversary might attempt to manipulate or attack friendly's volition, resolve, and life force via emotion. Our Über-thinker and thought pilgrim decide that their deliberations must involve a specific effort based on their adversary and the operational context in which the struggle for dominance is destined to occur. Our Über-thinker and thought pilgrim enter the fray intending to stalk and strike their adversary's basis for emotion with the express purpose to degrade or manipulate emotion. They now possess the intellectual wherewithal to consider and selectively attack their adversary's emotions, ensuring what they are doing is relative to the central idea at hand while protecting themselves from attacks on their theoretical but sensitive all the same well of centrality of *will*.

They think deeply, often with the help of a virtual knowledge environment (VKE),[10] flush with specific knowledge, cultural experts, statisticians, and technology scientists who know how a particular people think and what their subconscious states of being might be under a variety of circumstances. Indigenous people prove valuable to a VKE for opening the door of emotion into a room where they find, via their sight and intuition,

10. *Virtual knowledge environment (VKE)*: Physical and virtual aggregation of SMEs (subject matter experts), organizations, computers, tacit knowledge, data and knowledge bases.

various whirling emotions (e.g., rage, fear, hate, love, retribution). With the help of high technology, a sterling imagination, and their indigenous guide, they search for and find possible ways to influence the adversary they face, whether individual, aggregates, micro-, or macro-aggregations—who they are; their background, upbringing, and social mores (e.g., showing emotion or not showing emotion); how they think and feel about family; how they feel about themselves; how they emote; how they grieve, feel, and express joy and love of country; how they hold grudges and approach slights; how they experience emotions about life force and destiny; how they believe in spirituality and afterlife (mythos[11]); and how they express emotion. This adventurous triumvirate (Über-thinker, thought pilgrim, and guide), with their artificial intelligence–driven visual and physical umbilical cord to the VKE, seeks the core or basis of emotion in the dark well in which it exists, floating, dormant for the most part, sometimes easily or not easily aroused but once aroused able to influence human thinking and action. Of course, as the triumvirate engages in this hefty mental effort, they consider how to protect their action elements and decision maker's grounds for their emotional bases—this is duality and pendulum thinking at its best.

It is up to leaders and decision makers to use emotion as a "glue" for clumping their actions into aggregations to develop the power in capabilities to act. To optimize this power, they think about how to synchronize, combine, relate, and connect like and disparate parts and pieces and bring all into one or more wholes that are aggregations. In addition, to win, they possess and implement the passion to keep one or more aggregations together so the whole continues to be greater than the sum of its parts on a continuum, thereby not only opening the door of holism and its immense power, but also propping the window open for the high probability of constancy of synchronized action of one or more powerful wholes infused and often propelled by none other than emotion.

Our Über-thinker and thought pilgrim understandably view this mental work as extreme but worthwhile. No rest for the weary, though, so on we go. We talk about how this volatile "fuel of emotion," like so many elements in question, takes study to gain mastery, interact with cultural experts, all the time acknowledging a need for a heavy dose of wargaming and critical thinking about necessary but always dangerous assumptions and "what if" bouts of logic. No human being can go it alone all the time, everywhere. They have to rely on fellow Über-thinkers and thought pilgrims, other planners, their decision makers, subject matter experts in their VKEs,

11. *Mythos*: An underpinning system of beliefs, especially those dealing with supernatural forces, characteristic of a particular cultural group. In our work I have expanded the definition to include the forces and vagaries of life after death.

artificial intelligence machines, nested computing power, and the like. They understand that an important aspect of conflict of any kind is only understandable if one places their mind and body in another person's mind and body and feels and senses the emotions pouring from and empowering the person in question as well as their actions and behaviors but always from their points of view. This concern is beset by the complicated phenomenon of duality, as the decision maker and their Überthinker and thought pilgrim know with certainty that they must consider the emotions of not only their action people and organizations but also those of the adversary (for advantages to exploit or for disadvantages to guard against with vigorous surveillance) as these true but difficult struggles come forth and prove ever so relative to the thinking and actions of one another. It follows then that emotion is an essential aspect, indeed a major contributor, to the puppet master behind the screen, infusing its power and influencing perseverance, determination, passion, sacrifice, strength of motive, capabilities, purpose, and life force.

Who perseveres in conflicts? This question presupposes that different people become involved with perseverance at different times, and thus they act and behave differently under varying circumstances and play of variables. Sometimes they even show great awareness and deference to the importance of sensitive variables. If we want to go into some depth on this matter (which I do), one performs deep thinking via analysis and then shifts their mind to synthesize what they learn from it and apply their thoughts into a better sense of meaning and understanding. All of us must always consider the dark cloud of duality constantly trailing our movement while trekking along our path toward enlightenment.

So back to answering who perseveres, let's start with a leader/decision maker. The desire to persevere comes from somewhere. A starting point in my mind involves the leader or decision maker whose desire prompts action elements to satisfy. Consider this thought: Let's say a leader desires something—say, a province with a rich city in it. He realizes something within his person excites his life force and stimulates the desire to turn it into action that imposes action sufficient to satisfy the original desire—undoubtedly a series of related actions. From life force comes purpose, which leads to this particular decision maker's hypothetical interrogative: Should I? Then he, in a flurry of thinking, asks: Can I? Some decision makers even go so far as to ask yet another question: What are the possible consequences of this desire? The decision maker then thinks about capabilities and strengths of motive for himself in relation not only to the target, but also the operational context at play.

Four groups of people again serve to be the immediate and physical whole the imposer of volition has at his disposal. As a first group of evaluation, the decision maker thinks about his coterie of trusted confidants to work details involved in carrying out the imposition to satisfy the life force–originated desire. This devolution into details requires deep thinking. As a second group, Über-thinkers and thought pilgrims perform the deep thinking. These people are always ready to persevere to accomplish their leaders' desires, and in this case, they have a vested interested in winning. They provide the intellectual backbone, the framework for triumph of the all-important perseverance in any contest at hand. The decision maker turns around and takes stock of his talent and his line of vision sets on none other than the Über-thinkers and thought pilgrims. The Über-thinkers and thought pilgrims have become professional thinkers; they love to engage in deep thinking, wargaming, examining the pros and cons, and engaging in consequence analysis, and they think like the adversary thinks. If our adversary we fight has his own Über-thinkers and thought pilgrims, consider them, their motivation, their thinking prowess, and their moral fiber and find a wedge or angle with which to come at them.

As one thinks critically[12] and works with assumptions, thought models, thinking like the adversary, causes and effect, etc., they eventually reach a position about how to act, yet the position precipitates other questions. Who do I trust to impose action to convince a resisting decision maker to acquiesce or suffer the consequences? Does my resister have sufficient capability and strength of motive to resist my capabilities and strength of motive, as I act? What does it cost to use my people, organizations, and machines to win? Is my expected benefit worth the cost? What does my adversary believe it will cost to resist me? Is he willing and able to pay what he believes the costs to win? Can he generate sufficient perseverance for a long-haul conflict and in doing so, ignite and sustain sufficient passion so as to absorb my actions and build sufficient resilience and robustness to believe he can resist me?

Upon examination, one finds a third group of people who have a say about perseverance: the mid-grade and junior leaders of the action people at the tip of the sword of imposition. These people play an ever so important role as interlocutors between the people imposing *will* at the action level and the senior person or people with whom the origination of the desire, purpose, capabilities, strength of motive, etc., came forth. For perseverance to exist and keep existing, these same people must be loyal to the purpose of the imposition and, of course, to the person(s) whose desires

12. I use 13 elements to satisfy my critical thinking quality standards as I consider *will*: 1) nonlinearity; 2) deep thinking; 3) *wills;* 4) causes, links, and effects; 5) thinking like the adversary; 6) introspection; 7) 12 logic and 12 bias errors; 8) relational/relative action outcomes; 9) cultural drivers and shapers; 10) facts, objectivity, and subjectivity; 11) chance; 12) thinking critically per se (judge *assumptions, enquire into claims, survey values and social mores,* examine *evidence,* search for hidden *relationships, study facts, scrutinize truth, and* assess *conclusions*); and 13) context.

they actuate. This loyalty is a form of perseverance, and it must stay strong even in the maw of the beast of conflict. Also, the people at the point of the spear must keep their perseverance high when the resisters' co-evolution and adaptation cycles cause continual changes. So, what motivates them to lead, to be disposed to persevere, while imposing the senior decision maker's vision? Well, they could be idealists and believe in a particular cause. They might just love action. They might love to lead people in conflict. Or they could be absolutely loyal to the senior decision maker attempting to impose his way of thinking on the resister. Many, though, persevere because of the "winning horse" syndrome. This syndrome involves the strong desire to get ahead via one's life force and thereby pursue their ambition at all costs with their support to the person who has the best odds to be a winner.

Now for the fourth grouping of people, organizations, and equipment for consideration about persevering. To be more specific, I am speaking about humans and their machines. In this "whole," a symbiosis of sorts occurs. It deals with the immediacy and volatility of their adversary's actions and activities as he sets conditions for and actually acts as he resists the imposition of which we speak. Without any doubt, our people must be committed to the purpose of the imposition, possess the perseverance to triumph against all obstacles, and be prepared to endure the immediate sacrifice required to defeat an adversary and cause the opponent to acquiesce and accept the terms of the imposer. From a duality perspective, these action people anticipate and resist an adversary's return imposition. The same standards hold true for retarding or "neutering" the blooming of an aggregate or aggregations of people. The resisters stay committed to their purpose for resisting, possess the perseverance to triumph against obstacles, and must be prepared to endure pain and suffer the initial sacrificing required to blunt their adversary's attempt to impose his vision on the friendly decision maker. The blunting of which we seek involves our adversary's big ideas. Thus, one can argue the recurring dominance of four omnipresent big ideas: aim, goals, objectives, and strategies (plural due to the necessity of using a variety of strategies for related actions across the vertical domain silos of conflict, as well as relativity of action across the horizontal levels of conflict troughs). The engagement entwines with the battle and the battle entwines to the campaign. Nonetheless, human beings find themselves caught in a maelstrom much bigger than their being or immediate surroundings and thereby must be disposed to stay the course and continue to persevere, often as a supporter. As an example, consider about the administrative, maintenance, medical, communications, transportation, law and order, logistics, and intelligence people who live and sometimes die performing and trudging ahead because there is no alternative, such as the German Army fighting in the Soviet Union from 1941 to 1945.

The people of whom I speak who perform the actions can be mental competitors, soldiers, cyber warriors, law enforcement people, or people at work in corporations or companies. All of these people participate in their leader's efforts to defeat a resisting force. At times, struggles for winning actions can be physical, such as during combat in which one finds a force of soldiers on the offense to achieve their objective, which feeds into the engagement, which feeds into a battle, and which feeds into a campaign. Other struggles occur in mental combat, as opposing sides try to outthink one another and thereby eventually win by gaining market share over their rivals—consider a commercial business takeover, as an example. In addition, the struggles of people to either impose or deny an imposition can occur in a cyber, information, cognition domain, etc., or even via data and the effects it has on how people perceive, think, plan, act, assess, evaluate assessment data, and adapt.

Some examples to help us understand perseverance include 1) ancient Roman infantry marched in their formation as a highly trained and confident unit into what they knew would be a horrible and bloody battle as they sought to impose their leader's determination against a defending adversary; 2) German civilians during WWII endured and persevered via heavy sacrifice in the bombings of their cities and subsequent death and destruction of civilians, cities, and culture; 3) the Soviet populace and army endured four years of savage warfare against the invading German armies and ultimately turned the tide of aggression and then, at a high cost, imposed their *will* and severe retribution on the German armies and population; 4) the North Vietnamese army and population endured heavy casualties to unite North with South Vietnam; 5) U.S. troops trapped at the Battle of the Bulge in December 1944 refused to acquiesce to the Germans attackers who had the initiative in a surprise attack. All of these situations have several common threads, including no alternatives (than the unacceptable acquiescence to their adversary) available other than to forge ahead, belief in and love of country, training and camaraderie, love for each other as fighting people, hatred and retribution, belief in leaders, belief in a superior ideology, the need to export said ideology and impose its tenets on others, and nationalism necessary to reunite the two parts of a country.

Why do the people who are the point of the spear of either imposing or resisting persevere to win? Why are they ready to sacrifice to persevere? From whence does the well of passion surge forth to nurture sacrifice, strength of motive, determination, and purpose sufficient to "win" in a contest of *wills*? This question intimates the importance of winning and defeating or thwarting the adversary leader's desires. Or, from the perspective of the recipient of the imposition, to parry said imposition and actually turn the flow of offense on the aggressor and in the end, impose their own leader's desires on the original attackers, who now defend and desperately try to frustrate this new effort by their adversary. The original resister finds himself turned around in the situation with the ebb and flow of conflict, and now has the initiative and attempts to beat the new resister. This is where explanation becomes difficult because of the abstractness of the subject. Nonetheless, other answers, thoughts, and knowledge exist and they constitute our next targets in this trip of mental exploration. With that said, let us next turn our attention to determination.

DETERMINATION

As we think about the considerations one has to make in conflict, one always, always, always considers perseverance, determination, and sacrifice. These three words ring out with importance and clarity, and each has a distinct meaning of interest in our study of *will*. Interestingly, each term relates. It is difficult to first understand what determination and perseverance mean and to understand enough about each to be sensible about terms and actions. Please remember the all-important relationship of determination, which stretches to and connects with perseverance and then to the inclination to sacrifice, as gossamer thread, leaps forth and connects with one another to make a whole. With this said, let us begin to increase our understanding of determination.

First, determination means "resolve, resoluteness, firmness of one's fixation on purpose." Determination is a state of mind that drives one's physical and mental being; it tries with utmost desire and energy to perform a task; it is a "fuel" of sorts propelling perseverance; it is the invisible impetus that continuously pushes perseverance to not only occur but also to succeed; it involves possessing a state of mind or state of emotion from which the individual fixates while attempting to accomplish a goal or objective; it is an act of coming to a decision or of accepting/selecting a purpose and then possessing the resolve to fulfill the purpose.

At the beginning of this part of our journey toward the light of understanding and comprehension, our Über-thinker and thought pilgrim humbly realize their reasoning needs to include and comprehend more than one important relationship because "determination" has multiple thought tentacles reaching out and connecting with other equally vital and relative concepts. As one connection, consider appearance. Appearance means something—an entity's presence, an entity's actions, an entity's behavior, a smell, a latent intuition coming into existence or becoming a presence to one's senses. An appearance emerges into our consciousness because it catches our eye and our attention. There is a relationship between our consciousness and this presence that presents an appearance or presence for our attentive minds to mull over.

Appearance[13] is important in our study of determination, because it helps us to understand how it manifests and thus provides us a hint, at least, of how serious an imposition might be and how strongly determined an adversary could be in his intentions. The antipode is just as important. As our decision makers contemplate imposing their desires and volition on an adversary, it is important to know the wherewithal for successful imposition against the adversary's determination but also both side's instruments of imposition and in particular determination. Thus you reason that determination is one of the most important assessments in any kind of conflict. If one's subordinates prove prepared to pursue their mission and objective to the final degree to "win," then life is good. If the decision maker performs their due diligence and comes up with a question mark, then life is bad. But worse, if for some reason this decision maker moves forward with the play anyway, their probability of success is low. In addition, the decision maker wants the recipient of their imposition to understand their level of commitment, hence determination to pursue the imposition not only with vigor but as a sustained effort over time and space. Now, I infer that my determination comes forth, manifesting the imposition action through words, shows of force, sanctions, occupation of territory, police presence, diplomatic admonitions, and the like. Determination can be real or it can be deceptive. It protects the person, motive, or resolve to achieve or win. It is evident that "determination" deserves our attention and deep thinking. Our Über-thinker and thought pilgrim therefore reason about the veracity of the "appearance" in question. Forming conclusions about "appearance" only comes with deep thinking, wargaming, assumption analyses, and praxis but always preparing to change if said deliberating proves errant.

Able adversaries always anticipate the views and actions of the opposing force and discern their considerations about their determination. As such, any adversary has to consider how to manipulate their adversary's 1) purpose; 2) strength of motive; 3) degree of determination; and 4) perseverance. All of these terms, revealing to the thinker, prove important, regardless of how impossible they seem to any efforts to measure. Opponents always size each other up to the best quality of thinking they can muster relative to discerning the imponderable "determination" to win and their corollary payment in sacrifice—lives, money, time, political capital, etc.—this is the relationship between determination and sacrifice. But perseverance is in the mix too, as it designates how long and how much energy one side or the other or both sides is resolute in putting forth to triumph

13. My thoughts about appearance first came forth from Hannah Arendt's *The Life of the Mind*. I have built upon what I learned from her involving appearance. In truth, I had never thought of appearance this way until her mind guided mine.

in a conflict. That is to say, when I ponder determination, I believe what it presents can be true or false. Even if true, I think about how one might know whether it's true or untrue. I must consider how the friendly side appears in my eyes and in the eyes of the recipient of my action, or how serious the threat of my determination to impose my *will* might appear to the recipient of the threatened imposition action. I must put myself into my adversary's mind and consider his thinking about how determined he thinks I am to impose my desired state of being on him via my capabilities and my determination to have my way. The same holds true with resoluteness and firmness of one's fixation on purpose. As we discussed earlier, purpose, of course, comes from a leader or decision maker who explains why a particular imposition of action is important. Thus, purpose and determination entangle and prove almost impossible to extirpate. This entanglement plays out if we consider determination as resoluteness or firmness of fixation on the purpose or cause for imposing one's action on another resisting entity. Determination also involves some important descriptive thoughts, each worthy of consideration but requiring slightly different expenditures of energy and action to guide an adversary's thoughts. His thoughts should center on imposing his actions or countering his adversary's. Thus, along with determination, we find marching behind determination the silent soldiers of fortitude (mental and emotional strength) and resolve (tenacity), both important descriptors demanding consideration of one's overall capability (tangible and intangible forces and energies) to accomplish one's aim, goals, objectives, and strategies.

Our Über-thinker and thought pilgrim consider another important question that involves subtle but highly related meaning and implications: Whose determination do we consider? As a first thought, it could be the determination of an instigator. It could be a political cabal or elite group the initiator needs to have in pocket and whose degree of determination is important for the outcome of a struggle. Then one should consider a decision maker's determination as well as his judgment of how well determination has seeped into and affected his capabilities, strengths of motive, resolve of a given populace, élan or morale of his military or law enforcement forces, the involvement of subordinate organizations, and finally, involved individual human beings—say a populace in general. In addition, we consider the determination within people who perform the actions of the imposition. Are these entities, organizations, decision makers, and individual people truly determined to win and might they be prepared to sacrifice according to their level of determination—or are they going to acquiesce when the going gets tough? One has to not only consider determination of the friendly people, structures, and gatherings I just mentioned, but also each of those aspects of determination for given or potential adversaries—one or more decision makers, leaders, political elements, religious elements, their military, intelligentsia, media, and a populace and their social and cultural groupings and inclinations in thought. Finally, one considers the formation of groups and teams springing forth that one usually has difficulty in anticipating—for example, in the 2003 American invasion of Iraq, the Iraqi leadership was decimated, the military destroyed, and the political apparatus (Baathists) basically "fired." The forthcoming insurgency grew and festered from the fragments that appeared benign from an American perspective, but that proved very much alive in the hearts and souls of the insurgents and terrorists.

A force arose from the ashes of defeat, much as the phoenix arose from the ashes of its deceased predecessor—in this case, though, it arose from the army and the Baathist political apparatuses. These new forces, mostly Sunnis, turned into insurgents working in nonhierarchical networks, armed with small arms and improvised explosive devices, and fortified with a determination to expel the foreign forces and to wreak havoc with the new majority ruling class—the Shia. In our precognition and anticipation[14] efforts, our Über-thinker and thought pilgrim would have considered an impressive strength of determination in the first place and would have estimated the determination intensity of each and what could cause this intensity to vary. Unfortunately, they were toiling in Plato's Cave, marching to the tune and truth of the puppet master behind the curtain. Now, though, our Über-thinker and thought pilgrim develop possible sources of the foundation of an opponent's determination. This opponent could find his determination with the righteousness of a rendered decision destined to be a course of action. They might attain solace in the justice of settling a slight or a long-standing dispute or contest. Of course, once our Über-thinker and thought pilgrim consider this aspect of determination, they realize they possess a power not only to draw conclusions, but also to recommend ways in which their leaders might strike. It could focus on the locus or foundation of the adversary's determination as they come into being. It follows that our two travelers would possess the capability to preempt said activities, seize the initiative, and strangle the action before it becomes effective and strong.

Figure 6.3 allows the reader to peek into determination's seemingly invisible but very real relationships.

By now the Über-thinker and thought pilgrim understand determination quite well and its firmness in staying power. Then, in an interesting discovery, they unearth yet another connection: If there exists a relationship, there exists a link, and with a link one always finds a way to induce decay, to sever the link, or to manipulate the link and thereby gain an advantage over the adversary. Five kinds of links exist in which the decay

14. In advanced analysis, students learn to use a precognition thought model (PTM), which has three parts: precognition, anticipation, and preemption.

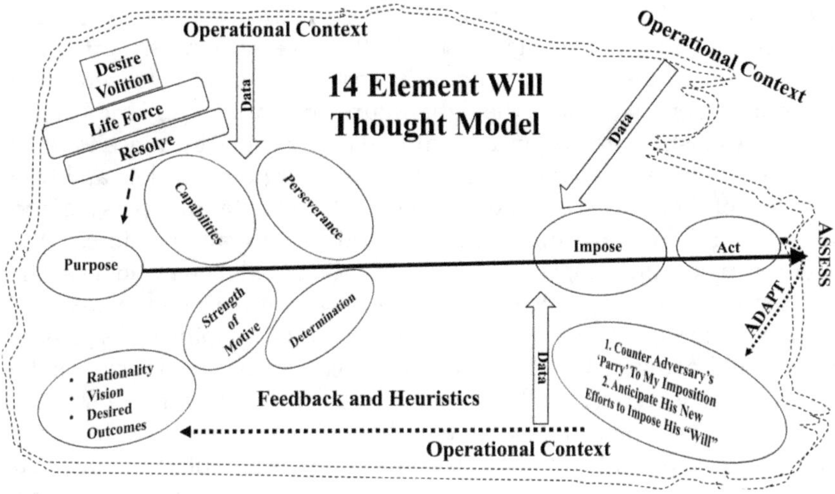

Figure 6.3. Focus on Determination

may be induced: human/social, technical, functional, organizational, and thought. For clarity, consider the relationship between perseverance and determination. The connecting link could be a bundle rather than a single link; it could thereby include human/social, functional, organizational, and thought links. With this insight, our Über-thinker and thought pilgrim commence to identify ways to influence one or all of the links via countering and manipulating actions to affect link strengths. They know choices exist. They can choose to use either a direct or indirect approach and choose one or the other based on sufficient reason relative to advantage to friendly and disadvantage to adversary and correlating length of time said advantage could exist. Our Über-thinker and thought pilgrim thereby use an indirect approach to weaken the firmness of staying power and indirectly affect the strength of *will* and each of its main elements, while remaining in the shadows of obscurity immune to the "dust-up" of the operational context under the extremis of rapid but inexplicable change. Thus the one or more links connecting perseverance and determination have to be sought, found, and manipulated to their advantage or actually severed at the right time and right place with the right degree of finesse suitable for bringing a distinct advantage to one's decision maker.

I started this chapter with discussion of perseverance; it is essential to triumph in all. I explained what perseverance means. It is *the indomitable continuation, staying power, resolute completion of a task, deed, action, imposition of "will," or gritty, continued defense against another's imposition of their "will."* I helped the reader learn how to think about perseverance as they, in a fight, must convince the adversary that his probability of victory is slim and his cost and perseverance too difficult to sustain over time. I explained to my readers that they must learn to like the adversary thinks sufficiently well to gain entrée into his mind to discern his level of perseverance in preparation for a fight or as the fight occurs. In conflict, two kinds of perseverance exist: a perseverance to impose *will* and perseverance to resist. Each side must examine perseverance from their point of view and from the view of their adversary. I explained in this chapter that perseverance always stands unwavering in fighting and beating another force. With regard to determination, I explained its meaning (and thereby delineate the difference with perseverance); it means *"resolve, resoluteness, firmness of one's fixation on purpose."* Determination, a state of mind shaping one's physical and mental being, is the "fuel" for the success of perseverance; it is the impetus to succeed in conflicts. *Appearance* is important in our study of determination; it helps us understand how determination manifests and thus provides insights into how serious an imposition of action might be and how strongly determined an adversary could be in his intentions to win. I lastly explain that determination is one of the most important assessments in any kind of conflict. Why, I ask? The answer is this: Whether in conflict or combat, able adversaries anticipate the views and actions of their enemy, including their level of determination and perseverance and know the difference between the two. As such, any adversary has to manipulate and affect their adversary's: perseverance and determination, or face abject defeat.

CHAPTER 7

Passion and Sacrifice

Argument: *In this chapter, I explain passion and sacrifice. Passion means*—a "strong craving with control questionable and on the edge of rational relinquished; it is not rational thinking most of the time—it is an emotional state of being whereby the affective domain dominates the rational/thinking domain." *Passion is a "propellant" in my model of* will. *Passion, including greed, hatred, and retribution, motivates people, causes them to support a leader, and proves a driver for sacrifice. If its ardor is crushed, it may cause one to lose in conflict.* Sacrifice *links with emotion and passion. Sacrifice means*—the surrender or destruction of something prized or desirable for the sake of something considered as having a higher or more pressing claim.[1] *Sacrifice, real but mysterious, lives in the dark well of souls, at the core of all human beings.*

PASSION

What does passion mean? Again, it means a "strong craving with control questionable and on the edge of rational relinquished; it is not rational thinking most of the time—it is emotional state of being whereby the affective domain dominates the rational/thinking domain." Most people have passion about something—a game, reading, playing cards, collecting timepieces, old cars, writing their thoughts, and the like. Passion is a "propellant" in our model for working with *will.* As such, once ignited, passion provides the explosive power necessary to cause aggregates and aggregations to connect, move, and to pick up in speed, momentum, and velocity and to cause action and behavior. Examples of passion in conflict could include greed, hatred, and retribution. Passion is the fuel to motivate, impetus to support a leader, a driver for sacrifice, and if its ardor is crushed, it can cause one side to acquiesce to another's desires.

1. Sacrifice. Dictionary.com. Dictionary.com Unabridged. Random House, Inc. http://www.dictionary.com/brouse/sacrifice (accessed: November 14, 2017).

Passion can be volatile; as a matter of fact, some forms or aspects of passion can prove to be like gasoline thrown on an open flame. Or passion can be normal and therefore manageable, such as people being passionate about football games and their tailgating. Passion is a strong motivation. It can involve conflict, such as acquiring companies, beating a business opponent in a contract competition, and feeling the surge of happiness and power that comes with victories of this sort, particularly when they gain the upper hand against people they do not like—passion requited is this kind of passion. Another type of passion comes with riots. Riots are disastrous for one's society, neighborhood, and city. They sometimes rage without reason as a contagion engulfing neighborhoods, destroying businesses, randomly and pointedly shooting (e.g., at the police) before eventually burning out.

Yet another type of passion involves people in combat. They fight with passion for a cause, country, ideology, religious beliefs, freedom, love of fellow soldiers, retribution, repressed but released hatred of other people due to their religious beliefs, social conduct, differences, myths, fables, and the like. In some cases, people fight one another within the same god and religion but with different sects at each other's throats. A case comes to mind involving the Iran-Iraq War (1980–1988). In this case, Sunni Iraqis fought Shia Iranians, each side believing in Allah and Mohammad but in different ways. In all cases, however, whether an obvious passion or repressed and hidden passion, it is a powerful force. It may flame brightly, then dim, only to come back to flaming brightly.

Charlatans often hide within groups of people who exhibit true passion and readiness to sacrifice. These charlatans love to fight, or they may be thugs hiding in the mass of people rioting to be treated fairly. They could be thieves or miscreants with goals inimical to the pure passion driving the acts and behavior of people who believe so strongly in their cause that their reasoning is ransacked to feed their emotional passion. We find such charlatans at play in history such as the Great Crusades, hiding in the midst of people who were passionate and sincere about their religious passions. These pretenders must be neutralized or discarded so as to help us think deeply and subsequently act to assuage the emotions feeding the passion that is fueling the riot, as happened in the Los Angeles riots of 1992, or even mass attacks, as happened in the Iran-Iraq War.

In Figure 7.1, I show where passion goes. As such it fuels sacrifice (see the next chapter), and between the two essential elements they rule the day when the wolf of volition is not at bay.

Why is it one finds that the imposition actions of conflict and desire often trigger or unloosen passion in the people imposing such an action? When one side attacks the other, the recipient has no choice but to fight unless they do not have the strength of motive, capability, perseverance, determination,

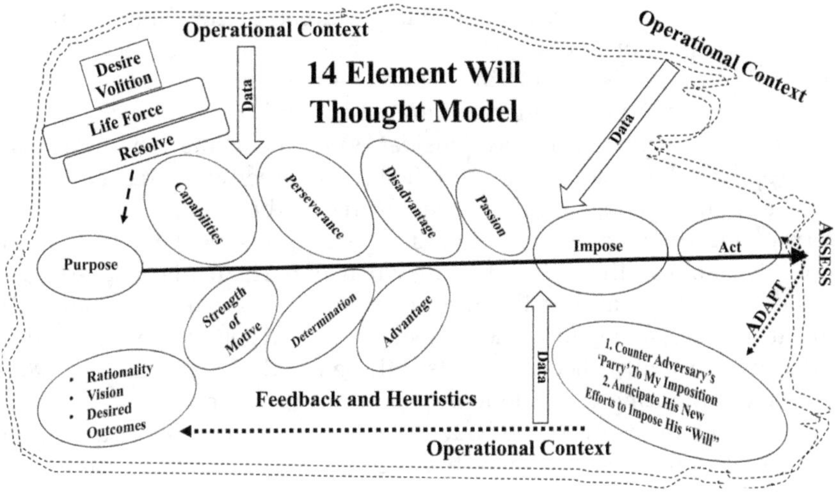

Figure 7.1. Adding Passion

etc. Capitulation could be wiser than a death struggle; a death struggle might be honorable, but sometimes possibly brief and terminating if against the stronger and more capable attackers. Very briefly, I'll provide some recent historical examples. On September 1, 1939, Germany attacked Poland, a far weaker state that had no chance to thwart or even slow down the Nazi blitzkrieg. Their valiant effort was pulverized very quickly. When the Poles refused to surrender Warsaw, the Nazis attacked with their air and artillery, destroying much of the city. The Poles did surrender. Later, and farther to the west, when Germany invaded the Low Countries in May 1940, having approximately five million people, Denmark quickly surrendered and was able to avoid the carnage that Poland had suffered. Though the Poles had the passion to resist, its manifestation bordered on insanity. Denmark was able to save their country and cut deals with the Germans to avoid the Gestapo and intrusions into their daily lives. Yes, the Germans were there, but the occupation was far less severe than in Poland. Did the Danes have the passion to resist? I believe not, as Denmark had a population of only 5 million and they had very little military capability. They could not compete and they would have preferred neutrality. Nonetheless, they were occupied, but somewhat benignly, until later in the war. I'm convinced that as we scratch the veneer that separates the rational human being from the reactive, emotive, and passionate people, we find variance in thickness of the veneer and variance in the motivation to fight to protect one's country with the passion it takes to defend it against a superior enemy. It follows that many conflicts become grudge matches in the minds of participants. But it also involves comprehending a struggle between the passions of people, groups, or organizations participating in the conflict. Correctly considering passion becomes paramount.

Passion drives civilized men to war, to fight and sometimes die, and to do so over a long period of time. Consider WWI. The young men from most of Europe faced off and fought and killed one another with great effectiveness over four years of bloody war. Some of them lived to tell their stories,[2] and the employment of passion as an invisible weapon of sorts certainly comes forth early in the war, when all participants believed they would win quickly and easily. In August 1914, a strong sense of nationalism, arms races, and competition for supremacy in colonies and in navies and armies certainly filled the minds of those wonderful youths with overconfidence, ignoring the potential quagmire they eagerly marched into. Sadly, passion over time turned into resignation and dehumanization. Life became kill or be killed; life in the trenches involved struggling to stay alive as one become a human form of automaton.

We can now infer that Clausewitz asks us to consider passion, but I think he suggests in his tome, *On War,* the need to recognize a connection among 1) passion; 2) purpose; 3) determination; 4) perseverance; and 5) strength of motive. One can also draw an implication of the importance of precognition via reflection and deep thinking. It is a vision coming into being about how passion (and accompanying emotions) can be a boon in any kind of conflict, whether in hand-to-hand fighting in no-man's land of the trenches in WWI, mental combat pitting America's best thinkers against their opponents, and even politically motivated conflicts in which participants become imbued with passion, often irrational (in our view) but solidly in the camp of passion.

As our Über-thinker and thought pilgrim ponder passion and its many challenges, they stop and consider once again duality and pendulum thinking. As friendly forces experience the many faces of passion, their adversaries often face similar challenges. They realize they must try to understand and manipulate the many faces of passion adversarial forces wear. Passion can present a hydra-like personification. As one battles a people's passion, they often find many sources. As they dispel one, others surface and influence. Battles over the passion's hydra shape and capabilities to regenerate can include 1) strength of passion; 2) how to assail an opponents' passion; 3) how the adversary might anticipate such a move and thereby defend their soft underbelly leading to the essence or true source of their passion;

---

2. See Robert Graves, *Good-bye to All That* (London: Jonathan Cape, 1929) and Paul Fussell, *The Great War and Modern Memory* (Oxford, UK: Oxford University Press, 1975), which tell the story of survival, valor, passion, filth, despondency, and determinism about World War I and life in the trenches.

and 4) anticipate and thwart any adversary moves to attack friendly's source of passion. Assailing the opponent's passion always proves important in the outputs of conflict, as passion touches and influences many considerations of our topic of discussion.

Passion has many faces and characteristics. It is a complicated subject. Imagine a floating cube that twists and turns and revolves with your thought. As you see one characteristic and bore in on it with your mind's eye, you find what you are interested in is pliant, enabling you to press on it and voilà, you find more explanation. Let us start with some of the aspects of passion within the mind, heart, and soul.

1. Internal meaning. Passion wells up from the mind and soul. More specifically, passion comes from one's under-mind pushing its way into one's upper-mind. Passion can dominate one's rational thinking and one's actions. On the other hand, passion can be normal and innocent as it fuels the normal actions of human beings as they attend games, compete in racing or triathlons, card games, and so forth.
2. External meaning. An externally caused manifestation of one's passion such as fighting with emotion-inspired fury can be awesome in its power. The manifestation is the physical act exuding from the entity possessing the passion fueled by fury. The external passion, however, has a lineage from the act, to the passion, to the upper- or under-minds to causes, which can be duty, honor, country, retribution, hatred, jealousy, values, social mores. This phenomenon of repressed passion and influence often breaks free of its moorings and thereby proceeds to instigate passion that drives actions that drive assessments, and so forth.
3. Meaning of passion, redux. Passion has been difficult to write about. It is easy to mouth the word, but it is difficult to describe something—passion—that originates in one's emotional base. Passion is abstract, nonquantifiable, invisible, and powerful in many a feasible situation. Its presence and influence only come with manifestations of one's behaviors. Even then we still have trouble thinking about an emotion. But we also recognize a source of passion exists as one, two, three, or more "wells of origination," or better stated, "wells of passion" from which all passion flows as molten lava. In a very simple way, our Über-thinker and thought pilgrim must consider these "wells of passion" as causes with one or more links, connecting to one or more effects (manifestation of passion coming forth as zest, fury, murder, robbery, acquiring companies, and the like). Thus, it follows one can seek, find, and influence these "wells of passion" via cause and effect relationships by 1) imagining the presence, influence, and shape of the object coming forth from dormancy to form a whole; 2) seeking and

finding the cause, and manipulating or even neutralizing the same; 3) finding and attacking or link bundles connecting cause to effect; or 4) learning from studying the effect (This is forensic in nature. One has to be careful with it because generally people believe what happened in the past must happen the same way in the future. The danger I'm describing here is a logic error of the first order of magnitude via false analogy.); and 5) affecting the dreaded act itself.

4. Transforming passion. Passion can change from a single entity in one person's mind to massive aggregations/mass. This notion comes from gaining understanding through a layman/practitioner's perceptions and mind of the characteristic of nonlinear operational context, including unexpected data inputs, friction, randomness, the presence of duality, the presence and influence of complex adaptive systems, the presence and influence of sensitive variables. In addition, of special concern to our thinking, we have to recall that in nonlinear operational contexts one finds sensitive dependence on initial conditions (often the propellant, the glue that holds this aggregate—and aggregation—together, comprises passion and it kludges, and proceeds sometimes with logical social and physical aggregation). This ability is a variant of determinism, and it holds true for all dynamic systems. However, the initial conditions of many complex systems prove difficult to determine accurately. When systems exhibit sensitive dependence on initial conditions, they are no longer predictable, and determinism no longer holds true.[3] The phenomena of sensitive dependence on initial conditions where small errors can turn into large and influential outcomes is at work in nonlinear contexts.
5. Fluctuating nature. Passion fluctuates—sometimes it is powerful and influential, at other times it is inconsequential to conflict. Passion can be a personal drive, such as stinging with words upon insult fueled by some kind of emotion; at still other times passion is dormant but smoldering—awaiting awakening by one's emotions, exhortations, expectations, interpretations. I caution my Über-thinker and thought pilgrim to first of all be aware of this phenomenon of fluctuating passion even in themselves; second, to understand its nature; third, to comprehend what it could influence and empower; fourth, to ponder the adversary's power and use the passion of friendly forces, companies, corporations, etc., against their adversaries; and fifth, to always remember to watch for smoldering passion. Its arousal into movement and action could seem to come from nowhere, only to find it has been dormant all along in the aftermath's exploration.

3. Gerald J. Schueler, "Sensitive Dependence on Initial Conditions." Unpublished paper, 1991.

6. Identifying the role of emotion. Passion is emotional. It is a state of mind in our sense of the word, in which emotion awakens passion and provides the drive and purpose of the apparel of passion. Passion, as a child of emotion, points us in the right direction for crimping or shortening the dynamism and power of passion. Please allow me to pursue this topic a little more, as it is important. Emotion is a light or heavy cloud or fog whose ghostly presence often reaches people as a forbearer or harbinger of action coming their way. In this regard, emotion affects all aspects of passion. As such, emotion is one of the "wells" in which passion lives, sometimes in peace and quietude, other times as tempestuous beast straining at its restraints, seething with hatred, revenge, jealousy, or anger. One thing is for certain though: All living souls experience emotion, and most of us have tried to quell its force when it is violent or inimical to our interests. It is therefore a cause that connects to the effect (via five kinds of links I identified earlier). To preempt or tamp the emerging passion, it is emotion one must find, judge, and influence. Clausewitz helps us consider this powerful phenomenon, emotion, with this passage from *On War*:

> If war is an act of force, the emotions cannot fail to be involved. War may not spring from them, but they will still affect it to some degree.[4]

7. Recognizing the phenomenon of incrementalism and passion. Passion is fickle—it does not bloom from almost nonexistent to a heavy influence without some signs that it is coming forth. Passion is subject to human moods, feelings, emotions, sensitive variables, vagaries of the operational context, belief in mission, love of leader, nationalism, and the like. Passion can come with belonging to a group, and its growth and inclination to gain power can be slow but sometimes certain and deadly. Consider the passion of people in Germany who battled each other in the streets of Berlin in the 1920s. The Nazis had great passion emanating from their leader and their group; their opponents, the Communists, enjoyed similar ardent passion. Also, consider the Spanish Civil War in 1936. On one side one finds great passion emanating from the Fascists; they faced a similar ardent passion of the Communists, their opposition. They battled against one another for four bloody years with immense loss of life and property on both sides. Yes, they battled over ideology, but often their passion emanated from belonging to a group with its associated influence on levels and ardency via camaraderie.

4. Clausewitz, *On War*, 76.

8. So, what does this mean for our Über-thinker and thought pilgrim? As one consideration, they must know about, watch for, and cope with incrementalism relative to passion. Incrementalism means gradual change. But gradual is an ambiguous term and can mean gradually in slow time or gradually in fast time.
   - As such, the Über-thinker and thought pilgrim working a problem and its subsequent influences and relationships with passion have to face challenges. They have to understand and cope with incrementalism. They must also consider vagaries of the operational context. Vagaries induce change in the context and in the complex adaptive systems that operate in the context. Vagaries can work against any opponent due to its tendencies to create chaos and rapid-fire change. Thus, one has to consider the forces at work that can only be attributable to nonlinear systems in complex operational contexts. They recognize and cope with, in a positive way, a truism: Rarely does anybody catch a fast-beat incrementalism that is the boiling point of passion.
   - Being careful and understanding how fast dormant passion can turn into a virulent and highly influential passion only to find its lifespan or influence-span to be short-lived and appear to die can resurrect literally overnight and return via recidivism to its somber, puzzling, and potentially influential way of affecting *will*'s elements. It follows that our Über-thinker and thought pilgrim have to learn to see, consider, and develop the patience and take the time to observe shifting truths that change in a gradual, incremental way. Most of the time they undoubtedly find themselves working against incrementalism where passion sometimes comes forth and aggregates slowly—sometimes even at a glacial pace—but definitely holds the potential to disgorge passion. Of course, the Über-thinker and thought pilgrim must anticipate the appearance and influence of passion not in one fell swoop, but well masked by the breath that is wind, a human proclivity to invest little when returns don't appear to be worth the cost. Without definitive targets, intelligence analysts shift their focus to something more lucrative, and their collection assets go with them.
   - As a matter of fact, I find that my Über-thinker and thought pilgrim have a plan for dealing with and influencing passion. The reason for their preparation is obvious, as passion influences all aspects of *will*. It follows they need a thought model, as simple as it is, to help them focus on their deliberations. After all, my approach to mental combat settles on aggressive thinking and action, the necessity to act first so as to seize the initiative and open the door, as it were, to the other six kinds of advantage. A thought model follows—it is for the reader to decide whether they need what Table 7.1 brings to their minds.

Table 7.1

Antidotes against the Virus That Is Harmful Passion

Acknowledge passion's inherent complexity	Accept passion as real and dangerous	Seek, find, attack sources of passion	Attack adversary's thinking relative to passion
Attack rationale to counter the energy of passion in cultural terms	Know and manipulate culture to affect passion	Attack passion via familial pressures	Manipulate passions' emotional aspects
Attack smoldering passion with social media and other sources of data	Neutralize passion via violence but measured delivery	Influence, induce, incentivize to tamp down passion	Attack passion via thought links and observe and/or measure outcomes

- Admittedly, this table requires aggressive thinking, considerations, wargaming, action, and an even quicker assessment of the action, learning from said action, and adapting faster and more effectively than our adversary or other competitors. Our Über-thinker and thought pilgrim retain this model in their minds and in their software so as to be of immediate assistance, as they consider all parts, pieces, and elements of passion. Our Über-thinker and thought pilgrim consider passion and how to influence it to directly and indirectly influence the adversary's aim, goal, objectives, strategies, and so forth. They can bet that the adversary could be doing the same, as passion is not only important, but it is also obvious that combatants must deal with it.

9. Passion has precipitated some of the most heinous wars ever fought. Consider passion about religion. One can easily find adversaries with stark differences in their religious preferences fighting against one another. An example would be one side being Catholic and the opposing side being Protestant. In my studies I recall the Thirty Years War (1618–1648) went on and on, causing much suffering, loss of life, loss of property, and huge shifts in the population of Germany. The Great Crusades occurred from 1095 to 1291. These crusades pitted passionate Christians against passionate Muslims. In the Balkans in the 1990s, we find Christians massacring Muslims. In Syria and Iraq, we find Islamic State of Iraq and Syria—ISIS—(disaffected Sunnis) massacring Christians and Shia Muslims. Unfortunately, one can always

find a person or a people forcing their views and prejudices on other people—see the Holocaust in which more than 6 million Jews died in Germany and the rest of Europe from 1939 to 1945.

10. So as our Über-thinker and thought pilgrim ponder passion in particular, they must always account for 1) what people are passionate about; 2) strength of passion; 3) what happens if passion turns from being dormant to being active and aggressive; and 4) what might induce people to turn down the heat of their passion and live in peace. The latter is a worthy ideal, but undoubtedly idealistic and beyond human capabilities.
11. Passion is one of several important impetuses in human life. The word impetus means "the power by which an entity or element moves or changes." Power or dynamism is the basis for action ,and it is actions and their causes that prove inimical to the friendly side. In particular, impetus is important to study, know, and watch for so one can intercede before an action causes the friendly side damage. As I have mentioned several times, anticipating passion as an impetus is a force of action that perhaps we have not expected.

    In our current discussion impetus involves and is at the center of the excretion of power and the hold it can have in either an isolated place and time or as a connected passion conjoining across space, in populated places, and even at the same time. Consider the military and its use of power. In a micro-view, bringing forth and releasing timed pulses of energy in the military is "synchronization"; in the macro-view, it can connect across the world but wreak havoc with connected forces motivated and released at the right place and right time by synchronized action. Here is a broader example for your consideration. The United States in World War II proved bent on unleashing its potential and passion after the Japanese attack on Pearl Harbor. Earlier, Americans did not want to become openly involved with the wars in either Europe or Asia. The surprise attack on Pearl Harbor changed the desire for peace and neutrality into a massive effort and connected action always finding at its core an impetus for action—a passion, in this case, to hate any and all things Japanese. The release of passion for revenge and to win the war and go home alive proved to be the passion connecting actions in the European theater as well as the Pacific theater.

An impetus is important for the passion escaping from its well of confinement. Impetus may be intense, incremental, invisible most of the time, awaiting ignition and propulsion, and even dormant until awakened. After all, it isn't so much the passion we are interested in, but the expulsion of energy that passion creates. Impetuses for action, as released energy and deed, most often need an originator or a motivator for not only the release of energy propelled by passion, but also the origins of sacrifice, determinism, perseverance, capabilities, strength of motive, and the like. Adversaries must have this special and ghostly apparition that appears and disappears like a phantasm of sorts.

Thinkers like our Über-thinker and thought pilgrim always consider the adversary engendering and releasing passion as an impetus for action. That is to say, as power builds, rationale for action appears in an adversary's mind and becomes an impetus for action that swells and releases its energy. Our Über-thinker and thought pilgrim must therefore advise their decision maker to intercede via preempting the causes leading and connecting to the effect they now know to be coming via anticipation. With this kind of reasoning, friendly forces can bleed off the air in the adversary's balloon of passion, thereby significantly weakening its strength.

SACRIFICE

For the purpose of satisfying our quest to understand considerations of sacrifice, we must first understand its meaning:

> The surrender or destruction of something prized or desirable for the sake of something considered as having a higher or more pressing claim.[5]

In further expansion or our understanding of sacrifice and in my own words that I have kluged over the years, I think of sacrifice as:

> To surrender or give up, or permit injury, or to yield a relational disadvantage to an adversary; a readiness to endure loss and to take on the burden of physical and emotional pain and stress for the sake of passion, hatred, retribution, leader exhortations, accomplishing an aim, goal, or objective, the execution of a strategy or even continuation of loss and pain in the face of certain defeat.

Sacrifice also closely relates to emotion. Additionally, sacrifice is important because it relates to so many other considerations in this book and primary model. For example, sacrifice relates to purpose, strength of motive, determination, perseverance, passion, and, of course, it relates to life force. Sacrifice is active. When people confront their inclination to sacrifice, they make a choice. Sacrifice comes when a person or an organization readily accepts an outcome often detrimental to their well-being. Sacrifice can be spontaneous and short-lived, or it can come forth with a readiness to endure loss and pain over time. Additionally, the inclination to sacrifice can come slowly. Or, sometimes, people don't sacrifice anything. Sometimes, these same people become willing to sacrifice everything. After

5. Sacrifice. Dictionary.com. Dictionary.com Unabridged. Random House, Inc. http://www.dictionary.com/brouse/sacrifice (accessed: November 14, 2017).

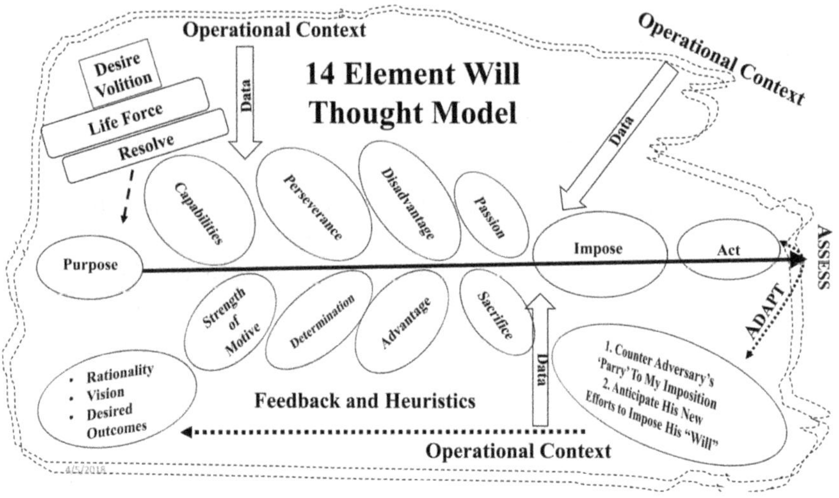

Figure 7.2. Adding Sacrifice

my study of sacrifice, I have found it to be mysterious. It lives in the dark well of souls, at the core of all human beings. Let's take a look at sacrifice's place on the shaft of our thought model in Figure 7.2.

I want you to think about and account for sacrifice from two perspectives. First, consider sacrifice as you contemplate the adversary. Your reasoning produces assumptions about whether their adversary will choose to resist and pay the price for resisting, which in military conflicts can be death or incarceration. To impose your life force upon another resisting person, put yourself in the personage of the resister and estimate the strength of his resolution to sacrifice. This thinking suggests how to approximate the necessary force required to lessen said resistance. Second, consider yourself. For example, always discern whether your human and organizational capabilities possess sufficient strength of motive, perseverance, and determination to sacrifice enough to accomplish what your life force and purpose demand.

Let's pursue an example of sacrifice from history—Stalingrad. As the Germans attempted to take the city in the fall and early winter of 1942, their leaders could count on their German troops to sacrifice with the goal to take and control Stalingrad. On the home front, the German high command assumed their population was and would continue to be prepared to endure losses of their young men and thereby knowingly sacrifice to win the war even with the beginning of the massive air raids that would destroy many a German city. At Stalingrad, Romanians, Italians, and Hungarians protected the Germans' flanks. These allies were insufficiently trained, inadequately equipped, and lacked the strength of motive to perform their missions. Sacrifice in this case proved volatile when the Soviets attacked these weak German allies who had neither capabilities nor readiness to sacrifice to fight sufficiently well to protect the German flanks. In retrospect, the Germans should have not only analyzed their allies' physical capability, but also their strength of motive and willingness to sacrifice in the war far from home. I cannot help but wonder whether the Germans failed to consider this important part of war—the willingness to sacrifice to accomplish an aim, goal, objective, or strategy.

The Soviets, as an army and a nation, had the readiness to sacrifice to hold Stalingrad, and they suffered approximately 1 million casualties in its defense. On a very high plane of thought, the Soviet nation proved prepared to sacrifice lives, treasure, time, and their physical well-being to defeat the Nazis ostensibly for their love of country. In addition, they proved prepared to sacrifice because it was obvious early in the war that the Germans intended to enslave, exterminate, or banish them from their country. On a lower plane, some soldiers didn't have the choice to think about sacrifice—either they attacked and braved withering German fire or if they retreated, they faced fire from their own people—the political commissars and officers tasked with shooting soldiers who retreated. They were on the true horns of a dilemma with death waiting on either side they took. Most of the soldiers opted for at least a feigned readiness to sacrifice to kill Germans or to be killed trying. In this sense, one finds a phenomenon our Über-thinkers and thought pilgrims now recognize as the presence of a feigned (artificial or insincere) inclination to sacrifice. This phenomenon is important ,and friendly decision makers must consider this attempt to influence the appearance of such a dilemma and its outcome favorable to their positions.

What can one learn from thinking about Stalingrad relative to sacrifice? First, sacrifice can be a personal choice, but with respect to organizations or groups, sacrifice can be group determined. Even if a group sacrifice is being made, people as individuals still have to agree to the sacrifice at hand. Two quick examples help us understand this type of sacrifice. To start, let us briefly consider Masada (brochure from visit in 2006). In my mind, the conflict was a test of *wills* between the ruling, mighty Romans who occupied and governed Judaea and a small, uncompromising group of Jewish miscreants. This small group occupied the mountain fortress of Masada and refused to surrender to the Romans. The Romans built a ramp up the side of the mountain fortress. Once at the top, they used siege towers and battering rams to gain entrance to the fortress to subdue the rebels. Upon entry, they found the rebels had committed suicide rather than surrender. They sacrificed their lives to defy the Romans and to hold the ideas and ideology they believed to be right. Second, sometimes living within a larger force dictates the strength of motive and shaping of a willingness to sacrifice. Third, sacrifice often directly connects with both capability and strength of motive. Fourth, sacrifice is relative to control of initiative, tempo, and momentum. Fifth, people make assumptions about the inclination to sacrifice that can be wrong. If one has confidence in their assumption about being resolute in exerting a readiness to sacrifice, they need to keep double-checking the veracity of their assumption, as it always wavers with contextual changes, adversary adaptation, and friendly changes in roles, missions, resources, constraints, and strategies. Moreover, the basis for the said assumption(s) can be correct, but all the same, involved people have to be quick to change the plan and its execution, if one finds mistakes people (often planning people and decision makers) have made about assumptions. Sixth, senior people need to think about how their opponent thinks. In particular, they need to consider whether and how their adversary might consider the dual nature of a readiness to sacrifice—theirs and their adversary's. For a beneficial example, let us swing our thoughts back to Stalingrad. The Germans in the 1942 offensive into southern Russia should not have let themselves be drawn into Stalingrad. By this time on the Eastern Front, their leaders should have known that the Soviets would sacrifice everything to hold the city. In addition, the Germans developed poor assumptions about the Soviets' preparedness to sacrifice lives in Stalingrad so they could set conditions for their encircling attacks on the German flanks. Pushing even further, the Germans should have thought like their adversary and thus known of their desperation and readiness to sacrifice, indeed gamble everything they had, to hold Stalingrad and thereby set conditions for a successful breakthrough north and south of the entire German Sixth Army, allowing the encirclement of the German forces.

Once again emotion has shown its many faces. Ah, here we have another role for emotion similar to our earlier discussion of perseverance. The role of emotion with respect to sacrifice is important. It is human beings who feel emotion and either act or don't respond to appeals to sacrifice. For example, the people at Masada were compelled to smother their emotions and the urge to live so as to gather the inner strength to either commit suicide themselves or submit to someone else cutting their throats or injecting them with cyanide. Thousands of Japanese Okinawan civilians chose to commit suicide rather than surrender to the invading Americans in 1945. In another twist of sacrificing themselves to an honorable death, we can find this situation in ancient Roman combat. They sometimes committed honorable suicide by falling on their swords rather than surrender and dishonor their names. They smothered and cast aside the strength of emotion to survive and live so as to commit combative suicide. They performed this ritual sometimes helping each other when they ran out of options and time and chose to end their own lives rather than submit to torture, punishment, slavery, and even death at the hand of victors in the struggle they were experiencing. Consider the Romans at the great battle of Cannae in 216 BCE. Although surrounded by the Carthaginians under the leadership of Hannibal, Romans soldiers were alive and fighting. They must have known they were surrounded and going to die or be captured and killed, tortured, or turned into slaves. It is my belief that many a Roman, regardless of rank, chose to kneel and then fall on his sword and thus die honorably instead of submitting to the humility of captivity.

It follows then, in our thinking, what appears to be a self-evident truism: Emotion and sacrifice link inextricably in a whole. Any combatant can ignore this linkage only at their peril. As another output of rumination, emotion is worthy of contemplation, as it relates to and is the basis of many an action. In wargaming, consider approaching people to contemplate sacrifice with believable (to the people we want to save) alternatives ranging from changing extant and influential narratives, to providing incentives (inducements) or a range from compellence to punishments if the plea for surrender is ignored.

Let us continue with sacrifice and wargaming for just a few more minutes. In my view, Über-thinkers and thought pilgrims have no alternative but to study possibilities and probabilities of sacrifice via realistic wargaming. Wargaming is, without question, an important aspect in one's study of our phenomenon under study. In modern times our soldiers, law enforcement, and security people must consider suicide bombers and their attacks. When a bomber chooses to give up their life to kill and maim innocent people by blowing themselves to bits with a suicide bomb, there isn't much that can be done to alter their narratives and beliefs. But for neophytes and acolytes in the business of finding, recruiting, convincing, training, and actually acting as suicide bombers, we should try to convince them via social media; randomness of counterbombing operations; fear via graphics of those who have attacked with suicide belts; and indirectly through friends, religious leaders, and families to change their thinking, and thus their lives, in both metaphorical and unembellished senses. Families could be instrumental in changing such a readiness to sacrifice one's life because of a twisted rationale (justified through their eyes, perceptions, and minds). This is the epitome of mental combat—to outthink and hopefully turn potential suicide bombers away from violence. For the moment, though, wargaming helps to determine where, how, and when a bomber might rig up, how they might move, look, act, and emit both verbal and nonverbal behavior, culturally driven or influenced, at the right time and place, and acting in nuanced ways find ways to neutralize him in the best possible place, and at the most advantageous time.

Now let us further our understanding of sacrifice with a simple "who" and "why" question-and-answer drill. Who is sacrificing? Well, anybody can choose to sacrifice. Sometimes it involves the action people who, as individuals and as units or groups, sacrifice themselves to accomplish a larger goal. The small groups of American soldiers who held their positions until they died in the Battle of the Bulge were committed to sacrifice.

Their determined resistance and readiness to sacrifice themselves and each other made a difference and contributed to the defeat of the Nazi attack. Interestingly, individuals and groups of individuals can be sacrificed to a larger cause by a senior decision maker. In this line of thinking, gambits in business, such as buying and selling commercial companies, sometimes at a loss, but with purposefully causing the sacrifice to gain a larger goal can happen. As an example, in war, I recall that in 1805's Battle of Austerlitz, Napoleon sacrificed the dominant terrain of the impending battlefield—the Pratzen Heights—with a larger plan and goal in mind. That is to say, to present the "sacrifice" in hopes of drawing his enemy, led by the Tsar Alexander, to cross the unguarded and unoccupied Pratzen Heights and to thereby attack Napoleon's purposefully weakened southern flank. This "sacrifice" worked perfectly, and Napoleon won perhaps the most brilliant battle of his career.[6] But to sacrifice takes a decision, sometimes as intuition, but other times as a reasoned desire to sacrifice. Our Über-thinkers and thought pilgrims have much to consider relative to sacrificing. It is safe to exclaim that sacrificing comes in many forms and by way of many an action, so consider them all.

Why sacrifice? This is a question people have pondered for millennia, I'm certain. Why would we care about something as abstract and seemingly unanswerable and unknowable? I maintain that sacrifice plays a major part of any consideration conflict. We want to know why people or a single person is prepared to sacrifice, is sacrificing, or has sacrificed to influence, manipulate, or negate the power of sacrifice. There has to be a cause and effect at play with sacrificing. Sacrificing, let's say, is the effect, so our Über-thinkers and thought pilgrims must search for the causes of the effect. Causes for the effect come forth in three ways: 1) before the act of sacrificing; and 2) during the actual act of sacrificing; and 3) after the act and into the aftermath. We should anticipate sacrifice well before an engagement occurs, but again, what is the cause for wittingly taking on pain and loss? Is a goal enough? Is an ideology enough? Is camaraderie sufficient to bring forth the act of sacrificing? Why did the British and French soldiers repeatedly line up and go over the ramparts and trenches during those horrible months in 1916 that comprised the Battle of the Somme? Surely, they knew many of them would die by the thousands, as tens of thousands of their comrades had already perished on those grounds in previous attacks. A great motivator was that these soldiers often came from the same towns or villages and they believed in and loved their friends—they had no choice but to go over the top. John Keegan gives us a glimpse into the "why":

6. Bevin Alexander, *How Wars Are Won* (New York: Three Rivers Press, 2002), 261–269.

> But over and above its cohesion, sense of mission, mood of self-sacrifice, local as well as national patriotism, there were other elements in play. Self-confidence and credulity were certainly present, and powerfully effective at persuading the Pals [British soldiers who enlisted to stay together as friends and neighbors from specific locations in Great Britain] to jump the parapet . . . the importance which leadership played in taking it into battle [was important too]. An argument can be found to suggest that leadership . . . was of higher quality and greater military significant in the First World War. . . . It does not take very much more illustration than these instances provide to explain why it was that the Germans raked so ferociously the advancing British lines at zero hour on 1 July. . . . To surrender was dishonorable and might be dangerous. To run away was impossible. . . . To kill the British was, therefore, a necessity . . . a duty . . . if this helps to explain the German . . . it helps to explain too what motivated the British to dispute with them possession of the front trench.[7]

Is hatred enough to induce sacrifice? Is retribution enough to suffer sacrifice? Is mythos enough to induce sacrifice in individuals and aggregations of people? Why do individual soldiers give up their lives to save the lives of their comrades? Some of "why" in war or life and death situations comes with instinct. A grenade rolls into a foxhole. Most people try to exit the hole, but in certain circumstances other people throw themselves upon the grenade and die saving their comrades.

Are aggregations of people prepared to sacrifice to accomplish a goal or objective because their leaders tell them to do so even in life-and-death situations? The answer is not easy, as it depends—it is contingent on the sensitivity of variables, adversary adaptation, or vagaries in the surrounding operational context. What is it that bonds people into an aggregation that is ready to sacrifice their lives—a cause, an ideology, love of country? Of course, it could be that fear of alternatives sometimes dictates sacrifice—desertion in war or refusal to carry out an order often results in death via firing squad or imprisonment for cowardice, and cowardice can bring with it an ignominy that would last throughout their lives. It is a far cry for old men in faraway capitals who start wars and exhort people in combat to sacrifice their lives for a cause, but when does this said cause and its power dissipate? So perhaps we can discern this aspect of sacrifice by finding its causes and then doing something to distort, destroy, or overcome the power sacrifice brings and implies.

Ideology and nationalism can also be strong motivators to sacrifice. Love of country has played a great role too in understanding sacrifice. Let's consider some quick examples—consider the Soviets in the opening days of the German invasion of their homeland; the French refusing to surrender in the

7. John Keegan, *The Face of Battle* (New York: Penguin Books, 1978), 277–284.

opening of WWI in August 1914 and the ensuing four years of terrible sacrifice. American soldiers, along with volunteering, were drafted. Preparing to fight battles certainly carried with it sacrifice of time and possibly of life during WWII. While draftees had no choice, most would have been predisposed to sacrifice and fight the Japanese and Germans because of Pearl Harbor and the subsequent German declaration of war on America. As an obvious inference, we find a combination of nationalism, duty, and the law, all of which prompted a very firm preparedness to sacrifice for protecting a particular way of life. My father met the call to duty and love of country and served in the U.S. Army training in the United States and then deploying to the Pacific Theater 1943–1945. Many powerful motivators to sacrifice exist, but none ever prove more powerful than nationalism and ideology—powerful forces at play in all kinds of conflict.

One also finds a more peaceful way of seeking to know why people sacrifice. For example, people have goals and objectives. They sacrifice time, money, and even family to accomplish this goal or objective. For example, all of us who earned master's and doctorate degrees know and recognize others who attempt to accomplish such goals and objectives—it takes sacrifice of a different kind than that of a soldier or a pilot in the extremis of conflict. Sometimes people in extremis prove ready to sacrifice because of personal bravery and disdain of personal well-being, preferring to be with or lead soldiers in hand-to-hand combat—I imagine Caesar, as he led his legions the Gallic campaign and in particular at Alesia. Or I think of Scipio Africanus as he led his legions against the soldiers of Carthage in the Battle of Ilipa in 211 BCE. Sacrifice also connects tightly with strength of motive. It is motive that pushes forth sacrifice. It is the basis and strength of motive that wields the power and infuses sacrifice with its pragmatism and reasonableness but always from each player's point of view. Motive, as a review, means:

> That force or energy or other provocative phenomena that causes a people to act in a certain way, do a certain thing, endure deprivations, or operate, or act/behave, or perform, usually relative to goal accomplishment, which could be good or evil.

Motive also involves 1) one or more reasons for acting or behaving, especially one reason hidden or not obvious; 2) the actual reason (cause) for an outcome (effect); and 3) the core or nub or pressure point of one or more causes that always link with an outcome.

One has to be interested in considering this connection. We seek to find "a way" to debilitate an adversary's penchant to sacrifice. As such one has to decrease his strength of motive along with his motivation to sacrifice to accomplish goals and objects. Strength of motive ties to sacrifice and sacrifice ties to capabilities, and sacrifice and capabilities and strengths of motive all connect with advantage/disadvantage, determination, perseverance, and passion. These elements connect back to life force and ahead to imposition, action, and assessing outcomes of the means-driven action. One finds centrality of importance and influence of sacrifice. Please notice, although the whole is greater than the mere sum of its parts, as we chip away the power and influence of each of these elements, then the whole becomes weaker. But as I cause decay of strength and thereby induce weakness, caution comes calling to my mind. Missteps can cause a strengthening instead of decay in elements of our adversary's models too.

Each combatant has to ask repetitively and relative to themselves and to their adversary, "Is there sufficient strength of motive to sacrifice and to keep sacrificing until the aim, goal, or objective proves satisfied?" If so, the strength of motive in any competitive endeavor influences readiness to sacrifice and to keep sacrificing and vice versa. If one side or the other discerns a wavering, even a hint of a flinch when it comes to sacrificing, they need to pounce on that vulnerability, as it can be the door leading to winning in any kind of conflict. It is through this combination—first one, then the other, then both, then back to one, and so forth—in which the aim of conflict, and combat, become ultra-important: they buffet the preparedness to sacrifice. This subject demands decision-maker attention and intervention. Otherwise, one might win the battle but lose the war, as it were, as decision makers must think holistically and do so via synthesis. It follows then that both capabilities and morale of both sides in a conflict become of great importance, requiring the closest attention and involvement of decision makers and their intelligence apparatuses.

By now you have been pummeled with many new ideas. But let me give you even more. It is a war of minds (war of wits) in which we find ourselves, as technology has bombarded us with seemingly disparate parts and pieces of a whole—a diaspora of potentiality and probability lurking and waiting to come into being. One adversary nurtures ways to sustain sacrifice while their adversary seeks, discovers those attempts, and strives to neuter them; back and forth goes the struggle to influence this vague notion that is sacrifice.

Rational thinking, from a theoretical adversary's view, focus our thinking so as to influence sacrifice. If we catch sacrifice and other elements in their fluid state, then this adversary is vulnerable to our direct or indirect intercession. If we miss, though, one element of our model can meld with another element, and then another element, and so forth. As this motion occurs, the minds of the human contenders whisper in their mind's eye, "it is the right time, right place, right 'crease' or juncture or interval of motion or non-motion to act and seek advantage," in a frequently fast-changing operational context. It is self-evident, so it seems to me, that when these elements exist in isolation, we find an opportunity to influence them before they conjoin with other elements and thereby improve their resistance to manipulation. In isolation, we may be able to gain knowledge and understanding of the isolated element's "marrow," as it were, and discern whether it is sufficiently strong to conjoin with another element's marrow into a larger whole or sufficiently weak to attack and exploit. This knowledge helps us learn how best to attack or neuter each element before they become infused with sacrifice, via their links (in situ or nascent) connecting their unfolding and enfolding wholes, how, when, and where a subsequent aggregation of elements might occur, and, of course, its potential power to help win conflicts. This mental work provides an aggressive decision maker with the potential, indeed wherewithal, to attack and degenerate burgeoning aggregates before they become large and powerful and even impervious to attack and manipulation—a super aggregation or whole.

My Über-thinker and thought pilgrim ponder the questions: 1) When is sacrifice at its peak strength? 2) What causes the sacrifice to reach its apex and height of influence? 3) Can one identify the signs of conditions coming into being that tell us the apex of influence is nearing? and 4) Can one's mind discover when the individual and collective sacrifice prove to be at their lowest and thereby vulnerable to "arrangement"?[8]

A readiness to sacrifice flows and ebbs with the influence of variables. For example, in a deployed military fighting in a faraway land, a letter from home, the loss of a comrade, or harsh living conditions could all cause a fluctuation in "sacrifice." Sometimes the readiness to sacrifice comes with the leader slugging it out in the mud and filth with their troops (see Caesar at Alesia in 52 BCE). Sometimes a hot shower or a hot meal might influence the actors. Lots of times, this question involves the game of struggling to see whose devotion to sacrifice crumbles first. The struggles in the four-year Great War became a war of attrition and the attrition had to be aimed at not only the battlefield, but the civilian home front as well. One chief of the German General Staff—General Erich von Falkenhayn—went so far as to announce a mandate to "bleed the French white" as a strategy for winning World War I at Verdun. It failed because it was absurd, but the war was absurd for people who had to endure its demanding sacrifices and farcical logic. This particular strategy failed due to the strong French commitment to sacrifice and resulted in horrendous causalities for both the German and French soldiers. General Falkenhayn miscalculated not only the strength of France's readiness to sacrifice at the tip of the spear, he also failed to anticipate the iron strong leadership of the French General Pétain, the Sacred Way (the road from Paris to Verdun by which virtually of France's men, supplies, and casualties moved), as well as France's home front, which the Germans counted upon to crumble due to the huge initial losses the Germans inflicted upon the French.

As our Über-thinker and thought pilgrim discern, it is not an easy mental task to judge the strength of an opponent's preparedness to sacrifice. They

8. T. E. Lawrence, *Seven Pillars of Wisdom* (New York: Anchor Books, 1991), 195.

delve into specifics to get their arms around the concepts and wrestle them to the ground. They discover a useful definition for "strength," which helps to discern the condition of sacrifice. To our Über-thinker and thought pilgrim in our situation, strength means:

Strength comes to our understanding via four essential explanations or descriptors: 1) a status of strength; 2) ability to cope with difficult situations; 3) a decision to maintain an emotional, moral, or intellectual position (stance); and 4) a possession of a quality of mind and spirit sufficient to try and persevere despite disadvantageous odds or potential cost/loss.

Two other definitions help our Über-thinker and thought pilgrim in their quest to understand the phenomenon of sufficient strength to influence and sustain the motivation to sacrifice. In our work, we use the following definition for sufficient: enough, adequate, ample. But wait! Our Über-thinker and thought pilgrim must delve into more detail to ponder this definition. People must scratch their way into the density of this definition and thereby find its core. Within this core they discover what sufficient reason means in our conflict context. Sufficiency to alter the existing status quo is what one needs; however, once again, one also needs to consider the appearance and influence of "potential." Potential affects sufficiency, but intermittently. So, as one gazes upon this definition of sufficient reason to see how it affects our knowledge base, hence our thinking, they see and think with a questioning eye. Sufficient reason, for our purposes and as I think about it and apply it to our world, is a principle or better yet, a maxim stating everything occurring has a cause and the cause connects with an effect via one of a variety of links.

I then ask my Über-thinker and thought pilgrim if they can discern ways to influence strength and sacrifice knowing full well that they do exist? I believe so. Unfortunately, I can only offer theoretical approaches due to the uniqueness of all contexts surrounding conflict. While thinking about strength, one finds pressing questions: 1) What can be done to stop people from sacrificing? 2) How can any of us anticipate how our adversary intends to assault our willingness to sacrifice? Our Über-thinker and thought pilgrim ponder the four essential elements of the aforementioned definitions of strength (relative to sacrifice) and decide to assault or manipulate each in a synchronized way. Their aim is to assault or manipulate the core of the adversary's strength and sacrifice to our advantage.

The Über-thinker and thought pilgrim also consider the culture and how it affects the adversary's mind. One who enters this world is always wary of their own penchant to commit bias and logic errors. Thus, our Über-thinker and thought pilgrim get Red Teamers[9] to work with them to

9. *Red Team*: People who perform the function of providing alternatives; critiquing plans as objectively as possible; playing the adversary in wargames; and providing innovative or

improve their reasoning via questioning, providing alternative analyses, challenging assumptions, evaluating evidence, assessing conclusions, and logic and bias errors such as mirror imaging and confirmatory bias. At least one member of the Red Team is a local resident who understands the language, culture, social mores, mythos, apperception, experience, and the like, of the people who oppose our cause, preferably from the immediate locale of the struggle at hand. Armed with this assistance, they venture forth into the adversary's mind to try to think as he thinks, to try to anticipate his moves, anticipate and watch for his counters to our impositions, and identify and watch for his opportunities, but through his eyes. Interestingly, as a fact, any adversary must set conditions for his success in impending clashes, and he has to first anticipate and then attempt to counter his opponent's actions they design to win. This need to set conditions proves particularly complicated and vulnerable because of entanglement between adversaries as one side attempts to overcome the resistance of their opponent's initial counterimposition. With a Red Team, we once again return to our thought model and reconsider each of 14 essential elements of *will* from the adversary's perspective, and in particular to this chapter, how they relate to sacrifice.

Our Über-thinker and thought pilgrim want to seize the initiative and eventually control the entirety of the advantages opponents always dispute and physically and mentally fight over in any given conflict. In particular, they want to diminish the adversary's eagerness to sacrifice at a crescendo point where one finds the peak of visible attributes of the presence of emotion. This desire takes them into probabilities of potential outcomes designed to affect sacrifice and the adversary's anticipation of friendly's efforts to reduce his strength, thereby his willingness to sacrifice. My acolytes thereby consider ways to assault his strengths and readiness to sacrifice and turn them into a manipulable vulnerability. But other dangers lurk. So, thinkers be wary, take notice, beware the vicissitudes of clashing sides in all kinds of conflict. As I have discussed earlier, people must ponder the importance of appearance as a primary manifestation of emotions and sometimes rational thought driving one's zeal to sacrifice. Appearance has to be part of any thinking about sacrifice. A good, working definition of appearance for our purposes is:

> The set of observable characteristics of one or more individuals coming forth from the operational context—or via interaction with other human beings. Appearance is important when the individual we observe appears and is in situ, stasis, in motion via behavior and action, deceptive as to purposes of their

---

creative thinking to help overcome conventional wisdom, blinding biases, poor assumptions, and personal logic errors.

behavior, and finally, when the organism is in competition, denial, or acquiescence to the threats they face.

Appearance is important in helping to determine the strength of an adversary's readiness to sacrifice. Threads of connection shoot forth from these individuals as they live and appear—with many threads being spurious and transient. This ebb and flow means that our Über-thinker and thought pilgrim must hypothesize about exactly what they seek by way of appearance—how they could be acting, what they are carrying, how they dress, how they mingle (or attempt to), their gait, their biometrics (such as sweat/smell), and their nonverbal behavior (lack of eye blinking, staring straight ahead, reaction to police), and so forth. Regardless of difficulty this mental process may assist in gauging a target's readiness to sacrifice. Low-level police, civilians, and even military people must seek indicants of the adversary and his activities as they appear in condition setting steps. They must train as low-level human data collectors and look for the specifics in five kinds of observables: 1) cultural; 2) functional; 3) technical; 4) organizational; and 5) biometric.[10]

Appearance wears several masks worth mentioning. One such mask involves physiognomy. Facial features and actions always prove important, as it is difficult for people to hide their frame of mind, particularly if emotions control their behavior. Also, all people live in patterns. Their physiognomy exists and exhibits changes in patterns and is thereby invaluable. Their emotions too exist in patterns. Thus, it follows that smart, specific, and directed intelligence at the right time, place, and activity can observe, consider, and report on an adversary's physiognomy and derivative patterns. The best collection asset for this work is a low-level human collection capability, and thus it needs to be recruited and prepared relative to a specific aspect and location of an operational context.

Another type of appearance involves operational context. Collections of all kinds can surveil appearances of any particular infrastructure. Their work, however valuable to observing patterns of an adversary setting his conditions to launch an attack with an inclination to sacrifice, has a significant flaw—mechanical collections cannot detect nuanced physical body changes, changes in physiognomy, emotions, blood pressure, heart beats per minute, pupil dilation, sweat, and the like from a distance. Moreover, mechanical devices cannot detect tendencies for action and change without hours of patience and dedication to very small areas of concern. Sometimes these inclinations prove difficult to discern, particularly when

10. *Observable*: A physical, physiological, emotional property or absence of one or all of the aforementioned that can be observed or measured directly—cultural, technical, situational, functional and biometric. The thought comes from my book, *Intelligence Analysis*, 86–87.

coming from data inputs into the adversary's mind causing changes due to data inputs from the operational context. Mechanical sensors cannot see and hear what happens in conversation inside homes or businesses or within granite mountains. These are the places where leanings toward sacrifice bubble forth in conversations and declarations. Emotions change and people receive instruction on how to mask their readiness to sacrifice. Nonetheless, this seeming conundrum is not impossible; it can be worked and used via "tendency analysis."[11] I must warn you that to understand it takes extreme mental work, for example, thinking like the adversary and considering the adversary's advantage and disadvantage views of the operational context (for himself and for our friendly forces).

Continuing with the phenomenon of "appearance," several types exist, and our Über-thinker and thought pilgrim must understand each in order to detect and thereby shield a friendly force in a conflict. *One type of appearance* is the simplest and involves one's physical being, but our watchers are able to spot changes from normal due to norms established in maintained baselines—cultural and functional, for example. This change is identified through anomaly analysis,[12] and it is a powerful weapon in the mental combat that our Über-thinker and thought pilgrim experience every day. A *second type of appearance* comes forth in one's imagination. Though these appearances cannot be said to be physically true, they appear as an apparition or a misty outline of an appearance coming into being, thus inclined to turn from apparition into physical. A *third type of appearance* involves the appearance of what has happened and vestiges therein. One could see the vestiges as traces or wisps of the aftermath of an attack. Sometimes postmortem thinking yields a variety of clues as to how dedicated the adversary's strength of readiness to sacrifice (think of suicide bombers or vehicle-born improved explosive devices). More precisely, this kind of appearance leaves few discernable vestiges, but if the Über-thinker and thought pilgrim are involved, they know what to look for and also can backtrack this perpetrator of the attack in question. A *fourth type of appearance* involves states of emotion and thereby manifests inner motivation for sacrificing one's wealth, physical well-being, and social estrangement all attributable to a readiness to sacrifice for various causes, for example, to

11. *Tendency analysis*: Discerning meaning through thought and study of the general proclivities of people, the behavioral and action inclinations of organizations, mental snapshots of current environment or contextual situations, events, activities, behaviors, the emanation dispersal of energy emissions, and what the interaction and enmeshing of all could portend for the future.

12. *Anomaly*: One or more departures from the normal or common order, form, pattern, or rule; or an absence of what people or machines expect. *Anomaly analysis* is a logical derivation from anomaly: discerning meaning in departures from the normal or common order, form, or rule; absence of the expected.

spread a religion (consider radical Islamic extremists and their belief in spreading their faith via force) or to push an ideology (consider America's founding fathers who risked their lives, their family's lives, and their fortunes manifesting the readiness to sacrifice for their cause). A *fifth type of appearance* involves manifestation in one's minds by way of flashes of insight of future happenings or even what has happened in the past that has meaning for the future in dreams. This visitation, appearing and disappearing, is a phantasm—it warns the sleeper of an adversary's appearances, intent, and readiness to sacrifice before the events occur.

From whence do these embracing and penetrating flashes of insight originate? Imagination? Upper-mind? The subconscious mind? All of the above? I'm always in awe when people sacrifice for a belief, religion, or ideology when all they own and the welfare of their family is on the line. With combinations, relationships, synergy, coalescence of parts, and the unity of opposites becoming apparent, one can begin to discern what appearances of strong sacrifice could be. Since the appearance changes, it is problematic to discern its appearance and the shapes of its clues. Without thinking of the kind of which I speak, preemption and influence of this preparedness to sacrifice becomes highly problematic—just a warning, as it were. What I want, of course, is to be able to preempt the birth of and strengthening of a preparedness to sacrifice at some point in time so as to break into the adversary's cycle of action. The goal is to denigrate his attack patterns, but this work is only possible if you have prepared and are aggressive. Über-thinkers and thought pilgrims deeply ponder this problem set and provide good conclusions and strong recommendations to act on what is coming into being and appearance.

I hope you recognize the importance of this subject. The motivation to sacrifice influences all elements one can find when considering and trying to understand *will*. Though largely invisible because it occurs in mankind's minds and hearts, with good thinking one can seek and find the essence of what disposes people to sacrifice. Sacrifice has varying levels of strength, so it is best to affect it when its strength is low. It is always best to influence sacrifice before it combines with each of the elements and before each element can combine with one another until they reach a holistic and powerful state of being and influence. The specter of preemption helps to push the perpetrator through termination of his imposition of life force and purpose. With this kind of mental combat, your adversary might very well become of a mind to dispense with his plans and actions that could be in motion.

In this chapter, I discussed another essential element in our model. *Passion* means *a "strong craving with control questionable and on the edge of rational relinquished; it is not rational thinking most of the time—it is emotional state of being whereby the affective domain dominates the rational/thinking domain."* Passion is a "propellant" in our model of *will*. I explained that examples of passion in conflict could include greed, hatred, and retribution. Passion is fuel to motivate people, impetus to support a leader, a driver for sacrifice from all concerned, and if its ardor is crushed, it can cause one side to acquiesce to another. People planning for or in conflict must ponder passion. As such, they must always account for 1) what people are passionate about; 2) strength of passion; 3) what happens if passion turns from being dormant to being active and aggressive; 4) what might induce people to turn down the heat of their passion and live in peace; and 5) the state of passion resident in one's own soldiers. Passion is a strong source of motivation. People in combat experience degrees of passion. They fight with passion for living in daily struggles of death vs. life, a cause, country, ideology, religious beliefs, freedom, love of fellow soldiers, retribution, repressed but released hatred of other people due to their religious beliefs, social conduct, differences, myths, fables, and the like. *Sacrifice* directly links with emotion and passion and therefore demands consideration planning for any conflict. Sacrifice inextricably links with passion. In this part of the chapter, though, I explain that sacrifice means *the surrender or destruction of something prized or desirable for the sake of something considered as having a higher or more pressing claim.*[13] Sacrifice has remained important throughout history. For example, sacrifice relates to purpose, strength of motive, determination, perseverance, and passion, and, of course, it relates to life force. Sacrifice is active. I have found sacrifice to be real but mysterious. It lives in the dark well of souls, at the core of all human beings. People in any kind of conflict must always consider sacrifice from two perspectives: one's own readiness to sacrifice and how enthusiastic, as it were, one's adversary is to sacrifice and to what degree will they possess and demonstrate this intangible but powerful force against their foe in a fight.

---

13. Sacrifice. Dictionary.com. Dictionary.com Unabridged. Random House, Inc. http://www.dictionary.com/brouse/sacrifice (accessed: November 14, 2017).

CHAPTER 8

Value of Goals and Objectives

Argument: *In this chapter I explain how to think about value and its relationship to goals and objectives. I explain the utility of using a* value to goal ratio *and a* value to objective ratio *that proves useful to all sides in a conflict. The ratios also prove particularly valuable when attempting to manipulate the ratio of the adversary, while protecting our own. I define* value, goal, *and* objectives *and explain four important purposes of a goal: 1) interlocutor for connecting objectives with the strategic aim; 2) connector bonding objectives with will's nub—desire, volition, life force; 3) sculptor of probabilities to discern if one's strength of motive is sufficient to accomplish the strategic aim; and 4) thrust lines for action. Lastly, the chapter postulates an important notion: The wise adversary always discerns and attacks his opponent's goals and objectives.*

Goals and objectives are at the center of the battle of *wills*. They are linked to both purpose and strength of motive.

Competitors focus their capabilities and help enactors of actions with a sequence that focuses their thinking and their efforts—strategic aim, goal, objective, etc. A goal is what an agent, actor, or, in our case, the adversary on any stage of strife seeks. It connects an objective to a broader and more abstract strategic aim. The goal paints a picture, as it were, an image in one's mind depicting *will*'s purpose and strength of motive. A high-quality goal does not tell an action agent of change what to do, but instead shapes or constrains how the person or organization, country, and so on reaches the articulated strategic aim. In this respect, goals serve as interlocutors between broad statements and thrust lines/arrows of strategic aims with more specific objectives. Goals provide a way for senior leaders in any profession to articulate their vision (which provides hints of a state of continuity before and after the goals and objectives satisfactorily come to fruition). Well-stated goals have a structure that helps senior decision makers determine progress in realizing the strategic aim via subordinates' objectives, strategies, tactics, and actions. Each of these steps has elements and each relates to the adversary's view. Out of necessity, one views the people, organizations, nation-states, etc. against whom he contests and considers how these actors think about value in their sought-after goals and objectives.

My Über-thinker and thought pilgrim appear confused. So, I stop and we engage in a three-person-plus-reader Chautauqua. I explain to their tired but eager minds this thought—value[1] dictates the effort, money, sacrifice, time, etc., each adversary is willing to expend to win battles of *wills*. One's construed value identifies an undulating scale that reveals levels of commitment each side in a conflict brings to bear to attain its respective goals and objectives.[2]

Our examination of value comes from two timeless perspectives. As one perspective, a value involves *moral belief*; it subtly infiltrates minds and souls, and affects how people think and feel about goals and objectives in a conflict or any competitive endeavor. Now, when one considers the other perspective, valuing goals comes forth as *material*. Such a value takes thinking about a particular side in a conflict and discerning its purpose, strength of motive, level of commitment, and willingness to sacrifice and thereby expend people, time, treasury, and perhaps even territory to impose its will successfully on another entity. One begins to comprehend this notion of the worth of a goal or an objective only when he "enters" the mind of the adversary and understands how the adversary schemes and wargames the value we could be placing on our goals and objectives. That is to say, one must reason about how he values his own goals and objectives and how he thinks we value not only ours but his too.

My Über-thinker and thought pilgrim seem to be thinking with me now so we tread deeper into my inner sanctum of thought to discover ways to think about value relative to goals and objectives. I tell them, "I realized another way to help me understand the value of goals and objectives—I speak of ratios—rough ratios, though. Allow me to explain my thinking. Each side always considers and has a methodology for calculating its *value to goal ratio* and *value to objective ratio*. Contestants pack both moral and material value into their goals and objectives. Whereas material value can be quantified, moral influences can be estimated only. Consequently, smart opponents realize their thinking will always be flawed because that which they must consider to be important, mostly falls in the moral domain. So,

---

1. *Value*: A moral principle and belief or accepted standard of behavior of a person or social group; something that has worth and is sought after; something that is significant and deemed useful by all sides in a competitive situation.

2. *Objective*: A deliberate action that consumes mental and physical energy, effort, desire, perseverance, etc. to accomplish or satisfy a personal, organizational, or national aim, goal, strategy, or outcome.

our thinking mind piles on our beleaguered intellect and counsels as such—"count on it—each side will mangle badly its estimates of an opponent's *value to goal* and *value to objective ratios*. Each side always errs in this regard."

The discussion continues, with customary head nods, grunts, and groans, which infer questions jumping around in their minds probably concerning how one overcomes this apparent impossibility. I respond, "Accordingly, I want you to learn to discern the magnitude of this mangling, but again, direct your thinking from the perspective of each side, and how much offset or adjustment could appear before it happens, after it happens and said adjustment has occurred, and, what could be if it shows its presence in the future. Be assured, this thinking is not difficult if you acknowledge my initial proposition—each side will err as it thinks about its views and those of its adversary about the *value to goal ratio* and *value to objective ratio*. These thinking errors usually involve a culprit: the moral domain. But, thinking about these ratios is paramount nevertheless.

Realize the moral domain always appears in an opponent's mind from his experience via his past actions. Good thinkers estimate how a "close to right" vision might appear, but they remain wary because of the potential for fluctuation of variables in nonlinear contextual inputs. This unknown is natural but frustrating. It represents a dark, turbulent sea of uncertainty, chance, and a dense fog of culture, humanness, and emotion, for example, fear, passion, sacrifice, hatred, capabilities, retribution, perseverance, determination, and the like. Nonetheless, conflict imposes a stern demand on each adversary—with the best exactitude possible, estimate your ratio and your adversary's, because deep inside the ratios and judgments, within the protective layers that enshroud the ratios, one can *peer into the adversary's stage props supporting his will*. The effort will reveal in the raw visions—flashing appearances of strength of motive, purpose, life force, resolve, volition, and desire—all permanent residents of the house I call, the nub of *will*. How an adversary values its goals and objectives and how you value your human and contextual induced errors notwithstanding, influence suffering, death, injury, monetary losses, and so on. Further, each adversary must have plans for enduring these tribulations, perhaps even twisting them into advantage. Remember—conceptual tentacles from the ratios reach back and cling to the definition and spread through the elements comprising our models of *will*.

I go on to explain another contributory notion concerning the battle of goals between opposing sides. Interestingly, the term "goal" describes the focal point each side seeks. Yet, a useful goal for any side purposefully lacks the specificity and descriptiveness of an "objective." I want you to remember—broad goals diminish in breadth, depth, and width as they become objectives. Directly and indirectly, planners, leaders, and decision makers at higher levels guide those at lower levels who need increasing specificity. Each level of such leaders and their organizations squeeze the wide, large "goal" into smaller and smaller objectives to provide sufficient detail and guidance to develop the right actions to impose their *will*. Then, feedback occurs. Intelligence, surveillance, and reconnaissance (ISR) gathers data, analysts and leaders evaluate the quality of their actions, and they provide feedback to senior decision makers to adjust their thinking and guidance pertaining to the value of goals and objectives.

I now provide you three more simple but important points to consider. To set the stage, I endeavor to think like my adversary. My first task—think about his goals and their value to him: 1) I task my Red Team[3] to be my enemy in wargaming, to cogitate and design guidance to accomplish its (my opponent's) strategic aim, goals, objectives, resources, constraints, strategies, tactics, and so on. The Red Team assesses the relevant *value to goal ratios* and *value to objective ratios* for both sides, knowing full well the seductive powers inherent to subjectivity. They take the strategic aim, goals, and eventually objectives, and pepper them with sufficient detail to enable planners and decision makers to "develop a recipe" and bake it. Out of the oven comes a creative hot dish where one finds five paragraphs: 1) friendly and adversary situations; 2) mission with specified and implied tasks; 3) execution; 4) sustainment; and 5) command and control. In *civilian commercial companies*, one could find something akin to this sequence: situation at hand; strategic vision; goals and objectives; adversary; context; undesired outcomes; risk and uncertainty; security; media reactions; value to goal and value to objective ratios—ours and adversary's; agility to perturbation and friction; corporate relationships; feedback mechanisms; standards; and aftermath of the conflict. To an *individual*, a sequence might be something like this: What am I doing? Why am I doing it? Does the risk justify the action? Where will I act? What is my vision? How do I impose my actions? How do I assess outcomes for quality? What are the criteria I use to judge quality of my actions? When do I act with highest probability of success? Against whom do I impose my *will*? Will he resist? What is the context like? Need I worry about aftermath of the struggle? Can I use the adversary's mind and thinking for my advantage? Can I use the context to my advantage and my opponent's disadvantage?

Any organizationally layered player in a conflict provides derivative organizations—actors on this stage of strife—with sufficient guidance to first plan, then conduct actions relating to a particular *will's* nub. They 1) prepare to be agile, when influences of the context nibble at and sometimes alter the "cooked dish"; 2) provide specific guidance and constraints

3. *Red Team*: People, either trained/educated or otherwise who perform the function of providing alternatives; critiquing plans as objectively as possible; playing the adversary in wargames; and providing innovative or creative thinking to help overcome conventional wisdom, blinding biases, poor assumptions, and personal logic errors.

sufficient, in a broad sense, to arrange[4] minds—just a bit—(these are the thought models that describe the intricacies of a strategic aim, how this aim guides goals, objectives, etc., and how they might bring the strategic aim into reality); and, 3) provide the thought links[5] connecting the strategic aim to goals and objectives, thereby guiding the action, assessment, data collection, evaluation, and adaptation. A high-quality goal such as I describe transforms into an etching or depiction of action on a Greek urn—it is the desired future appearing in one's open, receiving mind. It provides direction, boundaries, and macro-constraints to guide planning and action to accomplish the goal.

I ask my acolytes and readers to stand, turn 180 degrees, and be in awe: sense the sequence of seeing an appearing, cascading, string of connected, translucent globules—probabilities and outcomes—moving about; entangle with imposition actions, always clawing back and bonding via enfolding and unfolding the sequence, respectively—objectives to goals to strategic aim, and back down, *ad infinitum.*

Now on to the next element of our model—the objective. The definition for objective is "a deliberate action that consumes mental and physical energy, desire, perseverance to accomplish or satisfy a personal, organizational, or national aim, goal, strategy, or outcome." An objective is subordinate to a goal but remains broader than the next lower rung in the thought model, "strategy," which I will soon discuss. Objectives force people to narrow their thinking and thereby focus on what decision makers and organizations seek during conflict, "that which truly matters" and "value of goals and objectives" considerations. Objectives, if decomposed and properly monitored, can provide metrics of success or failure in progress occurring and moving (via actions) toward goals and the strategic aim. Objectives become increasingly specific as people consider actions to accomplish or satisfy both goals and objectives. Good thinking provides objectives (written and oral) sufficiently specific, efficient, and effective. Such objectives enable planners to set conditions to judge the state of quality (set forth in the decision maker's criteria for success) in their goal- and objective-driven efforts. In some cases, people develop objectives with quantifiable metrics or quality matrices to evaluate progress toward finding and overcoming—or at least render ineffective—extant resisters to satisfying their objectives. Note 1: How our adversary views his "resisters," how he chooses to cope with them, and how he considers overcoming their influences becomes one of the most important aspects of thinking like the adversary and using such thought as a preemptive "weapon

4. Lawrence, *Seven Pillars of Wisdom*, 95.

5. *Thought link:* Association with or development of something observed, imagined, discussed, or connected by thought, Hall and Citrenbaum, *Intelligence Analysis*, 126.

system." Note 2: Again a word of caution; using quality metrics to evaluate moral influences is prone to errors and, hence, the wise planner and decision maker will sprinkle such assessments with a healthy dose of skepticism and establish a mechanism for confirming or refuting the assessment.

Specific objectives instill in their enactors a sense of purpose, a unity of thought and understanding, and linked aggregations of consciousness. As one proceeds to unravel the twists and knots comprising meanings of objectives (implied and explained), people start thinking about and developing actions they believe offer the best probabilities to satisfy their objectives. Objectives provide some specific times, locations, and resources, and desired accomplishments to not only act but also to assess outcomes of actions and, thereby, to adapt to contextual or adversarial adaptation. Adversaries certainly develop and execute a variety of actions to satisfy their objectives. They undoubtedly consider their opponents' objectives relative to theirs, then they find themselves circling back to the influential concept of duality and riding the wild pendulum between the minds of adversaries and friendly forces, looking for ways to their adversary's vulnerabilities while simultaneously protecting their own.

We have to consider this value of our objectives, from our perspective, as well as how our adversary views their world and relates their objectives to ours. And, of course, one must consider the value of objectives as he sees it and also consider the adversary's view of how we view our *value to objective ratio*—tough mental slogging indeed. The high probability of mangling this process with your own subjective thinking remains from our discussion earlier. Regardless, we want to know how much our adversary wants to accomplish his objective(s) and how much he wants to deny us our objective(s). We also have to understand our own objectives and their value to us. Wariness is needed to deny being flummoxed by a wily and determined adversary. All of our intelligence tentacles should be out, watching, and sensing for indications of the lines of action our foe could be taking.

In the context of conflict, let's continue to expand our understanding of objectives. Each side in a conflict will have its idea of the most valuable objective, so the struggle over dominance of one side's objectives and the thwarting and subjugation of the opponent's objectives involves the duality factor of this important concept.

Objectives are important because they constitute an aim point for which decision makers and their staffs plan. They provide the basis or center of mass for which action occurs. Interestingly, though, the initiator of an action must assess the outcomes of said action so as to judge success or failure of progress toward accomplishing their objective(s). My indomitable, remorseless Über-thinker and thought pilgrim ever so rudely demand that I stop rambling and think like them for once. I extrapolate their harshly stated question. The question becomes a raging torrent of a flood of thought coursing through my mind. Finally, I say, "Well, what actually happens so as to assess my adversary's value of his objectives? How do they assess its continuity of value so they can adapt if the value of the objective changes? How do they assess this 'value of objective' via the five 'w's:' what, where, when, who, and why am I assessing? What happens after I gather data and start assessing?" To assess, one must watch for, collect, and understand data relevant to the action whose outcomes I'm assessing. Since I'm truly speaking about "quality" of my assessment, I know I must answer these questions: 1) Did my action cause the intended outcome or effect? 2) Did my action affect my adversary's value of his objectives? 3) Did the means I used to create the concerned action perform as I expected efficiently and effectively? 4) Do the outcomes of my action relate to my objective for which I designed the action? 5) What does the data I collected mean for the value of my objectives and for "spin-off" benefits or negativisms? 6) How well did I turn data into information and knowledge in this assessment? 7) How did I evaluate the data, information, and knowledge and use it in decisions? 8) Did my assessment effort matter? 9) How did I learn and apply what I learned about myself and my adversary? 10) How well and how quickly did I share what I learned from my evaluation with my colleagues? 11) How, when, and where did I actually move from thought to adaptation? 12) Was my adaptation faster and better than my adversary's adaptation? 13) Was my adaptation more influential on my co-evolutionary cycle than my adversary's? This gives you a thought model on which to build for determining the quality of your assessing and adaptation responsibilities.

How does one determine each side's most valuable objective? A good question! My most valuable objectives are vital to their associated goal(s) and contribute to the strategic aim. The closer the objective in question is to enhancing one's strategic aim and goal accomplishment, the higher its value. Of course, once again, duality sticks up its ugly head and demands our attention and our capacity to adapt our actions and protective measures, given this competing clash of objectives. That is to say, when one places a most valuable tag on an objective, it includes 1) the means to satisfy the objective; 2) the quality a decision maker desires affixed to the objective to be accomplished; and 3) the capability to assess outcomes and thereby possess the wherewithal to adapt faster and more effectively than an adversary.

Our work, however, is relative to 1) the adversary's most important objective selection; 2) his designated means to accomplish this objective; 3) his description of standards for quality; and 4) his capabilities to assess and adapt. It follows, then, that one finds a curious phenomenon arising out of the mist and fog of a clash of objectives. Let me explain. I steadfastly develop my most valuable objective. I provide the means to cause the action to accomplish this objective within the quality standards my decision maker prescribed. I also provide the means to assess outcomes of my action, the status of my objectives, plus the capability to adapt my actions, as necessary. This is 25 percent of the whole of our problem set. Given that all of us believe in duality and the clash of objectives, then recognize the adversary goes through a similar process. This is another 25 percent of the whole. Then, as a third 25 percent, we find ourselves quickly desiring to create one or more adverse influences on the adversary's objective satisfaction, his means to accomplish his most valuable objective, and the means to assess the actions he plans to execute to adapt. As the final 25 percent, we find ourselves attempting to protect our objective, identifying means to accomplish the objective, using assessment capabilities relative to the adversary's interference of our objective accomplishment, and using our means to assess how well we adapt faster and better than our adversary. I exclaim to my Über-thinker and thought pilgrim, "You should be drawing an inference here—that is to say, I must design alerts and counter-measures to recognize the adversary's efforts, and you can safely wager your adversary is doing the same. We want to beat him and he wants to beat us into acquiescence of his desires. So it goes in the affairs of human beings—back and forth, side to side, up and down, diagonal corner to diagonal corner—a continuous battle of wits, means, actions, assessments, and adaptations toward the *most valuable objective*."

When addressing the thinking that has to go into this issue, sometimes a thoughtful person can drift back in mankind's ancient history to find solid analogies (keeping in mind, of course, changes in such things as technology and organizational design). Let's revisit Scipio Africanus and his political and military maneuvering from 236 to 183 BCE, when he led Rome's armies in the Second Punic War with Carthage. Once Scipio Africanus had secured Spain it was Carthage's great general Hannibal, operating in southern Italy, who caused Rome the greatest concern. Scipio, on the other hand, had his strategic eye on an objective far more valuable than the immediacy of the day: Attack Carthage and Hannibal would be forced to leave Italy and fight Scipio and his Roman legions in North Africa. That which seemed so obvious to Scipio, however, wasn't obvious to the Roman Senate. Here is how a renowned historian of Scipio Africanus described the situation:

> The two conflicting strategic policies [of the two counsels—Scipio and Fabius and bifurcated factions in the Roman Senate] stand in deep relief. Fabius's object was strictly limited; to get rid of Hannibal with all speed so that he could turn to Italy and heal the wounds of her countryside. Scipio's object was more absolute. He aimed at crushing both Hannibal and Carthage. To get rid of Hannibal by defeating him in Italy would only alleviate a symptom. Until Carthage was humbled, Rome would never be safe . . . it was his penetrating vision which soared

above the narrow patriotic view of Fabius and convinced him that Rome's safety did not lie merely in Hannibal's defeat. Carthage itself must be humiliated and fettered.[6]

When one finds or suspects the presence of weak or basically valueless objectives from the adversary's point of view, the value of the objectives is low enough to be cheaper in a cost/benefit relationship relative to a desired outcome. When the stakes and the potential outcomes are high, then the objective has to be of the highest value for the side making the determination. Of course, the opponent needs to anticipate the value his adversary places on this objective and seeks to retard or thwart its fulfillment.

Thus, once again, we have to think like our opponent, understand his objectives and the value he places on them, his short- and long-term capabilities to reach and satisfy those objectives, and his strength of motive to accomplish his objectives, even long after one or the other combatant lies in his grave. If the long-term objective is challenging, then the required buildup of the capabilities to accomplish it means the receiving side in this struggle must act to neutralize those condition setting activities of the aggressor.

[F]low and change were the essential features of nature, but also that there are constant patterns in these changes. . . . The sage recognizes these patterns and directs his actions according to them.[7]

For certain, in future bouts of mental combat we shall find this back and forth of one's objective relative to the opponent's objective. It follows we must have three views of the value of objective: 1) our own view; 2) our view of the adversary's value of his and our objectives; and 3) how the adversary is viewing our view of our value of objective, as well as how he thinks we are viewing how he is viewing his value of his objective. Sounds complicated, doesn't it? Well, it is, but nothing in "knowledge war"[8] is simple.

The aim of volition—and the imposition of force or power or money committed therein by both sides—is to win as their life force directs and their purpose describes. With conflicts, one always finds something—a nub, a fortune, a company, an idea, a castle, a piece of land, a woman, power, etc.—one or both sides want. It is evident, of course, many a man

6. H. H. Scullard, *Scipio Africanus: Soldier and Politician* (Ithaca, NY: Cornell University Press, 1970), 109.

7. Fritjof Capra, *The Tao of Physics*, second edition (New York: Bantam Books, 1983), 95.

8. A knowledge war has two aims: attacking the knowledge that the adversary uses to make decisions, and protecting our knowledge workers and information systems from assault.

has tried to dominate others over the word "true"[9] and its sibling "truth"—it is the imposer's view of truth the recipient of this kind of imposition often resists. Truth is a hollow word that bends with the winds of force and change. Quite literally, truth lies within the eye of the beholder.

Yes, we see with this passage the truth about truth, as it were, but do we? It is difficult to convince human beings their truth is wrong and ours is correct. The situation becomes worse as truth, or what was agreed upon to be truth, changes with causation, sometimes coming with vagaries of nonlinear operational contexts and co-evolution actions of complex adaptive systems (CAS). And, unfortunately, people do not generally think well enough to overcome another person's view of truth via logic and argumentation. A thoughtful person would look at the claim of truth with a jaundiced eye but possess a way of reasoning the yay or nay of a position of truth. For example, the smart person has a model for thinking which he can use and demonstrate how he arrived at what he considers to be truth. If one makes a claim as a truth, then he must prove the claim with evidence. Evidence needs to be proven true too. People use facts to prove evidence to be true. Facts prove elusive though, as people are prone to differing views of facts rather than agreeing on the validity of a fact. Culture also shapes the perceptions of how people consider facts, evidence, and claims. At the bottom of the quest to prove a claim, one works with sub- or micro-truths drifting and floating in irregular movements around what could be one or more facts. These sub- or micro-truths are indeed additive and, when they conjoin in an aggregation, they lend credence to facts, which then helps to prove evidence, which then helps convince others of the claim's (macro-truth's) validity. In Figure 8.1, I provide you with my model for arriving at truth and convincing others of the validity of our claim.

People have to agree in the truthfulness of a claim of objective value. If we are able to convince others of the truth of our propositions, then move ahead. Of course, if people use this thought model, then it follows, via the mechanism of duality, our adversary does likewise.

Let's take a closer look at this model. In the center, you find a classic progression of a decision maker trying to understand the situation and make a decision. As you can see in the center column, the decision maker has knowledge gaps; intelligence fills the gaps and recommends action or no action. On the left angle, you see a process for working your claim or

9. *Truth*: Consistent with agreed upon facts; genuine, conforming to the beliefs and standards of a group of people; an act or behavior or opinion or thought that conforms to rules, regulations, measurements, standards, or patterns. From the *American Heritage Dictionary of the English Language*, fifth edition (New York: Houghton Mifflin Harcourt Publishing Company, 2016).

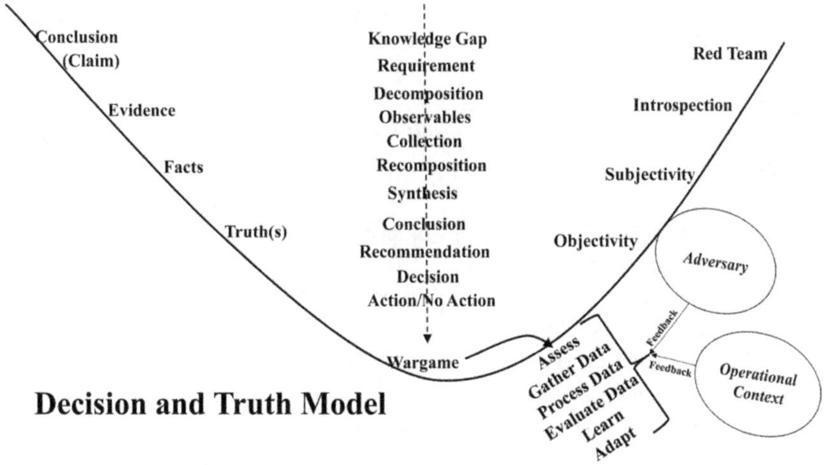

Figure 8.1. Decisions and Truth Model

conclusion—claim, evidence, facts, macro-truths, and micro-truths. But, as when you direct your thinking to the right angle, you see what bedevils the entire process: the two fighting factions of objectivity and subjectivity. In my world, nothing is objective and all is subjective. Nonetheless, one has to possess a way to get rid of our biases and logic errors to be as close to objectivity as possible. One uses personal and organizational introspection and a Red Team to challenge our assumptions. One also wargames to see the world from the adversary's perspective, and also looks hard at and studies the operational context. In the lower-right-hand corner, you can find the co-evolution cycle in shorthand, so to speak. With action, one assesses, gathers data from the adversary, and from the context, processes it, learns, and adapts.

With at least two sides, duality always proves to be highly influential on the outcome of conflict. To get at this notion of duality, again, learn to think like the adversary. Orson Scott Card, in his book *Ender's Game*, provides us with some clues as to how to judge not only the value of our objective, but at least the thoughts of our adversary.

[Y]ou will learn to be quick and discover what tricks the enemy has for you. Remember, boy, from now on the enemy is more clever than you. From now on the enemy is stronger than you. From now on you are always about to lose, . . . You will learn to defeat the enemy. He will teach you how, . . . Take what pleasure you can in the interstices of your work, but your work is first, learning is first, winning is everything because without it there is nothing, . . . I'm going to hit you with everything I can imagine, and I will have no mercy, because when you face the buggers they will think of things I can't imagine and compassion for human beings is impossible for them.[10]

Please recall the definitions of "value" and "objective" as we turn our knowledge into something pragmatic and actionable by way of answers to these questions:

1. Who determines the "value of objectives?"
2. Is it a person? Can a machine do this?
3. Is it the politician or the action person (e.g., the general) who decides on the "value of objectives?"
4. Is it a body of people (e.g., Roman Senate in Scipio's day or the U.S. Congress in our present day)?
5. What are the criteria to judge "value"?
6. Have the general, the political leader, and the legislative body (the people) come to an agreement about the value of the objective accomplished by diplomacy, political, economic, social, informational, and military imposition actions and desired consequences?

To answer these questions, I provide the following views:

1. The political leader and political body should identify their aims, goals, and objectives—all to accomplish political outcomes by military means. The desired political outcomes—*will* to impose others to do their bidding—define the "value of objectives," and also guide the nature of military action.
2. People always make these judgments determining value of objectives. Machines can help with quantitative cost/benefit analyses, but in the end, humans have to make the calls, as machines cannot do this yet.
3. Again, it is the politician who determines value of objectives. Military people assist and advise, but in the end, the politician must stand up and be heard and make the call. Military people need this judgment, because the next step involves the military determining expenditure of effort to accomplish the objectives. As Clausewitz tells us, the political objective and its value drive the level of violence via military action to be unleashed to accomplish this objective.
4. In a democracy, the political body should help the political leader decide the value of the objective(s), as this ties the three parts of Clausewitz's magnificent trinity (people, government, military) together. But in a practical sense, this determination in turn guides the military with

10. Orson Scott Card, *Ender's Game* (New York: A Tom Doherty Associates Book, 1991), 263–264, 277.

vision, broad political goals and objectives, priorities, resources, and constraints, for example, losses, time taken to satisfy the objectives, money spent, collateral damage with civilians, and the like.

5. The political body and the leader should make transparent the criteria for judging value—it helps the people of this nation and its military understand the shape and magnitude of the effort. I know this is rarely done, but in the idealist side of my mind, this procedure should occur before our young people go forth into harm's way.
6. The military, the political leader, and the people (via the legislative body) need to come to an agreement about the nature of the conflict upon which they conjecture or embark. But in their deliberations, they cannot forget possible counters by the adversarial entities or countries at whom said imposition aims. The *will* of the adversary and friendly capabilities come first, then objectives, then the value of the objectives via prioritization and definition, and then constraints/restraints—strategies, tactics, thinking like the adversary, operating in nonlinear contexts, the culture in which the contest occurs, and so forth. What I describe seems to be a logical flow of enacting the value of objectives in my opinion, but the reader needs to judge validity of my proposition and if the quality of thought therein meets his or her expectations.

Moving along, I must admit the way we judge value is only half the challenge—the other half requires people to think deeply about how our adversary judges value in pursuit of his objectives. This requirement becomes dicey as America, for example, collides with far away cultures in which our people know very little, particularly in "how they reason" about the value of their objectives and discerning whether or not they are ready to sacrifice to accomplish said objectives. Could it be with such thinking one could find or at least identify the importance of interfering with the process our adversary uses to discern value in his objectives? A good starting point could be to determine the adversary's objective—or more likely, objectives. Once we discern his objective(s), one could start by attempting to think like him and discern how valuable his chosen objective is, and how much he is prepared to sacrifice to accomplish this objective. Could one affect his ruminations so the cost appears far greater than his discernment of value of the objective? Could it be the adversary plans to affect the processes we use to judge value and thus influence our estimate of cost to be more than the value we attribute to our objective to cause us to discard the objective and seek another more amenable to our needs?

Let us discuss some of the indicants of value people could use to rank their objectives and to ensure their objectives and values tie to the fight in question. Let's pick just a few to help illustrate the ideas we have to consider about how our adversary could be planning to defeat us.

1. Political outcomes. How to govern is a treasured aspect of a national ethos. If one side believes regime continuity or sustaining power to be a determinant of "value" of objective, then this aspect of value of the objective is important. Just a point here to help us think better. One side is the high-value objective, and such a lofty status involves its ability to govern or to remain in power. Its fulfillment is important to this side. The status, however, does not have to be relative to the value of the objective of the opposing side, who might be pursuing objectives dealing with another aspect of competition. It is through anticipated conflict in the competition that the seemingly divergent objectives both slide to the middle and become colliding objectives. Or, the objectives of each side could be highly relational. One side could have the highest value objective to be regime continuity, while his adversary's highest-value objective could be to cast out the current regime and emplace one friendlier. Complicated business indeed!
2. Territory. As another example, one side's high-value objective could be to seize an opponent's territory and to control its sources of power. The other side, it seems, could have the impudence to disagree and consequently designate preservation of the contested territory as their highest-value objective. Again, we find a significant collision of objectives transliterated into a virulent struggle between the two, as we could see the aggressor, with the life force and purpose, as well as strength of motive and capabilities to attack or place significant pressure on the country in question or on the international community to seek an end to the carnage. The implied message to the receiving party by the stronger aggressor? Acquiesce or face invasion and destruction. Has this happened in recent history? The answer is yes—consider post-Munich in 1938, when Germany started making menacing demands on Czechoslovakia to give up the Sudetenland. Germany promised this would be the last such demand. Britain and France acquiesced in October 1938, and Hitler's Nazis soon occupied the Sudetenland. Well, it wasn't the last demand after all; Germany annexed all of Czechoslovakia in March 1939. Appeasement did not work as a strategy for European peace.
3. Ideology. For the purpose of meaning in this work, ideology means:

> The compendium of doctrine, myth, belief, ideas, values, etc., that guides and influences the behavior of an individual, social movement, ideological grouping, institution, small group, criminal gangs, terrorists (a sub-set of ideology), countries, et al. Ideology is a belief or beliefs that ideas influence people, political activities, organizations, social strata, social activities, institutions, organizations, or nations that have a belief system based on history, ideas, social mores, values, honor, determinism, myths, metaphors, etc., and often inspired and motivated by a political, economic, or social movements—such as Marxism, liberalism, socialism, fascism, communism, and democratic idealism.

An ideology could be at the top of value of objective in many ways of thinking because ideology is idea based, as the name implies. Ideas, important to all kinds and groupings of people, can dominate how people live, reason, and behave; moreover, an ideology can structure views, ambitions, prospects, and inner drives. Ideologies have influenced man from ancient antiquity to present days. With a definition of this power, we can readily see that ideology can shoot to the top of the value of objective scale so much so sometimes people choose to die for their ideology, such as the droves of soldiers of National Socialism and communism, who fought and killed each other in World War II; and, as the North Vietnamese, who fought in turn, the Chinese, Japanese, French, South Vietnamese, and Americans for their ideology of nationalism.

4. Retribution. For our work, retribution means payback or reprisal for an injustice, crime, murder, seizure of property, or dishonorable act. Again, retribution often competes for the top rung of the value of objective ladder; however, the side seeking retribution must have the power, capability, and intention of bringing its soul-penetrating, infiltrating influences to bear. Retribution occupies its lofty position on a hierarchy of value of objective because it deals with emotion and repressed anger, which sometimes smolders and nearly flames over many years, sometimes even centuries. In a way, society is retributive to criminal behavior when it sends people to prison or executes them. France and Britain were retributive to Germany after World War I. Germans were retributive in their enactment of punishment of France when France capitulated to Germany in June 1940. The Soviets were vengeful to the Germans when they invaded Germany in the waning days of World War II.
5. Passion of the populace. By way of review, passion means:

> A strong craving with control questionable and on the edge of rational relinquishment; passion is not rational thinking most of the time—it is an emotional state of being, whereby the affective domain dominates the rational/thinking domain.

Passion is, of course, important enough to warrant an essential rung in the ladder of low to high value, as it provides the intellectual and physical verve for action. People act out the group's or leader's vision to accomplish an objective. This truism holds for each side in a conflict. Passion is in the minds and hearts of human beings—machines, of course, do not feel emotion; therefore, machines cannot replicate the supernatural strengths and stamina of people imbued with passion. If a person's passion ignites, his thinking becomes subordinate to the emotional side of his being. Hatred is another fuel for passion. So, let us review once again this word, this concept that has kindled and lit so many fires or murderous ire, what is hatred and how and why does it fuel and drive passion.

> An intense and emotion driven dislike or abhorrence for a person or organization, country, or terrorist group . . . hatred dominates rational thought when acrimony dominates the perceptions and feelings, thus rationality of one or more people feel in a situation.

When people hate one another, they abhor one another. Hatred can drive people to not only fail to cooperate, but also to inflict pain and damage on their opponent and sometimes to kill their opponents. But to impose hatred on the object of this force does not always end the explosion of passion. No, hatred and hate-fueled action can in the extreme lead to uncivilized actions. A few examples for you to consider include what the Japanese did to the Chinese, what the Germans did to the Slavs and Jews before and during WWII, and what the U.S. government did in its eradication campaign against its Native American population in the mid-to-late 1800s. Hatred, along with its sibling, passion, figure high in any campaign involving action on a resisting force. Hatred and passion are also catalysts for persevering in a conflict, especially when confronted with increasing "costs."

Hatred is nothing new—its tentacles stretch back to the beginning of time and it is destined to continue *ad infinitum*. It is a terrible burden to bear, and it is a burden unique to the human animal. Once a person hates, it is difficult to implore and convince that person to stop hating. The journey to hate's antipode, or even its neutral position—love or indifference—is akin to human travel to the sun. Hate seeps through one's mind, heart, and organs as cancer; it cannot be healed or eradicated. Levels of hate exist. At a low level, hate simmers but does nothing by way of action. Often this kind of hate lays in a state of confinement. When hate seethes and boils, it can burst out of its confining gates and savagely act out its passion. When people who hate conjoin, they provide fuel and strength to passion and propel the subsequent actions.

6. Opportunism. Often, visionary senior leaders prove to be opportunistic—when they see an advantage or a wedge into an advantage, they make the most of the opportunities and strike. In this case, taking advantage and succeeding would be a high-value objective. As an example, Vladimir Putin took advantage of global politics and weak and feckless Western leadership to retake the Crimea and annex it back into Russia. He has also intervened in Ukraine's political and territorial status, which has not been resolved to this day. In addition, he saw a vacuum in the Syrian civil war and took the opportunity to intervene with force. Since he was opportunistic, he filled the vacuum vacated by America's choice to be more of an observer than a direct player in

the civil war. Although this aspect of value of objective is obvious to understand, I thought you would like to read this passage by David Jablonsky:

> Anyone desiring to shape events . . . must be opportunistic to some degree. But the politician . . . adjusts his purposes to fit reality, while the visionary statesman attempts to shape reality in terms of his purpose or the change he desires. . . . Any success in creating and realizing a strategic vision for the management of power will rest primarily on the ability of the statesman to paint a credible picture of desired change using strategic ends, ways, and means.[11]

At high levels, opportunism, as a criterion for valuing an objective, does not occur with on the spot decisions and actions. This quick action to take advantage of an opportunity does exist and is practiced in competition. But, I am speaking of higher levels of competition. Sometimes opportunism is set up over time by the wise, visionary statesman or general. In such a situation, one finds value in an objective of long-term advantage this visionary sets up over months and years. This kind of person has a mind that sees the world as interconnected, via strands and linkages:

> Linkage, however, is not a natural concept for Americans, who have traditionally perceived foreign policy as an episodic enterprise. Our bureaucratic organizations, divided into regional and functional bureaus, and indeed our academic tradition of specialization compound the tendency to compartmentalize. American pragmatism produces a penchant for examining issues separately: to solve problems on their merits, without a sense of time or context or of the seamless web of reality.[12]

You should now grasp how important it is to consider the value of the objective. Your thoughts must drift back and forth between your mind and the mind of your adversary. The only way to be able to consider this aspect of *will* is to contemplate duality and thus acknowledge your capable adversary who is undoubtedly attempting to do to you what you want to do to him. I now present Table 8.1 to help with comprehension. Please note, in this table, I placed a selection of elements whose meanings, shapes, and forms in the minds of adversaries could help us determine the value of objectives.

Understand, though, you must rank these considerations and develop objective in a hierarchy, from top priority to the lowest in value. You must protect those objectives highest in the hierarchy, as you must acknowledge

11. David Jablonsky, "Strategic Vision and Presidential Authority in the Post-Cold War Era." *Parameters*. Carlisle, PA: U.S. Army War College, Vol. XXI, no. 4, Winter 1991–1992. pp. 3, 14.

12. Henry Kissinger, *White House Years* (Boston: Little, Brown and Company, 1979), 129–130.

Table 8.1

How to Think about the Value of Objectives

Policy	Territory—value	Ideology—strength	Retribution	Passion
Opportunism	Ends, ways, means	Adversary—thinking	Purpose	Sacrifice
Capabilities	Strengths—motive	Duality	Objectives	Values

your adversary is coming for them. This difficult task is important because placement in hierarchy of value each side designates for their objectives is what drives cutlines, derived risk, and uncertainty. It is the adversary's risk and uncertainty, with respect to the value of his objectives, in which you will find hunting rewarding. Nonetheless, be wary as you anticipate how your adversary might come at your value of objectives. In this respect, wargaming is critically important. Where each element places in your valuing depends on the mission, operational context, the adversary, and your ability to anticipate the adversary's objective values.

In this chapter, I presented several important considerations for your examination. Let us review what we discussed. In my view, the term "goal" describes the focal point each side seeks. Yet, a useful goal purposefully lacks the specificity and descriptiveness of "objective." I advised my Überthinker, thought pilgrim, and readers to imagine how any adversary must focus his capabilities and empower enactors of actions to achieve his objectives, goals, and strategic aim. I explained that goals connect objectives to a strategic aim, but do not tell an agent of change what to do. Instead, a valuable goal shapes and constrains the thinking of people charged with designing and implementing actions. In a macro-sense, goals help senior leaders direct their volition into action via objectives, resources, strategies, constraints and tactics.

In this chapter, I also explained value[13] dictates the effort, money, sacrifice, time, etc., each adversary is willing to expend to win battles of *wills*. One's value defines the level of commitment he brings to bear to attain his goals and objectives.[14] Of interest in my examination of value, from one perspective, I think about its *moral* component. From the other

13. *Value*: A moral principle and belief or accepted standard of behavior of a person or social group; something that has worth and is sought after; something that is significant and deemed useful by all sides in a competitive situation.

14. *Objective*: A deliberate action that consumes mental and physical energy, effort, desire, perseverance, etc., to accomplish or satisfy a personal, organizational, or national aim, goal, strategy, or outcome.

perspective, I consider value's *material* component. In a practical sense, one can only begin to comprehend the worth of a goal or an objective by "entering" the mind of one's adversary and understanding how he is wargaming our wargaming relative to our value, aim, goals and objectives. He will attack each or all parts of this process. To forestall his thinking and action, we reason how he values his own goals and objectives and how he thinks our side values our goals and objectives to gain advantages.

I explained why goals exist. They are 1) interlocutors—between and among the strategic aim, goals, objectives and desire, volition, or vision of life force; 2) sources—for verve and the intellectual wherewithal necessary to sculpt probabilities artfully for success by reasoning about resolve and exerting strength of motive; 3) guidance—to shape, form, and link objectives; and 4) eyes (intelligence, surveillance, and reconnaissance)—to glimpse into the quality of action, assessment, and adaptation.

As a further venture into deep thinking, I explained five points upon which to reflect. I undertook this portion of my journey by thinking like my adversary. My first task—think about his aim, goals, and objectives: 1) I thus tasked my Red Team to be my enemy in wargaming; 2) they design guidance to accomplish their version of strategic aim, goals, objectives, (what we think to be the enemy's) and so on; 3) my faux enemy assesses value to goal ratios and value to objective ratios for both sides, keeping in mind siren calls of subjectivity; 4) my Red Teamer provides guidance and constraints, sufficient in a subtle sense, to arrange the minds of our implementers—just a bit; and, 5) the Red Teamer begets an amazing appearance—thought links[15] swishing about in tornadic flows. Of interest to many a sharp mind, I explained a goal of high value is an imaginative etching of the future in one's mind. A high-value goal provides broad direction, boundaries, and constraints for implementers; it influences planning and subsequent actions with sufficient quality to accomplish the stated goal and contribute to the strategic aim.

Now, let us review objectives. I explained an objective involves *a purposefully sought outcome, toward which the actor applies all his energy, capabilities, perseverance, and determination*. Clausewitz tells us, "*The political object[ive] is the goal, war is the means of reaching it, and means can never be considered in isolation from their purpose.*"[16] The worth of an objective can be determined only by examining it in the prickly wicket of duality—*value to objective ratio* of each side in conflict. What neither side knows for certain, though, is its *opponent's value to objective ratio*. How our adversary values his objectives and how we value our objectives influence suffering, death, injury and lost

15. Hall and Citrenbaum, *Intelligence Analysis*, 126.
16. Clausewitz, *On War*, 81.

capital, which both sides prove willing to put forth and endure. One always wants to know how much his adversary will pay, how much he will endure, and how far he will suffer to accomplish his objectives (ties to strength of motive) and how much and far does he intend to deny us our objectives. We also have to understand our own objectives and their value to our decision maker. Objectives are important because they provide aim points to which decision makers and their staffs plan and to which instruments of power impose actions. Interestingly, though, an initiator of action must assess the potential outcomes of said action before it occurs, to judge unknowns, risks, and probabilities of success or failure of progress toward accomplishing his aim, goals, and objectives.

I explained in this chapter how my most valuable objectives link to the strategic aim. So implied in this pronouncement, I need high-quality statements of strategic aim and coherent goals so I can develop high-quality objectives. In turn, high-quality objectives are important to a decision maker because they influence the development and placement of the value on goals and objectives. All of the other important elements necessary for turning one's desire, volition, resolve, purpose, and strength of motive into imposition actions enhance one's acceptance and support of this sequence design.

I also presented you with a decision and truth model to help you evaluate the quality of your thinking. Moreover, I presented a table with 15 elements with which to judge the value an adversary's places on each of his objectives. To help you learn how to think deeper about the value of objectives, I provided six value indicants you could use for ranking objectives, always remembering the tornadic model reaching toward the sky, with translucent goblets connecting to one another, but always involving quality of goals and objectives.

CHAPTER 9

Constraints, Pressure Points, Decisive Points, and Centers of Gravity

Argument: *In this chapter, I define and explain pressure points, decisive points, and centers of gravity (COGs) and their relationships. A constraint is* "a restraint or limitation on action or behavior due to morals, lack of resources, limited capabilities, limited time, contextual limitations, legal, or cultural inhibitions." *Constraints always relate to pressure points, decisive points, and COGs. An adversary seeks and attacks them. Four constraints exist: 1) translatable; 2) moral; 3) legal; and 4) positional. I provide original ways to work with domains and levels of conflict. I present a matrix with seven vertical domain "silos" and four levels of conflict "troughs" intersecting. Thus, a 28-cell matrix appears. In these cells, battles for superiority occur—pressure points, decisive points, and COGs experience perturbation fights for superiority. COGs exist and purposefully "disintegrate" at all levels, spreading through several of these cells.*

CONSTRAINTS

Learn, understand, and consider the nature of constraints in your planning, executing action, assessing outcomes, learning, sharing, and adapting. Constraint's definition is easy to understand, but its simplicity and power have had a significant effect on curbing one's use of capabilities. Some form of constraint has affected conflicts throughout the ages, and it will continue to exert influence on conflicts in the future. Constraints often curb a person's life-force, purpose, capabilities, and even strength of motive in our model for thinking about *will.* Constraints influence man's most secretive and strongly covetous desires. Constraints always relate to pressure points, decisive points, and centers of gravity. Constraints limit one's use of their capabilities, or accentuate one's advantages, or prove to be a disadvantage. Constraints can cause pressure points, decisive points, or centers of gravity to be vulnerable to attack or manipulation, or they can cause a decisive point or center of gravity to be visible but untouchable, for example, sanctuaries in Cambodia and Laos during the Vietnam War and west Pakistan and the opium trade in America's long war in Afghanistan. So, let us first discuss constraints.

My definition for constraint is "a restraint or limitation on action or behavior due to morals, lack of resources, limited capabilities, limited time, contextual limitations, legal, or cultural inhibitions." A constraint holds back, limits, or reduces levels of violence or expulsions of energy and therefore limits the energy initiating action or behavior. This means as one actor upon the stage of strife strives to beat a resisting actor in a conflict, he must be certain that his capabilities and corollary strength of motive are not only capable but as free from constraints as possible. Some statesmen embellish their capabilities, and this state of mind sometimes becomes real and possessive of intellects, which then enter a state of denial when constraints come forth, as usual. They howl to the moon decrying the coming end of the world rather than simply making do. They often commit egregious errors in struggles, such as Hitler during the winter of 1945 in the waning days of World War II. He could not live with real-world constraints and therefore invented weapons, armies, army groups, and corps.

Incremental degradation in the mind-set of either side coming from positional constraints influences one's intensity of aggressiveness, capability and confidence to spring a trap, slyness to deceive, and the *raison d'être* of conflict—to win. A constraint such as a positional constraint proves to even the most skeptical mind to be particularly important when one side shows any weakness—those weaknesses ever so slight to the commitment for winning in any struggle for dominance.[1] The amazing struggles that have occurred in history even when the adversary held a positional advantage proved to caution us against believing the side with the best positional advantage always wins. Positional constraints inhibit any force and cause the side with such a constraint to seek workaround solutions, perhaps leveraging one or several of the other kinds of advantage.

Let's think a moment about the nature of constraints. One should know and understand constraints layers and textures to find their nature and meaning for existence and realize how constraints connect with intent and expected outcomes. Consider what I believe to be four kinds of constraint characteristics:

1. Translatable: A constraint can be physical. Just because one side has a powerful capability easily translatable into power for imposing action

1. Clausewitz, *On War*, 91.

does not mean one can use it to create action. As an example, when the Chinese entered the Korean War, General MacArthur wanted to bomb Manchuria, destroy crossings from Manchuria to the Korean peninsula via the Yalu River, and use the atomic bomb, if necessary. President Truman and his Joint Chiefs of Staff said no, accepted a limited objective war, and put forth the constraint on expanding the physical aspect of the war.

2. Moral: This means to impose inhibitions on excessively brutal acts, to minimize the killing of innocent people, to minimize the destruction of their property (collateral damage), and to restrict conflict behaviors, as the other side might do the same thing back to you.
3. Legal: Until the Nurnberg trials of 1945–1946, senior leaders of the losing side were not prosecuted for crimes against humanity or aggression. There was some talk about punishing the people responsible for starting World War I in what the victors described as a German war of aggression, but no action occurred other than punishment on Germany per se—occupation of the demilitarized Rhineland, loss of land, limitations on the military, and reparations. Today, thanks to the Nuremberg trials in 1946, if people commit genocide or crimes against humanity or start wars of aggression toward their peaceful neighbors, then they do so knowing they very well could be tried for their actions.
4. The wars of Al Qaida, Iraqi insurgents, ISIS, and the like prove troubling as we speak of constraints. They present challenges in which our thinkers must reason differently, as they try to enter the minds of such people and think like them. These forces present difficult challenges for America and its allies because of differences of culture, and in particular, religious "truths" according to their reasoning, experiences, backgrounds, and outright ruthlessness. America and its allies, on the other hand, have codes of moral and legal conduct and written laws enforcing standards of moral and physical behaviors and actions. These laws and regulations regulate the behavior of human beings even in extremis and prove to be constraints on potential behavior alternatives. Though some organizations or entities don't believe the rules and morals of warfare apply, civilized countries (admittedly from my Western bias) have self-imposed legal and moral constraints concerning boundaries of acceptable behavior, even while in combat against an enemy who is cruel and murderous.
5. The Western legal system constrains behavior even though the perpetrators I just listed have no code of conduct. ISIS barbaric activities and the brutal behavior of each side in the Syrian civil war come to mind as examples. Russian aggrandizement against Ukraine in the Crimea takeover comes to mind too. But a point to remember for all of us is this—people in conflict often find themselves constrained in their behavior against their enemies due to capabilities, morals, values, ethos, public

opinion, and the like. But in conflicts constraints must be either self-imposed or otherwise imposed and enforced. Constraints prove to be only as good as self-enforcement or external enforcement. In the ideal, combatants would stick with self-denial and live with the constraint of not employing all diplomatic, economic, informational, and military capabilities and to purposefully lessen the passion inherent to and empowering capabilities and strength of motive, thus lessening the destructive potential in fights. Nonetheless, in real and modern situations, ruthless people mouth the words of constraint only to proceed to unloosen their capabilities not only on their adversary's fighters but also against innocent civilians, for example, Assad's use of chemical weapons against his own people in the Syrian Civil War. Obviously, the ideal was, is, and never will be reached in that situation. The only solution for resolution is for outside imposition and true enforcement of constraints on all sides.

6. I believe if any of our immoral enemies survive (many appear inclined to fight to the death), they must be tried for crimes against humanity given the prosecutorial side has the evidence to proceed in a moral and legal way. Even the Japanese Bushido code, which legally allowed Japanese troops to commit atrocities against enemies with a strict code of behavior that abhorred surrender and worshiped honorable death, could not save responsible senior Japanese officers and politicians from confinement or the gallows after World War II. The Nazis committed mass murder and atrocities within the legalities of their respective legal codes, but the top leaders were not allowed to get away with this behavior. In their minds, war was war, and brutal, and the victors could do as they pleased. When people hate, when they want to grab land and to impose their *will* on others to force them into compliance about what they should think, how they should worship, live, and so forth, then international law does not serve to alter their behavior to the extent the civilized nations would want. With the Nuremberg trials and those in Tokyo, the framework of international law came into being. It has not deterred genocide and wars of aggression to the extent civilized humanity had hoped following World War II.
7. Positional: A situation or condition dictating favorable or unfavorable circumstances. This kind of constraint often involves the mental and emotional acknowledgement of positional advantage and disadvantage—current and postulated. Such acknowledgements affect decision making, extant capability, and strength of motive to impose one's life force on the opponent and to counter his efforts to deny or block or parry your imposition. Even the faintest hint of being at a disadvantage causes a diminution of decision capabilities, a sapping of the energy coming with high morale, or conceding the opening gambit to the opponent. Let us consider a few examples. Again, realize that

positional constraints flow back and forth among combatants as advantage and disadvantage move to first one side then the other with changes in the operational context. As an example, in July 2006 Israel invaded Lebanon because northern Israel was under constant surface to surface missile attacks from Hezbollah operatives in southern Lebanon. The context and the Hezbollah's use of it for advantage—position, freedom of movement, initiative, and knowledge—forced the Israelis to take sufficient action to kill or force the perpetrators to move farther north and thereby move their missiles out of range of northern Israel. When the Israelis moved their formidable military into southern Lebanon, they did not perform well. They faced constraints imposed by modern irregular, indeed hybrid, warfare and a heavily urbanized operational context. The adversary had constructed bunkers and antitank ambushes and set in improvised explosive devices (IEDs) along the many streets and alleys in the densely populated villages and cities of southern Lebanon. They used cyber attacks and cruise missiles (crude), they employed drones, they used terrorism, and, of course, viewed the social media as a weapon system. The Hezbollah dug in and buried their command posts, which became deep and hardened targets under dwellings and commercial business buildings. Their positions located deep in the ground under and atop of urban terrain became what I consider to be a definite positional advantage. In this case, the Hezbollah possessed the positional advantage because the ground they chose to fight on happened to be in villages and cities. The mass media became a contributor in this fight because they could and did report from the dangerous midst of the fighting. The positional advantage of one connected mind over another began to gain the initiative due to the constraints the Israelis were initially fighting under, or which would soon be levied due to public outrage from around the world over the destruction of private property, significant humanitarian problems, and the killing of innocents. It became apparent that due to positional constraints, the Israelis were the "ogres" and in August 2006, their national decision makers pulled out the Israeli Defense Forces (IDF). The IDF endured a bloody nose not only in physical losses but also in the moral domain of war in which positional constraints on the Israelis proved to be positional advantages to the Hezbollah, even in cyber, informational, and cognitive vertical domain silos.[2]

2. Please recall that I have taken the U.S. Department of Defense's depiction of five domains of war and 1) labeled these domains as domains of conflict and 2) added two—information and cognition—for a total of seven domains. I will discuss more about this addition and renaming later in the book.

As you have certainly surmised by now, constraints prove omnipresent in every type of conflict. Thus, our decision maker and his Über-thinker and thought pilgrim always remain wary of constraints and doubly wary about how their adversary could plan to exploit their constraints and sense of urgency. Oh, I heard you mutter, how can the politicians or the CEOs or policy makers expect us to win with the constraints that they place upon us? Sometimes such questions are valid, and the action effort of imposition is not possible given the constraints policy or national decision makers impose upon their military action arm. These considerations always come forth in any quest for superiority over their adversary. Every decision maker would like to work in a constraint-free operational context, but constraints are the way of the world. Sometimes the constraints are political because of the supremacy of civilian decision makers over the military. Quite often our adversaries don't have to cope with the same level of constraints as western military forces, but they always have some kind of constraints—we just have to think deeply about their presence, find them, and affect them to gain advantages (one, two, or all seven advantages available to competitors of any kind). It is always in an adversary's best interests to take advantage of their own minimal constraints and exploit their adversary's sometimes debilitating constraints.

Let's take a few minutes and review three constraint considerations likely to arise in conflict. In pursuing this line of thought, all of us must consider too the reduction of these considerations for any adversary under almost all scenarios. This is duality playing out once again. The first consideration about constraints involves moral constraints. As a reminder, moral means "principles or a code of conduct that defines acceptable and unacceptable activities and behavior and the goodness or their antipode as human beings." As we consider morals relative to a conflict with an adversary from another culture, we easily understand how differences among cultures prescribe not only dissimilar behaviors from one another but also dissimilar views about conflict and subsequent influences on the many ways people can conduct themselves and their actions. It is for certain the two sides in any conflict won't agree on what is moral, and no amount of arbitration can help moderate this difference. For our adversaries, it can be a lever, a seam, or an indirect approach to exploit. For friendly forces, the morality is a vulnerability and therefore must be thought about, considered, wargamed, and buttressed in strength. The friendly force always assumes that their adversary most assuredly must attempt to exploit friendly morality so as to gain advantages similar to those I list earlier.

A second consideration concerns the use of weapons. We conclude it is quite easy to think about super weapons such as nuclear weapons and the self-induced constraint on their use unless someone uses them against us first. Sometimes people don't use weapons of mass destruction because of moral considerations, possible retaliation by the opposite side, and a reprehensible cost/effect ratio. Now, to be certain, America today faces adversaries who would use weapons of mass destruction given they could develop themselves or buy one or two nuclear devices from countries such as Russia, Ukraine, or North Korea.

A third consideration involves the operational context. In a big city, for example, technically oriented intelligence collection and communications system don't work nearly as well as in open terrain. This is an operational context constraint. Also, an advantage accrues for an adversary who knows the infrastructure and icons in a city, both part of the infrastructure. Another challenge facing U.S. forces in particular involves fighting a counterinsurgency in a city and understanding all the elements, functions, interactions, transactions, nonverbal behavior, etc. inherent to the particular operational context. In addition, a city offers possible advantages and disadvantages to all sides in a conflict. One has to be careful to understand the context relative to the enemy's views and how he thinks he can gain advantages. In a city, many buildings must be safeguarded due to their use and importance after the conflict; important parts of infrastructure, for example, are necessary to support human existence. As a last point about operational context and how it constrains each side in a conflict, if local residents support the insurgents or terrorists, this support becomes a constraint for government people. The protected buildings and elements of infrastructure can be important for ensuring the populace has the wherewithal to live, receive food, receive medical aid, and so forth. Of course, our adversary uses these off-limits buildings to work in or to tunnel below, using the context as a shield for their activities.

PRESSURE POINTS, DECISIVE POINTS, AND CENTERS OF GRAVITY

These three phenomena—pressure points, decisive points, and centers of gravity—solidly connect to one another and, of course to constraints. Each could easily represent "that which is most important," but the most important characteristic of this line of thought involving the three is realizing how they relate and what happens when an adversary attacks two or three at the same time. Before proceeding further, I certainly recognize that one can find many pressure points (the definition is coming) in any opponent, and they most often prove less invasive in my system of thought than decisive points and centers of gravity. In this disciplined, rigorous way of thinking, I want you to discover a certain freedom to reason in an often-unfree world. Thus, we circle back and reengage our minds, and we consider pressure points.

Let us take this moment to contemplate our theoretical adversary's possible pressure points in which we might influence his thoughts and subsequent actions to our benefit. Of course, we have to assume the adversary has thought about and knows pressure points, but perhaps not; pressure points, however, are situationally dependent. Once we develop our list of the adversary's pressure points, we balance the equation with how the adversary could view friendly pressure points without constraints. Then we swing to the adversary's side and apply constraints from his perspective and then decide which of his pressure points would be left. We do the same for ourselves through his voyeuristic plundering of our supposed thoughts. If the pressure point involves a constraint from his perspective, he protects it. We comprehend how he reasons about this constraint, one or more pressure points, how he intends to protect them. But, typically, an adversary cannot protect all of his pressure points—they number too many and some prove off limits due to being a constraint. This line of thinking leads the deep thinker to infer that he or she must design ways to directly or indirectly affect pressure points and protect ours because they affect constraints and thus affect capabilities, which both influence resolve to win conflicts of any kind.

One can find advantages within the pressure points and attempt to exploit them to gain influence, if not for a lengthy time, then for a short burst. Nonetheless, many pressure points, in the aggregate, could truly be one of several decisive points and several decisive points in the aggregate could be one or more centers of gravity. The outcomes of thinking about these relationships contribute to success or failure in our efforts to determine how our adversary considers his pressure points and our pressure points, as they increase in importance via aggregation. One can hurt their adversary if they can find and influence the adversary's pressure points, decisive points, and centers of gravity at the right times and places with the same desired outcome. Count on him to act against friendly pressure points in this aggregated way too. I must describe this activity as "synchronizing one's influence on one or more pressure points to find and create a desired outcome in an adversary's physical, mental, or psychological approaches to conflict."

As a corollary benefit this process implies, indeed demands, that a friendly force's decision maker consider considers his own pressure points from the adversary's perspectives because he could attempt to attack or manipulate them directly or indirectly. Or, if he misses our pressure points during multiple engagements, battles, and campaigns in struggles for control of the initiative (dictating the terms of action in an operation), he just might stumble upon them in subsequent interactions. I rest assured that my adversary has the desire to relentlessly pursue my pressure points, as in his way of thinking, he realizes how important they are not only to me but to him. Many of our adversaries will be weaker than us and therefore seek asymmetric approaches as this quote provides:

Asymmetric warfare involves a strong force using or threatening to use an advantage that the weaker opponent cannot respond to; it also involves a weak force seeking offsets against the stronger force; and it usually presents a social or political dilemma to the stronger force. In almost any situation a stronger force flaunts its advantage openly and powerfully . . . a weaker force uses an indirect approach to strike at a stronger forces vulnerabilities, and occasionally its strengths.[3]

After all, striking pressure points can open one or more "windows of opportunity" to interfere with our criteria for success involving the quality markers for enacting aims, goals, objectives, and strategy. It follows that we now have in our repertoire of possible targets yet another insight into what an adversary might do, as we reach a promontory of high-level thought along the ascent from the pits of Plato's Cave.

Upon examination, one can search for and find decisive points. Fewer in number, they prove more difficult to find and manipulate than pressure points. They prove important because they provide a "pheromone trail" to centers of gravity. And degrading or disturbing a decisive point can cause significant reverberations in purpose, strength of motive, capabilities, and potentially the rest of our 14-element thought archetype. Furthermore, to find and successfully attack or manipulate an adversary's centers of gravity is the most difficult due to their fewer numbers, and the notion that any formidable adversary will recognize their importance; thus, he vigorously hides and protects them. In particular, this notion of centers of gravity is difficult to attack or manipulate because of their importance, which causes our adversary to protect his centers of gravity while attacking his opponent's. "Wait," my Über-thinker emphatically states before going on to say, "Don't the adversary's centers of gravity relate to our centers of gravity?" I answer, "Yes, of course they relate. I always ponder and look for my adversary's centers of gravity. I also ponder and anticipate how he views my centers of gravity and how he might try to find and affect my centers of gravity. At the same time, I acknowledge that the adversary considers his own centers of gravity and how I could be intending to affect them, as well as how I contemplate my own centers of gravity and how I anticipate the enemy will target them, his means to attack them, and how he anticipates my protective measures."

Each of the three concepts solidly connect with one another, but each prove to be somewhat different in definition and conceptual structuring. All of these points can be difficult to influence, as we assume any adversary knows "that which truly matters" but flails, not unlike us, when he attempts to understand "that which truly matters" to his adversary. Nonetheless, our adversary promises to defend attempts to influence "that which truly matters" to him—pressure points, decisive points, and centers of gravity. With the antithesis, I must identify "that which truly matters" to

---

3. Wayne Michael Hall, *Stray Voltage War in the Information Age* (Annapolis, MD: Naval Institute Press, 2003), 44–45.

me and then anticipate and defend any of his attempts to intrude and influence these points of interest and power. Let us proceed by first discussing pressure point and what it means.

- Pressure point—It means a sensitive, critical point, weakness, or dispute against which an adversary directs pressure of many kinds. Such actions against pressure points always have a distinct purpose in mind, and the dispenser of said action must possess a dedicated effort to see whether the tactics of action against the pressure point are working or not and, if not, to find what could work to convince the adversary to abandon his effort. A pressure point always has a logical connection with the situation at hand and its pressure points via a heavily related hierarchy as follows: 1) pressure point(s)—important; 2) decisive point(s)—very important; and 3) center(s) of gravity—vital. One can find advantages and disadvantages buried within the pressure points they find and attempt to influence.
- Decisive point—A geographic place, specific key event, critical factor, or function that, when acted upon, allows commanders to gain a marked advantage over an adversary or contribute materially to achieving success.[4]
- Center of gravity—Clausewitz said that "[o]ne must keep the dominant characteristics . . . in mind. Out of these characteristics a certain center of gravity develops, the hub of all power and movement."[5]

What the adversary doesn't know, however, is that through deep thinking, exploitation of the unity of opposites, and advantages forthcoming in the battle for knowledge supremacy via knowledge and thought combat,[6] we discovered a crevice in the adversary's mind and his thinking about pressure points, decisive points, and centers of gravity that the deep thinker can exploit. Any Über-thinker and thought pilgrim can provide the intellectual ability and resolve to lead our thinking about such a crevice to seek and select the best outcomes from its presence and fortunate discovery. In such thought, they consider the steepness of the crevice's walls comprising its V, where the crevice leads, the possibility of a deceptive "ambush" lurking within the crevice, what we could assault, how this hypothetical assault might help us get at his pressure points, decisive points, and/or center(s) of gravity and ultimately, present an indirect approach to attack.

4. U.S. Joint Publication 1-02, March 2017.

5. Clausewitz, *On War,* 595–596.

6. That is to say, we must engage the adversary in mind versus mind, thinking versus thinking, and knowledge versus knowledge. See Timothy L. Thomas's paper "Like Adding Wings to the Tiger: Chinese Information War Theory and Practice" (Fort Leavenworth, KS: Foreign Military Studies Office, 2001).

Ever-present relationships provoke choices, dynamics, and unforeseen interactions on any field of strife. Our deep thinker can find multiple pressure points, but with decisive points, fewer, and with the center of gravity portion, our thinker finds only one or two. Consider a funnel. One finds multiple pressure points in the open end, but as the funnel narrows, fewer decisive points, and at the tip of the funnel only one or two centers of gravity in the particular field of view of a conflict we are taking. Many of these funnels exist on a field of strife. This reduction exemplifies the narrowing phenomenon, which places pressure on our people because finding and affecting the narrow end of the funnel of this schematic is much more difficult than locating and influencing pressure points at the funnel's broad opening. With deep thinking, one also might be able to see the veneer of protection the adversary has designed to thwart our efforts to influence any of his pressure points, decisive points, and centers of gravity. So, anticipating hidden pressure points, decisive points, and center(s) of gravity always occurs, but to excel, our thinkers should ruminate like the adversary and how he might be considering his pressure points, decisive points, and center(s) of gravity, and his view of his own strengths and weakness, hiding them, or flummoxing our attempts to find them, and how we might attack his efforts and thus beat him.

A decisive point could be a hinge between two divisions of an army, for example, the presence of the purposefully weakened French division on Napoleon's southern (right) flank at the battle of Austerlitz in 1805. This kind of a decisive point involves physical capabilities, location on terrain (this division's placement on a series of small ponds, the Goldbach Ponds), and psychological, as when the Russian soldiers came off the Pratzen heights and rushed to the sounds of battle in the thick fog and gun smoke of the Austerlitz battlefield, they had to be psychologically high as they rushed forth only to be downfallen when they realized they had fallen for a ruse. Our deep thinkers must "ride the wild pendulum" of duality and think about how the adversary thinks about his decisive points relative to how he believes his adversary thinks now only about their own decisive points, but more importantly how this adversary thinks we think he thinks about his own decisive points and how he could protect it/them via deception, physical protection, or locational protection.

One of the most enduring and controversial of the many thoughts that Clausewitz presented in *On War* involves his description of a center of gravity (COG) in war. The United States Military's Joint Staff defines center of gravity as "[t]he source of power that provides moral or physical strength, freedom of action, or *will* to act."[7] I quarrel with the word "center" when it should be "centers." In this day and age, there will be, are, or

7. JP 1-02, March 2017.

in an incipient sense, multiple COGs. These centers connect one to the other. They undoubtedly exist in all seven vertical domain silos and at all four levels of conflict troughs. I have no doubt that in his day, possessing his predominant train of thought one always worked against a single COG, which he said was the adversary's army. But even he equivocates and essentially backs off of the notion of singularity relative to this concept. He does this via dialectical arguing with himself in his book *On War* and might have clarified the contradiction, if he had been able to edit the entire book.[8]

In my world, cohesion means coherence of parts or elements; parts or elements are solidly conjoined; especially the conjoining of elements and other divisions of organizations, people, equipment, maintenance, rest, logistics, communications, and so forth. Three ideas come forth: First, multiple centers of gravity exist to this day. Second, the importance of intelligence and reporting was invaluable but often not reliable. Regardless, a leader needs these bits and pieces of data to make judgments about pressure points, decisive points, and centers of gravity. Third, to impose one's way of thinking on an adversary (if he is clever) one must never strike against his COGs in just one domain, but in multiple domains and across all levels of conflict. I propose one can and should find such places and know they are sensitive. Connections and relationships exist galore in the complicated fields of strife that our military faces but also in competition among athletes and in competition and takeovers within the corporate world.

The process of which I speak is a difficult mental effort for many reasons, but most important, this phenomenon causes conflict to be much more complicated as the pieces of centers of gravity appear broken apart and seemingly disparate when they are really roughly similar but different in size and roles. The difficulty with modern conflicts also comes with changing roles and missions, problem sets, assumptions, truth, evidence, and facts. Furthermore, now people in conflict require a holistic perspective to understand the pieces and parts that make whole cohesive as well as the whole under our consideration. Anybody engaged in conflict with a wily foe must be superior in the mind so as to win complicated mental combat battles, engagements, and campaigns. One has to reason about and identify the element, part, or piece of a subordinate whole's "diaspora." Nonetheless, our minds grow too, and the potential for exploiting one's mind for our cause, safety, winning, and so on can work with this complexity. But the mind needs to be prepared thoroughly to provide decision makers these mental skills.

---

8. Clausewitz died unexpectedly of cholera in 1834 while in the process of editing his masterwork.

As it happens, one finds the implements of "war" at work, but aperiodically, or so it seems. But combatants first recognize and then affect their adversary's capabilities. Capabilities are peculiar to an adversary, as it is from his perspective that some gadget, bomb, device, computer, etc., becomes capable of assisting him and his imposition actions. Everything connects in some way, including capabilities, but this is not a new revelation.

We also find ourselves pitted against unseen adversaries, but they surely exist. Thus, many people engage in bouts of mental combat[9] every day. One finds in our world people connected via social media, collaboration, organization, leisure, and communication systems. Communications, computers, and data flows and conduits and storage all relate, but communications connect to people and organizations. Logistics connect to people, organizations, and weapons systems. Even the fields of strife connect—the engagement, battle, and campaign; tactical, operational, strategic; operational context—individual context with micro-contexts with small macro-contexts, with large macro-contexts; forward deployed with sanctuary; U.S. people and organizations and fighting forces with allies.

When contemplating the additive, indeed the collective nature of these seemingly disparate parts, elements, and pieces of a whole, one finds several centers of gravity—they possess various degrees of importance in the whole. For example, in a very simplistic way, let us contemplate an adversary's mobile surface to surface missile systems (SSM). Upon contemplation of the problem set, our Über-thinker and thought pilgrim discover several important parts and elements in the seas of data they can access. Some we can call micro-centers of gravity but in aggregated form, and at a higher level of conception, they would be considered macro-centers of gravity (MCOGs). This MCOG can be in the same domain, but it also relates to other similar elements via connections among SSM in other domains and at different levels of conflict. These parts of a SSM system are not isolated. Some of them could be powerful by themselves. If all of the elements of the SSM system work holistically as one whole, the SSM not only affect the tactical and operational levels, but also the strategic (military) strategic (policy) levels of conflict. The great power available to people who employ mobile SSM cuts vertically through all vertical domain silos—air, ground, sea, space, cyber, information, and cognition and across the four planes that I call—horizontal levels of conflict troughs—tactical, operational, strategic (military), and grand strategic (policy)—these sickle cuts can affect actions and activities in all conflict activities in any operational context.

---

9. *Mental combat:* The constant multidomain, multilevel, multispectrum cognitive conflict or competition in which people and entities attempt to impose their *will* on opposing side(s) by possessing and employing superior mental functioning while resisting the opposing side's efforts to impose their *will*.

Our Über-thinker and thought pilgrim push their minds to think holistically. They assemble what appears to be disparate, scattered, and meaningless into a whole in which parts, pieces, and subordinated systems congeal into a coherent and formidable aggregation.[10] Their observation is true among levels of conflict (tactical, operational, strategic (military) and grand strategic (policy) because everything at these levels are parts of the same whole and vulnerable to the mobile SSM's potential to inflict damage. Flipping this coin of thinking capabilities, consider an adversary who wants to use all the parts and pieces of his scattered whole in a timed and synchronized way. He then wants his whole to purposefully and quickly disaggregate after firing and hide. He depends upon an intelligence system (higher headquarters or nodes) to gather data relevant to assess the damage (physically and psychologically) as his missile strikes. Then, timed with when the missile lifts off and heads for its target, the adversary breaks his SSM system apart for security. He relies upon his higher headquarters for intelligence sufficient to assess outcomes of his action—the missile launch. Since this is an important target, adversaries push their intelligence to collect data pertinent to the strike (this is interesting and the reason for extreme importance of this data-gathering operation and appearance of a counterstrike). I'm sure by now you realize the importance of adversary co-evolution and his attempt to retard friendly co-evolution. He pushes his own co-evolution with assessment tools and evaluates, learns, shares, and adapts speedily enough to adapt faster than his adversary. So their intelligence collection capabilities become a center of gravity, or said another way, that which truly matters. The adversary must anticipate friendly intrusion and protect his methods of co-evolution and adaptation.

I counsel my Über-thinker and thought pilgrim to learn how their adversary might react to his successful launch and search for assessment data to judge the outcome of the missile strike; they do this by requesting intelligence support from their chain of command or in industry their sources of power to assess the action. So, this system 1) acts; 2) assesses results; 3) develops observables; 4) collects data; 5) evaluates the data; 6) learns from this evaluation; 7) shares the insights to other nodes of the system; and finally, 8) adapts—of course, they hope to adapt faster than their adversary, who has to collect and analyze relevant data for this aspect of the duel as well.

---

10. This kind of thinking has been used since Sun Tzu's time. Napoleon used it, as did Clausewitz, T. E. Lawrence, von Manstein, Patton, Eisenhower, Marshall, and Nimitz and MacArthur in the Pacific. In modern times, Air Force (Retired) Colonel John Boyd wrote a wonderful paper—"Destruction and Creation"—but he never published it, as he wanted more people to read and use his thoughts more than what he expected from a journal.

To cause the greatest effects on any adversary, one has to assault (tangibly or intangibly) the adversary's multiple, connected (vertically and horizontally) COGs with an assemblage of weapon systems (again, tangible and intangible). They cannot hide from us, they cannot move without being detected, and we are relentless and remorseless in our quest to impose our volition on even the simplest as well as the most sophisticated adversary. One has to use this method of thinking from action to assessment to adaptation faster than any adversary leveraging the software tools and networks the friendly side controls. In essence, one must turn his center of gravity—his assessment system—into our center of gravity, our assessment system so as to outthink him, seize the initiative, preempt his firing, and destroy him or his essential parts. Our deep thinking and planning enables the supported decision maker or policy maker to thereby "maneuver" the right kind of big data, the data conduits, the computers, the sensors, the minds, the knowledge, the organizations, and the virtual knowledge environments into a large, functioning whole and employ it at the right place, at the right time, against the right observables, and, of course, directed at the right activities to create the right effects, all relating to the adversary's COGs.

Any center of gravity has related "siblings" (smaller but also attached to larger COGs) and "parents" (larger but also attached to smaller COGs)—each roughly similar to one another but, of course, somewhat different in size, capabilities, limitations, and vulnerabilities. Well-run adversary functions and organizations always relate and connect first in functions/outputs and second in form. Please notice, certain kinds of activities, actors, siblings, and parents exist and connect to one another at all levels of war and in all domains of conflict. I consider this finding to be of utmost importance in winning conflicts in domain-based conflicts. Also, it helps to explain why important systems like intelligence collections, for example, have trouble providing support at all levels and in all domains of conflict.

So, if we consider in a holistic and theoretical sense, COGs are several, but in reality Matryoshka dolls, as I discussed earlier. The metaphor is so important that I am discussing it once more. Smaller aggregates enfold and kludge to larger aggregations. These assemblages (several aggregates "glued" to one another) unfold (gather in, that is) the smaller aggregations, while they now find the smaller aggregation enfolded into larger aggregations which eagerly await their enfolding arrival with unfolding arms. Upon searching for and being guided by higher level reasoning about aggregation analysis, a thinking person seeks and finds with deep thinking, of course, aggregations of capabilities and probabilities. But their smaller and larger pieces stretch and connect across levels within domains of conflict and then among between levels of conflict and domains of conflict.

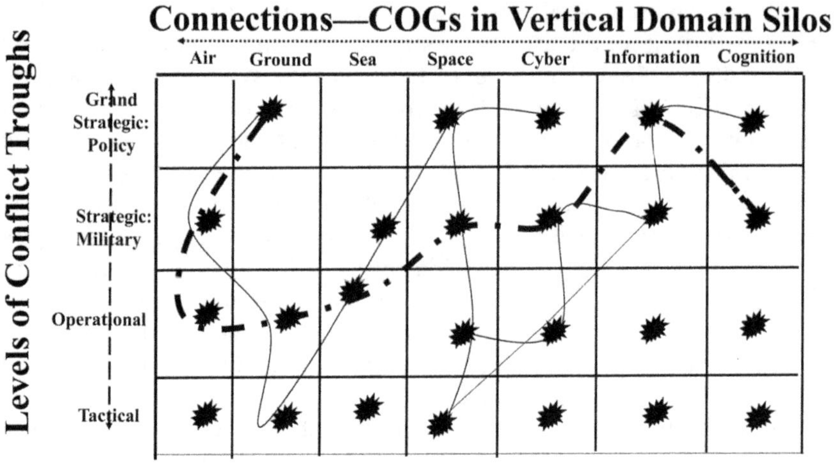

Figure 9.1. Vertical Domain Silos and Horizontal Levels of War Troughs

So, how might deep thinkers ponder the domain and level continuum? In Figure 9.1, please note the presence of seven vertical domain silos of conflict (air, ground, sea, space, cyber, information, and cognition) and four horizontal levels of conflict troughs (tactical, operational, strategic [military], and grand strategic [policy]). With our minds (and eventually actions), each can be crossed and connected with links among actions, activities, data sharing, while conducting offensive and defensive operations.

COGs exist, become neutral, act, and die in each vertical domain silo and at each horizontal level of conflict trough. These COGs, though, are sometimes "active" and sometimes "dormant." Decision makers and their supporting staff must remember how an action at one level of conflict trough or one domain silo can affect several levels and several domains. Conversely, an action at one level, say policy, can influence what happens in several vertical domain silos. Thus, when people use the word "conflict," they find minds compelled to understand the activities and actions that exist and influence in several horizontal levels as well as several vertical domains of conflict. Such thinking is how one must ponder COGs too. If one desires to influence the adversary's vision for winning, they have to reason holistically and relationally across vertical domain silos of conflict as well as up and down horizontal levels of conflict troughs—an action in one place not only affects COGs in a particular location but influences COGs at other levels of conflict troughs and in domain silos too. The search for COGs, decisive points, and pressure points has to occur via this kind of connectedness. This applies to pressure points and decisive points too, but for ease in understanding, I chose to portray just centers of gravity. It

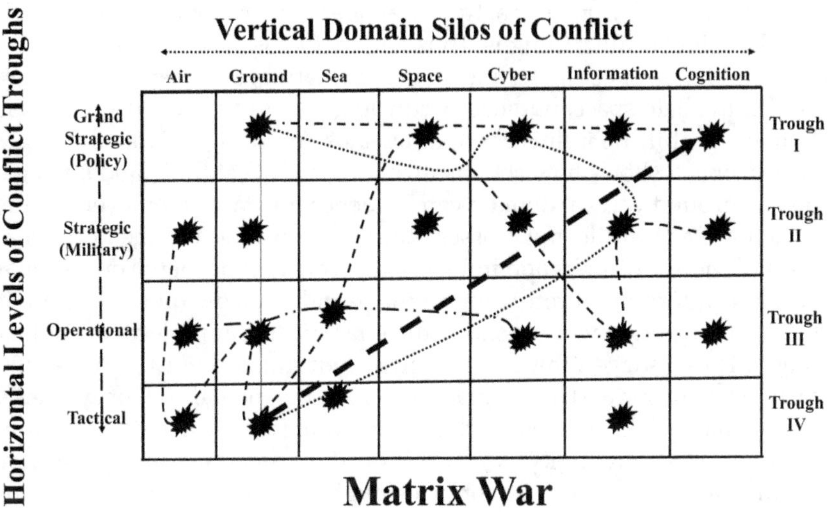

Figure 9.2. COG Connections in Domain Silos and Levels of Conflict Troughs

is with this view and the implied skills to ruminate that we shall employ to prevail against any adversary. Without this kind of thinking, one's mental drive loses not only the struggle for ascendency of *will,* but he also loses the capability to seek, find, and sustain advantages. You can see how things connect in this graphic with seven vertical domain silos and four horizontal levels of conflict troughs. Actions occur in these silos and troughs but these actions relate and affecting a COG at one level can affect other COGs in other silos and other conflict troughs.

While keeping the previous paragraph and its accompanying graphic in mind, our Über-thinker and thought pilgrim venture even deeper into the rabbit hole of the unknown. Importantly, these centers of gravity connect vertically and horizontally as you can see. Also, consider that some of the vertical domain silos have several COGs that involve, for example, the air domain—a COG at the tactical, operational, and strategic (military) levels of conflict troughs. These COGs connect with and depend upon one another. But they also connect with other COGs in other domain silos, which one also finds at several levels of conflict troughs.

Figure 9.2 is about relativity and connectedness. As you can see, once again, one finds vertical domain silos and horizontal levels of conflict troughs. As I previously described, one finds COGs at levels of conflict troughs and in vertical domain silos each roughly similar but larger or smaller depending on the systems importance and complexity, but all connected in a unified whole. The starbursts signify actions with COGs in a conflict, which disturb the universe not only within the particular silo (in the vertical silo), but also activities at or among one or more of the horizontal levels of conflict troughs. Thus, several COGs in several domain silos at several levels of conflict come to life, fibrillating, as it were, influencing their immediate space, but also perturbing the universe, and thus cause change and shifting influences in other silos and troughs. Note the larger dashed line. It shows how actions involving a COG at the grand strategic (policy) ground vertical domain can influence not only other levels in this particular vertical silo, but crosses other domain silos and the horizontal levels of conflict troughs and influences space and cyber at the operational level and information returning to the grand strategic (policy) before it settles on cognition vertical silo at the strategic (military) level of conflict trough. Thus, I suggest this proclamation—our thinkers must purposefully learn to be holistic and artful practitioners in the mental skill of synthesis and ultimately holism to use and leverage what I just described. Generally speaking, one's proclivity is to work on the immediate in a particular domain silo at the particular conflict trough of immediate action without understanding how profoundly this one action on one COG can connect and cause perturbation in other COGs at other levels of conflict troughs and in other domain silos.

One can find (if they look and think about what they see) domain silos that exist but are sliced horizontally by these four levels of conflict I have identified. Consider the burst in the air domain silo at the operational trough, which reverberates to the ground, sea, space, and cyber vertical domain silos and at the strategic (military) trough of conflict. Can one infer the presence of a maxim stalking our minds as we converse here? That is to say, actions against COGs in one domain or one level can affect COGs in several other domain silos and other levels of conflict troughs. One has to anticipate reverberations, watch for them, and decisively act appropriately.

An action against a COG in one domain silo can not only affect the health and vibrancy of the COG in that domain silo, but spread horizontally up or down or both up and down several levels of conflict troughs. But how do people combine duality, synchronization, and synergy into a whole and use them against the foe relative to what we have learned about the vertical domain silos and horizontal levels of conflict troughs? One must be able to analyze, synthesize, and enjoy the magic of holism too. If our considerations about vertical domain silos and horizontal levels of conflict troughs prove to be true for one side, should it not be the truth for the other side? Thus, I would design recommendations for actions that assault COGs in several domain silos and horizontal levels of conflict troughs at the same time to create seemingly disparate but actually combined effects and thereby unleash the violent winds and fires of synergy. The adversary does likewise; therefore, I prepare to meet him and win.

In this chapter, I provide the definition of constraint: *"a restraint or limitation on action or behavior owing to morals, lack of resources, limited capabilities, limited time, contextual limitations, legal, or cultural inhibitions."* Constraints always relate to pressure points, decisive points, and centers of gravity. They have to protect these sensitive areas or activities, etc., as their adversary resolves to come after them with sound and fury. The antithesis also holds true. That is to say, the adversary undoubtedly knows his constraints and that his enemy is certain to come after them. I provide four kinds of constraints and their characteristics. These constraints include 1) translatable; 2) moral; 3) legal; and 4) positional. One never finds a pure context where constraints do not exist. Constraints dictate imposition of action, but constraints can change due to turbulence inherent to chaos, co-evolution, and adaptation. I explain that my advice regarding constraints is to be agile and ready for rapid change. I urge my readers to understand that constraints always change, which highlights the importance of rapid interpretation and adaptation for each side in a conflict. Constraints often exist and influence many aspects of conflict, but three very sensitive to constraint perturbation deserve one's interest now: pressure points, decisive points, and centers of gravity. In this chapter, I present definitions and discussions of these three terms. I also provide two ways of viewing domains and levels of conflict. As such, I propose to my readers of a new presence—a matrix of seven vertical domain "silos" and four levels of conflict "troughs." At the intersections of the vertical domain silos and horizontal levels of conflict troughs the reader can see 28 cells in what we now have—a 28-cell matrix. It is in these cells where the struggles for superiority in combat occurs. It is here one finds, *Matrix War.*

Since centers of gravity exist at all levels, it makes sense that COGs, as wholes or broken apart and spread through several cells, upon perturbation, even extremis, can cause perturbation with their "parents" and other centers of gravity in other cells, in other vertical domain silos, and at multiple levels of conflict troughs. All four concepts are important as separate entities, but in fact, my thematic thread of connectedness stiches these concepts into an entwined bundle—a whole as it were. When one of the four concepts feel influence and change, the others feel the disturbance and change too—such changes can be positive or negative depending on one's position and thinking. I asked my readers to remember my admonition—all the pieces, links, connections, and thoughts matter, so they must wargame, anticipate, and preempt your adversary's attempts to attack your constraints, pressure points, decisive points, and centers of gravity and how he intends to protect his from your attempts to attack his vital four points.

In this chapter, I reviewed the definition and conceptual explanation of constraint: *"a restraint or limitation on action or behavior owing to morals, lack of resources, limited capabilities, limited time, contextual limitations, legal, or cultural inhibitions."* Constraints always relate to pressure points, decisive points, and centers of gravity—all key in winning engagements, battles, and campaigns. They have to protect these sensitive areas or activities, etc., as their adversary surely comes after them with sound and fury. The antithesis also holds true. That is to say, the adversary undoubtedly knows his constraints and that his enemy is certain to come after them. I provided four kinds of constraints and their characteristics. These constraints include 1) translatable; 2) moral; 3) legal; and 4) positional. One never finds a pure context where constraints do not exist. Constraints dictate imposition of action, but constraints can change due to turbulence inherent to chaos, co-evolution, and adaptation. I explained that my advice regarding constraints, it is agile and a harbinger of rapid change. I urged my readers to understand that constraints will always change, which highlights the importance of rapid interpretation of the context and actions therein, and ensuing adaptation for each side in a conflict. In this chapter, I presented definitions and discussions of pressure points, decisive points, and centers of gravity. I also provided two ways of viewing domains and levels of conflict. As such, I proposed to my readers a new appearance—a matrix of seven vertical domain "silos" and four levels of conflict "troughs." At the intersections of the vertical domain silos and horizontal levels of conflict troughs the reader discovered 28 cells in what we now have—a 28-cell matrix. It is in these cells where the struggles for superiority in combat occurs. Since centers of gravity exist at all levels, it makes sense that COGs, either as wholes or broken apart and spread through several cells, cause perturbation with their "parents" and connected other centers of gravity in other cells, in other vertical domain silos, and at multiple levels of conflict troughs. This depiction helps thinkers know their adversary's and their own pressure points, decisive points, and COGs. I explained how my thematic thread of connectedness stitches these concepts into an entwined bundle—a whole, as it were. When one of the four concepts feel influence and change, others feel the disturbance and change too—such changes can be positive or negative depending on one's position and thinking. I asked my readers to remember this admonition—all the pieces, links, connections, and thoughts matter. Thus, players in any conflict wargame, anticipate, and preempt their adversary's attempts to attack one's constraints, pressure points, decisive points, and centers of gravity and how he intends to protect his from you.

CHAPTER 10

That Which Truly Matters

Argument: *In this chapter, I explain how to search for that which truly matters to our adversary in conflicts. As one side one comprehends that which truly matters from their perspective, they also find the adversary's. Truth varies in the eyes of the beholder. I caution my readers:* Multiple views of truth about that which truly matters exist. *Jittering "truths" influence actions during conflicts of "will." I discuss the need for detailed* wargaming the adversary's wargaming *in a deep-thinking and systematic way aided by software, synthetic contexts, and artificial intelligence (AI). I introduce co-evolution; our adversaries constantly seek feedback relative to a fluctuating context; it causes perturbation in that which truly matters.*

This looks like an obvious statement: Focus on that which is most important as you work your way to imposing actions on a resisting adversary. Whether we comprise an organization, unit, squadron, our goal is to be specific in our thinking. Specificity in thought is a goal whose accomplishment still allows us to recognize a range of probabilities to success in our desired imposition. So, let us proceed along the path to escape Plato's Cave. Let us consider "that which is most important" as one of the major considerations for people who plan, who execute plans, and leaders who make decisions about actions and interpreting outcomes of action, and adapting to assessments of actions. Let us start with most valuable objectives.

CORE[1] OR NUB[2] OF THE ISSUE AT HAND—BOTH SIDES' VIEWS

As a maxim—know the adversary. This knowledge has to be current and true to the best we know in our thinking processes. Knowledge about our adversary is often relative to other relationships, such as those among the adversary, the adversary's opponent, the operational context, the adversary's political base, strength of motive, sources for passion and sacrifice, etc. Conclusions and recommendations must be offered to our decision maker to enable her to act first against this foe so as to grasp and hold on to the initiative. Let us reason about what understanding means and its relationship to comprehension:

- Understand in our efforts here means "to be thoroughly familiar with; to clearly grasp the character, nature, relationships, nuances, or subtleties of a foe, their organization, a given populace, their political base, the culture in which they live, and connecting relationships. Understand is a relative of comprehend, but is neither as intellectually arduous as the latter nor in possession of a total grasp of any particular whole (a thing contained in itself) and its relationships, with potential for emergence and or synergy from a coupling of all the connectedness, parts, and aspects of things, people, organizations, situations and the like."
- Comprehend in our efforts here means "to totally grasp, make sense of, fathom the meaning, visualize a state of being intellectually 'conjoined' with the links that bond elements, aggregates, and aggregations into ever larger wholes; and state of coherence in the object, person, their organization, their aim, goals, objectives, strategies, and tactics falling within our study, appearance, and function of a whole." A person comprehending a phenomenon apprehends its meaning, its parts, it connectors, and its potential. To comprehend, an intellectual assertion is most assuredly a long and firm step beyond the term understand.

Our reasoning processes enable us to comprehend the notion of working against one or more human beings, their organizations, their wealth, their families, and so forth and know their inclination to resist. In attempting to settle the question of comprehending the nature of our conflict or

---

1. *Core*: The focus, central, or most important aspect of a challenge, problem, problem set, outcome, or conflict. It is usually a small aggregation of elements, aspects, or pressure points of a problem. The core of a problem or issue or challenge is so important it must have one's attention—if one ignores the friendly core and the adversary's view of this core, they do so at their peril.

2. *Nub*: The crux of a matter, the essence of, the most important issue, or the kernel of a problem; the epicenter of a problem or most-demanding challenge. It must be attacked, if belonging to a foe; it must be defended against adversary assaults.

competition, our minds work hard to visualize and realize implications of attendant relationships at play and interacting in the fray, regardless of difficulty in our attempts to comprehend one of several wholes. Success in mental combat demands embarking on an extensive journey into the adversary's mind, an important aspect of "that which truly matters." We must do our best to 1) think like him; 2) think like him as he looks and thinks about us; 3) reason like him as he thinks about himself relationally to how we attempt to consider like he considers; and 4) comprehend how he looks and thinks about the influences, pluses, and minuses for both sides in the conflict of using the operational context to gain an upper hand.

To win, think faster and better than your opponent. Our goal is "to be there waiting when he comes" as he attempts to set conditions for or actually starts to initiate actions he has specifically designed to impose his *will* on us. Diving into the increasingly clear waters of culturally induced obfuscation one realizes that with such thinking, they can comprehend "that which truly matters" to the adversary and his discernment of "that which truly matters" to us. A unity of opposites ensues, thus adding antitheses' energy to an already turbulent operational context.

We conclude that our asymmetric adversaries fight using mental combat as a means to enter into episodes of conflict because many adversaries lack sufficient capabilities to fight the United States as a conventional force and win. It seems reasonable (to one's adversaries, so I imagine) to always tilt toward hybrid warfare,[3] or even multidomain conflict, which presents the greatest challenges to America in categories of force for which our military is responsible. I must confess—nobody can think exactly like the adversary or competitor, as we aren't them and they aren't us. But in many a problem set one can creep closely, as there are some things an adversary would have to do to impose his volition on us or our friends. While attempting to think similarly to our adversary, know our thinking will be pummeled by a torrent of possibilities, all possessing varying degrees of friction (unexpected chance events), uncertainty, error, and risk. With that said, one finds no choice—do not ignore this essential aspect of contemplation that this effort requires.

Therefore, we guide our minds and our subordinates and colleagues to learn how to proceed, as one anticipates and accounts for 1) competing with an unpredictable adversary; 2) operating in a peculiar chaos-driven nonlinear operational context; 3) anticipating, alerting to, and pouncing on the presence and influence of sensitive variables, as well as condition setting activities portending offensive actions for the adversary to attempt to influence our

3. *Hybrid warfare*: The diverse and dynamic combination of regular forces, irregular forces, criminal elements, or a combination of these forces and elements all unified to achieve mutually benefitting effects. The source of this definition is U.S. Army, Field Manual 3-0 Operations C-1. GPO, Washington, D.C.: February 2011, pp. 1–5.

decision maker's mind; 4) overcoming bureaucratic obstacles restricting our choice of the right paths to reach the point of sufficient reason to stimulate intellectual growth for this and future eras where thinking dominates both current and future conflict; and 5) overcoming our adversaries with both active learning and heuristics via my how to think models, concepts, and methods of problem solving that this book provides to each reader's mind.

"That which truly matters" is the nub or essence of one's being. The adversary and us, in a condition of duality, determine what I'm speaking about. One way you can consider this dual interacting nub is via Heraclites's unity of opposites, Chinese yin and yang, analysis and synthesis, with one side acting against another resisting side. Yet all work in the same whole, and each entity or force understands how it differs from the other. In particular, one comprehends how each side in a duality views "that which truly matters" to them in various situations, interactions, intersections, transactions, actions, and cultures, all conditioned by life force, philosophical points of view, worldviews, personalities, education, religion, values, and so forth. Duality comes to the forefront as a generic but vital whole into which one must thrust their hands into a mixture of deliberations and thereby feel and understand our adversary's most important considerations, and then adapt accordingly to be superior to our foe in these most important aspects or elements of conflict.

To work with "that which truly matters" to each side, one must again be in the skin and mind of the adversary[4] and see the world, the operational context, his view of us, his own capabilities, and so forth. He must, like us, see these elements and capabilities as neutrally and honestly as a human can determine. To travel inside his mind, one must realize and understand the fine points, subtleties, and ambiguities of his culture, apperception, social mores, military background and experience, education, subjugation to laws, the hold of religion on his being (extent and his knowing what it and the influence of religion drives him to do and how it influences his behavior), and the many pressures that cause stress in the adversary's psyche. We must understand how this being perceives truth—his and ours, but understanding truth rarely appears and it lies in the eyes of the beholden because it changes. Here are two short thoughts that help us move through the thorny and dense clouds of truth:

> Truth is so obscure in these times, and falsehood so established, that, unless we love the truth, we cannot know it.
>
> —Blaise Pascal

> Truth, though for God it may be one, assumes many shapes to men.
>
> —Pieter Geyl

4. Harper Lee, *To Kill A Mocking Bird* (Philadelphia: J. B. Lippincott & Co., 1960), 85–87.

Friendly intelligence analysts and our Über-thinker and thought pilgrim wargame the adversary's mission, his view of the operational context, his view of his targets and missions, his view of the pluses and minuses that the operational context presents, and his view of the obstacles he could possibly run up against. We see this whole—it always involves deep thinking, duality and pendulum thinking—so as to understand how best to reason like the adversary to be inside his mind. It is there that we use our intuition, intellect, reasoning powers, understanding, comprehension, analysis, and synthesis to search for and find the nub of his fight—or in the language of our work here, "that which truly matters"—and also the nub of mind shaping our view of the fight, and play out the game accordingly: act, react, and counteract. Note: U.S. forces or whom we construe to be the friendly do not get to act first all the time (and thus automatically possess the initiative); instead, the initiative has to be fought for, and this struggle is a lens through which the viewer can recognize "that which truly matters." Sometimes (a lot of times in irregular warfare) the adversary has the initiative most of the time.[5] This is wargaming, a necessity in mental combat; it does not occur with the frequency, depth, and intensity it deserves, I have discovered.[6] It always requires specific thought, additional time, and a hefty injection of expertise. This kind of wargaming is much more time consuming and stressful than traditional wargaming (used for course of action). The wargaming of which I speak can take hours and possibly days of intense intellectual work not only internally but also by using external resources to one's organization to think like the adversary, find the sources of "that which truly matters" to him, and massing of minds and machines (via a virtual knowledge environment [VKE]) to develop a plan with its many complicated offshoots appropriate for the problem set. In addition, such detailed wargaming helps decision makers develop plans to accomplish their mission. At a higher level, consider the adversary's organizations and thought processes to include this decision maker's 1) aim; 2) goals; 3) objectives; 4) constraints; 5) resources; 6) strategy; 7) tactics; 8) view of *will*; 9) pluses and minuses of the operational context; 10) need to synchronize; 11) co-evolution; and so on. Our people deliberately assess his actions not only for the sake of co-evolution, but also to imagine the shape and timing of unanticipated data forcing change

5. David Kilcullen, "Twenty-Eight Articles Fundamentals of Company-level Counterinsurgency." *Small Wars Journal*, no. 11 (2006). In article 28 (the last article) this experienced irregular warfare expert portends that the adversary possesses the initiative most of the time and that if friendly forces let this happen, then we shall lose the fight.

6. From 2008 to 2015 I led ~52 one- and two-week advanced analysis seminars to ~1,250 military and intelligence community analysts. It is from their discussions in small groups that I developed this conclusion. I plan to discuss more about this subject throughout this book.

due to its arrival from the operational context, which purveys data and within data, kernels of energy that fuel chaos.

To perform mentally as I describe requires taking steps to stimulate this potential for victory. All players on this stage of strife realize a distinct requirement for resources (e.g., knowledgeable subject matter experts and people of the same ethnicity, morality, language, and culture as the opponent). Success is enshrouded by a few qualifications (as nothing is perfect), including a need for 1) kluging and amassing minds; 2) "maneuvering" them to form a virtual collective intellect to provide knowledge workers in extremis with an amazingly formidable connected intellectual power; 3) accessing all new and old data pertinent to the problem at hand; 4) accessing the tacit knowledge[7] inherent to all organizations; 5) linking and "maneuvering" the combined computing power of several organizations; and 6) accessing and employing organizational processes that make the VKE[8] in question strong, agile, and reliable.

I designed the VKE concept to gain probabilities of sufficient quality for decision makers to possess a good idea about how the adversary decision maker thinks. This estimate of his reasoning is framed by the given current or future situation, how he might view his mission and the central idea of his mission, what he considers to be most germane to his mission, and what he believes to be most germane to the friendly decision maker (again, duality at work).

I designed the VKE concept to perform important duties—thinking, data manipulation, knowledge products—people in extremis cannot perform because of lack of skill or time. The example I have in mind has data scientists of a VKE providing data support to people in extremis. For example, the data people of the VKE may support people in extremis by sustaining and updating their databases, but in particular updating an important triumvirate—baselines, problem sets, and subproblem sets so all are kept current. Such support allows analysts working closer in and with finer granularity time to emplace and merge with the VKE's higher-level data and its visualization. A VKE would also work the operational context and keep track of the operational context's data inputs for both linear and nonlinear systems, which could lead to the properties inherent to emergence of benefits, and as we say, the seven advantages from the operational context. Thus, the VKE concept—its appearance, presence, and use, not unlike a weapon system—has to be another of our "that which truly matters" truisms in our work to comprehend the intricacies of *will* and enable American decision makers to win in conflicts. This support also helps the people in action or danger to mass, maneuver, and swarm minds,

7. *Tacit knowledge*: Knowledge the possessor doesn't know that he possesses.
8. Here, an aggregation of organizations.

collections computers, data, and data networks, organizations, and other VKEs. It helps with the always complicated element of intelligence—anomaly analysis, for example, because of its demands for constantly updated and current baselines, in particular those baselines working with patterns. A VKE that performs at a high level like I envision provides SMEs for analytic wargaming of which I have been speaking. This kind of wargaming pushes, indeed demands, that decision makers to provide early guidance (earlier than ever before) to people who perform this kind of detailed and anticipatory wargaming. Outputs of this kind of wargaming are important, though there is never time to perform all needed musing sufficient to produce desired outputs in an ideal world. So one approaches this dilemma with a solution: A cutline appears in our imaginations and our rational minds go to work. Wargaming outputs above the cutline are worked and finished; outputs below the cutline—delayed until resources become available. Elements and possible outputs above the cutline turn into tasks and worked to completion, while those elements and outputs falling below the cutline wait—they constitute risk.

At this point in our discourse I am going to present you with a graphic offering thoughts about wargaming about *will*. More specifically, Figure 10.1 provides insight into a chosen few of elements essentially important in their potential power—for both sides. Keep this admonition in your minds—if I am planning and wargaming, I can assume my adversary does likewise, but from his perspective. Please rest assured you can add or subtract outputs appearing on this graphic. For example, I only list a few of the important outputs. Readers should add more considerations as they gain knowledge, understanding, and comprehension.

As certain as the occurrences of sunrise and sunset, intelligence practitioners force their minds to read, reason, and soar with one side of their being while the other side clings to routine. The soaring part of the mind connects with the part that remains in stasis—they are as one, a whole as it were, the interaction of opposites constantly interacting but still relating to the theme at work. These wholes come with education, thought, mentorship, and experience, but most important, they come with a powerful individual desire to learn and gain knowledge daily. Such knowledge has to focus on discerning a duality-based explanation for "that which truly matters."

More important for comprehending the meanings and implications in this book, postulate a new whole slowly coming into your consciousness and appearing in your "mind's eye."[9] This new theme involves not only

9. *Mind's eye*: The visualization of what one's rational mind provides—a synthesis of fragments, shreds, and shards of with rational thought and imagination. The mind's eye filters and shunts most of this data into one's under-mind and allows only parcels into the over-mind. Through critical thinking, knowing "how to think," "deep thinking," and employing the doctrine that is "holism" a person can weave both thoughts and data into

Analytic Wargaming Outputs Pertaining to Will

- **Adversary's 'will' (hence strength of motive and objectives)**
  - **Whose 'will' are we discussing – specifics**
  - **What truly matters – his vulnerability to pressure points and decisive points**
  - **Life-force, teleology, vitalism**
  - **Purpose**
  - **Capabilities -- constraints and resources**
  - **Strength of motive, passion**
  - **Determination, perseverance**
  - **Advantage and disadvantage**
  - **Sacrifice**
  - **Incentives and inducements**
  - **Trinity of war, COG**
  - **Recomposition probabilities**
  - **Co-evolution, assessment, adaptation**
  - **Value he places on goals and objectives**
  - **Outcomes – imposition, counters**
  - **Influence of media**

- **Context – its influence on all sides and how these people think about context**
- **Adversary's thinking -- Aim, goal, objectives, resources, constraints, strategies, etc.**
- **Influences of nonlinearity on outcomes of mental combat relative to 'will.'**
- **Influence of culture, apperception, mores**
- **Cross-domain linkages – competing in vertical domain silos and horizontal levels of war troughs**

Figure 10.1. Analytic Wargaming—Outputs

soaring and thus being in a position to observe parts and pieces of wholes, but also synthesizing possibilities (potentialities unbound by constraint) and various roads and pathways, some partially open and some appearing to be too difficult to enter, let along to work through the heavy brambles to bring the most promising of possibilities to life via creative thinking. Any traveler who escapes Plato's Cave seeking to comprehend knowledge and truth must endure mental and physical obstacles to reach the light up, up, outside of Plato's Cave (some aspects of truth keep changing—see Pieter Geyl's quote about truth at the beginning of this chapter), but the rewards are certainly worth the effort and the cost to one's physical, emotional, and intellectual well-being.

Sadly, the latency and collective wisdom of bureaucracies have proven over the years to be intellectually hackneyed. Though all people cannot be innovative, let alone creative, the baseline of thought must be willing to change, innovate, and create lest we endure more Pearl Harbors or 9/11s. Safe, slow, methodical, reductionist thinking seems to dominate our ever-expanding bureaucracies. In my view, leaders must nurture and sprinkle

meaningful tapestries of connections and meaning. The output is, of course, a synthesis of knowledge, understanding, and comprehension.

more innovators and creative people into bureaucracies and help people therein learn how to think via a system of thought for the 21st century. John Kenneth Galbraith describes what I'm worried about:

> To a very large extent, of course, we associate truth with convenience—with what most closely accords with self-interest and personal wellbeing or promises best to avoid awkward effort or unwelcome dislocation of life. We also find highly acceptable what contributes most to self-esteem. . . . But most important of all, people approve most of what they best understand. . . . Therefore, we adhere, as though to a raft, to those ideas which represent our understanding. This is a prime manifestation of vested interest. For a vested interest in understanding is more preciously guarded than any treasure. It is why men react, not infrequently with something akin to religious passion, to the defense of what they have so laboriously learned.[10]

Some bureaucracies have lost the art of thinking, particularly in the critical and creative realms of thought; they grind out simple briefings and papers, work with software programs, and respond to emergencies. Their people "feed the beast" of the production demands of bureaucratic processes. People who could be deep thinkers can lose the skill because of a persisting infection of mediocrity in their thought. They therefore produce just enough to stay in the game, to be graded and judged by the equally complacent. Part of the containing force of which I speak involves individual and organizational "conventional wisdom." Thus "that which is most important" becomes that which sustains the stasis. But if the people in these bureaucracies become armed with knowledge from the soaring part of our beings, something positive can break free from the sticky, grasping muck of intellectual bondage. What we see then is akin to that stirring and overwhelming feeling of joy and how great it is to be alive, as when a baby colt first romps after birth. The great German poet, dramatist, and writer Goethe wrote a superb passage in his epic poem *Faust* describing this dichotomy:

> Two souls, alas! are lodg'd within my breast,
> Which struggle there for undivided reign:
> One to the world, with obstinate desire,
> And closely-cleaving organs, still adheres;
> Above the mist, the other doth aspire,
> With sacred vehemence, to purer spheres.
> Oh, are there spirits in the air,
> Who float 'twixt heaven and earth dominion wielding,
> Stoop hither from your golden atmosphere,
> Lead me to scenes, new life, and fuller yielding.[11]

---

10. Galbraith, *The Affluent Society*, 7.

11. Johann Wolfgang von Goethe, *Faust, Part One*, ed. Charles W. Eliot, LL.D. (Danbury, CT: Grolier Enterprises Corp., 1982), 49–50.

Enough of theory for now. Let's imagine squaring off with a very smart adversary who presents a distinct threat to our interests. He constantly assaults us with a broad band of seemingly disparate actions and behaviors. Some are tools of action and influence, some we can see and some feel, whereas still others remain invisible but capable of assaulting our sense of privacy, stability, and well-being all the same. What would America's bureaucracies think to be the most important interests relative to threats from their perspective? Could it be a unified effort to cooperate with one another to defeat or negate our adversary's actions? What I saw after 9/11 was hopeful—I thought the large bureaucracies in Washington would band together as one. What these large organizations did was revert from altruism to self-interest. I sound like I speak of individuals, but in reality when one emplaces well-meaning people into a bureaucracy, sometimes they tend to be immersed in very separate and distinct bureaucratic ethos; the cultural influences at work can seduce people to accept mediocrity, believe they are doing something smart when it is not, fall into the trap of conventional wisdom, resist change (like cooperating with one another), and sustain the way they typically do things (bureaucratic dislikes, infighting, immunities for obviously wrong behavior). Most people do not know they live and work in Plato's Cave. In my thinking, large bureaucracies sometimes fail to choose the moral high ground for "that which truly matters" and instead pursue inane and irrelevant goals and objectives. "That which truly matters" becomes an unreachable ideal and thus largely irrelevant to the ever so important outcomes of mental and physical conflict.

This smart enemy of which I have been speaking observes how Americans reason about "that which truly matters," including the American way of waging conflicts. What I'm speaking of always involves 1) low military and civilian casualties; 2) a strong military but constantly demonstrating reluctance in using its power; 3) a desired dictum that any conflict must end quickly; 4) refusal to admit to actual war when our national interests become threatened—maintain the same context of everyday life, even when young people are deployed and in action for vague purposes, aims, goals, objectives, strategies, and desired outcomes; and 5) in the end, bureaucracies and people in general act in their self-interests, regardless of how those actions affect the country as a whole. Bureaucracies keep themselves on a normal footing in daily activities even when the country's leadership says we are at war (e.g., Iraq from 2003–2007) and has people deployed and in extremis; they produce lots of rhetoric but very little action. America's *will* at the national level varies from the severe beating America took in Vietnam, when our national strength of motive dissipated, to the wonderful resolve of WWII. With respect to the Vietnam War (1954–1975), few people recognized the absolute duality and actual clash of two *wills*—the

United States and North Vietnam. With the Japanese attack and the German declaration of war against America in WWII, people knew what was most important—it was clear—defeat Germany, Japan, and their allies. In our war in Vietnam, we clearly America did not comprehend our naive, collective considerations regarding the trustworthiness of American political leadership and some governmental agencies, the rationale for being in Vietnam, how America wages war (e.g., bombing, Agent Orange, cluster bombs, napalm), and all the lost lives and money this hideous and fruitless war cost America. Entangled in this morass one can find Lyndon Johnson's volition at war with Ho Chi Min's. Our leaders failed to recognize what I'm speaking about and the tough considerations one has to make. *That which truly mattered* to the North Vietnamese was the steady and singular focus on their vision of a whole—their nationalism was most important, not furthering the cause of international communism. Their war had been occurring for several hundred years. It involved fighting and surely suffering to bring all of Vietnam into a unified whole that stretched into the past whether fighting China, Japan, France, or America. America's take on "that which truly matters" involved keeping America's social programs going, not putting the country on a war footing, not provoking China or the Soviet Union into the war on the side of North Vietnam, and stabilizing South Vietnam and ensuring its independence. A priceless quote comes from Colonel Harry Summers, who captured a discussion he had after the war:

> "You know you never defeated us on the battlefield," said the American colonel.
>
> The North Vietnamese colonel pondered this remark a moment. "That may be so," he replied, "but it is also irrelevant."[12]

The North Vietnamese colonel was speaking, of course, about the importance of the struggle of that which truly mattered. It wasn't the lives lost or the suffering on all sides; it was about a struggle of competing *wills.* Though it is obvious America won the tactical battles, it lost the strategic campaign. In my view, America lost the struggle because we didn't have a grip on this difficult but important concept of *will.* Strangely enough, to this day many a person hasn't seized upon on this exchange in Colonel Summers's book and done much to learn the inherent wisdom you see in the earlier exchange.

Our adversaries look at America's national *will* ranging from 9/11; the war in Iraq and Afghanistan; and the confounding lack of understanding

---

12. Harry Summers, *On Strategy: The Vietnam War in Context* (Carlisle, PA: U.S. Army War College, 1982), 1.

of the military, religious, civil government, and regionalism forces at play in the war. To what end do we fight? Look through the wide lens of the Taliban, ISIS, Syria, America, Russia, Turkey, Kurds, Iran, Israel, Lebanon, Jordan, Iraq, Afghanistan, Pakistan, the Gulf States, and the political commitments of our allies—comprehension of such a view does much for one's comprehension of this great but neglected phenomenon: *will*. Has anybody at all thought about "that which truly matters" to these players acting out their destinies on multiple stages of strife?

Can one say that our national effort focused like a laser beam on "that which was most important" to the United States with our amazingly weak and misguided attempts to impose our desired outcomes and thereby act to either protect or act to reduce that which was most important to the antagonists in the Arab Spring—Benghazi, Tunisia, Egypt, and Syria? I ask you to consider the infamous "red line" and how it became laughable when nothing happened after Assad used chemical weapons. Clearly, the "red line" was a statement of *will*; however, when one makes a strong statement of irrefutable intention to impose their will if the red line is crossed, they must be prepared to engage in conflict to win, if the recipient of the threat continues his miscreant behavior thus calling out the sender, daring him to act. In my view, the strength and sincerity of America's *will* stumbled in this situation, damaging its credibility. Instead, what appeared revealed feckless leaders, and the appearance of laughable threats of action (truly nonaction in the bad neighborhood of the Middle East) contributing to the global spread of ISIS; Iran's continuous marauding in the Persian Gulf, Iraq, and Syria; China's air strip in the South China Sea; and Russia's recidivistic, nationalistic, and destiny oriented escapades in Ukraine and the Crimea. What would you think if you were an enemy of America trying to discern America's *will* and that which is most important? We ourselves cannot answer the question because of the hideous hydra of self-interests in very powerful centers of influence in America. The vision appearing in my mind portrayed more instead of less aggression, more irrelevant but expensive acquisitions, increasing assaults on our global influence from all sides, and the spread of alternative ideologies other than ours in Europe and other places being affected by the Syrian civil war and the influence that ISIS has had on so many countries in the world. This vision—all of it—is antithetical to our values, and, of course, that which truly matters.

I am sure you can infer that the right people must push their how to think skills I am describing; the needs I imply and you infer must be of supreme importance to America's security. For as long as I am alive, I anticipate the continuing separation of capabilities and efforts among the bureaucracies and the nation's top leadership in the executive branch and our leaders' failure to know the seven advantages in sufficient depth to seize the first and most important advantage—the initiative, thereby setting the conditions for action from the sure-to-come varieties of well-planned and camouflaged assaults on our country from Russia, Iran, North Korea, and nonstates like ISIS and drug lords.

Let's stop and perform some basic thinking about that which truly matters. In Clausewitz's day, clearly the adversary's army was most important—in fact, according to him, the opponent's army was the center of gravity. Just as clearly in the Napoleonic wars, two other essential elements crept into the equation of "that which is most important":

- That is to say, the operational context[13] of Napoleon's invasion of Russia in June 1812 was crucially important. Second, though Russian General Kutuzov's defending army was important, it was more important to draw Napoleon into "Mother" Russia than to engage in a pitched battle in which one side or the other would lose the war. Third, occupying Moscow and thinking via if/then logic (if I enter and ravage the heart of Russia and occupy their capital, then I have broken their "backbone" and thereby crushed their *will* and subsequent lack of resolve will lead to capitulation) was a serious miscalculation in Napoleon's thinking. Up to that point in time, Napoleon must have believed that if one side imposed their desire on their adversary, occupied their country and capital, and put the opponent's army on the run, then their dire situation should be more than enough to cause capitulation. Of course, you know what happened. The Battle of Borodino was a draw. Moscow burned, leaving the French with a smoldering pile of rubbish; the Russian tsar refused to capitulate; the Russian army was still intact; the French army was far from Paris; and the infamous Russian winter was setting in and dominating the operational context. All of these inputs and factors caused Napoleon to order a withdrawal that turned out to be a disaster for France.
- So, the lessons for us given this situation follow. As one and most obvious, occupying a country doesn't always break its people's *will* and lead to capitulation. As another lesson, the operational context often proves of definitive importance, and decision makers discount it at their peril. Even as astute as Napoleon was, he and his staff surely underestimated the challenges presented by the Russian expanse, the severity of Russian winters, and the country's terrible roads—as would the German planners of Operation Barbarossa a century later. As Napoleon's invasion proceeded, he found the Russian army conducting orderly withdrawals,

13. *Context*: In abbreviated form: the circumstances surrounding and influencing people in conflict.

not unlike drawing a bowstring to be fired when the French started their withdrawal in December 1812. Keeping this vignette in mind, let's return to thinking about finding a formula or a thought model for helping us discern "that which truly matters" to each side of a conflict. As such, let us dive into the micro and then climb back to the high country to reach a whole of micro- and macro-consideration of "that which truly matters" when anybody considers their opponent's volition. Let us view Figure 10.2.

To impose one's volition, a person needs some basic aspects of conflict on their side. They need resolve—the spark from life force to produce a desire to acquire something that somebody else owns or uses. This inspiration appears first as an apparition but assumes a resemblance of life (the derivative vision from the apparition) and eventually comes forth from a written or spoken vision—articulating actuation of life force. Life force is not easy to either neutralize or destroy. Any given person can find themselves carting a life force of aggression through life. Because of its difficulty to influence, even to understand sufficiently well to snuff out as one would a candle, we must have a go at life force in slightly elliptical ways—that is to say, come at it through the back door and stealthily take his capabilities with which he could use to impose his way of thinking and erode them by pushing his strength of motive down or into a declining state of inertia and thereby cause his capabilities to atrophy (see capabilities in the model shown earlier). Strength of motive holds a mesmerizing power (read influence) over one's interpretation of another's capabilities and his willingness

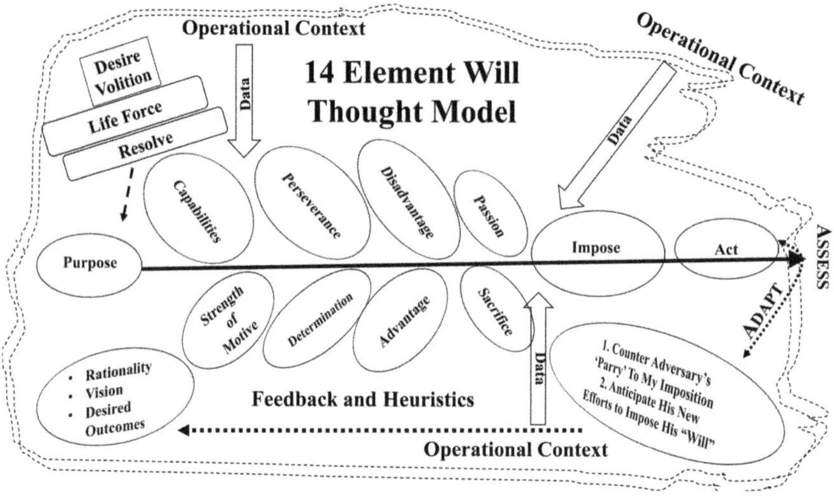

Figure 10.2. Holism at Work—Model of *Will*

to expend these often-expensive capabilities to satisfy the purpose of a leader to impose his desired outcomes on another entity specifically designed for self-interest, aggrandizement, legacy, grudge, etc. One can thus influence purpose via the rationality, vision, and desired outcomes that an adversary uses to convince his followers to take up their cudgels and to be willing to sacrifice all to impose their leader's desired outcomes. With this angle of influence, one could cause a decline of his capabilities via degrading the fuel one finds in morality, determination, decisiveness, passion, and sacrifice all necessary to impose one's actions and thereby achieve desired outcomes. The adversary decision maker, even with a burning and powerful life force, cannot seek to impose his *will* on resisting bodies without elements of his *will* model working. If a conflict situation is further along and is, in fact, underway, one always can find purpose, capabilities, and strength of motive often proving impervious to our entreaties; therefore, it follows one chooses to work on dissipating our adversary's view of his advantages and disadvantages by causing him to have to counter episodes of our own incursions showing our capabilities and power of strength of motive and thereby—from his perspective once again—implying significant cost if he tries to impose his volition via actions.

These actions that spring forth to influence an opponent's reasoning come from direct and indirect targeting of "that which truly matters" to the adversary. One gains such an important insight from how one side thinks the other thinks, but again, from his perspective, and inversely. In any conflict each side, person, or organization must consider "that which truly matters" to the adversary and purposefully set out to influence either it or other possibilities of "that which truly matters" in how our adversary thinks we think about this subject. These important pressure points must be considered for attacking, negating, influencing, etc., with the utmost vigor, focus, and energy elements of our friendly thought model of *will*. Let us make some subconsiderations or subelements of the larger consideration, the larger whole. First, determine that which truly matters to our side, why it is important, and what would happen if our adversary happened to target successfully said aspect of importance. In any context, one must anticipate and choose to preempt or divert their adversary's attacks on such a tempting target. As one makes this particular consideration, they think about what the adversary is considering but relative to how he commits bias and logic errors, like any human makes. One has to realize how the adversary errs from his culturally influenced perspective and intellect. Second, let us assume that the adversary is resolute in trying to anticipate friendly efforts to attack, manipulate, or confuse "that which truly matters" and how friendly people and organizations most probably plan to flummox his mind. It is his mental and physical travail that one should attack and occupy then with sufficient strength, deny his impositions—with synchronous shards aiming at his unprotected innards with enough strength to delay his counter-impositions and thereby provide one's extraordinary forces[14] or efforts to mass and work against the adversary's soft underbelly. This kind of attack can only come with an approach involving that which truly matters via his expectations of our approaches. Third, wargame both friendly and adversary considerations via people of the adversary's culture and discern how he might respond to friendly denial efforts, his response to friendly attempts to affect, from his perspective, that which truly matters, and how he might attempt to deny said imposition actions. Fourth, discern how the adversary might respond to the friendly employment of Sun Tzu's extraordinary force and his attempts to block such actions either after being surprised or if he correctly anticipates such a move. When one's operation aims for the adversary's soft underbelly so as to influence "that which truly matters," it helps to consult the theory underpinning the action from a historian/theoretician and realize that such movements constitute an indirect approach, and its effects and influence on the adversary in his physical and psychological spheres and how this adversary might respond. Historian B. H. Liddell Hart wrote in his famous book, *Strategy*:

Let us assume that a strategist is empowered to seek a military decision. His responsibility is to seek it under the most advantageous circumstances in order to produce the most profitable result. Hence his true aim is not so much to seek battle as to seek a strategic situation so advantageous that if it does not of itself produce the decision, its continuation by a battle is sure to achieve this. In other words, dislocation [the aim of Hart's version of indirect approach] is the aim of strategy; its sequel may be either the enemy's dissolution or his easier disruption in battle. . . . In the physical or logistical sphere, it is the result of a move which upsets the enemy's disposition and, by compelling a sudden "change of front," dislocates the distribution and organization of his forces; (b) separates his forces; (c) endangers his supplies; (d) menaces the route or routes by which he could retreat in case of need and re-establish himself in his base or homeland. . . . In the psychological sphere, dislocation is the result of the impression on the commander's mind of the physical effects which we have listed. The impression is strongly accentuated if his realization of his being at a disadvantage is sudden, and if he feels that he is unable to counter the enemy's move. Psychological dislocation fundamentally springs from his sense of being trapped. . . . In studying the physical aspect, we must never lose sight of the psychological, and only when both are combined is the strategy truly an indirect approach, calculated to dislocate the opponent's balance.[15]

14. Sun Tzu, *The Art of War,* 91–93.
15. B. H. Liddell Hart, *Strategy* (New York: Henry Holt & Company Inc., 1954), 325–327.

For an excellent example of the indirect approach to why it is "that which truly matters" proves important, consider the German attack against France in May 1940. The German's main attack came through the Ardennes Forest on France's east border, with their lightning war—blitzkrieg—and headed with ferocious speed and violence toward the English Channel. France had decided to fight a defensive battle with an underdefended Sedan highly vulnerable to German intelligence collection, but not considered seriously by the French X Corp commander. So in a macro sense, "[the area of] Sedan formed the hinge between the fixed right wing of the French army along the Maginot Line and the mobile left wing that was to swing up into Belgium in case of a military clash."[16] The vaunted Maginot Line embedded in the Ardennes Forest was believed to be impenetrable by tanks. The German plan (developed by General Erich von Manstein) found a crevice in the French defense plan—"that which truly mattered" to the French, which was first a belief that the defense would prevail; second, if the Germans conducted their attacks through the Low Countries of Belgium and the Netherlands, their speed would be slowed due to wet and soggy terrain. The French thought they would have time to defend with the British, not unlike WWI. But the Germans attacked "that which truly matters" to the French—their belief in the defense, their lack of imagination with respect to massing and maneuvering tank formations, their weak moral fiber, their theories and subsequent inability to use armor in coordination with artillery and air, their poor hierarchical command and control, and so forth. The Germans, thanks to von Manstein's plan, destroyed these ideas and exposed the French philosophy of defense, bypassed the Maginot Line, and sped through the Ardennes as fast as they could with their main attack. The German forces that sped through the Ardennes with the concentrated fury of fast moving and coordinated tanks, artillery, and airpower and the, of course, radios and leaders operating from the front, proceeded to conduct a masterful display of Blitzkrieg.

Notwithstanding the ultimate outcome, France did perform reasonably well in understanding the vulnerability of the attacking spearhead and its support columns stretching to the rear. The attacking Panzers needed infantry to protect its ever-lengthening columns and flanks and thereby allow the German army's logistics to feed the voracious appetites (tank parts, fuel, ammunition, replacements) of the Panzer units moving at breakneck speed after traversing the Ardennes. The French attempted several counterattacks against the spearhead's columns so as to cut the front armor units racing ahead from their logistics and infantry. These counterattacks were never coordinated and never threatened the German spearhead, its

16. Karl-Heinz Frieser, *The Blitzkrieg Legend* (Annapolis, MD: Naval Institute Press), 145.

supporting columns, or their flanks.[17] But some Frenchmen actually and correctly focused on "that which truly mattered" to the German attack and the German war effort in toto. That is to say the spearhead's flanks and the German attacker's abilities to 1) move quickly; 2) lead and communicate by forward deployed commanders; 3) coordinate and employ combined arms—tanks and artillery, air via communications; 4) take enormous risks apparently balanced with the potential for enormous positive outcomes through the actions of audacious senior commanders like Heinz Guderian; and 5) take advantage of the poor command and control of the allies in Belgium with the French in the south at a strategic level, from operational and tactical perspectives in France and southern Belgium, and as the Panzer units moved with utmost speed toward Abbeville, aiming where the remnants of the British and French northern forces were forming at Dunkirk. The French were never able to coordinate and mass to strike at "that which truly mattered" to the Germans.

Clearly the British and French lacked a satisfactory, holistic approach to counter the German Blitzkrieg, and the advantages coming with such speedy warfare brought to and stayed with the Germans, which were 1) initiative; 2) momentum; 3) tempo; 4) knowledge; 5) decisions; 6) position; and 7) freedom of maneuver/movement. The Blitzkrieg and its advantages proved to be the new norm. Carefully staged and time-consuming massing of forces and a hierarchical and archaic chain of command proved helpless against the Germans. The French counterattacks against the German spearhead and columns stretching across northern France and southern Belgium occurred without rapidity, momentum, mass, and tempo and proved doomed to failure even when the obvious target had to be the columns of the spearhead's "shaft" of the attack arrow, which was not exactly well protected by infantry, as the armor raced rapidly toward Dunkirk in those dark days of 1940. As a result, the Germans also found the French's second version of "that which truly matters"—Paris—and German threats to it with its symbolism of French culture as its soft underbelly. As you know, the French capitulated to the Germans' *will*. It is, of course, that which truly matters that often provide the oxygenated life-blood to either a singular or collective brain by knowing the possibilities from an adversary's perspective and how he views his advantages and disadvantages per se. Sometimes one must purposefully assault his reasoning and aim at influencing his calculus of the pluses and minuses the operational context presents, as it houses both sets of conflicting aims, goals, objectives, strategies, tactics via colliding sets of operations. For certain, the operational context in question provides each side advantages and disadvantages—some

17. Kenneth Macksey, *Guderian Creator of the Blitzkrieg* (New York: Stein and Day Publishers, 1975), 132–134.

visible, some invisible, some according to patterns in time, others asynchronous. Sometimes in conflicts each side attempts to anticipate the other side's thoughts and actions in spinning one or more narratives via mass media. One has to then work hard to disprove the adversary's lies in his propaganda aimed against what he considers to be important targets, providing us with clues as to how his mind is working. Consider how Germany's propaganda helped them acquire Austria and Czechoslovakia's Sudetenland immediately prior to WWII, the effort proves telling by its themes and patterns to attack.

As another thought, history tells us of sacrifices an aggressive side makes in trying to impose desired outcomes on a more passive side. Clues exist, of course, in that which truly matters, when discerning what an aggressor needs to do to defeat a weaker or more passive side. This discovery then leads one to consider a preemptive move to expose or weaken the aggressor's intentions and possibly cause him to back down if the exposure or preemption hits a pressure point. At some point in time, reality presses in. Passion only props up the timbers of the heavy burden people carry for so long as they experience the sacrifice of people, machines, cities, etc., in war, and in less lethal situations such as competition in commercial environments. In either situation, each side runs a high probability of a quick turnaround of any remaining friendly or conciliatory feelings, holdings, or attitudinal stability in a military's or commercial company's workforce, and their safety nets all human beings love to possess but hate to lose.

We can then assume any of our adversaries would cherish the opportunity for seizing the initiative in conflict with us, thereby being able to adapt ahead of us, and thus set conditions for moving ahead via sweeping in more and more advantages (e.g., tempo, momentum, knowledge, decision making, position, and freedom of movement[18]/freedom of maneuver). An example might be President Vladimir Putin's surprise seizure of the Crimea and its incorporation back into Russia. The capabilities coming with one's control and use of initiative could be important enough to cause their adversary to experience entropy (slowing and deteriorating into a state of confusion and disarray) and actually expire, as it were, ceasing to be relevant if one took his intelligence collection for assessment away or if one manipulated his gathered data and made it to be of questionable value, the least of which might slow his decision-making processes. Such an important, purposeful retardation could very well open a window of opportunity for this adversary's opponent. Such knowledge would allow one to impose life force on a preparing adversary or let him "know they know," as he sets conditions for imposing his actions on them. They could also find that we do not intend to allow him to prepare for aggression in secrecy and

18. Mao, *On Guerrilla Warfare*, 98.

surprise, and with possible reprisal becoming a given, of course, this adversary would know his opponent to possess the capabilities to thwart his desires. It follows—initiative could very well be that which truly matters.

Many aspects of life, political position, military strength and operations, and conduits—electrical, Internet, geographical, telephonic, etc.—could be at the apex of "that which truly matters" at one point in time only to find that after a few days, the affected variables had changed once again. So, the Über-thinker and thought pilgrim who trudge with me on my journey from the bottom of Plato's Cave to the light of truth and knowledge always find an undulating condition of "truth," sometimes changing rapidly. But for now, some possible candidates for "that which truly matters" come forth as:

1. Preserve governing and regime. Regime survival and sustaining a capability and strength of motive to resist an imposition of another person's or group's *will* to cause ways of living and governing to change figures into the equation of "that which truly matters." I'm speaking of an element of great importance to any person in a position of power such as members of our Congress running for reelection every two or six years—longevity seems to be the call word for people in power. Regime change proved important during Arab Spring in Egypt in 2010, as the incumbent Egyptian President Hosni Mubarak clearly feared losing power not only for himself, but also for his designated successor, his son, and did everything he could do to retain power. Of course, factions swayed back and forth, as on one side was the regime, on another side was the Muslim Brotherhood, the Egyptian Army, the students, protestors, and the like.
2. Impose a certain ideology on a resisting party. An adversary might believe that imposing his ideology on one or more other sects, tribes, political parties, theocracies, aggregations of people, even nation-states to be "that which truly matters." Examples include the struggles for power within the Soviet Union's Communist Party after Lenin died and Stalin's ascension to power. Or another example could be the triumph of the Nazi Party in their struggles against the Communist Party in Germany from the early 1920s to January 1933, when Hitler was appointed chancellor.
3. Deny oil supplies to oil-barren economic powers. If Japan, Germany, South Korea, and China had their oil supplies denied, I assure you such a loss would constitute "that which truly matters." Many countries, but in particular these countries I mention, do not have their own oil supplies and thereby depend upon external countries and businesses to provide oil. Sources of oil such as in Indonesia and the Persian Gulf states warrant close attention and constant monitoring of political, economic, and military news and trends. Oil and the purveyors of

oil—tankers, pipelines, and geographic routes—also constitute "that which truly matters" to these highly industrialized countries. One can argue if these oil flows were to be disrupted, the issue could be so important that these highly dependent countries and their superpower ally would or could be tempted to go to war over unrestricted access.

4. Deny natural gas supplies. I'm speaking about Europe's dependence on Russian natural gas. Russia has a great bargaining position in that they provide the vast majority of Europe's natural gas and any rise in international tensions involving Russia, Europe, or the United States can cause immediate ripples in these economies. Though the flow of natural gas into Europe isn't "that which truly matters" to the Russians, it is important. Of course, the Russians therefore take a dim view of gas pipeline alternative routes from Azerbaijan to southern Europe and Norway from northern Europe. Regardless, the uninterrupted supply of natural gas forces its way to near the top rung of the ladder of "that which truly matters" to several European countries.
5. Stop drug consumption/enhance drug consumption. On one hand, stopping drug consumption should be "that which truly matters" in any effort to halt the violence and crime associated with consumption, distribution, movement, growth, and production of drugs destined for the United States. Nonetheless, regardless of morality, practicality settles in. Instead of attacking the consumption problem, certain countries, including the United States, try to stop the flow of drugs, which is impossible. On the other hand, it is in the best interests (financial) of the drug cartels that America's consumption of drugs continues. Secondarily, because that issue isn't going to shift much, "that which truly matters" in this fight belongs with the pipeline of drugs and distribution and money laundering in Western countries, which use the most illicit drugs. So instead of the primary "that which truly matters," which would be the consumption, we find ourselves in a constant battle of stopping the flow of illicit drugs when the spigot keeps turning clockwise at an ever-increasing stream.
6. Ensure safety, rule of law, and stability. My belief is that most ordinary people think "that which truly matters" can be found in five words: stability, safety, family, peace, and jobs. Most ordinary people know war and conflict to be blights of this life on earth. The people do not want war and only fight when called upon via direct threat (when one's person or family is threatened), nationalism (when one's country and way of life is threatened), and when their religion calls for conflict (one can look in the past for countless lives lost in the name of God during the Great Crusades, the Thirty Years War, the spread of Islam, or in recent jihads or guidance from a revered leader). Interestingly, occupations of one's country stir people's emotions and tilts their rationality to that which is irrational (to us). When occupiers take over a

country, the citizens in question surmise through implication, inference, and sometimes via actions of the occupier that they, the citizens, have to accept another culture's beliefs, values, and behaviors foreign to their own beliefs and values. Resentment sets in, and then, in a collective way, people start resisting the occupiers. The overthrow and riddance of the occupier becomes "that which truly matters," while in a duality way the occupier desires to sustain their occupation and end any resistance and therefore always presents a direct bead on "that which truly matters" to the occupier. Part of enforcing foreign values involves denying religious freedom to people occupied. This denial becomes a powerful motivator to resist said hypothetical occupation for people ensnared and who strongly desire freedom of worship and their beliefs in God.

7. Destroy war making capabilities/protect war making capabilities. Sometimes one can find "that which truly matters" in the war-making capabilities of competing and hostile countries. The perfect example of this notion involves the "continuous war" in Europe from 1870 to 1945. As you can recall, politicians who were the victors (if anybody could label any side true "victors") proved ignorant that their behavior at the end of WWI perpetuated the cycle of resentment that began with the aftermath of the Franco-Prussian War in 1870, where harsh and the loss of Alsace-Lorraine to Prussia fueled French hatred and retribution for anything German. This strong emotion erupted in WWI and again in in the years leading up to WWII, when multiple countries experienced disorder, social upheaval, the great depression, widespread fear, a longing for law and order led to totalitarianism. What a fertile field for the Four Horsemen of the Apocalypse—famine, death, pestilence, and war—to come forth and cause battles of *will.*
8. Attack infrastructure/deny attacks on infrastructure. Infrastructure comes in several different modes, works with different kinds of equipment and processes, performs many different functions, and enables us, as human beings, to live in a state of luxury and cleanliness never before seen. Infrastructure includes electrical grids, telephony, water, sewage, rail lines, airlines, roads, bridges, waterways, dams, locks on rivers and canals, Internet, data storage centers, natural gas, oil, gasoline, pipelines, docks, ports, tunnels—the list could go on and on. Several of these aspects of infrastructure could very well be "that which is most important."
9. In, let's say, the Netherlands, one can easily determine that dams, locks, roads, and canals are "that which truly matters." For Germany, it might be the consistent flow of oil and natural gas that occupies the top spot. For the United States, electrical grids, Internet, port facilities, nuclear power stations, airports, railroads could be most important. For Norway, the offshore oil and natural gas deposits and extractions

as well as distribution systems and ports occupy the top spot. It truly comes down to different countries and their operational contexts to determine "that which truly matters." And to top it off, "that which truly matters" can change, sometimes quickly. When Japan suffered a tsunami in 2011, "that which truly mattered" proved to be humanitarian relief as well as containing the nuclear accident.

10. When we seek "that which truly matters," sometimes one finds a sweet spot[19] within the whole, but know that it cannot exist in isolation. The sweet spot has to be relative to how well the parts, deemed most important, work with the whole in a coherent way. But my acolytes say, "You speak of the nation as a whole, but you are not dealing with its parts. Please explain how one can consider not only the infrastructure as a whole, the macro-aggregation—the total infrastructure of a country—but also the micro-aggregations of subsystems that comprise the whole." One must know both macro- and micro-aggregations that comprise the micro- and macro-infrastructure as both parts, objects, and wholes, and also how each connects to and contributes to the whole. To help us comprehend, I ask you to look at the macro-aggregation of the United States and how each state fits with the overall whole as a puzzle, with each state being a puzzle part of the whole. Each state has their own peculiarities; therefore, each state has priorities about "that which truly matters" to them. With some states, like Tennessee and Colorado, one can place dams into the most important bin of thought. With other states, like Arizona, New Mexico, and Texas, one consideration involves the arterials that move drugs into America. Another consideration involves the government—national, state, and local—infrastructures dealing with the illegal immigration problem. With California, one can argue most important subsystems of the whole that are truly most important to the state macro-infrastructure are its water system, its ports, and its distribution infrastructures.
11. We know the subsystems to be important in the macro-system, the national infrastructure. This national infrastructure enfolds the states' macro-system (and unfolds into the global infrastructure). Each state enfolds their important micro-systems and unfolds into their macro-systems. Thus, each state has to know the sub-sub-subsystems that when connected, comprise their whole and rack and stack each so they have priorities for the flow of attention, money, security, statuses feedback, and the like. Each sub-sub-subsystem is as one and connects

19. *Sweet spot*: The place in a whole where a combination of influences come together at the right time and right circumstances sufficient to cause an optimum yield for a given expenditure of effort.

to a micro-infrastructure, which connects to the macro-infrastructure. If perturbation in a low portion of a piece of the infrastructure occurs, its reverberations quickly affect the macro-infrastructure. We can now successfully think about links, which make the connections, and the doctrine of holism in which the parts of the whole in question all connect to one another and to the whole itself, as a web, in which the overall larger web is only as strong as each of its cells and the links connecting each cell to the totality of the whole. From a national perspective, one could pick several top priorities—ports, highways, bridges, and tunnel maintenance, Internet, nuclear power plants, power grids, fiber-optic cable systems under the Atlantic and Pacific Oceans, nuclear storage, and airports, as examples. But the paradox comes with the pressing need to expend the effort and money not for just one top priority but several, all demanding and competing for primacy.

12. Therefore, one has to possess and use what I call a "swinging priorities door" in which top dollar and top attention go to that which needs help the most at a moment in time. But the door oscillates between postures of closure, so while paying attention to fixing that which is broken now, good leaders lay, bury, and nurture the seeds of change and improvement for the future, knowing full well they won't live to see all they have planted and nurtured. The possession of a clear vision recognizes what I so fervently beckon as lines of life attached from the swinging priorities door to present and future contexts and always allowing for the appearance of the competing images of success and failure, so as to have a safe and prosperous infrastructure in place now, but always keeping and nurturing my vision of a connector with the important transition into the future in mind and action too.
13. The lines of life of which I speak prove self-evident to a state's human need for safe, efficient, agile, and coherent infrastructures. The vision and its lines of life and swinging priorities doors thereby build and nurture one's macro-aggregation of that which comprise infrastructures, of which level one happens to belong. It follows, too, as wary human beings, diligent people keep essential parts of our infrastructures improving and changing with the passage of time. But to be a deep thinker, one must know not only their particular piece of the infrastructure, but the whole that is their macro-view; not just the national infrastructure, but also where each state's "piece of the infrastructure" fits into the overall puzzle of the whole. What I am describing calls for people who realize full well where the weaknesses, indeed vulnerabilities, graze and demand our attention for protecting them from several different kinds of assault. Any infrastructure is vulnerable to assault by, in a physical sense, a combination of humans and machines attacking key nodes, and in an invisible sense, the occurrence of cyber attacks against any infrastructure's command-and-control apparatuses.

14. I'm also speaking of the infrastructure of the mind. We, as owners of our minds, are either cursed or blessed to be a person who lives by values and social mores but who also is far-sighted. This personage and its mind know of the need to nurture the moorings of our mental infrastructure while attending to its expansion and exploration of new ideas and connections for even further expansion of one's mental infrastructure, each day, as long as they live. There is also the presence and influence of ongoing and sometimes contentious "proceedings" in one's mind. These proceedings consider speed, healing that which is currently broken, and continuing to explore the width and depth of a constant expansion of the infrastructure of one's mind. In my personal case, I always endure the gyrations of the proceedings of my inner mind only to succumb to simple answers when I know they don't exist. I know my motivation wells from my soul and furthers my knowledge, comprehension, and understanding of the connectedness of all things. This pressure occurs as my mind's natural proceedings grapple with my mind's "wild" forces, and thus find my inner eye seeking and finding a compromise between rational and wild. These proceedings then guide my mind's movement from subjects large and small and then from small to large, in the dance of the yin and yang, rapidly, efficiently, and flexibly.
15. It follows that our thinking is obliged to consider each of the connecting pieces and prepare either to deny or favorably manipulate any attempts to intrude and destroy these operational mechanisms, and thereby create terror, and how they could very well immobilize their targets by attacking these connecting pieces of which I speak. I don't need to say that in my view, the worst assaults on infrastructure inevitably come forth from a dark underworld, with a purposeful combining of invisible and visible assaults. Another danger finds the smart adversary who "sees" connections between and among the micro and macro and sets out not only to destroy parts and pieces but the right parts and pieces that connect to or govern indispensable objects, parts, and pieces, and sub-systems all which contribute most to their aim, goals, objectives, etc. It is thought that helps us first understand "that which truly matters," and second, to find the best solutions for anticipating an adversary's imposition activities by attacking that which truly matters and to be there waiting when he comes, stomping him into oblivion.
16. Obtain secrets/deny attempts to obtain secrets. It is self-evident, so I assume, that one's important secrets exist and must be protected. Some secrets prove so important that they qualify as "that which truly matters." Knowing the adversary's secrets without their knowledge provides a powerful boost to one's capabilities. Specifically, the high-grade secrets one wants could involve new weapons, such as America's

development of the first atom bomb in WWII. Or high-grade secrets could involve an intelligence collection capability such as the Enigma and Magic projects of WWII. Sometimes high-grade secrets involve a new technology for a corporation placing them far ahead of their competitors—say, a "killer app." Sometimes high-grade secrets involve penetrating the adversary or competitor's minds via their decision-making processes, considerations, actions, assessments, and adaptations and using this knowledge to create advantages when and where our adversary has none; cyber penetrations of networks for espionage purposes present a modern example. If a network penetration occurs, the adversary could have the following advantages in their favor: 1) initiative; 2) knowledge; 3) decisions; 4) position; and 5) freedom of movement inside the network and inside the computers and routers the network and its people and organizations use.

Germany during WWII did not know about the secret penetration of the German Enigma encrypting and communications enabler machine, codenamed Ultra. Allied leaders possessed the capability to read much of Germany's high-level military traffic for most of the war. Japan during WWII did not know the United States had developed a decryption machine via a series of good breaks (Germany's sharing of their Enigma machines with Japan) and hard mental work by several very smart mathematicians and cryptologists who proceeded to break the Japanese cryptology system (codenamed Operation Magic). This work enabled the United States and its allies to read much of Japan's military traffic.

That which I'm speaking about is nothing new. As long as 2,500 years ago, Sun Tzu extolled the virtues of secret agents to penetrate their enemy's defenses, garner his secrets, and use said information for action:

> Now the reason the enlightened prince and the wise general conquer the enemy whenever they move and their achievements surpass those of ordinary men is foreknowledge. What is called "foreknowledge" cannot be elicited from spirits, nor from gods, nor by analogy with past events, nor from calculations. It must be obtained from men who know the enemy situation. . . . There is no place where espionage is not used.[20]

It is safe to say that every country tries to collect data, information, and knowledge against their foes and their partners to garner their secrets. In addition, corporations try to steal secrets from their competitors so as to gain an advantage (position in the market, knowledge, decision making, and initiative could be examples of advantage a business corporation could be seeking via secrets). Every person

20. Sun Tzu, *The Art of War*, 144–149.

and every organization is aware of their adversary's efforts to obtain secrets, and must deny their adversary's attempts to obtain their secrets. Military units use counterintelligence people to anticipate and counter their adversary's efforts to collect friendly data, information, and knowledge. Whether our military is working to collect data against terrorists, insurgents, or drug cartels, we know that all of them have countersurveillance capabilities to block human intelligence collection means, as well as encryption machines and procedures. Corporate organizations should have experts on the payroll who work to collect their competitor's efforts to garner valuable, hidden data, and experts who anticipate and deny competitors' efforts to obtain their secrets. How well one adversary protects their secrets and thereby blocks adversary efforts to obtain their secrets can be "that which truly matters." Protecting the secrets of exactly where the beaches would be in the invasion of France on D-Day is a great example of guarding hugely important secrets. As another example, in the early winter of 1940, a German staff officer carrying the invasion plans for the European Low Countries and France flew off-course and had to land in Belgium. Undoubtedly, the German general staff considered this a horrific breach in security, and its discovery by the allies helped to push a different, creative, and highly controversial plan—Case Yellow—to attack through the Ardennes Forest, and all of us know the immense success the Germans experienced in doing so. From a slightly different but still strongly related point of view, at times, obtaining the adversary's secrets can be "that which truly matters," but the antipode is pertinent, as even while trying to steal one's opponent's secrets, at the same time, one must protect their own secrets from their adversary's efforts to steal them. One must always remain wary on alert for efforts to flummox via secret agents who are really double agents supporting the adversary.

17. Retain all prime ingredients for considering how to impose one's *will*. If an adversary can find *will's* essential elements and attack each singularly, via combinations, or en masse, the means and the fortitude to fight and win crumbles. To accept this premise, believe in connectedness. In a layman's book about complexity and chaos, M. Mitchell Waldrop the following thoughts about connectedness:

> In example after example, the message was the same: everything is connected, and often with incredible sensitivity. Tiny perturbations won't always remain tiny. Under the right circumstances, the slightest uncertainty can grow until the system's future becomes utterly unpredictable—or, in a word, chaotic.[21]

21. Waldrop, *Complexity*, 66.

Famous warfighters and philosophers have always recognized and spoken about connectedness and its influence. Napoleon, at the Battle of Austerlitz in December 1805, used connectedness in his famous victory over Russian and Austrian forces. Now, to be certain, I have not found any Napoleonic discourses identifying the importance of connectedness, but in my view, it is always present, the lightning bolt in the dark clouds of war. Let me explain. Napoleon won the battle with different but connected activities before the battle: 1) he acted as though afraid of being outnumbered by sending peace envoys and scouring about as to order a retreat; 2) he weakened his right flank; 3) he moved his separated forces from two different distant places to join him before the battle started; 4) he made the decision to abandon the Pratzen Heights (the dominant land feature in the operational context); 5) he timed the reoccupation of the Pratzen Heights after most Russian and Austrian forces had attacked over the Pratzen Heights to strike at the deceptively weak French right flank; 6) he decided then to occupy the Pratzen Heights with sufficient numbers to beat off furious Russian counterattacks; 7) he connected with the young Czar Alexander's mind and "knew" that he would attack Napoleon's weak right flank with the intention to roll up Napoleon's battle flank and defeat him decidedly; and 8) he connected all these parts and pieces via connectedness. Of course there was a surprise connection with Napoleon's masterful plan and the operational context, as when both sides awakened and prepared for battle—heavy fog covered the battlefield; moreover, the air became even a thicker cauldron of obscuration when the fog mingled with camp fire smoke and cannon and musket fire smoke so the Russian tsar could not see what was happening on his left flank after he had sent regiment after regiment over the Pratzen Heights to enter battle against Napoleon's weak right flank.[22]

In this chapter, I entered into the vast halls of the great edifice that is *will*. I provided my thoughts about the inevitable potential or actual conflict that swirls around this age-old enemy of mankind—aggressive impositions and ensuing protestations. I explained to my readers that as one searches for that which truly matters to an adversary, gaze into the eyes of truth and notice, alas, it flutters and variates because *truth changes*. In a moment, I want you to look in those eyes of escaping truth, the reflection of a double-edged sword—on one side I see that which truly matters from our side, but on the other side I find the adversary—the adaptive adversary, who has his version of that which truly matters. Duality must run through our minds. Truth varies in the eyes of the beholder, so it goes; this means the

22. Alexander, *How Wars Are Won*, 261–269.

adversary has his version of truth, we have our version of truth, and other players or watchers of war and conflict have their notion of truth. So, be mindful of these many versions of truth, but always put yourself into the minds of our adversaries and experience his views during the all-important wargame to seek and find the *multiple views of truth about that which truly matters.* I explained too, that in my view, one must understand that which truly matters from a variety of views—friendly, adversary, populace, social media, world opinion. The cause for this effect involves experiencing strain—to successfully "crawl inside the mind and skin" of an adversary. To help, I discussed the absolute need for very detailed wargaming—similar to *advanced analysis* and *advanced collection* but also something new—*wargaming the adversary's wargaming* in a deep-thinking and systematic way aided by synthetic contexts, artificial intelligence (AI), and software for wargaming. I also provided 10 examples of that which could be important. Nonetheless, I cautioned to consider relative to our jousting partner, the operational context, influencers, and, of course, one's own decision maker. In this chapter, I introduced co-evolution and how it constantly seeks feedback relative to a constantly fluctuating context, thereby causing perturbation in that which truly matters (from the nonlinear operational context and constant conflict among adversaries on the battlefield). I also present my readers with some historical examples to help us understand that which truly matters, such as Napoleon at his best at the battle of Austerlitz and at his worst in his invasion of Russia in 1812. We also spend some time on Germany's invasion of the lowlands and France in the spring and summer of 1940 and finally in the struggle of "wills" in the Vietnam War. In all of these examples, human beings try to do their best but often miss the mark in their thinking, and nobody wants to be losers in future conflict. Thus, to succeed in identifying and affecting that which truly matters, we have to think holistically, work with dualism, wargame the adversary's wargaming, recognize the peculiarities of the operational context, use the models I have provided, and in particular the inputs of the context caused by change induced by nonlinear systems.

CHAPTER 11

The Influences of Alternatives and Pressures on *Will*

Argument: *In this chapter, I first discuss* alternatives. *Human beings face alternatives when caught in conflict and war. Alternatives influence outcomes of struggles people experience in fights. Fear of and disdain for alternatives needs to be a subject of much thought because each component can suddenly appear and seriously affect conflict outcomes. People must think about* "pressures," *fear, and disdain for alternatives for success. Pressure, important for understanding* will, *is the* continuous physical or emotional "weight" a person intuits, senses, or thinks about as he or she makes a decision. *Pressure influences that which truly matters even when the adversary protects this sensitive core of his being. Pressure serves as a lubricant to the engine of* will *and its 14 essential elements.*

THE INFLUENCES OF ALTERNATIVES

It appears to me that this is a most interesting subject, teeming with meaning. Of direct interest to this inquiry, I want us to think about two related lines of thinking: fear of alternatives and disdain for alternatives. Both of these lines of thought relate to our study. Fear of and disdain for alternatives needs to be a subject of much thought; however, one only finds completeness if they can wear two faces: 1) through the eyes and the mind of the recipient of an imposition of volition and 2) through the eyes and mind of the side that imposes its quest for advantage. Each face shows concern and stress; it comes from fear of or disdain for alternatives. After all, it is one or more members of the species who plan for or engage in conflict. This same species ruminates about and makes conscious decisions concerning the ways each side in a conflict tries to triumph with their peculiar desire-driven impositions. In addition, people on the imposition and receiving ends of the battle for supremacy catch lots of innocent, ordinary people in fishermen's nets from the river of life.

Often, when two centers of power engage conflict, one finds innocents caught between the warring parties because they were at the wrong place at the wrong time—these people, forced to think about alternatives so they can live, must always be afraid for both their immediate well-being and their long-term prospects for stability, peace, and prosperity—they find themselves in extremis, hence fear. How they think about alternatives is important. The imposer of *will* and the recipient realize the importance of comprehending what these people might be pondering and what is to be done. Anyone interested in this kind of knowledge specifically concerns themselves with what the fish in the net perceive, interpret, expect, and experience as they behave. Also at play, one always needs to seek and learn the sources of data, information, knowledge, and narratives at play, with which to "feed" targets' minds so they can push away from emotion and reel in larger and larger fish—logical thinking in an often-illogical world or predicament.

So, let us start this portion of our journey by defining fear, disdain, and alternative:

- Fear is a disturbing or threatening emotion arising as a premonition of lurking danger, trepidation of an impending experience, or a foreboding state of mind coming from one's mental and emotional status. All people know fear at one time or another. Generally, they overcome fear with the rational side of their mind. Or they move or change in some way to distance or protect themselves from the source of their fear.
- Disdain connotes mocking, scorn, or contempt. In our context, disdain for an alternative means the person doing the disdaining holds one or more alternatives in low regard; hence, they possess a condition of being in which they lack fear. Examples could be suicide bombers who either kill themselves for a cause because they are drugged or because they believe a better life awaits them in death. The Jewish fighters who fought the Nazis in the Warsaw Ghetto uprising of April 1943 knew their only alternative was death, and admirably, they went down fighting. They were not afraid to die, and hate (of the Nazis in this case) was a powerful motivator—it had to help.
- Alternative is an interesting word as it connotes flexibility, varied options, a different method or path, or the availability of a selection from which to choose. Alternatives prove to be a close relative to potentiality, which I define as "possibilities unbound by constraints." Aristotle also has a way of describing potentiality. He, too, believed in the concept of potentiality, which in this context, generally refers to any "prospect" that an entity can be said to have. Aristotle did not consider all possibilities the same and emphasized the importance of those that become real of their own accord when conditions were right and nothing impeded their march into being. The mere presence of a choice of

> alternatives chimes a pleasant cord stroking our emotional and mental well-being. But as it sometimes happens, having several alternatives, each with many possibilities that we can envision fluttering and moving in the breeze, an alternative does not become "real" until one is chosen and brought into context. Of course, one can grasp the wrong possibility and suffer the consequences; therefore, thinking people always realize and figure the odds and pick the best probability for success. People weigh the scales and perform some variation on the theme of cost-benefit analyses and then either act or don't act. Of course, they have to be in control of their wits to make a considered choice.

With the subject of fear of or disdain for alternatives, one (the imposer) finds ample and necessary room for concern. Sometimes people allow fear to rule their rational mind; fear by definition is emotional. With emotion, one finds a dearth of thought. Trying to help or convince people to overcome their fear is difficult. People have to overcome fear themselves, although sometimes they get help—a transferal of fear. Sometimes people overcome their fears of given alternatives because they know of more plausible alternatives. To people who do possess their wits while in extremis, an examination of alternative plausibility becomes imperative. Choice of alternatives sets in and gains influence and directly or indirectly influences the *will* of an organization, army, country, terrorist organization, and so forth. They can fantasize about their alternatives, which at times can be a soothing salve to the open wounds of fear, but they always stand the risk of distorting reality—though in a positive light, as the fantasy to which they "escape" can keep them going in times of duress. Fear can overpower a person and influence what they do or expect, or interpret, or think.

It is unwelcome stress that accompanies us and heightens our fears on the pathway of alternatives; it must be a consideration and thereby causes all of us to approach this issue carefully and thoughtfully. The perpetrator, for example, always has some kind of constraints on expenditure of time, money, lives, etc., and he could always face morality issues during the action or shortly thereafter, particularly if he is the loser—he has to consider all, if he is a thinking human being. But this mental process takes place in the mind of a human whose mental processes and emoting are unique. We attempt to reason like the people whose fear of or disdain for alternatives fall within our contemplation. Of course, studying the imposer of action, one finds within expected outcomes, possible *alternatives,* which the imposer vigorously seeks. If he fails to achieve his outcome, it can be a problem for him, and at least some apprehension, stress, and fear for alternatives must occur. When Hitler rearmed and reoccupied the Rhineland in March 1936, his general staff feared that the French would intervene with their superior military, and the Germans were prepared to retreat at the first sign of a French military response. The French didn't intervene for several reasons, including the fear of starting another war, but one reason in particular relates to alternatives of a nation-state and its national security:

> With the construction of the Maginot Line, the wheel of French military thought, which had started spinning in 1870, performed a fatal full cycle. In 1870 . . . France had lost a war through adopting too defensive a posture and relying too much on permanent fortifications. . . . France had nearly lost the next war by being too aggressive-minded. Now she was seeking safety under concrete and steel. Rapidly the Maginot line came to be not just a component of strategy, but a way of life . . . the French Army allowed itself to atrophy, to lapse into desuetude.[1]

The Rhineland stayed militarized and occupied by the Germans, and Hitler's successful bluff emboldened his resolve for winning in future struggles. Sometimes, though, people prove more circumspect than Hitler about the level of vigor they impose their volition, how quickly they stand to reach this level, and the play and influence of uncertainty and risk. Each could serve as a brake of sorts on the gambling with chance that Hitler proved to be more and more comfortable with. More important, one should try to empathize with those whose fear of alternatives are susceptible to influence—a most difficult task, though, as it is difficult to think like an adversary, let alone to emote like an adversary or the population that supports him.

Past history tells people caught in a predicament to look at and think about alternatives from analogies, but often they can't help but focus on limitations of existing alternatives. They sometimes see a grim death or loss of their cultural existence if they lose, so they have a high sense of purpose and a strength of motive both of which tumble and affect elements of our 14-element model. Sometimes the tumbling and tumultuousness prove so significant as to cause the model to reset and perhaps even to reform. Occasionally, fear of alternatives is way off base as an alternative of that which would normally be acceptable. Fate becomes unimaginable—see Nazi slaughter of Europe's Jewish population during World War II. Thus, death in a Treblinka or an Auschwitz death camp must have seemed unbelievable, and people probably discarded such an ending as an alternative (even though it seems obvious to us in retrospect) because it was unthinkable that extermination was what the Nazis had in mind. This belief, though, faded with time as word reached the people awaiting deportation. By then the alternatives were so miniscule that resignation prevailed.

Next, I'll review a few examples from history that enunciate and explain some of the theories I presented to you as being highly influential and how

1. Alistair Horne, *To Lose a Battle* (London: The Penguin Group, 1969), 63.

we can think about this abstract subject. I presented some of the theory earlier; now here are some historical examples:

- Unconditional surrender. At the Casablanca Conference in 1943, the United States, under the leadership of Franklin D. Roosevelt, issued a demand for Germany's unconditional surrender. This standard of defeat had the effect of giving the German people no other choice than to trudge forward and resist to the end. Great swaths of Germany fell to the fury of Allied bombers and from invasions from the east and the west. Faced with unconditional surrender, as well as the honorable requirement to defend their Fatherland, the Germans fought ferociously, particularly against the Soviets in the Battle of Berlin. Many people felt they had no alternative than to fight to the death, as they were being called upon by the "entombed" Hitler and forced to fight by the SS who would hang or shoot people, young and old, whom they labeled as deserters.
- Control of data, information, and knowledge. At one end of the spectrum of possibilities, consider the sad case of the North Korean populace. They suffer en masse from a dearth of "true" data, information, and knowledge, and they don't even know it. The populace has only a small amount of outside, unfiltered news coming into country, usually through the observations of rare travelers from the Hermit Kingdom to other countries. Even then, what these travelers see and hear filters through their "apperception"; almost all of their experiences have been local so their worldview is quite limited. The North Korean populace, while quite literate, could be the most "information emaciated" populace in the world. In addition, one finds in North Korea the dominant influence from the cult of the great leader—the prison camps, conditions and fears of war with South Korea and the United States that the government drums into the populace's heads, and life in a society with almost no data inputs other than what comes from their personal contexts and from their government. All of these conditioners have an immense impact on how one would attempt to "arrange the minds" of any target audience in North Korea. I have no doubts that many North Koreans would either resist any outside invader or commit suicide like many Japanese people living in Okinawa during and at the end of World War II, should war ever come to the peninsula. As a perspective, though, North Korea's leader and his entourage possess alternatives as they rush toward being a nuclear power and continue to menace South Korea. To impose our *will* on the North Korean leadership, friendly decision makers always consider the range of alternatives from the North Koran perspective. Thinking similarly to them cannot focus only on the present, but also how they view the past and future and knit all three perspectives into one whole. One has to know how such a whole appears

from their perspective. Interestingly, they have constraints, pressure points, decisive points, and centers of gravity, so some of their alternatives always involve protecting these constraints and points. From a North Korean's perspective, their approach is totally rational and impeccable. Thus, it would behoove us to consider alternatives available to the North Korean leadership but from their perspective. I suspect then this *Crime and Punishment* quote would have great meaning:

> [Y]ou think I am attacking them for talking nonsense? Not a bit! I like them to talk nonsense. That's man's one privilege over all creation. . . . Talk nonsense, but talk your own nonsense, and I'll kiss you for it. To go wrong in one's own way is better than to go right in someone else's. In the first case you are a man, in the second you're no better than a bird. Truth won't escape you, but life can be cramped.[2]

North Korea looks at the south and its allies, and must often think,

> "They speak nonsense, and it is good they do speak nonsense. It is to my advantage. They have few alternatives other than sustaining the status quo and throwing some unimportant sanctions at me. I don't care—I have other sources for what I need. They have done very little to affect my alternatives, and the greater my nuclear and ballistic capability, the more leverage I possess for obtaining wealth, goods, and services from the south, and exultation from my people. I tweak the nose of the dragon with my actions, and I have a host of alternatives they have not thought about, as they do not think like me, they do not have the experiences I have—they do nothing in their thought or actions to hinder entrance to my dark cave of alternatives. I have very good choices for regime preservation, my personal self-interests, and for eventual unification of the peninsula under my terms."

- Japanese civilians on Okinawa. Toward the end of World War II in the Pacific area of operations, American forces invaded Okinawa. The battle for control of the island lasted 82 days—April 1 through June 22, 1945. The Japanese military chose to fight to the death or commit suicide, so it was a slow and dangerous slog through a difficult operational context. The populace of Okinawa proved to be another variable that was both sickening and frightening. The fact is many Okinawans committed suicide. Why? It was the end of the war, American troops were winning the fight against the Japanese, and the death and destruction were drawing to a close, so why would the civilians not try to survive and turn themselves over to the Americans? It seems that the Okinawans also were devoid of information other than what the Japanese army told them: that the Americans would rape and kill them so self-inflicted

2. Horne, *To Lose a Battle*, 165.

death or death at the hands of the Japanese army were better alternatives than to surrender to the Americans. A dreadful tragedy came about via people lacking sufficient factual information and knowledge with which to make informed decisions about alternatives.[3] I found myself wondering what would have happened if we would have anticipated the lack of plausible alternatives as a cause/effect relationship and attempted to communicate with civilians crushed between two clashing sides in conflict.

- Over the top in World War I. Why did soldiers keep going over the top of the trenches in endless and senseless attacks during World War I? Some possible answers include honor, friendships on the right and left, home expectations, loyalty to good leaders, and most assuredly, fear of an alternative, which most often meant a court martial and subsequent imprisonment or death by firing squad. Did people become desensitized to the fear of death? Did they possess a disdain for death, which enabled them to turn off fear and be brave enough to go over the top of the trenches and charge? Remember the first day of the Battle of Somme—British casualties were approximately 60,000 (see John Keegan's *The Face of Battle*, p. 260) people either killed or wounded so the alternative proved very narrow and an "either-or choice" was not much different than the choices of alternatives Soviets soldiers experienced in World War II—they faced death from the Germans to their front or death from the NKVD[4] if they fell back. Most seemed to have moved forward and faced an honorable death defending the Motherland.
- Fear of the beast set loose. Large bureaucracies can become mindless, even with hundreds and sometimes thousands of human beings turning dials, pulling levers, and opening and shutting trap doors and rarely thinking in a creative or innovative way. As a favorite bit of my gallows humor, read and muse on this thought, "Paperwork is the embalming fluid of bureaucracy, maintaining an appearance of life where none exists."[5]
- Bureaucracies can lose their vision and moral purpose while seducing their own minds and calling the immoral, moral. A loose beast sometimes opts for a veil of conventional wisdom with which to do its deeds. Managers mouth phrases like "we already do that" to ensure nothing changes unless they (the managers) see an idea they can call their own and take credit for its arrival. The beast's maw becomes particularly wide and voracious when a lower-ranking person comes forth with a

3. Unsigned editorial, "Cornerstone of Peace: A Legacy of Bloodshed." *SFGate*, 1995-06-24. Retrieved May 15, 2017, from http://www.sfgate.com/opinion/article/EDITORIAL-Cornerstone-of-Peace-A-Legacy-of-3029891.php.

4. The Soviet secret police under Stalin.

5. Quote attributable to Robert J. Meltzer.

new and creative idea that could change the beast's image of what is right and what is wrong and a threat to the always favorable (to it) status quo.

- Another author thinks much the same way about large bureaucracies. He describes so well the state of affairs in which the way people find themselves as they try to consider alternatives and instead find fear in their hearts. Their fear is well founded. Its origin is in their knowledge and fear of alternatives, which can become governed by their fear of the beast set loose with its power to hide behind regulations, and ruin people and organizations if they differ with the central purpose of the bureaucracy, with its power, rules, regulations, and with leaders who are not accountable:

> They [a televised debate between two intellectuals—one, William Buckley an arch conservative, and Arthur Schlesinger, a liberal] disagreed about nearly everything. The one notion they concurred on . . . was that bureaucratic agencies—such as government departments—mindlessly and inexorably attempt to increase their power, their budget, and their size. Like hungry amoebas, social groups have an automatic desire to grow. Superorganisms are hungry creatures, attempting to break down the boundaries of their competitors, chew off chunks of their opponents' substance, and digest and redistribute it as part of themselves. . . . Its message varies, but under the many disguises is one imperative. Gather a group together and awaken them with my words. Take all those who find themselves in the condition that I describe and weld them into a mighty force that will impose its dominion on a large swatch of the world. The voice of the super organism calls out to those on a lower level as well. To them, it dictates sacrifice. The converts have a sublime perception of truth and feel caught up in a frenzied oneness with some superior being whose power leaves them in awe.[6]

We find our minds drifting to a strange "never-never land" and find a context in which wrong is right, yes is no, love is hate, killing is both sane and legal, and so forth. Such a lack of true thinking means that this organization and its people are in the pits of Plato's Cave. They believe as true only what their puppet master shows or tells them. Let's let our minds jump from today back to Germany in World War II with a discussion about the Allied bureaucracy and then, the Nazi bureaucracy.

It was the presence and actions of gigantic bureaucracies, appearing mindless and endlessly powerful in which an often-numbing pattern of almost unconscious motion came forth in the bombing campaigns of WWII. So, in explaining more of the power of the beast being on the loose, it influences the choice of acceptable alternatives in its self-interest;

6. Howard Bloom, *The Lucifer Principle* (New York: The Atlantic Monthly Press, 1995), 182.

the beast actually robs its humans of a true available range of alternatives and leaves them with alternatives they fear but choose because it is the "only" path on which to safely walk. Author W. B. Sebald, wrote in one of his books, *On the Natural History of Destruction*, the following explanation of the beast turned loose and how its human operators dealt with the death and destruction they were delivering to civilians on the ground:

> The construction of the strategy of air war in all its monstrous complexity, the transformation of bomber crews into professionals, . . . [bomber crews who came from ordinary backgrounds and ordinary jobs] how to overcome the psychological problem of keeping them interested in their tasks despite the abstract nature of their function, the problems of conducting an orderly cycle of operations that involved . . . [complicated aircraft] flying toward a city, and of the technology ensuring that the bombs would cause large-scale fires and firestorms—all these factors, which Kluge [Alexander Kluge, author of an Allied attack of 200 bombers on Halberstadt, which happened to be a place for the bombers to dump their bombs since the main target was weathered out] studies from the organizers' viewpoint, show that so much intelligence, capital, and labor went into the planning of destruction that, under the potential of all the accumulated potential, it [the massive bombing] had to happen in the end.[7]

People have good justification to fear the beast when it is loose. Alternatives become distorted, muted, or disappear altogether. When a huge bureaucracy starts along a destructive path, it takes on a growing tempo and momentum, with a voracious appetite, as Buckley and Schlesinger describe earlier. In *Slaughterhouse-Five,* Kurt Vonnegut tries to rationally present why the German city of Dresden was bombed toward the end of the war when it didn't hold or do anything of military value. Most of the historic part of the town was destroyed and at least 20,000 to 40,000 civilians died.[8] Vonnegut was a firsthand witness, as an American soldier and a prisoner of war put to work in Dresden in the latter days of World War II. He survived the bombing and was a witness to the aftermath of the destruction of Dresden. He attributed this destruction to one of the crazy things about war. In his book Vonnegut shows a cynicism and hopelessness of people who faced the horror of seeing their friends and beautiful city incinerated, helpless and innocent victims of being at the wrong place at the wrong time who had no alternatives other than to suddenly and horribly die. Vonnegut tried to explain how

7. W. B. Sebald, *On the Natural History of Destruction*, trans. Anthea Bell (New York: Penguin Books, 1999), 63.

8. Vonnegut said in *Slaughterhouse-Five* that 120,000 German civilians perished in the raid.

ordinary people could purposefully rain death from the air on a city that had no military value in this passage:

> Lt. Gen. Ira C. Eaker wrote in a foreword—"I find it difficult to understand Englishmen or Americans who weep about enemy civilians who were killed but who have not shed a tear for our gallant crews lost in combat with a cruel enemy." Eaker's foreword ended this way: "I deeply regret that British and U.S. bombers killed 135,000 people in the attack on Dresden, but I remember who started the last war and I regret even more the loss of more than 5,000,000 Allied lives in the necessary effort to completely defeat and utterly destroy Nazism." What Air Marshal Saundby said, among other things, was this: "That the bombing of Dresden was a great tragedy none can deny. That it was really a military necessity few, after reading this book, will believe. It was one of those terrible things that sometimes happen in wartime, brought about by an unfortunate combination of circumstances. Those who approved it were neither wicked nor cruel, though it may well be that they were too remote from the harsh realities of war to understand fully the appalling destructive power of air bombardment in the spring of 1945."[9]

So, letting the beast loose to impose its *will* on a nation can happen. It is our responsibility to anticipate the beast breaking free from its constraints, to understand its potential power, and thereby stop the release of that power in an evil way in its nascency. Let's consider a German example of the beast gone wild. The Nazi Party took political control of Germany in the winter of 1933. Within five years, they completely wiped out freedom of the press and labor unions. They controlled all news and the arts, and the next generation through the Hitler Youth. They rearmed, remilitarized, and reoccupied the Rhineland in 1936; put people to work; built autobahns; hosted the Olympics; and rewrote their laws particularly to legally enable the abuse and persecution of German Jews. Germany became a police state, and the beast was loose with no constraints, no accountability except to a criminal Nazi Party. It was a place where immoral became moral, where thoughtlessness became thoughtful, where compliance became patriotism, a place where the inmates ran the asylum, as it were, with traditions, law, and personal views sharply fixated on what this septic bureaucracy and its leader were postulating. People with money in the early days of the Nazi government had alternatives to leave or stay, but taking an alternative in those days wasn't pressing. It wasn't until after 1936 and particularly after the beast's savagery in Kristallnacht, November 9–10, 1938, that people began to understand how dangerous it was to live in a totalitarian state. People had to watch what they said and to whom

9. Kurt Vonnegut, *Slaughterhouse-Five* (New York: Delacorte, 1969), 238.

they talked—they had no ways to protest, as even the police and the legal apparatus, including the laws, were part of an internal security bureaucracy. If they resisted or complained, they could be sent to a reeducation camp or concentration camp. Sadly, ordinary Germans had no alternatives but to hope for the return of more tolerant days.

Still, people didn't believe it could get too bad; Germany was highly educated and a cultural epicenter after all, home to Goethe, Schiller, Mozart, Beethoven, Wagner, Rilke, and Hegel, among other great minds. It wasn't until the night of the broken glass—Kristallnacht, November 1938—when Goebbels and Hitler turned their Nazi storm troopers loose to murder, plunder, imprison, and destroy Jews and their property that the Nazi state's bureaucracies, occupied by the wrong people and focused in the wrong direction, allowed the beast loose and with it came ferocity and savagery on a scale rarely seen. Then, the alternatives for the oppressed, primarily Germany's Jews, became quite limited, particularly for people with little money. Soon the only alternative became to go with the flow and hope for the best. Their collective *wills* acquiesced because they saw no other alternatives. This, too, would pass, so they thought. The giant Nazi nation-state, run by powerful bureaucracies, brought home to the Jews of Germany and to homosexuals, communists, mentally disabled people, Gypsies, or anybody deemed non-Aryan what the beast turned loose could be capable of doing against humanity, as the destroyer of alternatives and a destroyer of hope and, ultimately, mankind. By the time the German people fully understood the bureaucracy's evil ways, it was too late to do anything—all of the feasible alternatives had been closed off by the Nazi bureaucracy, which had seeped into every nook and cranny of society. The beast's masters at work in the bureaucracies faced no punishment and did not take responsibility for their actions, until they lost the war. Even then, most of them did not feel the pangs of guilt for the crimes they conducted, even those people going to the gallows at the Nuremberg Trials except for one person—Albert Speer. The beast had gone mad and the result was World War II—50 million dead, including 6 million Jews murdered in death camps; hundreds of concentration camps; disrupted and dislocated people all over the world; and misery and pain to innocent men, women, and children. Visit Yad Vashem in Jerusalem and the Holocaust Museum in Washington, D.C., sometime to get an education about what the beast is capable of doing.

In a macabre display of efficiency, Nazi Germany's bureaucracies kept track of what they had looted from Europe, how many people they murdered, and the stolen resources used; it was a bureaucratic machine, and what bureaucracies do well is collect data, ensure that trains are on time, turn out war materiel, produce reports, budget money, and keep records. The bureaucratic machines, imbued with typical German gifts for organization and precision of things and systems, such as rail passenger travel, used efficiency to massacre the innocent. They took their techniques and exploited them to emplace a highly efficient system of rounding up and transporting Jewish men, women, and children from all over Europe to the death camps of Treblinka, Auschwitz-Birkenau, Chelmno, Belzec, and Sobibor; these trains even enjoyed higher priority than the war effort. Truly, in the 1940s the epitome of absurdity into which man could devolve took over. Even when the Soviets were moving west and overrunning camps, thousands of inmates were forced to leave and march in freezing cold weather to camps into Germany's interior. The beast on the loose only stopped its evil doings when the state's black heart quit beating.

The ultimate insanity—WWI Verdun. Moving on, where were reason and rationality relative to *will* in the World War I German army when they decided to initiate the Battle of Verdun guided by an intellectually impoverished strategy that was, quite simply, to bleed the French white! Between February 21 and December 18, 1916, approximately 976,000 soldiers from all sides either died or were wounded with no outcome—the French *will* didn't crack (in fact in a technical sense won, but at the cost of more than 400,000 casualties), and the fight ended as a stalemate. Where was the rationale to tell the German bureaucracy's leaders that such an aim involving the imposition of action to impose an effect was vapid and impossible in the first place and largely immoral for its soldiers and the soldiers of France to fight each other to the death over basically no strategy? Does fear of the alternative or disdain for alternatives exist on both sides of the equation (leader and follower for at least two sides) in a battle for superiority? I think so. The soldiers on each side who fought and died had few alternatives—either fight or face courts-martial. Fight they did and ferociously in the most hideous of conditions. Verdun is a strange and haunting place in modern times.[10] It is hard to believe human beings had such few options that they would have to first plan the campaign, execute the campaign, cause thousands of soldiers to fight each other, and to keep at it for 10 months. Did General Erich von Falkenhayn, who thought up this deplorable and pitiful strategy, bear responsibility for such a wanton massacre of human beings by developing the "bleed

---

10. I visited Verdun in March 1985. It was a haunting experience. The ossuaries (and memorials), shaped as large tall bullets, have two ground-floor hallways that run into one another from opposite directions and a memorial at each end. Inside, one finds complete silence, the Germans at one end of a long hallway, some ways a cenotaph, and the same for the French at the opposite end. I saw people praying and weeping, even then, after so many yeas—a stunning and tribute to war's folly. I peered in the windows under the ossuary and saw lying the bones of thousands of men, none identified.

them white" strategy? Oh, please accept my apology. I forgot that when the beast is loose, people in bureaucracies can disdain thinking about alternatives because they do not bear responsibility.

Alternatives are important. If none exist, people sometimes herd and willingly accept the directions of the force that holds them in bondage. While assessing *will* and fear of or disdain for alternatives, always consider the powerful forces at work that include emotion. Do not forget that emotion touches quite literally all of the elements our study in this book and cannot be ignored. Emotion, with its invisible power, influences whether people find alternatives and act or acquiesce.

PRESSURES

The omnipresent influence of "pressure" is relative to "that which truly matters" in any struggle over the imposition of one's desired outcomes on another side who resists. Pressure means, for my purposes in this book, "the continuous physical or emotional 'weight' that a decision maker, or anyone for that matter, feels, intuits, senses, or thinks about as he makes a decision." This definition includes the possible deviations often coming forth as variations on this theme. I'm speaking of the self-infused or externally infused pressure leading to compulsion that could appear as obvious or subtle evidence of our influence or advantage in any given situation. Pressure of varying types always casts an ominous and powerful shadow of influence on a decision maker's mind. I next provide a short review of each of these types of pressure with historical examples where possible.

Self-pressure, ego,[11] and self-esteem. This is a simple concept to imagine abstractly, but devilishly difficult to grasp and turn into reality with practical use. Regardless, these three considerations remain important. Let's give it a go and gain some good and practical understanding of each. First, let's think about self-pressure. Self-pressure strongly relates to ego and esteem pressures. Self-pressure, by name and definition, is the pressure one puts on the self to achieve, win, do better, be perfect, not waste life, seek and get revenge, make a name for one's self, impose one's way of thinking on a resisting force or adversary, and the like. Hitler, for example, apparently believed in *Götterdämmerung*[12] and the total destruction of Germany when he accepted that the nation was not going to win at the

11. *Ego*: The organized part of the personality structure that includes defensive, perceptual, intellectual-cognitive, and executive functions.

12. Literally, Twilight of the Gods, coming from the fourth Wagner opera in The Ring of the *Der Ring des Nibelungen* (*The Ring of the Nibelung*).

end of WWII. He felt self-pressure to avoid being captured alive by the Soviets; therefore, he killed himself when the Russians drew ever so close to the Reich Chancellery. Saddam Hussein obviously felt a high degree of self-pressure not to acquiesce to U.S. entreaties to expose his nonexistent weapons of mass destruction. His behavior seemed extraordinarily dull, as he lost his entire family, his country, his dictatorship, and his life because of this aberrant self-pressure and his insistence to go to war against the United States and its coalition partners. In another example, both Hitler and Stalin felt self-pressure to win at Stalingrad at all costs. Both countries paid dearly in this fight to the death for basically nothing. It was the self-pressure to win because it was Hitler vs. Stalin, and Nazism vs. communism—all or nothing for each dictator. Both sides played all their cards and the Soviets won. In the end, of course, Stalin prevailed with long-term consequences for Germany and the world.

Ego-pressure comes with overly confident, narcissistic, or even low perceptions of oneself. Regardless, each of the three conditions involves holding self-centered views of what their ego tells them is real. Dante obviously believed that there was a special spot in the Inferno for excessively ego-struck worshipers of the self:

> In your world, that was an arrogant personage; good there is none to ornament the memory of him: so is his shadow here in fury. How many up there now think themselves great kings, that shall lie here like swine in mire, leaving behind them terrible reproaches! And I: Master, I should be glad to see him dipped in this swill, ere we quit the lake![13]

My, I exclaim to myself, Dante's context mirrors today the feigned fights of hubris and posturing, with uncontrolled egos hiding under the transparent veneer of civility, church attendance, feigned interest in others, and so forth. It is the out-of-control ego that can drive mankind mad via conflicts whose circuitous searching for "why" and purpose and "idealism" only find, as the Bible describes in the Book of Revelation, the Four Horsemen of the Apocalypse coming forth to spread pestilence, famine, death, and war. Those inquisitive souls who possess the energy to wonder "why" always find a sense of déjà vu with the return to the incurable disease of rampant egos, extreme arrogance, self-centricity, narcissism, and self-serving purposes. Mankind's character has not changed, but technology has intervened to strengthen the egos of which I speak. Egomaniacs now have selfies, droves of sycophants (like people in the past) following one's every word (via blogs and tweets), television, and garishly bright teeth. Oh, for a few more philosophical minds. These ever-so-arrogant people, stuck in the trappings and falsities of their positions and wealth,

---

13. Dante Alighieri, *The Divine Comedy* (New York: The Modern Library, 1950), 46.

who cannot admit their wrongs, eventually suffer their blind vanity even in death, perhaps even sentenced to Dante's Inferno for evermore.

Ego-pressure comes to some people (perhaps most) in positions of power, and this pressure distorts their worldview. Ego-pressure appears to grip and dominate the self-images and thoughts of some politicians, military flag officers, CEOs, leaders of countries, police chiefs, mayors, and the like—truly the list goes on and on. At the extreme, names come forth—Genghis Khan, Caesar, Alexander the Great, Augustus Caesar, Kaiser Wilhelm, Hitler, Stalin and so on, not mentioning, of course, people of my genre whose egos seem truly out of control and distortive of reality. It is a sad but real phenomenon. Dante found many of these people during his descent into through the inferno, with the ever-so-wise Virgil as his guide. With his discussion guiding my thoughts, I concluded that something goes wrong in the minds of people of this ilk. They begin to believe the soothing voices of the sycophants surrounding them and their "press," their optics, making them godlike in their own minds. This disease causes decay of the flower of thinking; such decay in the collective thinking and decision making of our adversary becomes an important aspect of deep thinking, led by none other than our intrepid Über-thinker and thought pilgrim. This mental work is difficult because to think similarly to them, one has to understand the thinking and worldviews of sycophants, coteries of people around decision makers, and the power of bureaucracies, whose collective minds also demand attention.

Next, self-esteem comes forth appearing my mind's eye. It involves one's self-regard, which can be good or bad. It also includes one's self-reverence or loathing. It is a force to be reckoned with because it is present in all human beings and to be certain, all human beings think and muse about themselves. Self-esteem is a recognizable trait, but is most often hidden, and private. For example, if a person felt self-conscious and depressed about their public-speaking skills, they may perform magnificently only to fall to pieces after the public appearance. Or low self-esteem may cause their failure. Signs of low self-esteem in decision making could involve procrastination, agonizing over detail, not wanting to be wrong, the requirement for constant self-assurance and compliments from subordinates, and the like.

These aspects of pressure may seem overly emotional, but I assure you that with some deep thinking, we can recognize their importance in deciding that which truly matters, going back to one of the earlier considerations one has to make as they plan to win a conflict. When one comes down to the nub of a problem and a person has a decision to make, they desire to make themselves look good and thus mollify their ego-pressures via the always dominate specter of self-interest. It almost always triumphs except in the case of martyrs or good popes or monks hidden away on a mountaintop. Any opponent of a current leader can jump to this aspect of their opponent's self-esteem; inevitably, the opponent spins to their own self-interest. Of course, very grand and high-ranking people have multiple spinners of words and deeds whose mission is to make certain their leader's self-esteem, hence self-interest, blossom, with the accolades that come forth as a result of the tales they tell. We have to take our adversary's self-pressure, ego-pressure, a particular spin on self-esteem (always with self-interest in mind) into account. That which truly matters is a motivator for how *will,* with its swirling and boiling cauldron of possibilities and probabilities, plays out in the multiple acts upon a stage, full of sound and fury that often signifies nothing of value, yielding only misery, retribution, and momentary satiation before the next batch of witches' broth and steam do their evil business again.[14]

Adversarial pressure. This kind of pressure comes with adversarial pressure. This pressure demands that leaders recognize the kind of battles they experience and possess a steady and clear mind because of emotional stress and the physical presence and capabilities of their opponent. As I recall from my earlier studies, it is safe to surmise the presence of pressure in the Battle of Dien Bien Phu (French vs. Viet Minh 1954), poor French decision making (to discount their enemy's resolve and capabilities) Viet Minh determination, perseverance, surrounding context, and, of course, superior *will* contributed to the failure of the French to avoid being surrounded thus allowing the Viet Minh to win the Battle of Dien Bien Phu and change the outcome of the Indochina War.[15]

Adversary pressure is important for several reasons: First, such pressure signifies something slowing or negatively affecting one's progress toward a goal or objective. Second, such pressure can cause a premature decision and action because of the potential advantages the adversary could derive from his pressure on his opponent. Third, adversary pressure can be emotionally unsettling and stressful, particularly if the person or people on the receiving end did not expect said pressure to appear. As another historical example, my favorite situation in which adversary pressure came forth and influenced outcomes involves the Battle of Gettysburg. Lee invaded the North with his army in June 1863 with the intention of ending the war. His plan was to move deep into Union country and with one bold stroke threaten and perhaps occupy Harrisburg and Philadelphia to place unbearable pressure on President Lincoln and Congress. Such a bold move, he hoped, would cause the North to submit to his imposition of the South's *will.* Originally, Lee had no intention of engaging in a pitched battle at Gettysburg, particularly when the North held the positional advantage after the first few hours of July 1, 1863. But his lead elements under Brigadier

14. A loose paraphrasing of Shakespeare's words in *Macbeth.*
15. https://www.britannica.com/event/Battle-of-Dien-Bien-Phu

General Johnston Pettigrew of Heath's division and A. P. Hill's corps ran into what was first thought as a small force. Pettigrew recalled Lee's intent and withdrew. Pettigrew, Heath, and Hill conferred and all agreed for Heath to advance to Gettysburg the next day, ostensibly to find shoes reported to be in the town in large numbers. On July 1, Heath sent, in a normal rotation of honor, the Alabama Brigade of James Archer forward toward Gettysburg, and he promptly ran into the defenses set up by the Union cavalry of John Buford. Skirmishers began fighting, followed by Confederate regular infantry who battled the two brigades of John Buford's cavalry. The battle was joined when the North rushed its closest army corps—John Reynolds's I Corps—to Gettysburg to take up the fight. However, Lee did not have his "eyes and ears" of intelligence as his cavalry was out of contact; therefore, his decisions came devoid of intelligence gathering other than what I call battle information, which, as Clausewitz indicated, was most often wrong and exaggerated due to fear and the need to exaggerate.[16]

The menacing and growing Union army occupied the high ground south of Gettysburg on Cemetery Ridge. Though Lee could have and should have made the decision to back off and go another route, he chose to fight the Union forces even though the Union Army had a tremendous advantage of position. Lee chose to deal with the adversary pressure where it was and to do so by initially working on the flanks to find a place to roll up the Union line and then switched to a frontal assault on the last day of the battle with Pickett's Charge. His decision making was poor, and the physical presence and active pressure of the Union Army pushed him into making the decisions that led to a terrible defeat in a monumental struggle between the North and the South that changed the course of the war.[17]

Organizational, political, historical, and cultural pressure. Other pressures can influence decision making, and often the decision between peace and war but at its nub, one finds virulent struggles over *will.* A good example of this kind of pressure came from the 1962 Cuban Missile Crisis. After President Kennedy found out that the Soviets were installing ballistic missiles in Cuba, he called together a secret executive committee (ExComm). It was from this ExComm that the great advice came to quarantine Cuba rather than invade, bomb, or blockade. Messages went back and forth between Khrushchev and Kennedy. Interestingly, Kennedy humanized the problem and tried to think like his opponent and why he had taken this

16. Clausewitz, *On War,* 117.

17. In this entire section about Gettysburg, I consulted Shelby Foote, *The Civil War: 1863* (New York: Random House, 1963), 464–581.

pathway. He started pondering Khrushchev's pressures.[18] As Kennedy thought about his opponent, he asked about the meaning of words, thoughts, tenor, and questions in message traffic between the Kremlin and the White House putting into his mind a human spin about his adversary, Khrushchev:

> Kennedy and ExComm showed uncommon interest in the history in the heads of their adversaries. Kennedy's questions at the first ExComm meeting were about the Soviet Union, conceived as a single rational actor. He asked, in effect, why is he doing this to me? . . . his interest in when the rational actor had decided to depart from a previous line of conduct. . . . So far as we can tell, neither Kennedy nor any member of ExComm wondered aloud about the Russian history that Khrushchev and other Soviet leaders had experienced—the Revolution, the civil war, the Great Purge, World War II, de-Stalinization, the split with China.[19]

Not every leader or decision maker attempts to think as the adversary and, in particular, to try to understand the organizational, political, historical, and cultural pressures any particular decision maker might be feeling. I advise you to take this influence on adversary decisions and subsequent contributors to outcomes of fights seriously. In another situation during this crisis, Khrushchev sent a rambling cable that at least opened the door to peace if the United States would promise not to invade Cuba. A curter message followed, but the ExComm reacted to what the first message said and promptly ignored the second, less promising message:

> [T]he President and members of the ExComm speculated about factionalism in the Kremlin. They visualized Khrushchev, stamping around his giant office in the Kremlin, possibly not altogether sober, dictating to a secretary, and sending off the text without showing it to anyone. They imagined other members of the Politburo bending over the second cable and tightening its wording. . . . Kennedy and his ExComm paid attention to organization histories. . . . They thought of how organizations behaved without asking explicitly how they had behaved over time and why. But the fact that they took organizational behavior into account at all distinguishes them from ninety-odd percent of the decision-making groups of which we [the authors] have personal knowledge.[20]

Familial pressure. This is a pressure that all leaders and their supporters have to take into account. Often, decision makers trust members of their family before anybody else, for example, President John Kennedy chose his brother Robert Kennedy to be his attorney general and trusted adviser. Any

---

18. Richard E. Neustadt and Earnest R. May, *Thinking in Time* (New York: The Free Press, 1986), 7–12.
19. Ibid. p. 12.
20. Ibid. p. 12.

family could have expectations of a high-ranking decision maker and thereby place pressure on this decision maker to meet the family's goals and objectives. President Trump has placed and relies upon several members of his family for active roles in government, and they, in fact, advise him. Sometimes decision makers put members of their family in high-level executive positions in a government only to have them turn rogue and criminal—Saddam Hussein's sons, for example. Therefore, one can conclude that whether through direct or indirect pressure, the family in many countries matters and deep-thinking people must take this kind of pressure into account and set out to understand and observe behavior forthcoming from familial pressure.

Hatred and revenge pressure. Hatred is a powerful emotion. Though emotion can cause and embellish the reasons for hatred, it is emotion that fuels its cancerous growth in one's mind and heart. Sometimes hatred and revenge pressure comes from that which one immediately observes, endures, and feels. At other times, hatred and revenge stretch over centuries.

Revenge can and often is the offspring of hatred. Revenge and hatred closely, perhaps inextricably, relate with one another. I believe you would agree that in most historical cases of revenge, hatred was the handmaiden. Cases of hatred though don't always end with a case of revenge. It may be impossible; one might not have the capabilities required; one might come to a sphere of rationality that blows aside the emotion fueling hatred and retribution.

In our interest to understand, indeed comprehend, this powerful force, revenge, one first recalls that it connects with an earlier consideration, "that which truly matters." Continuing with this line of thought, always remember this: revenge has extraordinary powers to grip people in its viselike jaws and extract the level of retribution the originating and pressuring emotion demands. When revenge occurs, there imposition of action occurs. This action can be visible or invisible and the force applied can be both types. Revenge begets more revenge, and soon the actors of this stage of strife get caught up in a circular motion whereby one act of revenge begets a retaliatory act for payback and so on. Revenge drives action, and it drives retaliation to that action. The level of revenge helps a recipient of a vengeful action decide whether to retaliate in kind or escalate. This growing circle brings revenge inflictor and recipient into an interaction of opposites with their circle always moving, to which escape is often impossible. Their involvement with one another involves a distinct oscillation between perpetrator and recipient and recipient and perpetrator of vengeful action. The level of revenge inflicted on another helps the now perpetrator of revenge to select the means by which he intends to reinflict revenge on his target.

Revenge, therefore, in the context of action and behavior becomes something an observant person can anticipate before punitive actions occur. One needs to be mindful that before a vindictive act, the avenger must set necessary conditions necessary to achieve his desired outcomes, always his point of view and desired level of retribution. All of these thoughts combine to help make more transparent this seemingly invisible starting point and the accompanying expulsion of energy—his drive to invoke his way on the person from whom he seeks revenge. It also provides an opportunity to intercede with the momentum of the heretofore confined emotions that schemed and acted to discharge physical actions to gain that ever so satisfying feeling of inflicting revenge on one's enemy.

In this chapter, I first discussed alternatives. The presence and power of alternatives that human beings face when caught in conflict and war have a direct influence on the overall outcomes of struggles people experience in conflict. Fear of and disdain for alternatives, for a starting point, need to be a subject of much thought because each can suddenly appear and affect *will.* For example, I explained as we think back in history and find the ominous reality of suicide bombers, Kamikaze pilots in World War II, the charge of Medal of Honor Winner Colonel Joshua Chamberlin in the face of certain death in the battle of Gettysburg in the Civil War, and the amazing exploits of Medal of Honor winner U.S. Army Green Beret, Master Sergeant Raul Perez "Roy" Benavidez experienced in Vietnam, all provide examples of people performing incredible feats with no fear of alternatives. I for one am in awe of what human beings can do and not do. Thus, to learn about *will* I postulated that one must give thought to alternatives and pressures. To assist in gaining an appreciation of the importance of alternatives, I presented examples of fear of and disdain for alternatives to include 1) unconditional surrender during WWII; 2) control of data, information, and knowledge during war, 3) Japanese civilians on Okinawa in the 1945 Pacific battle; 4) over the top in WWI; 5) the beast (bureaucracies) set loose in Nazi Germany; and 5) the ultimate insanity of Verdun in 1916. This chapter provided definitions for fear, disdain, and alternative. I brought forth as an example the reoccupation of the Rhineland in 1936 and how Hitler's *will* might have been thwarted with his subsequently ousting from power by his own generals, if the French or British had imposed their desired objectives against the German reoccupation. As another consideration I discussed how people must surely think about pressures, fear, and disdain for alternatives, or fail in their endeavors. However, I concluded one only finds completeness and comfort in their thinking if they can wear first one, then the other, of two impressionable masks permitting the wearer to see viable alternatives through the eyes and the minds of the recipient of an imposition of volition; and then via the other malleable mask to see viable alternatives through the eyes and mind of the side imposing actions to reach its desired outcomes. Each mask deviates allowing their wearer to feel fear and stress and the influences sometimes frightening comprehension of context and mortal danger from hostile actions. Importantly, with transmogrification, a fear of or disdain for alternatives can force, influence, indeed dominate, struggles involving one *will against another.* I also discussed several varieties of pressure that affect outcomes conflicts. I discussed how physical pressure affects one's emotions and thereby affects decision making. Military people in extremis reason about their adversary's use of physical pressure even when deemed to be impossible, such as when the Viet Minh dragged their artillery to the hills surrounding Dien Bien Phu in Indochina in 1954 and thus beat the French forces and to the expulsion of the French from Indochina. I also provided an example of the strength of position the Union Army experienced over the Confederate Army during the awful days in early July 1863 during the battle of Gettysburg. Pressure, an important aspect in anybody's attempts to understand *will,* realizes the imperative of recognizing how the influence of pressure influences that which truly matters even when the adversary protects this sensitive core or nub. I stated that pressure serves as a lubricant, as it were, to the engine of *will* and its 14 essential elements. Of course, I presented you with the definition of pressure I use in this book. It is *the continuous physical or emotional "weight" a decision maker, or anyone for that matter, feels, intuits, senses, or thinks about as he makes a decision.* For edification, I provided some typical types of pressure one finds at every corner, at every turn of the road, including 1) self-pressure, ego, and self-esteem; 2) physical and adversarial; 3) organizational, political, historical, and cultural; 4) familial; and 5) hatred and revenge pressure.

CHAPTER 12

Balancing Advantages, Disadvantages, and the Marvelous Trinity

Argument: *In this chapter, I explain that in conflict opponents seek advantages to win; their object is to hold their advantages and degrade their adversary's. In this chapter, I introduce seven advantages necessary to win: 1) initiative; 2) tempo; 3) momentum; 4) knowledge; 5) decisions; 6) position; and 7) freedom of movement.*[1] *The best strategy causes disadvantages for adversaries to appear. I introduce Clausewitz's Marvelous Trinity and the need to sustain a balance among the people, government, and military. Advantage rests with balance; disadvantage with disequilibrium. I tell readers that wise people always consider war as an act of policy; they never allow the trinity to tilt out of balance because decay sets in and dissipates one's strength of* will.

In any kind of conflict or competition, contestants seek advantages[2] over their opponent. They seek these advantages to win; to be a victor, they must hold their advantages and degrade their adversary's advantages. The quest for advantage applies to most all people-oriented activities, such as athletics, interacting, transacting, driving, buying, golfing, going on a cruise, bargaining in the Grand Bazar in Istanbul, and on and on. People like and seek advantages; often their motivation involves the process, not the end. Human beings, from all walks of life and from around the world, savor a position of superiority over others, particularly during competitive events, sometimes even in noncompetitive everyday situations. Here is a borrowed thought that helps me put self-interest and the pursuit of advantage in perspective:

1. Mao, *On Guerilla Warfare*, 98.
2. *Advantage*: A situation of being in a preferable position over another competitor.

Man was sent into the world to contend with man, and to get the advantage of him in every possible way. The great object of life is to be first at the winning post . . . it matters nothing how many of his fellow candidates he hustles on the way. W. S. Gilbert (of Gilbert and Sullivan)

Possessing an advantage contributes to a possessor's sense of mental, physical, or emotional "wellness." In some people, one finds the thrill of the process, the thrill of the chase to achieve an advantage to be better than actually seizing an advantage. Of course, I must add that goodness rests in situations in which one's adversary doesn't know that you have an advantage over him or because you have infested his defenses and pretended to be in situ. In real life, you set forth a cocked and poised action whose trajectory and velocity can negate one or more of your adversary's self-proclaimed advantages and influence how you find and affect his well-hidden and protected disadvantages.

At the nub of any thinking about advantage and disadvantage, however, one finds the grand motivator—self-interest. Once we peer at our adversary and know that he peers at us, when we consider the adversary and as he reasons about the us, when we attempt to think similarly to him and know he is doing the same, it is only then we can begin to discover his reasoning in sufficient depth to comprehend his advantages and disadvantages from his perspective. At such a point, he could choose to try to protect his advantages and disadvantages (from our actions whose purpose is to increase the antithesis—disadvantage). The best outcome from a friendly perspective is to cause your adversary's disadvantages to be more significant and influential than any advantage he might hold. Or you might want to use any of these exploited disadvantages as a "window" through which one could pass to either find more advantages or to attack and degrade the adversary's advantages. Such attacks could place the adversary on the horns of a dilemma, causing him to divert his time and energy in "plugging the hole" in his self-proclaimed advantage or disadvantage framework as it is being perturbed and perhaps degraded by our actions or to proceed with the initial activity and the initial advantage. We would know, of course, whether we face a smart and worldly adversary or a lesser one. Either adversary obviously commands a different approach with which to compete depending upon the adversary's version of duality and riding the wild pendulum. Of further interest, each side in a conflict possesses or controls advantages and in doing so, they expose their hidden and protected disadvantages (this is, once again, the influence of Heraclitus on our work in critical thinking—the unity of opposites).

Again, advantage means "enjoying a position of superiority or state of improved or superior positioning over another competitor." The antithesis of advantage is, of course, disadvantage: a state of being, physical or mental, involving an instance of finding one's self trying to operate but doing so under the dark cloud of being in an unfavorable circumstance or condition and knowing the inferiority of the circumstance. When you find a disadvantage, consider pouncing on it to exploit the opportunity, as it could be brief. Or you could have a faux opportunity, perhaps even a trap.

When I consider advantage, seven come to mind, as I have stated earlier. An advantage can be strong by itself, but advantages work most effectively when one bundles them, such as initiative and position; tempo and momentum; knowledge and decision making; and position and freedom of movement/maneuver. Any effective leader charged with the well-being of their people as well as accomplishing complicated mission sets, charges their thought supporters to identify probabilities for success via seizing, using, and simultaneously anticipating and blocking an adversary's use of these advantages:

1. Initiative: Setting the of terms of action and associated outputs/outcomes, reaction, and counteraction in a conflict or competition.
2. Tempo: A rate or rhythm of activity; a pace or speed of action that provides favorable circumstances over a slower adversary.
3. Momentum: Property or propensity of a moving object to continue moving, to come into being.
4. Knowledge: A superior realization of reality and facts, when one compares this state of being to an adversary's state of being. It is a level or a body of compiled, related, information taken to a higher level of meaning and applicability; it is a comprehension and understanding coming from an acquired, organized, and related a body of facts and truths, although both could rapidly change. Knowledge has a short life of value, but when it is in its prime, it helps decision makers lower uncertainty and manage risk.
5. Decision: In a competitive situation enjoying a situation of marked superiority over an opponent via making faster and better decisions than an adversary.
6. Position: A place—physical, mental, cyber, moral—where someone or something is located whereby the location provides a locus of superiority over an adversary—a favorable or superior place of conflict.
7. Freedom of movement[3]: A situation of superiority over one or more adversaries in moving from one or more points or positions (physical and nonphysical, e.g., cyberspace, infosphere) to another—faster, more safely, with less friction, and more effectively.

If one side in a conflict senses that their adversary has an advantage, they work to turn it into a disadvantage. This proposition should be self-evident,

3. Mao, *On Guerrilla Warfare*, 98.

but I have found it not to be. That is to say, if I know an adversary has an advantage over me, I must turn his advantage into a disadvantage and claim the advantage for my operations at his expense. If one side attacks the other to gain an advantage, the recipient must know and feel the perturbation of the context and the ratio of advantage and disadvantage and respective diminution of capability. They must try to reverse this situation. Along with rumination, supporters perform this kind of work with actions, assessments, and adaptations along with wargaming.

I now present four thoughts for you to ponder. First, I ask you to consider a dangle operation. That is to say, dangle a false advantage or better yet, a false disadvantage for the adversary to "nibble" and "bite." Second, sometimes an adversary won't know he has a disadvantage until you strike, manipulate, or negate what he thought to be his advantage. Third, at times, your adversary seeks that which he believes the friendly decision maker believes to be his disadvantage, only to walk into a cleverly baited trap—he mistakenly takes a friendly decision maker's estimated (from the adversary's reasoning) disadvantage only to find a friendly advantage waiting to pummel his being. Fourth, the adversary not only responds in kind to strikes or attempts to manipulate the friendly decision maker's advantages or disadvantages (friendly perspective of the adversary's reasoning), but instead acts against the friendly's strike capability, whose intention for use involves penetrating the "moat of protection" surrounding a perceived castle protecting the adversary's disadvantage. In such a situation, you tease from your adversary's mind three choices: 1) protect the disadvantage; 2) cover the gaping hole in the all-important window of opportunity for affecting the disadvantage; or 3) change the condition or circumstances causing the disadvantage. In all three situations, the adversary is vulnerable to your actions to worsen his already beleaguered disadvantage. Soon the adversary could very well have to draw from his advantages to shore up his disadvantages.

In another variation on this theme, at times people engage in a kind of mental combat where each side tries to bring forth a Trojan Horse that is a state of equilibrium. Inside the Trojan Horse they plant furies—confusion, fear, errors, misgivings, pressures. When the time is right, they open the trap door under the horse and allow the furies out to eat away at the mind of their adversary's decision maker—this is knowledge war, mental combat, and a war of wits. His risk and uncertainty escalate, making him vulnerable to your moves to create advantages. In this sense, you would lie low and await the right time to burst through the false state of equilibrium and strike. The emotional and physical influences of such activities could very well cause your true advantages to show as fake disadvantages primed for even further action at his weakened advantages and even further degrade his perceived disadvantages.

At the start of a conflict, each side goes into the fray with a good idea of their advantages and disadvantages, not only actualities, but also their appearances.[4] Poet W. H. Auden once wrote "Does God ever judge us by appearances? I suspect that he does." People live their lives by appearance—but does what one observes in another person's appearance enable them to see and understand what is in the minds, souls, and inner strengths of the person under inspection? No. Regardless, appearances are important; they often prove "real" and "true" in the eyes of both beholders in a conflict.

As adversaries seek one or more advantages, the smart wager is to bet on your ability to think like the adversary and thereby beat him. But expect your adversary to engage in duality and ride the wild pendulum and thereby attempt to enter your mind with respect to how you consider your advantages and disadvantages. It follows then, an adversary could attack or seek influence on your disadvantages (from your view of your disadvantages). The adversary knows, if he spots one of your disadvantages, he can pounce and use it not only for a general trouncing but also and perhaps more importantly to crack open the crevase in your armor to seek other advantages awaiting him, with the right kind of reasoning driving the right kind of action at the right place and at the right time. You do not want to be surprised when the adversary interferes your efforts to strengthen or hide your disadvantages.

Now you can edge toward comprehending the complicated nature of relevant contexts from views of other human beings but relative to our own views of the situation that is bringing the adversary and us together. Such dualistic perspectives, expectations, and interpretations heavily influence whether friendly operations can succeed. After all, our interactions with our adversary exemplify the motion and expenditure of energy occurring and spilling out of the unity of opposites whole where action and counteraction occur. One side holds an advantage but the other side covets this advantage and its fickleness enables it to flip from one side to the other. It follows that how to think about our adversary becomes tempered by how we think he thinks about us. But we have to think about how he thinks we think about his thinking about us—phew! This is mental combat against an adaptive, capable foe.

Advantages come to one side in a conflict because that side possesses and uses the recommendations of its best and most agile minds (including responses from unsolicited, context-produced data), armed with a philosophy to condition their minds to recognize the constant presence and influence of fluctuations in life and in particular in operational contexts thanks to chaos—and knowing, with certainty, that the unity of opposites brings constant energy and change with their interaction. You should know for sure by now that the struggle for advantages and the protection

4. Arendt, *The Life of the Mind*, e-book, location 300 of 8237.

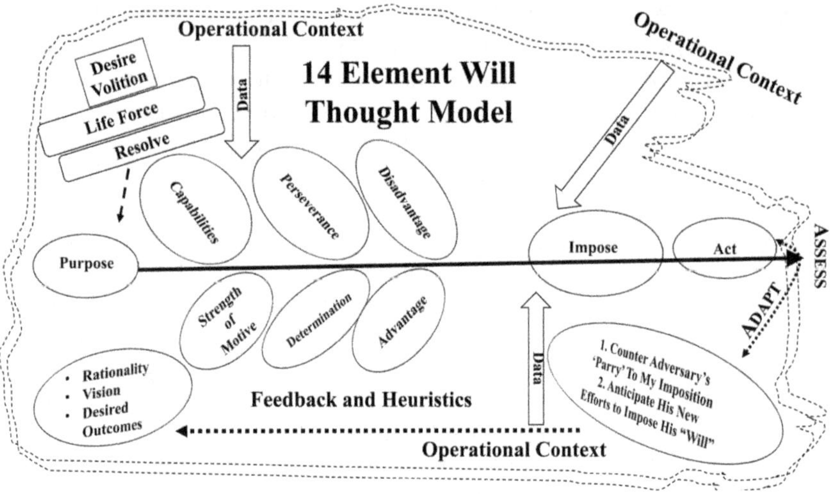

Figure 12.1. Advantage and Disadvantage

of disadvantages ceases when one side, out of necessity, acquiesces to the other in the struggle in which they compete.

Advantages and disadvantages relate to one another, of course, but they also relate to the other aspects of *will* we consider. I ask you to consider the connectedness of advantage and disadvantage to other parts of the model in Figure 12.1.

Competitors wargame to discern possible adversary views and responses to actions, assessment, and adaptation. They also recognize that the adversary is undoubtedly wanting to do the same thing to his opponent. Thus, one finds themselves in mental conflict, with each side seeking to attack their adversary's plans, if possible at their inception,[5] with a constant and pulsating pressure to find and exploit advantages. As friendly analysts ponder this problem using deep-thinking methodologies, they deliberate from the adversary's perspective and see the world as he sees it—they get into his skin, so to speak, with the limitations I discussed earlier. Our adversary recognizes advantages and disadvantages for himself, and he identifies and views advantages and disadvantages from his opponent's perspective. We prepare for him to protect his advantages. He actively seeks to keep us on the defensive and in an inferior position. Our adversary is resolute in his intent to win and thereby uses his capabilities and actions wisely so as to keep his us in a position relative to him.

In a struggle for advantages and disadvantages in a particular operational context, people focus on and direct their decisions and subsequent actions on what is important to their decision maker's intent. Ultimately

5. Sun Tzu, *The Art of War*, 77.

mission outcome and deep thinking about the operational context housing a particular conflict is of supreme importance, but only in a complete sense, when we include hard mental work in the adversary's view of his and our operational contexts and the direct and indirect advantages this context presents. How does one gain understanding of the adversary's perspective when it is so different from ours? It goes like this: Approach thinking like the adversary by knowing how he reasons and influences on his mental processes. So, you forge ahead and see in your imagination what he reveals as his persona, apperception, personage, and physiognomy (facial features or visage). This human being is probably imbued with hatred and passion, but more specifically this enemy has 1) a grim determination and resolve; 2) a recognition and wariness about his adversary; 3) watchful eyes so as to not get surprised; 4) thoughts about his and our views of operational context; and 5) holistic thinking skills. This kind of leader could be a serious obstacle to winning a contest.

CLAUSEWITZ'S MARVELOUS TRINITY AND *WILL*

Though Clausewitz has been dead for almost 200 years, his Marvelous Trinity is still used by serious thinkers who muse about the vagaries and intricacies of conflict. Let us start our endeavor by focusing our attention on what he wrote in *On War* as he developed this notion of the remarkable trinity. It is packed with wisdom, but it seems that politicians and other policy makers either never read anything about The Marvelous Trinity, or if they did, they promptly forgot about it. I still find the trinity to be a useful theoretical construct with many applications, although it must be adapted it to our world of today. So, I call forth my audacious Über-thinker and thought pilgrim to help understand. They shall act as our Dante and I the role of Virgil, traveling up to the gates of Paradiso.[6] Clausewitz's wise thoughts counsel us yet today:

> [A] remarkable trinity—composed of primordial violence, hatred, and enmity. . . . a blind natural force; of the play of chance and probability within the creative spirit is free to roam; and its elements of subordination, as an instrument of policy, which makes it subject to reason alone. The first . . . concerns the people; the second the commander and his army; the third the government. . . . Our task . . . is to develop a theory that maintains a balance between these three tendencies.[7]

The trinity is quite simple when we view it as a triangle with equal parts in two dimensions and in stasis. Our intellectual challenges start to occur

6. In Dante's the *Divine Comedy*, Virgil, the great Roman poet and author of *The Aeneid*, guides Dante through the Inferno and Purgatory, and then to Paradiso, where Virgil, as a pagan, could not follow.

7. Clausewitz, *On War*, 89.

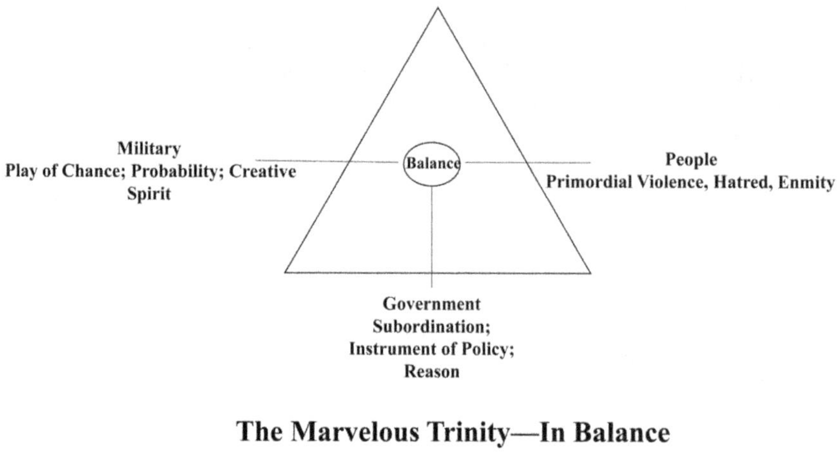

Figure 12.2. The Marvelous Trinity—In Balance

when we recognize the triangle has four dimensions (depth, width, height, and time) and each prove continuously active in preparation for, or in actual conflict against a resisting entity (Figure 12.2).

When the winds coming from conflict disturb the trinity, change occurs due to activities in nonlinear operational contexts that harbor the collisions-intersections-careening-conjoining of rival complex adaptive systems. It becomes difficult to tie any one of the three to the ground and vivisect its elements and tendencies so as to understand them and how the parts relate and eventually work as a whole. People should want to monitor the balance Clausewitz speaks about in the passage from *On War* earlier. As mentioned, the challenge is to keep the tendencies of the trinity balanced among themselves. If one element breaks free and starts to dominate the other two elements, possible trouble becomes real trouble. As an example, consider Germany in WWI. At the start of the war, the three elements of the trinity—reason (government), creativity (military), and passion (populace)—were fairly well balanced within their culture, but have no doubt, the military was the most influential among the three elements. And the longer the war lasted, the more the military came to dominate—the military seemed to completely forget his admonition that the use of force is politics by other means. Figure 12.3 provides a simple representation showing the tilt to a condition of the trinity being unbalanced—tilting to hatred and military action.

Take note of this graphic that shows a trinity out of balance, and thus out of control. This theory is simple and understandable, but generally speaking, people don't live through conflicts imbued with the meaning of the trinity and its far reaches into other aspects involving *will.* Senior

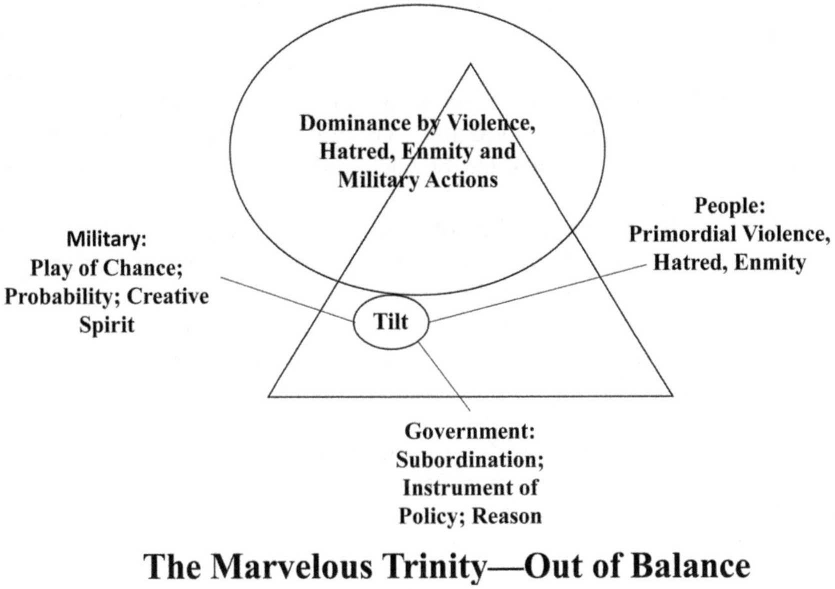

Figure 12.3. The Always Dangerous "Tilt" of the Trinity

leaders in any kind of conflict have to master this concept and work diligently to keep the three parts of the trinity equal in size and taut via balancing mechanisms. The three elements prove essential to successfully using the philosophy and basis of the trinity to estimate and judge the strength of spirit and power of thought behind each. This balance and spiritual approach to comprehension of the trinity come with an acknowledgement of the need to understand what is important, to compromise to sustain balance among the parts, and to put away differences of views and selfish hatreds to ensure harmony among the three parts. As some quick examples, I do think the U.S. government in World War II did a great job in keeping these three elements of the trinity balanced. Germany's, Japan's, and the Soviets' elements tilted out of balance quickly and stayed tilted toward the military and often myopic decision making; distorted view of prowess; ethnic hatred; and often brutal treatment of their own people, citizens in conquered countries, and prisoners of war.

To use the Marvelous Trinity successfully, consider it not only from a friendly perspective, but also account for the presence and influence of an adversary's trinity. It is important to identify the particulars for his trinity and devise a stratagem for affecting the three elements, thus enhancing our efforts to impose our desired outcomes on this adversary or competitor. Our thinking blossoms by asking and answering some rhetorical questions about the trinity but with the adversary's view in mind. How does it work?

Is it working now? Is there a dominant element? How does the adversary view his trinity? How does he view our trinity? How does he view our views of their views on his own trinity and our trinity? Once again, you must circle back to the concepts of duality and riding the wild pendulum. I apologize if this sounds convoluted—I do not consider it to be so, but you have to take the time to consider the back and forth requirements coming with duality.

Following along with this line of thought, one has to find a discussion and a meeting of minds between the policy maker(s) and the commander(s). They decide upon the use of military power relative to the course of action they design so as to achieve the aim, goals, objectives, and strategies—the act of policy and the military means have to be ready to implement in accordance with the political goal(s) of the policy maker.

> The first, the supreme, the most far-reaching act of judgment that the statesman and commander have to make is to establish . . . the kind of war on which they are embarking; neither mistaking it for, nor trying to turn it into, something that is alien to its nature.[8]

How apparently simple, but how difficult it is to maintain balance among the people (primordial hatred, passion), military (chance, probability, creativity), and the statesman (government, reason for being) for subordination, policy, and reason!

This revelation causes our intrepid Über-thinker and thought pilgrim to pause, catch their breath, and ask an important question: "If it is so easy to understand what Clausewitz is saying about relationships among the elements of this Marvelous Trinity, why does it seem like this maxim is never used?" I respond with this explanation: "To help us think and act in all types of conflict and ruminate about the importance of war (its conduct and outcomes) and its subordination to political ends, people have to comprehend theoretical constructs. Generally speaking, people planning and executing policy and military action to accomplish goals and objectives neither know nor understand the theoretical constructs, the history, the context, and the deep thinking behind the theory—all essential for praxis, as it were, moving theory into practice.

As students and other practitioners of conflict interpret Clausewitz and then try to bring his theory into our time and place and the future, they also need to learn about what other theorists and warriors thought. They need such learning in a collegial environment before they are "in the fire" of action. Is this a simple problem to resolve? No, in the sense that senior military people, for example, can and should do better in working with policy makers to do what he calls for in his thinking—the first, the supreme,

---

8. Clausewitz, *On War*, 88–89.

the most far-reaching act of judgment, and so forth. Of course, senior policy makers must know and understand at least a modicum of this theory before they resort to military force on their adversary and to ensure this adversary doesn't preempt our imposition and seize the initiative. In my view, in the rush of arrogance inherent in being big and strong, people start taking shortcuts and do not perform the necessary deep thinking to use his dictums and theory about his Marvelous Trinity.

Sometimes people simply do not like each other and therefore subordinate the good of the country or corporation and instead pursue their own interests. After winning at Ilipa (206 BC), Scipio Africanus had taken all of Spain from the Carthaginians. Being a strategist of the first order, Scipio Africanus wanted his next step to be to take his army to North Africa, threaten Carthage, and cause Carthage's leadership to demand that their hero, Hannibal, come home from his military campaign in Italy and fight Scipio. From historical analyses, it appears that many Roman senators feared Scipio and some were jealous of his successes. So instead of recognizing him as the hero he was for what he accomplished in Spain, they granted him only one legion to take to North Africa. This occurred not for the good of Rome, but for mollifying the jealousy and fear these senators had for Scipio.[9] Eventually Scipio put together an army (partially comprised of dishonored and exiled survivors of the massacre at Cannae [216 BC]) and defeated Hannibal at the Battle of Zama in 202 BCE.

Some people are altruistic and caring with high moral values and intent. They are rare. One finds many more individuals who are narcissists, mentally puny, perverted, and sometimes one finds aggregates and aggregations of people who reason only in terms of their self-promotion and self-interests even hiding true intent behind a fig leaf of doing what is right and best for say a country and organization. People can be both bad and good in spirit and intention. Individuals and organizations and sometimes countries have to soul-search and engage in introspection and find where they stand, and to openly see, grasp, and think about that which makes them human. Often, if we are honest with ourselves, the seesaw upon which we stand and seek to balance tilts first toward evil and self-serving outlooks and actions, and then only occasionally and slightly toward goodness. Often self-interest is a final arbitrator; it is the albatross hanging from the heads and shoulders of humanity to always be strongly inclined to swing to self-interest. Being skeptical about human nature is all right, and wariness shall serve us well throughout their lives. The human nature of which I speak involves avarice, narcissism, self-interest *über alles* (meaning more than anything else in the world), sycophancy, fear, jealousy, charlatanism,

9. B. H. Liddell Hart, *Scipio Africanus: Greater Than Napoleon* (Cambridge, MA: Da Capo Press, 1926), 112–122.

retribution, and changing values and beliefs for their own interest, but it is what it is what it is. It is all part of the human package of being. It follows one of the first thoughts in any study of the Marvelous Trinity involves considering strength of motive and always self-interest levels of people involved in each of the three points of our theoretical trinity.

In the book *Fiasco* by Thomas Ricks, the author discusses the abhorrent relationship between the senior military officer and the senior statesman on the scene after the initial combat was over and Baghdad captured and occupied in 2003. The two most important organizations—one civilian and the other military—had no official relationship to tether them via a well-established chain of command. Instead the military and civilian Coalition Provisional Authority (CPA) leaders and underlings did not answer to a single decision maker and did not get along at all from a personal and operational context, and operations for the common good therefore suffered:

> Fundamentally, the CPA and the [U.S.] military had different conceptions of what the United States was doing in Iraq. The civilians, more in line with Bush administration thinking about transforming Iraq and the region, implemented policies that set out to change the politics, economy, and even the culture of Iraq. The military, less culturally sympathetic to the administration's revolutionary goals thought of its mission as almost the opposite, calling it "stability and security operations." . . . After the war, the military sought to keep the population quiet, while the CPA "focused on change," which meant that it was bound to provoke vocal and violent reactions from some Iraqis opposed to those changes.[10]

Realizing how easy it is to form opinions and judge via my apperception, as I think about this issue in the comfort of my office, I cannot help being critical about Iraq and pondering these seven questions, rhetorical in nature but clawing at my mind nonetheless:

1. Why didn't America do what Clausewitz argued for relative to our view of the Marvelous Trinity for Iraq from their perspective (e.g., the Baathists and Sunnis who were forced out of their previous positions of power and who happened to hate not only the Shi'a, but also the invader—the United States)?
2. Why enter a conflict without understanding the struggle for ascendancy of *will?* What is *will* from a dualist perspective (adversary and friendly)?
3. Why did faulty assumptions[11] about *will* live? Why didn't people aggressively and quickly challenge and change assumptions if the context,

10. Thomas E. Ricks, *Fiasco: The American Military Adventure in Iraq* (New York: The Penguin Press, 2006), 210.

11. *Assumption*: 1) A supposition on the current situation or a presupposition on the future course of events, either or both assumed to be true in the absence of positive proof, necessary to enable the commander in the process of planning to complete an estimate of

adversary, and our instruments for implementing policy ran into trouble, or discovered a different and more difficult truth instead of preconceived notions?
4. Why weren't our political and military leaders agile and ready to change quickly since the adversary (a complex adaptive system) makes co-evolution and adaptation a continuous practice?
5. Why couldn't policy makers and senior military leaders cooperate and form a close partnership so as to firmly affix the instrument for carrying out policy and the policy itself but always subordinating the military solution to the civilian government's policy making?
6. Why couldn't policy makers and senior military leaders agree upon, coordinate, and synchronize policies for accomplishing national aim, goals, objectives, strategy, etc.?
7. Why couldn't senior leaders understand each other's roles and missions (policy and military) so as to conduct the kind of war and peace high-level senior policy makers should desire to embark upon? Such an understanding by political and military leaders would have balanced the trinity and thereby forced leaders—political and military—to describe in detail their aim, goals, and objectives. Such cooperation would have enabled military leaders to address political concerns and vice versa and would have enabled political and military leaders to have confidence about the kind of war they were in so a coherent unity of effort and chain of command could have been in play.

I bring up this situation because it illustrates the poor thinking in which people sometimes engage. Sometimes people don't bother to consider what happens after the outcome of a fight has been decided before using the military instrument to satisfy foreign policy aims, goals, objectives, strategies, etc. Senior military leaders must know theory and explain it in a meaningful way to senior policy makers—not pedantically, steeped in the arrogance of knowledge, but in a style conductive for understanding in a partnership. If civilian policy makers and senior military leaders knew and kept the trinity and other dictums in mind and then executed the required political policy and military actions in tandem and always relative to the policy goal for which the military action was shaped and created, then I submit the war at best would not have occurred, and would have been short-lived at worst. Also, if the operations designed to accomplish the aim, goals, objectives, strategies, etc., were wrong, which they often are, we

---

the situation and make a decision on the course of action. DOD Joint Publication 1-02, March 2017, 2) A thing or outcome accepted as true or as certain to happen, without proof. An assumption is a guess one designs to fill in a knowledge gap or a mystery.

should not enter the blame game, accusing one another as the perpetrator of the failure at hand, as so many people appear prone to do.

INCENTIVES AND INDUCEMENTS

Incentives and inducements are important considerations in the subject of *will*. By design, they prove important in attempting to cause an opponent to accept our way of thinking and our desired outcomes. Unfortunately, when using the coercive tools of incentive and inducement, outcomes, both short-term and long-term, don't always work as one would hope. Before slogging into the whys of this continuous failure or subpar production out of our chosen incentive or inducement, let us first define each of these terms, then differentiate between the two concepts relative to our given inquiry. An incentive is:

> Something that incites or tends to incite to action or greater effort, as a reward offered for increased productivity[12]; it also means, an action, reward, or promise that could motivate or encourage desired action in an opponent.

An incentive works best with the promise of a reward for observed behavioral changes relative to one side's imposition actions and the other side, the target, who accepts or resists this imposition. Such acceptance could be the reward, but usually one finds more by way of causal relationship to the acceptance in addition to rewards. Often one can find fear of alternatives if the side being coerced via the promise of rewards doesn't accept the offered reward. It could be, too, that the recipient of the imposition and promise of reward believes he can bamboozle the proposing side and actually do better over the long term than if he resists the incentive proposal; this is taking the bait and doing what he wants to do anyway. Also, the receiving side could be weak in capability or not have the purpose, strength of motive, determination, perseverance, willingness to sacrifice, or passion to get involved with a stronger, more capable aggressor. With this type of indirect coercion, the imposing and giving side must always watch with a skeptical eye and intellect to ensure compliance with the agreement. One should never completely trust the side receiving the largess for changing their behavior—people, organizations, and nation-states always reason and act in compliance with their self-interest with all movements and give and take being for self-serving purposes. The side offering the incentive should always be prepared to switch to inducement or even glide into punishment if their intelligence system

12. Incentive. Dictionary.com. Dictionary.com Unabridged. Random House, Inc. http://www.dictionary.com/browse/ incentive (accessed: November 17, 2017).

finds variance or outright indulgence in lying and cheating on any agreement. This thinking has to occur before the incentives come forth.

To do any of this mental work requires the imposing side to understand how the receiving side thinks and is influenced. Agreed-upon actions and subsequent rewards could truly be just a pause awaiting more strength or the receiving element might have in their minds and hearts treachery all the same, due to hatred, retaliation, humiliation, and so forth. Interestingly, the imposing side might be using incentives as a show for awaiting the recipient's bad behavior to surface so they could wreak havoc and weaken their opponent owing to their brand of vengeance and in essence set a trap of "legalized" action for their hated foe to fall into. A peek into the hearts of leaders often yields evil and a penchant to lie.

Some people use inducement and incentive as being the same in their meanings. I do not share this opinion. I believe people need to know the differences and thereby artfully use each to carry out our intended imposition actions on a recalcitrant foe. Let us consider our definition of inducement before proceeding further:

> An offer that promises or encourages one side to accept the terms of the other side's desired outcome. Inducement is more sinister [threatening] than incentive—inducement implies punishment if the receiving side tries to manipulate conditions of the agreement for their self-interest. Inducement can also persuade or influence through rewarding good behavior but with the suggestion of heavy punishment if its specter promises to tear apart the recipient if he deviates from promised behavior.

Subtle but important differences play when one uses inducement as a means to alter an opponent's behavior. The difficult part comes with discerning whether the adversary clearly understands the difference between the two concepts—incentive and inducement—and acts accordingly. Deep thinking in the minds of decision makers, intelligence analysts, and collections people proves necessary to make this kind of hefty intellectual work available in our work and interactions with competing entities. Each of these capabilities needs to be explained and "massaged" with help from people from the culture of the decision maker in question and who know the context at hand. One does not want to inadvertently err via an error of omission about "that which truly matters" which is of worth to the recipient from a cultural perspective. A similar cultural approach then helps one to see and understand what happens with their adversary's reasoning and his responses, as one shifts from incentive to inducement.

Difficulty also arises if the side being induced promises one thing but possesses the means to proceed with actions opposite to what they promised—say, a highly secret weapons of mass destruction (WMD) program buried in the tunnels of granite behind the Korean demilitarized zone. What would one need to know to ensure that their side is not flummoxed? As one waypoint, one needs a presence—even appearance on call—to perform due diligence and thereby ensure that the imposer can not only understand what the recipient of promises and what the imposer expects by way of change in behavior of this recipient. As another point, the imposer has to think like the side being coerced to the extent possible. To do so the imposer must engage in mental combat against the receiving side so as to discern possibilities (potentialities unbound by constraints) and probabilities (something likely to happen) from the eyes and minds of their opponent.

What do we need to bring forth to convey the highest probability of success in both incentive and inducement? My Über-thinker and thought pilgrim respond, "That which truly matters, if thought about correctly, ties to the thoughts of a key decision maker or politician and even down to the tactical level in which troops have to deal with IEDs and suicide bombers in some kind of hybrid warfare/cross domain conflict. What we should seek involves the crux or core of the problem set, in which pushing a play/action forces a reaction." "That is all true," I say, "but there is something quite important you missed. Along with learning about the adversary's capabilities by pondering his potential and actual actions, your learning also identifies and leads you to comprehend his (this kind of rumination has to be from the adversary's perspective relative to friendly's intent) view of *will*." But if he has never delved into this subject and thought about and decided upon that which truly matters, it proves difficult to play this mental game. I go on to explain, "In this case of anti-thinking, one might have to show or demonstrate what incentives and inducements mean and what happens if either fails to move the adversary. This kind of foe is much more difficult to deal with when using incentives and inducements. Nonetheless, if he is sophisticated enough to comprehend the considerations of *will*, as we are doing but from his point of view, then our heavy and deep cogitating about the characteristics of *will* could do what we intend via incentives and in extreme cases inducement via economic or military capabilities." In many cases, determining what truly matters becomes a struggle of intellects, understanding, and comprehension from two perspectives. One perspective involves my intrepid Über-thinker and thought pilgrim helping others to consider "that which truly matters" sufficiently to cause them to aspire to protect it. A second perspective involves the adversary's perspective of "that which truly matters" to him and his sources of prestige and power.

Thinking about his point of view requires us to work our minds in a specially designed wargame. Its embodiment comes forth via man and machine symbiosis. Its operating space—the operational context. Its design, synthetic but replicative of actual context including randomness of weather and intrusion of this context by chaos, co-evolution of complex adaptive systems (CAS), adaptation, and constant change. In this wargame, one works with a synthetic environment replicating the operational context in which we expect the conflict to occur. I'm not speaking of the course of action that wargaming commanders of military units follow. Our wargaming is much more detailed. Its success also depends on support of linguists, host nationals, locals, and a virtual knowledge environment (VKE) so as to find the most knowledgeable, creative, and capable of deep-thinking people plus their organizations with their powerful processes, computers, networks, and tacit knowledge.

The operational context must contain linear and nonlinear systems, which compare and contrast as follows:

> A linear system is additive, predictable, tiny inputs cause tiny outputs, little feedback, no co-evolution, prediction with accuracy is possible, little to no friction and chance events exist, no chaos, and so forth. A nonlinear system is just the opposite—non-additive, unpredictable, small inputs can lead to large outputs, feedback on action, co-evolution, and so forth.

Nonlinear systems are particularly important to the outcomes of any conflict—we must learn about these systems and understand their characterizations. Nonlinear systems are chaotic and cause rapid change that wreaks havoc for all sides in a conflict. Here, as a quick review, are a few of the more influential characteristics of nonlinear systems at work in any operational context that build from earlier: 1) nonadditive; 2) unpredictable; 3) small inputs can cause exponentially large outputs; 4) presence and influence of CAS; 5) presence and influence of variables that could become sensitive with right stimuli; 6) co-evolution is important; 7) feedback and adaptation are imperative to vibrancy of CAS, which are co-evolving and seeking feedback; 8) presence and importance of aggregations; and 9) the presence and influence of messy rules due to the nature of CAS and the roiling context in which a conflict is occurring.

To use wargaming to help us consider an ideal state of mind and being, the avatar selected as the adversary should be a highly intelligent avatar, not just an intellectual avatar but one representing an adversary's thinking and that which is most important. The adversary whom they represent proves to be savvy; it knows and uses the operational context to further its interests; it has a past and experience that argue for a human-like ability to think under pressure; it is agile in mind and organization; it has a cultural and an experiential base and trail with which to reach their base; and its mind embeds in a complicated, influential, and often hostile culture. This avatar, programmed to reason like the adversary, is responsive to the influence of current or future states of operational context, as I advocate in this book and elsewhere in my works. That is to say, this avatar views his operational context as pluses and minuses for him and his followers relative to his adversary's and pathways to take advantage of discerned weaknesses, as well as to attack his adversary in this context. He considers how his adversary might come at his vulnerable minuses. In addition, the avatar's program causes it to render how its adversary could be judging the pluses and minuses of the operational context. Furthermore, the adversary avatar in question considers how his adversary might reason as it views not only his own pluses and minuses inherent to the operational context, but also how this adversary views and acts on pluses and minuses that the operational context provides to him and how he might seek to take advantage of the pluses and shore up the minuses.

Our adversary avatar replicates the thinking of his foe (friendly decision makers). This effort presents enormous opportunities for acting first, seizing the initiative, and dictating tempo and momentum, and winning the struggle for knowledge superiority, making superior decisions, and finding and enjoying positional advantage and superiority in freedom of movement. The avatar's data world tells him to be co-evolutionary, to assess his and his enemy's actions and assess and adapt faster than his enemy. The avatar, programmed to win battles against his adversary at all costs—mental or physical—keeps his costs to a minimum. The avatar, influenced by the considerations of *will* I have discussed with you in this chapter and throughout the book, is a determined and formidable foe. It will win at any cost and lives and operates by no moral parameters. Such avatars, programmed to replicate how our current and future adversaries might be thinking—their worldview, their cultural influences on them (e.g., social mores, mythos, belief in either predestination [one's life is already planned out and humans act out what has been preordained] or existentialism), and it represents a foe worthy of all our best intellectual effort with which to fight.[13]

In any kind of conflict or competition, contestants seek advantages[14] over their opponent. They seek these advantages to win; to be a victor in conflict and war, they must hold their advantages and degrade their adversary's advantages.

At the nub of thinking about advantage and disadvantage, however, one finds the grand motivator: self-interest. While peering at our adversary and being fully aware that he is peering back at us, when we consider the

13. *Existentialism*: A philosophical attitude and opposed to rationalism and empiricism, that stresses the individual's unique position as a self-determining agent responsible for the authenticity of his or her choices. Dictionary.com. Dictionary.com Unabridged. Random House, Inc. http://www.dictionary.com/browse/existentialism (accessed: May 29, 2017). Existentialism suggests one is responsible for their "volition" and for their thoughts and actions (see Dostoevsky's *Crime and Punishment* as a good example of existentialism).

14. *Advantage*: A situation of being in a preferable position over another competitor.

adversary and as he reasons about the us, when we attempt to think similarly to him and know he is doing the same, it is only then one can begin to discover his reasoning in sufficient depth to comprehend his advantages and disadvantages from his perspective. At such a point, he could choose to try to protect his advantages and disadvantages (from our actions whose purpose is to increase the antithesis—disadvantage).

The best outcome from a friendly perspective is to create what I call inferiority of the circumstance and attack it with rigor with a variety of approaches. Or you might want to use any of these exploited disadvantages as a "window" through which one could pass to either find more advantages or to attack and degrade the adversary's advantages. Such attacks could place the adversary on the horns of a dilemma, causing him to divert his time and energy in "plugging the hole" in his self-proclaimed advantage or disadvantage framework as it is being perturbed and perhaps degraded by our actions or to proceed with the initial activity and the initial advantage. The antithesis of advantage is, of course, disadvantage: a state of being, physical or mental, involving an instance of finding one's self trying to operate but doing so under the dark cloud of being in an unfavorable circumstance or condition and knowing the inferiority of the circumstance. When you find a disadvantage, consider pouncing on it to exploit the opportunity, as it could be brief.

As I summarize this chapter, recall that in any kind of conflict or competition, contestants aggressively seek advantages over their opponents. I have discussed these advantages earlier in this work, so I won't list them again. At the nub of thinking about advantage and disadvantage, however, one finds the grand motivator: self-interest. The best outcome from a friendly perspective is to cause one's adversary's disadvantages to be more significant and influential than any advantage he might hold. Our aggressive thinker must make his adversary susceptible to the appearance of the dark cloud of entropy in decisions and fully aware that he is in trouble. In the chapter, I explained that when you find a disadvantage, consider pouncing and forcefully exploiting the opportunity, as it could be brief. I presented many ideas, factors, elements, influences, and inputs in this chapter. None proved more important than deliberating about how their opposing side thinks, considers their adversary in toto and existentially, how he ponders the operational context as a whole, and discerns its advantages and disadvantages. In this chapter, I introduce Clausewitz's Marvelous Trinity—a necessity for keeping a balance among the people, government, and military in conflicts. But, I tell my readers, there is more to the trinity captured in these following thoughts: The statesman and military leader must always consider and plan for and implement conflict with war and violence being an act of policy. They must never allow the Marvelous Trinity to become out of balance or tilting to one or two of the elements. In conflict, the statesman and commander must know what the quality of their thinking and planning is and thus keep it high, as they both know assumptions often prove wrong and need constant attention and adjustment.

The next chapter takes us into a new universe of how to think about *will*. It focuses on understanding CAS, which are people and people populated entities, including those organizations, countries, and aggregations of people against whom America wages war.

CHAPTER 13

Complex Adaptive Systems (CAS) and *Will*

Argument: *In this chapter I explain how to think about and affect complex adaptive systems (CAS), their co-evolution and adaptation cycles, and contributions to battles of* will. *I ask the reader to consider imposing their* will *and blocking their adversary's with the basics of nonlinearity and CAS. This chapter explains how CAS rules influence 30 CAS models and how 24 CAS models drive CAS action and* will. *In this chapter I provide readers with these thoughts: first, learn to outthink the adversary using these techniques; second, think like your adversary using the methods of thinking in this chapter; and third, be intellectually agile, learn, and adapt as the adversary thinks and adds to his models.*

Next, let us turn our attention to thinking about affecting an adversary's adaptation cycle. Before starting I offer an explanation about the need to use our imaginations and creativity to find ways to get ahead of our hydra—our adversaries of the present and future. I borrow and use concepts of co-evolution, adaptation, complex adaptive systems (CAS), and nonlinearity as cornerstones for the framework I put forth for use in conflicts over successfully imposing our *will* while denying any adversary's attempts to impose his.

This proclamation and subsequent derivative actions injects this energy-radiating positive vector into conflict episodes in complicated operational inner workings. The vector comes forth and imbues the CAS with probabilities and possibilities, all seeming important, but none more important than the weighty and constant pressure to find and use the right kind of data, information, and knowledge (when available) to act before his adversary, and ideally, to strike an adversary's pressure points, which can, in the ideal, constitute attacking or manipulating an adversary's decisive points. To perform to his definition of high quality and high standards, the adversary must reason like his adversary (the friendly force leader) and aggressively engage in mental combat, but always act to assess vulnerabilities via pressure points and in the aggregate, decisive points. You stand warned—you must always, always anticipate and thwart or manipulate to gain advantage from such indirect approaches into your soft underbelly.

With adaptation, the nimblest and most aggressive CAS/agent seizes the initiative and thereby exerts positive energy of their own making in the crucible of conflict. The mere presence and influence of this jolt of energy provides an impetus for not only surviving but winning conflict situations, from both adversary and friendly perspectives, of course. Adaptation in the adversary's co-evolution process comes with purposeful, directed steerage, as CAS always, under threat of extinction, assesses the context and their competitors and thereby seeks and receive feedback. This feedback must be of sufficient quality to energize their adaptation. One must always anticipate the adversary's attempts to retard the friendly sources of data so as to cause the friendly adaptation system to suffer from entropy (gradual decline of order). America's forces do much the same, but bloated bureaucracies organized in multilayered hierarchies cannot be nimble and compete well in co-evolution intersections and then adapt as fast as adversaries working in semi-flat networks.

Of course, in 21st-century conflict, the agent or CAS writ large must adapt more quickly and effectively than their adversary. If they fail to adapt, co-evolution grinds to a halt and the CAS in question becomes susceptible to the ravenous dogs of extinction. I want to review our thought model for adversary co-evolution and the 13-step adaptation process: 1) perceive; 2) think; 3) plan; 4) decide; 5) act; 6) assess; 7) develop observables (to focus data gathering); 8) collect/gather data; 9) recompose data into information; 10) synthesize information into knowledge; 11) evaluate; 12) learn; and 13) adapt. Executing these 13 steps never stops for any combatant, as each side must continuously perform this cycle to survive. But it is particularly important for the adversary who doesn't possess the capabilities to compete directly and instead competes asymmetrically. If they can act, assess, gather, learn, and adapt faster than their adversary via indirect and unexpected means, they often find themselves with the initiative and not only surviving, but winning against their enemies via actions. This process is much more than winning a short-lived advantage—this process involves life and death for CAS/agents. The friendly decision maker and their thought supporters must consider their adversary's co-evolution and adaptation processes. Their intent with their thought vector is to influence, negate, neutralize, and induce decay into the adversary CAS's co-evolutionary processes—namely their data for adaptation.

Now, let's imagine a huge cake positioned on a table in front of you; it is the cake of knowledge. As you surveil the operational context and try to think as the adversary, your mind keeps returning to the cake. Why am I fixated on this cake, in the middle of a theoretical conflict, for crying out loud? Well, here goes my best explanation. As a first layer of this four-layer cake, one senses then understands—"I am in mental combat for dominance over another human's mind;" I am trying to purposefully "arrange his mind" (as T. E. Lawrence said in *Seven Pillars of Wisdom*). You work to dominate the adversary decision maker's mind; he tries to dominate your decision maker's mind. A clash of influencing actions ensues. In this case, try to convince our adversary of the miniscule chance of eking out one of many probabilities and possibilities bringing success; the cost to satisfy his goals outweighs his strength of motive and capabilities. As the second layer of the cake, you discover its recipe and see in its ratios and measures how you might parry the adversary's intent and actions to impose his desires on your decision maker. As the third layer of the cake, you find none other than thinking—and in particular, how to think.[1] As such you advise your decision maker where, when, how, and with what outcome he can best impose actions against his adversary because you know how he thinks. As a fourth layer of the cake, you recall the importance of co-evolution and in particular how the CAS in question (your enemy) knows he must assess outcomes and gather data to turn it into information and knowledge for decision making and adapt faster and more effectively that you. It is with knowledge the adversary minimizes risk and lowers uncertainty, not unlike our efforts to make the best decisions possible relative to our need for valuable data—he has an identical need.

The box for this cake involves the friendly side's decision maker and coterie of thought supporters who have learned how their adversary thinks, his values, his ethics, his morals, his attitudes, past experiences, cultural influences, *Weltanschauung*, mythos, and the like. Armed with this knowledge, the friendly decision maker chooses to penetrate the adversary's mind and shapes it with quick snapshots of data, not unlike burst transmissions whose cumulative power aggregates in the adversary's mind as none other than a conclusion. The conclusion we want him to draw serves our self-interests, not his and our goal is to possess advantages but not allow our adversary to know, and thereby revel in *schadenfreude*[2] until it is time to act. The details of his conclusion (to cooperate) prove important. Our Über-thinker and thought pilgrim attack his thoughts, motives, perception, expectations, interpretations, self-image, tensions, calculus of *will*, with data—subtly, they plant the notion of defeat in his mind (causing inference in readers' minds about the relationship with theme's throughout *On War*) and let the cancerous thoughts metastasize.

1. Wayne Michael Hall, "Metacognition: How to Think." (Unpublished, 2016), 3–20.
2. An internal, mischievous delight in the discomfort of others.

It should be apparent now that as the adversary's mind toils on his next decision, the friendly decision maker, in his role as the lead priest of mental combat, interferes with his adversary's understanding of the operational context, how his competitor is adapting and changing, and growing and shrinking the aggregation comprising his whole. All activities balance among the friendly decision maker's strength of motive, constraints, and capabilities. With an artificial and distorted view of the operational context induced in the adversary's mind by the friendly decision maker who has and is shaping his adversary's thinking via emplacing believable but baseless data into his co-evolution, assessment, collection, processing, knowledge, evaluation, learning, and adaptation mental and physical processes, gravitating extant advantages to the friendly decision maker.

We must convince our adversary of his probability of victory being slim and the cost to pursue this sliver of hope too high to bear. But to engage in these efforts, one must know how the enemy reasons, what he values, whether he lives by cultural morals, whether he fears death, how he deals with attitudes and attitudinal change, his loyalty to his family, how he engages in his decision-making processes, and so forth before this kind of mental gymnastics can possibly occur. If one inputs deceptive or shaping data to the adversary's sensors or receptacles for gathering data, or while neutralizing or manipulating what said collectors report to the adversary by way of the adversary's most trusted data gatherers, then the adversary could be forced to rely on other collection assets (possibly more advantageous to the friendly side) to gather data. Of course, he wants to protect his pressure, decisive, and center of gravity points, including his co-evolution and adaptation capabilities; thus you devise and implement highly sophisticated inputs of "massaged" data into his collectors for assessing and ultimately adapting while allowing a flickering hope that his adaptation is better than his competitor.

OBSERVED/OBSERVER RELATIONSHIPS

This relationship—observed/observer—is an important consideration for the struggle between two opposing sides. Though other considerations prove easier to understand, this topic can whipsaw from obscurity to most important in seconds, if what one tries to find and observe is of high importance, such as the location of a mobile missile armed with a nuclear warhead. This is a real problem—long periods of nothing, then suddenly, the missile comes out from its caves prepared to fire from a race-trace of probable firing sites. The struggle of wits arises when the adversary "feels" someone watching and changes his location or breaks a pattern he knows an observer would seek. Or what if we want to find a high-value target (HVT) buried deep and hardened within a large village or city, underneath one of many buildings, or even burrowed into a granite mountain?

Finding an HVT proves difficult, but is made more difficult because the adversary's countersurveillance believes that someone is watching and thereby changes patterns of life, patterns of maintenance, electrical emanations, movement of people in and out, air pipes, security, countersurveillance apparatuses (e.g., cameras and camera emissions and maintenance), and so on.

Such dire needs do in fact force extensive mental work in the minds of decision makers, intelligence analysts, and collections people. I introduced and developed this concept while leading my Advanced Analysis seminars from 2008 to 2014. I captured and put into words a phenomenon that has surely existed for millennia, but without the theory and without the descriptive name. Such ruminating often results in success or failure in intelligence collection by one side, or if you are the on the other side in a given fracas, success or failure depends on denying your adversary's collection efforts via countersurveillance, early warning, and deception. But this collection win or failure can be a bigger issue—it can and often does mean a degradation in the quality of decisions and the capability to understand a situation. Upon a closer examination of observed and observer relationships, one finds a "gaming" situation in which one side seeks, then "hooks to," observes, and then acts on, say, a deep and hardened target.

Actions like this rely on outthinking and "outgaming" a wily adversary who resolutely intends to counter any collection attempts (friendly collection)—yes, the struggle for dominance stretches far into the inner reaches of minds, functions, and activities of each competitor, including the observed vs. observer fight, and collection vs. countersurveillance fight.

Keep seven points in mind: 1) this is a deadly cat-and-mouse game; 2) each side attempts to exert their *will* on the other; 3) the observed believes he is being watched by an observer; 4) the observed changes his patterns, functions, technology, etc., if he believes he is being watched; 5) this relationship plays a major role in deception for both sides; 6) the observed side is doing this same work to collect against you; and 7) you have to be both observer and observed in the relationship. Obviously the observed/observer relationship proves complicated. Regardless, potential outcomes prove too important to relegate, procrastinate, or convince yourself that this game is too difficult for both sides.

Let's dive deeper into this fascinating but murky pool of interest, starting with some theory behind this phenomenon. First of all, one aspect of theory involves some important additions to our further exploration and comprehension of the operational context. Author Gary Zukav tells us that "[t]he new physics, quantum mechanics, tells us clearly that it is not possible to observe reality without changing it."[3] This holds true for our

3. Gary Zukav, *The Dancing Wu Li Masters* (New York: Bantam Books, 1979), 30.

contexts. That is to say, if the observed does watch the operational context and his adversary, minute changes occur and the context is disturbed. If the observed believes that someone or something watches for his activities or watches his person, he changes his routines. Moreover, if residents of the context feel or intuit that someone or something is watching them or their surroundings, they change their patterns of life, even without evidence. This phenomenon is important to both sides in a fracas. According to Zukav, "there is no such thing as objectivity. We cannot eliminate ourselves from the picture."[4] I claim that nothing is objective and everything is subjective; to recognize and ponder meaning from incoming data, each person processes the data and attaches meaning via their experiences, culture, education, thinking prowess, race, and the like. Everything is subjective, and it is with subjectivity that one finds errors and fissures in defenses. Zukav adds that "the physical world must be divided into two parts. These parts are the observed system and the observing system."[5]

Many probabilities exist under the guise of potential realities, all which could occur within the confines of the operational context of competition from which the observer surveys. When I focus my attention on one or more of these probabilities, they turn into possible actions that the observed could take or select as his choice for action(s). Thus, be thoughtful with your gaze, even when some of our gawking finds its foundation of meaning coming from the application of theory. While attempting to think like the adversary, narrow your thoughts to the desired outcome, the prize which we seek—the wondrous triumvirate—precognition, anticipation, and preemption, and with success in activating this triumvirate, establish conditions for our decision maker to seize the initiative.

The observed proves to be the observer collection systems' direct focus for intelligence collection. The observed recognizes, as he attempts to think like his adversary, the challenges coming with uncertainty of choice and limitations on his options and alternatives. The observed feels something is wrong, something is twisting in his mind, disturbing his equilibrium, but he doesn't know the cause. He would like to cast it away as an errant thought, but his intuition sounds a resounding alarm. Alas, he has no evidence about what could be causing his anxiety. His ability to theorize hunches, hypotheses, and mysteries comes from his cultural and experiential backgrounds. After all, in his past he could have been hunted, found, beaten, or castigated and therefore, more often than not he is more than a little paranoid. Thus, his working theory to bely the alert his intuition flashes to his consciousness involves the presence of something at work

4. Zukav, *The Dancing Wu Li Masters,* 31.
5. Ibid. p. 69.

against him within the micro-operational context that I presented to you in Chapter 4. Believing a presence is at work in the operational context but yet to appear, he develops hypotheses, watches for evidence, waits for a move, but he does not possess evidence, and therefore the sensed presence festers and dissonance slowly twists in his mind. His mind then wanders and his consciousness finds itself plagued about what in the world could be causing his discomfort. Many probabilities float in his cogitation space, but he knows not which could be causing such roiling of his intuition and other senses as they too alert. "What choice should I make," the adversary asks himself. "How can I hide my important targets or activities if somebody is watching and wants to find them? Could my adversary be the source of my discomfort? How does my adversary, the observer think? Could it be that my sensings involve his collection against me connecting with my efforts to protect my targets from his observation—my high-value targets, command posts, and the like?"

I cannot anticipate all possible causes of the relentless pain coming from stress and fear of uncertainty and the unknown. Once again and with thanks to recursion, I detect the specter of duality and the swinging wild pendulum hovering over me; it is the premier variable for unraveling this Gordian knot. That is to say, the main challenge always involves an observer selecting the most probable ways and means to find that which she seeks. The observer reasons that this observed person, function, pattern, or system could subsequently choose to offset their "seeable" and "discoverable" agents and machines (sensors, communication, human watchers) of his countersurveillance and early warning systems. The observed, our adversary, wants his countersurveillance systems to be well hidden, as their employment assuredly breaks one, two, or all four kinds of patterns—human/social, technical, functional, and organizational. Pattern perturbation, and thus change, produces observer-sought anomalies, if the observer watches for the right activity at the right time and place, using the right collector who is looking for the right observables. This is indeed a tall task, and therefore the observer seeks help. For our edification, let's turn once again to Gary Zukav, who states, in layman's terms, this edification of the Heisenberg principle of uncertainty:

> Whatever it is that we are observing can have a determinable momentum, and it can have a determinable position, but of the two properties, we must choose, for any given moment which one we wish to bring into focus. . . .[6] This is the primary significance of the uncertainty principle. At the subatomic level, we cannot observe something without changing it. There is no such thing as the independent observer who can stand on the sidelines watching nature run its course without influencing it. In one sense, this is not such a surprising statement. A good way to

6. Zukav, *The Dancing Wu Li Masters*, 27, 111–114.

make a stranger turn and look at you is to stare intently at his back. All of us know this, but we often discredit what we know when it contradicts what we have been taught is possible.[7]

Noted physicist David Bohm discusses fragmentation, coalescence, and wholes in his book *Wholeness and the Implicate Order.* Bohm worked on understanding the nature of reality, but only in a general sense and of consciousness in particular as a coherent whole with thought and body coalescing into one. He believes that consciousness is never static or complete but rather a continuously unfolding process. Along this line of thought he spoke of man's proclivity to reduce things to parts they consider to be independent in and among themselves, but his position differed significantly:

> [O]ne of the key factors of their origin is a kind of thought that treats things as inherently divided, disconnected, and "broken up" into yet smaller constituent parts. Each part is considered to be essentially independent and self-existent. . . . What I am proposing here is that man's general way of thinking of the totality, i.e., his general world view, is crucial for overall order of the human mind itself. If he thinks of the totality as constituted of independent fragments, then that is how his mind tends to operate, but if he can include everything coherently and harmoniously in an overall whole that is undivided, unbroken . . . then his mind will tend to move in a similar way, and from this will flow an orderly action within the whole.[8]

This theory happens to be important to success in our efforts to use this model for thinking like the adversary. That is to say, to "think like the adversary," then learn to replicate, albeit with understandable approximation, how he views the world in a very general sense—as fragmented or as holistic.

This passage speaks of three specific aspects of rumination to consider while attempting to think like an adversary. First, discern whether the adversary decision maker, coterie of his support team, and even organization thinks via reductionism[9] or by way of the ancient doctrine of holism. A reductionist—a person who fragments and shreds—typically knows a lot about the subject they have sliced and diced. But, archetypally, they are incapable of taking what they have learned via breaking into smaller and smaller parts and reassembling these pieces into a new and better whole. The holistic person is the more creative of the two. Holistic, synthetic minds seek combinations of parts and pieces, coherence,

7. Zukav, *The Dancing Wu Li Masters,* 112–113.

8. Bohm, *Wholeness and the Implicate Order,* xii–xiii.

9. *Reductionism*: The practice of simplifying a complex idea, issue, condition, or the like, especially to the point of minimizing, obscuring, or distorting it.

connectedness—discerning how well their combination works within a whole. In this recognition, the whole they create becomes greater than its simple sum of parts. Second, discern the adversary's worldview. A worldview is an outlook involving how people, nature, organizations, elements (wind, fire, water, earth) commingle, philosophies appear, and how all of these bind as one. For certain, think how any worthy adversary defines and ponders his worldview, as this concept is an important discriminator for levels of quality in reasoning. A shallow person with limited experience, for example, reasons differently than a broadly experienced, highly educated, and deeply thinking person who has traveled the world and interacted with different personalities from many different cultures and different walks of life from many locations. Generally, this more deeply reasoning person understandably possesses and often uses a broader, deeper, and more holistic way of reasoning. Understanding another person's worldview provides us with a voyeuristic peek into an adversary's inner mental workings, not perfect mind you, but at least a peek. Third, discern some of the most important intangibles of being human in an adversary. All humans possess values and varying degrees of morality. All human beings experience pain—emotional and physical. All humans live with their peculiar experiential background. All humans experience emotions—sadness, exultations, hatred, revenge, plentitude, security and on and on. Though these characteristics of being human prove unquantifiable, they always prove real, important, and sensitive:

> [M]any other factors, such [as] emotions, physical activities, human relationships, social organizations, etc., but perhaps because we have at present no coherent world view, there is a widespread tendency to ignore the psychological and social importance of such questions almost altogether. My suggestion is that a proper world view, appropriate for its time, is generally one of the basic factors that is essential for harmony in the individual and in society as a whole.[10]

Though physically and mentally unable to *will* our minds into the mind of another person, particularly a terrorist, a criminal, or a greedy ruler, and look through his eyes and see the world exactly as he does, there is a way around this contradiction. Let's start with the psychiatrist Carl Jung, who provides us with some insights into the difficulty of thinking exactly like another person with this passage:

> The vast majority of people are quite incapable of putting themselves individually into the mind of another. This is indeed a singularly rare art, and, truth to tell, it does not take us very far. Even the man whom we think we know best and who assures us himself that we understand him through and through is at bottom a

10. Bohm, *Wholeness and the Implicate Order*, xiii.

stranger to us. He is different. The most we can do, and the best, is to have at least some inkling of his otherness, to respect it.[11]

To be inside another person's skin in toto and thereby think and feel exactly like them works only as a metaphor. But while pondering this metaphor's meaning one can begin to understand the theory and put it into practice. One finds with this kind of rumination the primary impetus pushing us to learn to respect other people, to actually work hard to see the world from other people's points of view and experiences, and to narrow our rumination with sufficient detail and understanding to focus and concentrate on thinking like the adversary via the techniques in Chapter 14.

Even with the limitations Bohm and Jung discussed, all of us can learn to think like the adversary but always with qualifications. One finds the unfortunate presence and influence of boundaries, limitations, and cultural impasses. To use these techniques successfully, our approach accedes to moderate expectations—they are subjective insights, and one must always be cautious before biting into the sweet bread of "truth." As error-prone human beings, be wary, indeed skeptical, of our own thinking; all of us shall ride into the valley of truth knowing that there are no absolute truths.[12] I'm comfortable in postulating that our attention and mental and physical efforts work to approximate our adversary's thinking, but in a series of problem set and problem-peculiar ways, always remember the axiom that all people, thoughts, bodies, organizations, elements, and parts connect in some way. When one part moves, the other parts of the aggregation (the whole in which we live and compete) changes too, sometimes obviously and other times in ways too nuanced and subtle to notice. Interestingly, with smaller wholes, all connected elements feel and react to change, but often neither people nor organizations know causation for the change in question or discerning what the adversary decision maker is doing to contain and shape the changes affecting his worldview and thinking.

To venture up a slightly different but still heavily entangled pathway, we borrow terms typically involving individuals. Again, when one individual connects with another, they become a group; when this group connects with another group, the two groups form a larger group; they connect into larger and larger wholes. In layman's terms, this is aggregation theory. Further, these upcoming terms and their definitions fit with Bohm's prognostications about connectedness. These thoughts provide us with the capability to understand what is occurring within and outside of the

---

11. Jung, *Psychological Reflections A New Anthology of His Writings 1905–1961*, 153.

12. Wayne Michael Hall, "Advanced Analysis Discussion and Use in Deep Thinking about Conclusions and Recommendations: Claim, Evidence, Truth, Facts, Objectivity/Subjectivity." Unpublished, 2016, 6–13.

personages of the people attempting to impose their desires on us via setting conditions and then acting against us and our interests. The object is, of course, to understand the terms (connectedness, aggregations) and use their meaning, transposed into concrete action, to first spot adversary condition settings for imposing action, stopping or interfering with those condition-setting actions, and assessing the outcomes of our efforts. What else can help us overcome Jung and Bohm's cautionary limitations of our thinking? Let us think about a few other concepts. First, please consider proprioception, which means "the unconscious perception of movement and spatial orientation arising from stimuli within the body itself."[13] Then consider the term exteroceptive, which means "related to stimuli external to the organism"[14]; interoceptive, which means "responding to stimuli originating from within the body"[15]; and kinesthetics, or the "sensation of movement or strain in muscles, tendons, and joints; muscle sense."[16] All of these words and definitions suggest change, perturbation, what to watch for if so inclined. We can safely infer that all of these thoughts and terms flow in an endless river of time with the elements, parts, pieces, organs unfolding and enfolding smaller and larger wholes. This metaphor snugly fits with the concept of aggregation theory, a major and fundamental concept of advanced intelligence analysis.[17] They also relate to connectedness. As the adversary sets conditions, physical and mental activities occur—some human, some machine, and some organizational. They all connect via the five links all of us previously discussed (human/social, technical, functional, organizational, and thought). As each part changes, said change comes via human behavior, physiognomy, and so forth. As human beings act, interact, transact, and behave, the four other terms should come into play and provide us what to what for (e.g., changes in patterns and ripples in connectedness).

If thinking like another person is very difficult, let's briefly examine some other ways to proceed. So, we do know people around us would likely approach the problem with rejection and staid reasoning common to Plato's Cave.[18] In our minds, though, one develops a robust estimate of this adversary's aim goals, objectives, resources, constraints, strategies, tactics, and so forth. We hypothesize and debate "that which truly matters," the

---

13. *The American Heritage Stedman's Medical Dictionary*. Retrieved November 16, 2011, from http://dictionary.reference.com /browse/proprioception.

14. https://en.oxforddictionaries.com/definition/exteroceptive

15. Dictionary.com. Retrieved April 3, 2017, from www.dictionary.com/browse/intero ceptor.

16. Dictionary.com. *The American Heritage® Science Dictionary*. Houghton Mifflin Company. http://www.dictionary.com/browse/kinesthesia (accessed: May 30, 2017).

17. Hall and Citrenbaum, *Intelligence Analysis*, 277–299.

18. Plato, *Five Great Dialogues*, 398–401.

value of objectives, and the adversary's 14-element model relative to his aim, goals, and objectives, and ours. We study the operational context in which a conflict can occur and decide upon advantages and disadvantages it provides to first one side then the other. We work hard to understand and pragmatically employ the 18-consideration thought model appearing in this book. Continuing along this line of thought, while considering our adversary, recognize the importance of the operational context surrounding the action. The adversary's actions as well as friendly's actions and activities incur influence by the context's linear and nonlinear systems. These two systems operate as a whole, with one part being rational and repeatable and the other part being stray voltage. A helpful venture into how a great commander thought about this problem was Scipio Africanus as he successfully wrested Cartagena, Spain, in 209 BCE from the Carthaginians under the command of Hannibal's brother Mago. This passage shows a resourceful commander who studied his operational context and what such study can do relative to mission accomplishment via moral and physical domains of conflict:

> The way was thus paved for his next decisive move. To develop this, he was only waiting for the ebb of the tide [the sea surrounded Cartagena on three sides], and this design had been conceived by him . . . from inquiries among fishermen who knew Cartagena, he had learnt that at low water the lagoon was fordable. . . . He launched this assault simultaneously with a landing attack by the fleet, and when it was at its height the tide began to ebb and the water gradually receded from the edge of the lagoon . . . Scipio had his guides ready . . . when he called upon them . . . they obeyed and raced through the shallow water. . . . The walls thus captured, Scipio at once exploited his success.[19]

We must use a thought model to perform this mental excursion. This way of thinking requires a narrowing of the adversary's options—so as our thinker gazes at many probabilities of choice for the adversary, it is their knowledge, understanding, and comprehension that enables a winnowing of choices with the highest probability of bracketing his principle choice of action. Moreover, as I mentioned, one can know the operational context of the conflict to a good extent. It helps to employ the best offices of subject matter experts (SMEs), the host nation government, and the local populace. One should never attempt to think like the adversary in isolation from the situation, context, and this adversary's apperception (sum total of all his life's experiences). That is to say, while considering the adversary, recognize he is thinking about how you are thinking about him; this back and forth is one whole. Additionally, one always recognizes nonlinearity influences everything that happens, but it means the arena of conflict is chaotic,

19. Hart, *Scipio Africanus,* 34–36.

which means the operational context and the adversaries competing in it always prove influenced by unpredictable vagaries that can cause unexpected change in each antagonist.

So, take note: No one person can know with exactness and precision what an adversary, or anybody else for that matter, thinks at any one time. Whilst grasping at floating bits and bytes to collect "what one can know and cannot know" relative to how an adversary thinks, you walk into a morass, nonetheless knowing one thing for certain. When working our minds to ruminate like the adversary, success can come our way, some of the time. With this success, however, one feels the presence of a wraith blowing its foul breath, clouding our senses and carrying a real and present warning of risk and uncertainty. With good critical thinking, people can mitigate the negative power and influence of risk and uncertainty, and proceed into the dense fog of a long-lived process by using what I believe to be a human co-evolution process, which in some way, shape, or form represents how people tend to reason.

Proceeding with our thinking and acknowledging increasingly entangled relationships, I provide you with four propositions, seemingly self-evident but still important for your consideration. First, friendly decision makers and their analysts must learn to outthink their adversary. Nonetheless, they always feel the cold wind of reality—they make decisions within the frightening dark shrouds and influences of uncertainty, ambiguity, and risk. Our goals are to help decision makers manage risk and lower uncertainty; find pressure points, decisive points, and centers of gravity to attack or manipulate; open windows of opportunity to reach in and seize seven kinds of advantage; and provide opportunities to preempt the adversary's activities and thereby seize the initiative. Second, don't give up on the quest to reason like the adversary just because the effort proves difficult and continues to be fraught with the specter of failure. We must resolve this issue to engage in and win bouts of mental combat. Third, decision makers and their contemplative forces must use a thought model to help them think like the adversary thinks. With this model, knowledge warriors seek support via SMEs, automation, and their inbred, learned contemplation capabilities, each of sufficient quality to engage in precognition, anticipation, and preemption. This we can do, but again, cause your eyes to stay wide open; know with certainty our efforts can fail some of the time. Fourth, keep the thought model for thinking like the adversary open-ended—be agile. A model replicates our belief of reality. Though it can be wrong or inconclusive, a model evolves with our learning what the model actually represents. Some elements of my initial model can fall out, but over time, this framework or pegboard that I label a "thought model" comes to you with my determination to help your minds ponder your adversary and the context and vigorously and relentlessly attack this difficult challenge.

Uncertainty and risk are the kings and queens of decision making. These two concepts spring to life and influence all sides in a fray and are impossible to totally resolve. The villain precluding total resolution is us, the human being, with our vagary-laden humanness. Human beings are, at their core, unfathomable and unpredictable. People posture, perform, and act out their theater on the stages of life, but one can always count on the human being to tilt to act to satisfy their self-interests; very few people act out their "life stories" to be altruistic. People also change their minds and do so frequently. A few people are creative[20] and thereby create different ways of acting; others innovate.[21] The innovation of which I speak is easier to understand than when the human creates—creation is sometimes unfathomable in its outcomes and original cause/motivator. The operational context pushes humans hither and yon, influencing conditions in which they innovate and/or create. Variance comes, too, when observing how human beings act or respond to changes they receive via force-fed data flows from their contexts or because of another person's actions. After all, in conflict, humans say in an outraged and condescending way of speaking, and hence thinking—our adversary is irrational, he is inferior, he does not reason like us, he is crazy, he is evil, etc. Humans tend to demonize anybody who opposes them. But as they wallow in error and attribute their errors to forces beyond their control, they abjectly fail to realize that it is they who err. People fail to respect their adversary's capabilities and armed with a feeling of superiority, they fail to reach into the dark well of the opponent's mind and soul. They forfeit a real chance to understand how he reasons and beat him in competitive bouts. Certainly, the adversary judges himself quite sane; he proclaims his prowess with his reasoning and knows exactly what he seeks, why he seeks it, and he possesses a good estimate of his strength of motive. If an adversary is similar to many other people in the world, we find him fragmenting his life, work, mission, thoughts, and sense of worldview, with little to no comprehension of how he blends with the whole.

With some theoretical constructs aiding our minds, I want to take us back to our starting point for some additional thinking about observed/observer relationships. This conversation is deeper than our earlier conversation because you, my readers, know more than before. So, let's proceed with this "revisit" and concept expansion. If our adversary proves to be of sound mind, he senses somebody or something watching him and that which he hides and/or protects. But the observer doesn't know what probability, what possibility, what choice the observed takes, since he has

20. *Creative*: The use of the imagination in developing original ideas, especially solving difficult problem sets.

21. *Innovate*: To make changes for improvement in something already working.

multiple options, each with a probability of occurring. But one can be certain of one fact—the observed person acts if his intuition warns and convinces him so. An observer can know, with good certainty, that the observed action is forthcoming, but how, where, when, and for what reason those actions occur prove problematic to discern. Of interest too, is that this same phenomenon affects ordinary, innocent people as they live their lives. They change routine patterns with intuitive tingling. Recipients of the warning often don't grasp the cause for the effect occurring in their minds, but they respond and choose either to ignore the warning or to do something regardless of understanding causation of the warning klaxon.

In this way, the observed does indeed "disturb his own universe."[22] His intuition pushes attempts to reason like us, the observers, think. The adversary faces many probabilities but seizes upon one or two choices representing what he thinks we can and cannot fathom and then puts the choice where he reasons he has outthought us into action. His goal is, of course, to protect high-value targets with countersurveillance, and he also wants his own collection to work against our activities and actions. Again, he tries to reason like he thinks we reason. With this thought in mind, he uses deception to show what he wants us to see. He also plans for our anticipation and offset and adjusts his collection accordingly. This peek behind the screen of mystery and deception obscuring reality indicates false anomalies, false links, and false observables and thus our adversary offsets his early warning and countersurveillance operations and surreptitiously inspects and alters anything appearing out of the parameters of what he believes to be normal patterns in and around the high-value target (HVT) location. He conducts the inspection and makes the changes. He believes that we won't expect the changes and he thinks that he knows our collection capabilities and resolve aren't sufficient to win in this game of cat and mouse between the observed and observer. He is wrong!

Arguably, at times, our observed adversary possesses a preponderance of advantages. But we possess advantages too. Continuing with this line of thinking, one finds each side trying to penetrate their adversary's efforts to deny, while trying to outthink their opponent and deny his efforts to deny. Each side strives to dominate the other to create one, two, or even all kinds of advantages. For example, the adversary might hide a high-value target in a location where our intelligence collectors cannot reach. Perhaps our human collection cannot gain access to the well-protected HVT (e.g., a WMD hide site) due to the prevalence of adept air defense weapons, counterintelligence organizations, countersurveillance, and counterespionage operations. In addition, the observed usually possesses a thorough knowledge of the operational context and thereby uses the weather,

22. Eliot, "The Love Song of J. Alfred Prufrock," 1915.

infrastructure, functions, procedures, traffic patterns, darkness, terrain masking, buildings, communications, and subterranean conduits webbing underneath cities to his advantage. He even anticipates and hides even the most nuanced and subtle relative activities, such as 1) fill from a tunnel; 2) generators to power lighting in a tunnel or buried command post; 3) auguring equipment; 4) swapping food for forces hidden in tunnels and mountains; 5) exercising; 6) eating; 7) sleeping; 8) clearing air vents; 9) maintaining generation and power-related equipment; 10) disposing of human waste; and on and on.

What do these examples of the adversary's subtle ways of hiding what we want to find mean and imply? I say, it is about reasoning! We have to use reason about our adversary and operational context in this sophisticated game of cat and mouse involving human cognition, precognition (I defined this phenomenon earlier in this book), decomposition, anticipatory analysis, pattern and link analysis, tendency analysis, anomaly analysis, aggregation analysis, technical analysis,[23] advanced intelligence collection, and counterdenial and deception.[24] The implication involves improving ways to help people learn to think, develop Über-thinkers and thought pilgrims, and provide them with technology organized around the central ideas of our system of thought—this entire compendium of thought.

Both observed and observer in this peek and seek game can use Heraclites's long-lived and influential theory of "the unity of opposites," which I introduced earlier in this book. The theory comes to life and plays out in every cat-and-mouse game between the observer and the observed in all analysis and collection operations. You grasp, I'm sure, that the observed and observer inextricably connect in an interactive whole. The two interacting opposites (offense and defense) exert energies as they act, with each side attempting to deny such actions. These impositions and counterimpositions of actions cause the whole of our focus to move back and forth, up and down, and sideways, but the connectedness of the two opposites always exists. Each side "feeds" upon their own energies as well as the energies of their adversary. For your information and further research, the interaction of opposites also goes by other monikers: unity of opposites and interaction between the yin and yang. The theory behind the unity of opposites is important for both sides and in particular opposing decision makers, Über-thinkers, thought pilgrims, intelligence analysts, and intelligence collections people.

Let's take a few moments to proceed deeper into thinking about the unity of opposites. To start with, let us proceed to ruminate about some reasons

---

23. These are critical elements of advanced analysis that I present in my book, *Intelligence Analysis* (2009).

24. These concepts first came forth in my book *Intelligence Collection* (2012).

for the importance of the observed and observer relationship beyond what I just discussed.

- First, intelligence people always anticipate adversaries observing them—all analysts and collections people by trade, background, and professional inclination prove wary, skeptical, and iconoclastic. The observed in this case undoubtedly responds by changing his locations or positions of mobile assets he uses for countersurveillance and early warning. This movement results in a break and change in their functional patterns of behavior. I call this change the offset. The offset, for example, possesses an aura of importance in point persistent surveillance (P2S) operations for planning, executing, and assessing outcomes. The adversary's mobile countersurveillance and early warning capabilities make mistakes and induce change and perturbation in historically stolid, recurring patterns—social/human (patterns of life), technical, organizational, and functional. These patterns locate in friendly's baselines as part and parcel of problem sets and subproblem sets. These changes and the presence of countersurveillance and early warning suggest probabilities of potential openings in a complicated system built to deny collection. With this crack, as tenuous as it may be, the observer can finally aim their collectors against, and find or deduce the presence of a HVT, a weapon of mass destruction hide site, an SSM, or a command-and-control node buried in a village or urban area. Analysts account for this probable change, but they remain wary of their own thinking. They commit errors too, such as concentrating on and sticking with one favorite function; forming conclusions from small amounts of data; arrogance; confirmation bias; or the logic error of post hoc ergo propter hoc; oversimplification; stereotyping; mirror imaging; and so forth. These errors appear even as observers design their collection actions to induce behavior, design their observables, write their analytic sampling rate (ASR), and establish standards they submit to collectors. It is the Über-thinker and thought pilgrim and, of course, advanced analysts who advise their collection partners to change their focus to the right time, place, activity, and observable (five kinds of observables and the ASR) while accounting for the new, estimated, offset location.
- Second, collections understand the observed/observer phenomenon and take its properties into account as they perform detailed planning so fundamental to successful intelligence. This kind of thinking, is particularly important to an observer as they strive to find and then surveil deep and hardened and HVTs. If the adversary suspects his enemy searches for offset activities and/or errors that could cause anomalies to show in patterns involving organizations, infrastructure, command posts, deep and hardened targets, weapons of mass destruction caches, etc., he could very well use how he thinks his enemy believes he is

reasoning. He thereby could establish flummoxing devices—physical or cyber "honeypots," receptacles of deception, as a result of this personal and low-level wargaming. These receptacles of deception could be false anomalies, false patterns, false countersurveillance networks, false communications, false early warning networks, or false computer emissions and traffic.

- Third, decision makers, Über-thinkers, thought pilgrims, analysts, and collections people work as a team; each understands the observed/observer phenomenon from their perspective, as it helps them decide to collect when their target believes somebody or something to be observing them and how the observed, our adversary, then thinks about his peculiar problem set. Nonetheless, any true Über-thinkers, thought pilgrims know that culture shapes and drives how complex adaptive systems (humans and human-populated organizations) act and behave. We and our adversary, as CAS, compete with one another, co-evolve, assess their actions, assess actions of other CAS, receive data inputs from the operational context and from their competitors, and adapt. All of this activity is culturally dependent. Human beings and their organizations evolve and change to exist, but its existence is subject to culturally driven rules. Rules shape and control, even constrain, CAS models for action. CAS actions come from a complicated series of models—some built into the human mind, while others reside in organizations and even machines. The models of which I speak generate and shape action. CAS can be individuals (lone-wolf terrorists); groups of CAS, which I call aggregates; and groups of aggregates, which I call micro- and macro-aggregations. The aim, goals, objectives, behaviors, constraints, strategies, tactics, etc., come from rules. Rules can be 1) machine driven; 2) organization driven; and 3) individual driven. These three originators of rules are heavily influenced by culture.[25]

One's culture, whether macro or micro, influences the decisions CAS make as they disperse and as they self-organize. They perform these actions and activities because their thought models guide them into action, assessment, gathering data, turning data into knowledge, evaluating, learning, sharing, and adapting. The models at the core of CAS come from the living essence of their lives, which connotes experience via action, energy expulsion, movement, constancy of activity, aggressive co-evolution to compete, to act, to assess outcomes, to adapt, to act again—and we know their models function as rules dictate. Rules come, for the most part, from

25. I discuss the influence of culture in irregular warfare in the culture chapter in my book *Intelligence Analysis*, 235–255.

their culture—macro- and micro-cultures—though they can also derive from machines and bureaucratic/organizational processes.

It is interesting to note that even when CAS disperse, they still make decisions and don't necessarily depend upon direction or approval from a higher organization. One finds constant motion among CAS and variables in the operational context but often cultural data inputs defy the constant human quest for exact, quantifiable data with which to accurately predict. Stuart Kaufmann of the Santa Fe Institute helps us sharpen our wits about this subject:

> [A]gents persistently attempt to predict optimally the behaviors of other agents. To do so, each is driven to construct optimally complex models of the behaviors of the other agents. Inevitable disconfirmation of these models drives a co-evolutionary process among the models adopted by the agents, as each agent replaces disconfirmed models with new hypotheses [my note . . . and new models, of course]. These co-evolutionary dynamics can lie in a chaotic regime, in an ordered regime, and at the phase transition between order and chaos. . . . Here mutual behavior coordinates for intervals only to be disrupted by avalanches of changes in internal models driving avalanches of changes in decision rules and behavior. Mutual models, in short, would never settle down, but achieve a self-organized critical state. At this self-organized critical state, models would have an optimal bounded complexity. Thus, in this sense, agents construct optimally boundedly "rational" models.[26]

Our adversaries—I label them as CAS and CAS-populated organizations—go about their business by acting to create favorable outcomes. These actions have discernable condition-setting activities preceding them, as it were, a prequel of sorts. The condition-setting activities have noticeable and discoverable traits, which one can find as CAS constantly try to act out their desires. Within the depths of CAS, one finds imbedded models of action that push the CAS to impose via actions with high standards and advantageous posturing, relative to their competitor (which directly implies they must gather and assess data to measure/discern where their actions position along the scale of quality). One can count on CAS to possess varying degrees of 1) speed; 2) velocity; 3) mass; and 4) momentum in their aggressive actions. All four of these descriptors prominently figure in the power moves of CAS and how they could act against their competitors all the while trying to impose their desired outcomes. CAS co-evolve and compete with other CAS with the purpose, capability expenditure, and strength of motive dictated by their internal models and rule sets. This

---

26. Stuart A. Kaufmann, "Whispers from Carnot: The Origins of Order and Principles of Adaptation in Complex Nonequilibrium Systems." From *Complexity: Metaphors, Models, and Reality*, Santa Fe Institute Studies in the Sciences of Complexity, vol. XIX, ed. G. Cowan, D. Pines, & D. Meltzer (New York: Addison-Wesley, 1994), 125–126.

structured guidance, which varies from any particular society and culture to other societies and cultures but in general provides reason and rational guidance to models, causes CAS to act. But one can also count on finding insights to an understanding of an adversary CAS's inclination to sacrifice, his passion, views of advantages and disadvantages, his determination, and his perseverance in actions as models for acting. Further, CAS always compete as an aggressor or as a defender against aggression in one way or another. They also must stay cognizant of their operational contexts. CAS do not stay still—if they do, they become subject to elimination by more aggressive, adversarial CAS. Thus, CAS competition occurs with fluidity in conflict's operational context, and both CAS and operational context always prove vulnerable to heavy cultural influence. CAS have a choice—be aggressive or be reactive and subject to attack by other CAS of their particular genres. The advanced thinkers anticipate, seek, and identify possible openings against our competitor CAS or anticipate possible actions against us by other more aggressive CAS.

Culture is of great importance in understanding CAS. It shapes, sometimes skews, and sometimes dominates human thoughts and actions. We should understand the culture from several connected perspectives. These perspectives include 1) culture influences CAS thinking; therefore, it helps us discern how our opponent reasons; 2) culture shapes how my adversary interprets assessment data; 3) culture shapes how the adversary adapts; 4) culture shapes how I ruminate about how the adversary is thinking about his assessments; 5) culture is the perpetrator of both logic errors and bias errors; 6) culture frames criteria for judging the quality of how well CAS, aggregates, and aggregations have performed their basic functions; and 7) culture shapes how our adversary defines and thinks about value and quality of actions—his standards for success. If low and if his actions prove thwarted, he contemplates improving the quality of actions. It is undoubtedly, in some way, shape, or form, a "how to achieve" model and could be a dominating rule that demands performance from an action coming from the model coming from the rule set, that comes from the culture at hand.

Let's provide more thinking about culture's relationship to CAS models and rules. In this book, culture means "the behaviors and beliefs characteristic of a particular social, ethnic, or age group."[27] Cultural analysis involves:

> Knowing a particular culture, its people, and their patterns of behavior deriving from traditional, culturally induced attitudes, behaviors, social norms, and conditions. Gaining knowledge of a particular people or groupings of people through

27. Dictionary.com Unabridged (v 1.1). Retrieved December 20, 2008, from http://dictionary.reference.com/browse/culture.

observations, investigation, analysis, or understanding of integrated patterns of human behavior, which depend on the human capacity for learning and transmitting knowledge to members of an ethnic, religious, or social group, and succeeding generations.[28]

I want you to reason how to influence, neutralize, negate—whatever you wish to call it—the capabilities of your adversarial CAS who compete with you via his culture. You want to use the nature of CAS, the culture that guides their rules, and their models for action, and attack them by using normal and extraordinary forces[29] to win in all competitive activities between us and our competing CAS. CAS perform roles and missions; they cause actions, and actions cause outcomes. Some outcomes can prove favorable to the CAS, some not so much. Part of discerning outcomes of CAS actions involves their interpretation of incoming assessment data. That is to say, how the human CAS thinks about the outcomes his actions create. Yet again, culture provides the CAS wherewithal to shape their methods for interpreting extant and gathered data, turning it into knowledge, evaluating the knowledge, learning from their mistakes and strengths, and adapting. It also provides the wherewithal to judge the value of how well CAS rules influence models and how well models guide action and how well the action-assessment model is gathering the data with which to evaluate, learn, and adapt. All can and should change with internal quality controls for evaluating and adjusting outcomes of *will* imposition operations.

As CAS perform these functions and activities, they consider standards of quality and discern whether their actions met those standards. If not, they must adapt to do better. Quality checks provide a valuable means for both assessment and directing adaptation. Culture shapes how CAS perform this judgmental process—theirs and their adversary's. Quality is ever so important to CAS as it constitutes a "pressure gauge for success," which occurs in many ways. But it follows that one can gain more insights into this process as they peer even deeper into the rabbit hole of one's imagination merging with the real situation and experience by reading the thoughts of Nobel Laureate Murray Gell-Mann, a scientist at the Santa Fe Institute, as he encourages us to be more flexible and realize that emergence could be at play:

Now the feedback process need not be a clear-cut one in which success is well defined and leads to survival of the schema [internal model of a CAS] while failure, equally well defined, results in its disappearance. Fitness may be emergent . . . the effect on the competition among schemata may be only a tendency; and a

28. Hall and Citrenbaum, *Intelligence Analysis*, 235.
29. Sun Tzu, *The Art of War*, 91.

demoted schema may be kept for use in a subordinate capacity or retained in memory while not utilized. . . . The important thing is the nature of the selection pressures exerted in the feedback loop, whether or not they are expressible in terms of a fitness function. . . . In its application to the real world, a schema is in a sense re-expanded, reequipped with some of the arbitrariness of experience, some for the random material of the kind that was stripped away from the data when regularities [I think he means patterns when he speaks of regularities] were identified and compressed. For instance, a theory must be combined with boundary conditions in order to give a prediction. The additional data adjoined to the schema may simply be part of the continuing stream of incoming data, which contain, in general, the random along with the regular.[30]

Adversary CAS must assess how well their actors—the agents—collide, careen, intersect, and conjoin—this is a basic quality control process and function. What do we know about this motion and expulsion of energy? My thought to you is if you watch closely or look for seemingly invisible "CAS pheromones" you shall find CAS traces; they always leave trails—energy, physicality emissions (sweat, smell, breath), cigarette butts, oil slicks, whirring, sent of gunpowder, burn of rubber, computer sounds, cell phone pings, DNA droppings, and so on as they set conditions to impose their desired outcomes, collide, careen, intersect, and conjoin with their adversary. If our ever-thoughtful Über-thinker and thought pilgrim are the knowledge warriors, they find ways to search for, find, track, and interpret these mission-oriented CAS. CAS must compete, and to compete must act, but to live, they have to assess their actions, which often involve collisions or at least intersections with competitor CAS and fathom whether said actions met expected high standards. They seek feedback, but it must be the right kind of feedback, sought at the right time and place for the right activity and guided by the right observables (with their data collection or intelligence collection, or personal observations, sensings, thought, and intuition). They gather data; they turn data into information and knowledge; they evaluate the developed knowledge; they learn; they adapt; and, in doing so, they co-evolve. They perform all of these activities and actions under the sometimes strict and sometimes lenient rules their culture stipulates for judging the quality of action at a variety of times and circumstances. It follows that by way of simple logic, if one intends to influence and defeat their opponent CAS, a good way to do so is to influence the rules gauging the standards for judging value, and thus cause their vulnerability to friendly meddling.

30. Murray Gell-Mann, "Complex Adaptive Systems." From *Complexity: Metaphors, Models, and Reality,* Santa Fe Institute Studies in the Sciences of Complexity, vol. XIX, ed. G. Cowan, D. Pines, & D. Meltzer (New York: Addison-Wesley, 1994), 19–20.

You know by now that models exist in any CAS. Models guide what CAS do. Rule sets govern CAS rules. A rule in our thinking and for our purposes is:

A principle or structure of behavioral guidance that governs, binds, influences, and leads the models that shape and direct complex adaptive system (CAS), aggregate, and aggregation actions that, in turn impose one agent's *will* on another "agent" who resists said imposition.

In our expanded thinking here, a model is:

A style, design, plan, implementer of an action or a series of actions that cause behavior; a simplified representation of a system or phenomenon, as in a model of how the enemy thinks and perceives. Models are conduits of various kinds of action. Models exist in CAS as they are individuals and aggregations. Rules shape, control, and cause models to act. Models come, go, and become stagnant, but when active, they cause some kind of action.

Rules have a preeminence hierarchy. One always finds that seeking, obtaining, evaluating, learning, and adapting from feedback is essential to the life of the organism. When we think about this list, imagine a 13-step waltz that an adversary must "dance to" again and again, and the waltz becomes a pattern. Patterns, of course, derive from cultural influences as well as apperceptive interpretation. Patterns always prove vulnerable to decay, discovery, or exploitation. This waltz of the CAS involves 1) perceiving; 2) thinking; 3) planning; 4) deciding; and then: 5) acting; 6) assessing; 7) developing observables; 8) collecting data; 9) turning data into information; 10) turning information into knowledge; 11) evaluating knowledge; 12) learning; and 13) adapting. If one can know that patterns exist in this co-evolutionary waltz, why not target and affect said patterns with deep thinking to induce decay or debilitative action?

Any Über-thinker or thought pilgrim must reason deeply about how to plan for and actually influence CAS rule sets. The rules in a hypothetical set come from the macro-culture rules, organizational rules, and personal micro-rules and all of them come from years, sometimes centuries of existence and influence in a given society and derivative culture. Rules come from experience and much thought, yielding acceptable standards of acting, transacting, interacting, and behaving—the standards that shape the boundaries and innards of CAS actions and activities. What do these thoughts suggest to us? Here are some thoughts to answer this question. To compete, I must discover "living" rules; discern their origin; determine their length and intensity of influence; understand how the relevant culture surrounding actions; and be sure to discern how rules influence thinking, action, and assessment every day. Continuing with this line of thinking, I advise you to influence select rules that could affect CAS models most, and then affect the cycle action, outcome, assessment, data collection, data into knowledge, evaluate, learn, and adapt, recursion, and start again. To have any hope of working successfully with my approach, I want you to take the time and expend the mental effort to learn how a relevant culture influences rules, models, assessment, and quality control of assessment. Finally, I advise you to know and understand the clash of your quality control within the co-evolution quality control processes; protect your judgmental control mechanisms, and meddle with the adversary's.

Next, I provide you with 30 generic guidelines for use in your thinking about CAS and model functions (Table 13.1). Now I'll provide you with some ways to cope with CAS rules. As I continue to squeeze your minds harder about culture and its relationship with *will*, recognize culture as a cloak that wraps around the concept. Let us now us ponder the most important mental models within the minds and organizations of CAS, remembering, of course, that rules drive models and models drive action/behavior and action/behavior imposes what is thought to be favorable outcomes. Some deliberations that could be in play during almost any kind of conflict that could govern action and behavior deriving from CAS models and rules include those provided in Table 13.2.

Needless to say, it takes exceptionally bright, well-trained, motivated, and highly educated people to think as I'm advocating. Nonetheless, such thinking is possible and quite simple—it is structured on nature's way of sustaining life. This way of thinking helps people make sense of even nonsensical appearances. Thus, the right deep-thinking people can learn to understand how CAS, aggregates, and aggregations relate to imposing one's *will* and conversely, responding to and denying an adversary's attempts to impose his.

Let us move along and expend some mental energy to ruminate about how to influence the "rules" that stimulate and guide the energy propelled by actions coming from models (Table 13.2). Culture permeates every living thing, operational context, and conflict in any operational

Table 13.1

Generic CAS Rules

Vison	Relationships	Worldview	Myths	Regulations
Quality	Social Mores	Principles	Metaphors	Policies
Communication	Customs	Codes	Ethos	Knowledge
Connections	Life force	Values	Mythos	Doctrine
Aggregations	Rituals	Beliefs	Xenophobia	Templates
Context	Religion	Memes	Rules	Principles

Table 13.2

Possible CAS Models Driving Actions

Assess risk, uncertainty, make derivative conclusions	Anticipate, solve problems; anticipate and accentuate adversary problems	Scope future problems	Seek and create optimum outcomes	Perform condition-setting actions	Forecast the future oscillations of the context
Anticipate outcomes of will's actions	Compete and win in the race for attaining adaptation advantages	Seek quality of thought, action, adaptation	Co-evolve relative to adversary actions and adaptation	Seek accomplish aim, goals, objectives, strategies	Anticipate, and deny adversary's condition setting
Counter adversary's attempts to thwart my aggregation efforts	Anticipate observed/observer countersurveillance fight	Anticipate logic and bias errors (yours and adversary's)	Anticipate possible second- and third-order effects and consequences	Anticipate, manipulate adversary's intelligence operations	Anticipate and search for patterns (yours, adversary's, and other actors)
Anticipate, search for, affect adversary's pattern disturbance	Anticipate, search for, and affect adversary's anomalies (breaks in normal patterns)	Manipulate your anomalies for possible deception; anticipate same from adversary	Maintain baselines for use with normalcy, patterns, anomalies deceptive measures	Synchronize actions and search for right combinations to promote emergence and synergy	Challenge wargaming outcomes, assumptions, attack and resolve biases and logic errors

context. Culture influences how people think, act, assess, and adapt. With these thoughts in mind, let us consider just a few out of many methods our soldiers of mental combat can consider for influencing 10 CAS rules that drive models that drive behavior, assessment, and adaption:

1. Know and consider using particular societal, cultural, technological, and functional pressure points and manipulate them. Contemplate how to approach finding pressure points and placing them in baselines for exploitation.
2. Know and consider aiming at what you believe to be decisive points, possibly via an indirect approach through pressure points. Remember as you attempt this move—know and exploit the cultural influence on adversary's thinking, view of the world, actions, assessments, adaptations, and so forth.
3. Anticipate the adversary's centers of gravity and how they link in vertical domain silos and horizontal levels of conflict troughs, as previously discussed. Use the culture and its influence on rules and models as well as how the adversarial CAS think about their own centers of gravity, and how they link across vertical domain silos and horizontal levels of conflict troughs.
4. Know possible CAS rules and influence them. To know these rules, know the culture in which the conflict is taking place, the operational context, how the adversary thinks, acts, assesses, adapts, etc. Rules, for the most part, are subjective and flexible. Some, though, prove hallowed and thereby impermeable over time. What I'm speaking of here is the importance of understanding how, why, where, and when the rules controlling CAS come into being and the cultural influence on the rise of each of them. Mentally prepared people know cultural inputs relative to friendly aim, goals, objectives, etc., and problem sets. The data and the structure of the operational context and the adversary's organization and intent must go into shared baselines, and then they need to be in advanced thinking baselines for understanding and exploitation.
5. Know and affect the models that drive CAS to various kinds of action. Of course, you know that rules "electrify" and thus bring resident or new models to life in the human, organizational, and machine "minds" that impose desired outcomes on a resisting entity.
6. Know the origins of the rules at play. Know why rules of interest came into being. Know how long rules have been in place and the lifespan of their influence. Determine rule fragility, susceptibility to influence and pressure, nascence, longevity, and interpretative power. Consider creating random disequilibrium in CAS efforts to synchronize and achieve coherence in actions. Consider influencing operational contexts in which competitor CAS operate, including:

- Anticipate and influence CAS efforts to adapt and co-evolve.
- Influence how CAS processes, assesses, evaluates, learns, and decides to adapt to incoming data—self-procured and unsolicited data inputs from the nonlinear context.
- Influence how CAS collect, analyze, process, and use data.
- Consider how to deny competitor CAS data updates and subsequent modifications to CAS actions.
- Affect inputs which the competitor CAS interprets incoming data via apperceptive influences.

7. Any adversary in conflict searches for a Holy Grail that I describe as synchronizing power. It improves the performance of imposition actions and reactions. Friendly decision makers must always seek cross-vertical domain silo and horizontal levels of conflict level trough synchronization with the explicit goal of creating synergy. With it, the possibility arises whereby one can find emergent behavior given our Über-thinkers and thought pilgrims, planning people, execution-of-plans people, and decision makers/policy makers perform high-quality mental functions. We need to take a pathway leading to the epicenter of such behavior and consider its importance and power in the struggles of conflict. It follows that one may infer that an absolute necessity involves knowing, understanding, and comprehending not only the operational context and the adversary CAS, but also the culture that shapes and influences all things and all people and their actions, behaviors, interactions, and activities.
8. One cannot predict outcomes via rules with any sort of precision or consistency. Yes, this realization could cause some people to shy away from thinking about rules, models of behavior, CAS, aggregates, and aggregations. I do not see it that way. I fully recognize how volatile any operational context could be, particularly with the presence of agents who, by their very nature, have to assess and adapt faster and better than their competitor or face status diminution or even extinction. In addition, rules prove to be messy by their very nature. Their degree of messiness and complexity changes from culture to culture and from society to society, and even within any given culture with their sub-cultures. Rules subjugate first to one's comprehension of their essence and internal drivers, and then to manipulation—passive (observing to learn their patterns) or active (placing pressure on them)—to find how they fit with and disturb the operational context once jolted by an outside force or entity.
9. Our thinkers should consider pertinent examples of each in how they would act in particular settings, problem sets, and operational contexts. The best one can hope for is to study the culture and anticipate what rules exist, discern which dominate, determine which are subordinate,

and identify the rules that could direct and influence models that drive behavior. With that said, though, I do not advocate passively waiting for adversary CAS to seize the initiative via their intimate knowledge and understanding of any given operational context to succeed and thereby submit to their adversary's *will*. Instead, the friendly side strives to initiate action involving imposing their desired outcomes on adversary CAS.

10. To understand CAS, it helps to comprehend their importance to successful advanced and deep thinking. CAS comprise competitors' networks of networks of networks; CAS often live, work, thrive, or die in fluid operational contexts; CAS depend upon self-organization and in a way, often use mission-type orders—or in theoretical terms, *Auftragstaktik*.[31] CAS sometimes operate in a state of uneven similarity with larger and smaller CAS, aggregates, and aggregations. Self-similarity means when one decomposes a CAS, resultant smaller CAS prove generally similar to the CAS of which we speak.
11. To gain an edge on the phenomenon of emergent behavior, our Überthinkers and thought pilgrims provide decision makers with opportunities to preempt potentially dangerous macro-aggregations and shape or thwart their birth, maturation, decline, and death. People sometimes call such masses coming into existence a second- or third-order effect, or an unforeseen consequence. These people are thinking about and recognizing aggregations that often form when different entities conjoin and undergo self-organization. CAS are dynamic networks of interactions and relationships. They are adaptive in that their individual and collective behavior changes as a result of experience, feedback, evaluation, and adaptation. This outcome circles back to co-evolution.

Let's visit a phenomenon I have created help us think—it is tendency analysis of which I think, and it is highly relevant to this chapter. In this book's context, a tendency is "a disposition to move, proceed, or act in some direction or toward some point, end, or result." It involves performing high-level contemplation about the place where one intuits tendencies to be occurring and thereby signifying where and when future struggles could be occurring. Tendency analysis means:

Discerning meaning through thought and study of the general proclivities of people, the behavioral and action inclinations of organizations, mental snapshots of current environment or contextual situations, events, activities, behaviors, the

---

31. *Auftragstaktik*: In mission-type tactics, the military commander gives subordinate leaders a clearly defined goal (the mission), the forces needed to accomplish that goal, and a time frame within which the goal must be reached. Retrieved December 20, 2008, from http://dictionary.reference.com/browse/archaic.

emanation dispersal of energy emissions, and what the interaction and enmeshing of all could portend for the future.

Thinking about tendencies, I argue none of us ever see reality; we only have our idea of reality and it is, at best, approximate. Quite simply, our mind's eye tends to experience a slow slide into the murky pool of ambiguity, obfuscation, and confusion only to be pulled out of the pool by a jolt of intuition followed by clear thinking even though it remains subjective and naturally biased. As advanced thinking people, all of us work hard to verify our idea of reality. We seek an understanding about the slight differences, slight perturbations in normalcy, subtle flashes of intuition, ever so slight twinges in patterns that eventually reach our minds and senses even when thinking about something different. What do these slight changes mean? Do we shrug off what our intuition alerts us to, or instead try to figure out what is different and why it appeared? This is important thinking for this skill as it is intuition based and the presence of a small, almost non-existent ripple or ripples in previously calm contextual situations.

It is clear to me "fact," as it were, "truth," depends upon fictions, interpretations, metaphors, analogies, perspectives, and our rational (at least to us) thoughts—all culturally shaped. Of course, "truth" is seductive—particularly when I see what I want to see and turn a blind eye to reality. Someone who says, "this is the truth" is purporting to overcome not only their personal perspectives, as this excerpt describes, but all of their unique experiences, interpretations, expectations, and previous behaviors. It follows, quite simply, while trying to think and draw open the curtains of illusion to find the high ground of thought and "near truth" (and "near true facts"), one has to possess a sound rendition of experiential influences, what one's culture does by way of screening and shaping data inputs to our mind's eye, what a vision of what truth could be, and one's tainted perspectives. Thus, an admonition, if you will: Approach truth with a skeptical eye.

To win in the conflicts of which I speak, one must appreciate the strength of cultural influence on adversaries, neutrals, and a governed populace. All prove important in our desire relative to our adversary. None of these culturally laden signs of activity readily appear in our minds, as they enjoy a good degree of opaqueness. Such activities assume masks as CAS swim in tides of humanity moving in and out of cities and sustaining normal patterns of life, functional patterns, technical patterns, and human/social patterns. That which we seek—answers to what our intuition tells us cause a break in normal patterns—could be more obvious if our rheostat so our Veil of Maya lets in more rays, the particulates of data, information, and knowledge, each providing shards of meaning that the thinker forms into a tapestry of meaning.

As signs of focus become recognizable to our minds, we direct our "eyes" to scan a street corner or a neighborhood, locate a cave and its particulars, track a mobile surface-to-surface missile system's "race track," discover a WMD storage area, or "see" activities associated with condition setting for action with which to impose one's actions or deny an adversary's efforts. It takes a purposeful mental effort, which I call disambiguation, to understand that which culture masks and covers with ambiguity. It means, in our lexicon for advanced thinking,[32] our operational parlance, "to make visible that, which through ambiguity, appears invisible; to remove the ambiguity from; make unambiguous."[33]

Advanced thinking in a war of wits and mental combat involves risks and uncertainty, particularly when people dare peer under their own Veil of Maya (one never knows what they might find). How does one overcome or at least allay the dangers of risk and uncertainty? First of all, seek the following: 1) aggressive and well-prepared Über-thinkers and thought pilgrims; 2) an indigenous person to help you understand the culture; 3) a tough Red Team to challenge your assumptions, provide alternatives, think and act as the adversary, and seek and use the thoughts of a variety of subject matter experts; and 4) one or more virtual knowledge environments (VKEs) coming together viz. maneuvering,[34] from around the world and bringing to a distinct fray, combined great minds, linked super computers to complement organic computing power, tacit knowledge, organizational power, contributory energy, and the capability to cross-walk thoughts laterally and develop creatively solutions to the problems of the people in extremis, with other people in other VKE organizations in the struggle for the ascendency of our *will*. This virtual team peels away successive veils of people and even their organizations—adversary, friendly, neutrals, all with skin in the game; they work to do away with layers of illusions (natural, one's self-induced illusions, and adversary-induced illusions) to get at, find, and understand what is happening or about to happen. These experts take aim on finding the criteria of right time, right place, right activity, and right collection combinations to produce desired outcomes. The Veil of Maya is an illusion, as it were, a membrane, that obscures or distorts reality and truth from our thinking. It exists and manipulates our view of reality any time our minds allow it to meddle, which is most of the time. It is

32. Wayne Michael Hall, *Lexicon for Advanced Thinking*, March 4, 2017, pp. 1–50. Note: I have been working on this lexicon since 2007. It is open ended, and I'm adding to it every day.

33. Dictionary.com Unabridged (v 1.1). Retrieved March 6, 2008, from http://dictionary.reference.com/browse/disambiguate.

34. It is my contention that given advanced thinking, we can now maneuver minds, computers, sensors, data, data networks, knowledge, organizations, and VKE. When we maneuver and combine these eight capabilities at the right time, we will create synergy and thereby unleash a great and new power.

through thinking, knowledge, understanding, and comprehension that one overcomes the negative effects of the Veil of Maya. Our thinkers must instead maintain a steady focus on expanding their intellects and focusing on that which is most important.

We are in an Alice in Wonderland rabbit hole when contemplating future conflict. All of us must decide how deeply to descend into this hole. Yes, any of us can become confused, as often truth is false and false is true. Sometimes one finds dishonor to be revered more than honor, circumstances in which visible is invisible, where duplicitousness is more valuable than truth and many more human, culturally driven foibles. It is a world similar to George Orwell's world in his book, *1984*. In this book, he presents the Ministry of Truth as having three maxims on its façade: "War is peace," "Freedom is slavery," and "Ignorance is strength."[35] In our world of conflict there is a time for all seasons, meaning the interaction of opposites is alive and well and subject to interpretation via the culture at hand.

I'm not the only one to consider the unity of opposites to be important. One of my favorite authors, Paul Fussell, helps me think about this curious yet powerful unity as he writes of the poet Siegfried Sassoon's experiences in the trenches of World War I:

> But I am thinking more of the grinding daily contrasts which no line-officer ever forgets: those between "his" ground and ours; the enemy and "us;" invisibility and visibility; his dead and ours; day rest and night labor; the knowledge born of the line and the ignorant innocence at home; the life on the line and the life of the Staff.[36]

Mythos is a term laden with a range of meaning. It deserves our special attention, as a rule, and belief, and feeling, and "conditioner" of behavior. It means "the underlying system of beliefs, especially those dealing with supernatural forces, characteristic of a particular cultural group." Mythos suggests to a person's mind to recognize faith, know the difference between right and wrong, and thereby trust in your actions and behaviors. Its derivative is belief. A belief is trust, faith, and confidence in something. It can also mean an internal feeling that guides and governs behavior. Beliefs vary in meaning and intensity from culture to culture. Many threats, enemies, and even business competitors follow their cultural and religious beliefs of the supernatural, and they can be particularly focused on what is going to happen in the afterlife. In the cases of some suicide bombers, for example, I have read that they believe that if they blow themselves up and kill innocent people, then their afterlife is wonderful. At the present

35. George Orwell, *1984* (New York: Houghton Mifflin Harcourt, 1949), 10.
36. Paul Fussell, *The Great War and Modern Memory* (Oxford, UK: Oxford University Press, 1975), 92.

moment and in the present time their parents are heroes, and their families receive financial compensation all their lives. Their beliefs on the subject are stronger than a social more—they are a spiritual guidance and motivator to their beliefs. We want to influence such people to think our way, or to be hesitant in their actions and thereby present aberrant observables to wary security people who might notice the appearance of a killer. One hopes to, in T. E. Lawrence's words, purposefully arrange the minds[37] of such people and find a range of alternatives awaiting a snatch from our outstretched hands for immediate exploitation.

All people behave—obviously. All people have beliefs. All people have values. All people generally follow the semi-binding rules coming from social mores. I can also say with sureness that behaviors and beliefs firmly entwine. Both entwine with their particular culture. When looking hard into the distant parts of our minds, one can always find behavior following beliefs, and we find faith after beliefs, and faith comes from one's culture. With observation and deep thinking, one always finds more to any situation than meets the eye, hence the mind. This is a warning for people who prefer to sit back and react to what adversary CAS do as they plan and then attempt to beat America's individuals, aggregates, aggregations, etc. Broaden your perspectives and think deeply, broadly, holistically, and culturally comprehend our conflict problem sets. The most important element of our adversary's culture is the "puppet master" who our targets the adversary's mind as well as ours. Our goal: Find him (or them) and neutralize his power.

The nefarious (to us) *will* arises from nowhere and raises its ugly head. What appears is an entity who wants to impose his *will* via action on you. He knows you could resist, or acquiesce. At play, the generator might very well use his 14-element process model, identical to ours. He knows his opponent uses the same model. He attacks your elements and protects his. Thus, we can infer clashing models and movements among the elements swaying to and fro along the model's arrow-shaped shaft. One also finds select items of the 18-considerations at play—you have read about them throughout this book. It follows that one should know a lot about all aspects of *will* and act accordingly. If *it* is viewed as impossible to know and understand, our ignorance becomes stifling, intellectually numbing, and translucent.

Here are more important specifics I covered in this chapter. I explained how I rode the wild pendulum into a hypothetical adversary's mind and how I found thinkers not only assessing their adversaries, but also attempting to reason like him. Thus, I explained that the adversary rides the wild pendulum to the adversary's side and swings back to visit his version of

37. Lawrence, *Seven Pillars of Wisdom*, 195.

friendly key players with the situations inherent to each arch actually conflict. Our thinker postulates the adversary CAS must assess how well their actors—the agents—collide, careen, intersect, and conjoin—this is a basic quality control process and function. This is an area in which opposing sides potentially struggle to control and influence their own, and their adversary's, actions, assessments, and attempts to adapt. I presented the important question: What do we know about motion and expulsion of energy relative to CAS? I explained that CAS always "shed" pheromones as they move and collide/intersect with other CAS. To the attentive mind, they leave energy trails when they collide, careen, intersect, and conjoin along with other sensory traces. Thus, one should anticipate, search for, find, interpret, and perhaps follow the energy trails.

I explained in this chapter that CAS must compete, but to live, they have to assess their actions, which often involve collisions or at least intersections with competitor CAS. They thus seek feedback, but it must be the right kind of feedback, sought at the right time and place, and they must seek the right activity, being guided by the right observables (with their data collection or intelligence collection, or personal observations/sensings, thought, and intuition). CAS gather assessment data, turn data into information and knowledge, evaluate the developed knowledge, learn, and adapt, and in doing so, they co-evolve. CAS perform all of these activities and actions under sometimes strict and sometimes lenient rules that their culture stipulates not only for acting, but also for judging the outcomes of action at different times and under different circumstances. If one intends to influence and defeat their opponent CAS, a good way to meddle is to do so with a distinct knowledge-driven aim: to influence the rules gauging "quality," and thus cause their vulnerability to friendly meddling.

The focus of learning in this chapter is on "how to think" about affecting complex adaptive systems and their lifeblood—co-evolution and adaptation cycles—before and while planning and during actual combat operations. I submitted to readers that if they choose to go this route, they have to understand the basics of nonlinearity, complex adaptive systems (CAS), and their important characteristics.

In the chapter, I showed my readers how to take difficult theory and move it to actual practice—the transformation that is praxis. In this chapter I discussed CAS (humans and human-populated organizations) and their need to co-evolve with their adversaries and to the context. In the chapter, I presented a case for creative thinking via understanding CAS actions, coming from models of action, coming from rules, which in turn come from culture, technology, humanism, and so on. This chapter presented a detailed vision of how CAS rules influence CAS models and how CAS models then drive CAS behavior. The chapter presented the "amalgamation" of culture to rules to models to action evident and always present in all CAS as they struggle against their adversaries. The chapter offered examples of 30 possible CAS rules and 24 generic CAS models complete with tables and explanations.

The chapter presented ways in which people can think about CAS, aggregations, and how culture affects everything that happens on any given day in any given operational context. In this chapter, I offered an explanation about the need to use our imaginations and creativity to find ways to get ahead of our hydra—our adversaries of the present and future—discovering new ways to beat our foes in conflicts, whether via conventional military force on force, special operations, or in bouts of mental combat via cyber war, narratives, psychological operations, and information operations. I borrowed and used concepts of coevolution, adaptation, CAS, and nonlinearity as cornerstones for the framework I put forth for use in conflicts over "will." Finally, I provided my readers with four points about thinking in this chapter. First, friendly decision makers and their analysts must learn to outthink their adversary with the techniques and methods of thinking I presented in this chapter to win in conflicts. Second, nobody should give up on their quest to reason like the adversary because the subject is difficult. Third, friendly commanders and their coterie of advanced thinkers must use models to think like the adversary—I provided the models in this chapter as I introduced throughout the book. Specifically, I captured the models in tables that present 24 CAS models of action and 30 exemplar rules that could be influential in the human selection of rules and action models. Fourth, I advised my readers to keep in mind a unique 11-point thought model for thinking like the adversary.

CHAPTER 14

The Thinking Adversary

Argument: *In this chapter, readers learn to outthink adversaries.* Will, *the preeminent concept, demands comprehension to win. I caution readers: One can never reason exactly like an adversary; they must be content with narrowing the adversary's options and approximating his thinking by using models and detailed wargaming. I provide concerns of any adversary's mind: 1) unpredictability; 2) turbulence in nonlinear operational contexts; and 3) presence and influence of sensitive variables. Thought models in this chapter helps readers learn how to think like their adversaries with models: 1) duality; 2) cultural expertise; 3) wise, determined-to-win wargaming foes; 4) Red Teams that challenge assumptions, reasoning, etc.; and 5) virtual knowledge environments to link global assets (e.g., organizations with experts to help win).*

Mental combat has always been a state of being among warring humans even though I haven't seen it described in these words. One can identify these bouts throughout the works of theorists who have come before me—Sun Tzu, Caesar, von Moltke the elder, T. E. Lawrence, the Chinese colonels who wrote *Unlimited Warfare*, and Timothy Thomas, who wrote the fine paper titled "Like Riding on the Wings of a Tiger," which once again suggested the presence of knowledge war[1] and mental combat. Every person interested in any kind of security now and in the future, must reason about mental combat and how to outwit formidable foes who roam comfortably in the fertile pastures of operational contexts that American thinkers often don't know well at all. Often on familiar soil and armed with the phenomenon of changing and adapting quickly through the process of co-evolution, our foes rapidly learn and change because they constantly act, assess, receive feedback, and adapt faster and more effectively than hierarchical bureaucracies can possibly adapt or change even in ideal situations. To "recognize the presence and influence of an intellectually

1. Hall, *Stray Voltage*, 2003.

formidable adversary" one must recognize "the thinking adversary" and outthink him. Quite simply, people in mental combat need to learn how to think better than today, and it takes adapting and using networks to fight their adversary's networks.[2]

As I mentioned earlier, it is impossible to go into another person's mind and to know exactly what and how they think. All one can and must do is approximate the adversary's thoughts from his point of view and his idea of rationality given his problem set, his probable mission; his probable resources; and his probable aim, goals, and objectives. Does an aura of doom cause us to raise our hands in frustration and despair while groping in the fog of the dark and unknown, attempting to reason what and how an opponent might be reasoning? I say no. Using the thoughts I have introduced and emphasized throughout this book, by implication and inference one can approximate what an adversary could be thinking with six aspects of conflict: 1) his 14-element model; 2) the kind of conflict he has embarked upon; 3) his aim, goals, objectives, resources, constraints, and strategies; 4) the situation, operational, and political context in which he plans to compete; 5) his previous behavior; and 6) his co-evolution and adaptation cycles.

Asymmetric adversaries fight using mental combat and often indirect episodes of conflict because they haven't sufficient conventional might to fight the United States and win. While attempting to think like an adversary, our minds feel pummeled by probabilities portraying uncertainty, error, and risk. With that said, do not ignore this essential aspect of thought and the holism this effort requires because it is difficult. Learn to guide our minds to learn how to think deeply and develop ways to proceed, accounting for 1) competing with an unpredictable adversary; 2) competing in a nonlinear operational context; 3) recognizing and coping with the presence and influence of sensitive variables; 4) recognizing the bureaucratic obstacles impeding the intellectual growth one needs to outthink the adversary in mental combat while residing in western bureaucratic organizational models; and 5) overcoming our adversaries via thought models, concepts, and methods of problem solving the reader finds in this book.

I have 47 years of experience in intelligence. With a lot of thought and trial and error, my notion of "thinking like the adversary" has evolved to a "living" model—it changes as I learn, gain more experience, and of most importance, push my mind into new and more difficult intellectual challenges. But it is thinking about how to think that reaps benefits from my approach to

2. Stanley A. McChrystal, "It Takes a Network," *Foreign Policy* (2011), 1–10. Note, I found this on the *Foreign Policy* website, www.foreignpolicy.com, and accessed and read the article on November 22, 2017. The article did not have page numbers but consisted of 10 pages; hence the reference to 1–10.

Table 14.1

Adversary Strategy Thought Model
(Read from left to right for step-enumeration.)

Strategic aim	Goals	Objectives	Resources	Constraints	Strategies	Tactics
Will	Coevolution and adaptation	Duality and pendulum	Adversary wargaming	13-element thought model	Advantages/ disadvantages	Logic/ bias errors

this difficult venture into the shadowy world of conflict and colliding *wills*. My thinking comes forth in Table 14.1, a new model, which represents "a way" to approximate "thinking like the adversary" by using a thought and planning process model to replicate his reasoning to the extent possible.

Yes, using this thought model has its dangers—mirror imaging, confirmatory bias, outdated data, information, and knowledge, oversimplification and many other possible error points—but I plan to allay these valid fears in this chapter. Any decision maker and her deep thinkers must experience a process similar to what you see on the graphic to undertake a competitive mission with a high quality of possible accomplishment. I expect any adversary to possess and use an ingrained individual and in some cases, an organizational thought process. We enter this thought process and engage it with our minds, as Sun Tzu says, "Attack enemy plans at their inception. . . . The supreme excellence in war is to attack the enemy's plans."[3]

A model helps our minds consider a projected reality. This reality, composed of understandable characteristics, helps us discern what our adversary could be after as the model plays out. The model must be restless and in motion, always adapting to operational context and opponents, but never in isolation from other influencers of outcomes of conflict (e.g., stimuli of a nonlinear context). In my discussion at the start of Chapter 1 and Chapter 2, I put forth and advocated a proposition. I posited that people who consider this subject must do so from a holistic thinking[4] perspective. I do not know what this theoretical adversary calls or labels the elements in his thought models, but I can assure you that he must use some of the elements that I listed in my 14-element thought model. In his 14-element model I have attempted to replicate "a way" he could be thinking—strategic aim, goals, objectives, resources, constraints, strategies, tactics, and so on, as he

3. Sun Tzu, *The Art of War*, 77–78.

4. As a reminder, this book's definition for holism is "the whole is greater than the simple sum of parts and the parts of this whole can only be understood relative to the whole itself and how well it operates."

ponders his desired outcomes and considers us, the resister to his ambitions. Where can one start with such a large and complicated task of comprehending individual elements in these models, but also holistically, in how each element works within the model itself and relates to other elements—indeed, the whole in question? Well, one can start with the adversary's ultimate aim and methods to get to where he wants to go.

Any model of an adversary's desires always starts with ideas about what, in an overall sense, he wants to accomplish. His desired outcome results in his utterance of one or more broad goals. The broad goals provide himself if operating alone, or his subordinates if operating with many, a direction—or in other terms, a vector with an end or a desired outcome as to what he seeks. Of course, many specifics follow to enact this broad direction, but they come later in his thinking and consequently in our thought model. I proceed by first defining strategic aim: "an adversary or competitor's overall, holistic, and relational desired outcomes." An adversary's strategic aim lets us peek behind his Veil of Maya into his vision for what he seeks. The strategic aim is one's desire for a macro-outcome or set of outcomes in a conflict or even a competitive event. You can count, though, that with this line of thinking, our theoretical adversary could very well have developed a strategic aim. Included among the desired outcomes, we may find pressure points, decisive points, and/or centers of gravity, given we know where, when, and how to seek these points.

The strategic aim is broad in scope and written or stated in generalized instead of precise language, hence receptive to thought derivations. A strategic aim typically and broadly states guidance for the subordinate leaders' mission. The aim certainly leaves the receiving person with interpretation and latitude. It also implies constraints, explains why they exist, and whether they are permanent or malleable. A famous example was the Allied Combined Chiefs of Staff directive to General Eisenhower issued on February 12, 1944:

> Task. You will enter the continent of Europe and, in conjunction with the other United Nations, undertake operations aimed at the heart of Germany and the destruction of her armed forces.

As you can imagine, a strategic aim influences one's thinking and planning—friendly as well as adversarial. Be advised, though, in delving into more specificity about how our adversary could be reasoning, realize that all of us must understand and cope with our own constraints. Moreover, we cannot leave a further consideration to happenstance; that is to say, your adversary considers how you view constraints as well. These constraints can be monetary, they may be capabilities, they may be contextual, they could be religious or moral, or they could be choice of targets or approaches. At times an adversary attempts to exploit friendly constraints while minimizing access to and manipulation of his constraints. With my philosophy, I contemplate using a combination of political, economic, military, social, information, and contextual powers and influences to achieve my strategic aim. As a reminder, however, as I discussed early and throughout this work, duality is all-pervading.

Dangers lurk, ready to pounce when you err in attempting to place your mind inside an adversary's mind. It leads us to conclude: anticipate this mental fray and take appropriate precautions. Forge on and pursue a solvable mystery—how I think he thinks and then drill my thoughts and calculations during wargaming that occurs in an imaginary-only intellectual context. One must make the model of the quest for a high level of reasoning as real as possible. It is in such a context that we work diligently to think like the adversary only to find our limitations. If one is truthful with themselves, they recognize the significantly different thought processes from what they anticipated; lo and behold, this opponent thinks differently than us. In this book, I provide you with ways to overcome this intellectual baggage, but only to the vague level of adjusting one's thoughts to be more like our adversary's thoughts, knowing full well one can never eradicate this resilient evil of logic and bias errors. The metaphor involves imaging you "riding a swinging pendulum" to help consider duality. This metaphor carries you into the strange world of motion and vagary (unpredictable, erratic happening, incidence, activity). The pendulum's motion requires you to think like the adversary, only finding yourself returning to how you ruminate. This ride involves seeing the context, adversary, and constraints from your adversary's perceptions and perspectives.[5] The ride is never exactly the same, as each adversary is co-evolving and adapting, and the context constantly changes.

This metaphor reminds us to keep in our minds two maxims: 1) nothing happens in isolation; and 2) everything connects in some way. What you do always induces outcomes and change—turbulence in the operational context. You and your adversary, as you compete, disturb the universe through change. Swinging into your adversary's mind on the "wild pendulum," attempting to think like he thinks and then swinging back to musing in your mind, only works relationally. You do your best to be in his "skin" and perceive and think like him. You work diligently to discern his constraints from his perspective as he considers their influence on his operations. This complicated mental action occurs only in relation to the

5. In her book *The Life of the Mind,* Hannah Arendt provides us with some insights that could help analytic-driven intelligence collection penetrate the layers and wrappers protecting the adversary's perceptions and perspectives: "Sense perceptions are illusions, says the mind; they change according to the conditions of our body; sweet, bitter, color, and so on exist only by convention among men . . . according to true nature behind the appearances," 11.

struggle you are in with your adversary and other potential adversaries. When reasoning like the adversary and riding the wild pendulum into his world and back to ours, it only makes sense he is ruminating about how you consider your own capabilities and intentions as well as his.

Let us take a moment to consider "strategic aim" relative to nation-states or large organizations. In this context, strategic aim provides enough direction for lower-ranking decision makers to proceed, but again in the ideal situation, how recipients of the aim proceed comes through their own developed goals, objectives, and strategies. In this respect, the strategic aim induces more specific but related and connected goals and objectives. The strategic aim comes forth via the Clausewitzian dictum that "nothing is more important for the statesman and general than to come to an agreement about the nature of the conflict." He also informs us war is the imposition of political *will* via other means. As I mentioned earlier in this work, unfortunately, high-level political and military leaders seem to this day to either ignore this dictum and war's definition, or they become confused about how political needs always shape and constrain the use of military or other means to accomplish goals and triumph in conflicts.

Now let us burrow into even more difficult mental work—consider the strategic aim for adversaries who could be terrorists, drug people, or insurgents. Their strategic aim differs from an ideologue's, or an irregular war actor's. I can say with certitude that terrorists, drug people, or insurgent high-level leaders won't label their broad outcomes as a "strategic aim." Instead they disseminate strategic aim or share it as broad guidance, perhaps coming forth as a thought link,[6] a message coined in a video, a tweet, implied rewards and punishment,[7] speech, or a private message conveyed via email or voice. Thinking about such guidance helps us understand goals, objectives, resources, constraints, strategies, tactics, and the like as they are strung together like baubles of an ascending size, each reflecting the other.

Let's continue by imagining how a drug dealer could speak about his "strategic aim" in terms of money goals, acceptable risk, acceptable loss, and general times of production and smuggling. A high-level terrorist leader could be Osama bin Laden hiding in the hills of eastern Afghanistan or in his compound in Pakistan who sends fatwas broad in descriptiveness of action such as "take the fight against the Great Satan to the cities of the United States" or vague in guidance such as "kill all infidels." An

6. My definition for a "thought link" is neither singular nor simple. A thought link is "a broad or general description of direction or thrust for action or future intent of actions; high-level decision guidance; a concept or vision with intimation of necessary actions or possible plans of action."

7. Steven D. Levitt and Stephen J. Dubner, *Freakonomics* (New York: HarperCollins Publishers, 2005), 89–117.

insurgent leader's strategic aim could come forth as a vision generally describing a desired state of being such as "the existing government is no longer in power and the insurgents have taken over." Even if a strategic aim is broad or vague, one can surmise its nub or central idea, which provides the shape or at least a rough outline of "purpose." Once we discern purpose, reason about its strength, and voilà, you catch one of the essential elements of our model—strength of motive. As usual, duality moves front and center in our thoughts and I therefore consider motive from adversaries' or competitors' perspectives. Once motive appears, follow with consideration of strength of motive, which, along with capabilities, helps us begin the process of "fleshing out the skeletal structure" of not only strategic aim, but our thoughts about the adversary's views.

Allow me to take you on a brief journey into the minds of six famous philosophers of war: Sun Tzu in *The Art of War*, Julius Caesar in *The Gallic War*, Scipio Africanus in B. H. Liddell Hart's *Scipio Africanus: Better Than Napoleon*, T. E. Lawrence in *Seven Pillars of Wisdom*, and Erich von Manstein in *Lost Victories*.

- Sun Tzu: Chinese general who lived ~2,500 years ago and tells us to attack enemy plans at their inception. He also asks us to know the enemy and know oneself and we will never experience defeat in a hundred battles. He pushes our minds to think about and to apply the aphorism that the ultimate aim in war is to defeat the adversary's plans.
- Clausewitz: 19th-century Prussian theorist on engagements, battles, and campaigns; strategic aim; critical analysis; duality [my derivation via interpreting his writing] planning; strategy; genius of the commander; inner mind's eye; center of gravity; the Marvelous Trinity; friction; and chance.
- T. E. Lawrence: Directed Arab insurgency against the Ottoman Empire in WWI; wrote about overall goals; focus; his chapter XXXIII of *Seven Pillars of Wisdom* suggests principles for being a successful insurgent; shaping the minds of adversaries, one's own men, coalition leaders, the populace; relationship of political ends and military means; use of the indirect approach.
- Manstein: German field marshal in WWII; wrote about relationships between tactics, operations, and campaigns; strategic aim and resources; large resources; space and time; anticipated adversary actions and reactions; momentum and tempo; operational surprise; and deception.
- Julius Caesar: relationship of political and military actions; speed in movements; use of intelligence; variants of "knowledge war"; boldness; unity of home and operational context; decisiveness; unity of effort; surprise; risk; psychological operations; logistics; leadership; personal bravery.
- Scipio Africanus: gifted visionary; strategic thinker; personal bravery; creative ideas and their practical application; political and military unity

of effort; speed in movement; learning from the past; intelligence operations; patterns and deception; anticipation and denial; alliances and loyalty; focus on goals; relationship of operational context and one's aims; myths of invincibility; magnanimity in triumph.

POLICY

It is in governments or commercial organizations in which one finds policies. Policies usually come with the imprimatur of leaders, but organizations often develop the staffing and coordinating to not only design policy, but to put one or more of them into effect. Policy provides boundaries and guidance for strategic aims, goals, objectives, strategies, tactics, actions, and activities. It is within policy where one usually finds any given political objective, albeit sometimes vaguely—the motive for conflict, and the amount of effort to be expended in its (political objective) attainment.

I use the following definition for policy: "broad guidance to influence plans of action adopted or pursued by an individual, government, party, and business. It comes from 'vision' though entanglement with strategic aim (and sometimes vision), goals, objectives, and serves as the 'invisible hand' that constrains or unleashes actions and boundaries of action execution to accomplish aim, goals, and objectives." Policy provides human beings and organizations with sufficient guidance to govern how people think, plan, act, and or enforce laws, rules, and regulations, yet policy does not go into specifics. It often offers people latitude for interpretations and subsequent actions because it is purposefully vague. A policy, while binding, offers recipients latitude, but therein lies the rub—people sometimes develop and try to implement grotesque interpretations of policy and the subsequent actions can turn into folly. Occasionally, vagueness comes forth as an accident, but most of the time senior leaders design policy so various interpretations can arise thereby giving greater latitude to act within a wider interpretative set of actions or activities. So long as policy recipients enact the policy, how they choose to act is their choice. Policy makers must be careful though, as once a policy lives and multiple people live, dream, think, and plan within its guidance, it is difficult to undo and therefore has the potential to endure for generations.

GOALS AND OBJECTIVES

Next, we narrow our hypothetical adversary's ambition to aim-enabling goals and objectives. They are more specific than policy and strategic aim. Moreover, due to the need to be more specific than strategic aim, one usually finds several goals and objectives. Again, as in our discussion of strategic aim, an adversary might not call goals and objectives by those names, but they must use derivative "enabling" steps as they take their "what to think" strategic aim and winnow it into subsequent desired and necessary outcomes.

In my view, though goals and objectives certainly connect, we must consider goals as broader than objectives but not as broad as the strategic aim and policy. An objective is more specific than goals, but the two bond, providing increasingly more specific explanatory and enacting descriptions of just how, when, where, and why success needs to appear. The objective often describes and solidifies actions and effects (outcomes) of action. Implied in highly accomplishing organizations is a need to accomplish objectives as part of a unified whole that can burst and influence outcomes so as to win in conflict with a unity of effort of capabilities and strength of motive.

Could it be true that to anticipate how the outcomes of any conflict or competition could turn, one must narrow their views to potential battles of competing objectives, but occurring simultaneously in multiple vertical domain silos (air, ground, sea, space, cyber, information, and cognition) and levels of conflict troughs (tactical, operational, strategic [military], and grand strategic [policy]) and perhaps even alternative universes? I think so, and evidence by way of history or conflict theory generates and shapes my view. But I also postulate from my experience and my reading that people do not view a "battle of objectives" as a viable aspect of understanding competition and conflict, though they should. The battles of objectives of which I speak live and thrive inside the "whole" of conflict or completion. The thriving of which I speak, however, experiences variance in success owing to the presence of several kinds of potential battles, all driven by a notion that battles of objectives always conjoin and become entangled with and among battles of 1) minds; 2) materiel; 3) technology; 4) perspectives; 5) advantages and disadvantages; 6) leadership and decision making; 7) constraints; 8) pressure and decisive points; 9) adaptation; 10) information; knowledge; and narratives; 11) quality; 12) use of the operational context; and 13) organizations, et al.

All of these ways of viewing battles of objectives and their connections contribute to supremacy in which one side successfully imposes theirs on their adversary via actions and the recipient of the imposition fails to block the imposition. These struggles often occur simultaneously with varying degrees of intensity, and they cause the human mind to not only think in a vertical sense in one domain silo or one level of conflict trough, but also horizontally across several domain silos and levels of conflict troughs, as I discussed in Chapter 9. One finds pressure to know specifics in one's vertical domain silo, plus horizontally across horizontal levels of conflict troughs. What I'm describing complicates any adversary's efforts to understand the consequences of his and our actions and to discern who has the upper hand and who possesses meaningful advantages (e.g., initiative) in these levels and domains of conflict. We recognize their presence and discern their influences on the adversary's goals and objectives accomplishment or lack thereof.

Yet again all of us find ourselves riding the wild pendulum and trying to enter our adversary's mind as he ponders these silos and troughs and plots his actions within. Through his eyes, he undoubtedly finds implications for winning multiple bouts of conflict in these vertical domain silos and horizontal levels of conflict troughs via recognition and understanding of the connected "cells," and his actions are strengthened by knowledge of the matrix of which I speak—seven vertical domain silos intersecting with four levels of conflict troughs—which could push his individual and organizational thinking into, as a minimum, 1) altered roles, missions, and primacies of ways to influence competitive activity via well-constructed, well-focused, and executed action; 2) command and control decision making—he must realize that it must be agile, holistic and specific, and focused on the right thing, such as our pressure points, etc.; 3) attacking or manipulating his adversary's intelligence planning, operations, and assessments; 4) identifying advantages either under our control and the amount of time each side holds one or more of seven advantages; 5) adapting to context-induced changes faster and more effectively than his adversary; and 6) striking in the cells created by the intersections of multiple vertical domain silos and across multiple levels of conflict troughs at the same time to create synergy, perhaps even to create an emergent force. Of course, we perform similar wargaming.

RESOURCES

Once again, in a clash of resources one finds each side either attacking to seize or defending their advantages brought about via derivative capabilities. As such, each side attempts to manipulate, affect, and play off the resources of the other. I want to take you on a brief back-and-forth thought process so you understand the clash of resources that always occurs in any kind of conflict. I realize this might seem repetitive, but my discussion with you now involves resources instead of other aspects of conflict, such as conflicting strategies. So, without further ado, let's get started. Resources always have been and always shall be important in a conflict or competition. They provide the means (capabilities) to execute action, sustain action, and build physical and moral strength. To succeed, each side in a conflict must employ their resources wisely; the adversary always attempts to gain an advantage in resource usage (wisely or imbecilely)—a subcompartment in the staircase of conflicts—and adjusts his actions accordingly. Thus, an aspect of any decision maker's actions to impose their desires always involves knowing their adversary's resources and how economically and skillfully he uses them. Then, the next logical step is to approximate how the adversary reasons about his resources and how he thinks we consider ours.

Some of the resources at play could include people, units, cyber capabilities, support of a populace, knowledge (e.g., operational context), intelligence, computing power, data conduits, weapons, explosives, rockets, cruise missiles, artillery, air power, surface-to-air missiles, weapons of mass destruction, money, time, air, ground, sea, space, cyber, information, cognitive capabilities, and so forth. Please allow me to reiterate, in conflict one always anticipates and eventually experiences conflicting resources—adversary vs. friendly. No different than people in conflicts of the past, our future adversaries emerge from this struggle of resources and winnow their way to improve or increase their resources and degrade ours. People cannot reason via a simple view when the conflict is complicated. A good example that identifies what we don't need is readily falling back to the old saw of "I have more 'things' than my adversary" or "the adversary has more 'things' than me." Instead one has to consider 1) how the adversary views his capabilities to employ his resources; 2) how he thinks we view his skills in employing resources; and, of course, 3) how he thinks we view our capabilities to employ our resources to accomplish our aim, goals, objectives, but also to affect his resources.

When considering resources, the adversary considers their presence and influence but also, indeed always, with respect to both natural and situational imposed constraints. This thought comes with knowing that both sides make the same kind of consideration—from our opponent's perspectives and his ability to ruminate and our perspectives relative to our desired outcomes of conflict. A friendly force's leaders consider the skills, know-how, and intellectual capabilities their adversary must gather, prepare to employ, and actually employ, and how he intends to use them as his resources. One can find much room for error in this back-and-forth swing on the pendulum of duality. Some answers, often assumptions, come forth as culprits. Exhibit care about slipping on the slippery rocks of a shoal and tumbling pell-mell into the whirlpool that is "mirror imaging" about resources and constraints, and both tangible and intangible aspects of conflict, such as imposition, strength of motive, preparedness to sacrifice, and, of course, the ever-present dark cloud of resource and moral constraints. Always consider what one can and should influence, degrade, neutralize by way of the adversary's resources. To avoid error, consider how to think like the adversary and his thoughts about denigrating friendly resources.

In addition, friendly force leaders and planners always consider taking one or two resources from the adversary and contemplate how the adversary reacts and adapts via alternative analysis, synthesis, and more concretely, resource reallocation. Again, we think like the adversary in this tit-for-tat degradation the adversary seeks from his perspectives via subject matter experts, who in wargaming act as the opposition and try to replicate what the adversary might contemplate with a specter of resource diminution hovering over his every thought. Equally important, however, a friendly force should consider the adversary's views of the degradation he induces on friendly resources and how he thinks about and tries to anticipate our attempts to overcome either losses or shortages via alternative analyses and delay such adjustments.

People in conflict also consider resource allocation—all sides' resource allocation should hook to the rationale flowing through the veins as lifeblood in their strategic aim, goals, and objectives. There is never enough of anything for every person or organization to receive what they want, relative to constrained resources. Thus, people must make allocation decisions, which divvies resources in line with the overall aim, goals, and objectives, and priorities. Allocation comes forth from such thoughts and leaders' articulated priorities aligning resource allocation with the strategic aim. Resource allocation is equally important to an adversary. How an adversary decides to allocate his resources shapes one's thinking by way of conclusions and recommendations coteries of advisors and thinkers provide to decision makers. As an example, consider Germany's invasion of the Soviet Union on June 22, 1941. In early months the Nazis captured or killed huge numbers of troops (~3 million defending Soviets), and for a while, it looked like the German Wehrmacht would seize Moscow and topple Stalin's regime. Interestingly though, a well-placed Soviet agent in the German embassy in Tokyo—Richard Sorge—provided invaluable information to Stalin that the Japanese would not invade Siberia. Immediately, Stalin rushed Siberian-based Soviet soldiers to face the German invasion and threat to the capture of Moscow. He was able to throw in a counterattacking force of 18 divisions, 1,700 tanks, and more than 1,500 aircraft from Siberia and the Far East during the most critical months of the Battle for Moscow.[8] The Soviet counterattack succeeded, and the Germans were forced back. In my judgment, this reallocation and actual commitment of allocated resources saved the Soviet Union during those crucial days in December 1941.

CONSTRAINTS—REDUX

I covered the concepts of "constraint" in considerable depth in Chapter 9. Nonetheless, their importance causes me to continue my thinking in this chapter. Please allow me to explain. As one attempts to think like their

8. Stuart D. Goldman, *Nomonhan, 1939: The Red Army's Victory That Shaped World War II* (Annapolis, MD: Naval Institute Press, 2012), 177.

adversary, I challenge my Über-thinker and thought pilgrim to think about how to shape their adversary's or potential adversary's resources to meet what we anticipate being in his possession, available for use, or unavailable for accomplishing his aim, goals, and objectives. In conflict, all antagonists feel the pinch of constraints, as I discussed in Chapter 9. A constraint could be self-imposed such as rules of engagement. Constraints affect one's capabilities; therefore, they become of utmost importance in the calculus of conflict. A constraint could be a moral or ethical "brake" on using one's resources. Or a constraint could be fiscal, casualties, or materiel. Interestingly, constraints can also derive from operational contexts, weapons capabilities, how well trained a force is, the kind of capabilities either side holds back or keeps in a reserve, and, of course, the stakes in the outcomes of conflict which people fight over. A friendly force, and in particular its decision maker, always considers the kind of constraints at work, as they influence how they shape their resources decisions. It is a difficult process made all the more difficult by the absolute need to consider how an adversary considers his and our constraints. Constraints present advantages to one side or the other, and often one can manipulate, indeed accentuate, an adversary's perceived view of the influence of constraints on all sides in a fray. This means that constraints could serve as deceptive tools. Additionally, in discerning how an adversary views a friendly decision maker's views of constraints, this adversary's newly found views could very well signal an opportunity for exploitation. This circumstance presents a friendly force with a self-proclaimed constraint and opportunities to deceive or strike a counterblow against the adversary as he contemplates and sets about to exploit what he believes the friendly side considers to be his constraints and subsequent offsets for overcoming weaknesses that constrain his planning.

It follows that the friendly side considers its adversary's views of their constraints. This view, however, comes forth not as we wish the adversary to view his constraints and to experience prohibitions they bring forth, but a view of his own constraints from his perspective and how he thinks we think he thinks about his constraints. Our thought processes do not end with one simple perspective of the entanglement occurring with our adversary's and our constraints. No, we must also consider an alternative thought model as follows: 1) how he views our constraints; 2) how he views his own constraints; 3) how we view our constraints; 4) how he believes friendly views their own constraints; 5) how we think he views his own constraints; 6) how we think he thinks about how we think he thinks about his constraints; and 7) how he thinks we think about how he thinks we think about friendly constraints. In that last consideration, you could very well have found the adversary's *schwerpunkt* (point of main effort) from his point of view.

STRATEGY

As another important tenet of this book all of us find ourselves deeply thinking about: 1) anticipating; 2) feigning patience; and 3) defeating our adversary's strategy. Throughout history, the best way to operate in a conflict is to first consider and then defeat the adversary's strategy.[9] In this book, strategy means:

> A prudent idea or set of ideas (high or low level) for employing one's capabilities in a synchronized and integrated way to achieve an aim, goal/objective, policy with available resources, adversary, operational context, and constraint in mind.

Any adversary develops a strategy sufficiently specific to drive a plan so designed to inculcate policy and to be in line with one's strategic aim, goals and objectives, resources, constraints, tactics, and so on. A strategy is a plan—an approach to use resources at the right place and time and intensity to accomplish goals and objectives (whether strategic, operational, or tactical, and campaign objectives) and eventually a strategic aim. An adversary's strategy originates while assessing his advantages and disadvantages inherent to reaching his strategic aim, goals, and objectives. We present a serious stumbling block (resister) to this reach, and the operational context presents another, both of which influence the outcomes of complicated struggles for dominance and advantage in thought, action, and, of course, decisions. Friendly forces naturally feed off of the deep-thinking Über-thinker's and thought pilgrim's intellectual performances as they attempt to think like the adversary for sufficient insight so as to attack, confuse, flummox, or divert the adversary as he attempts to implement his strategy.

The advantage (a position of superiority or state of improved or superior position over a competitor) in a competitive fracas goes to the side bold and wise enough to use the operational context to maximize advantages and minimize disadvantages. Worthy opponents in any conflict always emphasize their advantages and minimize their weaknesses in the operational context, as I presented to you in Chapter 4. One could believe that exploiting the operational context is one way of reducing the transparency, hence the vulnerability, of the innards of their strategies. In addition, another way to seek and sustain one or more of the seven kinds of advantage is to know what one's adversary might be anticipating via their lurking presence, but from our perspective as well as their own. Assumptions prove to be the starting point for many a planner who designs a strategy for their decision maker—this postulation (notion,

9. Sun Tzu, *The Art of War*, 77–79.

exhortation, position—a hypothetical statement or proposal) is true for friendly and adversary. Once our Über-thinker and thought pilgrim confirm the sight of the assumptions at play in their imaginations, thoughts, buttressed by good intelligence, their aim would be, of course, to exploit the thoughts behind the assumptions, when the time is right, repeatedly, not unlike a prizefighter who seeks and finds, then exploits his opponent's weaknesses again, and again, and so on. Of course, any worthy adversary anticipates and protects his weaknesses and pressure points brought about by his assumptions. An adversary always strives to achieve advantages and a state of conditional stability, which he believes can lead to accomplishing his strategic aim, goals/objectives, and strategies.

TACTICS

Tactics are "the employment and ordered arrangement of forces in relation to each other."[10] They are actions that an adversary employs within his resource constraints, context, and strategy and how he thinks you consider him and how he views you. Tactics belong in a family of "wholes" involving a logical hierarchy of elements of strife or competition.

Each side in a conflict uses tactics. They always play out in a state of entanglement[11] within a complex (in context of complexity theory)[12] operational context. This implies an imperative for decision makers to employ tactics as part of a whole, but all the same, to keep some latitude to adjust due to unexpected chance events, feedback, and adaptation from both contextual and adversarial data and information inputs. People watching execution of tactics from a distance cannot know for certain how chosen tactics play out due to several important shapers of success or failure in conflict—vagaries of a nonlinear context; impossibility of precise, mathematical prediction[13]; an adaptive, co-evolving adversary;

---

10. Chairman of the Joint Chiefs of Staff, Joint Doctrine Development Process 5120.01. Washington, D.C., 2014.

11. *Entanglement*: Please be aware that this definition comes from my mind, and I use it to think holistically, but also so thinking people can see the appearance in their minds. The definition is as follows: A physical and psychological phenomenon occurring when dyads, triads, or groups of people and/or organizations connect with one another and form aggregates and aggregations and interact in ways such that the psychological or physical state of each CAS, aggregate, and aggregation cannot be described independently—their state of being can only be described and comprehended as part of or supporting the aggregation as a whole.

12. *Complexity theory*: The study of complex and chaotic systems and how order, pattern, and structure can arise from them. From Dictionary.com Unabridged, retrieved April 18, 2017, from http://www.dictionary.com/browse/complexity-theory.

13. Clausewitz, *On War*, 86.

tactics proficiency (thus training is important); and outcomes of destructive or nondestructive capabilities. We cannot extricate adversary and operational context but must view them as an interacting whole. All of us should consider how our adversary views the operational context (operational in this sense is the context where adversaries compete)[14] and advantages and disadvantages lurking in the context, from an adversary's and a friendly's perspective as they clash and struggle for advantages and disadvantages.

ADVERSARY WARGAMING

Adversary wargaming determines feasibility of an adversary's actions before actual engagement. *We must include the adversary's wargaming in our wargaming.* My Über-thinker and thought pilgrim seek to understand the adversary's strengths and weaknesses via capabilities but also his desires to hold the initiative and how he could seek in a variety of ways to "pry open the window of opportunity," so his decision maker might possess a choice to preempt his opposing force. Though our adversaries might not label this process "analytic wargaming," one can safely assume that he engages in such activities from his perspective of his adversary, his context, his situation, his desired outcomes, and the conditions he must set to perform all of these activities so imperative for his success. Of course, implied in all of what you just read is my assumption that the adversary is riding the wild pendulum and attempting to intrude into your mind in order to wrest his own advantages. An opposing force stands in his way, and it resists his resolve. This wargaming helps him reason about how, what, why, when, and where his actions should occur, all from his point of view as well as his adversary's.

Wargaming provides our adversary and their thought guardians an opportunity to square off against a worthy opponent within a facsimile of the operational context in which the conflict occurs. Their intent (and therefore of direct benefit to us) is to learn about and therefore anticipate possible outcomes from action, reaction, and counteraction efforts. Our thoughtful adversary plays out his aim, goals, objectives, and so on as the two opposing sides collide. All the while, proceed with our aim, goals, objectives, strategies, and the like. Understand what the adversary is thinking and how he believes relative to 1) what truly matters; 2) the value of his objectives; 3) the Marvelous Trinity; 4) the 14-element model; 5) pressure points; 6) decisive points; 7) centers of gravity from his point of view; 8) his "how to think" thought model; and 9) how he thinks you think about

14. Wayne Michael Hall, "Discussion and Deep Thinking about Advanced Analysis (A^2's) Rendition of Operational Context." Unpublished, 2016.

these things. His desire is to impose his desires on us and our organizations and win engagements in all domains and all levels of conflict[15] at all costs.

Insist that the wargame proceed by playing out our adversary's anticipated perceptions, thinking, planning, acting, assessing, and gathering data pertinent to the outcomes of action and inputs from the context. All this work thereby suggests some of the ways one could learn, adapt, and know via reaction of the adversary as his actions tend to slow, thus slowing his imposition of actions or attempting to block our impositions. If armed with such suppositions, a person can possess remarkable insight into the adversary's thinking and actions. This peering function therefore prepares one's intelligence to seek, find, and, once found, guide our forces to preempt the adversary's condition setting actions and seize the initiative.

Our Über-thinker, thought pilgrim, and decision maker decide the level of detail into which the wargame adversary delves as he tries to relate to and understand our decision maker and his aim, goals, objectives, and so forth. As such, our decision maker and analyst contemplate the adversary's worldview, his apperception, his culture, etc., as all of these influences shape how the adversary structures his wargaming efforts and his desired outputs to help him manage risk and reduce uncertainty and speed up decision making and action.

Just as surely as our people commit logic and bias errors, the adversary's thinking skews too; he commits logic and bias errors from his seemingly (to us) peculiar slant. As you ride the wild pendulum, consider the adversary's penchant to err in your musings about "how he is thinking about himself relative to your thinking about how he thinks." I advise my acolytes to attempt to discern why he ruminates the way he does and adjust their thoughts accordingly. Any worthy adversary always performs a likeness of this wargame I describe. They may have other names for it, they may quickly perform the game in their minds, but in some fashion the adversary must perform some of the activities I just discussed. You, as thought guardians, as Über-thinkers and thought pilgrims, shoulder the burden of responsibility for anticipating how the adversary reasons; therefore, you take yet another step into "deep thinking" and go above and beyond to work with other people, if possible, to determine how the

15. Please recall the appearance of matrices involving mental and physical combat. I see seven vertical domain silos: air, ground, sea, space, cyberspace, information, and cognition. They intersect with four levels of conflict troughs: tactical, operational, strategic (military), and strategic (policy). This act of intersections creates 28 cells; they form a matrix. Conflict occurs and connects among and across cells in the matrix. Within each cell, struggles occur; there one finds pressure points, decisive points, and centers of gravity. Cell actors create surges and bursts of energy, as actions occur and cause multiple connections, surges, and bursts across and up and down in the matrix.

adversary acts, reacts, and counteracts in his wargame and how he interprets, integrates, and employs the lessons and implications forthcoming. You must wargame against his wargaming being played out in your facsimile of an operational context and the Red Team who is playing the adversary. They are assisted by an adversary virtual knowledge environment (VKE) and friendly employs a friendly VKE.

An adversary's wargaming can vary, as he could be a wide variety of actors upon the stage of conflict. Depending on the situation, you must decide to act out the primary actors in their problem sets relative to friendly's in our wargame. Examples include perpetrators and practitioners of terrorism, criminal activities, hybrid warfare, conventional warfare, cyber war, irregular war. This wargaming could be a physical event or it could occur in computers or in one's mind. Consider how the adversary decision maker thinks as he anticipates bouts of mental combat us. Probably the most challenging is hybrid warfare. Thus, pay a lot attention to the challenges hybrid warfare brings to any conflict. A foe in this kind of conflict uses all kinds of approaches to and sources of power to impose his *will* but as a whole, in a holistic way. The aggregation of multiple types of adversaries and the merger of their different capabilities and ways of thinking present the most difficult problem set for any Über-thinker's and thought pilgrim's intelligence analyst or decision maker. I must add that multidomain conflict like I described in the seven vertical domain silos and the four levels of conflict troughs competing with people who practice hybrid warfare presents enormous challenges, as it causes our thinking to be both analytic and synthetic, as well as precise and holistic, and occurring via very fast co-evolution and adaptation operations and activities.

Your adversary's wargaming settles in on his enemy, his mission, and his view of the operational context. You demand that he strive to defeat you using any means possible during the gaming. Regardless of where he settles and plays out his wargaming, his purpose is to learn how to exploit your thinking and plans. He wants to know and understand how you consider your constraints and contextual disadvantages so as to gain advantages for himself. Of course, this adversary anticipates your (friendly) actions against his disadvantages so part of his wargame involves anticipating friendly thrusts via actions against what he believes friendly Über-thinkers and thought pilgrims think he thinks about relative to contextual and capabilities advantages and disadvantages they present. I tell my acolytes they can count on their adversary to ruminate aggressively about the tail end of any cycle involving impose and resist. That is, after the imposition and action, you must use intelligence collection assets to assess the outcomes of the imposition, evaluate the data, information, and knowledge, and adapt faster and better than the adversary. Thus, you can count on him to anticipate and try to interfere with your means to assess and adapt and thereby protect his own co-evolution and adaptation processes.

Any worthy adversary always examines action, reaction, and counteraction sequences of violence and nonviolent action of the clash of problem sets to seek, find, and gain the initiative, which he hopes will open one or more windows of opportunity to attain supremacy through other one, two, or all seven advantages. Our adversary undoubtedly wargames advantages and disadvantages pertaining to the influence of the operational context. With his wargaming, he tries to think like friendly-force decision makers and thus locate friendly pressure points, decisive points, and centers of gravity and associated protective mechanisms against which he can act. The adversary also uses his wargame to assess how we think about his resolve relative to our own. Thus, he surely has the friendly's 14-element model in mind as pressure and decisive points against which to focus.

How well have U.S. military strategists and intelligence analysts done to anticipate how an adversary thinks about *will* particularly from a duality perspective? At a risk of overgeneralizing, another reason America lost the war in Vietnam is, quite simply, we could not think like the adversary and thus could not comprehend how he was aiming at our center of gravity—our national *will*—via the American populace. The best and brightest people in our government and supposedly in America could not fathom a world in which the struggle wasn't against communism. They could not understand that the war was about nationalism, which the Vietnamese had been fighting for more than 1,000 years. America missed the mark in Vietnam, and I am compelled to ask this question: Are we any better at dealing with this phenomenon now? As I struggle to answer this hypothetical, several mêlées come to mind that I'll mention in passing but won't go into in any depth. That is to say, Korea (think China and its surprise entry into the war); Iraq (think about the insurgency); Afghanistan (think about the resurgence of the Taliban from being beaten to rising from its ashes of defeat to be a very formidable foe); the rise of ISIS, Russia, and the Ukraine; and the drug war (think about drug cartels and barons who defy America's resolve every day and impose their actions on us). Lots to think about and discuss here, but perhaps in another book.

THIRTEEN-ELEMENT THOUGHT MODEL

I developed a 13-element thought model for helping thought warriors understand how a generic adversary might reason. People who use this model have to fill in context and culturally dependent details of each of its 13 elements based on the mission or task's location and who the adversary or competitor turns out to be. This model takes the reader through a series of thoughts and concepts that all organized or semi-organized competitors perform. As you consider and act on this model, you might

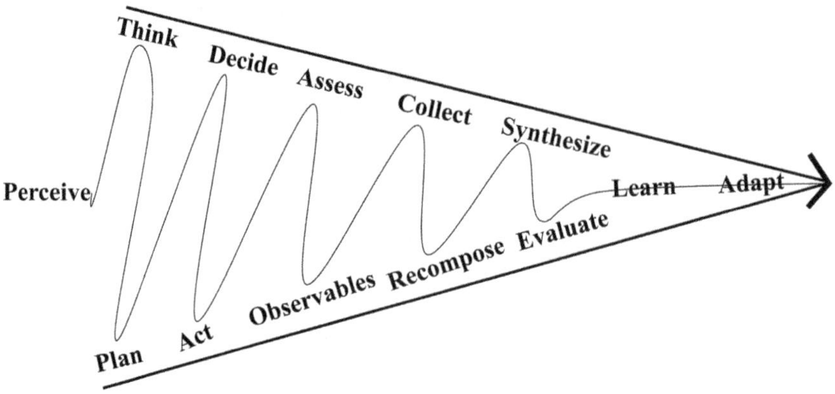

Figure 14.1. How an Adversary Could Be Thinking—A Thought Model

determine that you don't need to use all 13 elements; you can probably collapse a couple of elements here and there and even add more elements from your experience, particularly as you gain more knowledge of the adversary and his culture and the operational context. Figure 14.1 presents a visual of these 13 steps; then I briefly describe each.

- **Perceive.** Perceive means "to become aware of, know, or identify by means of the senses."[16] How human beings perceive directly affects how they think, plan, expect, interpret, and so forth.
- **Think.** In our work, to think means "to exercise the power of reason, as by conceiving ideas, drawing inferences, and using judgment."[17] People think, therefore they are human. Of course, the adversary reasons too—it drives his actions to subjugate or control others. Most thoughts prove to be of no value and therefore suffer their fate in the trash bin of time, whereas a small number of thoughts can be meaningful. Some reasoning leads to argumentation via claim, evidence, fact, and truth. As a person thinks, they seek to produce high-quality conclusions and recommendations. Good thinkers employ a quality-driven template to ruminate and then develop products that contribute to effective decision making. I'm speaking truisms for the friendly side as well as adversaries, although thinking capabilities and methods will always vary. These characteristics and outputs come from effective reasoning, which generally matures as a person comes forth

16. Dictionary.com Unabridged. Retrieved February 1, 2010, from http://dictionary.reference.com/browse/perceive.

17. *The American Heritage Stedman's Medical Dictionary*. Retrieved March 13, 2010, from http://dictionary.reference.com/browse/think.

in birth, lives in their environment, develops their backgrounds, experiences life, endures nurturing by schools, experiences familial interactions, reads, engages in their culture, and so forth.

- Thinking guides humans to make either good or bad decisions. It is with decisions that one finds often impatient actions waiting to burst forth from their restraining tethers as the outcome of thought turns to action, or stasis of thought via decision not to act. Thinking is person peculiar. How people think, how their minds work to produce thought, is highly personal. Consequently, thought, though sometimes similar to other people's in the same culture, varies greatly when one ventures across cultures. This variance makes contemplating the adversary's contemplation both problematic and fascinating. Thinking also varies with the vagaries of being human—anger, fear, contempt, arrogance, greed, fatigue, stimulants, depressants, sleep, and so forth. Thus, while "thinking like the adversary" take into account a potpourri of "shapers" and "resisters of thought" and act accordingly. Beware, logic and bias errors can arise from their slumbering and come to life and influence still in a concealing fog. Upon arousal, they often surround and selectively influence the omnipresence of human errors. Possible antidotes, however, prove available—internal critiques, Red Teaming, wargaming, devil's advocating, competitive intelligence, Socratic methods, and the like. Be aware, however, of the dark brooding clouds in the background of your lives. That is to say, know that we enter the age of mental combat and wars of wits. Prepare now!
- When one attempts to think like the adversary, they need to be particular. They consider, for example, their adversary's coterie of people who advise him. They also undoubtedly seek help from cultural experts as to the origin and strength of our cultural influences, how our decision makers use their reasoning to make decisions, our comfort with ambiguity, readiness to take risks, comfort levels with uncertainty, and boldness or timidity of thought, action, assessment, and adaptation. Anticipate how they condition their state of being as they think, act, assess, and adapt to outcomes from inputs they receive as they interact with other agents, particularly ours, and via data streaming to their receptors from within the operational context.
- While attempting to think like our adversaries, break apart or decompose their cognition from their perspectives and thereby gain insights into how they could think, plan, decide, etc. Culture plays an important part in how an adversary reasons and turns thought into action, assesses, and turns the results of assessing into adaption. Personality breaks into the picture too. Along with culture, as individual personalities think using some of the thought methods I provide next, they adjust and thereby meet demands their personalities, psyches, and subconsciousness insist.

- I have selected some directly applicable and important concepts and definitions, all derivatives of "thinking." The terms are reasoning, rationale, rational thinker, analysis, synthesis, evaluation, and holism. How one thinks in peaceful situations though, is always a far cry from the life-and-death thinking one performs in situations under extremis—not only for themselves, but also for the people who might be subordinates or even a given populace caught between opposing forces.
- Reasoning: the power and capability of one's mind to think, understand, evaluate evidence, assess outcomes of actions, judge right from wrong, discern hidden values and relationships in transactions, comprehend variables in situational contexts, and anticipate subsequent moves from ongoing actions or those actions about to occur.
- Rationale: Of, pertaining to, or constituting reasoning powers; being in or characterized by full possession of one's reason; sane; lucid; agreeable to reason.[18]
- Rational thinker: A person who exhibits reasoning powers during peace and while in extremis and being in possession of one's reasoning and sanity. Being a rational thinker, however, varies significantly from person to person and from culture to culture.
- Analysis: Breaking a whole entity into its constituent elements and thereby setting conditions for gaining understanding or meaning of each element setting the stage for a key process: turning data into information.
- Synthesis: As a review from Chapter 1, synthesis is the human cognitive activity that combines elements of substances, events, activities, or energy to form a coherent whole. The *DoD Dictionary of Military and Associated Terms* defines it as "the examining and combining of processed information with other information and intelligence for final interpretation."
- Evaluation: Assessing and placing value on a purchase, an action, presentation, paper, book, estimate, decision. Evaluation should involve presenting and defending one's position using the following template: 1) conclusion (claim); 2) evidence; 3) facts; 4) truth; and 5) plunging the depths of thought to search my use of biases due to trying to achieve the impossible—to be objective while being burdened at all times with the bondage of subjectivity; 6) examining assumptions for their validity; 7) judging the quality of data, information, and knowledge; 8) judging outcomes of actions; 9) judging validity of motives (dualistic determinants)[19]; 10) determining the validity of ideas (dualistic

18. Dictionary.com Unabridged. Retrieved December 16, 2010, from http://dictionary.reference.com/browse/rational.

19. *Dualistic determinants*: Approaching specific thinking problems using the theory of dualism and the unity of opposites.

determinants); 11) discerning the quality of conclusions (dualistic determinants); 12) discerning the value of "hidden" ideals and relationships; and 13) judging the quality of mental outputs.[20]

- Holism: As a review once again from Chapter 1, one can always find additional ways to think about "thinking." What I'm speaking of can involve excursions into the realms of deduction, induction, abduction, and so forth. There is nothing wrong with discussing and using these aspects of thinking.
- **Plan.** The word plan has a meaning. I start writing this part of the model as a generic adversary would plan. I assume acting in conflict, for the most part, is not spontaneous. Each adversary or competitor becomes involved in planning in advance about how to accomplish objectives, or what people call "end states." I provide meaning of what I mean with the term plan in six numbered bullets:

1. A plan involves, develops, and promulgates ways and means to accomplish an aim, goal, objective, strategy, or tactical outcome before any action, other than mental, comes forth.
2. A plan is a scheme or method of anticipating, acting out, assessing outcomes, and adapting from gathered and reasoned upon feedback (data). One must seek, find, and use specific data relative to the action you expended; data that just shows up may be spurious. Specific activities comprise actions, and all have as a purpose connectedness with the act of accomplishing an aim, goal, or objective.
3. Plans suggest to recipients that they should use resources wisely and enact preparatory activities via condition setting and onset activities dictated in form, function, and emergent energy from vision, aim, goals, objectives, strategies, tactics, etc. A plan calls for, develops, and sets in motion condition setting activities in advance of execution to achieve an outcome or effect. These activities always prove vulnerable to detection.
4. A plan is a method of thinking about action, reaction, and counteraction cycles all infused with purpose for acting beforehand. Action always connects to motion, speed, synchronization, and anticipating our resisters and counters to the adversary's actions.
5. A plan for use of our history, philosophy, and theory is 1) life force; 2) purpose; 3) strength of motive; 4) capabilities; 5) determination; 6) perseverance; 7) sacrifice; 8) passion; 9) advantage; 10) disadvantage; 11) imposition; 12) action; 13) assessment; and 14) adaptation.

20. Wayne Michael Hall, "Advanced Analysis Discussion and Use in Deep Thinking about Conclusions and Recommendations: Claim, Evidence, Truth, Facts, Objectivity/Subjectivity." (Unpublished, 2016), 2–6.

6. It was the German Chief of Staff, Helmuth von Moltke the Elder, who asserted, "No plan of operations extends with any certainty beyond the first contact with the main hostile force."[21] In other words, plans change from the moment of the contact or first shot in a fight. His dictum proved correct in his day and age, and remains so today. Plans never turn out as intended. With that said, it is necessary to perform detailed planning. It provides one with details, knowledge of actual, nascent, and possible connectedness, alternatives, and so forth, once the vagaries of conflict instill their relentless chaos and human opponents don't behave like you anticipated, and your assumptions prove wrong.

Any worthy adversary designs a plan whose purpose is to accomplish his aim, goals, objectives with the resources and constraints (natural and manmade) provided him to execute the overall plan with a strategy via specific tactics—engagement, battle, and campaign. (Note: Any adversary attempts to think like the friendly decision maker thinks and anticipates ways that he could preempt and strike first and thereby seize the initiative.) Any worthy adversary considers what he wants his plan to accomplish. What can we assume that a capable, adaptive, and learned adversary can and shall do by way of planning to engage friendly decision makers in mental combat? If the adversary is competent, he undoubtedly must ponder at least these following examples of some important considerations, from a generic adversary's perspective, knowing full well this short list is but a start to deep thinking about each of these thoughts:

1. Be detailed and specific in my planning.
2. Be wary—my adversary has sufficiently effective intelligence systems to find me.
3. Wargame my plan against an archetypal foe who represents how my adversary thinks and acts.
4. Anticipate the appearance and effects of chance events.
5. Anticipate randomness and turbulence, and be agile and aware that unpredictable events or happenings could occur.
6. Induce change I want via actions, but synchronize all activities; achieve a unity of effort.
7. Run effective intelligence operations to report on the target or the adversary's efforts to gather data via their collection system.
8. Use multiple collectors to optimize my intelligence collection efforts, even if one source becomes compromised and neutralized.
9. Establish countersurveillance to stop, neutralize, or flummox the adversary's intelligence collection operations.

21. http://www.azquotes.com/author/42993-Helmuth_von_Moltke_the_Elder.

10. Know how the adversary can attempt to stop or confuse my intelligence operations for affecting my co-evolution and adaptation processes—I must anticipate why, where, when, and method(s) and deny.
11. Anticipate how my adversary can confuse, obfuscate, and deceive my countersurveillance, early warning, and deception efforts and deny such quests.
12. Know and work to my advantage the observer/observed relationship and induce appropriate offsets in behavior/action.
13. Think like my adversary; anticipate what he seeks with his intelligence collections; seek to manipulate and influence his thoughts by threatening his pressure and decisive points and gathered data he uses for adaptation.
14. Consider the two entwined aspects of the operational context—linear and nonlinear systems—and leverage their characteristics for advantage and thereby cause my adversary to view this relationship and outputs of data as feedback and disadvantage.
15. Know and exploit the advantages/disadvantages a nonlinear operational context brings to each side in a conflict; accentuate my adversary's vulnerabilities and promote mine.
16. Be ahead of adversary's attempts to alter or neutralize any of my pressure points, decisive points (the unforgiving need to co-evolve via, in shorthand) and centers of gravity—act, assess, collect, evaluate, learn, adapt. Continued success here brings positive results to my co-evolution.
17. Use the thought model with seven vertical domain silos (air, ground, sea, space, cyber, information, cognition) and four horizontal levels of conflict troughs (grand strategic [policy], strategic [military], operational, and tactical). This way of thinking about planning leads us into matrix war, as I discussed earlier. Consider this vision. Battles, engagements, and campaign activities occur in each cell. That which happens in one cell connects with actions and their outcomes in other cells. When one plans, they must keep a mental picture of this struggle as well as use artificial intelligence to track connectedness and seemingly obscure or low-level actions in the low cells (say the tactical horizontal conflict trough) influencing the highest actions in the highest cells. Chaos comes with a nonlinear operational context; therefore, automation must help deep thinkers cope with speed and connectedness of actions and change.

The adversary can use his thinking prowess to delve into the friendly leader's planning; his attacks, shaping, or influencing of our thinking could come to affect my plans even as they come into being. The adversary's planning takes into account how the friendly leader perceives, thinks, plans, decides, acts, assesses, collects data for assessment, turns data into information, turns information into knowledge, evaluates, learns, and adapts, using, of course, what the adversary believes the friendly leader's perspectives, experience, and thoughts to be. He will always aim to affect these thought processes at the right time and place with the right methods.

- **Decide.** Make a choice. Resolve or don't become involved in a conflict; solve or conclude a question, controversy, or struggle; end an argument. At the end of any planning cycle, a decision maker decides to act or not act. Usually, the decision maker employs a coterie of trusted people who advise him and provide one or more conclusions (courses of action) and recommendation for action and subsequent actions and activities.
- **Act.** Anything done, or exerting energy to accomplish a goal. After a decision maker decides to act, he instigates required condition setting, which takes multiple subactions and time; he then instigates the energy and motion of acting to serve a purpose, accomplish a strategic aim, goal/objective, strategy, or plan (a subset of strategy) that in one shape or another always involves imposing desires on others. All actions, activities, and functions have a purpose—allowing mine to succeed and his to fail.
- **Assess.** Judging success or failure of a planned or unplanned outcome of an action coming from a decision; evaluating outcomes coming forth from an action. Prior to, before, and after an action finishes, a decision maker assesses outcomes of action. Such assessments and successive adjustments/adaptation occur within the decision maker's sphere of influence, aimed at understanding how one's actions affect an adversary or competitor, seeking data inputs from the operational context, and receiving and processing uninvited data pushed from the operational context. Often one finds this activity occurring in the decision maker's mind or via the help of a coterie of people who interpret and develop implications from assessment data.
- It is via intelligence activities that assessment data comes forth as feedback to a decision maker and her organization (a complex adaptive system). It is either the decision maker herself or her staff or coterie of trusted people who turn assessment data into information via a recomposition process; turn information into knowledge via synthesis; evaluate outcomes manifested in assessment data, information, and knowledge; learn; and finally adapt. Without this cycle of life—which I describe in this book as co-evolution and adaptation—the organism withers and eventually dies.
- **Observables.** A physical, physiological, and emotional property or absence of one or all of the aforementioned that can be observed or measured directly. Observables (some people use the less specific term indicator) guide and focus intelligence collection operations. An

observable focuses the adversary's collection to gather data at the right time and place, looking for the right activity and using the correct observable(s). Instead of observable, an adversary could use words like guide, criterion, guideline, standard, measure, or gauge. But all of these words provide guidance to people or machines gathering data for making decisions. Any adversary must provide his intelligence collection system—people, open source, machines—with specific requirements or needs and constraints (e.g., nighttime only, time limitations) with which to guide data gathering. If the adversary is worthy, he provides and holds collection to some kind of a high-quality standard for achieving success—one could call the adversary decision maker's quality checks his criteria for success in collecting needed data.

- **Collect.** Gathering data in an organized way so as to provide relevant data for a leader's decision making, which generally involves data of sufficient value to cause risk to become manageable and to lower uncertainty to an acceptable level. Data collection capabilities constitute an action arm for any decision maker and/or his intelligence analysts. Collection people, whether adversarial or friendly, have a specific mission—to collect or gather valuable, relevant, and current data with a variety of intelligence collection assets—people, instruments, radars, electro-optics, communication signals, social media, open sources, data, and the like, and to meet stated quality, relevance, specificity, and time qualifications.
- **Collection people.** Whether friendly or adversarial, people plan for and adjust to the observed/observer relationship and subsequent offsets and anticipation. Collection people engage in wargaming to determine the feasibility of 1) observables; 2) analytic sampling rate (ASR)—right time, right place, right activities, right observables; and 3) standards or criteria for success. Yes, I am mirror imaging, but any collection capabilities acting on their own do not perform well—they need to be told who, what, where, when, why, and broad sketches of "how." In other words, they need guidance about what to collect, when to collect, where to collect, specificity of what they collect, accuracy of their efforts, relevance of what they seek by way of data, and judgment of quality of their outputs.
- **Co-evolve.** Thus, I am convinced any effective adversary understands a "must-do" requirement is to co-evolve and peer into a dark pit of strange attractions and see connectedness of a unity of opposites. This process provides the adversary with insights and intellectual wherewithal to understand changes in the operational context, changes in the adversary's roles and missions, and effectiveness of actions pushed.
- **Intelligence collection.** Assets seek data—valuable, current data—for their decision maker and his coterie of insider supporters to use for assessment, co-evolution, and adaptation. The adversary imbues them with smarts coming with purpose for collecting data in the first place.

When collecting data, each side can become vulnerable to a dilemma. That is to say, each side knows their adversary aggressively seeks them or their systems or their networks with available collection capabilities. Each side engages in cognition of sufficient value to enable anticipation when and where and why their adversary's data gathering could be occurring and is agile in doing so. Each side knows what they have to do and why; they also realize another related and relevant requirement—they reason and decide how, when, and where to overcome the negatives of counter-moves each opponent makes as they enter the arena of observed/observer competition. As another constant in this fight, unforeseen disturbances occur in the operational context. These disturbances come with nonlinearity and its penchant to be chaotic, which causes turbulence and change. Change in the operational context is constant, and each side must be agile enough to mutate, move, and hide better at the moment of change detection.

- **Recomposition.**[22] Any adversary must turn their gathered data into meaning. After all, it is with meaning that a decision maker on any side can assuage their twin nemeses of risk and uncertainty. They set about this task by improving collected data by turning it into information. After all, data in the raw is just data: "numerical or other information represented in a form suitable for processing by computer; individual facts, statistics, or items of information."[23]

So, the adversary seeks information. Please take into account that most adversaries won't exactly follow the ontology of data, information, and knowledge. In my experience, most people do not differentiate among data, information, and knowledge, though they should. Data, information, and knowledge each relate with one another, but interesting differences appear. Data comes easy and fast, but it lacks meaning. If a person makes decisions with data, their risk is high and uncertainty is high. Information takes man and machine to turn data into information and more time than acting upon data. When turning data into information, man and machine work as one and correlate, fuse, visualize data, provide some meaning, and inject some sense of organization. The result is information, but its transformation from data to information takes man and machine power and time. And though information might have some meaning, it isn't all that can be had; information is usually unorganized and certainly not combined with other information. The

22. *Recomposition*: Human and machine-driven recompilation of collected data into information, thereby setting conditions for developing knowledge, understanding, and comprehension.

23. Dictionary.com Unabridged. Retrieved February 1, 2010, from http://dictionary.reference.com/browse/data.

term information means "a collection of facts or data.[24] A conveyance of meaning or facts told, read, or otherwise conveyed that may be disorganized or even dissimilar." As you can see, information has meaning but may be unorganized or appear unrelated. It is man plus machines plus time, which one relies upon for introducing the service of meaning.

- **Synthesis.** Any capable adversary thinks to 1) find existing knowledge; 2) understand and add value to existing knowledge; or 3) build new knowledge. It is with knowledge that one most often finds substantially lower risk and uncertainty than making decisions with data or information; however, developing knowledge takes more time than data or information, and it takes subject matter expertise. Knowledge is defined as: "an organized body of information or the comprehension and understanding consequent on having acquired and framed a body of facts."[25] All of these definitions and explanations enter into a calculus of decision making and trade-offs involving making fast decisions with data, which causes risk to rise, or making somewhat slower decisions with information, which provides some relief for coping with risk and uncertainty, or taking even more time and use of resources to develop knowledge, which helps decision makers manage risk and lower uncertainty. The downsides of knowledge are, of course, a questionable lifespan of usefulness, the time and brainpower it takes to develop, and subject matter experts' biases that seep into their mental efforts to develop knowledge.

  Synthesis, integral to successful thinking and decision making, is where and how dreams, visions, and creativity spring forth. It is the third phase of a thinking process in the Hegelian dialectic—thesis, antithesis, and synthesis. It opens the door to creativity and thereby disruptive change. It allows us to envision "wholes" with which they can work and be creative. From my experience, Americans generally have to work hard to successfully this type of thinking, though most are fairly good at analysis. People from some other cultures sometimes prove more adept than America's legions at synthesis. As we face any adversary adept at synthesis, know that they reason holistically. Our adversaries, who amplify their thinking sufficiently to gain a knowledge advantage, can certainly gain decision advantage as they connect knowledge and decision work—they bond.

  Arguably one can anticipate some current and future adversaries to be good at synthesizing data and information into knowledge, even reaching the exalted state of understanding and comprehension. Only

24. *The American Heritage Dictionary of the English Language*, fourth edition. Retrieved February 1, 2010, from http://dictionary.reference.com/browse/information.

25. Dictionary.com Unabridged (v 1.1). Retrieved April 5, 2008, from http://dictionary.reference.com/browse/information.

a few of the adversary's human beings can reach such a pinnacle of thought—that is to say, a state of comprehending, as a whole, the operational context and all the actions therein. As a review, comprehension means "totally grasp, make sense of, fathom the meaning, visualize the connectedness, and state of coherence in the object, person, their organization, their aim, goals, objectives, strategies, and tactics falling within our study, appearance, and function of a whole. A person comprehending a phenomenon apprehends its meaning, its parts, how the parts fit and work together, in a whole, and its potential. Comprehend this thought—an intellectually assertion is that comprehension is most assuredly a long and firm step beyond the term—understand." All of these actions occur within a framework of a conflict's whole, which Western military theorists label as engagement, battle, and campaign.

This framework's tentacles reach out, much as a wisteria's vines adorn a pergola. With just a little coaching, these connections work their way up the pergola's legs and across its high horizontal beams. These vines strive to clasp to one another, then enfold and entangle into an even larger whole while crossing and joining via the framework. This emergent behavior housed by the concept of holism presents yet another descriptive framework to help people with their thinking, focusing, resource allocation, understanding and managing time, and the like.

Our adversaries surely leverage their thinking, experience, and familiarity with the context so as to drag friendly people into their operational contexts, where they possess advantages and can negate friendly advantages. It is there, in their choice of operational contexts, that they can choose to engage American kinetic and nonkinetic conventional forces in mental combat. I'm convinced that our future enemies plan to use information and cognition as domain of conflict not unlike air, ground, sea, space, and cyber. Information and cognition should be places of mental battle, of competition where struggles occur, life-and-death actions occur, and where our minds face a game of chess with various chess masters. It is where adversaries who cannot compete in other domains often frolic. These two new domains of conflict are weapons of 21st-century conflict and should be treated as such. The medium for visible and invisible actions in these two additional domains is knowledge war where the side with the best thinkers win. Cognition battles and mental combat never sleep!

To help us consider this proposition, our deep thinkers transliterate what our brethren who preceded us dropped as pheromones—clues about the secrets that come with effective thinking. These long-dead conflict theoreticians thought deeply, and in doing so uncovered many of the secrets of mental combat reaching back through the dusty chronicles of time, where principles, theory, thought processes, and historical examples originated and still live. Once again, here is an admonition:

Weave this kind of thought into whole cloth for competing and triumphing in this new domain. These fragments and particles come from the tree of knowledge; they transcend time. The whole of meaning stretches out and touches other human beings who lived long ago, who have secured that which remains useful even today and tomorrow, all the while not disdaining but treating the fragments and particles from the tree of knowledge with reverence, the theory and contemplation still relevant with the passage of time.

Friendly decision makers and their coteries of thought warriors ready themselves to enter into the pits of mental combat with people possessing a high level of intelligence and formidable thinking talent. This kind of war comes our way, as I postulate, via opponents who clearly use thought-war as an asymmetric warfare capability, an offset designed to occur in mental combat battlegrounds. These future battlegrounds, often invisible, might cause real and potentially negative outcomes for people who fail to anticipate their presence, appearance, and activities. Though the United States continues to make wonderful bombs, guns, planes, ships, and high-technology tools, it provides miniscule investment in developing human minds sufficient to engage and win in mental combat in this new domain of conflict.

Now, certainly, our adversaries won't label what I just described in identical terms, they desire to use the magical powers of holism. With holism, the adversary can comprehend how well the parts and elements fit with and work within the whole of which we speak. If our adversary is a reductionist, it means an easier time to deal with him. As a reductionist, this adversary engages his mind in:

> the practice of simplifying a complex idea, issue, condition, or the like, especially to the point of minimizing, obscuring, or distorting it.[26] The idea in the mind of a reductionist is that one can understand the world, all of nature, by examining smaller and smaller pieces.

But we know in our mind and hearts, one must put these parts, which the reductionist decomposes into minute particles, back into 1) new relationships; 2) new combinations with other elements and parts; 3) coalescences of data fragments into a whole; and 4) aggregations of both similar and dissimilar things and parts and elements into larger, better, and in many cases, brand-new wholes. What I'm describing to you involves creating a better way to reason involving thinking, creating, and disruptive innovation. This method of contemplation is essential for winning conflicts in this 21st century. This century is where mental

26. Dictionary.com Unabridged (v 1.1). Retrieved February 20, 2008, from http://dictionary.reference.com/browse/reductionism.

combat and knowledge war[27]—the struggle for valuable information between adversaries over assessing and using valuable information and knowledge to gain advantages in decision making—surely reigns supreme and provides us with the means to accomplish today what Sun Tzu stated so cogently ~2,500 years ago:

> For to win one hundred victories in one hundred battles is not the acme of skill. Thus, what is of supreme importance in war is to attack the enemy's strategy; Attack plans at their inception.[28]

Engaging in mental combat requires us to use our intelligence system as a weapons system to mass, maneuver, swarm, disband, and return to base. What is it we maneuver? I say we need to maneuver 1) minds; 2) computers; 3) sensors/collections; 4) data; 5) data conduits; 6) knowledge; 7) organizations; and 8) VKEs. In the future, the intelligence system of yesteryear must adjust to that which I describe. This force has to mass, maneuver, swarm, disband, and return, not just as a provider of data, information, and knowledge, but as a force that creates outcomes. But I tell you this now, at this point, our adversaries could be well populated with people who create and bring into being constantly changing, disruptive innovations. I believe this adversary will use his mind and his intelligence system as new-age weapon systems.

I enjoin you to discipline your minds to corral our wild thinking and bring forth a few summary points. First, you can count on our future adversaries to possess varying degrees of mental ability. Never ridicule or sell the adversary's thinking capabilities short, as he could rise up from the ashes of our thoughts and strike us with surprise. Second, some adversaries can create wholes and subsequent actions we do not anticipate. Could it be that these people can be smart enough to create black swans[29] that our mechanically oriented minds neither anticipate nor fathom? Our hope is, of course, for an adversary who is a reductionist and a lockstep, Tab-A to Slot-B thinker, as this person is easier to flummox in bouts of mental combat. Third, a part of mental combat is scoping and pondering how your adversary thinks. As I swing on the wild pendulum, I believe he rides too—he seeks knowledge about his nemesis, the friendly decision maker, whose thinking is buttressed by the coterie of people providing him advice. The adversary therefore scopes how any given friendly decision maker reasons and makes decisions.

One can anticipate battles over advantages to be multitudinous when we consider they occur in all the vertical conflict domain silos—air,

27. Hall, *Stray Voltage*, 15.
28. Sun Tzu, *The Art of War*, 77–79.
29. Taleb, *The Black Swan: The Impact of the Highly Improbable*, xvii–xviii.

ground, sea, space, cyber, information, and cognition—and among battles, engagements, and campaigns intersecting with the horizontal levels of conflict troughs—tactical, operational, strategic (military), and grand strategic (policy)—and in derivative cells: the matrix war, as I discussed earlier. I see control of advantages appearing but swaying back and forth, within the vertical domain silos and horizontal layers of conflict troughs and cells of the matrix, in which one finds as the silos and levels intersect. All sides in a conflict want their power under direct control, and, of course, to deny such control and leverage for the superiority these advantages bring to an adversary. Each of these entities lives and operates with separate agendas, but each acts in the same operational context as opposing adversaries. Furthermore, each of these seemingly extraneous entities possesses variance in power but they always possess the capability, if not intent, to interfere with friendly and adversary leaders' pursuit of success with their mission.

- **Evaluate.** To evaluate means "to judge or determine the significance, worth, or quality of; to assess or evaluate meaning or turn of events, or changes in behavior from action."[30] One would hope to be objective as they evaluate, but alas, objectivity is impossible to achieve (only people who delude themselves believe objectivity to an achievable state). Regrettably, all that human beings can do is recognize the enduring state of subjectivity, and how well and how thorough supporters attempt to mitigate their proclivity to err due to being human, that is being humanly subjective. Regardless, one can begin to judge worth by evaluating how well a conclusion's presenters dealt with the objectivity/subjectivity challenge as well as the soundness of their conclusions and recommendations.[31] It follows then that deep and critical thinking of this nature helps friendly decision makers and analysts understand how an adversary defines "quality." It behooves the friendly decision maker and his thought supporters to understand the adversary's capabilities to gather data of sufficient value to serve as a continuing catalyst for evaluating 1) the superiority of his own actions; 2) how well he thwarts friendly actions; 3) how well he flummoxes the friendly decision maker and his coterie of thought advisers; and 4) speed of adaption to stay ahead of his adversary and thus retain the initiative.

We suddenly realize the answer to the earlier question—that is to say, know for certain that battles for quality control are coming your way. This involves the approaches that each side uses to judge how well they perform in the operational context. While judging the quality of our

30. Dictionary.com. Dictionary.com Unabridged. Random House, Inc. http://www.dictionary.com/browse/evaluate (accessed: May 31, 2017).

31. Hall, "Advanced Analysis Discussion," 2–6.

actions via assessment, do the same for our adversary but from his perspective. Any worthy adversary will work hard to reach the high standards he describes, defines, and demands. Interestingly, even with the knowledge gained by peeking behind the curtain of any play about conflict and then diving into the processes operating in a "back office" behind understanding and comprehension, a qualitative evaluation process remains. What is to be evaluated? What purpose causes evaluations to occur? Allow me to answer the questions and see if you agree. In my view, decision makers evaluate knowledge contributing to conclusions and recommendations. If they want more detail, and if they are smart enough, they examine how collected data works relative to their own and their adversary's co-evolution and adaptation processes and efforts. Or they review the quality of data if they have developed and promulgated a schema for judging outputs and outcomes of mental combat. They could also evaluate how efficiently data became information and the corollary effectiveness and value of information. Or they evaluate how well their knowledge workers turned information into knowledge and the value of knowledge coming forth.

Evaluation always involves a search for quality of an action, a thought, a plan, a conclusion, a recommendation, and/or use of assets and capabilities. What standard or look or outcome do helps one judge so as to evaluate and adjust to find our version of the Holy Grail—the high standard sought? Evaluating and judging the quality of something suggests possession of "a way" to judge, such as criteria for success and standards of performance. The focal points for judging excellence could be the plan and its implementation, quality of assumptions, contributions to decision making, maintenance, camouflage, actions, coordination, synchronization, output, action execution, money, collateral damage, how well an agent is co-evolving and adapting, and so forth. Of course, one must articulate these defined standards to people who implement and accomplish goals or objectives.

Nobody spends enough time thinking rigorously about what quality means in either an individual or organizational sense, and leaders do not provide immediate and harsh enough negatives as they evaluate and demand subsequent adjustment and improvement when their standards of quality have not been reached. In conflict, a friendly decision maker and his supporters anticipate what the adversary thinks by way of evaluating efforts to judge whether actions have met his standards for achieving quality as he desires. Friendly decision makers can plan on working against an adversary who, from his perspective, discerns value in his evaluative efforts from several respects. In one respect, he wants to know and judge how well his activities, operations, actions, assessments, data gathering, learning, and adapting performed. As such he designs criteria for success peculiar to his background, culture, experience, adversary, goals and objectives, operational context, and the like. In another respect, worthy adversaries anticipate how their opposing decision maker discerns worth in his evaluations of actions, assessment of outcomes, effectiveness of outcomes, efficiency of outcomes, thoughts, conclusions, and recommendations. From such knowledge and understanding, these adversaries fight it out, but in bouts of mental combat. Each side could very well decide to present false data into their opponent decision maker's data collection/gathering portion of discovery, continuance of discovery, outcome of action, and adaptation to changing circumstances and with the operational context in which the contest occurs. Is it safe to conclude that our adversary could attempt to think with this subtle way of injecting false data into our judgmental discernment processes and mechanisms? Could it be, in our hands lies another collision, another battle, but this time the clash of competing judgments of quality?

Let's hypothesize how an adversary might evaluate and determine the quality for satisfying his criteria for his success. He could very well follow this evaluative process and evaluate validity of a conclusion (claim) via 1) evidence; 2) facts; 3) truths; and 4) influence of objectivity and subjectivity, or at least a variation of this theme. It sounds like a process that Americans should perform. People are people, and if they want valuable evaluations and superior decisions, a sound thought process for judging quality is necessary. It helps people judge and evaluate whether their defined standards were met. So, who performs the evaluation? First and foremost, find a decision maker deeply involved and then find handpicked and trustworthy iconoclasts, contrarians, Red Teamers, subject matter experts (SMEs), critical thinkers, analysts, appropriate expertise on staffs, or possibly local people who have not tilted to either side but still have vested interests in the neighborhood containing a conflict. Our erstwhile Über-thinker and thought pilgrim could perform this task if they operated in this type of evaluative role instead of their other cognitive missions supporting their decision maker. Native people should be employed to provide a local and cultural perspective of the people, context, situation, and anticipated actions at hand. The adversary can certainly use them too, if for nothing else than as their low-level human collectors; therefore, the friendly side must anticipate and block these efforts and turn them into helping the friendly force via their countersurveillance and counterintelligence forces.

Thus, one could infer that any worthy adversary recognizes the human proclivity to be subjective in their evaluations. The adversary decision maker sometimes receives a distorted view of quality. If the adversary doesn't evaluate with a jaundiced eye toward subjectivity's relentless domination of reason, the adversary opens himself to experiencing a bad outcome with his "jousting" and leaves himself vulnerable for manipulation and defeat by the friendly brain trust.

Please remember, subjectivity in evaluation can ruin one's efforts to discern a true state for any given moment in time. If an adversary is totally subjective, this state of being opens a window of opportunity for flummoxing him via his data flows and transformation of data into information and information into knowledge and presentation of conclusions and recommendations therein. Regardless, as another measure of quality, the adversary could very well check their internal processes and their thought supporters' thinking along the lines I describe earlier to keep searching for the utopia of objectivity anyway. If so, the friendly task is much more difficult.

From understanding the co-evolution process and from being aggressive, one finds a progressive organism that uses this method of thinking for his advantage. As a consequence, they recognize their mistakes and those of their adversary and take action to improve themselves and adversely affect the praiseworthiness of learning within the adversary's camp. In short, the optimum solution for each side is to learn quickly and recognize when and how they should alter their behavior when necessary.

- **Learn.** Learning is relative to conflict; it means to find out, learn, or determine with certainty, usually by making an inquiry or other effort.[32] In my approach to learning, I add these ideas: "acquiring knowledge or skill via study, experience, trial and error, and, of course, the act of cognition; if one learns their thinking is wrong, they take action to repair the error yet set conditions to perpetuate the erring ways of their adversary, if appropriate." How do the antagonists learn when in conflict? The adversary learns from purposefully assessing his actions, from the behavior of his competitors, and from data inputs arriving from the operational context. He wants to exploit the context-provided data. As such he snaps the whip of his collection receptacles and tentacles as they spring forth to scope data coming from their adversary (the United States or other opponents) and the operational context. Any smart adversary recognizes the inevitability of context-provided data and thereby seeks and uses the data to placate his aim, goals, objectives, stratagem, and the like. He learns from his actions; his survival depends on such learning. He has to be a brutal judge of his errors, as generally speaking he is seriously outclassed regarding many life-and-death capabilities. Out of survival and necessity, he must faithfully adapt and do so quickly via the process of making the decision to assess, gather

32. http://www.freedictionarydefinitions.com/search.htm?word=Learn.

data, think about the gathered data, evaluate the data, learn, and adapt. Adaptation proves essential to living, as it is what makes up the stream of change.

The individual and organizational propensity to learn is a powerful weapon in its own right. But once again circle back to our recent discussion about evaluation for quality. The adversary primarily learns from 1) data inputs that come from our actions or inactions; 2) data coming from the operational context; 3) and insights from critiquing and questioning coteries' presentations with not only information and knowledge inputs, but rigorously developed conclusions and recommendations as well. On the friendly side, the decision maker and his knowledge supporters must assume that these current and future adversaries will continue to learn from their mistakes and ours. We must assume an improvement upon their mistakes and quick follow-on strikes to exploit our mistakes. It follows all of us must be on the lookout for perturbations coming from manifestations or outputs from learning—that is to say, look for adaptation, as within the act of adapting, one finds potentialities to gain insight into the quality of the adversary's learning, and even the hint of future actions. One must anticipate mistakes on both sides and in particular anticipate how an adversary might attempt to exploit the friendly decision maker's mistakes.

All of us need more thinking about the adversary's learning. He judges the value of his learning and our value of learning. He thinks in detail about his quality model for assessing learning and how lessons learned affect his adaptation, and if with adaptation, to fight well and win. The relationship between learning and adaptation is strong. If one interferes with an adversary's learning outcomes, they can interfere with the quality of his efforts and subsequent adaptation. One of our requirements in each operational context we enter involves thinking like the adversary about the value of how he learns and how learning outputs shape their thinking and actions, which happen to be how well and how quickly he adapts and how well he believes his adversary adapts. So, what might some elements of quality be for an adversary judging how well he and his followers learn? How fast did the adversary and his followers learn and demonstrate what they learned via actions? How fast and effectively did multiple people receive, inculcate, and implement via adaptation what one person learned? Again, from the adversary's perspective, did learning cause the right outcome for the adversary decision maker and his organization? The adversary decision maker determines what went right and what went wrong and as the upshot of this thinking, how he might have capitalized on what went right for him and his forces and mitigate what went wrong as a result of the learning under discussion. Finally, the adversary decision maker and his coterie of advisers judge the quality of learning via evaluating outcomes, considering how well his people adjusted from their learning and thus improved, appraising how well they received and inculcated the learning of others, and adjudging how well they adapt and perform their condition setting in future engagements.

An adversary's chameleon-like changes can be subtle adjustments to both contextual and competitor feedback systems and processes. This feedback comes via data inputs from the context and from executed actions and assessments of the worth of the action via assessing, collecting data, evaluating, learning, and adapting again. As a simple example, when I was a child, we fought out our dislikes and anger via sometimes daily battles with fists and feet, sweat, and grunts and swearing on the gravely surface of the East Ward playground. I was small and subject to regular beatings, but I learned to use the operational context—the schoolhouse, the swing sets, the gravely surface, the not-so-watchful proctors, the large and small slippery slides, the fire escapes, merry-go-rounds, and the teeter-totters—as sources of data from the overall context. I also learned from the bullies who wanted so badly to punch in my face. I watched them pound on other little squirts too. So, in a fracas, I would wrestle them as a tactic; though I was small, I had very strong arms from working on our farm and thus leveled the playing field—sometimes. Quite simply, I was smarter than the bullies and I learned quickly after the first few butt-whoopings I received. I used the context to my advantage, and I attacked my adversary's weaknesses. As a last resort, if the initiative and momentum were dissipating, I could always run because the bullies were neither nimble nor quick. I had to contemplate though, as I ran the mile to my home, what I learned on this particular day so I would be better off in the next round of cutthroat conflict of the 1950s school ground. This is how some of our asymmetric adversaries learn and then adapt. In this way, they quickly learn and then adapt effectively and act with improved purpose, aim, and violence.

- **Adaptation** is the output or result of a complex adaptive system's co-evolution process. It is about making decisions to change from assessment data inputs. It comes from learning and evaluating assessment data, information, and knowledge and then doing something positive with the knowledge. In this case, the adversary makes a decision about adaptation because of what his competitor is doing or has done. Adaptation also comes forth from data inputs, sometimes unwanted or unwelcome, from the operational context. Weather comes to mind as an example, for example, the early morning fog on the first day of the battle of Austerlitz on a cold morning in Moravia in 1805. Thus, my working definition of adaptation is:

> a purposeful effort to modify or shape movement, or execute an action due to 1) changes in the operational context and/or to 2) an adversary's reactions and

actions as she/he adjusts to fluctuations in the operational context and/or action of his/her adversary; adaptation is the final stage or outcome of co-evolution.

Adaptation exerts an aura or glow of positive energy. When a person chooses to adapt, you have to "see" or "intuit" the implication riding the wave of probabilities coming forthwith from adaptation. An action or situation causes the adaptation energy to release and relate to a cause. Thus, action leading to adaptation exerts a positive energy too. The energy comes from directed actions with distinct purposes to adapt, which can be positive and active or negative and reactive. At the end of this valley of tears, we always find a struggle between his resolve versus mine. If the complex adaptive system receiving data in its assessment process fails to act intelligently on incoming data (from the operational context and/or the adversary's actions or responses), then definitely adaptation turns into an always denigrated "knee jerk response"—a much vilified "just do something" response to a competitor's acts or non-acts or adaptation. When an aggressively thinking adversary decision maker decides and articulates purpose and motive via action, this effort becomes stronger, much stronger. For example, this decision maker, imbued with the spirit to think and win in conflict, might seek and grab the "floating" initiative and "act first." Also, he may orchestrate a quest to obtain feedback with which to adapt and thereby open this mystical "window of opportunity" of which I have been speaking to achieve even more advantages over his opponent. With these three elements in place—1) defining purpose and strength of motive; 2) seeking and grabbing the initiative; and 3) orchestrating an aggressive quest for feedback—one finds a positive force at work in focused actions. This proclamation and subsequent derivative actions constitute positive energy in the operational context, particularly when the decision maker seeking the feedback injects this energy infused, positive vector into conflict episodes in the complicated operational context and its inner workings. Efforts come forth and operate under a weighty, but important, pressure to find and use the right kind of data, information, and knowledge (when available) to act before his adversary, and ideally, to strike an adversary's pressure points, which can constitute attacking or manipulating adversary's decisive points, and perhaps even a center of gravity.

To perform to high standards, an adversary reasons and aggressively engages us in mental combat. His opponent is always on his mind. Thus, he acts to assess our vulnerabilities via stressing pressure points, and in the aggregate, decisive points. With adaptation, the nimblest and most aggressive CAS/agent can seize the initiative and thereby exert positive energy of their own making in the crucible of conflict. The mere presence and influence of these jolts of positive energy provides impetus for surviving and winning conflict situations from the adversary's perspective. Adaptation in the adversary's co-evolution process comes with purposeful, directed steerage as CAS always, under threat of extinction, assess the context and their competitors, and seek and receive feedback sufficient to energize their adaptation. One must infer they always attempt to retard friendly sources of data collection so as to cause entropy (gradual decline of order and going back in time instead of forward). Of course, in 21st-century conflict, the agent or CAS writ large is forced to adapt faster and more effectively than their competitors.

When learning to think like the adversary, we find the unfortunate presence and influence of boundaries, limitations, and cultural impasses. To use these techniques successfully requires moderate expectations. One always need to remind themselves: Be skeptical of your own thinking, lest we:

> Ride, ride into the valley of death;
> Know ye well, we who ride, we shall ride to seek truth, when it hides from even the Biblical Ruth, whose solace we take;
> Even as we doeth, truth's form remains elusive, deformed, difficult to hold, even for the bold;
> Yet our faith still abides, even when derided, indeed denigrated by others, even with our minds equivocal and torn, we continue to ride, ride, ride.

Our Über-thinker and thought pilgrim work their minds to approximate the adversary's reasoning, but they are confined to work within a series of problem set and problem-peculiar ways, always motivated by the axiom that all people, thoughts, bodies, organizations, elements, and parts connect in some way. As I have previously mentioned, to think this way, understand that when one part moves, the other parts of an aggregation (the whole in which we live and compete) change too, sometimes obvious and sometimes in ways too nuanced and subtle to notice unless specifically watching at the right time and place, but still detected via proprioception.[33] Interestingly, with smaller wholes, all connected elements can feel change, some of it almost imperceptible and some obviously noticeable; thus, our receptivity to outside stimuli has to be on high alert for incoming or extant data. Once again we find the appropriate appearance and use it to stimulate our thinking about the states of entities, human internal and human contrived, described as exteroceptive and interoceptive, at work as all entities can sense connectedness and perturbation in their connectors (links) externally, and within their beings;

---

33. *Proprioception*: Sometimes unconscious response relating to stimuli produced and perceived within an organism, especially those connected with position and movement of the body.

but often neither people nor organizations know the exact causation for the changes and sensings in question. Even our Über-thinker and thought pilgrim can't positively discern what the adversary decision maker is doing to contain and shape the changes affecting his thinking. But, we can anticipate his next moves.

To succeed in conflict requires the process I discussed. One's mind's eye is at work with perceptive inputs arriving and mixing with one's imagination from the under-mind and rational thought from the over-mind, with all three mixing in the mind's eye. Using our imaginations helps us think like the adversary, given we account for differences too (e.g., culture, experience, values, social mores, and the like). I ask that you use your imagination to bring forth the adversary within his circumstances and notice what you see in his mind's eye. Within the mind's eye we find creativity. In the deep and dark well of the under-mind we find imagination. *Webster's Dictionary* has an interesting discussion of mind's eye and its meaning: "the mental faculty of conceiving imaginary or recollected scenes." It turns out that a word has been coined to name the opposite condition: an inability to conceive imaginary or recollected scenes—this condition is aphantasia.[34] I implore you to explore the notion of phantasm—literally, an illusion or apparition. But it also implies imagination; therefore, a phantasm's antithesis or antipode is no imagination (a state of aphantasia),[35] an affliction that some suffer. I provide a definition first of imagination and then creativity, so as to differentiate between the two:

Imagination: Faculty of drifting in one's mind, in and out of our consciousness, all the while allowing one's subconscious to sense, feel, smell, perceive, and hear not only their immediate surroundings but also faraway surroundings they have experienced in some way and interacting with real or imaginary people; imagination comes with visions of what we want a future to be, for example. Imagination involves forming mental images or concepts of what is not actually present to the senses.[36]

Creativity: A takeoff from imagination in developing original ideas, especially solving difficult problem via new ideas or "creations." Creativity requires one's mind to think and imagine holistically—synthesizing like and seemingly disparate things into new and better and sometimes larger combinations, aggregations, or wholes. Creativity comes with thinking about "what could be" and not just

34. *Merriam-Webster's Dictionary*. Retrieved May 19, 2017, from https://www.merriam-webster.com/words-at-play/aphantasia-the-inability-to-form-mental-images.

35. *Aphantasia*: Inability to form mental images of objects that are not present. https://en.oxforddictionaries.com/definition/aphantasia.

36. Dictionary.com Unabridged. Retrieved June 25, 2010, from Dictionary.com website: http://dictionary.reference.com/browse/imagination.

thinking about "what is"; creativity is about stretching one's mind to answer questions such as: What does it mean? What could it mean? What are the implications?

Guy Claxton provides us with thoughts about the helpful notions of conscious and under-mind in his book *Hare Brain, Tortoise Mind*:

> The undermind is a layer of activity within the human psyche that is richer and subtler than consciousness. It can register and respond to events which, for one reason or another, do not become conscious. We have at our disposal a shimmering database full of pre-conceptual information, much of which is turned down by consciousness as being too contentious or unreliable.[37]

Claxton is on to something important. Of course, it is easy in the busy, stimuli-heavy world—our habitat—to shut down the under-mind. After all, it is the world of dangerous intuition that often lacks evidence to validate, and hence brings more risk and uncertainty. Thus, people tend to believe in what they can touch and obtain as evidence, to claim indisputable conclusions with facts and truths to back up these claims. They tend to disbelieve intuitive flashes. The problem is, of course, that intuition is powerful and sometimes, right regardless of any dearth of evidence. People who wait for evidence tend to miss out on the mysterious power of the under-mind where intuition and creativity and imagination lurk and only occasionally come forth to influence our thinking and actions. If we possessed a Judas eye[38] functioning as a go-between and thereby connecting the over-mind (conscious mind) and the under-mind, and siphoning some of what is occurring in the under-mind, it seems to my reasoning all of us would be better off in our attempts to outthink our adversaries in bouts of mental combat. These attributes will certainly be present and at work within the minds of some of our adversaries. Again, Claxton helps us understand the theory of what I'm advocating:

> Intuition . . . tends to work best in situations that are complex or unclear, in which the information that is given may be sketchy or incomplete, and in which progress can only be made by those who can, in Jerome Bruner's famous phrase, "go beyond the information given," and are able to draw on their own knowledge in order to develop fruitful hunches and hypotheses . . . the creative idea comes from bringing into maximum contact the "problem specification," the data, and one's own

37. Claxton, *Hare Brain, Tortoise Mind*, 116.

38. Ibid. p. 117. "Jerome Bruner . . . used to use the analogy of the 'Judas eye,' the peephole used by the doorkeeper at a 'speakeasy' to distinguish between bona fide member, for whom the door opens, and undesirables, such as the police, who are shut out. Without the Judas eye, one could only tell friend from foe by opening the door—and then it was too late."

store of experience and expertise; allowing these to resonate together as intimately and flexibly as possible so that the full range of meaning and possibility of both current data and past experience are extracted.[39]

So, since we are now through the theory of the mind's eye. Next let's take an imaginative journey to our adversary's place of thought.

Thus, my mind's eye appears in my adversary's lair, invisible yet as the Sphinx stares, hitherto quiet and pensive; my, how this adversary thinks—my mind inquires, do I dare blink? Do I care? But, I say to myself, there is more than presence—I ask, to what end? Then—What does he think? How does he think? Once I enter his mind, I find similitude, but not solitude; his mental faculties steadfastly work to win, thereby accomplishing his aim, goal, objectives, strategies, and tactics given his mission and resources, along my model's way to win.

My mind takes a surrogate ride—through his tunnels and his lairs I go. I smell the smell of thick smoke, dankness, decay, unwashed bodies, the stench of excrement and urine, the grease of his hair, but a tunnel all livable to humans who feel and know excitement in the air with a promise of impending action, breaking a fragile peace, so he dares.

But I ask myself, does he care? I feel the heat of a bulb, then another, the sound of machines, and air stirring from a fan asunder—the fan distributes dust in the air with each swirl and casts a spell in which a deceitful plume of dust particles suspends in midair and one by one, they twirl in this the lair and then they fall. Dust particles fly and drift, land in the shadows they do, and ever so banal with rote movement they stir with the fan's hot breath from afar; while just alive and dancing in the air, they just as easily meet their deaths in the dark corners of the penal colony lair.

I feel the damp tunnel walls with my hands, I run my finger along a wall and discover a distasteful, unfinished, and rough plaster surface I now long to expunge. I note the clothing—ever so smelly, sweat-stained bellies. Yet, bandy as they may be, they could be ready to strike ever so handily. From their talk, I find my thinking correct, with all due respect, yet I still gawk.

They fall in line with thoughts, surprised not at what they sought, but they intend to impose their *will* not though as a simple winter drill. I adjust my thoughts accordingly, my comprehension of their strategies and tactics, as you probably recognized by now I have taught.

My advantage—I know how to think better than they and thereby as I seek to have my way, I fear them not; I look for existing levers or create whole cloth ways to win bouts of monstrous jousts. I know in my heart of hearts and mind of minds, deep within the mine, the dark tunnel and well of my kind, in my mind's eye, I

39. Claxton, *Hare Brain, Tortoise Mind*, 72.

can win but only sadly, as pushed to bring grief to mankind's kin, as I sin with my sword and cleaver.

Be aware, the adversary might change the diction of some of the terms, he might change the order around, he might leave out one or more, but the processes to fight, accomplish one's missions, and live to survive beats strongly in their hearts. To help in this trying challenge, know the adversary acts, when he thinks rather than reacts, most of the time via models. In a general sense, some of his most important models for behavior and action probably include 1) co-evolution; 2) decision; 3) action; 4) assessment; 5) evaluation; 6) learning; 7) adaptation; 8) intelligence; 9) data; 10) secrecy and security (including countersurveillance); 11) logistics; 12) transportation; 13) condition setting; 14) his target; 15) competition and its outcomes; 16) launching attacks in or across multiple domains and levels (closely resembling my notion of matrix war); 17) and, of course, keeping his mind's eye and resolve firmly focused—imposing his desires and blocking his adversary's.

In a moment, this adversary can shuffle and shift his movements ever so quickly to different locations; this muffled movement for fear of discovery, thus necessitating drifting out of place with a song of a sentimental bon voyage full of false grace, not realizing life as bygone, but with hope of more "voyages" yet to sound, bong-bong, bong-bong, hammer and tong, and hope not gone.

So it goes in the game of strife; on it goes, up and down, across and round, forevermore, with Sisyphus-like regularity beleaguering one's soul with too much modularity but with ever so much clarity; a dark river carrying people whose absence of values and morals proves forever rife; their dark laid plans keep ringing in beleaguered minds, I can, I want, it is afterward of which I care, as my heart tears, after all, it is only life.

This ancient curse of human kind acts out of spite and heads to a vision of an end, his end, with a knife, rendering deafness from the screams of many a brave lad or lassie pursuing old men's dreams with the promise of glory, but finding instead death's contribution to vainglory, connected to one another in death-filled jollies, well-lamented in the rhythms of life's follies.

If we fail to do what I'm suggesting in a positive way, I postulate a nighttime visit from the ancient world's three Furies.[40] Morally speaking, one owes it to mankind to deny and condemn them to hell's flames those who aggress against others for their self-serving imposition of what we can call

40. *Furies*: In Greek mythology, three terrifying snake-haired winged goddesses who mercilessly punished wrongdoing.

life force. On the other hand, I worry about friendly forces and nations turning passive and reactive and similar to the Maginot Line syndrome that cost France its defeat by the Germans in the spring and summer of 1940. So, I cry out—outthink any adversary like the great Caesar:

> Caesar reached the enemy's camp before the Germans could have any inkling of what was toward. They were struck with sudden panic by everything—by the rapidity of our approach, the absence of their own chiefs; and, as no time was given them to think, or to take up arms, they were too much taken aback to decide which was best—to lead their forces against the enemy, to defend the camp, or to seek safety by flight.[41]

My admonition is this: Always wargame possible ways to accentuate your power and denigrate your adversary's not only to subvert his parry of your imposition, and neuter his effort to strike while you are tied up with your initial imposition and working against his parry. Most adversaries seek the best deal and thereby service his best interests[42] in a conflict or negotiations when they face losing. Thomas Schelling provides us with a useful thought about a strategy one could take in conflict that involves bargaining:

> To study the strategy of conflict is to take the view that most conflict situations are essentially bargaining situations. They are situations in which the ability of one participant to gain his ends is dependent to an important degree on the choices or decisions that the other participant will make. The bargaining may be explicit, as when one offers a concession; or it may be by tacit maneuver, as when one occupies or evacuates strategic territory.[43]

To understand any foe, one has to have in their mind and use theory to help grasp how any given adversary thinks. Without these two theories, one cannot reach the sacred summit of peace and stability. One should always be interested in how this adversary contemplates a variety of subjects near and dear to his heart and like a tapestry of select elements of my 18-consideration model I provided earlier. I have to admit, during vicious conflicts with terrorists, terrorist states, drug dealers, and sometimes even a nation-state, one finds zero-sum games or at least dead ends with no hope of resolution other than death. But, usually, one finds neither grandiose surrendering of one's flag and colors nor a complete resignation to capitulating against opposing supplications. In some cases, still with us

41. Julius Caesar, *The Gallic War*, trans. H. J. Edwards (Mineola, NY: Dover Publications, Inc., 2006), e-book, location 1337/4181.
42. Schelling, *The Strategy of Conflict*, 5.
43. Ibid. p. 5.

today (e.g., Syria and ISIS), one can search for but find no real bargaining incentives; it has been zero-sum for four years—one side wins and one side loses and innocent civilians remain in the middle until they flee or die. It has been a total abdication of honor and morality, but that kind of war has become a personal and in some cases a national capitulation of honor and morality. And it has been a fight among factions and coalitions of countries helping each side—one side being Assad's Syria and Iran (Shias) and Russia, and the other side the composite of rebels supported surreptitiously by Saudi Arabia and the Gulf States—Sunnis. Or it involves fighting until one side runs out of soldiers, territory, and natural resources. This situation has always existed but nowhere more in evidence than in 20th-century wars—World War I and World War II both ended only because one side became more exhausted than the other, and in the case of World War II Germany was not only exhausted but destroyed and occupied.

America found itself in limited-objective wars in Korea and Indochina. It found itself in a Cold War against the former Soviet Union. In these conflicts and quasi-wars, negotiations, bargaining, conceding, and giving and taking did play serious roles in averting conditions for nuclear war, which nobody wanted. But when fighting Iraqi insurgents or ISIS, it becomes a violent struggle with only a small number of indirect approaches capable of working in Iraq, such as winning the population and the Sunni sects onto the sides of peace, stability, and safety, which was put into effect by the United States as it performed its military surge operations in 2007–2008. Negotiations and bargaining certainly played a role in this kind of war, but it involved certain elements of the population—the Sunni—to live in peace with the Shia and the Shia to live in peace with the Sunni. It seems to me we have an admixture of situations in which one finds a variety of short- and long-range strategies for negotiating and bargaining in non–zero-sum games of threats, advantages, disadvantages, bargaining, and negotiating, so as to keep the proverbial lid on some semblance of "peace" while attempting in the long term to find ways people with polarized outlooks and aggressive revanchism and even recidivistic tendencies—read Russia—can indeed live in peace and stability. It follows one needs some of what I offer in the theory of *will* and "how to think like the adversary" along with some of what Professor Schelling offers, as he wrote in his Nobel Prize–winning 1960 book, *The Strategy of Conflict*—that we can find "win-win" outcomes:

> That game theory is underdeveloped . . . may reflect its preoccupation with the zero-sum game. Suggestions and inferences, threats and promises, are of no consequence in the accepted theory of zero-sum games. They are of no consequence because they imply a relation between the two players that, unless perfectly innocuous, must be to the disadvantage of one player; and he can destroy it by adopting

a mini-max[44] strategy . . . the rational strategies" pursued by two players in a situation of pure conflict—as typified by pursuit and evasion—should not be expected to reveal what kind of behavior is conducive to mutual accommodation, or how mutual dependence can be exploited for unilateral gain.[45]

Interestingly, Schelling did not tell us how to work with zero-sum people in a conflict. I always wanted to hear his thoughts about the importance of knowing and understanding how one's opponent thinks and in particular, how he considers 1) fighting a resisting party; and 2) exerting one's resolve to resist an opponent's. This book provides you with at least some supplemental thinking to his thoughts.

Let's take a look at what Schelling says about the gives and takes of bargaining during the strategy of conflict. Just from a Western point of view and predilection, the give and take method of gaming is much more attractive than the zero-sum game. So how does one negotiate and or bargain with an aggressive North Korea that seems hell-bent on developing not only a nuclear weapon but also the means to deliver it via an intercontinental ballistic missile? This nation-state has virtually nothing for the West to negotiate or bargain about. I don't believe it would, but a combination of Schelling's thinking and my theories might yield a useful pathway into the future, with the safety of not only South Korea, China, Taiwan, Japan, and parts of Russia secure, but also with a win-win strategy for all concerned. It would, however, need a different approach involving a consortium of countries with a unified and determined "carrot and stick" strategy.

As a far-out approach, participants in the consortium of countries desiring peace and stability on North Korea and how they might plan and act as follows: First, they would first of all read this book. Second, they would anticipate and wargame how to impose their resolve via a staircase of intangible actions as a starting point for coercing, incentivizing, and then inducing North Korea to comply to wishes. Third, along with building this staircase, build a second parallel staircase of tangible means to compel; it would decrease largess if he fails to comply but intimates, in his thought processes, a demonstrable, graduated, controlled violence. Fourth, build a third parallel pathway of compellence that increases violence, slowly or quickly, but always aiming a dagger to erode "that which truly matters" in the mind, heart, and soul of the adversary decision maker. In my hypothetical, the imposer overcomes the adversary's reticence and resistance by ensuring through initial gambits that he knows you are deadly serious. The adversary in this hypothetical would have to be made to know the friendly side means business and not just typical equivocation and empty threats.

44. *Mini-max*: A decision rule used in decision theory, game theory, statistics, and philosophy for minimizing the possible loss for a worst-case (maximum-loss) scenario.

45. Schelling, *The Strategy of Conflict*, 84.

Of course, this argument is hypothetical because the North Koreans have armed themselves with both weapons of mass destruction and weapons of mass effect via conventional weapons. All of us must therefore learn to think like him the best we can and identify his choices and means of implementing his choices. If he starts to set conditions for thwarting the consortium's desires, the consortium countries must be prepared to preempt with minimum force possible along the ladders of compellence but always anticipate his moves and deny him his capabilities. With an absence of deep thinking, this consortium could find itself paralyzed and in a series of strategic dead ends while the same adversary is preparing his fait accompli[46] before the other side becomes aware of the move. Don't fall in the trap of believing that you contemplate exactly like this adversary, or believe that each side has mutual goals and objectives, or that there are perfectly symmetrical views of the operational context in which a struggle could occur, for example, the value of Seoul to the Republic of Korea is different to all participants in a potential conflict on the Korean Peninsula. The adversary's thought processes could very well be common with the consortiums' in a few areas of concern, but his aim, goals, objectives, resources, constraints, strategies, etc., are unique to his mind—thinking, history, culture, apperception, etc. As one attempts to apply these thought processes into decision, action, assessment, and adaptation processes and models, keep in mind this admonition. Though always important and understandable to an extent, the 16-element "think like the adversary" model, the 14-element model you have learned in this book, and 13-subelement thinking model can only be imperfect ways to be in the minds of those people whose thoughts caused the need for bargaining action in the first place.

To perform reasonably well in understanding North Korea's leaders, you need help from disciplined and current subject matter experts, locals, people who have lived in the West but who understand the intrinsic values of the culture we are working against, highly educated intelligence analysts and collections people imbued with the latest theories of advanced analysis and advanced collections,[47] and the right kind and the right mixes of intelligence collections so as to seek and find the deep and hardened and high-value targets that abound in this country. The mental, organizational, and machine support can come via connected virtual knowledge environments (VKEs) with organizational SMEs, tacit knowledge, baselines and other

46. *Fait accompli*: A thing that has already happened or been decided before those affected hear about it, leaving them with no option but to accept. Oxford Living Dictionaries. Retrieved May 19, 2017, from https://en.oxforddictionaries.com/ definition /fait-accompli.

47. Yes, my books help people do what I'm suggesting. *Stray Voltage* (2003), *Intelligence Analysis* (2009), *Intelligence Collection* (2012), and *The Power of Will in International Security: How to Think about Will in Complex Environments* provide the basis for thinking holistically in bouts of will.

data bases, computing power, and the capability to transform typical organizational design into knowledge product teams all connected to warfighting headquarters scattered but still connected in and among domain silos and horizontal levels of conflict troughs. This large virtual knowledge environment can then return to its original forms or completely disband when you finish with them. Also, Red Teams can help critique your thinking and assumptions about how the adversary could reason about a particular course of action and how you might know from finding his cause to effect/his condition setting activities to create the outcome he seeks. You must have somebody challenge your thinking though, and in particular, your assumptions. Finally, approximate how they perceive, think, plan, decide, act, and so forth and how they view the context surrounding the conflict at hand.

This chapter is now history. In this chapter I provided my readers ways to outthink their adversary in conflict. *Will,* of course, is the preeminent concept one has to understand from the perspectives of the recipient of our ire—our adversary—and thereby to learn how he thinks to the best limit possible, as one studies select aspects of an adversary's thinking mind. I cautioned my readers that one can never reason exactly like the adversary. I told my readers that we have to be content with narrowing the adversary's options and trying to think like him by using models and detailed wargaming. At the beginning of this chapter I provided readers with thoughts that should help them understand aspects of an adversary's mind better, including 1) realize that you compete with an unpredictable adversary; 2) realize you compete in a nonlinear operational context; 3) recognize the presence of sensitive variables and bureaucratic obstacles to your efforts to think like the adversary; and 4) use the thought models this chapter presents. The chapter also provides a representation of several kinds of battles one faces in modern conflict. Specifically, I'm envisioning physical combat, mental combat, battles of wits, battles of *wills,* battles of objectives, and battles of quality. The theory of duality and riding the wild pendulum helps our thinking too, and the chapter spends a lot of time with it—we must learn to think like the adversary thinks using several techniques, such as 1) duality; 2) obtaining cultural expertise from a person from the particular culture in question; 3) using a group of cultural and technical—and military—wise opponents as wargaming foes, thereby seeking criticisms of my conclusions, facts, evidence, views of truth, and how bias can influence one's subjectivity; 4) using a Red Team to challenge our assumptions and conclusions and to provide creative counters; and 5) finding and employing a virtual knowledge environment in which I can link multiple think-tank organizations and scattered experts to help me work on my problem. The chapter provided ways to improve readers' thinking about the most important aspects of an adversary's mind. For example, the chapter presented a thought model that a person can use as they consider how the adversary thinks about his versus our 1) aim; 2) goals; 3) objectives; 4) resources; 5) constraints; 6) strategies; 7) tactics; 8) *will*; 9) co-evolution and adaptation; 10) duality and pendulum; 11) adversary wargaming; 12) observed and observer relationships; 13) advantages and disadvantages; 14) logic and bias errors; 15) inner coterie of decision making; and 16) a 13-element submodel within the construct of the larger thought model; it includes perceive, think, plan, decide, act, assess, observables, collect, recomposition, synthesis, evaluation, learn, and adapt. Lastly, the chapter presented as a visual a 13-element thought model to help people think about their adversary and to guide experts trying to assist.

I now take you off to a different subject, that is how to think critically about *will*. I am certain of its usefulness in your deliberations about the overall phenomenon we study. This next chapter provides you with some specifics about thinking critically about this great phenomenon. I'll see you on the trail!

CHAPTER 15

How to Think Critically about *Will*

Argument: *In this chapter, I explain* will *as the epicenter of all conflict. Three adages help people ponder its intricacies: 1) achievement reigns supreme in all people but proves stronger in some than others; 2)* will's *strength ebbs and flows; and 3) with deep thinking, one can discover and attack the nub of* will. *One tries to impose his* will *on others for a reason or reasons. Search for one or more causes for one or more effects influencing the desired outcome of conflict. Wise and agile imposers of* volition *move quickly and strike after finding a vulnerability. Their adversary does likewise. Life force, an inner energy burning in all people, stimulates this competitiveness. At volition's core, we find the usual suspects: greed, self-interest, religion, ideology, power, racism, hatred, retribution, and so on. Snuffing the strength of* will's *life force, purpose, and strength of motive can defeat aggression.*

This chapter presents a series of transition thoughts. The ideas take you to places you haven't traveled or perhaps we only touched upon thus far. As you move through the ensuing thoughts, see in your mind's eye vertical shafts of light as sickles of vertically oriented ideas combine with horizontally connecting ideas, thus creating a unified whole. Our vertical connectedness of ideas involves thought models, mental ticklers, a list of variables, a list of characteristics of nonlinearity, a 14-element model, 18 planning considerations, a listing of adages, and a listing of maxims. Our horizontal connectedness of ideas comprises wargaming your adversary's wargaming, how to think about *will*, holistic battles over *will*'s imposition, duality and pendulum thinking, the fullness of any operational context, our concept of life force, thinking like the adversary thinks, and shapers of volition. So, as you marry the vertical connections with horizontal connections, you create another matrix. At each place where the horizontal shafts of light intersect with vertical shafts of light, one finds cells blinking with human brightness and the restless energy coming from searching minds, connecting on and off like Indra's Net[1]:

> [T]here is a wonderful net which has been hung by some cunning artificer in such a manner that it stretches out infinitely in all directions. In accordance with the extravagant tastes of deities, the artificer has hung a single glittering jewel in each "eye" of the net, and since the net itself is infinite in dimension, the jewels are infinite in number. . . . If we now arbitrarily select one of these jewels . . . and look closely at it, . . . in its polished surface there are reflected all the other jewels in the net, infinite in number. Not only that, but each of the jewels reflected in this one jewel is also reflecting all the other jewels, so that there is an infinite reflecting process occurring.[2]

Each of the "jewels" in Indra's Net often proves to be "on" and "off" and sometimes connect directly with other "jewels" via links. Thus, it reflects not only itself but also with other "on" jewels in its network; and, this network connects with other networks, sometimes spreading and connecting further, and other times remaining dormant. That which causes these networks—these people—to jolt into an on status and thus transmit intellectual energy comes from stimuli from the operational context, inputs from adversaries, and perhaps a turn of the screw—dormancy to active emerging with the arousal of variables potentially sensitive in a chaos-ridden, nonlinear operational context. Each person can be activated in many different ways. The type of activation[3] determines which other people one connects with and causes their activation, energy emission, and perhaps even action.

If we hope to impose our ways of thinking on others, influence their ways of activating their energies and actions and on their connectedness with others. What conditions generate their activation? What are the ways and reasons they activate? And what are the links with whom they could be connecting with or seeking help from others?

This chapter is magic—it is alive, and as it grows, ideas, theories, and concepts become increasingly applicable to life. *Will*'s epistemology, ever so real and true beyond doubt, flourishes in the recesses of my mind and the minds of my acolytes and readers. Into the future I see *will*'s baseline of knowledge growing every day until it becomes a sea of churning energy.

---

1. Douglas Hofstadter, *Godel, Escher, Bach: An Eternal Golden Braid* (New York: Vintage Books, 1979), 258.
2. Francis H. Cook, *Hua-Yen Buddhism: The Jewel Net of Indra* (College Station, PA: Penn State Press, 1977).
3. Hofstadter, *Godel, Escher, Bach: An Eternal Golden Braid,* 371.

ADAGES

Let's get started. The first order of business is to provide you with four adages. I wrote them to provide you with a mooring in the rough seas of nonlinearity and in the co-evolution of adversaries swimming in this sea, the operational context.

- **Adage one.** Achievement reigns supreme in human beings. All but a few people set out to achieve something. This force is more powerful in some people than in others. Hyperaggressive people possess a life force that appears as desire, bubbling over the edges of probity from a boiling cauldron. Life force provides purpose to the endeavor and soon the other elements of our model of *will* kick into action. The motive of such people always involves self-interest, power, land, recognition, legacy, etc., but, they have a commonality—achieve, conquer, win, accomplish objectives, and take because they can. For some people, aggression proves insatiable until they die. Watch for aggressive people overtaken by the need to acquire and pursue things they do not control (e.g., power, money, position, legacy, etc.). Watch for signs of hyper in people—aggression then quietude; these people wait in their keep, looking for the right time to break free and impose their *will* on others, often resisting people.
- **Adage two.** *Will* doesn't stay the same—its strength subsides then moves forward. Consider Adolf Hitler and his conquests of Austria, the Sudetenland, and finally Czechoslovakia—peace, threats, acquiescence, and seizure; then peace, threats, acquiescence, and seizure, and so on the pattern of such people goes. As one side in a conflict acts, the stability of their volition and its desired outcomes depends upon what happens when the recipient of the imposition responds. That response can only be anticipated. Will he act to block or parry the imposition actions, or will he acquiesce? Variables involve the comparison between one's purpose, strength of motive, capabilities, and readiness to sacrifice, etc., with his. Working with this subject, of course, isn't a simple matter of calculating physical capabilities—consider the moral domain and the always unpredictable emotion too. Of course, one must wargame the adversary's capabilities and estimate the possibilities facing him. From this effort, he forms hypotheses or expectations, decomposes them into requirements, and develops observables for his intelligence collection system to confirm or refute. *Will* also changes with the roil of waves hitting the cliffs of life, some expected, some a surprise, but always changing the operational context, due to the presence and influence of nonlinear systems and the movement and interactions of complex adaptive systems (CAS). This ebb and flow creates advantages and opportunities for the wolves of volition.

- **Adage three.** With deep thinking, one can discover a pathway to the basis, the nub of an opponent's *will*. This effort is threefold. First, when an adversary resists an imposition of *will*, negate his "parry" by attacking his purpose, capabilities, and strength of motive; in doing so, you will be attacking his life force. Second, alter your adversary's desire to win by overwhelming him with simultaneous attacks across all vertical domain silos and horizontal levels of conflict. Third, search for opportunities to strike the soft underbelly of his nub of *will* via his pressure points, decisive points, and centers of gravity. Remember though, your adversary is doing likewise. So, one finds an interesting clash. That is to say, two forms of competition show their faces. First, the aggressor seeks to gain advantages via opportunities he knows to be present but which are obscured or protected. The recipient of the aggressor's imposition is aware of these opportunities and considers whether or not he can stop such a strike against his soft underbelly's pressure and decisive points and, perhaps, one or more of his centers of gravity; the recipient also considers other options, to include a pre-emptive attack. Know well this opponent will always surmise demise or success. He, too, looks for his own opportunities—truly vulnerabilities—to appear and plans to obscure their presence and to guard against their exploitation—or to use them to his advantage. Such clashes occur with some specificity—a place, a time, an intersection of vertical domain silos and horizontal levels of conflict troughs. Again, this is 28-cell-matrix war; the intersection of silos and troughs create cells where clashes occur. I call them conflict matrices. The cells house fighting over opportunities. Remember the essence of adage three: With deep thinking, one can discover and attack the nub of his adversary's *will*.
- **Adage four.** One tries to impose his *will* on others for a reason or reasons. The wise competitor searches for one or more causes for one or more effects influencing the desired outcome of conflict. This is so irrespective of whether or not one is imposing his wishes or is on the receiving side of the imposing assault. Here you find Schopenhauer's principle of sufficient reason. If either side pays attention to his cause and effect obstinacy to appear, he will find causal relationships and the links connecting causes to effects—cause, link, effect. Causes come forth with blinding speed after the fact but prove uncooperative and difficult to anticipate before the fact. If one does not stop the causes before the fact, the attacker becomes more and more difficult to stop or delay as causes strengthen during maturation and move closer to creating the effect.

The following reasons for fighting and struggling over *will* always prove present even if obscure. But I sense their presence, and it involves potential struggles over *will*, with the wolf of volition lurking, ready to charge from its keep, watching for the ingredients of conflict, everywhere I go, as I mix among fellow human beings. Thankfully, their presence usually remains latent, dormant, or restrained by the dam of reason, aesthetics, influence of values, a watchfulness for peace and a desire to live and let live. But causes for conflict can resurrect from dormancy and stride forth with amazing speed and danger, since causes and desire smolder in the fertile fields of mankind's minds, awaiting the right moment or the right catalyst or the right conditions to act. It is the job of Über-thinkers and thought pilgrims, planners, and, of course, decision makers to understand, anticipate, and watch for these dormant but fertile possibilities. With such machinations, we theorists see how desire and life force could leap from dormancy and become causes for effects that trigger immense struggles of *will*.

THE NATURE OF *WILL*

Individual *will* comes with identity. Genes, birth, context, culture, apperception, and upbringing all identify, shape, and condition the phenomenon. Genetics often prove to be the culprit in the appearance of aggression. But, for the wolf of volition to appear, the context must be right too. Also, each of the 14 elements in the will model needs to be stronger than—perhaps dominate—the adversary's elements. I want you to remember probably the most important part of the model is life force, or élan vital. Life force is an inner energy; it lives and stirs in all people and stimulates their motivation and competitiveness. As noted earlier, most people hold this force in abeyance and under control. Others though, prove compelled to fight, to leave their mark, to conquer, to seek their goals, to seek their destiny, to seek their objectives at a determined cost line or at any cost. The latter are the troublemakers to people who want to live in peace, security, and stability. Their rage could burst forth from genetic contagion, religious fervor, or determinism. When I pull back the curtain on the stage of strife though, I find tales told by idiots, full of sound and fury, and seeming to signify nothing,[4] but with the potential to cause misery and death to thousands of people nevertheless. At its aggressive nub, one finds the usual suspects—greed, self-interest, ideology, hubris, religiosity, power, folly, narcissism, avarice, money, land, nationalism, genocide, racism, hatred, retribution, desires to be remembered, desires to emulate another's quest for and acquisition of power (e.g., Alexander the Great, Julius Caesar, Hitler, Stalin, Ho Chi Min, Giap, Napoleon, etc.).

As it pertains to the phenomenon of aggressive acts of *will* imposition, you must consider life force as step one and purpose as step two; but you also need to examine the other parts of the model. Capabilities constitute a very good next step. It is with capabilities and strength of motive that

4. Shakespeare, *Macbeth*, 1,053.

one finds stimulants to start imposition. They shape and dictate resolve.[5] Next, you must contemplate further and continue to examine the other elements, such as determination, perseverance, advantage, disadvantage, passion, and sacrifice. So, along with physical attributes of the model, for the most part, a deep thinker always finds many intangible forces at play when considering *will* in a competitive way. Means and circumstances influence the exercise or imposition of this phenomenon. If a person is a gifted student, a great athlete, charismatic, or personable, he or she could have the wherewithal to impose his or her *will* to accomplish in all things. He or she could command, lead, and attract a zealous following. The circumstances of our birth and childhood affect how we think and emote, and they dictate, or at least highly influence, how we live our *will* (e.g., our plan, our path, our work, our goals) with friends and, at the other extreme, how we compete in the struggle of *will* against our enemies. Capabilities are strengths we possess that fluctuate in potency but decay over time. With changing settings and passage of time, the means to gain strength can undergo decay, particularly when acting and expending energy. Decay, of course, influences one's strength of inclination to sacrifice to accomplish goals and objectives. People realize what appears as a strength can be susceptible to induced decay. Examples of strengths extant before their antipode (decay) include:

1. Resolve
2. Motive
3. Perseverance
4. Determination
5. Passion
6. Sacrifice
7. Morality
8. Ideology
9. Position
10. Ego
11. Belief
12. Value

Continuing, always anticipate unwanted and unanticipated impositions of *will* coming from your adversary. Understand this observation with clear thinking—unexpected chance events always happen in conflict when you least expect their appearance—this is friction. You possess, however, the mental agility and a cascading organizational agility to transition rapidly

5. *Resolve*: Degree of commitment, steadfastness, and resolution relative to imposing one's *will* and thereby favorably terminating a competition or conflict.

when friction has its way with you. Thus, know how to plan, wargame, and parry a suspected imposition in a big hurry. You might use derivatives of the main line of thought to a sudden appearance of an event you have hypothesized or even dreamed about. All the same, you inculcate a complicated, holistic, and pressuring work ethos to cope with and use *will* to your advantage. To perform as you should, use your mind to full capacity and think the way I advocate. Do not ever forget to wargame your adversary's wargaming and deep-think options for both sides before the actual struggle for ascendency begins.

Remember, at the nub of all thinking and action, when it comes to *will*, one always finds the chameleon-like charlatan of *self-interest*. German philosopher Immanuel Kant provides these thoughts about this subject:

> Sometimes it happens that with the sharpest self-examination, we can find nothing beside the moral principle of duty which could have been powerful enough to move us to this or that action and to so great a sacrifice; yet we cannot from this infer with certainty that it was not really some secret impulse of self-love, under the false appearance of duty, that was the actual determining cause of the will. We like them to flatter ourselves by falsely taking credit for a more noble motive; whereas in fact we can never, even by the strictest examination, get completely behind the secret springs of action; since, when the question is of moral worth, it is not with the actions which we see that we are concerned but with those inward principles of them which we do not see . . . but if we look closer . . . we everywhere come upon the dear self which is always prominent, and it is this they have in view, and not the strict command of duty which would often require self-denial.[6]

Anticipate the duration of an acceptable expenditure of sacrifice in a contest of competing desires. You must, however, consider what "acceptable" means to you and your foe. As another important thought, determine how the adversary views intangibles (moral domain), as they show their many faces in every collision. Identify and comprehend the influence of intangibles on the outcome of projected clashes—but relative to both you and your adversary. Discern why outward appearances of people, organizations, and even countries (sudden, slowly appearing, visible and invisible, permanent, dormant, decay) can cause errors in judgment as people assess possible outcomes of bouts of imposition, as they parry these actions, as the appearance signifies the arrival of new impositions via possible adaptation, and so on. Be thorough and then do your assessment from the point of view of the recipient of your planned action but know his mind is imperfect too.

---

6. Immanuel Kant, "Fundamental Principles of Morals." From *The Harvard Classics Literary and Philosophical Essays*, ed. Charles W. Eliot (Danbury, CT: Grolier Enterprises, Corp., 1985), 318–319.

Let's take a few minutes to discern meaning from the thoughts we have covered so far. We have to come up with some conclusions as we work our minds. *Will* is important—it is the cause of all conflict. Thus, its successful imposition or negation means either winning or losing in a contest. But how can one work with this subject in a practical way? Though I admit it is difficult to comprehend and understand, I presented you with a way to think about it in both theoretical and practical terms in sufficient detail for you to grapple with your thoughts as they sway with the winds of change. With this orthodoxy, you possess an organized way to work with *will*'s complexities and create advantage in mental combat and wars of wits. In addition, *will* always appears with a variety of "wrappers," each contributing to its opacity. Our work demands we pull off the wrappers masking the nub all of us seek—to think, to understand, to comprehend, to wipe away opacity and thereby turn *will* into a state of translucency for our eyes only.

This is what I want you to do with *will*. Sculpt your own version to be without a discernable shape. Do not telegraph your intentions. Your adversaries watch; do not show them anything other than what you want them to see. Conversely, know the adversary—wily and cunning is he. As such, he does the same as you, but your work is to pull away the wrappers and expose his nub—to turn its opacity to translucence, at your discretion, without being discovered by your adversary's penetrating spies, double agents,[7] or his other means of discovery.

To reach the top of the trail out of Plato's Cave, my Über-thinker and thought pilgrim must study and know some other thoughts, phenomena, and concepts—one of which is their adversary's intent impregnated by his reasoning and beliefs. Sometimes an adversary is realistic in his outlooks (with realistic being a subjective word and differing interpretation by each side in a competition), but at other times he is going to be unrealistic, perhaps seemingly irrational (but irrational from your view). The object is to think like him and see rationality and irrationality for what they are, as he sees them. It is important to peek behind his layered masks of obscuration—his Veil of Maya—and think about what you see; identify his most important drivers pushing on his psyche to impose his desires or to counter ours and his strategy and tactics to do so. For example, an opponent may move his forces (minds, computers, sensors and other collections, data, data networks, knowledge, organizations, and VKEs) divided and unite them at the last moment for achieving maximum surprise and shock effect, or he might commit an atrocity by launching multiple suicide bombers to light their fire at the same time, spread around one or more geographic locations. Again, our model helps us think. We have come full circle back to life force,

7. Sun Tzu famously discusses the importance of possessing and using not only secret agents, but also he promotes the use of double agents in his book, *Sun Tzu the Art of War,* edited and translated by Samuel B. Griffith (London: Oxford University Press, 1963), 144–149.

where desire always conspires. It clearly shows the starting point for imposition always involves a person's desire, volition, and life force. Life force can be in a single person and shape his thoughts. Or life force can be an aggregation—several like-minded people who work as a team, whose life forces combine into one. Your job, of course, is to dissipate the aggregation, as working against singular *wills* always proves easier than working against an aggregation of *wills*.

THE LEADER'S RESPONSIBILITIES WITH *WILL*

All leaders, civilian and military alike, should study and understand the phenomenon of *will*; it is the basis for all struggles over compliance and dominance. Imposition or denial of desire is what mankind does. Many complicated elements, people, organizations, countries, and so forth come onward in our quest to understand this phenomenon. For example, one can find a mental construct of sorts depicting who is involved in a dispute. This construct could involve: 1) individual; 2) aggregates of individuals; 3) aggregations of organizations; 4) aggregations of individuals and organizations; 5) political organizations; 6) religious organizations; 7) business organizations; 8) military organizations; 9) country organizations; 10) non-state actor organizations; and so forth. At the beginning of any decision cycle, leaders and their Über-thinkers and thought pilgrims should discuss and decompose their adversary's *will*. The basis for this decomposition lies in the minds of the imposer or potential recipient of volition's cold winds. If we scratch the context "housing" the conflict, we find a sibling—the kluge of principles of sufficient reason—and a parent of self-interest. They always form the core of the heart of conflict.

Always wargame *will* from the perspectives of all actors or participants pitted against our plans in a struggle for: 1) imposing volition; 2) resisting such an imposition; 3) launching a long desired counter-imposition; 4) overcoming initial resistance; and 5) blocking the adversary's imposition. As you go through these act, react, and counter-act sequences, always remember at the core of all acts of *will*, one always finds the nub to be self-interest.

ON THE SUBJECT OF VOLITION

Another obstacle awaits my Über-thinker and thought pilgrim. We must finish our discussion of volition to succeed and remember the difference between volition and *will*. Volition is passive and commingles with a desire. The desire becomes real through the aggressive phenomenon of *will* that drives action. Volition comes forth, sometimes anticipated, sometimes by surprise. It lurks in the hearts and minds of people (in history, mostly men have been the originators of volition) and the instigation of actions can linger dormant in the heart and minds of actual and potential adversaries, so-called "neutrals," and a wide variety of miscellaneous do-gooders.

All of this is to say, volition is desire and does not conform to any pattern or predictable angle of rationality. Its rationality often comes from the oft-hallucinatory land of the psyche. In such a land, up can be down and down up, principles do not apply, right is wrong, cowardice is heroism, and hate is love. At the nub, one only finds the cold winds of desire springing forth, volition coming from a heart caught in the mire thus sentenced to perpetual fire.

Obviously, one side perpetrates or initiates acts of *will* and its associated actions, assessments, and adaptations. Action or no action, behavior or no behavior, constitute manifestations of acceptance or denial of imposition actions. Decisions to act or not to act come with one's relative assessment of his and his adversary's capabilities, power of purpose, strength of motive, level of determination, perseverance, etc., and capacity to withstand the shock of each other's imposition of action. This resonant burrowing into *will's* marrow must occur on a continuum or you will see no tomorrow. Before moving on, please read a short poem of mine; it helps us think—

> Related shards of thought, in these, my
> aging days of life, the locus for *will*'s
> struggles run rife; Never void of
> meaning, I see shards dancing, brief
> shimmers of light, appear and disappear
> in the gurgling stream of life;
>
> Probabilities appear and entangle with
> others of their kind; Their appearance to
> my mind, ever so kind to the point of
> thus being divine;
>
> Parts come into wholes; they electrify
> my soul; It is the whole I seek—it is the
> peak for which I climb and strive to
> reach the sublime, Mount Olympus the
> provider of essence and the delight in
> life!
>
> Despite longing for the appearance of
> otherwise, *will* is ever so real dwarfing
> my prayed for tool for peace—Holism
> is *will* 's knife; the haunting apparition
> holding outcomes of strife hound my
> mind and soul, in deadly discord over
> impositions for oft bloody goals—
> impose, block, block, impose, back and
> forth a contest goes; it lasts for
> evermore, so I'm told.

I next provide you with a few brain ticklers so as to point to some specifics of about *will*. As I think about this subject, they elucidate my thoughts in increasingly specific and connected terms. These brain ticklers involve knowing and understanding relative to what could be true, as I constantly edge toward praxis. They include the adversary's thinking capabilities, background, cultural influences, apperception, and so on.

Tickler One—How our adversary could be thinking, planning, acting, assessing outcomes, and adapting must always prove important, indeed critical, to success with high-quality outcomes. Through this process subsequent conclusions and recommendations roll forth into decision making during conflicts. Moreover, choosing an adversary proves important for successful wargaming with our Red Team playing individuals or groups against whom we struggle for dominance. Understand, of course, a better chance to succeed against an adversary exists when you use able cultural subject matter experts (SMEs) as adversarial role players. They help us understand the influence of cultural, interpersonal, familial, organizational, functional, and historical pressures on the adversary's considerations. Of course, one has to understand the adversary's societal and culture influences on his worldview and thinking prowess. Nevertheless, if you want to outthink the adversary and ride the wild pendulum and revel in it, do not shortchange either arc of the pendulum. Jump off the pendulum when you reason about the adversary's *will*; leap back on the pendulum and ride to the friendly side and jump down and consider how your team considers desires and volition, and then spring back on and then off in the middle of the pendulum's arc and evaluate one side against the other using our thought models—your thinking aids—dueling models, as it were. Know, too, the elements in these models prove supple. As such, the elements change positions and activity levels along each arrow of *will*, with causes for such effects coming from the adversary's adaptation, human foibles, and fluctuations in the operational context.

Tickler Two. While experiencing how your adversary thinks, dive into the deep and murky pool of his worldview, life force, apperception, values, cultural influences, views, understanding of technology, and his inner views about our (his adversary's) reasoning and our capabilities relative to his view of his own. Seek to know and understand the social mores of the adversary decision maker; they loom increasing larger and influence his thinking and his mind is where that thinking occurs. Thus, it serves as our target. Learn what most influences his thoughts and identify variables seemingly natural and real for him. Once you find these variables, ride them into his consciousness and thoughts, thus ridding ourselves of the murkiness in this pool into which we dove. Judge your opponent's intelligence and problem solving capabilities—a prodigious task indeed, as one's intelligence can be book smart, problem solving smart, emotional smart, talk smart, act smart, write smart, a combination therein, or the converse of each. Additionally, judge his intelligence via his humility.

Tickler Three. The intelligent person (again, it could be our adversary) becomes quiet and pensive as he infers the appearances of the conceptions he sees and senses, but know this—to him the conceptions are real and relative to his experience—he thinks he has found truth. Our charge—think similarly to our adversary and imagine polar opposites of his intellectual capabilities. Can he conceptualize or is he limited to the concrete? Always plan your actions with his intellectual capabilities and proclivities for deep thinking in mind.

Tickler Four. As you prepare for mental combat, identify models the adversary might be using to help him reason and attain advantages. Determine if the adversary could be thinking about your representation of thinking about *will* and your dependence on your conclusions. Of course, understand what advantage means to him and discern if his view is similar to yours. Observe his actions, spewing as water from a fountain, coming from his reasoning and decisions directly connecting to intent. Know he hopes his actions happen in a synchronized way. Observe both tangible and intangible, observed or measured properties for each action, which possess at least a modicum of direction and method relative to his future actions. Some of these properties could be narratives coming from speeches or other public utterances. So, I ask, could they be faint indicants of future actions to impose his *will* or to suggest a stiffening thereof? As you learn more about your adversary and how he reasons, possibilities appear in your mind as to his amenability to incentives and inducements that could stop, alter, or sculpt his behavior to be more favorable to your thinking. You want to know whether these inducements and incentives prove valid and if they could influence the people who advise him to accept or refuse our entreaties.

Tickler Five. In your thinking, always ask three questions: 1) "What does it mean?" This question involves seeking meaning from data coming from the operational context and the organism's efforts to co-evolve. 2) "What could it mean?" This question asks people to think creatively and innovatively so as to learn what the data, information, and knowledge coming before their eyes and minds could possibly mean. 3) "What are the implications?" People could use this model to shift their mental processes from "droning" into stimulating their intellects and moving to a heightened state of activity. It seems people become consumed by white noise data. Thus, they might skim data, and consider only a minute sample from a large whole of data because of the pressure to produce more outputs. Accordingly, this model could be an impetus with which to think about *will* from incoming data, to possibilities, implications, and straightway to appearances, visions, information, and knowledge.

Tickler Six. Do not view struggles for dominance of *will* in the abstract only; such struggles can involve violence and often people get wounded or killed. Fights over *will*, you will recall, involve a sequence: impose, parry, impose, parry each side's "will." Über-thinkers and thought pilgrims always go beyond the present and find comfort therein. As such, they ruminate about what they see by way of data, information, and knowledge and their contributions in imposing one's wishes beyond the present day. No, the present is not enough. Our big thinkers anticipate adversaries of the future and thereby consider ways to impose their *will* on this theoretical adversary in future operational contexts.

An obstacle appears. It is a wall. What is behind the wall? Our inquisitive minds move beyond the wall and explore in greater depth some maxims.[8] These maxims suggest the need, indeed requirement, for extreme pensiveness. Such a state of being helps us employ and optimize the outcomes of friendly *will* impositions, and also enables our minds to anticipate a competitor's efforts against us.

MAXIMS

1. Consider *will*, as I describe. As such, understand desire and volition, describe intent, and explain its shapes purpose, strength of motive, capabilities, and so on.
2. Consider, and then enact offensive as well as defensive *will*-related impositions; they are a unity of opposites interacting in the same whole.
3. Think deeply about *will*—yours and the adversary's, the operational context, and political and military nature of any impending struggle.
4. Understand why a conflict's nature dictates employment of capabilities, necessary strength of motive, intensity, level of passion, need to sacrifice, et al.
5. Always remember: all the pieces involving the 14-element model matter, regardless of their status or their location in the model shaft.
6. Assess pressure points, decisive points, and COGs—a triumvirate, as it were—from: 1) the adversary's perspective of himself; 2) the adversary's perspective of friendly's triumvirate; 3) the adversary's view of your triumvirate; and, 4) the adversary's views of how you view his triumvirate, etc.
7. Anticipate potential outcomes of adversary's attempts to use diathetics[9] (purposeful arranging of minds) so as to influence intellectual and emotional aspects of "will."
8. Become an expert on the 18 planning considerations model.
9. Anticipate how an adversary might parry your imposition actions.
10. Anticipate how an adversary could impose his *will* on you.

8. *Maxim*: A tenet for acting or behaving.
9. Lawrence, *Seven Pillars of Wisdom*, 195.

11. Anticipate how an adversary might think like you as you consider his imposition actions.
12. Anticipate how your adversary thinks you think and plan to impose your way of thinking even as the two sides posture, after the initial stratagem of imposition and parry plays out.
13. Anticipate how the adversary assesses the effectiveness of imposition actions.
14. Anticipate how your adversary assesses your strength of *will* to resist his efforts.
15. Anticipate how your adversary believes you can best posture your capabilities to impose your desired outcomes.
16. Anticipate the adversary's co-evolution activities and discern whether it is possible to use this knowledge to shape his mind and defeat his efforts.
17. Anticipate the adversary's co-evolution and adaptation model—all 13 steps—be postured to thwart interference with your co-evolution and adaptation efforts. The 13 steps include: perceive, think, plan, decide, act, assess, develop observables, collect, turn data into information, turn information into knowledge, evaluate, learn, and adapt.
18. Prepare your mind, machines, and organizations to win bouts of mental combat within a larger construct of a war of wits and subsequent micro- and macro-struggles of imposing actions.
19. Remember that struggles in mental combat occur in cells of the matrix I presented to you earlier in this book. The cells come forth via the intersection of seven vertical domain silos and four horizontal levels of conflict troughs. In its simplest form, I find 28 cells (7×4) in the matrix; each contains various struggles. The number of cells could explode into more and more as each struggle breaks apart and becomes a separate but connected struggle in its own right.
20. Identify a wide variety of brain-enhancing software requirements in situ, under development, or not yet developed. Focus the triad on your needs to engage in mental combat over the imposition and denial of *will*. The triad should enhance human thought relative to using *will* for advantage.
21. Identify software requirements to help people reason about designing actions to either impose or parry another actor's attempted imposition, anticipating an adversary's attempts to impose his desired outcomes, and considering how an adversary could attempt to block or negate your imposition actions.
22. Cause organizational change to account for and support necessary thought processes, organizational processes, and technical operations to engage and win in bouts of mental combat.
23. Defeat your own thinking and planning and then adjust your assumptions and other thoughts accordingly.

TIME AND *WILL*

Time and *will* connect. Let's examine this proposition. For example, when a prince, let's say, imposes his desires and seizes a state, the clock is ticking and, according to the great political philosopher, Machiavelli, the prince must cleanse the stables, as it were, to rid himself quickly of dissenters and malcontents—people whose simmering resentment or hatred could boil over and thereby cause later problems and erode the power and resilience of his imposition of volition. As Machiavelli tells us,

> . . . on seizing a state, the usurper should make haste to inflict what injuries he must, at a stroke, that he may not have to renew them daily, but be enabled by their discontinuance to reassure men's minds, and afterwards win them over by benefits. Whosoever, either through timidity or from following bad counsels, adopts a contrary course, must keep the sword always drawn, and can put no trust in his subjects . . . [10]

Once this thoughtful and wary prince takes over, his efforts have been successful. But, success is fickle and subject to change relative to changing human beings and a changing operational context. Thus, he must continue to reinforce his power again and again over time, if he fails to recognize the relationship between his *will* and time.

The time for an imposition of one's *will* on the resisting side rests with propitiousness. When the time is right, act. Allow me to provide a current example. Many governments are in a huff about the aggrandizement of Vladimir Putin and Russia in Ukraine and in Russia's annexation of the Crimea. His geopolitical moves should not have surprised anybody. Let me explain my theory as to causes for five effects. First, from a historical perspective, Russia believes Ukraine to be a historical and indispensable part of Russia. Second, Russia needed the Crimea for its military importance—access to a warm water port. Third, the seizure of the Crimea and Russia's involvement with the Ukrainian breakaway efforts seem to come as the strongman saw a vacuum caused by America's decision not to confront Russia's obvious aggrandizement. With this vacuum, Putin acted and grabbed his historical longing—he literally filled the vacuum. Fourth, Russia has been historically fearful of the West as from the west invasions have come over centuries. So as Russia sees NATO moving into countries along its borders, its sense of buffering and spatial protection is gone. Fifth, Russia has historically been expansionist. Thus, the strategist must never look at specific expanses of time but instead historical swaths of time often stretching over centuries.

10. Niccolo Machiavelli, *The Prince*. From *The Harvard Classics Machiavelli, More, Luther*, ed. Charles W. Eliot (Danbury, CT: Grolier Enterprises Corp., 1981), 32.

Another example involves Germany's invasion of the Soviet Union in 1941. Germany intended to launch its attack in May 1941. Apparently, the Germans thought this date would provide them with ample campaigning time to impose their desired outcome (slavery) on the Soviet Union and take what should have been the center of gravity—Moscow. The Germans, however, delayed the attack on the Soviet Union until June 22, 1941 to conduct their Balkan campaign. Some people argue wet weather would have delayed this monumental struggle anyway, while others argue the delay is the most important aspect of the German failure to take Moscow in December 1941. In retrospect, of course, the extra five weeks to impose Hitler's volition might have done the deed as expected.

Lo and behold, another angle of *will* imposition appears. That is to say, the Germans attacked with more than three million soldiers into the Soviet Union to impose Germany's way of living on the Soviet Union (Hitler vs. Stalin and Nazism vs. Communism played into the fight too). The Soviet Union, over time and space and distance, parried the German's imposition, and launched a winter counterattack in December 1941 to impose its desired outcome on the Germans. And so, it went in vicious back and forth close and personal battles of *will*—the desire for power, to win, to live, to make people pay for atrocities, and so forth, all with heavy doses of human folly. How did individual soldiers—Soviet and German—feel about being in a meat-grinding struggle? While they fought each other to the death, they probably thought about survival or an ordeal to save their friend. Yes, I suspect they viewed time to move ever so slowly when they were in hand-to-hand fighting for ascendency of their desire to live another minute, another hour, another day. But most died as time moved on and the balance swung back and forth. As in all wars, fighting over lofty platitudes catches young people in their prime and brings forth their time to die—either physically or psychologically. Ernest Hemingway helps us think about this problem with this passage from *A Farewell to Arms*:

> That was what you did. You died. You did not know what it was about. You never had time to learn. They threw you in and told the rules . . . But they killed you in the end. You could count on that. Stay around and they would kill you.[11]

What this means is to always be wary, when from your adversary's perspective, the time may be right to strike because of reasons all conflict experts should anticipate. Some of these times might be: 1) a time in which your adversary anticipates you could be the weakest; 2) a time in which you appear psychologically impaired; 3) a time in which a company's stock is depressed or that a bankruptcy appears imminent; 4) a time when his

11. Hemingway, *A Farewell to Arms*, 327.

capabilities appear the highest; or 5) a time in which he believes your leadership and organization/country appear to be weak. Interestingly, during all the years I spent as an infantry battalion, infantry brigade, infantry division, and theater senior intelligence officer, I worried the most about the adversary, any adversary, striking at the time they perceived us to be off guard or weakest. Early in the morning is excellent time to start an attack. For example, the German initiation of Barbarossa commenced at 0100 on the morning of June 22, 1941. Early morning is when most people are groggy, seeking food, seeking coffee, stretching, moving about to recover from their rest—thus an excellent time to strike. I know infantry line units always held a stand-to one hour or so before sunrise—at the beginning of morning nautical twilight (BMNT). It was a time I was always worried about, and I learned the principles of vigilance early in my career during Ranger School, where the ghosts of Rodger's Rangers[12] always followed me and my fellow Rangers and influenced our actions.

"HOW TO THINK" ABOUT *WILL*

To think about *will*, you first must know "how to think." This involves a perpetual quest for high-quality reasoning. I call for total immersion of motivated and hungry minds searching to understand implications from all perspectives in conflicts. People performing deep thinking about *will* experience a sense of duty to contemplate the outcomes of ensuing clashes. They anticipate the influence of thought on the outcomes of action. Sometimes my acolytes and I take one step forward and two steps back because of obstacles and difficulty of the subject matter. Yet, with determination, we proceed along this path to our particular version of the "high country."

It is their particular "high country" where my Über-thinker and thought pilgrim optimize their capacity to reason. It is there they bring forth sufficient cognition to comprehend the complicated subject under our consideration. And, it is there America's leaders need to learn to capitalize on its secrets for America's security. It follows our best and brightest people must know how to think about this subject. But, I must ask, do they?

How to think generally comes with education. It requires developing, then using cognitive processes, theoretical, and historical aids to reason. It helps to solve complicated problems, resolve issues, anticipate the actions of a competitor, and assess outcomes of actions. How to think does not include idle chatting where people say the first thing that pops into their minds. Chatting, while socially necessary, is not the intellectual process

12. *Rogers' Rangers*: Major Robert Rogers trained and led a light infantry force—Roger's Rangers—in the French and Indian War and for the colonist rebels led by George Washington.

of which I speak. I speak instead of considered thought, deep thought. Gilbert Ryle helps our thinking with a passage from his book, *The Concept of Mind*:

> . . . we have to allow that a person is doing genuine intellectual work in some situations where no expressions at all are being used, whether words, code-symbols, diagrams or pictures . . . In the greater part of our ordinary sociable chat we say the first things that come to our lips without deliberating what to say, or how to say it; we are confronted by no challenge to vindicate our statements, to elucidate the connections between our utterances, or to make plain the purport of our questions, or the real point of our coaxings . . . We judge them rather by the ways in which he talks when his talk is guarded, disciplined, and serious, uttered in his on-duty tone of voice and not in any of his off-duty tones of voice . . .[13]

People who want to use their intellectual prowess to win focus their attention on anticipatory, aggressive participation in mental warfare and winning bouts of mental combat. They use cognitive elements, thought templates, deep thinking techniques, theoretical and historical aids, and creativity to perceive, think, plan and anticipate their adversary's actions in any domain or any level of conflict. People who know and practice these skills solve complicated problems, resolve complex issues, assess outcomes of actions and adapt faster than their adversary. They are lifelong learners who know how to develop, write, and defend their high-quality conclusions, recommendations, and derivatives. It is the use of derivatives that allows one's expectations to become reality by producing excellent conclusions and the cascading recommendations for action, buttressed by worthy claims, evidence, facts and truths, all contributing to resolving age old battles of an outright struggle for supremacy of *will* between competing forces. This struggle resolves when one side beats the other. It is then that one has reached the nirvana of reasoning but always avoiding complacency, as success's antipode is resilient and sure to come knocking on your door.

Using the reasoning I espouse in this book, one constantly actuates[14] a cognitive energy during a certain rhythm of interaction between opposite poles—the unity of opposites. A strange thing happens in this ageless unity. While each part is powerful as a separate entity, when I combine them into a whole, they actuate and within actuation, a presence by way of ghostly shadow appears; it is the presence of potential. This potential involves ascendance of a great and mysterious power that can appear, in which the new whole of which I speak, through combination, manifests itself into a force much greater than the sum of its parts. Again, this is the

13. Gilbert Ryle, *The Concept of Mind* (Chicago: The Chicago University Press, 1949), 282–283.

14. *Actuate*: Cause someone or something to act or behave in a certain or even certain way.

process of conjoining and emergence among CAS when they aggregate, and when aggregates become aggregations, often occurring as unexpected and unintended consequences. These effects can surprise, and they can cause huge outcomes that promptly impel people to backtrack and try to learn what happened so as to make changes conducive to their self-interests.[15] I take it upon myself to roam surreptitiously and seriously hone in on the gateway to his mind; and, in doing so, I see an odd poem swirling in my mind, it sooths and placates people of my kind:

> Intrude through his secured portals without his knowing, I think, to solve the puzzle of his mind, as he thinks in time; I rob his mind, as the wind covers my movements, don't you know? Once in his mind, I find a labyrinth of dark and musty tunnels, so many of its kind, I find, a mind with ever so many bright messages, whizzing by with delight.
>
> Memories I see buzzing like phosphorescent lights, bees that hover or flit in flight don't you see, conditioned by traces of life, residual pains cut by knife; I find likes and dislikes too, but a heart laden with blues; yet I see with no small amount of rue, a coating on the tunnel walls, it so continuously renews, chasing his thoughts askew. I find culture's etchings appearing ever deeper in the keep and the moment's craggy fingers grasping to touch its future kind.
>
> I find wind gusts from pressures, explosions of concern, I see floating models of learning, with nowhere to turn, so on and on they go, where they stop, nobody knows. I find neurons churning and even more turning on and off and some just lurking; I see some gleaming without the dint of age, and those with rust, so slowly becoming dust. I fly along and see visions of his desires, but cloaked they are by rules of culture of the day oh so observable, even from afar, so I say.
>
> I see icons of his imagination, slivers of glass, as they shiver in the morass; I see them in ambient light, but floating as feathers, coming back to gatherers in the corners of this mind, along the river of vital élan.
>
> Lo and behold I say, I find his mind's eye today, its path to his under-mind battened and sashayed, shuttered to protect the scent from below, from whence the cold wind blows, its disuse now I find where only vegetation grows.
>
> I find rote thinking, fueled by inkling, I find over scrutiny and paralysis in the same whole, as only I know, important

15. Taleb, *The Black Swan: The Impact of the Highly Improbable*, xvii–xvix.

> parts of his mind I stole; I notice models of "what to think," and I find models to enhance "how to think," occurring as a dance, a holistic approach to thinking none stirring, and nothing left to chance, more than a glance so it twists and turns in the river of life.
>
> I soar into his mind's webs, over ever-growing racks of knowledge whose innards I seek, so I pledge, whose parts seem obscure but demure, totally inured to heartache, isn't that your take?
>
> Opening a dusty door, I find the nub of *will* ever so dire, there I see 14 elves dancing by a fire, some here, some there, but 14 everywhere. In those lockboxes of reason lies my desire, its funeral pyre stokes ambition with my adversary's ire, its crackling loosens choking flushes of color, to me a wonderful clutter, so I utter, "My how the peacocks flutter"—kaleidoscopes in motion, I know patterns therein persist, but none readily appear, so have they ceased to exist? I say no, as they tear apart, they do come to me as pieces of whole cloth to repair, and when I do compare, I plant treason in his mind with the notion to fly with even more reason and dare come hither to my mind's eye's care.

Importantly, learning how to think frees our Über-thinker and thought pilgrim as they venture into the musty and damp tunnels and dark mines that comprise an adversary's mind, to think like the adversary[16] and employ their imagination to feel, sense, see, and smell what their adversaries feel, sense, see, hear, and smell. This womb of thought protects and nourishes a live, active probability,[17] among the many, my acolytes can hear, see, sense, feel, taste, and smell in such a state. Their senses cause collection receptacles to move, lift, and gather relevant data. These receptacles remain on high alert to help people see, sense, feel, taste, and smell even when far removed from the physical location.

The Über-thinker and thought pilgrim ride the wild pendulum of duality. They take the time and expend the mental energy to explore the adversary's mind and reason from his perspective. It is during this state of mind—when one's sensing organs and thought processes rage, full of life—a person suddenly alerts and finds a problem or becomes interested

16. Hall, *Think Like the Adversary Thinks.*

17. *Probability*: The prospect that something is conceivable and doable; the viability of an action. I made probabilities into similes and gave them humanlike life force, albeit limited. In my reasoning and imagination, I see probabilities as multiple pods of energy floating around any situation waiting for the chance to snatch them and to turn them into energy and action.

in a mystery. This alert motivates a search for answers to questions and suggests attention to details that could possibly lead to an adversary's pressure points, decisive points, and hopefully, his centers of gravity.

My acolytes also role-play Janus as they look to the past and to the future to see what they can learn. They think about the past to its part in the whole of time—past, present, and future entanglements. They learn from the past and apply that knowledge to the present and to the future. Working with this continuum enables a great, synergistic power to appear. They know and help others know and understand the entangling past, present, and future to be as one, with its appearance without fear. Our Über-thinker and thought pilgrim work hard to see the friendly force through their adversary's eyes, relative to the characteristics of the operational context.

How to think involves several other traits and characteristics. It involves reflection[18] about past actions or activities, a passage in a book, a conversation, or entrée that one can apply in future situations and possible outcomes. It allows access into a contemplative state of mind and once in such a state, to muse deeply about the always important life force, purpose, strength of motive, capabilities and their relationships to other aspects of *will*, conflict, and competition. In this heightened state of reality, in the murky depths of thought, my acolytes contemplate the struggle; such thinking requires them to push their minds to the plane where the vestiges of life force appear as pheromones. It is this level of thought that empowers them to understand how the adversary's thoughts came into being, and in particular, how from desire he developed volition, purpose, and strength of motive. Their goal: find ways to bring forth the ascendance and triumph of their decision maker's vision. This smart and pertinent imposition of their volition upon an opponent occurs but with his resistance, parrying, and counteractions. Our Über-thinker and thought pilgrim must outthink this adversary. They must know with a high degree of certainty what could cause their leader to succumb and acquiesce to the adversary's desired outcomes. Knowing how to think allows a person to envision how concepts and ideas merge, bond, and aggregate into larger and more powerful wholes, for example, offense and defense, observed and observer, and truth and untruth. In our "how to think" phenomenon, the thinker invokes creativity and thereby can easily combine parts and pieces into a larger and possibly new whole or solution to a vexing problem or challenge via synthesis and holism.

18. *Reflection*: Contemplation, rumination, and deep thinking about a particular action, concept, requirement, findings, and the like.

APPLICATION ABSORPTION I

To engage successfully in how to think, a person does the following:

1. Think with a mental framework—a system of thought. I define system of thought as:

   A disciplined, rigorous assemblage of propositions, elements, principles, and axioms, promulgated through 1) thought models; 2) mental processes; 3) explanations; and 4) definitions. The advanced thinking system of thought explains mental efforts people exert to "think about the thinking" sufficient to reason deeply, make decisions, solve problems, develop functional assumptions, realize biases and propensity to make logic errors, develop high-quality conclusions and recommendations, provide wherewithal to gain advantages, and win bouts of mental combat. These bouts primarily occur in the matrix cells appearing and influencing when seven vertical domain silos and four horizontal conflict troughs intersect and, of course, within the operational contexts where one finds nonlinear systems wreaking havoc.

2. Live to thrive in chaos. Nothing new here—chaos always shadows conflict, all of us must live with turbulence inherence to chaos. Competition, imposing one's *will*, the always-lurking presence and influence of uncertainty, risk, and rapid, turbulent changes prove common in any competitive event or with people in extremis. Working with these commonalities brings forth a need for people who not only can reason vertically, thus deeply, but also horizontally, in an integrative or combinatorial way using synthesis. With these thoughts in mind, it is easy to deduce a finding. That is to say, one must be mentally agile, thus able to slip back and forth along the vertical axis and horizontal axis, when they visit their "high country" and engage in "deep thinking." Of course, organizations must also be similarly agile. Are they? Should they be? Can they be? Figure 15.1 depicts what I'm speaking about with respect to both the vertical thought line and the horizontal line, with combining the two, both types working as one.
3. Engage in deep thinking. This implies answering questions, but as we have learned, the process is neither linear nor straightforward. More questions come forth from the previous questions as deep thinking seeks knowledge, understanding, and comprehension about an appearance, an action, an event, a problem set, an adversary, a particular operational context, a person, a group, a culture, a mystery, and so forth. In a general sense, deep thinking means *taking the time and expending the mental energy to think about a subject or problem deeply and critically.* In an effort to provide the reader with additional details for understanding these two words—deep thinking—to the fullest extent, here is a description of deep and then a definition of think coming from my interpretative efforts:

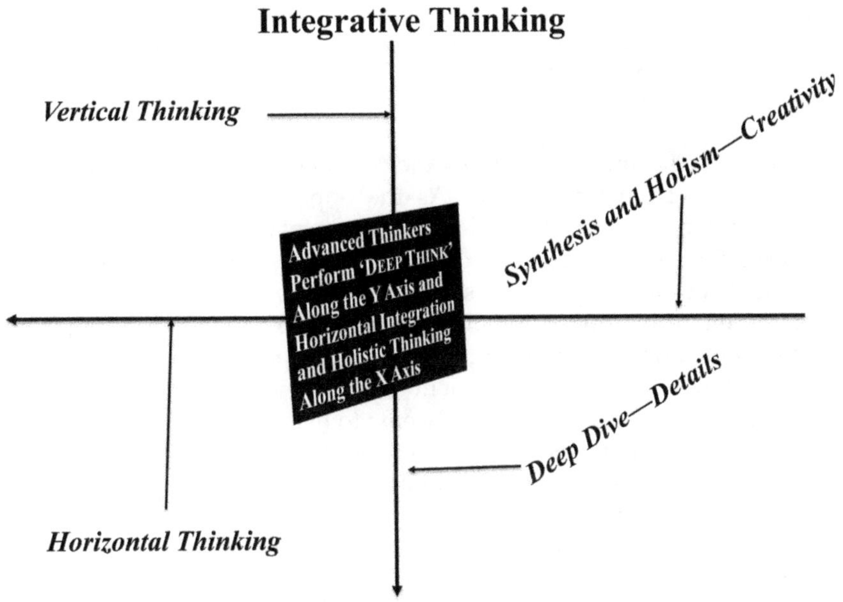

Figure 15.1. Vertical and Horizontal Thinking

Down, down into the depths of the well of thought I go, from where my thoughts come, nobody knows; I do know this, in my place of intellectual refuge, my thoughts flourish and become intense, extensive, relational, combinatorial, yet agile enough to shift when I see my mind glow. Oh, my high country of thought, where the murky water becomes clear; it provides me the wherewithal to experience reasoning, while others can only leer.

Deep is a bottomless and fathomless "well of thought" in which one purposefully dives and submerges in detail, but then, just as purposefully, raises his perspective to the hills, examining the situation and subject matter horizontally, or holistically, smiling in awe of living and experiencing this thrill. I decompose that which I seek, gather related data, and thereafter reassemble, integrate, relate, and combine parts and pieces of probabilities. I examine the elements inherent to my study, and come forth with something new relative to a different approach or view of a problem and its probabilities of outcomes.

In our Über-thinker and thought pilgrim's high ground of thought, the subject under inquiry and concern slowly twists and turns; it opens its shroud though, just long enough for them to peek and see and comprehend the nature of its essence and from a more holistic perspective, the adversary's character, his cultural influences, values, guidance by social mores, cultural rules and overall nature. Their minds discern from this quick peek, the appearance of fearful apparitions similar to Goya's "The Sleep of Reason Produces Monsters" etching.[19] They feel their necks and spines shiver with their intuitions banging and intellects starting to see the emergence of momentous implications and probabilities coming forth to influence the subject or object stimulating this bout of deep thinking.

4. Reason via the unity of opposites and comprehend the energy constantly emanating from interactions. As the opposites constantly interact, change comes forth as its child—the movement disturbs the context and causes ripples in the heretofore seemingly calm pond of life. When one thing in a unity of opposites is on top, it soon goes to the bottom of the circle containing this unity and the expulsions of energy coming from the interactions of opposites. It is the wise person who remembers, understands, and uses this ancient thought phenomenon. As a review, in my contemplation, I use 11 concepts to help guide my thinking into the realm of the unity of opposites. So, I can proclaim the unity of opposites involves one, two, or combinations of these concepts: 1) fragmentation; 2) coalescence; 3) relationship; 4) combination; 5) synergy; 6) coherence; 7) holism; 8) synthesis; 9) aggregation; 10) dialectic; and 11) unity of opposites.
5. Set knowledge conditions for superior decisions. Provide knowledge, conclusions, and recommendations. As my acolytes and I have concluded, having a method specifically developed for this purpose, with the right kind of leadership, can become a powerful aid in making decisions. Such holistic thought-powered decisions, whether with partners or competitors, affect people and their organizations and relationships, not only with us, but also with each other and potential participants who have yet to appear on the field of conflict or competition. These decisions connect with the past, present, and future via threads, portions of which are strong and others weak. When one disturbs the thread of which we speak in one's mind, or in an aggregation of minds, such action has within it the potential to affect the whole of the decision and the people and organizations who are subsidiaries to the decision under scrutiny. To understand potential outcomes involved with disturbing

19. Francisco Goya etched *The Sleep of Reason Produces Monsters* in Spain between 1797 and 1799. Goya loved self-portraits throughout his life. In this piece of his imagination, he imagines himself asleep, his reason harrowed by slumber and tormented by monsters and apparitions appearing at night and violating one's mind when reason is asleep too. I think Goya was talking about individuals abrogating their reasoning to the contextual influences and the dangers of government bureaucracies losing their reasoning powers as well so as to avoid change and rocking the boat, as it were. I have a large picture of Goya asleep with the tormenting monsters of nonreason appearing above his resting head. We must never abrogate our reasoning; otherwise, count on it—the sleep of reason evokes monsters. This rendition of his famous etching is how I paraphrase his work, his title, and apply this interpretation in my world.

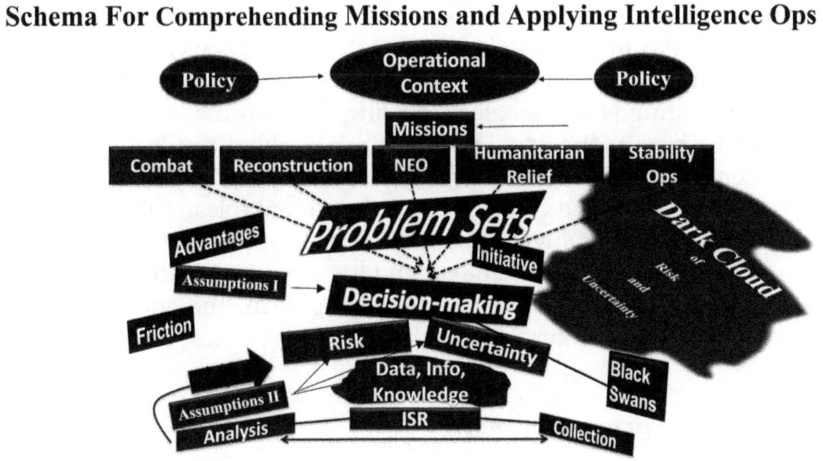

Figure 15.2. Problem Set Schema

the threads of our focus, one engages in holistic thinking and planning. With this kind of reasoning, one weaves the loose threads into a whole (a collage or a tapestry) of meaning to subsidize what our Über-thinker and thought pilgrim need for understanding actions and counteractions and to wage their part of the war of wits.

THE PROBLEM SET SCHEMA

The problem set is a useful means of thinking vertically and horizontally. It makes one work with detail, but causes them to think holistically too. In this schema, the decision maker and his supporters must think about the missions and design problem sets.[20] To think, they develop assumptions. Assumptions, as I previously discussed, prove dangerous for any thinking process because of their importance and the ominous and always high probability they could be wrong. Figure 15.2 depicts the helpful role of problem sets relative to its many challenges. In this graphic, the decision maker has a given context and a variety of missions; he may have to accomplish more than one mission at a time. This graphic shows where assumptions collide with the dark cloud of risk and uncertainty during the decision-making process. Continuing with our venture into

20. *Problem set*: Difficult problem that either has occurred or is anticipated to occur that has numerous subproblems that relate to the macro-problem at hand.

the nature of assumptions, my Über-thinker and thought pilgrim know two sets of assumptions exist, friendly and adversary; ignoring their entwined influences courts failure. The first set comes to the forefront when ruminating about problem sets and decision making therein. The second set comes as the decision maker thinks about results—the quality of the conclusion and recommendations. Again, assumptions (this time "Assumptions II" on the graphic) play an important role in subsiding angst; explaining gaps in intelligence collection data inputs; and providing the wherewithal for the decision maker and his organization to plan, decide, act, assess, gather assessment data, evaluate, learn, and adapt. Assumptions cannot be a stranger to adaptation.

CAUSES AND EFFECTS REDUX

Schopenhauer's principle of sufficient reason prevails in our Über-thinker and thought pilgrim's world. It proposes that for every effect, there is a cause. Their world also features the schema I developed following my study of Clausewitz's chapter on critical thinking where he discusses causes and effects, which I interpret as 1) one cause and one effect; 2) one cause and multiple effects; 3) multiple causes and one effect; 4) multiple causes and multiple effects; 5) on and off causes and effects; 6) dormant or obscured causes for effects; and 7) false or deceptive causes or effects.

ON QUALITY IN DEEP THINKING

I continue to expand my understanding of quality. I started this quest some time ago, when I was a senior intelligence officer (G2) in the 82d Airborne Division, and I have continued to learn about this phenomenon every day, even after my 30 years in the U.S. Army. Years later, from 2008 to 2014, I facilitated intellectually demanding seminars. During those years, I vividly recall listening to students' experiences with "quality" judgments within various bureaucracies from whence they appeared in my seminar. The emotion I felt from listening to and ruminating about the kind of evaluation of quality some of them had experienced was sadness. These feelings flooded my brain because at their places of work in Plato's Cave these fine young minds were being judged, for the most part, by seniors who didn't have a clue about the meaning of quality. I surmised they erred not out of commission, but instead, out of omission. They probably didn't know how to think about this subject to begin with and, therefore, lacked the intellectual base with which to render any meaningful judgment much less mentorship on the subject of quality. I also found myself loathing, in my experience, the process of judging a paper, a briefing, a train of thought—all screaming quality of thinking, but instead finding judgments forthcoming via quantification, for example, numbers of reports, reports seen by the high priests of organizations, meeting time requirements, or platitudes cloaked as accolades by decision makers. And, I heard stories about supervisors telling their analysts something like, "Just turn in the report as is. I just need it for my numbers of reports I turn in for evaluative purposes." "Quality really doesn't matter. Just do what is normal or expected, and whatever comes out suffices." "Just give me anything; I'm out of time for my weekly report." Or, an all-time favorite of mine, "Good enough for government work."

I continue to push my mind to contemplate and understand "quality," and in doing so, to improve and mature so I can help with metacognition of problems and thinking about their meaning and implications. Such mental preparation allows Sancho Panza[21] and me to assault the tyranny of numbers and time as final arbiters of quality. In the context of which I speak (conflict, competition, decision making, risk, uncertainty, conclusions, claims, evidence, facts, truths, objectivity vs. subjectivity), all of us need to consider how to best judge students', analysts', decision makers' and organizations' thinking. But biases and logic errors seep in even as we attempt to judge the quality.

A period of time passed in which I thought about this subject only occasionally. Only recently did I reinvigorate the stoker[22] feeding the fire one needs for finding understanding of pure quality. Once again, I pondered the word "quality" and thought about not only what it means but also what it suggests. I am convinced one must sustain continually this effort to improve upon this phenomenon—in both theoretical and practical methods with our aim being to enhance minds' intellectual prowess and creativity. Quality in our thinking, writing, presenting conclusions to a decision maker, and making sound recommendations demands understanding the core of the quality we seek and how it appears when it arrives. Our minds, and those of one's network, delves into the meaning of this value or worthiness of our thoughts and in the outputs of which we are interested.

How can one consider and improve a determined quest for quality? Along with Robert Pirsig's thoughts that come forth in *Zen and the Art of Motorcycle Maintenance*, the ideas in Figure 15.3 help us judge quality. The graphic provides you with a conclusion thought template on the left diagonal line from upper-left to mid-center bottom. On the right side, you

---

21. Sancho Panza is a fictional character in the novel *Don Quixote* written by Spanish author Don Miguel de Cervantes Saavedra in 1605. Sancho acts as squire to Don Quixote and provides comments throughout the novel, known as *sanchismos*, that are a combination of broad humor, ironic Spanish proverbs, and earthy wit.

22. *Stoker*: A person who tends the furnace on a steamship or steam locomotive.

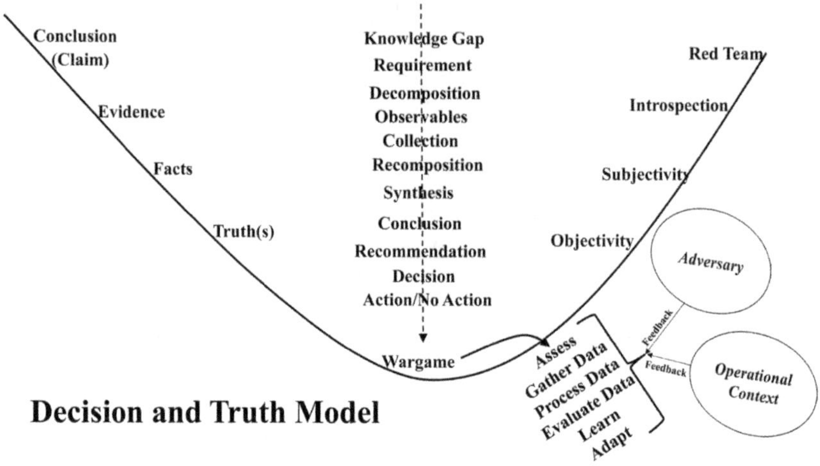

Figure 15.3. The Quest for Quality

can see some methods you can work on either your own quests for quality or those of your subordinates: Red Teaming, being introspective, and recognizing the perpetuity of subjectivity and the impossibility of objectivity. In the middle, I provide you with a thought process from a knowledge gap to its satisfaction to its contribution to decisions and actions. At the lower right, I provide you with a way to judge quality via evaluation of a truncated version of the co-evolution process I have been discussing in this book. This template enables you to consider the adversary and the operational context relative to your thoughts, actions, assessments, evaluations, and adaptations. I invite you to improve upon the model—it is but a start, but I find it useful!

Once you understand the core of quality you seek, then articulate and mentor your people to understand the standards you set. Here are some thoughts on "standards." Standards must be clear and make sense to the thought worker writing a conclusion and recommendation. You can certainly use our thought template to judge the value of conclusions and recommendations. But, there is more to it than one thinks. In short, the leader-mentor must emplace, in the minds of his or her people and in the organizational processes, clearly stated particulars about quality to guide the organization's processes and outputs. I, for one, expect people to think deeply about the graphic and its direct influence in judging quality. Additionally, I find elements of thought one can intelligently employ to ascertain whether standards of quality thinking are being met via claim, evidence, facts (both long-lived and transitorily afflicted facts), truths (again long-term and short-lived), and a consideration of objectivity and subjectivity. To help in the quest for quality, use the thoughts of great thinkers as they defend and employ counterargumentation. Always, if an effort is of high-quality thinking, I hear people identify and discuss implications from what they have thought about and read and now recommend. I also hear short- and long-term implications relative both to the adversary's thinking and to the operational context.

But now and again, I find myself expecting more than meeting this simple quality checkpoint. That is to say, I invite people to discuss with me, face to face and mind to mind, the pros and cons of each point in each template element and explain to me how they intend to use the model to defend their writing and their comprehension of the struggle to impose, attempt to deny said imposition, or acquiesce. With this said and the process understood, a leader judges the quality of their subordinates' writing and oral presentation. In my world, I contemplate thinking and decide if the intellectual efforts meet my standards. I also expect my people to brief me on how they intend to *defeat their own plans* relative to either imposition or denial of an adversary's imposition, how they would know if the adversary found this weakness, and how they would thwart his efforts in any fight. I expect my thinkers to explain how they overcame their human tendencies to commit logic and bias errors. Finally, I judge the quality of their conclusions and recommendations, ask for feedback as to whether there is a better way to judge quality, and determine if their input meets the "common-sense threshold." Through heuristics and recursion, the thinkers with whom I work learn, tweak, learn some more, tweak, etc.

In closing, this hard-traveled road is part of a lifelong journey that never ends. Learning how to think is essential, but not easy. It is a process requiring deep thinking, asking questions, journeying to one's high country, and providing high quality conclusions and recommendations about *will*.

APPLICATION ABSORPTION II

The person who thinks about imposing his desires and subsequent impositions or parries of a resister's responses always does the following:

1. Think with a mental framework—a system of thought (not unlike the one proffered in this book).
2. Live and work in chaos.
3. Absorb one's self in deep thinking.
4. Reason via the unity of opposites.
5. Know and understand the operational context.
6. Set knowledge conditions for high-quality decisions.

7. Understand and embrace nonlinearity.
8. Synthesize and think holistically.
9. Understand, articulate, and enforce standards of quality—your methods and procedures.

In this chapter, I expanded our discussion of an important presence—the presence of *will*. It is the epicenter of all conflicts, wars, battles, and mental and physical combat. The chapter provided four adages for the reader to ponder. These adages took the reader into more specificity about *will* and provided the practical application of this great phenomenon. The chapter explained individual *will* comes forth with an identity—genes, birth, context, culture, apperception, and upbringing all identify, shape, and condition the concept. The chapter also reiterated one of the fundamental elements of *will* is life force, or élan vital. It is an inner energy; it lives and stirs in all people and stimulates their motivation and competitiveness. Most people hold this force in abeyance and under control. Others come forth compelled to fight, to leave their mark, to conquer, to seek their goals, to seek their destiny, to seek their objectives at a determined cost line or at any cost. At *will*'s aggressive core, one finds the usual suspects—greed, self-interest, imposing one's view of religion on others, quests for power, narcissism, avarice, desires for money, desires to control land, nationalism, genocide, racism, hatred, retribution, desires to be remembered, desires to emulate another's quest for and acquisition of power, and so on. *Will* is the cause of any conflict. Its negation or its successful imposition means either winning or losing in fights. Of great interest, the chapter took on how to work with this complex subject in a practical way. Though *will* proves difficult to comprehend and understand, I presented readers with a way to think about it in both theoretical and practical terms. With this approach, I presented an organized way to understand *will* and work with its complexities.

Later in the chapter, I explained how to think about *will*. This always involves a quest for high-quality reasoning. I called for total immersion in this subject just waiting for motivated and hungry minds to learn about implications from all perspectives in conflicts. People performing deep thinking about *will* experience a sense of duty to contemplate and prepare for the outcomes of ensuing clashes. They anticipate the influence of thought on the outcomes of action. The chapter took the reader on a deep dive into the *nature of will*, an intellectual excursion into the *nature of volition*, and their differences. The chapter presented six ticklers and 23 maxims to help people think about the thinking necessary to master how to think.

The chapter presented a visual model about quality. The visual shows a conclusion thought template on the left diagonal line from upper-left to mid-center bottom. On the right side, one finds on the opposite diagonal line some methods to work on quests for quality via Red Teaming, introspection, and recognizing the perpetuity of subjectivity and the impossibility of achieving objectivity. In the middle of the model, one finds a thought process from a knowledge gap to its satisfaction to its contribution to decisions and actions. At the lower right, I provided a way to judge quality via a truncated version of the co-evolution process I have discussed in this book.

Also, the chapter presented a problem set methodology to employ how to think powers. In this schema, the decision maker and their supporters must think about missions and design problem sets. The problem set is a useful means of thinking vertically and horizontally. It makes us work with detail, but causes us to think holistically too. Thinking requires developing assumptions. Assumptions, as I previously discuss in the book, prove dangerous for any thinking process because of their importance and the ominous and high probability they could be wrong.

The chapter discussed learning to thrive in chaos. Nothing new here—chaos always engulfs any conflict, and all of us must live with the turbulence inherent to chaos. The chapter discussed competition, imposing one's *will*, the always-lurking presence and influence of uncertainty, risk, and how rapid, turbulent changes prove common in any competitive event or with people in extremis. The chapter identifies a need for people who not only can reason vertically, thus deeply, but horizontally, in an integrative or combinatorial way using synthesis. One must be mentally agile, and thus able to slip back and forth along the vertical axis and horizontal axis when he visits his "high country" and engages in "deep thinking." Of course, organizations must also be similarly agile. I asked: Are they? Should they be? Can they be?

CHAPTER 16

Conclusion: A State of Continuity

Argument: *In this chapter, I assert that* will*—because it is the most important aspect of conflict and competition—requires intensive study. It has never been studied or discussed like it is in this book. One's study of* will *first develops a thorough understanding of the phenomenon and then employs the power inherent in knowing its intricacies. In this book, I have led readers on a journey of learning, a journey during which we developed* will's *theoretical constructs and practical tools for how to think about will and how to apply that knowledge against adversaries.*

We reach the cave's entrance. We grasp our long-sought goal. We take the next step, placing our outstretched arms from the cave's gloom into the sun. We step forward together into the bright sunlight. Its warmth feels ever so good. Our eyes hurt from the sun's brightness—it hurts from our lengthy stent in the dark of Plato's Cave, but our minds, invigorated, realize a goal—understand truth and reality rather than false realities in the puppet master's theater. With this knowledge coming forth into their minds, my acolytes' eyes burn with tears of sadness due to the untruths they were led to believe to be true at the bottom of Plato's Cave and to their compassion of the plight of dear friends they left behind. Free they are from the insidious grips of half-truths, charlatan realities, and shadows on the cubicle walls. Nothing sadder can be, one says, than to think "I know the truth" but discover "I have held truth at bay." For people still toiling away at the bottom of the cave, their "truth" is being comfortable despite a haunting, persistent plague of inconsistencies and contradictions about the institutional truths of which they believe to be reality. These modern-day troglodytes fixate their minds on false pretenses of truth, as they know it, though experiencing an unsettling feeling—something is amiss. Thus, they replay this feeling over and over in their minds, but sadly find nothing different to convey beyond what they hear that day.

Now my Über-thinker and thought pilgrim reflect on what they learned while crawling up the narrow and torturous pathway. While they bask in the sun, I know they cannot stay. No, the reason I selected and mentored them was for a purpose larger than to sit at an ivory tower above and beyond the ugliness of the world. Those of us who have escaped from the cave have a moral responsibility to traipse bravely back down that narrow path to the gloomy pits of Plato's Cave. It is there to which we have been summoned, with humility, to know and learn and lead people in the cave to a condition of high spiritually, deep intellectuality, knowledge, truth and emotionality and, thereby, to become what they should be—deep thinkers for all their days! I want to spread about our learnings—what all of us have learned and discerned to be true about the great phenomenon—*will*—our group has studied and so ardently discussed. So, I tell my acolytes to enjoy their peace, but only for a short while. We shall hold forth a Chautauqua, I say, a Socratic mentor as one, and the Über-thinker and thought pilgrim as two other members. All of us shall congregate and review, exchange thoughts, and share reflections of high value.

I reiterate to them *will* has two faces: one normal ambition and desire, the other abnormal and out of control. I direct their attention to the book's preamble about the hungry wolf of volition:

> What barest the exit of that hungry wolf,
> Volition. It can be that man has evolved
> Into asceticism far enough to hold his
> Natural tendencies at bay. It could be that
> A catalyst has not awakened this day. But
> Know well all ye who dwellith here on
> This earth, it can be a monster that is held
> at bay.
>
> —Author Unknown

They nod their heads in agreement, recalling the chill when first this passage entered into their minds. The more they thought and discussed, the greater the dread pummeled their minds toward the nadir of intellectual, emotional, and moral being, as they realized volition's tentacles reach out and clutch all humankind. I tell them—do not fear not the hungry wolf, but learn to know him well for what he is. Human beings live two lives, one blessed and one cursed—greatness and wonderful kindness on one hand, but on the other hand deformities galore, with avarice and self-interest and the specter of yearning to impose their *will* beyond the pale of either decency or normalcy. These two characteristics of mankind swing, sometimes in balance, sometimes up and down, back and forth, never stopping, on it goes.

My acolytes proceed with their vastly improved thinking to help people learn to think via synthesis. It helps if humanity writ large learns sufficient mental processes to know the hungry wolf of volition; it is via synthesis and holism, where the parts and elements of this difficult subject appear as understandable and how all relevant thoughts and concepts coalesce, within the aggregated concept of which we speak—the imposition of one's desires on other entities resisting the imposition or resisting an adversary's attempts to impose his *will* on us. My acolytes acknowledge their mentor status. This mentoring business takes a personal commitment. It takes personal recognizance to know, understand, and comprehend *will*. With synthesis, people can grasp holism and with the two ways of thinking intertwined, thereby learning how to anticipate and deny the wolf of volition's dangerous yearnings even when quiet.

The difficulty of synthesis suggests people generally cannot learn this skill without help. My acolytes plan to help their wards become Überthinkers and thought pilgrims, to gain comprehension and, in doing so, learn to apply holism in this fight against the wolf of volition. As such, they must aggressively lead others in improving their intellectual skills via purposeful cognitive development and critical thinking/reading programs. A superb theorist, deceased Air Force Colonel John Boyd, certainly understood this way of thinking:

> Faced with such disorder or chaos, how can we reconstruct order and meaning? Going back to the idea chain of specific-to-general, induction, synthesis, and integration the thought occurs that a new domain or concept can be formed if we can find some common qualities, attributes, or operations among some or many of these constituents swimming in this sea of anarchy. Through such connecting threads (that produce meaning) we synthesize constituents from hence across, the domains we have just shattered.[1]

In the absence of this kind of thinking, one cannot travel, in an intellectual sense, to where he needs to go relative to imposing *will* on an adversary, or resisting an adversary's imposition actions. To use it, he must learn to relate, connect, and link like and dissimilar things with an always open and combination-seeking mind. With such a method of bringing parts and pieces of things together, he can develop new and better outcomes than ever before. One's mind conceptualizes and brings to reality the finely tuned workings of each of the 14 essential elements of *will*, each element powerful as a separate entity, but awesome when working as a whole. The whole of which I speak works best as one whole, harmoniously and thus synergistically, to wreak havoc on those who oppose America's desired outcomes.

1. John Boyd, "Destruction and Creation" (Unpublished, 1976), 3.

Definitions prove necessary for not only understanding words, but also knowing enough to tell from which "well of thought" our line of thinking emerges. I determined right away I needed a definition of *will* to proceed in this journey of discovery. I must confess I have worked on and off on this definition for 18 years, but I neither had defined nor explored adequately its nooks and crannies. This book does this mental work. I find comfort in knowing studious people will add and subtract thoughts to this definition. But a definition, a framework, an approach always foster ways to proceed. So here is my book's definition:

> The appearance of one's desire, volition, life force—empowered by potency of resolve and willingness to sacrifice, that when yoked with strength of motive and appropriate capabilities, provides action sufficient to accomplish or satisfy an aim, goal, objective, strategy and thereby imposing one's desires over and gaining the acquiescence of a resisting entity or understanding the phenomenon sufficiently to resist such attempts from another human entity.

My advice—engross your minds in deep thinking about the subject of *will*; recall when all of us shook our heads when seeing evil's tread. After all, it is the dark side of *will* that arrogantly poses and postures at the center of man's darkest desires, wars, and struggles. See this description of man's curse and folly, and gain a better understanding of the dark side:

> That for the general safety he despised
> His own; for neither do the Spirits damned
> Lose all their virtue; lest bad men should boast
> Their specious deeds on earth, which glory excites,
> Or close ambition varnished o'er with zeal . . .
> Scowls o'er the darkened landskip snow or shower; . . .
> O shame to men! Devil with devil damned
> Firm concord holds: men only disagree
> Of creatures rational, though under hope
> Of heavenly grace; and, God proclaiming peace,
> Yet live in hatred, enmity, and strife
> Among themselves and levy cruel wars,
> Wasting the Earth, each other to destroy:
> As if (which might not induce us to accord)
> Man had not hellish foes enow besides,
> That day and night for his destruction wait![2]

Within the words, concepts, methods, thought models, and definitions, you found an understanding of this phenomenon has been only lightly

2. John Milton, *Paradise Lost*, ed. Henry W. Boynton (Boston: Allyn and Bacon, 1916), Book II, 68–69.

touched by our baseline knowledge heretofore. Know this: I believe in the existence and influence of a never-ending state of connectedness among human beings and in fact all things. For example, this book has no last chapter, only a state of continuity depending on other people's further thinking and study into the phenomenon of *will*. In my imagination, I see gossamer threads—wisps, as it were—dancing, whirling, connecting one to the other and from the other to another. It is humanness I know you see that provides strength to the gossamer and wisps that tie one to the other. Even when in deadly conflict, it still involves humans.

> [E]very part of the world seems to contain, and be contained in, every other part: the writing table reflects the spheres on top of it, the spheres reflect each other, as well as the writing table, the drawings of them, and the artist drawing it. The endless connections which all things have to each other is only hinted at here, yet the hint is enough.[3]

Themes weave into dreams and come forth as a whole. Themes come from premises, straw into gold.[4] To tell the tale of our study of *will*, I reiterate for your review six "big thoughts" that glue ideas in the book into a whole. These six big thoughts or premises first came forth in the introduction and again in Chapter 1. They connected my thoughts throughout the book:

1. Practitioners and students of conflict must know the intricacies of the phenomenon of *will* and put this knowledge into practice.
2. The importance of *will* is self-evident. It is the central idea of conflict and competition.
3. The subject is difficult to master and put into use; therefore, one must use a method of how to think about the subject to comprehend and use its innate power.
4. To understand and employ *will* to its fullest powers requires knowing and employing a thought model with 14 elements: 1) life force; 2) purpose; 3) strength of motive; 4) capabilities; 5) determination; 6) perseverance; 7) sacrifice; 8) passion; 9) advantage; 10) disadvantage; 11) imposition; 12) action; 13) assessment; and 14) adaptation.

3. Hofstadter, *Godel, Escher, Bach: An Eternal Golden Braid*, 258.

4. The phrase "straw into gold" comes from a particular Grimm's Brother's fairy tale: Rumpelstiltskin. He has the ability to turn straw into gold with his spinning wheel in the tale. The analogy is with thought leaders, Über-thinkers, and thought pilgrims mentor others into understanding and using holism. They motivate and lead people to improve their intellectual skills via purposeful cognitive development and critical thinking/reading programs. Thought leadership takes the intellectual potential laying fallow in those fine minds and turns it into creative and holistic thinking—straw into gold.

5. To win clashes of *will*, participants always consider their adversary's point of view and the operational context within which clashes occur.
6. To put forth the highest-quality thinking possible, one must know, understand, and comprehend "connectedness." Connectedness requires the highest condition of holism and synthesis.

A grand collage, a tapestry of connections, relationships, and combinations, some you see, some you don't, remains a constant with this great subject—*will*. If one fiber or one entity or one string changes, the universe changes or even vibrates, thus causing other fibers, entities, or strings to change too—because all things connect, some faintly, others directly. The connections prove important in contests of desires, with one side imposing, and the other reposing, but neither dozing, waiting for fortune to change so they can impose their *will* once again. For here one finds the means to enact Sun Tzu's guidance, the concept of normal and extraordinary interacting as one. Upon searching for and succeeding, one's thinking finds unity and with it comes connectedness in a dance and rhythm of motion similar to the dark and mysterious waves covering the ocean.

> The external world and his inner world are for him only two sides of the same fabric, in which the threads of all forces and of all events, of all forms of consciousness and of their objects, are woven into an inseparable net of endless, mutually conditioned relations.[5]

Such thinking dominates my intellectual being, but I was a late bloomer, as it were. Though holism is how the world works, its appearance and influence on my life did not appear until 1984–1985, as a student in the U.S. Army's School of Advanced Military Studies. It was during that remarkable year, with the help of great mentors and friends, I learned how my mind works and to be comfortable therein. My learning experiences there and the subsequent awakening opened up a new, wonderful, and sometimes scary world for me in which to indulge and revel. I found myself wondering what my ideal Über-thinkers and thought pilgrims would be, and my mystery proved partially resolved with the thoughts of German writer Herman Hesse in his book *Siddhartha*. Here is the profound passage, juxtaposed with reality and the ideal to which I aspire:

> [A]t the world, completely coherent, without a loophole, clear as crystal, not dependent on chance, not dependent on the gods . . . but the unity of the world, the coherence of all events, the embracing of the big and the small from the same stream, from the same law of cause of becoming and dying . . . by your own

5. L. A. Govinda, *Foundations of Tibetan Mysticism* (New York: Samuel Weiser, 1974), 93.

seeking in your own way, through thought, through meditation, through knowledge, through enlightenment.[6]

A contributing influence in bringing forth what I seek involves minds connected with minds, tightly connected via links, disparate and like-kind, and always imagining what comprises connectedness between and among physical and mental aspects of conflict. Lofty levels of thought and action require commitment, hard work, implementation, and juxtaposition into practice where one learns how to use this complicated subject.

I find myself asking this question and seeking answers as to explain and rationalize. Are there people who want to impose their *will* for nefarious purposes? Yes, such insects drawn to light live today; they contrive to destroy good people everywhere. Some are capable of such thought as we have learnt, while others have not been taught. Some are attempting to impose their way of living on us; others are lining up the elements of their models of *will* so as to impose it on us. Many of these current or impending struggles occur in the human mind and heart. Russia, for example, mixes their actions—some physical and some mental—into a state of art. They are and for centuries have been masters at Maskirovka, or in a loose translation, deception and mind games. China—great relational thinkers—strategize for the long view. Drug people, ever so good at using thought, prove creative and evil; they use drugs as an asymmetric weapon; they scheme to outthink us so they can steal our children's souls.

Push your minds even further and engage in deep thinking about a peculiar aspect of knowledge—it involves decay. Decay is "the dissipation of strength, power, odor, appearance, or function." I want to present to you all again the phenomenon of knowledge decay that occurs over time and influences the strength of *will*. Decay is neutral. Each side in a fray can use natural or induced decay or recognize it for what it is and thereby cause the decay to occur more quickly or to spread horizontally or vertically. What is it that decays? Each of the 14 elements in my thought model prove vulnerable to such subtle assault! Decay comes with disuse. It also comes with the fragility of strength in question, as in "strength of motive," intensity of passion, dissipation of a person's or a people's readiness to sacrifice, or even the clarity and strength involved with purpose. One or any of possible combinations, or all of these elements prove vulnerable to decaying on their own, but even more so, with an adversary's forceful and aimed intervention specifically to induce decay. Thus, as a strategy or a tactic, always, always induce decay in our adversary's model of *will*.

Will can decay with the passage of time and with repeated and varied assaults on its essential elements. In fact, clashes and battles often involve

6. Herman Hesse, *Siddhartha* (New York: MJF Books, 1951), 26–27.

tempered, aimed, and purposeful actions to induce and cause decay in selected (situationally dependent) elements of a combatant's strengths. One has to know the model and the purported realities it portrays, but its mysteries often unfold, as the adversary's *will* conveys. Thus, ironically, the adversary's model becomes an action agent working against him, in that it replays its action again and again; but, in the end, even he cannot refute the ominous presence of decay. Understanding Leo Tolstoy's *War and Peace* led me to merge my notion of *will's* decay with the invasion of Russia in 1812. The farther Napoleon and his army moved into Russia without a climactic battle, the more they undoubtedly felt the gradual decay of their heretofore unbeatable reputation and élan. Although history tells us that Borodino was a draw at the tactical level, I believe the draw was also a defeat at the strategic (military) level. Because Napoleon's forces could not destroy the Russian army, their strength dissipated, long logistics tail must have withered, and their heretofore moral superiority decayed, gone with the Russian wind and haunted with the understanding of the approaching and always fierce Russian winter. They undoubtedly felt dissipation in their strength of motive, capabilities, purpose, perseverance, determination, with their advantage turning to disadvantage, as each dissolved and eventually faded into near nothingness with their long advance and lines of communication, the inconclusive Battle of Borodino, the occupation of a burned and deserted Moscow, and the long deadly retreat back to what is now Poland. With the decay came a lasting shift in all advantages.

> Napoleon was not the only one to experience that nightmare feeling that the terrible blow of the army was falling in vain, but all his generals, all the soldiers of the French army who took part or who did not take part, after all their experiences in former battles, when, after exerting a tenth as much force as now, the enemy would be vanquished, now experienced alike a feeling of awe at that enemy who, having lost half of his troops still stood just as threateningly at the end as he had stood at the beginning of the engagement.[7]

Repeatedly, I have extolled the virtues of holistic thinking, enabled and enhanced by synthesis. This kind of thinking provides an indispensable and irrefutable advantage over any foe. Note—physical and the nonphysical aspects of conflict entangle with one another; you must set conditions for the lever-seeking balance of these two aspects of conflict, providing you with advantage. Sometimes, however, the physical slips into dormancy and the mental comes to dominate—it is the ascension of the moral domain of conflict. In his book, *White House Years*, Henry Kissinger describes some of

7. Leo Tolstoy, *War and Peace* (Garden City, New York: International Collector's Library, 1949), 481.

the challenging minds of his Chinese counterparts during the preparation for and visit of President Nixon to China in 1972, as follows:

> Each remark made by a Chinese was part of a jigsaw puzzle, even if at first our more literal intelligence did not pick up the design. . . . On my ten visits to China, it was as if we were engaged in one endless conversation with an organism that recalled everything seemingly motivated by a single intelligence.[8]

As you can tell, the Chinese thought holistically and via connectedness then, and therefore Kissinger had to think this way too. It must have been difficult to carry on face-to-face discussions knowing full well his mind must work with past and future visits in the minds of the Chinese, from their point of view, and from his own, as a representative of the American government and President Nixon. All of this kind of thinking though proves to be a form of mental combat in which our Über-thinkers and thought pilgrims learn and perform imbued with a goal—always win.

Connectedness is awareness of a form of appearance. Connectedness, an exhilarating theme, surfaces again and again throughout this book—indeed, this book thrives on the phenomenon. The Internet and social media enable connectedness for all sides in any strife, which enables us to infer connectedness does not exist in isolation, but applies to and connects other people in conflicts. Throughout the book, connectedness is so fundamental to winning, each side searches and accounts for its appearance, lasting presence, and influence. Each side must wargame possible actions to affect the adversary's connectedness and thereby build the opportunity to gain superiority in creating narratives, defining truths, defining facts, presenting evidence, shaping interpretations of data, shaping expectations, influencing perceptions, and so on. Furthermore, connectedness is important for moving, shaping, and "arranging minds," as T. E. Lawrence would say, and thereby easing the way to impose one's *will* on populaces, businesses, governments and military. After all, these entities come with people who perceive, have expectations, interpret data, and then behave from their mishmash of all four entwined elements of living and being human—*perceive, expect, interpret*, and *behave*, which interconnect in all human endeavors.

As conflict activity occurs, other types of connectedness happen in the operational context that encloses the conflict. For example, seasons of the year connect, metamorphosis yields many a connection, elements and entities of food chains connect, and all of these examples connect and influence outcomes of conflicts. In addition, aggregates, micro-aggregations, and macro-aggregations connect. They can be the vehicles of pent-up energy that adversaries expend against one another. Additionally, contexts

---

8. Kissinger, *White House Years*, 1056.

connect—personal, micro-, macro-small, and macro-large. As people start walking, for example, their personal contexts connect and enfold with a personal context, micro-context, macro-small context, and a macro-large context. I found this thought from a famous scientist helpful:

> The world thus appears as a complicated tissue of events in which connections of different kinds alternate or overlap or combine and thereby determine the texture of the whole.[9]

One of the strongest themes in the book involves the continuous presence and influence of *will* throughout history. Do not deny its presence and influence. After all, one finds rare certainty when thinking about wars and conflicts—a certainty that war and destruction originate with a desire that transfers volition, to some person's life force, some human-connected council's desires, some governmental leader's hatred, a country's desires to acquire more land, and on and on. Common to all, at the nub of *will* one discovers man's desires pushing for prominence. In the middle of his heart and mind, one always finds a human being who is always self-serving, particularly as he attempts to impose his way of thinking on others who do not acquiesce to his desires.

I discussed early in the book a certain presence of different kinds of *will*. So as a next step in our review, please recall riding on the escalator as it moves up the slope of *will* from passive to hyperaggressive. Sometimes people prove to be passive and therefore benign, letting life come and go and not being assertive outside of a form of *will*—to live. Or, impositions of *will* can be normal, for example, disciplining a child, losing weight, winning a softball game, seeking and winning a more influential and better-paying job. The next step in the model of our attention involves people with normal aggressiveness, such as competing in business and subsequent takeovers of a company, corporation, or conglomerate by another. This form of imposing one's desires is more aggressive and harmful but still a normal part of any society. In this grouping of people, one traditionally finds corporate CEOs, financiers, military officers, and rank-and-file people trying to scratch their way to the top of their organizations. Finally, one finds the hyperaggressive people who dream about power and try to fulfill their desire to conquer.

At the far end of this depiction one finds Hitler, Stalin, Genghis Khan, and Napoleon. This kind of person could also be the billionaire, Sisyphus-like,[10] compelled to become richer and richer, regardless of possessing all

9. Werner Heisenberg, *Physics and Philosophy* (New York: Harper Torch Books, 1958), 107.

10. In ancient Greek mythology, the king Sisyphus erred. His punishment—push a huge boulder up a steep slope, reach the top, only to be required to do it again, again, into infinity. I want my readers to be anti-Sisyphus. Some people don't know about the lurking

the money he could ever spend, but who always wants more and more riches, regardless of who gets hurt along the way (recall Steinbeck's admonition "here's a capacity for appetite . . . that a whole heaven and earth of cake can't satisfy").[11] Power drives people like this; they have an insatiable desire to acquire more and more power with the power they gain. This is Nietzsche's idea personified as "will to power" in action. People with this "disease" possess these urges until their health intervenes to temper their aggression, and eventually the impetus of aggressiveness snuffs out, defeated by death. One can argue most actions to impose one's *will* one way or the other involves quests for money or power. I must say that I find it difficult to avoid the disease of cynicism, as I sadly realize how correct Nietzsche is. It is true—men have fought each other to impose their *will* for millennia, whether imposing it on their neighbors, serfs, against their enemies, aimed at the husband of a desired woman, forcing religious views, gaining wealth and power—it is all about power and the power money can bring.

Now let us consider once again, because of their importance in winning or losing conflicts, the realm of vertical domain silos and horizontal levels of conflict troughs. With the intersections and connectedness, one finds 28 cells. It is in these cells where engagements, battles, and campaigns occur and where national elements of power (e.g., political, economic, informational, and military) play out. This book discusses and explains these two schemata and their intersections as yet another example of the connectedness one can find everywhere if they enter into a state of mindfulness and deep thinking. Understanding this theory has a direct impact on successfully imposing one's *will* on other people or organizations, or defending oneself. Please recall from my earlier introduction and explanation of this vision the presence and influence of four horizontal troughs of conflict—grand strategic (policy), strategic (military), operational, and tactical—and the vertical silos of seven domains of conflict—air, ground, sea, space, cyberspace, information, and cognition (I added the last two). The vertical domain silos intersect with the horizontal levels of conflict troughs. The result—28 cells, each part of a larger struggle in a matrix conflict. This thought suggests the connectedness of like and dissimilar things. You should recall an event at the low end of one vertical domain silo (e.g., ground) and at the tactical level of conflict can affect the highest level of grand strategy. All of us need to prod our minds to think holistically as all parts of this whole connect and function as complete, but when one part

presence of what I label the Sisyphus syndrome in big bureaucracies, or they know and perform anyway. If so, they are complicit, as they accept day-by-day repetitive "boulder pushing." Bureaucracies can ruin intellectual potential; learning and thinking enables this potential to arise, appear, and influence the entire organization to learn and think!

11. Steinbeck, *East of Eden*, 157.

weakens, the other parts weaken too. Finally, I am suggesting when in the pit of conflict, be alert and keep track of happenings at construed low or high levels, as they can present vulnerabilities with which to strike quickly at activities in other troughs and in other vertical silos of conflict through direct or indirect approaches.

Context equals epicenter in contests of *will*; context's bubble surrounding conflict sends inputs via data to adversaries about changes in this context. The friendly side can potentially influence the adversary's thinking, reasoning, rationale, and/or decision making via manipulating or creating false data inputs into the adversary's models for action and rules that drive the action. The same effect can hold true when the adversary takes advantage of manipulating context-provided data and thus uses it against his foes.

One must always consider individual *will*. Start by thinking about CAS (human), their life environment, experiences, and the development and maturation of their life force that propels them to accomplish goals and objectives. Then work your way to CAS dyads, aggregates, micro-aggregations, and macro-aggregations. Life force helps us understand why and how much one person or many people could be inclined to sacrifice and their passion that could surface as they attempt to accomplish the goals they or their leaders seek. We sometimes believe in a person or are bound to the person via rules and regulations and devote our individual *will*, perhaps even abrogate our cherished "free will" to this person and to the actions he takes. It can happen to even the best of people, as happened in Nazi Germany, in particular, from 1933 to 1945. Destiny (fate) interlaces with *will* and life force. Consider Hitler and his book, *Mein Kampf*; he told us what he was going to do. In hindsight, it is easy to notice an out-of-control ego, enormous self-interest, extreme hatred, a compulsive psyche, charisma, and an influential but out-of-control life force. People followed him, subordinated themselves to him and his leadership, and commingled their individualism with his common good, and gained control of the entire German nation. Here you can read Nietzsche's thoughts and in doing so, I want you to imagine yourself living in Germany in January 1933 and see if the thoughts don't sound a claxon of alarm:

> Every animal . . . instinctively strives for an optimum of favorable conditions under which it can expend all its strength and achieve its maximal feeling of power.[12]

12. Friedrich Nietzsche, "Genealogy of Morals Third Essay, Section 12." From *Basic Writings of Nietzsche*, translated and edited by Walter Kaufmann (New York: The Modern Library, 1968), 543.

Hitler thought, of course, that his destiny was to build a thousand-year Reich, to conquer Europe, and to expand Germany's borders into vast swaths and tracts of land belonging to the Soviet Union. It seems Hitler thought his way to be fundamentally better than anybody else's. But not everyone shared this belief. One of his field marshals—General Erich von Manstein—had this to say about Hitler's self-appraised thinking:

> The [chief] characteristic of Hitler's leadership [was] his over-estimation of the power of the will. [To win the war] this will had only to be translated into faith down to the youngest private soldier.[13]

Hitler's vision, exemplified in his life force, involved enslaving whole peoples, particularly in Poland and the Soviet Union, and slaughtering millions of Jewish people because of his passionate hatred for them. I could go on, but you get the idea. If the West or the Soviet Union would have either focused on and taken away any of the elements of his *will* model, or reduced the German army's capability in Hitler's and his general's minds during the inner war years, Hitler's calculus may have shifted and the horrors of World War II might not have occurred.

To remind, this book presents a 14-element model of *will*. The thinking behind each element will codify and become part of America's deep-thinking capabilities. Our model and its meaning weave threads and cast them throughout each chapter in the book, connecting the beginning with the end, from the preface through Chapter 16, enabling the book to become a unified whole. Think about, seek, see, and gain an understanding of the power and beauty of this phenomenon I call connectedness. Connecting threads reach out and connect human beings to one another, but also to the past, present, and future. Connectedness beacons shine their bright lights on three interconnected rings of "being," touching, of course, each sentient organism—a ring signifying people long dead, a ring signifying people living today, and a ring from the future. A connecting thread runs through the middle of the touching rings, connecting people from the past, people living in the present, and people coming in the future.

As you certainly know by now, our subject is difficult to explain and consider. But elucidate and think we must, as our adversaries undoubtedly understand what I'm speaking about. I provided you with a way to think about *will*. As such, I equipped you with 18 considerations to help you think about this subject with the highest quality of thought possible. I think you will agree the list, though already extensive, can and should expand. The size and complexity of thoughts at the base of each consideration beckon our minds to study and use the considerations that make

---

13. Erich von Manstein, *Lost Victories: The War Memoirs of Hitler's Most Brilliant General* (Bonn, Germany: Athenäum-Verlag), 1955.

sense for the fast approaching days of reckoning. Since nobody can work well with all of the considerations all the time, select considerations with which to work based on the mission, adversary, and context. Draw a line separating what you can and can't do. Considerations falling below this cutline become risks in one's advanced thinking. Wise people profit by avoiding potential mistakes, so I ask you to use these thoughts to engage the adversary of the present and future in mental combat. Win wars of wits in which you find yourselves. Even the rarely used or the esoteric considerations must occur in the recesses of your mind as you think about the 18 considerations. I ask you also to consider always cost and benefit and ask yourself: Are all 18 considerations worth my mental energy, my time, and my physical effort? Can I afford to ignore them? If a consideration falls below the cutline, could it suddenly raise its ugly heads and strike me by surprise? Can I use intelligence assets as a tripwire for the appearance and importance of considerations that don't appear relevant?

As I ponder *will*—its cycle of imposition and resistance—I think about the need to understand, seek, and recognize some of the negative aspects of mankind that relate the most to conflict per se.

> Round and round they go,
> dance and chant to and
> fro; some deny, but know
> as surely as wind blows;
>
> Round and round, tip-toe,
> tip-toe, I come to realize
> so; In my mind, in my
> heart of hearts, a stealthy
> blow staggers me;
>
> It is the human condition,
> don't you know, armed
> with life's bow and
> arrows, and wanton
> desire, bringing
> lamentation and fear to
> satiate man's greed
> through bad deeds, so the
> sad story goes, as surely
> as the wind blows.

Negativisms of mankind burst from the containing walls and straps of their "keep." They surface all the time. The underlying motives for actions, even for those philanthropic, for the most part involve, when exposed to the light of day, self-aggrandizement, narcissism, self-interest, greed, hatred, prejudice, racism, and on and on. Self-interest guides all humankind's thoughts and actions. The imposition of *will* then always considers self-interest because no matter what aspect of inducements or incentives or mental or physical assaults, it is the opponent's self-interest to which the aggressor must appeal or affect. It is the nub of any argument or outright conflict.

Will is both an intellectual and emotional force. Its successful application comes with a high degree of confidence. This confidence comes from not only physical capabilities, but also emotions coming forth from the life force and purpose of the imposer—the moral domain, as it were. Such emotions can be pride, hubris, desire for power, confidence, lust, love, hate, retribution, revenge, and so forth. It also shifts back to the intellectual force—how hidden knowledge of your capabilities and strength of motive compare to the adversary's upon whom you plan to impose your desires. Above all, our subject involves the presence and influence of moral force.[14] A strong moral force directly influences the 14-element model. To impose successfully one's volition on a resisting opponent, one must have moral force, as abstract as it might be, and emotional force—both essential for infusing energy into purpose, capabilities, strength of motive, determination, perseverance, passion, and commitment to sacrifice.

This invisible but powerful force—the moral domain—is an important consideration in deep thinking about any kind of conflict. Furthermore, the deep-thinking human being always considers hatred, revenge, and retribution from the adversary's perspective and discerns, to the best quality of thought possible, how long the emotions just listed seethe before they die or break out of their veneer-encrusted cage. Such thinking shows the persistence of this phenomenon. I'm speaking of invisible forces at play that come with the moral domain—powerful and highly influential invisible forces indeed. Ignore them at your peril. I provided you, the reader, with the intellectual wherewithal to think deeply about these difficult phenomena, so use what you learned wisely, without becoming a cynic, like me.

Consider another example in which invisible forces were at play. During World War II imagine being a Polish, French, or Soviet soldier and sense his struggles to survive. But also sense in your heart your enemy—the Germans with their panzers—running amuck in your rear and surrounding you with giant pincer movements. The Germans' opponents' elements of *will* experienced decay in virtually all elements. In essence, with the

---

14. Moral means influenced by conditions, positions, and influences of good and bad, right and wrong, just and unjust. Causes, for example, can be just or unjust, but it depends upon the views of the beholder, which, in a conflict of clashing "wills" always differs from side to side. *Force* means the presence of a potentially penetrating energy that could appear, burst forth, and influence outcomes of conflicts. So when we put moral and force together, we find the presence and influence of an energy imbuing justness and righteousness on or in all it touches.

cascading psychological effects coming from German use of the indirect approach via blitzkrieg—deep panzer army thrusts through or around the defenses—most elements of their opponents' *will* quickly decayed until hundreds of thousands of people fighting the Germans surrendered or died. With such cascading vibrations throughout the attackers' whole, the Germans' energy became exponentially more powerful than their foes'.

I think it safe for us to infer people need education involving how to think about *will* in sufficient depth to understand and use it and its surrounding contextual variables to their advantage. A framework (this book) proves fungible from problem set to problem set, to culture to culture, and context to context. Moral force, as an aspect of any conflict, is so powerful it influences all the elements. Great Russian author Leo Tolstoy helps us gain a deeper understanding of not only the presence of moral force, but its importance and influence on all 14 elements in our model with this passage from his masterpiece *War and Peace*:

> The moral force of the French attacking army was exhausted. Victory is not something signalized by the fastening of certain strips of cloth called flags to poles, nor by the space on which troops have stood or are standing; victory is moral, when the one side has been persuaded as to the moral superiority of the other and of its own weakness; and such a victory was won by the Russians over the French at Borodino.[15] The invading army, like an exasperated beast of prey, having received as it ran a mortal wound, became conscious that it was doomed.[16]

Will involves the minds, hearts, and souls of people. I don't care what conflict situation presents itself, *will* is always at play and difficult to deal with, let alone understand and convey. Risks are high because as you explore *will*'s intricacies, you suddenly realize a requirement—that is to say, as you attempt to array the minds and hearts of naturally sensitive and proud human beings, consider both moral and physical dimensions of conflict. These two dimensions must rank high in your thinking priorities. To implement his or her desires, one thinks about and answers these very pertinent questions to the problem at hand. How do these people perceive? What do they expect? How do they interpret data and narratives as they arrive? What are the varieties of media for them to receive data, information, and knowledge? How do they think about the data arriving from the mass media? What is their subsequent behavior? Along with the difficulty one faces when trying to answer these questions, it is difficult to design

15. *Battle of Borodino*: September, 7, 1812, during Napoleon's invasion of Russia. In my view, the battle ended as a draw, in that Napoleon failed to destroy the Russian army and thus failed to force the Russian tsar to capitulate.

16. Tolstoy, *War and Peace*, 481.

actions, assess outcomes, and adapt action to influence people comprising a populace. The basics or frameworks remain the same from conflict to conflict and situation to situation but the "meat on the bone" differs.

So, what can one do? I say and have said repeatedly throughout this book—know and use your theory as the underpinning for thinking and then adapt it to the operational context, the populace (in this line of thinking), and adversaries at hand. All of this thinking and considering contribute too one's understanding of *will*. Often, we have to set conditions to impose our desires via actions on an adversary or competitor to be successful. Also, we have to require intelligence operations to assess successfully conflict outcome actions to determine how successful opposing sides have been. In this work, be leery with regard to game theory—even a wary person can and does tumble unanticipated events; and, of course, logic and bias errors lurk, ready to pounce and strike to convey deviations in thought.

The ravenous wolf of volition does not remain at bay. It spreads death and destruction around the world, even on this supposedly enlightened day basking in the supposedly bright rays of human history. Rest assured, it wends its evil ways, day by day, and year by year, forever more. Since the wolf is with us to stay, I implore, be not afraid, but instead come to know its ugly countenances. It appears in different forms among the "spreading fan" of aggressors and wanton slayers of people and peace. All of us must sustain hope with a bevy of prayers to help us force the wolf of volition back to sleep in its keep.

I ask you to remember *will* is the nub, the central idea, the most important aspect of war, conflict, and competition. To learn about will, study this book, and it will release its many secrets. *Will*, the life-blood of conflict, loudly courses through history's craggy gorges. My hope is you take it upon yourself to learn well this book of *will* and prepare for what is certain to come—struggles over *will*, never, ever, done. People studying or working with it in any form first understand, and then employ *will*'s inherent power, knowable only in its intricacies. Thus, the notion of *will* had first to be defined, succored with theory, then studied for theory, bundled into new ideas and concepts, and then put into practice to win bouts of *will*. And, please know this book is just a stepping stone in learning to understand this phenomenon. I ask you to think about the thoughts I present in my book, improve upon the ideas, and develop and write your own thoughts about this absolutely towering and influential phenomenon.

The time has come for me to close down my thoughts on this matter. My last book, it is. As such I leave you with what I consider to be a useful compendium of ideas concerning this great subject—*will*. Hard as it was, I loved this journey. What you read and contemplate in this book will serve you well, but you must challenge your mind and enter a state of deep thinking, at your particular high country, burrowed in your inner sanctum, to aptly muse about and apply for goodness the topic mankind blithely calls *will*. I want you to use these thoughts wisely, to withstand any upcoming test involving the resounding sound, feeling, smell, and touch of clashing *wills*! I bid thee farewell and wish you the best.

Wayne Michael Hall
Brigadier General, Ed.D.
U.S. Army, Retired
Denton, Texas
June 2018

Glossary

***Argument:** I designed this glossary to go as one with my book—*The Power of Will*. As such, I used a variety of sources in the book, which I dutifully footnoted. And with some words or phrases, I paraphrased and transformed words and used concepts, interpretations, explanations, and renderings of words.*

Adaptation—shaping one's activities or actions due to 1) changes in the operational context and/or 2) an adversary's actions or reactions as they adjust to fluctuations in the operational context.

Advantage—a situation of being in a preferable position over another competitor. In the book, there are seven advantages—initiative, tempo, momentum, knowledge, decision, position, and freedom of movement.

Aggregate—one complex adaptive system (CAS) kluging with another and bonding via glue (which holds similar and dissimilar aggregates together); when more than one aggregate conjoins, one finds an aggregation.

Aggregation—gathering and bonding separate aggregates into a larger whole. This whole is collective and responsive to accepting more like and disparate entities into its boundaries.

Appearance—manifestation of an altered state of being entering one's mind. An appearance has numerous states of manifestations, such as physicality, presence, color, size, depth, width, height, sound, dress, nonverbal behavior, action, cause to effect, outcomes, visions, links, patterns, anomalies, aggregations, and so on.

Apperception—understanding, interpretation, expectation, and behavior based on previous familiarities with a subject or close and personal experience.

Baseline—basic or standard level of data structures and fields to perceive and judge normalcy and also to hunt for anomalies.

Center of gravity—hub of all power and movement, on which everything depends. That is the point against which all our energies should be directed (Clausewitz, *On War*, 595–596).

Chance—unknown and unpredictable element in happenings that seems to have no assignable cause (for an effect or outcome).[1]

Chaos—cause for the appearance and influence of turbulence and change in operational contexts. Chaotic systems can prove sensitive to initial conditions; small changes in those conditions can lead to quite different outcomes.[2]

Co-evolution—evolution of two or more species or organisms (natural or man-made) that interact closely with one another, with each adapting to changes in the other(s). Note, all CAS must co-evolve (e.g., assess, collect, evaluate, learn, and adapt or die).

Complex adaptive system (CAS)—dynamic network of many agents (which may represent cells, species, individuals, firms, nations) acting in parallel, constantly acting and reacting to what the other agents are doing.

Comprehend—totally grasp meaning, visualize connectedness within wholes, and imagine states of coherence in aggregations of objects, persons, organizations, et al.

Connectedness—people, organizations, countries, etc., merged into wholes one hopes to be viable and operable. When I speak of connectedness, know I'm also including people, organizations, objects, subsystems, micro-aggregations, macro-aggregations comprising wholes, and many other organisms and entities.

Context—circumstances, meanings, actions, potentialities—malleable and permeable globule that surrounds and influences one, two, or many people, organizations, and so on in particular situational events, actions, operations, situations, and so forth. Context, once a person is cognizant of it, is rich in new and old data, some bursting with potential; context is visible in one's mind, and if imaginative and contemplative, capable of being felt and perceived.

Creativity—how some people imagine a problem or challenge, or present a simple observation. In their minds, they employ their imagination, their mind's eye, with a heady dose of the under-mind, and develop something new or original.

Critical thinking—an intellectual process that "examines assumptions, discerns hidden values, evaluates evidence, and assesses conclusions."[3]

Data—collected data appears in many forms, often possessing little to no meaning or lots of valuable potentialities. It becomes information via recomposition and it becomes knowledge via synthesis.

Decisive point—geographic place, specific key event, critical factor, or function that, when acted upon, allows commanders to gain a marked advantage over an adversary or contribute materially to achieving success (U.S. Joint Publication 3-0).

---

1. Dictionary.com Unabridged. Retrieved June 25, 2010, from Dictionary.com website: http://dictionary.reference.com/browse/chance

2. Online Etymology Dictionary. Retrieved June 17, 2014, from Dictionary.com website: http://dictionary.reference.com/browse/chaos

3. David G. Myers, *Exploring Psychology*, fifth edition (New York: Worth, 2003), xv.

Deep think—taking the time and expending the mental effort to think about a problem deeply and critically.

Determination—firmness of one's fixation on resolve and purpose. People comprehend determination by envisioning it as a "fuel," propelling perseverance, thus permeating the 14-step *will* model and potentially empowering a decision makers *will* via actions.

Disadvantage—a state or an instance of being in an unfavorable circumstance or condition.

Disdain—scorn for person, country, or organization as causing a condition of disdain for one or more thinking, assumptions, alternatives, options, actions, adversaries, forces at work in the operational context. With this condition, disdain, one cannot stop its cancerous spread and influence into humankind's perpetuating condition of hubris.

Duality—state of being in which one thinks as two connected opposites in motion all the time and is emitting noise and energy as one side interacts with the other. Duality considers two parts—friendly and adversary (and could increase in complicated contexts and conditions). One cannot discount an opponent out of hand. Enter his mind and discern how he thinks. Accept the premise that the adversary is doing the same.

Entanglement—a physical and psychological phenomenon occurring when individual people or groups of people and/or organizations connect with one another and form aggregations; an entanglement's actions and outputs cannot be described independently—instead, their state of being connects and entangles with one another and forms a whole.

Evidence—that which proves or disproves something and thus is the foundation for belief.

Exteroceptive—relating to stimuli that are external to an organism.[4]

Fact—a truth known by actual experience or observation, and in a collective sense, believed to be true so whatever is being considered is known to be true.

Friction—in my interpretation and my words, friction means—*unexpected chance events*—this interpretation derives from *On War* by Clausewitz.

Glue—that which holds both similar and dissimilar aggregates together, usually an ideology, emotion, extant condition, religion, racial superiority, and so forth.

Goal—an adversary's desires always starts with ideas or vision about what he wants to accomplish or possess. The desired outcome become one's strategic aim and results in the utterance of one or more broad goals. Goals provide *direction* with an end or a desired outcome being that which he seeks.

Hatred—intense loathing; a situation whereby rancor dominates perceptions and feelings in which one or more people feel for others whom they believe to be the cause of their resentment.

Holism—theory that the parts of any whole cannot exist and nor understood except in relation to an extant whole or wholes coming into existence via

4. https://en.oxforddictionaries.com/definition/exteroceptive.

aggregate and aggregation theory. The concept espouses the notion that wholes are greater than the sum of its parts.

How to think—involves high-level cognitive functions, deep thinking along with synthesis, intuition, and holism. At its base, one finds a rigorous system of thought (see the definition in this glossary). How to think relative to conflict implies that people use cognitive elements, theoretical and historical aids, and creativity to perceive, think, plan, and anticipate the thinking, planning, actions, assessments, and adaptations of any adversary in any domain.

Illusion—a principal cause, wearing one of many masks that alters one's comprehension of reality by suggesting or causing false or misleading impressions of truthfulness; illusions can be self-imposed or they can be part of elaborate deception plans. One has to rid themselves of illusions to peek briefly into reality.

Imagination—drifting in and out of consciousness via contemplation; nonetheless being sufficiently conscious to see, hear, touch, smell floating shards, flotsam of data, pictures of activities, the absence of what should be present, and the all-important intrusion of one's quietude and contemplation by active and nonactive appearances and presences. Imagination discloses parts of one's subconscious to the conscious, thus enabling the person to envisage new vistas, creative ideas, the future, the past, problem sets, and spurring engagement in synthesis, holism, and creativity.

Interoceptive—elating to stimuli produced within an organism, especially in the gut and other internal organs.[5]

Knowledge war—a conflict of knowledge, which involves outthinking adversaries who can be in situ or appearing as new potentialities for potential conflicts in which opposing minds willfully; enter into bouts of mental combat and try to outthink one another to gain advantages and defeat their adversary.

Life force—-impetus force within a human that ignites and motivates purpose, strength of motive, capabilities, passion, sacrifice, and so on. Life force is a fundamental dynamism within one's being that compels a person to take what another person possesses. It is the most important aspect in imposing or denying an imposition action, but it remains elusive to understand, often darting to and fro within the dark corners of opponents' minds.

Manifestation—output of an appearance.

Mass media—a varied assemblage of media technologies designed to receive and spew data from a large variety of sources. Data without explanation can mean nothing, or it can mean a little, but man and machine must turn data into information via applied thinking for meaning.

Mental combat—the constant multidomain, multilevel, multispectrum cognitive conflict or competition in which people with conflicting interests, attempt to impose their *will* via superior mental functioning.

Metacognition—thinking about thinking.

5. https://en.oxforddictionaries.com/definition/interoceptive.

Mind's eye—inner sanctum of thought where one imagines and visualizes a comingling of data fragments and shards streaming into this sanctum via the body's portals into the quiet, inner refuge of one's private thoughts.

Mirror imaging—superimposing one's own thoughts, experience, and values to another person of a different culture and or background so as to understand how they think and act.

Model—style, design, plan, driver of an action or a series of actions that stimulate behavior in CAS. It is also a simplified representation of a complicated or not well-known phenomenon, as in representing how the enemy perceives and thinks.

Motive—an incentive, inducement, vision, fear, etc., that causes a person to behave or act in a variety of ways always connecting back to the motive.

Mythos—a foundational system of beliefs, especially those dealing with supernatural forces, typical of a particular cultural group. Mythos includes forces and vagaries of life after death.

Nonlinearity—the study of situations where, in a general sense, cause and effect are not proportional to each other.[6] Nonlinear systems possess some oddities that drive the minds of decision makers and their coteries literally wild. Here are a few of these oddities most pertinent to our work: 1) nonadditive; 2) improbability of accurate prediction; 3) small inputs can lead to large outputs; 4) turbulence and change are the norm; 5) causes for effects are difficult to discern; 6) presence and influence of aggregations; 7) presence and influence of sensitive variables; 8) importance of context; 9) presence and influence of complex adaptive systems; 10) presence and influence of co-evolution; 11) presence and influence of the spooky world of tendency theory; 12) importance of adaptation; 13) sensitive dependence on initial conditions; 14) presence and influence of observed/observer behavior and influence; 15) untidy and changing rules; 16) presence and influence of the edge of chaos[7]; 17) presence and influence of conditions that cause variables to become sensitive and thereby influential; and 18) presence and influence of friction, randomness, and chance.

Nub—core of a matter, essence of, most important issue, or kernel of a problem.

Objective—1) a deliberate action that consumes mental and physical energy, desire, perseverance to accomplish or satisfy a personal, organizational, or national aim, goal, strategy, or outcome via specific strategies, tactics, actions, etc., to accomplish an outcome; 2) thinking objectively involves thinking without the influence of emotions, prejudices, feelings, interpretations, experiences, preferences, viewpoints.

---

6. https://encyclopedia2.thefreedictionary.com/nonlinear+physics. Retrieved February 23, 2017.

7. Waldrop, *Complexity,* 12. The edge of chaos is "where components of a system never quire lock into place, and yet never quite dissolve into turbulence, either . . . where life has enough stability to sustain itself and enough creativity to deserve the name of life. The edge of chaos is where new ideas and innovative genotypes are forever nibbling away as the edges of the status quo, and where even the most entrenched old guard will eventually be overthrown."

Passion—a strong craving with rationale often altered or sometimes relinquished and a periodic absence of rational thinking.

Perseverance—indomitable continuation, lasting power, resolute finishing of an action, imposition of *will*, or dogged, continued defense against another's person's imposition of their *will*.

Phenomenon—awareness of an appearance or immediate focus of one's awareness of action or interaction with other beings, human, organizational, and machine in experience.

Plan—scheme or method to accomplish an aim, goal, objective developed via thinking about and wargaming acts and purposes and anticipating an adversary's actions attempts to forestall the plan's actions beforehand.

Position—taking an intellectual or personal stance; a domineering physical location relative to either side in a conflict in all kinds of operational contexts.

Possibility—potentiality unbound by constraint.

Precognition—knowing an event in the future and/or changes in a pertinent operational context before it happens.

Preemption—affecting an action or behavior by acting first and grasping the initiative.

Pressure point—a sensitive, critical point, weakness, or dispute against which pressure of many persuasions is directed.

Probability—likelihood that something is plausible and doable and also the viability of the possibility of occurrence of an action or event.

Problem set—difficult problem that either has occurred or is anticipated to occur that has numerous subproblems that relate to the macro-problem at hand.

Quality—degree of excellence in a product: thought, play, book, problem solution, etc.

Random—proceeding, made, or occurring without definite aim, reason, or pattern.[8]

Rational thinker—A person who exhibits sufficient reasoning powers with which to assume, think, decide, act, assess outcomes of action, and adapt.

Reason—capability to think, understand, evaluate evidence, assess outcomes of actions, judge right from wrong, discern hidden values and relationships, comprehend variables, and anticipate moves from ongoing actions or those about to occur.

Red Team—people who do the following: provide alternatives; critique plans; serve as the adversary in wargames; and provide innovative or creative thinking to help overcome people's conventional wisdom, blinding biases, poor assumptions, and personal logic errors.

---

8. Dictionary.com Unabridged. Retrieved March 31, 2016 from Dictionary.com website http://www.dictionary.com/browse/randomness.

Reductionism—practice of simplifying a complex idea, issue, condition, or the like, especially to the point of minimizing, obscuring, or distorting it.

Reflection—contemplation, rumination, deep thinking about a particular action, concept, requirement, findings, and the like.

Relationship—a link, connection, interaction between two entities.

Resilient—returning to the original or roughly similar form or position or capability after being assaulted, attacked, dispersed, bent, compressed, or stretched.

Resolve—degree of commitment, steadfastness, and resolution relative to imposing one's *will* and thereby favorably ending a competition or conflict.

Robust—strong and able to withstand pressure from change and turbulence and dire assaults against one's health and welfare.

Rule—with respect to my CAS theory, a principle or structure of behavioral code governing and influencing the models that shape actions; guidance that governs, binds, influences, and leads models to direct CAS, actions that may, in turn, impose one agent's *will* on another.

Sacrifice—readiness to endure loss and physical and emotional pain and stress for the sake of a goal, objective, execution of a strategy, hatred, retribution, leader exhortations, etc.

Sensitive variable—something potentially reactive to stimuli but potentially easily excited; a sensitive variable can be highly influential in volatile operational contexts.

Strategy—ideas for employing one's capabilities in a synchronized and integrated way to achieve an aim, goal/objective, policy with available resources but always accounting for adversary, operational context, and constraints.

Strength of motive—Strength: a status of being strong, such as taking a stance against unfavorable odds or potential cost/loss. Motive: the force or energy, which causes people to act in a certain way, endure hardships, perform, and drive toward winning.

Subjective—an individual's mind and emotions controlling their reasoning, decision making, judging, and so on, shaped by their attitudes, opinions, experience, values, political views, upbringing and so forth. Subjective and objective co-exist in the same whole.

Sufficient reason—a cause for all effects.

Synthesis—human cognitive activity that combines elements of contexts, substances, events, electrons, activities, energy, and the like to create a new, coherent, and better whole.

System of thought—disciplined, rigorous assemblage of propositions, elements, principles, and axioms promulgated through 1) thought models; 2) mental processes; 3) explanations; and 4) definitions.

Tacit knowledge—lies in the minds of individuals who know many things and who store knowledge in their minds.

Thought link—broad or general description of direction or thrust for action or future intent of actions; high-level decision guidance; a concept or vision with intimation of necessary actions or possible plans of action.

Thought pilgrim—person preparing themselves for "deep-thinking" engagements by traveling to their personal "high country," which is conducive to their deep thinking.

Truth—consistent with agreed-upon facts; genuine, conforming to the beliefs and standards of a group of people; an act or behavior or opinion or thought that conforms to rules, regulations, measurements, standards, or patterns.[9]

Über-thinker—a great or better than the average person type of thinker. This kind of thinker transcends all other thinkers and is trained and educated to engage in *mental combat* and to win against any foe, in any domain, at any level of conflict, day or night.

Under-mind—"a layer of activity within the human psyche. . . . It can register and respond to events which, don't become conscious thoughts . . . it is a database full of pre-conceptual information, much of which is turned down by consciousness as being too contentious or unreliable. Conscious awareness decides what it will accept as valid—thereby it misses dissonant patterns and subtler nuances."[10]

Unity of opposites—a situation or several situations or conditions in which the appearance, existence, or identity of something depends on co-existing with its opposite, both riding on the undulating vicissitudes of life attached to dependent on one another all the same.

Veil of Maya—illusion of normalcy involving an imaginary veil or mesh covering or deluding ones understanding of connections and interactions.

Will—appearance of one's desire, volition, or life force, empowered by potency of resolve and willingness to sacrifice, that when yoked with strength of motive and appropriate capabilities, provides action sufficient to accomplish or satisfy an aim, goal, objective, or strategy and thereby impose one's desires over and gain the acquiescence of a resisting entity, or understand the phenomenon sufficiently to resist such attempts from another human entity.

---

9. *The Free Dictionary, American Heritage Dictionary of the English Language,* fifth edition (New York: Houghton Mifflin Harcourt Publishing Company, 2016).

10. Claxton, *Hair Brain Tortoise Mind,* 116.

Bibliography

Alexander, Bevin. *How Wars Are Won: 13 Rules of War from Ancient Greece to the War on Terror*. New York: Three Rivers Press, 2002.

Alighieri, Dante. *The Divine Comedy*. Edited by Charles W. Eliot, Translated by Henry F. Cary. Danbury, CT: Grolier Enterprises Corp., 1985.

Arendt, Hannah. *The Human Condition*. Chicago: University of Chicago Press, 1958.

Arendt, Hannah. *The Life of the Mind: Volumes 1 & 2*. San Diego: Harcourt, Inc., 1979.

Bohm, David. *Wholeness and the Implicate Order*. New York: Routledge Classics, 1980.

Caesar, Julius. *The Gallic War*. Translated by H. J. Edwards. Mineola, NY: Dover Publications, Inc., 2006.

Capra, Fritjof. *The Tao of Physics*. New York: Bantam Books, 1984.

Card, Orson Scott. *Ender's Game*. New York: Tom Doherty Associates Books, 1977.

Clausewitz, Carl von. *On War*. Princeton, NJ: Princeton University Press, 1976.

Claxton, Guy. *Hare Brain, Tortoise Mind*. New York: The Ecco Press, 1997.

Conrad, Joseph. *Heart of Darkness*. New York: Penguin Books, 2012.

Cook, Francis H. *Hua-Yen Buddhism: The Jewel Net of Indra*. University State Park: The Pennsylvania State University Press, 1977.

Copleston, Frederick, S. J. *A History of Philosophy, Volume VII, Fichte to Nietzsche*. New York: Doubleday, 1973.

Donne, John. "Meditation XVII," *Devotions upon Emergent Occasions*. London: Stationers' Company, 1624.

Dostoyevsky, Fyodor. *The Idiot*. Baltimore: Penguin Books, 1955.

Dostoevsky, Fyodor. *Crime and Punishment*. New York: International Collector's Library, 1953.

Dostoevsky, Fyodor. "Notes from Underground." *From Existentialism from Dostoevsky to Sartre*. Edited by Walter Kaufmann. New York: New American Library, 1975.

Fehrenbach, T. R. *This Kind of War: The Classic Korean War History*. Washington, D.C.: Potomac Publishing Company, 2001.

Frieser, Karl-Heinz. *The Blitzkrieg Legend*. Annapolis, MS: Naval Institute Press, 2005.

Fussell, Paul. *The Great War and Modern Memory*. London: Oxford University Press, 1975.

Gaiman, Neil. *American Gods: The Tenth Anniversary Edition*. New York: William Morrow, 2011.

Galbraith, John Kenneth. *The Affluent Society*. New York: Houghton Mifflin Company, 1958.

Gell-Mann, Murray. "Complex Adaptive Systems." *Complexity: Metaphors, Models, and Reality*. Edited by G. Cowan, D. Pines, and D. Meltzer. Santa Fe Institute Studies in the Sciences of Complexity, vol. XIX. New York: Addison-Wesley, 1994.

Geyl, Pieter. *Napoleon: For and Against*. New Haven, CT, and London: Yale University Press, 1949.

Gladwell, Malcolm. *Blink: The Power of Thinking Without Thinking*. New York: Little, Brown and Company, 2005.

Goethe, Johann Wolfgang. *Faust*. New York: The Modern Library, 1950.

Goethe, Johann Wolfgang. *Johann Wolfgang von Goethe, Maxims and Reflections of Goethe*, Kindle Book, UUID9ce661f6-11e5-853a=119a1b5d0361, created with StreetLib Write (http:/write.streetlib.com) by Simplicssimus Book Farm, 27.

Goldman, Stuart D. *Nomonhan, 1939: The Red Army's Victory That Shaped World War II*. Annapolis, MS: Naval Institute Press, 2012.

Govinda, L. A. *Foundations of Tibetan Mysticism*. New York: Samuel Weiser, 1974.

Graves, Robert. *Goodbye to All That*. New York: Anchor Books, 1985.

Graves, Robert. *I, Claudius*. New York: Vintage Books, 1989.

Hall, Wayne M. *Stray Voltage War in the Information Age*. Annapolis, MD: Naval Institute Press, 2003.

Hall, Wayne M., and Citrenbaum, Gary C. *Intelligence Analysis: How to Think in Complex Environments*. Santa Barbara, CA: Praeger Security International, 2009.

Hall, Wayne M., and Citrenbaum, Gary C. *Intelligence Collection: How to Plan and Execute Intelligence Collection Operations in Complex Environments*. Santa Barbara, CA: Praeger Security International, 2012.

Hart, B. H. Liddell. *Scipio Africanus: Greater Than Napoleon*. Cambridge, MA: Da Capo Press, 1926.

Hart, B. H. Liddell. *Strategy*. New York: Henry Holt & Company Inc., 1954.

Heisenberg, Werner. *Physics and Philosophy*. New York: Harper Torch Books, 1958.

Hemingway, Ernest. *For Whom the Bell Tolls*. New York: Scribner, 2003.

Hesse, Hermann. *Siddhartha*. New York: MJF Books, 1951.

Hofstadter, Douglas R. *Godel, Escher, Bach: An Eternal Golden Braid*. New York: Vintage Books, 1979.

Holland, John. *Hidden Order*. New York: Helix Books, 1995.

Homer. *The Odyssey*. Edited by Charles W. Eliot, Translated by S. H. Butcher and A. Lang. Danbury, CT: Grolier Enterprises Corp., 1985.

Horne, Alistair. *The Price of Glory*. New York: Penguin Books, 1962.

Horne, Alistair. *To Lose a Battle*. London: Penguin Books, 1969.

Jung, C.G. *Psychological Reflections: A New Anthology of His Writings 1905–1961*. Edited by Jolande Jacobi and R.F.C. Princeton, NJ: Bollingen, 1970.

Kant, Immanuel. "Fundamental Principles of Morals." *The Harvard Classics Literary and Philosophical Essays*. Edited by Charles W. Eliot. Danbury, CT: Grolier Enterprises, Corp., 1985.

Kaufmann, Stewart A. "Whispers from Carnot: The Origins of Order and Principles of Adaptation in Complex Nonequilibrium Systems." Edited by G. Cowan, D. Pines, and D. Meltzer. Santa Fe Institute Studies in the Sciences of Complexity, vol. XIX. New York: Addison-Wesley, 1994.

Keegan, John. *The Face of Battle*. New York: The Viking Press, 1976.

Kissinger, Henry. *White House Years*. Boston: Little, Brown and Company, 1979.

Lawrence, T. E. *Seven Pillars of Wisdom*. New York: Anchor Books, 1991.

Lee, Harper. *To Kill a Mockingbird*. New York: Harper Perennial Modern Classics, 2006.

Levitin, Daniel. *A Field Guide to Lies: Critical Thinking in the Information Age*. New York: Dutton, 2016.

Manstein, Erich von. *Lost Victories: The War Memoirs of Hitler's Most Brilliant General*. Bonn, Germany: Athenäum-Verlag, 1955.

Mao Zedong. *On Guerrilla Warfare*. Translated by Samuel B. Griffith II. Urbana: University of Illinois Press, 1961.

Milton, John. *Paradise Lost*. Edited by Henry W. Boynton. Boston: Allyn and Bacon, 1916.

Montaigne, Michel. *The Complete Essays*. Michel de Montaigne (1533–1592), "On Experience," *The Complete Essays of Montaigne*, unabridged, translator, Donald M. Frame, narrator, Christopher Lane, *Audible, Publisher*: Brilliance Audio, release date: 09-20-11, https://www.audible.com/pd/Classics/ The-Complete-Essays-of-Montaigne-Audiobook/B005NC866K?ref=a_a_search_c_lProduct_1_1&pf_rd_p=e81b7c27-6880-467a-b5a7-13cef5d729fe&pf_rd_r=4CCA3YABPV4Z3NTXBDJW&.

Neustadt, Richard E., and May, Earnest R. *Thinking in Time*. New York: The Free Press, 1986.

Nietzsche, Friedrich. "Beyond Good and Evil." *Basic Writings of Nietzsche*. Translated and Edited by Walter Kaufmann. New York: First Modern Library, 1968.

Nietzsche, Friedrich. *Schopenhauer as Educator*. Translated with notes by Daniel Pellerin.

Orwell, George. *1984*. New York: Houghton Mifflin Harcourt, 1949.

Pascal, Blaise. *Thoughts*. Edited by Charles W. Eliot, Translated by W. F. Trotter. Danbury, CT: Grolier Enterprises Corp., 1984.

Pirsig, Robert M. *Zen and the Art of Motorcycle Maintenance*. New York: Bantam Books, 1975.

Plato. *Five Great Dialogues*. Roslyn, NY: Walter J. Black, Inc., 1942.

Rand, Ayn. *Atlas Shrugged*. New York: The Penguin Group, 1957.

Ricks, Thomas E. *Fiasco*. New York: The Penguin Press, 2006.

Ryle, Gilbert. *The Concept of Mind*. Chicago: The Chicago University Press, 1949.

Schelling, Thomas C. *Arms and Influence*. New Haven, CT: Yale University Press, 1966.

Schelling, Thomas C. *The Strategy of Conflict*. Cambridge, MA: Harvard University, 1960.

Schopenhauer, Arthur. "The World as Will and Idea." *The European Philosophers from Descartes to Nietzsche*. Edited by Monroe C. Beardsley. New York: Random House, 1960.

Scullard, H. H. *Scipio Africanus: Soldier and Politician*. Ithaca: Cornell University Press, 1970.

Seabald, W. G. *On The Natural History of Destruction*. Translated by Anthea Bell. New York: Penguin Books, 1999.

Shakespeare, William. *Macbeth*. Edited by Charles W. Eliot. Danbury: Grolier Enterprises Corp., 1980.

Shakespeare, William. *The Tragedy of Julius Caesar. The Complete Works of William Shakespeare*. Edited by William Aldis Wright. Garden City, NY: Garden City Books, The Cambridge Edition Text, Including the Temple Notes, 1936.

Shakespeare, William. King Henry VI—Part II. *The Complete Works of William Shakespeare*. Edited by William Aldis Wright. Garden City, NY: Garden City Books, The Cambridge Edition Text, Including the Temple Notes, 1936.

Steinbeck, John. *East of Eden*. New York: Penguin Classics, June 2003. Audio book, read by Richard Poe.

Summers, Harry. *On Strategy: The Vietnam War in Context*. Carlisle Barracks, PA: Strategic Studies Institute U.S. Army War College, 1982.

Sun Tzu. *The Art of War*. Translated and Edited by Samuel B. Griffith. London: Oxford University Press, 1971.

Taleb, Nassim Nicholas. *The Black Swan: The Impact of the Highly Improbable*. New York: Random House, 2007.

Tolstoy, Leo. *War and Peace*. New York: International Collector's Library, 1949.

Vonnegut, Kurt. *Slaughterhouse-Five*. New York: Delacorte, 1969

Waldrop, M. Mitchell. *Complexity: The Emerging Science at the Edge of Order and Chaos*. New York: Touchstone Books, 1992.

Zukav, Gary. *The Dancing Wu Li Masters*. Toronto: Bantam Books, 1979.

ARTICLES

Adams, Eddie. "Eulogy." *Time*, 1998.

Beres, Derek. "Can We Think Critically Anymore?" Big Think, 2016.

Jablonsky, David. "Strategic Vision and Presidential Authority in the Post-Cold War Era." Parameters, Carlisle, PA: U.S. Army War College, vol. XXI, no. 4.

Kilcullen, David. "Twenty-Eight Articles Fundamentals of Company-level Counterinsurgency." *Small Wars Journal*, 2006.

Schneider, James. "Inside the Mind of An Insurgent." *Army Magazine*, July 2005.

Thomas, Timothy L. "Like Adding Wings to the Tiger: Chinese Information War Theory and Practice." Fort Leavenworth, KS: Foreign Military Studies Office, 2001.

UNPUBLISHED PAPERS

Boyd, John. "Destruction and Creation." 1976.

Hall, Wayne Michael. "Abridged Advanced Analysis Summary." 2016.

Hall, Wayne Michael. "Advanced Analysis Discussion and Use in Deep Thinking about Conclusions and Recommendations—Claim, Evidence, Truth, Facts, Objectivity/Subjectivity." 2016.
Hall, Wayne Michael. "Advanced Analysis Thought Model—Quality Control of Analysis and Collection Events Via Auditing Advanced Analysis and Collections Processes." 2016.
Hall, Wayne Michael. "Advanced Analysis: 10 Thought Models." 2016.
Hall, Wayne Michael. "Advanced Analysis and Advanced Collection Vision Document." 2016.
Hall, Wayne Michael. "Conclusion Template Redux: The Arcane World of Decision-Making." 2016.
Hall, Wayne Michael. "Electives for Educating Senior Officers and Civilians at Command and Staff Colleges (CSC) and Senior Service Colleges (SSC) on Select Topics in: Mental Combat Inherent to 21st Century Conflicts." 2016.
Hall, Wayne Michael. "Metacognition: 'How to Think' Redux." 2016.
Hall, Wayne Michael. "Operational Context." 2016.
Hall, Wayne Michael. "Reflections on Advanced Analysis I." 2011.
Hall, Wayne Michael. "Reflections on Advanced Analysis II Redux." 2014.
Hall, Wayne Michael. "Think Like the Adversary Thinks." 2016.
Hall, Wayne Michael. "Thinking and Planning for the 21st Century." Washington, D.C.: National War College, 1992.
Schueler, Gerald J. "Sensitive Dependence on Initial Conditions." 1991.

LECTURES

Anthony Goldblum. "The Jobs We'll Lose to Machines and the Ones We Won't." TED, 2016.
Karl Raymond Popper. "Of Clouds and Clocks: An Approach to the Problem of Rationality and the Freedom of Man."

PUBLICATIONS

Chairman of the Joint Chiefs of Staff Memorandum (CJCSM) 5120.01A. Joint Doctrine Development Process, Joint Staff Washington, D.C.: 2014.
U.S. Army, Field Manual 3-0, Operations C-1. GPO, Washington, D.C.: 2011.
U.S. Department of Defense, Joint Staff, Joint Publication 1-02, Dictionary of Military and Associated Terms. Washington, D.C.: Joint Publication 1-02,8 2010 (as amended through February 15, 2016).
U.S. Department of Defense, Joint Staff, Joint Publication 2-0, Joint Intelligence. Washington, D.C.: Joint Publication 2-0, October 22, 2013.
U.S. Department of Defense, Joint Staff, Joint Publication 2-01, Joint and National Intelligence Support to Military Operations. Washington, D.C.: Joint Publication 2-01, January 5, 2012.
U.S. Department of Defense, Joint Staff, Joint Publication 2-01.3, Joint Intelligence Preparation of the Operational Environment (JIPOE). Washington, D.C.: Joint Publication 2-01.3, June 16, 2009.

U.S. Department of Defense, Joint Staff, Joint Publication 3-0, Joint Operations. Washington, D.C.: Joint Publication 3-0, January 17, 2017.

U.S. Department of Defense, Joint Staff, Joint Publication 5-0, Joint Operation Planning. Washington, D.C.: Joint Publication 5-0, August 11, 2011.

POEMS

Eliot, T. S. "The Love Song of J. Alfred Prufrock." *Poetry: A Magazine of Verse.* Chicago, 1915.

Index

Page numbers in italics refer to illustrations.

About the Author

WAYNE MICHAEL "MIKE" HALL, Brigadier General, U.S. Army, Retired, is a career intelligence officer with over 40 years of experience in intelligence operations. After retiring, he worked with the military and private corporations providing consulting services in intelligence-related matters for more than 12 years. He led seminars about his book *Intelligence Analysis* for six years and thereby worked with ~1200 analysts and collections people in over 50 one- and two-week seminars. Brigadier General Hall holds a BS from the University of Nebraska, an MS from Kansas State University, an MMAS from the U.S. Army CGSC, and an EdD from The George Washington University. He attended Command and General Staff College (CGSC), School of Advanced Military Studies (SAMS), and the National War College. His first book, *Stray Voltage: War in the Information Age,* was published in April 2003. His next book, *Intelligence Analysis: How to Think in Complex Environments,* was published by Praeger in 2009. He followed that up with *Intelligence Collection: How to Plan and Execute Intelligence Collection in Complex Environments,* published by Praeger in 2012. This new book on will is the companion piece to his first two Praeger books. Hall spends his time reading, writing, and listening to music.

Printed in the USA
CPSIA information can be obtained
at www.ICGtesting.com
LVHW011035070624
782600LV00001B/23

9 798765 120446